Cosmic Wit

Juan de la Cuesta Hispanic Monographs

SERIES: *Homenajes*, 53

FOUNDING EDITOR
Tom Lathrop
University of Delaware

EDITOR
Michael J. McGrath
Georgia Southern University

EDITORIAL BOARD
Vincent Barletta
Stanford University

Annette Grant Cash
Georgia State University

David Castillo
State University of New York-Buffalo

Gwen Kirkpatrick
Georgetown University

Mark P. Del Mastro
College of Charleston

Juan F. Egea
University of Wisconsin-Madison

Sara L. Lehman
Fordham University

Mariselle Meléndez
University of Illinois at Urbana-Champaign

Eyda Merediz
University of Maryland

Dayle Seidenspinner-Núñez
University of Notre Dame

Elzbieta Sklodowska
Washington University in St. Louis

Noël Valis
Yale University

"Cosmic Wit"

Essays in Honor of Edward H. Friedman

Edited by

VICENTE PÉREZ DE LEÓN
University of Glasgow

MARTHA GARCÍA
University of Central Florida

G. CORY DUCLOS
Colgate University

Juan de la Cuesta
Newark, Delaware

Photograph of Edward H. Friedman courtesy of
the Department of Spanish & Portuguese at Vanderbilt University

Copyright © 2021 LinguaText, LLC. All rights reserved.

Juan de la Cuesta Hispanic Monographs
An imprint of LinguaText, LLC.
Newark, Delaware 19711 USA
(302) 453-8695

www.JuandelaCuesta.com

Manufactured in the United States of America

ISBN: 978-1-58871-346-9 (HB)
E-ISBN: 978-1-58871-370-4 (PDF)

Edward H. Friedman

Table of Contents

I. Introduction 11

II. Breaking Away, circa 1993
    Vicente Pérez de León 25

III. Back in 2000 and Beyond
     Martha García 29

IV. A Comedy of Editors 1999-2017
    G. Cory Duclos 33

V. Synopsis of articles 37

VI. Articles

   Too Near the Bone: Translation, *Los melindres de Belisa* and the
   Problem of Proximity
   Mindy E. Badía 45

   Quijotes transatlánticos and Golden-Age Latin Americanism
   Robert Bayliss 60

   Terceras and pandering wives in Tirso's *El pretendiente al revés*
   Kathleen Costales 78

   Well-Behaved Panzas Rarely Make History: Teresa Panza and the
   Metafiction of *Don Quijote*
   G. Cory Duclos 92

Miguel Manipulated: Metatheater and Social Critique in Two Quixotic Puppet Operas
TIMOTHY M. FOSTER 108

La desordenada codicia de los bienes agenos: El doctor Carlos García ante la tradición picaresca aurisecular
ANTÓN GARCÍA-FERNÁNDEZ 126

Atenea y Minerva en la temprana edad moderna: Teresa Sánchez de Cepeda & María Isidra de Guzmán
MARTHA GARCÍA 135

Anacaona and the areito: A Generative Model for Pro-indigenous Discourse in Lope de Vega's *El Nuevo Mundo descubierto por Cristobal Colón*?
JEANNE GILLESPIE 150

El gran prodigio de España: Joanna Theodora de Souza's Performative Convent *Comedia*
ANNA-LISA HALLING 170

De Lisbeth Salander a la Ertzaintza: Fantasías neoliberales en la serie procedimental de Eva García Sáenz de Urturi
SALVADOR A. OROPESA 182

Juanita versus Cecilia: Competing Allegories of Cuba by Mary Peabody Mann and Cirilo Villaverde
JULIA C. PAULK 200

La superficie cóncava del primer cielo. Sobre la liminalidad de los periplos angulares al Lago Español de Álvaro Mendaña, Isabel de Barreto y el don Quijote portugués, Pedro Fernández de Quirós
VICENTE PÉREZ DE LEÓN 218

"Melancólico espejo": From Garcilaso's "Églogas" to Luis Cernuda's Égloga, elegía, oda
DAVID F. RICHTER 240

Returning Home in Juan Ruiz de Alarcón's Plays
GLADYS ROBALINO 254

El poder de las palabras: la percepción de los conversos en la literatura del Siglo de Oro
TUGBA SEVIN 268

Family Functions and Dysfunctions: Secrecy in *La vida es sueño*
GWEN H. STICKNEY 279

Copying the Unreal: The Multiple Imitations in the Balcony Scene of *Don Gil de las calzas verdes*
ROBERT L. TURNER 297

La comunidad morisca del siglo dieciséis se enfrenta a los horrores de la tumba
MIGUEL ÁNGEL VÁZQUEZ 311

Poéticas profanas de lo sagrado. Intersecciones culturales en torno a la construcción del predicador barroco. Dos propuestas teóricas
JUAN VITULLI 330

Tilting at Relevance: The Quixotic Enterprise of Portuguese Authors of the Iberian Union
JONATHAN WADE 348

The Importance of Humor in Recent Translations of *Don Quijote*
STEVEN B. WENZ 361

Don Quijote and the Construction of Dulcinea
HABIB ZANZANA 379

VII. Tuits/Tweets dedicados al Profesor Edward H. Friedman 401

TABULA GRATULATORIA 405

Introducción

PROFESSOR EDWARD H. FRIEDMAN: AN INSPIRING LIFE

THE DISCRETE READER WILL certainly understand the difficultly inherent in summarizing the academic achievements of Edward H. Friedman. As a scholar, his research has a lasting and long-reaching impact. As professor, he has taught and mentored countless students. But most importantly, as a kind and generous person he has given of himself to anyone fortunate enough to have worked with him.

In recent years, Ed has been asked to write autobiographical reflections on his life and career, providing insight into his upbringing and motivations for his academic work. Here we provide a brief summary of Ed's life based on those pieces, followed by three short, personal essays from each of the editors touching on our work with him through three pivotal points of his career: as a professor at the University of Indiana, as a professor at Vanderbilt University, and as the Editor of *Bulletin of the Comediantes*. We hope these more intimate portraits accurately depict the type of friend that Ed has become for the authors of this collection, who, at Ed's request, are all his former students.

Ed was born in 1948 in Richmond, Virginia, the home of his mother Sara Sherman Friedman. His father, Joseph Friedman, was from the Bronx, New York. Arthur Friedman, Ed's twin brother, was born four minutes later, and, as Ed notes, despite being labeled "identical," they had quite contrasting personalities. Ed credits his parents for providing him with a strong sense of moral character and instilling within him a sense of social justice. Having themselves seen the persecution leveled against their own Jewish community, Ed was taught the inherent immorality of segregation and racism.

As a student in the public schools of Richmond, Ed first learned of his interest in literature and theater. Although he was unable to attend many productions, he recalls mentally reconstructing the plays as he read, staging them in his mind. His academic interest in literature led him to the University of Virginia, where he decided, luckily for all of us, to study Spanish literature. While at UVA, he traveled to Spain for the first time to spend an academic year studying in Madrid. There, his linguistic skills grew along with his desire to know more. Upon returning home, he decided to apply for doctoral programs and was accepted at Johns Hopkins, where he studied and wrote a dissertation about Cervantes's *comedia* as a fellow at the Folger Shakespeare Library in Washington, D.C. He completed his dissertation in April of 1974 and married his lifelong companion Susan Krug in May of the same year.

Ed's career has taken him all over the nation and the world. After three years teaching at Kalamazoo College, he accepted a position at Arizona State University. He went on to teach at the University of Indiana, Bloomington, and in the new millennium at Vanderbilt University. During his time at those schools, he has participated in a variety of teaching and research opportunities around the globe, allowing him to work and study in Spain, Portugal, and throughout the United States. In addition to undergraduate and graduate students, Ed has taught in programs for young gifted children, high school teachers, and working professionals. He has served the profession in academic publishing in numerous capacities, most notably as the long-time editor of *Bulletin of the Comediantes*. In addition to his countless academic articles and excellent monographs, Ed has produced creative writing pieces inspired by Golden Age literature.

Throughout Ed's life, he has used his knowledge and positions to guide others and inspire them. As the editors of this volume, we believe that the articles herein reflect an ongoing legacy of excellent scholarship that is the direct outcome of Ed's generosity. In closing this section of this volume, we leave you with Ed's own words of advice to serve as inspiration for all of us:

1. Make a determination to be continually on the move, intellectually speaking. Never be complacent. Never be satisfied with prior achievements. Never be satisfied at having achieved the goals of the past. Never stop creating new courses or new research topics. Never think that you have mastered your field.

2. Texts are stable; criticism and theory are unstable, in the best sense. That keeps us on our toes and in business.

3. Teaching should be interactive. Dialogue should never be missing from the classroom or from engagement with texts and colleagues.

4. Students are, in the overwhelming majority, smart, kind, and generous. They also are vulnerable, so one should try to be understanding of them, should treat them with tolerance and an open mind, and should give them the benefit of the doubt. Especially as the generation gap grows wider, students will know many things bout which their teachers are ignorant. Give them the chance to make the acquisition of knowledge a two-way street.

5. Teaching is a vulnerable and venerated profession. We should take our disciplines and our students more seriously, but we should not take ourselves too seriously. Our task challenges us to be models of excellence, and we should try as hard as possible to reach that objective, which generally will mean casting the spotlight away from ourselves and onto our texts, our pedagogical methods, and our students.

6. An indisputable way to learn is keep up with what students are reading for their research.

7. The profession is, like life, a dialectics of good and bad. The good far outweighs the bad, but the bad can be intrusive, distracting, and harmful. Some people function on negative energy. One needs to work toward minimizing the ability of these individuals to hurt others and toward protecting, to the extent possible, young scholars and students from their abuse of authority. It may be quixotic, but a belief in poetic justice can be an asset.

8. What do I want students to learn from taking classes and/or working with me on their projects? To read carefully, analytically, and creatively. To seek points to praise before seeking points to criticize, and to be respectful (rather than dismissive) in their criticism. To find impetus and subjects for future work. To work tirelessly, but with enjoyment. To develop a spirit of collaboration. To be sympathetic toward others, in narrow and broad terms. To become advocates for the humanities and, needless to say, for humanity.

9. On the fairly rare occasions in which I may be inclined to tout my self-sufficiency, I think of all the people who have watched over me at home and abroad, and I strive to emulate those mentors, guides, and good citizens. Remember that it takes—evoking Thomas Jefferson and Hillary Clinton—an "academic village" to prepare a teacher.

10. Having grown up in the period of "massive resistance" to integration and having observed the strides made by women and minorities—and the impact of these civil rights movements on the academy—I feel that the humanities are more important than ever, because the struggles have not ended. High technology and core principles can, and should, coexist. ("Center of Gravity", 16)

Works Consulted

Friedman, Edward H. "Centers of Gravity." *Letters*. Robert Penn Warren Center for the Humanities, 2016. 12-17.

———. "La verdadera historia, más o menos." *¿Por qué España?* Edited by Anna Caballé Masforroll and Randolph D. Pope. Translated by Oriol Porta. Barcelona: Galaxia Gutenberg, 2014.

EDWARD H. FRIEDMAN

SELECTED HONORS AND GRANTS

Grants from the Newberry Library Center for Renaissance Studies, the Harry Ransom Center (University of Texas at Austin), the National Endowment for the Humanities, the Eli Lilly Foundation
National Humanities Center Academic Year Fellowship
Fulbright Lecturing/Research Grant, Madrid, Spain
Fulbright Lecturing/Research Grant, Lisbon, Portugal
Sigma Delta Pi National Spanish Honor Society "Orden de Don Quijote" Award
Vanderbilt University College of Arts and Science Graduate Mentoring Award
Vanderbilt University Jeffrey Nordhaus Award for Excellence in Undergraduate Teaching (2006, 2012)
FACET Teaching Award, Indiana University
Burlington Northern Foundation Faculty Achievement Award for Excellence in Teaching, Arizona State University
School of Criticism and Theory postdoctoral fellowship
Folger Shakespeare Library Dissertation Fellowship
Gilman Fellowship, Johns Hopkins University
Institute of European Studies Academic Scholarship, Madrid
Phi Eta Sigma, Phi Beta Kappa, Cultura Hispánica Prize in Spanish, University of Virginia

PUBLICATIONS:
BOOKS

Love and Pedagogy; Or, How to Create a Genius. An Adaptation of *Amor y pedagogía* by Miguel de Unamuno. Newark, DE: Juan de la Cuesta, 2019.

Pedro the Schemer: A Work in Progress. An Adaptation of *Pedro de Urdemalas* by Miguel de Cervantes. Newark, DE: Juan de la Cuesta, 2018.

Trading Up: A Comedy of Manners. Suggested by Juan Ruiz de Alarcón's *Mudarse por mejorarse*. Newark, DE: Juan de la Cuesta, 2015.

Quixotic Haiku: Poems and Notes. Newark, DE: Juan de la Cuesta, 2014.

The Labyrinth of Love. Inspired by *El laberinto de amor* of Miguel de Cervantes. Newark, DE: Juan de la Cuesta, 2013.

Crossing the Line: A Quixotic Adventure in Two Parts. A play inspired by *Don Quixote*. Newark, DE: Juan de la Cuesta, 2012.

Into the Mist. A play based on the novel ("nivola") *Niebla* (1914) by Miguel de Unamuno. Newark, DE: Juan de la Cuesta, 2011.

The Little Woman: A Liberal Translation of Leandro Fernández de Moratín's El sí de las niñas. Newark, DE: Juan de la Cuesta, 2010.

Cervantes in the Middle: Realism and Reality in the Spanish Novel. Newark: DE: Juan de la Cuesta, 2006.

El caballero de Olmedo by Lope de Vega. Ed. Edward H. Friedman. Newark, DE: Juan de la Cuesta, 2004.

El cuento: arte y análisis. Upper Saddle River, NJ: Prentice Hall, 2003.

Wit's End: An Adaptation of Lope de Vega's La dama boba. New York: Peter Lang/Ibérica, 2000. Presented as part of the 2006-2007 season of Vanderbilt Theatre (six performances in November 2006, under the direction of Jeffrey Ullom). Revised version reprinted in *The Mercurian*, 2013.

The Antiheroine's Voice: Narrative Discourse and Transformations of the Picaresque. Columbia: University of Missouri Press, 1987.

Aproximaciones al estudio de la literatura hispánica. With L. Teresa Valdivieso and Carmelo Virgillo. New York: Random House, 1983. 7th ed., McGraw-Hill, 2011.

The Unifying Concept: Approaches to the Structure of Cervantes' Comedias. York, SC: Spanish Literature Publications, 1981.

Selected Edited Essays

Studies in Honor of Robert ter Horst. Eds. Eleanor ter Horst, Edward H. Friedman, and Ali Shehzad Zaidi. Fair Lawn, NJ: TSI Press, 2017.

Confluencia, special number in memory of Professor Elias L. Rivers (30.3, 2015) [guest editor].

Miríada Hispánica (Valencia, Spain), special number on early modern Spanish literature (no. 4, spring 2012) [guest editor].

Calíope, special number on the teaching of Golden Age Spanish poetry (11.2, 2005) [guest editor].

Hispania, special number on *Don Quixote* (March 2005) [guest editor, with James A. Parr].

Vanderbilt e-Journal of Luso-Hispanic Studies, Metafictional Crossings (2005) [guest editor].

"Never-ending Adventure": Studies in Medieval and Early Modern Spanish Literature in Honor of Peter N. Dunn. Ed. with Harlan Sturm. Newark, DE: Juan de la Cuesta, 2002.

A Society on Stage: Essays on Spanish Golden Age Drama. Ed. with H. J. Manzari and Donald D. Miller. New Orleans: University Press of the South, 1998.

Brave New Words: Studies in Spanish Golden Age Literature. Ed. with Catherine Larson. New Orleans: University Press of the South, 1996.

SELECTED ARTICLES AND BOOK CHAPTERS

"The Women of Spanish Baroque Literature: Finding a Place." *Itinerarios de lectura / A Journey in Readership: Homenaje a Cathy L. Jrade.* Eds. Christina Karageorgou-Bastea, Fátima R. Nogueira, and Leila M. Lehnen. Vigo, Spain: Editorial Academia del Hispanismo, 2019. 145-63. (197)

"Grotesque Visions: Irony and the Distorted Image in *Don Quijote*." *Hispania Felix: Revista Hispano-Romana de Cultura y Civilización de los Siglos de Oro* 7. Ed. A. Robert Lauer (2016 [2017]): 47-72. (190)

"Artful Resources: Adaptation and Reconstruction in Drama." *Hipogrifo* 5.1 (2017): 211-32. (186)

"Assault and Flattery: *Don Quixote* and Jaime Manrique's *Cervantes Street*." *Bulletin of Hispanic Studies* 92.8 (2015): 913-31. (169)

"The Quixotic Template in Contemporary American Theater." *Confluencia* 30.2 (2015): 2-16. (168)

"Voice in Context: Writing Women in Early Modern Spain." *Perspectives on Early Modern Women in Iberia and the Americas: Studies in Law, Society, Art and Literature in Honor of Anne J. Cruz.* Eds. Adrienne Martín and María Cristina Quintero. New York: Escribana Books, 2015. 575-95. (167)

"The Baroque Picaro: Francisco de Quevedo's *Buscón.*" *The Picaresque Novel in Western Literature: From the Sixteenth Century to the Neopicaresque.* Ed. J. A. Garrido Ardila. Cambridge: Cambridge University Press, 2015. 75-95. (165)

"Roads Untaken: The Spanish Picaresque Novel." *A History of the Spanish Novel.* Ed. J. A. Garrido Ardila. Oxford: Oxford University Press, 2015. 96-121. (164)

"The High Anxiety of Influence: Caro, Zayas, Sor Juana, and Their Models." *Shakespeare and the Spanish* Comedia: *Translation, Interpretation, Performance.* Ed. Barbara Mujica. Lewisburg, PA: Bucknell University Press, 2013. 89-103. (155)

"Picaresque Partitions: The Material World and Quevedo's *Buscón.*" *Objects of Culture in the Literature of Imperial Spain.* Eds. Mary E. Barnard and Frederick A. de Armas. Toronto: University of Toronto Press, 2013. 159-80. (150)

"Cultural Buddies: Text and Context, in Context." *Hispanic Issues* 8 (2011): 204-21. (145)

"From the Inside Out: The Poetics of *Lazarillo de Tormes.*" *Philological Quarterly* 89.1 (2010): 13-30. (142)

"Collaborating with Lope de Vega; or, Wit's Friend." *Hispanic Studies in Honor of Robert L. Fiore.* Eds. Chad M. Gasta and Julia Domínguez. Newark, DE: Juan de la Cuesta, 2009. 209-26. (135)

"Rewriting Honor: Jacinto Benavente's *La otra honra* and Its Precedents." *Hispanic Studies in Honor of Daniel Eisenberg.* Ed. Tom Lathrop. Newark, DE: Juan de la Cuesta, 2009. 91-120. (134)

"The Peninsular *Amphitruo*: The Plautine Adaptations of Juan de Timoneda and Luís de Camões." *Hecho Teatral* 5 (2005) [2007]: 13-35. (128)

"Offensive Hermeneutics: Fiction as Critique in Avellaneda's *Quixote.*" *Central Institute of English and Foreign Languages (CIEFL) Bulletin* (India), 15.2 (2005)-16.2 (2006) [2007]: 103-19. (127)

"The Culture of the Comedia: The Interplay of Text and Theory." *Critical Reflections: Essays on Golden Age Spanish Literature in Honor of James A. Parr.* Eds. Amy Williamsen and Barbara Simerka. Newark, DE: Juan de la Cuesta, 2006. 189-203. (124)

"'El pobre servicio de mano': *Lazarillo de Tormes, Don Quixote,* and the Design of the Novel." *1605-2005: Don Quixote across the Centuries.* Ed. John

P. Gabriele. Madrid and Frankfurt am Main: Iberoamericana / Vervuert, 2005. 29-50. (122)

"Discourses on Spain: Gerald Brenan and Cervantes." *Cervantes y su mundo*, III. Ed. A. Robert Lauer and Kurt Reichenberger. Kassel: Reichenberger, 2005. 167-88. (120)

"Afterword: Redressing the Baroque." *Hispanic Baroques: Reading Cultures in Context*. Eds. Nicholas Spadaccini and Luis Martín-Estudillo. Nashville: Vanderbilt University Press, 2005. 287-305. (119)

"Fame and Misfortune: The Cost of Success in *Don Quixote*." *Bulletin of Hispanic Studies* 82.5 (2005): 649-69. (115)

"Women in *Don Quixote*: The Master Plan," *"Corónente tus hazañas": Studies in Honor of John Jay Allen*. Ed. Michael J. McGrath. Newark, DE: Juan de la Cuesta, 2005. 205-29. (114)

"Redressing the Trickster: *El burlador de Sevilla* and Critical Transitions." *Revista Canadiense de Estudios Hispánicos* 29.1 (2004): 61-77. (112)

"Living History: Gamel Woolsey's *Death's Other Kingdom*." *Letras Peninsulares* 17.1 (2004): 159-80. (110)

"Realities and Poets: Góngora, Cervantes, and the Nature of Art." *Calíope* 8.1 (2002): 55-68. (106)

"Dioses y monstruos: El espacio trágico en Lope y Calderón." *El teatro del Siglo de Oro ante los espacios de la crítica: Encuentros y revisiones*. Ed. Enrique García Santo-Tomás. Madrid: Iberoamericana, 2002. 115-38. (105)

"Constructing Romance: The Deceptive Idealism of María de Zayas's *El jardín engañoso*. *Zayas and Her Sisters, 2*. Eds. Gwyn E. Campbell and Judith A. Whitenack. Binghamton, NY: Global Publications, Binghamton University, 2001. 45-61. (100)

"Sign Language: The Semiotics of Lope de Vega's *El perro del hortelano*." *Hispanic Review* 68.1 (2000): 1-20. (96)

"The Golden Age Sonnet: Metaphor and Metonymy, with a Difference." *Calíope* 5.1 (1999): 47-58. (93)

"*La Comedia* at the Border: Francisco Manuel de Melo's *O Fidalgo Aprendiz*." *Bulletin of the Comediantes* 49.1 (1997): 5-14. (86)

"The Fortunes of Chivalry: António José da Silva's *Vida do Grande D. Quixote de La Mancha y do Gordo Sancho Pança*." *Cervantes* 17 (1997): 80-93. (85)

"Constructing Gracián." *Rhetoric and Politics: Gracián and the New World Order*, ed. Nicholas Spadaccini and Jenaro Talens, Hispanic Issues, 14. Minneapolis: University of Minnesota Press, 1997. 355-72. (81)

"Enemy Territory: The Frontiers of Gender in María de Zayas's *El traidor contra su sangre* and *Mal presagio casar lejos*." *"Ingeniosa invención": Essays on Golden Age Spanish Literature for Geoffrey L. Stagg in Honor of His Eighty-fifth Birthday*. Eds. Ellen M. Anderson and Amy R. Williamsen. Newark, DE: Juan de la Cuesta, 1999. 43-68. (80)

"Theater Semiotics and Lope de Vega's *El caballero de Olmedo*." *El arte nuevo de estudiar comedias: Literary Theory and Spanish Golden Age Drama*. Ed. Barbara Simerka. Lewisburg, PA: Bucknell University Press, 1996. 66-85. (75)

"Theory in the Margin: Latin American Literature and the Jewish Subject." *The Jewish Diaspora in Latin America: New Studies on History and Literature*. Eds. David Sheinin and Lois Baer Barr. New York: Garland Press, 1996. 21-31. (74)

"Trials of Discourse: Narrative Space in Quevedo's *Buscón*." *The Picaresque: Tradition and Displacement*. Ed. Giancarlo Maiorino. Minneapolis: University of Minnesota Press, 1996. 183-225. (72)

"Creative Space: Ideologies of Discourse in Góngora's *Polifemo*." *Cultural Authority in Golden Age Spain*. Eds. Marina S. Brownlee and Hans Ulrich Gumbrecht. Baltimore: The Johns Hopkins University Press, 1995. 51-78. (70)

"Postmodernism and the Spanish *Comedia*: The Drama of Mediation." *Gestos* 9, no. 17 (1994): 61-78. (65)

"Rhetoric at Work: Celestina, Trotaconventos, and the Persuasive Arts." *Fernando de Rojas and Celestina: Approaching the Fifth Centenary*. Eds. Ivy A. Corfis and Joseph T. Snow. Madison, WI: Hispanic Seminary of Hispanic Studies, 1993. 359-70. (62)

"Angelina Muñiz's *Tierra adentro*: (Re)creating the Subject." *Tradition and Innovation: Reflections on Latin American Jewish Writing*. Eds. Robert DiAntonio and Nora Glickman. Albany: State University of New York Press, 1993. 179-92. (60)

"Deference, *Différance*: The Rhetoric of Deferral in *La vida es sueño*." *The Prince in the Tower: Perceptions of "La vida es sueño"*. Ed. Frederick A. de Armas. Lewiston, PA: Bucknell University Press, 1993. 41-53. (59)

"The Novel as Revisionist History: Art as Process in Mario Szichman's *A las 20:25 la señora entró en la inmortalidad* and Isaac Goldemberg's *Tiempo al tiempo*." *Modern Jewish Studies* 8.2 (1993): 24-33. (53)

"Reading Inscribed: *Don Quixote* and the Parameters of Fiction." *On Cervantes: Essays for L. A. Murillo*. Eds. James A. Parr. Newark, DE: Juan de la Cuesta, 1991. 63-84. (52)

"Cervantes' *La fuerza de la sangre* and the Rhetoric of Power." *Cervantes's 'Exemplary Novels' and the Adventure of Writing*. Eds. Michael Nerlich and Nicholas Spadaccini. *Hispanic Issues*. Minneapolis: The Prisma Institute, 1989. 125-56. (50)

"The Writerly Edge: A Question of Structure in the *Poema de Mio Cid*." *La Corónica* 18.2 (1990): 11-20. (49)

"The Spanish Golden Age Sonnet and the Semiotics of Poetry." *Studies in Honor of Elias Rivers*. Eds. Bruno M. Damiani and Ruth El Saffar. Potomac, Maryland: Scripta Humanistica, 1989. 94-104. (47)

Romeo and Juliet as Tragicomedy: Lope de Vega's *Castelvines y Monteses* and Francisco de Rojas Zorrilla's *Los bandos de Verona*." *Comedias del Siglo de Oro and Shakespeare*. Ed. Susan L. Fischer. Lewisburg, PA: Bucknell University Press, 1989. 82-96. (46)

"Narrative Discourse in Juana Trullás's *Una mujer*: A Poetics of Alienation." *Letras Peninsulares* 1.2 (1988): 168-81. (43)

"'Cherchez la femme': El lector como detective en *50 vacas gordas* de Isaac Chocrón." *Discurso Literario* 4.2 (1987): 647-56. (36)

"Perspectivism on Stage: *Don Quijote* and the Mediated Vision of Cervantes' *Comedias*." *Ideologies and Literature* Nueva época, 2.1 (1986): 69-86. (35)

"Poetic Discourse and Performance Text: Toward a Semiotics of the *Comedia*." *Journal of the Rocky Mountain Medieval and Renaissance Association* 5 (1984): 7-18. (32)

"Toward a More Perfect Union: Art and Craft in Calderón's *Saber del mal y del bien* and ¿*Cuál es mayor perfección?*" *Bulletin of the Comediantes* 35 (1983): 51-67. (30)

"*Don Quixote* and the Act of Reading," *Approaches to Teaching Don Quixote*. Ed. Richard Bjornson. New York: Modern Language Association, 1984. 87-95. (29)

"The Validity of Contradiction: Narrative Art in the *Libro de Buen Amor* and the Spanish Picaresque Novel." *Rivista di Letterature Moderne e Comparate* 35 (1982): 111-23. (25)

"The Other Side of the Metaphor: An Approach to *La devoción de la cruz*," *Approaches to the Theater of Calderón*. Ed. Michael D. McGaha. Washington, D.C.: University Press of America, 1982. 129-41. (22)

"Chaos Restored: Authorial Control and Ambiguity in *Lazarillo de Tormes*." *Crítica Hispánica* 3 (1981): 59-73. (20)

"'Folly and a Woman': Galdós' Rhetoric of Irony in *Tristana*," *Theory and Practice of Feminist Literary Criticism*. Ed. Gabriela Mora and Karen S. Van Hooft. Ypsilanti, MI: Bilingual Press, 1982. 201-28. (19)

"The Thorns on the Roses: A Reading of Jacinto Benavente's *Rosas de otoño*." *International Journal of Women's Studies* 4 (1981): 168-72. (18)

"From Concept to Drama: The Other Unamuno." *Hispanófila* no. 68 (January 1980): 29-38. (13)

"Tragedy and Tragicomedy in Ruiz de Alarcón's *El dueño de las estrellas* and *La crueldad por el honor*." *Kentucky Romance Quarterly* 22 (1975): 429-44. (3)

"Conceptual Proportion in Cervantes' *El licenciado Vidriera*." *South Atlantic Bulletin* 39 (1974): 51-59. (2)

"Dramatic Perspective in Calderón's *El mayor monstruo los celos*." *Bulletin of the Comediantes* 26 (1974): 43-49. (1)

Selected Book Reviews

Luis de Góngora and Lope de Vega: Masters of Parody by Lindsay G. Kerr, *Hispanic Review* 86.4 (2018): 514-17. (260)

Cervantes y su época by Francisco Olmos García and *Intención y silencio en el 'Quijote'* by Ricardo Aguilera, *MLN* 88 (1973): 448-51. (1)

Selected Conference Papers

"Golden Stages: The Dialectics of Adaptation," Association of Literary Scholars, Critics, and Writers, Vanderbilt University (November 2018). (198)

"Elements of Unity in Cervantes' *Rinconete y Cortadillo*," Midwest Modern Language Association (November 1975). (2)

Selected Professional Activities

Editor, *Bulletin of the Comediantes* (1999-2017)

President, Cervantes Society of America (2001-2004), Vice-President (1998-2001)

General Editor, *Yearbook of Comparative and General Literature* (1997-1999)

Editor, *Indiana Journal of Hispanic Literatures* (1993-1997)

Book Review Editor, *Yearbook of Comparative and General Literature* (1994-1997)
Book Review Editor, *Cervantes* (1991-2000)
Book Review Editor, *Hispania* (1984-1987)
Associate Editor, Purdue University Monographs in Romance Languages (1991-)
Editorial Board: *Letr@s Hispanas* (2005-), *Hispania* (2004-), *Hispanófila* (2002-), *Revista de Estudios Hispánicos* (2002-), *Arizona Journal of Hispanic Cultural Studies* (1996-), *Confluencia* (1993-), *Hispanic Issues* (1987-), *Discurso Literario* (1984-1989), *Cervantes* (1984-), *Bulletin of the Comediantes* (1983-99), *Chasqui* (1982-1995), *Rocky Mountain Review* (1981-1999)

Breaking Away, circa 1993
Vicente Pérez de León

Back in 1993, during my last year at Villanova, I was forced to make a life-changing decision. On the one hand, one option was returning to Madrid and rejoining my family and friends. In Spain I had two job offers; one at a language school, another one at the Spanish Swimming Federation. On the other hand and alternative option was to stay longer in the States and continuing studying a PhD in Spanish literature. This was my true passion, after having completed two postgraduate degrees in English and Translation in Madrid. Randomly, I came across Ed through my admired Harriet Goldberg. I still remember my short conversation with her:

— Harriet, si volviera a España para hacer un doctorado, ¿Dónde...

Before I finished my sentence, she said...

— Barcelona, con Francisco Rico.
— ¿Y si me quedara aquí?
— Indiana con Friedman, Edward Friedman.
— ¿Por qué?
— Ya lo sabrás.

Although I had been accepted to several East Coast Grad Schools, I would choose to attend Indiana University, even though I was soon discouraged by several of my Villanova colleagues. "Indiana? What is (it in) Indiana?"

Other than Kinsey, the IU little 500, James Counsilman and Bobby Knight, my only other references about Bloomington and Indiana University were through *Breaking Away*, a movie which I had seen, I remember now, in a double feature at the *España* cinema in Marqués de Vadillo, a few years before my arrival to America. It was about this crazy guy, Dave, who pretended to be Italian, a kind of *Quixotic* character. The film included a mythical scene where Dave's father, while claiming to eat "true American food," a "hamburger" and some "French fries," complained about his son's obsession with Italian cuisine. A Bud Spencer-Terence Hill kind of brawl, an exciting race against the national Italian cycling team, high jumping at the quarry lake, academic love . . . this place seemed fun! Why not? Then, I discovered that, on the one hand, Indiana was one of the few universities combining two very strong programs in Spanish and Comparative Literature. Ed was Professor in both Departments. Luis Beltrán was a Medievalist, but also a football, Real Madrid supported. As Head of School of the Department of Spanish and Portuguese, he claimed to have attracted the two best "academic players" in the Latin American and Iberian Studies league at the time, Ed Friedman and Gordon Brotherston. I felt then and I can confirm it now, that I was studying Golden Age Spain during IU's own Golden Age period! How self-reflective and Cervantine!

I had no further doubts. In fact, Ed being one of the best Cervantes scholars and my passion for Golden Age Theater, was a perfect match as well. Then, fitting in at Indiana was easy, Ed's true passion for Madrid and Spain, his captivating and encouraging personality, his vast literary knowledge, his passion for literature, his creative writing interest, his editorial talent shown at his work at the *IJHS* and *Cervantes* . . .

Ed, together with Gordon Brotherston, Catherine Larson and Willis Barnstone composed my dissertation committee. I was able to become friends with Juan L. Alborg during that period too. Can you imagine any better place to study literature than Indiana? I heard so many anecdotes and experiences about Picasso, Julian Marías, Carmen Laforet, Borges, Mao Zedong, Allen Ginsberg, Ana María Matute, Gustavo Sainz, Carlos Fuentes, Rafael Sánchez Ferlosio, just to name some. Literature became real for the first time in my life. So fascinating fellow graduate students, with some of whom I keep several life-long friendships. My wife Alicia, Juan Manuel, Adrian, Martha, Melissa, Carlos, Eric, "el otro Vicente", Miguel, Julia, Mindy . . . so many great memories.

Thanks to Ed's tireless support, I was able to complete my PhD and dissertation on Cervantes' *entremeses* in just four years. He was always present. He was early at his office at the end of the corridor in Ballantine Hall every morning, and he was often the last person leaving the building. His generosity was and continues to be mythical. I remember the many instances when he tirelessly supported me in preparing my conference papers, my first MLA interview, when he and Susan were patiently listening to my lecturing about

Calderón's *entremeses*... I am sure that all colleagues collaborating in this volume have tens of similar anecdotes and life lessons.

I had so many opportunities to progress in the profession with Ed: presenting my early essays at panels, put together by him at the Purdue RL conference, meeting unique scholars such as Ganelin, Mancing, Hart, and other early career colleagues such as Oropesa, the Castillo brothers, Moisés and David, together with Nelson and Egginton from Minnesota. Superb Cervantes and Comparative Literature classes by Ed included that unforgettable one on Zayas' and Cervantes' *novelas*. My best class ever. His support and clarity for our understanding of so many head-aching literary theories in that period was invaluable. I cannot imagine my academic career without my years at Indiana. I would be somewhere else, very far from Ed's superb values and inspirational exemplary actions. I like it here and now, very much. Thanks again Ed.

Ed is not only a model as a scholar and teacher. He is a true academic gentleman. When in difficult life situations, I often ask myself: what would Ed do now? The preferred option is always the most moderate, empathizing one. Ed is a unique, harmonizing, academic light. Easy-going, but much disciplined and seriously respectful of each of our individual free will.

Cervantes was illuminating about the fact that mortality is relative to memory. We, as humans, are barely nothing more than meaning, with the added responsibility of making sense of it. Ed means sharing, encouragement, support, appreciation, high excellence standards, and patient understanding... always living and celebrating academic life. Working hard without noticing it. Such as when I instantly felt transformed into one of Tom Sawyer's curious friends while at Bloomington. I was so naturally persuaded about trading my best years for painting that intriguing academic fence! I feel grateful to belong to one of the most solid and long-standing traditions ever. I am so privileged to be part of Ed's legacy, together with my twenty-four colleagues plus collaborating in this volume in his honour!

Harriet, thanks for your best advice ever, which informed my confused free will, when I mostly needed it. *Ya lo sé.*

Gaudeamus igitur, Ed! Here's to your *Cosmic Wit*!

Back in 2000 and Beyond
Martha García

Since I was a child my family taught us the value of education over any other tangible good. Being raised in a home that respects and supports higher education contributed to my passion to reading and writing. I went to private school and private and public universities. When I received the news that I had been accepted into Vanderbilt University in the year 2000 for my doctorate degree, I certainly did not take it for granted. I was going to have the possibility to study the literature of early modern Spain and Cervantes at my first-choice university. But wait, it gets better.

Not only did I meet an exceptional group of faculty members, caring administrators, welcoming classmates and excellent staff, but my first year at Vanderbilt was also the first year of a new member in the Department of Spanish & Portuguese: Professor Edward H. Friedman (I cannot still call him Ed). Since I took my first course with Prof. Friedman, I knew, I had found a mentor for a lifetime. It is not only how brilliant, talented, and intellectual Prof. Friedman naturally is, it is that we can converse with him about any existing topic in the universe and he will delight us with a well-versed dialogue. As the years go by, Professor Edward Friedman, and his wife and life companion, Prof. Susan Friedman, have been role models within the academia enlightening successfully the path of those who have had the privilege to get to know them.

Since I was introduced to Prof. Friedman, I noticed the genuine joy that he experiences in his dedication to his students and to his research undertakings. Even though, the word *research* may be intimidating for new undergraduate students and even for graduate students, Prof. Friedman presents it to us like part of a life activity and inspires us to lose ourselves into new paths of exploration and surprising findings. Sometimes the exploration would lead us to another territory that we did not have in mind, but that is part of it, and Prof. Friedman allows us to discover, or rediscover, our own thoroughfare.

Reflecting about it, the academia enhances our lives since we can interact and create a *convivium* with individuals that probably we would have never had the opportunity to meet outside of this unique world called university. My years at Vandy made me realize that in the classrooms and in the virtual learning environment, honestly, miracles can happen in front of our eyes. Being Prof. Friedman's graduate student assistant during the NEH Summer Seminar that he directed at Vanderbilt in 2003 made me meditate about the real value of higher education. Ed's (I am trying here to call him Ed!) incredible humility, leadership, and generosity showed me the intrinsic significance of humanity. At the end of the summer seminar, I wished I could be his graduate assistant forever! I could not, he said: "you will graduate successfully with your doctorate degree and you will be a brilliant faculty member and researcher". You can notice here one of many examples of his generosity, kindness, and best wishes for his students!

Prof. Friedman believes in people over any other good because, like Ed and Susan would remind us, we, the people, see how lives can be transformed for good, we, the people, participate in activities that will change the world in all aspects, we, the people, can be part of solutions and contribute to eradicate needs—or at least to alleviate them—and we, the people, found the capacity to become better people. Both of them understand indeed these true values and live up to these noble standards each day.

Ed's (I keep trying here!) career and research is internationally well-known and recognized and it does not need much introduction, so as an anecdote, from many that his students may remember as well, I will share this vivid fond memory at Vandy. I led an interdisciplinary workshop and gave a presentation aimed to graduate students as part of the Center for Teaching at Vanderbilt in the spring of 2003. It turns out that on the weekend of the workshop, we enjoyed an unprecedented snowfall that practically neutralized the city. Vanderbilt never closes and this was not going to be the exception, so I had to be at the forefront of the event that Saturday in the early hours of this very, very, very, cold morning. José Antonio, my husband, my tireless and admirable knight, took me on-campus on a journey that lasted almost two hours due to the accumulated snow (allow me to explain here that our home base is in Florida, consequently, for us the word 'snow' is not part of our daily linguistic inventory!). We thought that we wouldn't have many participants under those circumstances. We were pleasantly surprised. Graduate students were enthusiastically waiting on the front line to participate all together in this event. Professor Friedman was the first to come to my presentation on that cold and snowy Saturday. That day I learned a life lesson that reconfirmed why I had chosen this profession.

When I have the opportunity to visit Vanderbilt University after my graduation (like the grownup that anticipates with joy visiting home), I always feel like a part of me never left it. A part of me is still there (metaphorically speaking of course!). I remember with gratitude my hours at the Jean and Alexander Heard Libraries with archives and books (yes, tons of books!) and their patient librarians. I feel so fortunate for the precious years in the Department of Spanish & Portuguese in Furman Hall, the majestic medieval castle building in the middle of campus, with the remarkable people that I had the honor to get to know well. There, miracles happen every academic semester. Being a Vanderbilt alumna has been, without any doubt, a lifetime opportunity that I treasure immensely. All of the faculty members during my graduate studies at Vandy are irreplaceable in my academic preparation and each of them has been important part in shaping my whole persona.

Our cherished Professor Friedman deserves this recognition because of his teaching example, inside and outside of the classroom, his pedagogical gift of counseling and advising, his tireless dedication, and his care in directing and mentoring represent a vivid example of the essence of the chosen profession. I have a lot more to say, but we do not have the space on these pages. We are infinitely grateful that Professor Edward H. Friedman has listened to his calling in life and followed his indispensable mission in the academia. And I am extremely grateful that Ed (do not get used to it is just for this introduction!) had accepted coming to Vanderbilt University, not only for my own good, but for the unlimited benefit of all the students that would validate this truth and for each of the students that one day will have the unique opportunity of calling themselves a *student* of Prof. Edward H. Friedman.

Gratias tibi ago pro omnem hoc homenage Cosmic Wit!

A Comedy of Editors 1999-2017
G. Cory Duclos

MY FIRST INTERACTION WITH Ed Friedman was a nervous and excited phone call I took in a small apartment in Reno, NV. In that conversation, I learned from him that I was on a waitlist for acceptance to the doctoral program in Spanish at Vanderbilt University. As a first-generation college student, I realize now that I had somewhat haphazardly stumbled my way into an M.A. program at the University of Nevada, Reno with the hope of going on to receive a Ph.D. I owe a debt of gratitude to my former professors Judith Whitenack and Darrel Lockhart for, among other things, making it clear that Ed would make a wonderful graduate advisor. Despite their assurance, and after my formal acceptance came through, I was nervous to take the leap in to a Ph.D. program with a cohort of fellow students with much more prestigious academic backgrounds than mine.

My insecurity manifested itself in trying to be what I imagined was the ideal academic: serious, disciplined, and above all critical. During that first semester, I scoured the assigned articles, at times struggling to grasp meaning, but always, as I believed was my duty, to find flaws in arguments and ways to refute the authors. I was eager to show my knowledge and prove that I belonged at Vanderbilt. Ed was offering his *Don Quijote* course that semester, and I felt confident, having taken undergraduate and MA level courses on the novel, that it was my best opportunity to shine. During one class session, we were discussing an article "de cuyo nombre no quiero acordarme," and I offered a rather critical take on its premise. Without dismissing my comments, Ed gracefully pointed out some of the salient points from the article that I had missed in my critique. I realized that I was in a rush to be a cynical scholar, while Ed had gotten where he was by always trying to find the best in others' scholarship.

I have seen this same attitude time and again with Ed over the years. He can find the merit in any academic contribution, whether it be an undergraduate's comment in class, a graduate student's seminar paper, or an academic manuscript. Ed's desire to lift others up and help support their scholarship was always apparent in his work as editor of *The Bulletin of the Comediantes*. Ed served as the editor from 1999-2017. As a graduate student, I helped proofread manuscripts for the journal, and during his last years there, I filled in as the interim Managing Editor, giving me further insight into Ed's editorial approach. During his tenure, Ed made a concerted effort to encourage new scholars to publish in the journal. He took time to personally help younger scholars improve their articles for publication and navigate the publishing process. He was able to appreciate new and different critical approximations, even if they differed from his own. And he used his position as a tool to help me and other graduate students gain insights into the inner workings of an academic journal.

Ed has never pretended to be an expert in technology, but perhaps one of the most impressive aspects of his editorial career is his seemingly effortless ability to manage emails. While many journals, for good reason, pay for expensive proprietary software to manage the tangle of article submissions and peer review responses, Ed was able to do it all from his own email account. Despite what I imagine is an overwhelming amount of electronic correspondence he must receive, anyone who has ever communicated with Ed knows that he responds to emails with an uncanny speed. I once asked him how he was able to respond so quickly. He said that his computer chimes every time he gets a new email, and that when it does, he reads the email and responds (such a simple solution that evades so many of us!). But I imagine there is another explanation Ed left out. I think that Ed's emailing abilities come from his natural respect for other people, their time, and their goals. He is generous with his time, because he values what everyone else can do with theirs.

Another thing that makes it such a joy to work with Ed as a professor, an editor, or a friend, is his keen sense of humor. His creative writing projects play off Golden Age humor in truly delightful ways. His quick and cosmic wit often leaves me in stitches. In one instance I can recall, during an event focused on Golden Age literature in Vanderbilt's Warren Center, I was choosing from a selection of lunch options and quipped, "I'll take the bacon sandwich so that you all know I'm a *cristiano viejo*." Ed, without hesitation, responded, "And I'll take the same to make you all *think* that I am." Ed's humor and joviality are woven into all that he does. These traits are emblematic of the man who understands the need to temper the drive for professional achievement with human connection. The academic life can often be mentally isolating, with our best work confined to the pages of scholarship. But Ed is a person who shows that reaching out with compassion to others always has value. Or as he said once, and I paraphrase, so many people in academia can do the hard things but forget to do the easy things, like being courteous and kind.

Ed used his time as Editor of *Bulletin of the Comediantes* to lift up other scholars and help promote their work. His unpaid service in this area was fueled as much by his academic interests as by his desire to assist others in furthering their own research and contributing to a collective advancement of the field. The quality, depth, and breadth of work produced in the pages of the journal during Ed's tenure attest to its incomparable value for current and future generations of scholars.

Resúmenes de los artículos

In "Too Near the Bone: Translation, *Los melindres de Belisa* and the Problem of Proximity" **Mindy E. Badía** argues that the way we translate metaphors in early modern Spanish drama influences audiences/readers' understanding of *comedias*. Using a Translation Studies perspective, Badía acknowledges the complex process of translating metaphors: "On the one hand, metaphor identifies a thing by something other than what it is, an instance of dissociation; on the other, it does so in a way that brings us closer to understanding the nature of that thing." Badía's own experience translating *Los melindres de Belisa* illustrates her support of an approach which sacrifices the synchronic meaning of the original play's metaphors by focusing instead on establishing a closer proximity to contemporary readers' understanding of the *comedia*'s allegories.

"*Quijotes transatlánticos* and Golden-Age Latin Americanism" by **Robert Bayliss** is a panoramic study of contemporary reception and impact of the *Quijote* in Latin American cultural production. The essay shows how "'Quijotes transatlánticos' have (and more recently, how they have *not*) been studied by Hispanists throughout the Americas." Although the *Quijote* has been traditionally very popular among Latin American authors, "recent scholarship dedicated to the *Quijote*'s broader cultural ubiquity in Latin America has been comparatively scarce." Using the case study of Mexico, including the Guanajuato drama festival and the political use of the myth of Don Quijote by both EZLN leaders and current president of Mexico López Obrador, Bayliss demonstrates that the appropriation of Cervantes's most famous knight continues being polemically latent in Latin America cultural reality today.

The historical and literary precedents that inform matrimonial relations are studied in **Kathleen Costales**'s "Terceras and Pandering Wives in Tirso's *El pretendiente al revés.*" Her analysis shows that the practice of alachuetería was common in both Spanish literature and society of the medieval and early modern periods. *El pretendiente al revés* challenges this tradition, adding to it the complication of beginning the play with the main romantic interests already wedded, thus foregoing the possibility that a final nuptial ceremony might resolve the conflict. This backward order is reinforced through the addition of the figure of the wife as procurer, something Costales demonstrates is Lope's innovative contribution to the literary tradition.

In "Well-Behaved Panzas Rarely Make History: Teresa Panza and the Metafiction of *Don Quijote*," **Cory Duclos** analyzes the various female characterizations within *Don Quijote*, exploring and dedicating more attention to the character of Teresa Panza, Sancho's loyal wife, who Cervantes baptizes with several names throughout the entire novel. This study emphasizes that the nexus of this female character with Spain's countryside reveals the need to embrace fantasy and realism in the first modern novel. Duclos acknowledges that to fully understand the interface between historical context, cultural influence, and the emergence of modernity, it would be necessary to approach the presence of the Cervantine characters that are *not* considered protagonists from a new lens of scrutiny.

"Miguel Manipulated: Puppet Play, Self-Referentiality, and Social Critique in Two Plays Inspired by *Don Quixote*" by **Timothy Foster** explores the different artistic manifestations of key characters in several Iberoamerican recreations of Cervantes's text in the form of visual art, classical music, film, and literature. This essay particularly concentrates on the *Vida do grande d. Quixote de la Mancha e do gordo Sancho Pança* (1733) by Brazilian/Portuguese playwright António José da Silva and *El retablo de Maese Pedro* (1923) by Spanish composer Manuel del Falla. Foster's meticulous appraisal of self-accountability provides contemporary readers a better understanding of the art that resides in the metafiction and density of Cervantine narrative. The author highlights the transferability from narrative and prose to a realm of artistic productions without overlooking the essence of the original work within the practice of constructing textuality.

"*La desordenada codicia de los bienes agenos*: El doctor Carlos García ante la tradición picaresca aurisecular" by **Antón García-Fernández** explores the life and works of Carlos García, a Spanish Golden Age author who lived in Paris for most of his life, where he published two early seventeenth-century texts: *Oposición y conjunción de los dos grandes luminares de la Tierra* (1617) and *La desordenada codicia de los bienes agenos* (1619). García Fernández argues that, although *La desordenada codicia* is written with a picaresque tone, it was influenced by *rogue pamphlets* of authors such as Walker, Thomas Harman, and Robert Greene, and by related French texts such as *Vie généreuse* *des mercelots* as well. The author demonstrates that Carlos García himself might have been incarcerated and thus would have had firsthand experience on several autobiographic events described in his own narrative.

"Atenea y Minerva en la temprana edad moderna: Teresa Sánchez de Cepeda & María Isidra de Guzmán" by **Martha García** focuses on the cultural outreach of two classic myths, Athena and Minerva, allegorically associated with knowledge, wisdom, civilization and scientific discovery. The author explores the presence of some of these mythological features in the lives of two Spanish female intellectuals: mystic sixteenth-century author Teresa Sánchez de Cepeda y Ahumada (1515-1582) and eighteenth-century scholar and academic María Isidra Quintina de Guzmán y de la Cerda (1767-1803). García defends that whereas Santa Teresa personifies Athena's religious devotion, María Isidra represents Minerva's search for knowledge, even though, as the author probes, unfortunately these female authors may not have counted with the same realm of opportunities as their male counterparts in order to fulfill their respective spiritual and intellectual aspirations.

Jeanne Gillespie's article, "Anacaona and the areito: A Generative Model for Pro-Indigenous Discourse in Lope de Vega's *El Nuevo mundo descubierto por Cristobal Colón*," analyzes Lope's representation of Amerindian women's role in the Spanish colonial enterprise. She argues that the figure of Anacaona (and not Malíntzin) is a more apt historical analogue to the characters Lope creates in his representations. The play's use of the areito shows Lope's familiarity with the chronicles of the conquest along with his willingness to forgo historical accuracy to create a dramatic text that inscribes within it theatrical tropes in the context of a cross-cultural encounter.

Anna-Lisa Halling in "*El gran prodigio de España*: Joanna Theodora de Souza's Performative Convent *Comedia*" explores the reception of this, potentially, *intramuros* piece. Halling defends its dual categorization. Existing between a *comedia de santos* and a *comedia de capa y espada*, this play is considered within the structure of conventions that resonates with the secular on-stage performance. This diversity of theatrical practice is examined through the light of extant sources found in convents from Portugal, Spain, and Latin America. This essay argues that the relevance that Dona Joanna's *El gran prodigio de España, y lealtad de un amigo*, deserves consideration within the key canonic scholarly creative works by women writers of the period.

"De Lisbeth Salander a la Ertzaintza: Fantasías neoliberales en la serie procedimental de Eva García Sáenz de Urturi" by **Salvador Oropesa** evidences how neoliberal ideology is present in the *noir* narrative trilogy by Eva García Sáenz de Urturi, *La Ciudad Blanca* (the eponym of Vitoria-Gasteiz, the capital of the Basque Country). The main characters of *El silencio de la ciudad* blanca (2016), *Los ritos del agua* (2017), and *los señores del tiempo* (2018) include investigators Unai López de Ayala, alias Kraken; Alba Díaz de Salvatierra; and Estíbaliz Ruiz de Gauna. Serial killings investigated are related to city monuments in the first volume of the trilogy and to Celtic mythology in the second part. Finally, neo-medievalism serves as the source of inspiration for the serial criminal in the last volume of the series. Influenced by Steig Larsson's deconstructive noir approach, *La Ciudad Blanca* trilogy shares his same de-structuring social context, which Oropesa contests is ideologically neoliberal and is evidenced by, among other exclusive sophistications, the Michelin-star restaurants and the display of exotic vacations enjoyed by the main characters.

"Juanita Versus Cecilia: Competing Allegories of Cuba by Mary Peabody Mann and Cirilo Villaverde" by **Julia C. Paulk** explores the polemic topic of slavery life in plantations, taking into account opposite perspectives from the North and South of the United States. Two novels by the mentioned authors are approached within the context of the European reformation and counterreformation movements. Paulk questions the historical prevalence of slavery in the United States and the Americas, providing a new approximation to the complexity of slavery between Cuba and the United States. Even though they are very close geographically, they seem to be very far apart in the arena of international and diplomatic relations.

In "*La superficie cóncava del primer cielo.* Sobre la liminalidad de los periplos angulares al Lago Español de Álvaro Mendaña, Isabel de Barreto y el don Quijote portugués, Pedro Fernández de Quirós," **Vicente Pérez de León** explores how the undefined distance between earth and sky awakened the fantasy about mystical phenomenology of the first Spanish travelers to Oceania, over-feeding their imagination when describing this unusual phenomenon. Informed by Gustavo Bueno's philosophy, Pérez de León considers the three journeys to the Pacific led by travelers such as Álvaro de Mendaña, Isabel de Barreto, and Fernández de Quirós during late sixteenth century and the threshold of the seventeenth century as *periplos angulares*. The conclusion validates the honest and legitimate actions by Fernández de Quirós, recognizing him as one of the most ethical Catholic humanists in his Quixotic existential aim of returning to Oceania to continue supporting and integrating Spanish and South Pacific indigenous societies.

"'Melancólico espejo': From Garcilaso's 'Églogas' to Luis Cernuda's *Égloga, elegía, oda*" by **David F. Richter** reflects on the heritage of the literary production from early modern Spain and later poetry from the Iberian

Peninsula. This study takes into account a poetic trajectory coming from the Renaissance period into the Avant-garde movements. It concentrates on Cernuda's "Égloga" in reminiscence of Garcilaso's second "Égloga." It reveals the implicit value perceived by the early modern heritage. The essay acknowledges the innovation in the creation of new poetic structures and utterance style that takes place in Avant-garde movements. In addition, Richter invites readers to reconsider the measure of melancholy in the artistic construction of the *self* and its respective context that constantly influences the existent distance that interplays between truth and aspiration.

In "Returning Home in Juan Ruiz de Alarcón's Plays," **Gladys Robalino** uses a new approach to study the figure of the indiano. Using the notion of "root migration," in which the children of immigrants return to the home of their parents, she explores the difficulties facing five of Ruiz de Alarcón's characters who attempt to return to Spain after living in the Americas. Despite the initial joy these characters feel upon returning, they ultimately find home to be a dangerous place. Feelings of doubt and suspicion coupled with economic insecurities intensify the social isolation felt when trying to adapt to life in the Spanish court. These characters represent the estrangement felt by those considered forasteros by the Spanish natives and the difficult, if not impossible, task they face at reintegration.

"El poder de las palabras: la percepción de los *conversos* en la literatura del Siglo de Oro" by **Tugba Sevin** explores the presence of the *converso* archetype in two Spanish Golden Age texts: *Las paces de los Reyes y judía de Toledo*, an early modern *comedia* written by Lope de Vega in 1610-1612 and *El diablo cojuelo* (1641) by Luis Vélez de Guevara. Sevin defends that whereas *conversos* are not positively portrayed in Lope de Vega's historical *comedia*, *El diablo cojuelo* shows a much different approach to these key Spanish Golden Age archetypes. In fact, Vélez de Guevara's only narrative work makes an effort in presenting the complexity of integrating *conversos* into his contemporary society in a much more realistic way.

In "Family Functions and Dysfunctions: Secrecy in *La vida es sueño*," **Gwen H. Stickney** approaches the complexity of the dynamics of family's inter-relations (nuclear) and extra-relations (extended) in Calderon's most famous play. Contemporary theories, used in modern counseling, are effectively used to identify how interpersonal relations in the structure of this *comedia* are directly associated with the preparation and formation that Segismundo receives from his immediate and extended relatives. The way these interrelations affect the potential leadership expected from the protagonist, which is greatly needed for his country, are explored as well. Finally, Stickney defends that both in Segismundo's and Rosaura's characterizations, the promise of a better future should be aligned towards new life structures and more stable functionality in order to overcome the danger of emulating the previous patterns observed in their respective family configurations.

Fractured and invented identities provide a frame of reference for **Robert Turner** in "Copying the Unreal: The Multiple Imitations in the Balcony Scene of *Don Gil de las calzas verdes*." As the author notes, although the play begins in a typical fashion, it is soon complicated, first by placing Don Martín's father as the cause for the broken marriage promise and the creator of the imagined Don Gil, leaving the typical *galán* figure as nothing more than a passive recipient of the other characters' actions. Turner focuses on the splits of selves within Doña Juana herself, including the written text, the historical actor playing the role, the character Doña Juana, Don Gil, and Elvira. This proliferation of identities continues, spreading to further imitations, each subsequently more abstract in form, dramatizing the difficulties inherent in defining a true identity.

"La comunidad morisca del siglo dieciséis se enfrenta a los horrores de la tumba" by **Miguel Ángel Vázquez** includes both an essay and an edition of a "literatura aljamiada" text called a "carta morisca para el muerto" or "*morisco* letter for the deceased ones." The *aljamiado* corpus, although written originally in Spanish, was transliterated in Arabic characters during the Spanish Golden Age period. This cultural production supposedly lasted until most *moriscos* were abruptly expelled from Spain in 1609. But many of these texts secretly survived afterwards, as the deposit containing manuscripts found in 1884 in Almonacid de la Sierra proves. The "cartas moriscas para el muerto" are religious advises placed in *moriscos*' coffins before they were buried. Their purpose was for friends and relatives to provide support to their deceased ones in their process of coming face-to-face with angels during their translife experience. The author defends the importance of these extant texts as unique sources of pre-modern Spanish *morisco* communities' beliefs and religious practices.

In "Poéticas profanas de lo sagrado. Intersecciones culturales en torno a la construcción del predicador barroco. Dos propuestas teóricas," **Juan Vitulli** defends the importance of the academic discipline of Catholic Preaching in Spanish Baroque culture, not only as a scholarly field, but also related to the value of its potential use in the classroom. Vitulli's approaches to study catholic preaching include material culture, with a focus on exploring efficiency in predication and liturgy. At the same time, the author defends the use of sonic studies in support of a better understanding on how acoustic impact is key in deciphering the extant self-conscious preachers' practices of testimonials and sermons.

Jonathan Wade brings to light the often-ignored Spanish literature coming from Portugal's Dual Monarchy period in "Tilting at Relevance: The Quixotic Enterprise of Portuguese Authors of the Iberian Union." Wade employs Cervantes's fictional tale as a frame for understanding the lives of these writers within Portuguese literature. Just as the Manchegan knight seeks out new armor in which to attire himself, these Portuguese authors used the Spanish language to position themselves both politically and culturally. More importantly, in a similar fashion to Don Quijote's adoration of Dulcinea and imitation of Amadís de Gaula, literary works of the period show a tendency to idealize Portugal and hold Camões as a literary paragon to be emulated.

The complicated task of translating the humor of *Don Quijote* into other languages is explored in **Steve Wenz's** "The Importance of Humor in Recent Translations of *Don Quijote*." Wenz's discussion of translation theory helps frame an understanding of the issues translators must consider when approaching a text as complex as *Don Quijote*. The key types of humor that are particularly salient to the discussion are emphasized through studying the reviews of eight translations, two in each of four languages: English, Portuguese, French, and Italian. This evaluation shows word choice, rhetoric, diction, and readability are a chief concern among reviewers in popular publications, while they dismiss the impact of the novel's humor on a modern audience. The article shows how translators of *Don Quijote* must be close readers of the humor in order to understand it and bring it forth in a new linguistic register and a more modern historical context.

Habib Zanzana adds a new dimension to the understanding of the disembodied Dulcinea's importance within the narrative structure of *Don Quijote* in his article "Don Quijote and the Construction of Dulcinea". The work explores the interplay between the chivalric code and the gendered creation of Dulcinea, noting that naming his lady allows Don Quijote to create a new idealized and fictional feminine figure separated from the embodied Aldonza Lorenzo. Don Quijote's thoughts and actions regarding Dulcinea reveal his inner motivations and how the protagonist inscribes the ideals of chivalry onto his imagined quest. The resulting conflicts with those who refuse to participate in this ideal motivate and propel the novel's plot while the idea of Dulcinea ties together the various narratives and levels of fictional reality within *Don Quijote*.

Too Near the Bone: Translation, *Los melindres de Belisa* and the Problem of Proximity
Mindy E. Badía
Indiana University Southeast

THE ACT OF TRANSLATION is often characterized by metaphors that evoke distance, that is, as an effort to bring a text closer to its intended audience. As an ambivalent device that expresses conceptual complexity, metaphor itself engages the interplay of separation and approximation fundamental to translation. On the one hand, metaphor identifies a thing by something other than what it is, an instance of dissociation; on the other, it does so in a way that brings us closer to understanding the nature of that thing. In the specific case of early modern Spanish drama, scholars and translators typically comment on the degree to which today's audiences are chronologically, linguistically and culturally removed from those of seventeenth-century Spain, and within this framework the translator's job becomes one of reducing distance or, as Michael McGaha puts it, of functioning as a bridge (86). Although the perceived remoteness of the *Comedia* certainly does pose challenges to its meaningful reception by contemporary spectators and readers, and anticipating and understanding these challenges is an important step in producing a successful English rendering of a *Siglo de Oro* play, I would like to propose that we view the translation of early modern playtexts from an opposing angle. Using my own experience translating Lope de Vega's *Los melindres de Belisa*, I consider the matter of a text's cultural translatability, arguing that, with respect to distance and proximity, and in certain instances, proximity may pose the greater challenge.

In one form or another, the matter of propinquity informs most academic discourse about translation. Scholars agree that Translation Studies emerged as a distinct field in the 1970s with the publication of James Holmes's seminal article "The Name and Nature of Translation Studies"

(Venuti 124). Holmes's paper responds, in part, to disagreements about the degree to which translation scholarship ought to maintain critical distance. He proposes the formation of a distinct discipline that would span the chasm between linguistic approaches to translation, which treat translation as a scientifically objective undertaking, to literary ones, which acknowledge the subjective nature of translation as an aesthetic activity. With respect to the first approach, Mostafa El Dali writes:

> Translation was initially studied as a linguistic phenomenon, as a process of meaning transfer via linguistic transcoding, and consequently, translation studies was conceived as a linguistic discipline. Attempts were made to develop a 'science of translation' (e.g. Nida 1964), or a linguistic theory of translation (Catford 1965) whose aim was to give a precise description of the equivalence relation between signs and combinations of signs in the source language (SL) and the target language. (TL) (32)

During the nineteenth-century, there emerged

> two conflicting tendencies: the first considered translation as a category of thought and saw the translator as a creative genius, who enriches the literature and the language into which he is translating, while the second saw him through the mechanical function of making a text or author known. (El Dali 31)

Lawrence Venuti describes the state of translation theory upon the publication of Holmes's defining article as a

> heterogeneous field throughout this period. It encompasses both linguists like Catford... and the eclectic Levy, who synthesizes psycho-linguistics, semantics, structural anthropology, literary criticism, and game theory. George Steiner's magisterial 1975 study *After Babel*... opposes modern linguistics with a literary and philosophical approach.... (124)

Whether mechanical or muse-inspired, these approaches all share a belief, at least implicitly, that good translating brings a text closer to non-readers of the original language and, consequently, that the primary challenge of translating is overcoming distance.

The expected nearness of a translation to its source, its equivalence (or fidelity, for the romantics among us), remained relatively unchallenged until the 1980s, when critics began to prioritize a translation's purpose over its proximity to an idealized original. In the last two decades of the twentieth century, Translation Studies experienced a "cultural turn" approximating other emerging academic fields such as gender, cultural, and postcolonial studies. Consistent with this paradigm, critics such as Susan Bassnett and André Lefevere explore directly the relationships between language and culture brought to the fore through the process of translation, addressing explicitly the ways in which the subjectivity of the translator engages power relationships. In the preface to their book they write, "Through the concepts of rewriting and manipulation, this series aims to tackle the problem of ideology, change, and power in literature and society and to assert the central function of translation as a shaping force" (Bassnett and Lefevere viii).

This notion of translation as a subjective process is manifested in much of the scholarship focused on creating English renderings of early modern Spanish drama, in which the overwhelming tendency has been to conceptualize translation as an endeavor bound intimately to the experiences of the individual. In fact, many published essays about the process of translating the *Comedia* exhibit an openly introspective, even mystical tone illustrative of this persistent inward turn. Catherine Larson writes of the frequent use of the first person in scholarly accounts of Golden Age drama translation and ends her critical discussion of the process of crafting *Friendship Betrayed* (*La traición en la amistad*) with a reference to a popular hymn, an intertextual maneuver that emphasizes the ways that translation, always a process of change, transforms its agent, "I once was lost, but now I'm found" (93-93). Both David Gitlitz and Dakin Matthews begin their analyses of creating English versions of *Siglo de Oro* plays with a confession; Gitlitz openly admits that he is "adicto a la traducción de comedias," (45) and Matthews, a bit more subtly, writes, "There are a number of things about which I can claim to be moderately knowledgeable; unfortunately, Spanish Language and Literature are not two of them" (37). Similarly, David Johnston likens the *Comedia* translator to a "shaman" (70) capable of "reviving dead authors temporarily" (70). He argues that, in tandem with this fleeting resurrection of an author from the past, "translators must necessarily incorporate a heightened and explicit sense of their own situatedness in the present into their working practice" and "cannot simply decontextualize themselves" (70). In these examples, an acute self-awareness emerges, what Larson describes as an inevitable feeling of alienation ("Translator's Note 28), as scholars examine the intellectual and affective responses stimulated by their interaction with the translated object, a convergence of history and the here and now. This linking of opposites, of self and other; of art and science; of mind and heart; and of past and present, illustrates once again the notion of reducing distance as translation's primary mediating function.

Los melindres de Belisa offers examples of a similar melding of opposing elements whereby meta-dramatic excess and representation of another casts light on the self. Written just before the 1609 expulsion of the Moriscos, the drama, like the typical *comedia de enredo,* satirizes the urban, aristocratic milieu of contemporary Madrid, confronting spectators with a representation of marginalized characters, in this instance, two Morisco slaves, that is, from the outset, an established fiction. Lope's eponymous protagonist has earned a reputation for her eccentricities, among them her capricious rejection of any man who seeks her hand in marriage. Eliso, one of Belisa's here-to-fore unlucky suitors, has borrowed money from her mother, the recently widowed Lisarda. Unable to return the money, Eliso pays his debt with two Morisco slaves, Pedro and Zara. Unbeknownst to the family, Pedro and Zara are actually Felisardo and Celia, noble characters who have disguised themselves as slaves to escape arrest for a prior act of aggression committed by Felisardo. The complications mount when both Belisa and Lisarda fall in love with Pedro, and Belisa's brother, Juan, falls in love with Zara, and it is only due to the repeated interventions of Tiberio, Belisa's uncle, that dramatic and social order are restored.

As a student, teacher, and, more recently, a would-be translator of this *comedia*, I have grappled with the text's heavy reliance on wordplay and have found the experience both delightful and infuriating. The play's very title alerts the translator to the sort of linguistic battle he or she should be prepared wage. *Melindres* can refer to a sweet treat or a personality flaw, an ambivalence that parallels audiences' experiences as they partake of the character's delicious wit but also her whimsical wielding of power, even to the point of aggression. Belisa is at her best when avoiding marriage and at her worst when seeking it with the reluctant Felisardo or, as she knows him, the Morisco slave Pedro. She defends as her right the choice not to wed and, in the case of her infatuation with Pedro, to wed whomever she chooses. Through verbal virtuosity, Belisa turns her family's constant questioning about her refusal to marry on its ear, begging the implicit question: why would *any* reasonable woman want to choose one of these gold-digging suitors as a mate? However, when she falls in love with Pedro and he refuses her advances, Belisa resorts to lies and violence. She falsely accuses Zara of stealing jewelry, demands that both Zara and Pedro be branded on the face, orders that the object of her affection wear shackles around his neck, and commands that Zara be basted in a hot liquid. The way Belisa uses language often seems strange and out-of-place, in dire need of translation even for other characters and within the context of the play. An effective English rendering of her dialogue ought to be nonsensical, but meaningfully so; it must communicate her *melindres* and her progressive descent into violence and make her engaging nonetheless, and the difficulty balancing these competing demands could well account for the fact that, to my knowledge, no published English translation of this *comedia* exists.

Among the gallants who come courting, most of whom we only experience through Belisa's hyperbole, figure: a man with enormous feet, a bald man, a man with excessive facial hair and a very old man. To illustrate the complexities of translating this play, I offer four examples of Belisa's descriptions of her suitors, along with drafts of my translations of three of these passages in the endnotes. First, the bald man, about whom Belisa complains:

BELISA: Un letrado me traían calvo.
TIBERIO: ¿Qué importa la calva?
BELISA: Cuando yo fuera mujer
espiritual y santa,
y para vencer la carne
—gran enemigo del alma—
quisiera una calavera
tener de noche en la cama,
lindamente me venía
un hombre al lado con calva.
LISARDA: Era muy rico.
BELISA: Ya quise
asir la ocasión; estaba
sin copete por la frente
y volvióme las espaldas.[1] (vv. 201-14)

---

[1] BEL: They brought me a lawyer who was a bald.
TIB: What does being bald matter?
BEL: Imagine me, a spiritual, saintly girl. Now, in order to triumph over the flesh
—that great enemy of the soul—suppose I decided to take a skull to bed with me.
How could I lie with a skinless head bone and a hairless bonehead?
LIS: Well, he was very rich.
BEL: I tried to seize opportunity by the hair, but since he didn't have any...

The man with big feet does not fare much better:

> LISARDA: ¿Y aquel caballero rico
> de aquel lugar de la Mancha?
> BELISA: Tenía los pies grandes.
> LISARDA: ¿Esa es falta de importancia?
> BELISA: No, madre, que sobra era,
> y temí que, si se enojaba,
> que era sepultarme en losa
> y cubrirme de una patada.[2] (vv. 237-44)

Nor does the dashing young knight of the Order of Santiago:

> LISARDA: Pues, dime. ¿En qué hallaste falta
> en don Luis, mozo y galán,
> cuyos pechos esmaltaba un lagarto de Santiago?
> BELISA: ¡Calla, madre, que me espantas!
> ¿No dicen que las mujeres,
> a sus maridos abrazan?
> Con un lagarto en el pecho,
> En mi vida le abrazara.
> TIBERIO: Sobrina, llámase así
> aquella cruz colorada
> que es espada y no es lagarto.
> BELISA: Bastaba la semejanza
> para matarme de miedo.[3] (vv. 252-66)

---

2   LIS.: And that rich gentleman from La Mancha
    BEL.: He had big feet.
    LIS.: And that shortcoming was important?
    BEL.: *Shortcoming*? Oh no, they were terribly long. Why, I was afraid that, if he ever got mad and stomped his foot, I'd end up six feet under with a size 12 boot for a tombstone.

3   LIS.: And what was wrong with don Luis? Young, dashing, his noble breast adorned with the blood-red sword of Santiago...
    BEL.: Shush, mother, you're scaring me! Aren't wives supposed to embrace their husbands? Coming at me sword-first... I wouldn't go near him, much less hug him.
    TIB.: Niece, the sword it just an emblem. It means that he's a knight in the Order of Santiago.

Perhaps the most difficult passage for this translator is Belisa's depiction of a one-eyed (though high-ranking) soldier described in the following exchange between Belisa and her mother:

LISARDA: ¿Por qué dejaste al maestre
             de campo?
BELISA: ¿No es casi nada
             faltar un ojo?
LISARDA: ¿Qué importa?,
             pues se le pone de plata.
BELISA: Yo te diré la ocasión.
LISARDA: Dila.
BELISA: Si este hombre jurara,
             "como a mis ojos te quiero",
             y le costaba el de plata
             dos reales, en otros tantos
             mi amor y vida estimaba.
             Fuera deso, no podía
             llamarle "mis ojos".
LISARDA: ¡Calla!
BELISA: Pues llamarle yo "mi ojo"
             era ser negra. (vv. 215-29)

This last example, in particular its last two lines, poses significant challenges for the translator, not the least of which is the difficulty that he or she faces with Belisa's mimicry of Black speech. Although this particular retort presents an instance of wordplay for which no easy English equivalent exists, overcoming its linguistic obstacles creates an even stickier wicket. Making audiences laugh, a measure of the translation's success, risks assumed complicity among translator, author, and spectator with respect to the unproblematic interpretation of a racially insensitive joke, a gamble that few contemporary adaptors of the *Comedia* appear willing to take. Indeed, while a fair number of Golden Age plays do feature parodic representations of Africanized Spanish, such texts are not among the most frequently translated or performed, and I would venture that far fewer staged *comedias* depict white characters imitating Black Spanish.[4] *Out of the Wings*, a project on which King's College Lon-

---

    BEL.: The resemblance to the real thing is enough to scare me to death. (She swoons.)
4   I am not familiar with any.

don, Queen's University Belfast and the University of Oxford collaborate in order to "to make the riches of the theatres of Spain and Spanish America accessible to English-speaking researchers and theatre professionals" includes an annotated bibliography of translations that does not list a single Golden Age play depicting Afro-Hispanic speech ("A Contextualized Resource"). John Beusterian envisions his "Talking Black in Spanish: An Unfinished Black Spanish Glossary," as "an aid to theater troupes" (85) wishing to stage *Comedias* that contain examples of Black Spanish. Yet, in spite of Beusterian's note of "a growing interest in Afro-Hispanic Black representations not just among Hispanists in the Academy, but among the community of those interested in presenting classical Hispanic plays," (85) my research found no documented performance or published translation of the texts listed in his glossary. Further, John Lipinski's observations about the function of Black speech in early modern Spanish literature places Beusterian's translations in the midst of a quandary. Lipinski likens the use of Africanized Spanish to the "outlandish costumes and humiliating dances forced upon African actors by the Spanish public, eager to bury its own (Moorish) African roots and laugh heartily at Africans culturally and racially at safe remove from Golden Age society" (10). Though the glossary may well constitute an affirmation of the cultural validity of Africanized Spanish (85-6), as its author asserts, one has to wonder what occurs with such representations of Black speech in performance, when the success of a comic production hinges on its ability to make spectators laugh, perhaps at the expense of Black characters.

Dean Zayas, a professor of drama at the University of Puerto Rico, Río Piedras has directed *Los melindres de Belisa* several times. In response to the question of how to go about rendering Belisa's questionable quip in English, Zayas has stated informally that he would simply remove it and, in fact, did just that in his own 2012 Spanish staging of the play. For Zayas, mimicry of Black speech would stand in the way of a sympathetic response to the character, which would, in turn, jeopardize the success of the translation or restaging. Although this is but one piece of anecdotal evidence, it is a good illustration of Henry Niedzielski's argument that translators of comedy "must consider the culture of the target audience and the acceptability of the original text" ("Cultural Transfers in the Translating of Humor" 141). As an extreme example of where such considerations might lead, he queries, "Should the interpreter transfer a racist joke?" ("Cultural Transfers in the Translating of Humor," 141) Should she, indeed?

Although someday I will be forced to respond to Niedzielski's rhetorical question, an attempt to answer it definitively, or to prove or disprove the validity of Zayas's judgment, misses the point of this essay. Within the context of my argument, the value of these two examples lies in their illustration of how scholars and theater practitioners imagine the relationship between translator and author, and between text and audience, with respect to distance and proximity. In the first instance, Niedzielski posits that the translator and author tread similarly unethical ground in the case of transferring racist humor, and in this respect, their nearness to one another poses a threat to the translator's sense of self as a non-racist individual. In the second, Zayas imagines today's English-speaking audiences as so offended by the stereotypical depiction of Black speech that they would reject outright a character such as Belisa and, by extension, a text in which she figures so prominently (not to mention the creator of said text). In each case, what is really at stake is the self-image of the mediator—the translator, director, or adapter—caught between the exigencies of a source and those of its audience, both of which come into being by means of this very same mediator's conceptualization. In light of this, and given the many other instances of Belisa's speech and behavior that would likely fall outside the bounds of most twenty-first century spectators' horizons of expectations, why does Zayas imagine an audience for which this particular line would constitute, in Katherine Faull's words, an instance of "dangerous mobility" (25) too threatening to include?

Intersecting at the grotesque, notions of the carnivalesque and the abject provide a theoretical framework for understanding Belisa's confounding characterization as it relates to Zayas's resistance to transferring her racist speech. *Oxford Reference* defines the carnivalesque as "writing that depicts the de-stabilization or reversal of power structures ... by mobilizing humour, satire, and grotesquery." Abjection shares with the carnivalesque an emphasis on the body's transgressive potential, but unlike the carnivalesque, it is not located within the comic realm, but rather is "one of those violent, dark revolts of being, directed against a threat that seems to emanate from an exorbitant outside or inside ... it cannot he assimilated" (Kristeva 1). It is through the convergence of these two theoretical concepts that the translator finds herself at the limits of what can (and ought) to be translated in light of what Gabriela Carrión describes as the play's "startling juxtaposition of comedy and violence" (15).

Mikhail Bakhtin writes of the centrality of the carnivalesque in early modern European ("Renaissance") literature, noting its presence in Lope's work and centering on its interconnectedness with idealistic literary traditions:

> Carnival imagery was used by Erasmus, Shakespeare, Lope de Vega, Guevara, and Quevedo, by the German 'literature of fools.' Without an un-

derstanding of it, therefore, a full appreciation of Renaissance and grotesque literature is impossible. Not only *belles lettres* but the utopias of the Renaissance and its conception of the universe itself were deeply penetrated by the carnival spirit and often adopted its forms and symbols. (11)

This interdependence of the sublime and the grotesque appears in the convergent polarities that structure *Melindres*. Although Belisa's use of language illustrates Renaissance ideals of wit and individual (in this case, female) agency, her verbal virtuosity also turns her "model" suitors into hideous caricatures, bearing the primary responsibility for the upturning of her household, its carnivalesque undoing. For seventeenth-century audiences, this tension would have been expected, and it would have been resolved by the revelation of Pedro and Zara's real identities and the marriage of Belisa to the money-hungry Eliso. Nevertheless, the play's dénouement would likely leave the very contemporary spectators who had most heartily applauded Belisa's rhetorical resistance to marriage feeling the most dissatisfied, and her assertion of hegemonic authority over "slaves" could lead these same spectators to adopt a suspicious stance with respect to her previous attempts to disrupt power relationships.

Further, Belisa's linking of the marvelous (with respect to her linguistic prowess) and the monstrous in describing her suitors paves the way for her slippage into the abject, connecting her conduct to the translator's dilemma. Belisa's imagery illustrates the role of the grotesque body in the carnivalesque mode, about which Bakhtin writes "the grotesque body . . . is not a closed, completed unit; it is unfinished, outgrows itself, transgresses its own limits" (26). Belisa uses her way with words to render her "ideal" suitors hyperbolically monstrous, expanding their "faults" and drawing an implicit line in the sand with respect to the expectation that she will marry. However, when she becomes enamored of "Pedro," and resorts to branding him on the face when he rejects her, his feigned disfigurement makes him even more handsome in her eyes and results in her breaking her own "no-marriage" code and actually wanting to wed him. Her *melindres*, which began as a means to avoid marriage, have exceeded their own limits. In the case of the translator, the rendering of Belisa's outrageous language, which sometimes refers to actual physical disfigurement and sometimes is simply an instance of verbal distortion, reaches its own line in the sand with a racist play on words that forces a choice between excision (which can seem like giving up) and inclusion (which is both technically difficult and politically problematic). Ironically, the closer an English rendering approximates the exact wording of Belisa's wit (one measure of a good translation), the further it finds itself beyond the boundaries of what would ensure a successful reception by today's audiences.

As Belisa's quirks become increasingly threatening to social and familial stability they become, according to Julia Kristeva's theory of the abject, that which must be broken away from ("expelled" in Kristeva's words) "within the same motion through which 'I' claim to establish myself" (Kristeva 3). Understood within this framework, Belisa's assertion of her identity has an uncanny relationship with her socio-political environment. When she converts her suitors into distorted manifestations of her own linguistic prowess, she enters the carnivalesque realm, humorously inverting hierarchies, undermining masculine privilege, subverting the power of titles and wealth, and asserting her independence in the face of her family's insistence that she marry; in sum, her recourse to the carnivalesque undermines the exigencies of the dominant culture which demand a socially acceptable pairing with a Christian gentleman. At the same time, her movement into the abject (her commands to brand, chain, and burn characters she believes to be Morisco slaves), at least for contemporary audiences, aligns her with the status quo insofar as they constitute an assertion of her power as a wealthy Christian aristocrat. When she demands that Pedro and Zara be branded, her acting out, a term I use mindfully, falls outside the boundaries of the comic genre. The resulting physical disfigurement marks the once-beautiful characters for exclusion from the social and affective sphere that Belisa inhabits through a process of differentiation, excision, and casting way that would serve to reinforce her position of dominance. It is also at this point that Tiberio, fully aware that Pedro and Zara are actually Felisardo and Celia, must intervene, not in order to address the injustice of Belisa's demands (since he allows her to believe that the two have been branded by applying fake scars), but, rather, to ensure that the noble body, in both its individual and social sense, and of which he forms a part, remains intact. The convergence of the carnivalesque and the abject occurs when Belisa's behavior risks becoming a bit too eccentric for audiences, both dramatic and real. At the same time, it is what enables spectators to contextualize her comedic lines (among them, her racist joke) within the context of hegemonic discourse about the religious and ethnic other in early modern Spain, a particularly poignant situation given the play's composition shortly before the 1609 expulsion of the Moriscos, and to connect this discourse to a history of racism and enslavement beyond Golden Age Spain.

Suppressing Belisa's use of Afro-Hispanic speech through zero translation establishes a boundary that would confine her to the comic realm of the carnivalesque by eliminating words that, in the wider context of the play as a whole, and for contemporary U.S. audiences in particular, place her in dangerous proximity to the abject. For these English speaking spectators, even if her violent treatment of an early modern Spanish religious and ethnic other seemed far-removed, her mocking of Blacks, in the context of a play about enslavement, one rife with descriptions of horrific violence committed against slaves, would not. When delivered in a familiar language and, in the case of performance, uttered by individuals who share our present-day reality, her words recall the institutionalized slavery of Black Africans, a specter from a not-so-remote past that reappears provocatively in contemporary public discourse as we attempt to come to terms, literally and figuratively, with its consequences.[5] And although we cannot comment definitively on the responses of individual spectators, we can consider the matter of a national or cultural sensibility and assert, as Arthur Neal does, that the institution of slavery exists as one of the "major traumas that are deeply embedded in the American conscious" (x). Further, in spite of Neal's problematic use of the adjective "American" to refer only to the United States, his slip of the tongue extends the reach of my discussion of translation to encompass Zayas's Spanish adaptation of Lope's play, a production staged at the University of Puerto Rico and performed before an audience made up of diverse identities, Hispanic, Afro-Hispanic, and Caribbean, whose shared histories would also include the legacy of slavery. I would submit that Belisa's mimicry of Black speech, in conjunction with the references to slavery in the play, rather than being too far-removed from these contemporary worldviews, may well hit just a bit too close to home. As such, excising her lines actually functions to create space, keeping the *Comedia* at a safe distance by affirming its otherness and eliminating a reference that would engage tensions about race and rhetoric, and race *as* rhetoric, that continue to seethe.

Because Belisa's words disrupt the illusion that theatrical manifestations of *habla de negros* faithfully represent Black speech, the play dramatizes unambiguously the manner in which literary depictions of Africanized Spanish, even when placed in the mouths of Black characters, refer back to the mimicking agent.[6] Translation, understood as process, product, or hypothetical

---

   5   As I finalize this essay in July 2020, while protesters in many U.S. cities continue their fight for justice in response to the killing of George Floyd and Breonna Taylor (among other instances of police violence committed against people of color), I am struck by the poignancy of this statement.

   6   This is akin to Kathleen Lennon's contention that through the abject "we are reminded of the constructed nature of the self as positioned in the symbolic

construct, seems to oblige a comparably self-conscious bent that returns to fore in recent discussions of the role of individual human subjectivity in light of technological advances in machine translation.[7] Likewise, scholars and translators of the *Comedia* who write about their experiences recasting the texts that they love and study as a transcendent process of personal transformation exemplify this same tendency. It is perhaps fitting, then, that I come back to my own attempts to translate *Los melindres de Belisa*, the results of which will remain hidden in recesses of my laptop, at least for now, and to a summary of how practice has allowed me to theorize about translation.

While I have chosen to look at the problem of proximity, my efforts to translate Belisa's line do certainly reveal the difficulties that linguistic distance poses. The aspirated word-final sibilant in "mis ojos" simply does not connote Black speech in English, so the joke cannot transfer without significant changes to the form and content of the utterance. Nevertheless, "talking Black" is a cultural construct with a rhetorical function, an observation as true here and now as it was in early modern Spain, and it is this functional similarity that, as I argue, tightens the bind. While scholars have generally accepted the cultural turn in translation studies, the predisposition to think about the problem of *cultural* translatability in *linguistic* terms persists. This is understandable because, in its most basic sense, translation presupposes linguistic difference; we simply would not need *Friendship Betrayed* if Zayas had written *La traición en la amistad* in English. Nevertheless, an utterance's full resonance emerges in the context of culture, and cultural translatability cannot be assumed on the basis of likeness. The unexpected proximity of a classical play can stimulate a particularly pointed self-awareness. In some instances, such as the examples of translator-scholars and theater professionals whose work connects the *Comedia* to a wider audience, this sharpness is productive. In others, as the line from Lope's play illustrates, it cuts too near the bone.

---

order." In early modern Spain, depictions of marginalized people (Blacks, religious minorities) functioned to affirm hegemonic notions of national identity. Revealing portrayals of the other as obvious constructs destabilizes the sense of self.

7   See, for example, Heather Connelly's discussion of "mistranslations that occur in Machine Translation (MT) and Back Translation (BT) within art practice to draw attention to the subjectivity of the translator and translation's creative potential" (43). Back Translation is the process of verifying the accuracy of a translation by translating it back into the original language using a different translator.

Works Cited

"A contextualized resource of Spanish-Language Plays for English-Speaking Practitioners and Researchers." *Out of the Wings.* Queen's College London, http://www.outofthewings.org. Accessed 7 April 2019.

Bakhtin, Mikhail. *Rabelais and His World.* Translated by Helene Iswolsky, Indiana University Press, 1984.

Bassnett, Susan and Lefevere, André, editors. "Preface." *Translation, Rewriting, and the Manipulation of Literary Fame,* Routledge, 1992, pp. vii-viii.

Booker, M. Keith. *Techniques of Subversion in Modern Literature: Transgression, Abjection, and the Carnivalesque.* University Press of Florida, 1991.

"Carnivalesque." *Oxford Reference.* Oxford UP, http://www.oxfordreference.com/view/10.1093/oi/authority.20110803095550811. Accessed 20 April 2019.

Carrión, Gabriela. "'Burlas en tiempo de tantas veras': Violence and Humor in Lope de Vega's *Los melindres de Belisa.*" *Bulletin of the Comediantes,* vol. 67, no. 2, 2015, pp. 15-31.

Connelly, Heather. "Speaking Through the Voice of Another: Amplifying Subjectivity Through Machine Translation." *Salford Working Papers in Translation and Interpreting,* 1, 2014, pp. 42-56. Accessed 7 April 2019.

Edwards, Justin and Rune Grauland. *Grotesque: The New Critical Idiom.* Routledge, 2013.

El Dali, Hosni Mostafa. "Towards and Understanding of the Distinctive Nature of Translation Studies." *Journal of King Saud University-Languages and Translation,* vol. 23, no. 1, 2011, pp. 29-45.

Faull, Katherine. "Performing Translation: The (Dangerous) Mobilities of Cultural Identity." *Shakespeare and the Spanish Comedia. Translation, Interpretation, and Performance: Essays in Honor of Susan L. Fischer,* edited by Barbara Mujica, Bucknell, 2013, pp. 17-27.

Gitlitz, David. "Confesiones de un traductor." *Traducir a los clásicos,* special issue of *Cuadernos de teatro clásico,* no. 4, 1989, pp. 45-52.

Johnston, David. "Lope de Vega in English: The Historical Imagination." *The Comedia in English: Translation and Performance,* edited by Susan Paun de García and Donald R. Larson, Tamesis, 2008, pp. 66-82.

Kristeva, Julia. *The Powers of Horror,* translated by Leon S. Roudiez, Columbia UP, 1982.

Larson, Catherine. "Found in Translation: María de Zayas's *Friendship Betrayed* on the English-Speaking Stage." *The Comedia in English: Translation and Performance,* edited by Susan Paun de García and Donald R. Larson, Tamesis, 2008, pp. 83-94.

———. "Translator's Note." *Friendship Betrayed,* Bucknell, 1999, pp. 28-9.

Lennon, Kathleen, "Feminist Perspectives on the Body." *The Stanford Encyclopedia of Philosophy,* edited by Edward N. Zalta, https://plato.stanford.edu/entries/feminist-body/. Accessed 7 April 2019.
Lope de Vega, Félix. *Los melindres de Belisa,* edited by Francisco Crosas, Rialp, 2017.
Matthews, Dakin. "Translating Comedias Into English Verse for Modern Audiences." *The Comedia in English: Translation and Performance,* edited by Susan Paun de García and Donald R. Larson, Tamesis, 2008, pp. 37-53.
McGaha, Michael. "Building Bridges." *Prologue to Performance: Spanish Classical Theatre Today,* edited by Louise Fothergill-Payne and Peter Fothergill-Payne, Bucknell, 1991, pp. 85-92.
Nieddzielski, Henry. "Cultural transfers in the Translating of humor." *Translation: Theory and Practice, Tension and Interdependence,* edited by Mildred L. Larson, John Benjamin, 2008, pp. 139-56.
Venuti, Lawrence, editor. *The Translation Studies Reader,* London, 2000.
Vice, Sue. "Bahktin and Kristeva: Grotesque Body, Abject Self." *Face to Face: Bahktin in Russia and the West,* edited by Carol Adlam, Sheffield Academic Press, 1997, pp. 160-74.

Quijotes transatlánticos and Golden-Age Latin Americanism
Robert Bayliss
University of Kansas

IN ONE OF HIS final public appearances before his death, Carlos Fuentes was asked to recommend five novels for aspiring writers to read. His response was to repeat five times: *Don Quijote de la Mancha*. During the same appearance, Fuentes reflected on his long friendship with Gabriel García Márquez and noted that upon reading the first completed draft of *Cien años de soledad*, he praised his friend by calling it "El *Quijote* de América Latina." The esteem and admiration for Cervantes's novel among writers of the 20th-century Latin American "boom" are well known, as are the multitude of intertextual references to and cultural invocations of *Don Quijote* throughout the literary history of Latin America. And yet, if we were to rely only on academic scholarship for information regarding cultural production in Latin America, it would appear that the importance of the *Quijote* has declined precipitously there among the post-boom generations.

This essay examines the question of how these "Quijotes transatlánticos" have (and more recently, how they have *not*) been studied by Hispanists[1] throughout the Americas. While scholars of Comparative Literature continue to examine the novel's literary and cultural influence in North America and Europe, Hispanism has had a more complicated relationship with the cultural legacy of the *Quijote* and its author in the Spanish-speaking world. As the most canonical text ever written in the Spanish language, its disci-

---

1 A brief but important terminological clarification is necessary: by Hispanism I refer to scholarship of the cultural production of the Spanish-speaking world. This "pan-Hispanic" use of the term contrasts with its use by others, including some scholars cited in this essay (e.g., Faber, "Hispanism"), to denote only European Spanish studies. My pan-Hispanic usage is indebted to Mejías-López's *The Inverted Conquest*.

plinary shadow is immense, as is its influence on Latin American authors from Lizardi to Vargas Llosa. Excluding the work of Hispanists from North America and Europe (in particular, those specialized in "peninsularist" Spanish studies), however, recent scholarship dedicated to the *Quijote*'s broader cultural ubiquity in Latin America has been comparatively scarce. Indeed, if our knowledge and awareness of the cultural realities of contemporary Latin America were limited exclusively to scholarship identified by the disciplinary label of "Latin American cultural studies," we very well might think that *Don Quijote* is no longer read, studied, adapted, invoked or even remembered in the region by anyone younger than Fuentes's generation.

Given the fact that countless examples of such deployments of the *Quijote* are in fact ripe for discovery across Latin America, as indicated by the small sample examined in these pages, the most logical way to account for this disconnect between "theory and practice" (if we take "theory" to mean the published scholarship of Hispanists and "practice" to mean the cultural production that they study) is to consider how developments in our fields of study might have brought us to it. Especially in North America, the field of Latin American literary and cultural studies is now positioned as the principal driver of Hispanist scholarship—a striking reversal from the state of the field five decades ago, when the study of "Spanish American literature" struggled to receive critical attention within a midcentury Eurocentric critical paradigm naturally predisposed to treat it as derivative or secondary, just as many would argue that the label "Spanish America" implies. With good reason, the praxis of Latin Americanism has not privileged the study of cultural production with overt intertextual ties to Spain, including the ways in which the Spanish Empire's most enduring cultural product remains an object of imitation and veneration in the region. This essay aims to show, however, that we all stand to gain from resisting traditional, (pen)insular disciplinary demarcations, and from instead considering more open-ended modes of inquiry, so that our work can more nimbly address the transnational complexities and cultural ambivalences that neither Eurocentric nor Decolonizing critical paradigms can hope to address on their own. If a common suspicion among critics of transatlantic scholarship is that it "runs the risk of reimperializing, as it were, both the field and its object of study," as Alejandro Mejías-López describes it ("Hispanic Studies," 212), a means to move beyond such an impasse is to show what we stand to learn from removing such disciplinary barriers. In other words, Latin American Quijotes promise to teach us about pan-hispanic cultural dynamics in a way to which our institutional and ideological structures remain resistant.

Transatlantic Quijotes, Literary Canonicity and Extra-literary Cultural Capital

The approach to such a solution proposed here is only now possible because of a broader methodological shift in our field, from a philologically oriented approach to "Literature" to a more interdisciplinary mode of Cultural Studies, which permits the study of a wider array of cultural products and resituates itself, post-Barthes, to depend less on original authorship as the guiding principle for studying cultural activity. It is certainly difficult, as we will see, to disentangle questions of authorship from questions of cultural identity and authority, but the lens of Cultural Studies permits a broader view of the forms of cultural expression through which Spaniards and Latin Americans engage with *Don Quijote*. In the spirit of Linda Hutcheon's *A Theory of Adaptation*, which argues against dismissing adaptations of literary texts as valid objects of study (because they are derivative, secondary, "unoriginal," and so forth), we can look to invocations and deployments of the *Quijote* as a process of intercultural exchange, whose study can shed new light on all cultures involved in that exchange.

Since at least the rise of Cultural Materialism in late-1970s England, literary and cultural scholars have understood that the literary canon can assume a life of its own, and that the readings, recastings and deployments of canonical texts can constitute a cultural narrative in their own right. Alan Sinfield has explained this narrative in the context of England in this way:

> Shakespeare is a powerful cultural token, such that what you want to say has more authority if it seems to come through him. That is how Shakespeare comes to speak to people at different times: the plays have been continuously reinterpreted in attempts to coopt the bard for this or that worldview. This is not surprising or illegitimate; it is a key practice through which cultural contest proceeds. (Sinfield 11)

By virtue of the cultural authority of its very canonicity, *Don Quijote* has been deployed along the lines that Sinfield describes. The enemies against whom Don Quijote has fought since his initial appearance in the two installments of Cervantes's novel (1605 and 1615) have indeed been diverse, including what was perceived by 19th-century Spanish cultural purists to be the invasive cultural influence of France, fascism, communism, capitalism, consumerism, neoliberalism, U.S. economic and military hegemony, and even illiteracy.

It is not surprising that the most-studied and best-documented instances of these uses of Don Quijote and *Don Quijote* to tilt at post-cervantine windmills have occurred in Spain. Since "classical" Spanish literature was identified by German Romantics as a model for their institutionalization of national literary traditions, cultural critics within Spain have heralded Cervantes's novel as the crowned jewel of its cultural splendor, and as a source of national pride. By the turn of the twentieth century, as the last vestiges of the Spanish Empire were ceded to the U.S. after the Spanish-American War, Spanish intellectuals like José Ortega y Gasset and Miguel de Unamuno found the novel to constitute a map for recouping the nation's lost glory and for distilling an essentialist national character. These "Quixotists," as Christopher Britt-Arredondo explains, would unwittingly sow the intellectual seeds for a nationalist-fascistic deployment of Don Quijote that would persist through the waning years of the Franco regime. Recent Spanish celebrations of the novel's fourth centennial in 2005 and 2015 show that despite its current economic and political complexities, Cervantes's novel and hero remain natural points of pride and inspiration. To be sure, these deployments are not without their ironies: despite the fact that a comprehensive survey in 2005 revealed that only one in five Spaniards have actually read the text in its entirety, the international "Día del libro" (Day of the Book) is observed on April 23, the anniversary of death for both Cervantes and Shakespeare, and it is celebrated in Spain by the public oral recitation of *Don Quijote* from cover to cover. Indeed, throughout the many twists and turns of post-imperial Spanish history, Don Quijote has been a mainstay of articulating Spanish national identity and of confronting nefarious cultural agents that would undermine it.

Ample evidence of Don Quijote's persistent cultural ubiquity can be found in contemporary Latin America as well—even if, for reasons tied to the history of the field of Latin American literary and cultural studies, they are less often synthesized and studied. The first documented appearance of Cervantes's hero in the Americas came as early as 1607, as part of a parade and cultural spectacle in Peru to celebrate the appointment of the Marqués de Montesclaros as Vice Regent. Even as Cervantes was still writing the novel's second installment, *Don Quijote* was deployed by the Spanish Empire in its efforts to establish a regulated colonial culture in its own image. Spanish Golden Age literary, visual and performance texts were indispensible tools for colonizing the indigenous communities of the Americas after their conquest; they facilitated the evangelization, regulation and education of newly conquered colonial subjects, and they were equally valuable to the many religious orders and missions that served the empire's interests. As colonial societies developed in subsequent centuries and through the empire's 19th-century collapse, these cultural landmarks continued to circulate and resonate in the many emerging "imagined communities" that now constitute the nations of Latin America, and chief among these agents and vestiges of colonialism was *Don Quijote*.

To be sure, acknowledgement of Cervantes's influence by intellectuals and especially authors in Latin America has been continual since the end of the colonial period. Nineteenth-century authors like José Joaquín Fernández de Lizardi (Mexico) and Juan Montalvo (Ecuador) forged explicit intertextual dialogue with *Don Quijote*, and the degree of adulation has only increased since those foundational texts. Jorge Luis Borges, Julio Cortázar and Alejo Carpentier are among the most prominent authors of the twentieth-century Latin American "Boom" who openly praised Cervantes and considered his work foundational to their own craft. Carlos Fuentes describes the moment when Don Quijote sets out on his first adventure as the moment when the modern world was born. In a 1997 interview, nobel laureate Gabriel García Márquez admitted that "Cuando voy a empezar a escribir, pienso que soy Miguel de Cervantes. Y cada que me pongo frente a una máquina, pienso que voy a escribir como Cervantes" ("Whenever I'm getting ready to write, I think that I am Miguel de Cervantes. And when I sit before a typewriter, I think that I'll write like Cervantes."). In his prefatory essay ("A Novel for the 21st Century") to a new commemorative edition of *Don Quijote* published by the Spanish Royal Academy, Mario Vargas Llosa claims that the novel anticipates virtually all of the best fiction written in the twentieth century, in terms of its exploration of the lines between fiction and reality, its manipulation of language, time and point of view, and the complexity of its narrative voices.

Not surprisingly, this literary reverence runs parallel to the extraliterary dimensions of Latin American cultures, in other words to the cultural presence of Don Quijote beyond the level of literary influence. Upon winning the Cuban Revolution, for example, Fidel Castro seized control of several newspapers hostile to his cause and directed their raw materials (ink, paper, printing presses) to be redeployed in a massive new edition of *Don Quijote*, edited by Alejo Carpentier. Hundreds of thousands of copies were distributed at no cost to the Cuban people in a gesture meant to underscore the regime's prioritization of literacy and education in the new socialist state. Decades later, Hugo Chavez would launch a similar program under the name "Operation Dulcinea" (in reference to the imagined lady to whom Don Quijote's efforts were dedicated), with an estimated 500,000 free copies of the text distributed to the Venezuelan people. In a press release announcing Chavez's program, Don Quijote's struggle against windmills (which he mistakes for evil giants) is referenced as an unironic allegory of Venezuela's struggles against American hemispheric hegemony. Kristine Vanden Berghe studies a similarly allegorical use of Don Quijote by "Subcomandante Marcos" in the context of the Zapatista movement's conflict in the Chiapas region of Mexico during the 1990s, as the most recent in a series of explicit political appropriations of Cervantes in that country dating back to its original struggles for independence from Spain.

Transatlantic Studies and their Discontents

The disconnect between the reality of these Latin American Quijotes and their absence in the pages of Latin Americanist scholarship is not specific to *Quijote* studies: to name one related phenomenon, contemporary performances of Spanish Golden Age theater throughout Latin America are now far less likely to be treated as cultural production within the purview of the field of Latin American theatre studies than was the case in the 1970s, as that field was emerging through new critical venues for scholarly exchange like the *Latin American Theatre Review*. While some of the developments contributing to this shift are specific to theater studies—the shift away from more traditional modes of textual analysis centering on the playscript and towards the cultural and material analysis of performance and spectacle, for example—I would argue that the Spanish *Comedia*'s exclusion from the field is primarily due to institutional circumstances that are shared with the critical myopia regarding Latin American deployments of *Don Quijote*. In both cases, the critical tipping point occurs during the last two decades of the previous century, when both the scholarship and the curricula shaped by it become increasingly less focused on Spain and much more concerned with cultural products from Latin America. As poststructuralism prompted a broader reboot of literary studies, underwritten by a systemic questioning of the Eurocentric master narratives upon which departments of "national" languages and literatures (including English) had been founded, the study of Latin American literatures would find in Postcolonial theory a compelling intellectual framework for rethinking the study of texts pertinent to a field that was known at the time as "Spanish" (with the implication of defining the field as the study of "Spain and its former colonies"). That label (and its attendant term, "Spanish America") became an inapt descriptor of the field, and indeed the reversal of its implicit "verticality" (to use Walter Mignolo's term) or eurocentric hierarchical orientation continues to animate some of the most important scholarship being done by Hispanists today.

Regardless of one's personal stake in these developments, it is safe to say that especially in the North American Academy, they have occasioned some clear tensions within the intellectual community of Hispanism, not the least of which is a dynamic in which "Peninsularist" and Latin Americanist scholars often view themselves as competing for scarce resources and institutional support. To further the cause of diminishing these tensions and their implicit view of Hispanism as a zero-sum game, this essay proposes a collaborative framework of comparative cultural studies through the example of *Don Quijote*, whose contemporary Spanish and Latin American deployments evince the potential for more synergistic and mutually beneficial modes of transatlantic scholarship. Comparing the uses of Cervantes's hero and text in Spain to those in Latin American cultures promises to shed new light on the underlying cultural, political and ideological dynamics informing cultural programming on both sides of the Atlantic. Beyond offering a more comprehensive understanding of Cervantes's global cultural legacy, this framework can lead to the discovery of gaps or blind spots that are difficult to perceive from an exclusively "Peninsularist" or "Latin Americanist" perspective. Ultimately, we may even find that this framework reveals how the Hispanic world is less divided than the current praxis of Hispanism would have us believe.

A first step towards such a project is to acknowledge the ideological parameters that our fields of study have inherited from previous generations. Sebastiaan Faber, for example, sees Hispanism itself as an ideology, and Iberian Cultural Studies in particular as "the construction of the cultural history of the Spanish-speaking world through a Castilian- and Spain-centered lens" (23). For Faber, the philological tradition of the Spanish Academy (by which I mean both the *Real Academia Española* and especially universities in Spain) continues to affirm a kind of academic insularity that necessitates the exclusion of any Latin American writers in its conception of Spanish literary history, regardless of how absurd such exclusions might appear. This inscription of Spanish culture into a national-cultural identitarian discursive space known as "Spanish" is further problematized in the context of the North American Academy, where the same "Spanish" label denotes academic units whose intellectual energies are clearly trending away from Spain and towards Latin America.

If we probe a bit further back into our field's North American institutional history, however, that postcolonial exclusion is revealed to be the product of a dynamic that for most of the twentieth century would be better characterized as colonial appropriation, in part stemming from the European paradigm of national literary traditions but also reinforced by the midcentury arrival of a number of important Spanish scholars in the wake of the Spanish Civil War. Regardless of how one chooses to read the history behind it, the ideological footprint of Eurocentric Hispanism has proven to be far more resistant to erasure than the geopolitical Spanish Empire was by the end of the nineteenth century. In North America, the emergence of Latin American studies—and especially the dearth of studies on subjects like the present one, Latin American Quijotes—is difficult to understand without taking that ideological footprint into account: if the earliest articulations of Latin Americanism were inscribed in an identitarian space in contradistinction to an iberocentric field of "Spanish" with a long legacy of treating "Spanish American Literature" as derivative and subordinate, it should come as no surprise that the "decolonized" field of Latin Americanism would be less interested in studying the reception and reproduction of literary figures like Don Quijote than their peninsularist colleagues.

The unfortunate consequence of these disciplinary developments, however, is the gaps or blind-spots that they have created. When addressing the problems that have arisen with the development of transatlantic Hispanic studies, Alejandro Mejías-López refers to the bifurcated fields of Peninsular and Latin American studies as a case of each field having turned its back on the other ("Hispanic Studies," 217)—a metaphor that indicates mutually exclusive fields of vision, but that also suggests a demarcation of the fields resistant to those cultural events and practices that resist such exclusivity and would find it impossible to disentangle the "Spanish" from the "Latin American." As we will see, the case of Don Quijote's reception since the Latin American "boom" (if not before) offers ample evidence of such entanglements. To avoid broad generalizations regarding the diverse communities, cultures and political systems that constitute Latin America, I will delimit my analysis to the concrete example of Mexico, with the caveat that its cultural entanglements with Spain do connect to broader regional efforts by the former empire to engage with its former colonies.

OPPORTUNITIES LOST (AND FOUND?)
In a letter delivered in March 2019, Mexican president Andres Manuel López Obrador requested a formal apology from both King Phillip of Spain and the Vatican for the Spanish conquest of the indigenous communities of what we now know as Mexico. Despite Spain's recent divisive culture wars tied to questions of cultural memory and the legacy of its imperial and colonial his-

tory, which included a law passed in 2015 extending rights of citizenship to descendants of the Sephardic Jewish communities forced into exile in 1492, the request for a Spanish apology to Mexico occasioned a rare moment of consensus among Spain's otherwise polarized political class. While conservative pushback was to be expected, even Pedro Sánchez's socialist PSOE administration was quick to respond with a definitive "no," on the grounds that it would be anachronistic to apply twenty-first century standards for human rights and national sovereignty to events that occurred five centuries ago. In a moment in Spanish political history that might be characterized as a passage from what Luisa-Elena Delgado refers to as an *estado de consenso*[2] to a more divided and polarized climate (as evinced by the inconclusive general elections of Spring 2019), López Obrador's transatlantic claim was resisted in Spain with a consensus recommendation that, rather than litigate the past, the two nations look towards the future.

Perhaps more telling is the criticism that the Mexican president received from voices from within his own, supposedly aggrieved, country and from elsewhere in Latin America. The Peruvian novelist Mario Vargas Llosa opined that "López Obrador se equivocó de destinatario; se la debía haber mandado a sí mismo. ¿Por qué tiene México tantos millones de indios pobres, ignorantes y marginados?" (Camps). Vargas Llosa's critique is especially noteworthy in light of the context in which it was offered: the opening speech of the eighth *Congreso Internacional de la Lengua Española* [CILE], held in Córdoba, Argentina. While López Obrador's gesture was likely driven by domestic political concerns beyond the scope of these pages, Vargas Llosa's reply indicates the extent to which it has taken on transnational implications. Regardless of the president's intentions, the myopia cited in its critique—that Mexico's indictment of Spain fails to acknowledge its own perpetuation of the systemic inequality along racial and cultural divides that the colony inherited from the colonizer—is not unique to one specific former colony, and the CILE is but one of the many fora for international intellectual exchange in which prominent artists and intellectuals have addressed the problem on a regional scale.

---

2 In her monograph *La nación singular*, Delgado develops the notion of an *estado de consenso* based in part on, among other sources, Guillem Martínez's concept of a *Cultura de la Transición* to describe a post-Franco cultural dynamic that prioritized national cohesion and stability over dissent and ideological pluralism. For Delgado, this *estado* persisted well into the turn of the current century, until its destabilization during Spain's economic crisis (2008-2014).

The CILE is one of several international cultural and political fora for transatlantic exchange in which one can perceive what Mejías-López might call the "ghost" of the Spanish Empire: since Spain's return to democracy, its economic, political and cultural ties to Latin America have been carefully curated by institutions funded by the Spanish government. The highest-profile of these institutions—which happens to underwrite and archive the proceedings of the CILE—is the *Instituto Cervantes*, a state-funded network of more than 80 cultural centers strategically located around the globe. The *Instituto* has been described as an outward-looking and "evangelical" cultural analogue to the Spanish Royal Academy, in that it aims to set standards for second-language Spanish instruction worldwide and foster international appreciation of Hispanic cultures. One can see in its cultural programming that the *Instituto* (and presumably the Spanish state funding it) embraces a pan-hispanic view of its evangelization project, featuring Latin American cultural production alongside its own. In the last several years, it has invested in and developed its online presence to facilitate the dissemination of pan-hispanic cultural production to the rest of the world, including a newly curated, open-access digital edition of *Don Quijote*, edited by the Spanish philologist Francisco Rico.

The *Instituto*'s mission is to promote global appreciation of the Spanish language and Hispanic cultures—a scope that immediately echoes colonial verticality by appropriating all Spanish-speaking cultures within its purview. To foster this mission within Latin America while carefully avoiding charges of cultural imperialism, it has depended on the enlistment of prominent Latin American voices to articulate the same message—let's not litigate the past, but instead look to the future—that was communicated in response to López-Obrador's controversial letter to Spain and the Vatican. At the 2004 CILE in Rosario, Argentina, Enrique Krauze (author and editor of the Mexican magazine *Letras Libres*) demonstates how this messaging can even explicitly invoke discourses of empire:

> Hay un imperio bienhechor en el que no se pone el sol. Es el imperio del español; un dominio antiquísimo y moderno, cultural y espiritual, una nación virtual, sin fronteras, múltiple, compleja, variada, cambiante y llena de promesas. El español se expande ufano, y ya no es sólo de España, ni principalmente de España: tiene muchos más hablantes fuera de ella. (Krause)

Those echoes of empire resonate even more loudly in light of Spain's other Latin American entanglements, including those that are economic. Spain is now the single biggest investor in Latin America: its private-industry investment steadily increased since the return to democracy after Franco's death in 1975, and its economic development has become increasingly tied to the region ever since. Investment in Latin American real estate and other industries played a pivotal role, for example, in how Spain recovered from its own experience of the global financial crisis that began in 2007. As Emma Martín Díaz, Francisco Cuberos Gallardo and Simone Castellani explain, these economic entanglements are further complicated by transatlantic migration, which had never really stopped after the geopolitical end of the Spanish empire. For most of the twentieth century (and especially during the years before and after the Spanish Civil War), Latin America absorbed millions of Spanish immigrants. With Spain's economic expansion in the 1980s and 1990s, this dynamic reversed directions, especially after reforms to Spanish immigration policies went into effect in 1985. Whereas migration patterns prior to Spain's financial crisis (2008-2014) consisted primarily of human capital flowing into the Spanish labor market from Latin America with a corresponding return of economic capital (in the form of remittances) in the reverse direction, the crisis-induced spike in Spanish unemployment (which at its worst point approached 30%) proved disruptive to the economies on both sides of the Atlantic.

In this economic context it is noteworthy that Spain is now making its most significant effort since the Colonial era to promote the appreciation of its linguistic and cultural heritage across the world, including in its former colonies. The Spanish Ministry of Culture funds a number of initiatives aimed at promoting the study and consumption of Spanish culture in Latin America, including annual tours by the National Classical Theater Company (*Compañía Nacional de Teatro Clásico*) to perform plays written by Cervantes and his contemporaries, as well as several stage adaptations of *Don Quijote*. The machinations of the Ministry are complex and fluid, as political turnover has involved its continual restructuring (for example, the *Partido Popular* administrations of Aznar and Rajoy combined Culture and Education within the same ministry, while the PSOE-led governments of González, Zapatero and Sánchez have preferred to separate them), and its emphasis on *patrimonio cultural* has involved coordination with the EU and UNESCO. Since its founding in 1991, the *Instituto Cervantes* has remained a stable and consistent cultural institution working behind the scenes to promote and archive this cultural ambassadorship.

This broader context of postcolonial (or neocolonial?) entanglements certainly illuminates López-Obrador's formal request for an apology from Spain and the Vatican, but Vargas Llosa's retort that Mexico would do well to address its own role in perpetuating the injustices of colonialism points to deeper entanglements with Spain that in fact are as old as the Mexican State itself—the first in Latin America to publish an edition of the *Quijote* (in 1833). As the *metrópoli*'s most famous cultural narrative during the colonial era, *Don Quijote* served as a point of reference for interpreting the events leading to Mexican independence in the early nineteenth century. Miguel Hidalgo y Costillo, a Spanish priest generally regarded as a key instigator of the independence movement in 1810, was satirized by Agustín Pomposo Fernández de San Salvador in a short dramatic piece titled "Las fazañas de Hidalgo, Quixote de nuevo cuño, facedor de tuertos, etc." Here, we should note, the *Quijote* intertext is bound to the "hard" or satirical reading of Cervantes's novel that prevailed among readers on both sides of the ocean before the so-called "Romantic" or "soft" approach to the novel would develop later in the century.[3] By this reading, Don Quijote was a ridiculous madman and, for those opposing Hidalgo's movement, a perfect analogue for attacking this enemy of the colonial state.

Don Quijote would appear as foil, analogue or intertext throughout Mexican literary history, but it is especially worth noting here that his enlistment amid times of political instability and national crisis forges a fascinating transatlantic dialogue. Spain's appropriation of Cervantes's narrative and protagonist is of course well known in the context of the so-called crisis of 1898, when Spain's loss of the Philippines, Cuba and Puerto Rico effectively ended the Spanish empire. Freshly rehabilitated from the buffoonish "hard" reading noted above into a Romantic hero, Don Quixote would be proposed as a kind of national allegory by Spain's leading intellectuals (including Azorín, Miguel de Unamuno and José Ortega y Gasset). Both the Mexican Revolution (1910-1920) and this Spanish re-engagement with Don Quijote in the early years of the twentieth century would gather steam at the same time, and ample evidence exists of an awareness among Mexican revolutionaries of Don Quijote's political-allegorical utility, but with a key difference: the Quijote-as-fool "hard" or satirical reading appears to have prevailed in Mexico, rendering him an inversion of the Quijote-as-hero being heralded contemporaneously across the ocean.

If a romanticized Don Quijote worked as a kind of spiritual elixir for Spanish intellectuals to prescribe for a national readership in existential crisis, his transatlantic functionality during and after the Mexican Revolution would necessarily be different, insofar as Revolutionary discourse identified

---

3   See Close and Russell.

its mission as a correction to the vestiges of colonialism embodied in the policies and power structures of the *Porfiriato*. It is a testimony to the discursive complexities of Cervantes's novel that the same protagonist can be Spain's hero and Mexico's fool, as when Martín Luis Guzmán's 1928 novel *El águila y la serpiente* draws explicit intertextual comparisons between Don Quijote and the Mexican revolutionary Venustiano Carranza, officially the first president of the Mexican Republic before his assassination in 1920; both are idealistic dreamers whose foolhardy missions, noble as they may be, could not withstand the windmills of reality. In "calavera" illustrations by José Guadalupe Posada published by Antonio Vanegas Arroyo for cheap distribution to the public during the buildup to the Revolution, a foolhardy, skeletal Quijote wreaks havoc, charging into a defenseless crowd and leaving scattered bones in his wake.[4] Along similar lines, the parade celebrating the inaugural *Día de la Raza* in 1919 featured a procession of Latin American national flags, preceded by two allegorical representatives of the former colonizer, still in convalescence from the wounds of 1898: Don Quijote and Sancho, described by José Rojas Garcidueñas as "el Manchego inmortal con sus ojos alucinados en contemplación del eterno ideal" (18).

While our understanding of the *Quijote*'s rich reception history has largely been built upon notions of a simple dichotomy—Close's "Romantic" reading vs. Russell's "hard" approach, also neatly packaged by John Jay Allen as a hero/fool binary—my reading of these Mexican Quijotes suggests far more nuance than such an either/or choice would imply. While the politics informing revolutionary discourse would make a complete absorption of Spain's Romanticized and rehabilitated Quijote-as-hero impossible, the satirical Quijote of the Mexican Revolution does reflect a degree of sympathy and respect for his idealism (misguided though it may be) that is absent from the "hard" presentation of him on both sides of the ocean prior to the Romantic period. This more nuanced and complex Quijote anticipates the development of a transatlantic appreciation for *Don Quijote* (the novel, rather than the character) as an exemplary representation of the complexity of the human condition and progenitor of the modern novel, bolstered by scholars writing from outside the Hispanic world (Bahktin, Auerbach, Spitzer, Bloom, Foucault, and so forth). In Spain, a midcentury philological tradition of *cervantismo* would eventually develop a greater interest in the novel's artistic achievement and discursive complexity than on the protagonist's

---

4   Posada's drawing is available digitally at the British Museum's online collection, hosted by Google Arts & Culture. Its caption reads "Don Quijote y Sancho Panza / Se presentan altaneros / Arremetiendo su lanza / A todos lo embusteros."

heroism—a shift that would lead us to better understand how Cervantes's text eludes facile readings and simple (hero/fool) binaries.

Beyond the realm of scholarship, Mexico's relationship with Don Quijote (and with *Don Quijote*) would persist throughout the twentieth century, stimulated at least in part by the Civil War-era arrival of exiled Spanish philologists and other intellectuals to universities in Mexico and throughout the Americas. Mexico, second only to France as a destination for the Spanish Republican diaspora, would refuse to recognize Franco's regime and only reestablished official diplomatic ties with Spain after his death. Because the pre-war ideological formation of these exiled intellectuals coincided with the nationalistic deployment of a Romanticized Don Quijote prevalent in Spain since the Generation of 1898, their absorption into Mexican society (and especially into Mexican universities) would inevitably affect the novel's reception and interpretation there, as Piñero Valverde explains. This influence would gradually "soften" the stubbornly "hard" reading of *Don Quijote* in the era of the Mexican Revolution.

In the 1950s, the local troupe *Teatro Universitario de Guanajuato* began staging Cervantes's *entremeses* for theatrical performance annually in the city of Guanajuato, under the leadership of Enrique Ruelas Espinosa. Ruelas, by virtue of his minimalist approach to the production (taking advantage of the Plaza de San Roque's colonial architecture) and his enlistment of local residents in the production, created a degree of cultural identification between the Spanish author and the Mexican community that for Barrera-Fernández and Hernández-Escampa is unique. By 1972 the activities surrounding the cervantine spectacle would be officially rebranded as the *Festival Internacional Cervantino*, with administrative control assumed by the federal government. Enthusiasm for this annual event would later develop into a number of permanent fixtures of the region's cultural programming, including a *Museo Iconográfico del Quijote* launched in 1987 after the exiled Republican Eulalio Ferrer bequeathed his extensive private collection of *Quijote* and Cervantes memorabilia. An annual academic conference coinciding with the *Festival* now provides scholars from all over Latin America an important opportunity for *cervantista* intellectual exchange. Guanajuato, the parish from which Miguel Hidalgo began his revolutionary campaign in 1810, was named (by the Spanish government) the official international *Capital Cervantino* in 2004.

While space here does not allow for a more detailed analysis of the Guanajuato phenomenon, the sheer scope of the event (statistics from the 2015 edition indicate that the small city of 180,000 residents accommodates as many as 400,000 tourists during it) is indicative of how important *Don*

Quijote remains to the community, beyond the obvious economic benefits that such tourism brings for it. Across Mexico the deployment of the novel extends to the political sphere, most recently in the context of the *Ejército Zapatista de Liberación Nacional*. As Kristine Vanden Berghe has shown, the EZLN's Subcomandante Marcos has drawn upon the *Quijote* since the movement's anti-NAFTA launch in 1994 to guide his unique approach to the role of spokesman for the movement. Through a series of short vignettes centering around a quixotic beetle named Don Durito, Marcos inverts the paradigm of politicizing literature by embedding his political message in cervantine literary discourse. In an interview published in 2001, the *subcomandante* referred to *Don Quijote* as "the best book of political theory" (Marcos), followed by *Hamlet* and *MacBeth*. The cervantine lens allows for a satirical critique of neoliberalism while acknowledging both the impossibility of defeating the Mexican military and the high idealism of the EZLN mission.

While the EZLN applauded the electoral defeat of López Obrador's predecessor, it has thus far remained reluctant to trust that the new government would negotiate with them in better faith. The indigenous communities to whose quixotic defense the Zapatista movement is dedicated remain threatened by federal plans for development in Chiapas, including new infrastructure initiatives launched by López-Obrador's administration that (according to the EZLN) promise to displace indigenous communities and bring lasting environmental damage.

It is in this context, replete with uses of *Don Quijote* as a symbolic tool and discursive model, that Vargas Llosa's admonition to the Mexican president resonates most loudly. The call for a formal apology from Spain, ostensibly on behalf of the indigenous communities who were decimated by Spanish conquest and colonization in the era of Cervantes, fails to acknowledge that throughout the history of the Mexican republic *since* gaining its independence, many of the same problems for which an apology was sought have been perpetuated by its own government. It is a critique that echoes arguments made by cultural historians in Mexico like Hector Aguilar Camín, who distinguishes between the current Spanish state and an imaginary Spain that haunts would-be revolutionaries like López-Obrador. This imaginary Spain, Camín argues, is a scapegoat that allows the Mexican ruling class to excuse the rampant social and economic inequalities for which it only has itself to blame.

The fact that *Don Quijote* continues to speak to López-Obrador's diverse constituents, and that his administration supports and subsidizes cultural programming tied to it and its author (in Guanajuato and elsewhere) with the support of the Instituto Cervantes and other Spanish agents, is suggestive of how cultural narratives imported from Spain can illuminate cultural and political tensions in contemporary Mexico from fresh angles. The kind of transatlantic work outlined in these pages might be seen to constitute a step in this direction, but only so much can be accomplished by scholars like myself, who work from outside of Latin America and, more importantly, from outside of the field of Latin American studies. Without the assistance of scholars working within that field, however, such transatlantic gestures can only posit tentative suggestions for future research. Until the complex and persistent entanglements between Spain and Latin America are engaged by "peninsularist" *and* "Latin Americanist" scholars—and especially until that work circulates in a mutually informing community of Hispanist scholarship—admonitions of "imperialization" voiced by Mejías-López and others remain valid. In the absence of full engagement by both fields, Spain's heralding of Latin American Quijotes at the service of its own cultural imperialism will likely stand unquestioned and unchallenged. Like Don Quijote, scholars of Iberian cultural studies will tilt at windmills we imagine to be giants and attempt to rescue damsels who in reality are not in need of rescue. In the meantime, the cultural ubiquity of Don Quijote in Mexico, as seen in his deployment in educational curricula, cultural programming and political discourse, constitutes a missed opportunity to illuminate the vexing cultural problems that should concern us all.

Works Cited:

Barrera-Fernández, Daniel, and Marco Hernández-Escampa. "Events and Placemaking: The Case of the Festival Internacional Cervantino in Guanajuato, Mexico." *International Journal of Event and Festival Management* vol. 8, no. 1, 6 Mar. 2017, pp. 24-38, doi.org/10.1108/IJEFM-05-2016-0041.

Berghe, Kristine Vanden. "The *Quixote* in the Stories of Subcomandante Marcos." *International Don Quixote*. Brill-Rodopi, 2009, doi.org/10.1163/9789042029187_005.

Britt-Arredondo, Christopher. *Quixotism: The Imaginative Denial of Spain's Loss of Empire*. SUNY Press, 2005.

Camps, Magí. "Vargas Llosa: 'López Obrador se tenía que haber enviado la carta a sí mismo." *La Vanguardia* 27 Mar. 2019, lavanguardia.com/cultura/20190327/461298506337/vargas-llosa-pedir-perdon-espana-lopez-obrador.html.

Camín, Héctor Aguilar. *La invención de México: Historia y cultura política de México 1810-1910*. Planeta, 2008.

César Carrillo, Pablo. "García Márquez, quería ser como Cervantes." *Milenio*, Grupo Milenio, 22 Apr. 2014, www.milenio.com/opinion/pablo-cesar-carrillo/reporte-de-inteligencia/garcia-marquez-queria-ser-como-cervantes.

Close, Anthony. *The Romantic Approach to* Don Quixote. Cambridge University Press, 1978.

Cruz, Anne J. "Golden Age Studies in the 21st Century: A View of the Culture Wars." *Debating Hispanic Studies: Reflections on Our Disciplines*. Ed. Luis Martín-Estudillo, Francisco Ocampo, and Nicholas Spadaccini. *Hispanic Issues On Line* 1.1 (2006): 81-86, hiol_01_10_cruz_golden_age_studies_in_the_21st_century.pdf.

Delgado, Luisa-Elena. *La nación singular. Fantasías de la normalidad democrática española (1996-2011)*. Siglo XXI de España Editores, 2014.

Faber, Sebastiaan. "Hispanism, Transatlantic Studies, and the Problem of Cultural History." *Empire's End: Transnational Connections in the Hispanic World*, eds. Akiko Tsuchiya and William G. Acree Jr. Nashville: Vanderbilt University Press, 2016, 17-33.

Garcidueñas, José Rojas. *Presencias de don Quijote en las artes de México*. Instituto de Investigaciones Estéticas UNAM, 1968.

González Echevarría, Roberto. "Cervantes and the Modern Latin American Narrative." *Ciberletras*, vol. 1, no.1, Aug. 1999, http://www.lehman.cuny.edu/ciberletras/v1n1/crit_07.htm.

Hutcheon, Linda. *A Theory of Adaptation*. Routledge, 2006.

Krauze, Enrique. "El imperio del español." Congreso Internacional de la Lengua Española, 2004, Rosario, Argentina, congresosdelalengua.es/rosario/plenarias/krauze_e.htm.

"La última visita de Carlos Fuentes a Colombia." *Dinero* 15 May 2012, dinero.com/actualidad/articulo/la-ultima-visita-carlos-fuentes-colombia/151036.

Lindstrom, Naomi. "Twentieth-Century Latin American Literary Studies and Cultural Autonomy," *Studies in 20th Century Literature* vol. 19, no. 2, 1995, pp. 207-221, https://doi.org/10.4148/2334-4415.1371.

Marcos, Subcomandante. "Punch Card and Hourglass." *New Left Review* vol. 9, 2001, newleftreview.org/issues/II9/articles/subcomandante-marcos-the-punch-card-and-the-hourglass.

Martín Díaz, Emma, Cuberos Gallardo, Francisco and Castellani, Simone. "Latin American Immigration to Spain." *Cultural Studies* vol. 26, 2012, pp. 814-841.

Martínez, Guillem (ed). *CT o la Cultura de la Transición. Crítica a 35 años de cultura española*. Debolsillo, 2012.

Mejías-López, Alejandro. "Hispanic Studies and the Legacy of Empire." *Empire's End: Transnational Connections in the Hispanic World*, edited by Akiko

Tsuchiya and William G. Acree Jr., Vanderbilt University Press, 2016, pp. 204-221.

———. *The Inverted Conquest: The Myth of Modernity and the Transatlantic Onset of Modernism*. Vanderbilt University Press, 2010.

Piñero Valverde, José María. "*Las Españas* y la presencia del *Quijote* entre los exiliados en México." *Biblioteca Virtual Miguel de Cervantes*, 2005, pp. 1-14, cervantesvirtual.com/research/las-espaas-y-la-presencia-del-quijote-entre-los-exiliados-en-mxico-0/00760334-82b2-11df-acc7-002185ce6064.pdf.

Pomposo Fernández de San Salvador, Agustín. "Las fazañas de Hidalgo, Quixote de nuevo cuño, facedor de tuertos, etc." *Biblioteca Virtual Miguel de Cervantes*, cervantesvirtual.com/nd/ark:/59851/bmc416v4.

Posada, José Guadalupe. Calavera image of Don Quijote, *British Museum*, Google Arts & Culture, https://artsandculture.google.com/asset/la-calaveras-de-don-quijote-from-the-portfolio-36-grabados-jos%C3%A9-guadalupe-posada-jos%C3%A9-guadalupe-posada/dgGkL3PVXo9HFA?ms=%7B%22x%22%3A0.5%2C%22y%22%3A0.5%2C%22z%22%3A9.5934983738 94318%2C%22size%22%3A%7B%22width%22%3A1.3202940673828132%2 C%22height%22%3A1.2375000000000005%7D%7D.

Resina, Joan Ramón. *Del hispanismo a los estudios ibéricos: Una propuesta federativa para el* ámbito cultural. Biblioteca Nueva, 2009.

Russell, P. E. "*Don Quixote* as a Funny Book." *Modern Language Review* vol. 64, no. 2, 1969, pp. 312-326.

Sinfield, Alan. *Faultlines: Cultural Materialism and the Politics of Dissident Reading*. Oxford University Press, 1992.

Vanden Berghe, Kristine. "Sobre armas y letras. El Quijote como intertexto en los relatos del Subcomandante Marcos." *Boletín AFEHC* vol. 33, 2007, afehc-historia-centroamericana.org/index_action_fi_aff_id_1785.html.

Vargas Llosa, Mario. "Una novela para el siglo XXI." Real Academia Española, 2005, rae.es/sites/default/files/Mario_Vargas_Llosa_Una_novela_para_el_siglo_XXI.pdf.

Terceras and pandering wives in Tirso's *El pretendiente al revés*

KATHLEEN COSTALES
The University of Dayton

TIRSO DE MOLINA'S PALATINE comedy *El pretendiente al revés* is among his lesser known works. It was first published in 1627 in the *Primera parte* of his comedies, but the date of composition is unclear. María del Pilar Palomo Vazquéz dates the play to a four-year period between the years of 1608 and 1612, but Eva Galar Irurre, in her critical edition of the work, suggests a later date of composition, and situates *El pretendiente* between 1615 and 1625. It is in any case a complex, nontraditional play, in which—as its title suggests—the theme of a world upside down or backwards is central. As Peter Evans has noted, this theme is reflected even in the structure of the play, as the four lovers involved in the comedia's action are already married, thus eliminating the possibility of the traditional marriages that function to restore order in the dénouement.

> *El pretendiente al revés* invierte el orden de las estructuras típicas de lo cómico. Como ya se han casado los amantes, la comedia no puede terminar tradicionalmente con las bodas acostumbradas del género. Filipo, el Duque de Bretaña, se ha casado con Leonora recientemente, mientras que Carlos y Sirena llevan un año casados. Este es el más significativo de los reveses estructurales dentro de un ambiente donde los comienzos son finales, y viceversa (Evans 270).

The Spanish director José Maya staged the play in 2014 at the Teatro Fernán Gómez in Madrid and then again that same summer at Almagro, and has commented on the transgressive nature of the action. While discussing *El pretendiente al revés* he described the play as a "carnaval de deseos irrefrenables y pasiones al límite." He further expressed his surprise at how infrequently the play has been brought to the stage for he described it as "absolutamente transgresora para su tiempo y pone "patas arriba" el orden moral establecido, a través de la historia de celos y enredos que encabezan los personajes del duque de Bretaña y su esposa Leonora" (El Diario).

A quick run-down of the complicated plot: Sirena is the orphaned Marquesa de Belvalle. As the name suggests, Belvalle is a beautiful country valley where Sirena lives happily with her *villanos*. She is in love and has been married to her cousin Carlos for a year at the play's start; theirs is a clandestine marriage, and it must remain so because of her guardian the Duque Filipo de Bretaña's sexual obsession with her. The Duque, after having his advances repeatedly rebuffed for a period of over two years, has now married Leonora, the daughter of the Duque de Borgoña in an attempt to "cure" himself of this love sickness from which he suffers; and—even more importantly to him, at least—to make Sirena jealous. Rather than curing his sexual obsession, however, it has only grown; and his marriage has not caused Sirena to feel jealousy, only relief, as she hopes he will now leave her in peace and cease to harass her. His thwarted sexual desire has driven him mad, and in desperation, as her guardian, the Duque insists on bringing Sirena to his palace under the guise of offering her his protection. In reality, of course, he desires only to keep her close at hand to facilitate his efforts to woo her. This move to the corrupting environment of the palace, and away from the idyllic simplicity of life in the countryside, introduces the commonplace of *menosprecio de corte y alabanza de aldea* and further highlights the notion of a world turned upside down.

Once he has Sirena safely ensconced in his court, the Duque then turns to his new wife for help. He explains to the Duquesa Leonora that he cannot love her, nor can he be faithful to her, as he knows he should, because of his obsession for Sirena, leading him to exclaim: "¡Oh mi bien! ¡Quién pudiera, / para amarte / mejor, desocuparte el alma toda, / Que hospeda y acomoda ingratas prendas!" (1616-18). He then asks his wife to be his *tercera*, helping him to seduce Sirena, with the idea that once possessed, he can finally put an end to his obsession, claiming that "Ya suele la experiencia haber mostrado / causar odio y enfado, si se alcanza" (1706-07). Leonora reluctantly agrees to become "la primera / mujer que sea tercera de su esposo / seré, mas si es forzoso el agradarte" (1752-54) as she feels, as a wife, it is her duty to obey her husband. However, she in turn determines to seduce Sirena's secret husband/ cousin Carlos—who has followed Sirena to the palace—in revenge for the Duque's attempted infidelity. As part of Leonora's machinations, and to complicate the situation further, Leonora convinces Filipo to enlist the younger man's help to carry out his planned seduction of Sirena by suggesting that the Duque order Carlos to serve her, purportedly to assist in her efforts to persuade Sirena of the Duque's love. Thus, the Duque unwittingly becomes his wife's *tercero* in her attempts to sleep with Carlos, and Carlos is now forced by the Duque to pander his own wife: "dile que, si desea / servirte y tenerte grato, / con mas frecuencia me vea" (2279-81). At the same time Sirena unwillingly becomes the Duchess's accomplice in Leonora's endeavors to seduce Carlos, for, unaware that Sirena and Carlos are husband and wife as well as cousins, Leonora blackmails her with the threat of dishonor by allowing her husband to seduce Sirena unless the younger woman helps her to win Carlos:

> Si por aqueste camino
> no me ayudas, con mi fe
> tu honor a riesgo pondré,
> dando a mi enojo motivo,
> pues cuando mi honor derribo
> no ha de haber honor en pie.
> Los ojos ha puesto en ti
> el duque, para cegarlos,
> y yo los he puesto en Carlos,
> tu primo. (1886-95)

In this way, each character is both spouse and panderer of their respective partner leading Raúl Galoppe to compare the play to Mazursky's sexual boundary-pushing movie *Bob & Carol & Ted & Alice* from 1969 (2).

Given the centrality of the themes of pandering and *terceras* to the play, for this paper, I will be touching on some of the famous *alcahuetas* and *alcahuetes* in Spanish literature from the Trotaconventos, through to poor Sancho Panza in *Don Quijote*. I will also compare these literary creations to some real-life panderers as described in Tomé Pinheiro da Veiga's chronicles of life at the Court in Valladolid. The Portuguese diplomat claimed in his *Fastiginio o fastos geniales* that it was not uncommon, apparently, for Spanish noblemen to pander their wives:

> Por lo cual decía un amigo mío: «Mohíno el hombre que no es cornudo, porque tiene mala cama y mala mesa, mujer fea y poco regalo.» Y por eso quedó el proverbio de llamar á los dichosos cornudos, porque no hay mejor ventura que tener mujer hermosa, y sin poner nada de casa, tener

por tributarias las ajenas y la mujer alegre, que, porque calléis, os hace mil mimos (114).

The practice was so common—according to this saying—that cuckolded men were considered fortunate, and those who did not have a cheating wife were unlucky, as they had to endure bad food and few luxuries. In *El pretendiente al revés*, however, the main panderer is not the husband, nor is she the servant, but rather the wife herself. I will examine, therefore, the role of wife as procurer, for it is my contention that Tirso's Leonora is an original addition to the corpus of the panderer or *alcahueta* in Spanish Literature.

Now, the figure of the *alcahueta* or *tercera* is familiar to any student of Medieval or Early Modern Spanish literature, and they can be broken down into types. The earliest example of which is the Arcipreste de Hita's Urraca, otherwise known as the Trotaconventos, from *El libro del buen amor*. Fernando de Rojas, with his Celestina, fleshes out the basic pattern established in the earlier work; both characters are older women of low social standing who rely on their wits, their words, and a little bit of witchcraft to help young men seduce young women. If at one end of the scale you have this first "puta vieja" type, as Celestina is so lovingly referred to, other female characters who perform the same role of *tercera*, according to Augustín Redondo's ranking of them, would be *dueñas*, *criadas*, and *doncellas medianeras*. Although these last three types differ, perhaps, in age and social standing, they are all female confidants of the object of the *galán*'s affection, and all work as go-betweens, with or without the knowledge of the lady in question. Examples of these are numerous and range from the doncella Darioleta who facilitated King Perión's union with the infanta Helisena—resulting in the birth of Amadís de Gaula—to the parodic Maritornes in the *Quijote* (Redondo 685-86). These female go-betweens are frequent in Tirso's plays as well. We have the examples of Doña Juana from *El vergonzoso en palacio* who facilitates her cousin Antonio's seduction of and eventual marriage to Serafina, the daughter of the Duke of Avero, as well as the unnamed "mujer" who unwittingly assists Don Juan Tenorio in dishonoring her mistress Doña Ana de Ulloa in *El burlador de Sevilla*.

Their male literary counterparts run the gamut from poor Sancho Panza who acted as *medianero* for the Caballero de la Triste Figura, to Mateo Alemán's *Guzmán de Alfarache* in which the rogue served as *tercero* for the ambassador while in Rome. In Cervantes, notably, the figure of the ruffian or *alcahuete* is a recurrent one, and two examples from his theatrical works would be Trampagos from the *entremes El rufián viudo* and Cristóbal de Lugo from the more serious *comedia de santos*, *El rufián dichoso*. In the first instance, Pericona, a prostitute, has died of syphilis and her pimp Trampagos mourns her passing, as she was his principal source of income. In this satirical work, the other prostitutes now vie for Trampagos's approval and the honor of replacing Pericona. The second is a full-length play about the life of Cristóbal de Lugo, a young pimp, and his penitence and conversion to Fray Cristóbal de la Cruz, and eventual canonization. Perhaps Cervantes's most famous pimp, however, is the *alcahuete* condemned to the *galeras* in the *Quijote* who affirmed that his profession was "necesarísimo en la republica bien ordenada" (269; part 1, ch. 22). There is, in fact, a legal and moral basis to the *alcahuete*'s argument, for, according to Mary Elizabeth Perry in her study of legalized prostitution in Sevilla, there was a long-standing belief that prostitution was a necessary evil to protect society against what was perceived to be the greater sins of male homosexuality and adultery. Furthermore, brothels, and legalized and well-regulated prostitution, were thought to protect honorable women from being propositioned and potentially dishonored. Clerics, such as Francisco Farfán, based their support of prostitution on the writings of Saint Augustine and Saint Thomas Aquinas, arguing that: "society needed brothels just as a palace required a cesspool" (143).

In spite of these examples mentioned above, male literary *alcahuetes* are, perhaps, less well-known in Spanish literature than women, but in legal terms *alcahuetes*, and not *alcahuetas* seem to be more concerning to the authorities. In Partida Séptima, "Título 22: De los alcahuetes" in the *Las Siete Partidas*, for example, there are five types of panderers listed:

> Y son cinco maneras de alcahuetes, la primera es de los bellacos malos que guardan las putas que están públicamente en la putería, (tomando su parte de los que ellas ganan;) la segunda es de los que andan por trujamanes que de ellos reciben; la tercera es cuando los hombres crían en sus casas cautivas u otras mozas a sabiendas porque hagan maldad de sus cuerpos, (tomando de ellas lo que así ganaren;) la cuarta es cuando algún hombre es tan vil que él mismo alcahuetea a su mujer; la quinta es si alguno consiente que alguna mujer casada u otra de buen lugar haga fornicio en su casa por algo que le den, (aunque no ande él por trujamán entre ellos.) Y nace muy gran daño de estos tales pues, por la maldad de ellos, muchas mujeres que son buenas se vuelven malas, y aun las que hubiesen comenzado a errar, hácense por el bullicio de ellos peores (129).

This legal text seems to suggest that the majority of woman are not given to misbehaving of their own accord, but are, unfortunately, easily manipulated and led astray by corrupting male influences. Woman are presented here as susceptible and in need of protection, for otherwise, their moral purity easily could be debased and they will "become bad" (se vuelven malas). Even those women who already have begun to err ([han] comenzado a errar) will apparently venture further down the road to perdition under the guidance of a bad man than they would have on their own. The *alcahuetes* are condemned in the eyes of the law for their role in corrupting and exploiting decent women who would otherwise not have sinned. This perception of women as weak or vulnerable was further reflected in the legal codes of Sevilla regarding prostitution. As Perry notes, in 1570, the city passed an ordinance prohibiting "ruffians" from pawning their women, and brothel owners were specifically forbidden from employing a pawned woman, even if she were a willing participant in the financial arrangement (Perry 149). There were, in fact, formal procedures in place for a woman to become a licensed prostitute at an official brothel: she had to appear before a magistrate, and, among other things, swear that she understood the purpose of a brothel, and that she was entering into prostitution of her own volition.[1] Female agency, at least in this regard, was considered an important factor in permitting a woman to legally enter the sex trade (Perry 145). Women, therefore, were allowed to sell themselves, but men were forbidden by law from selling these same women, at least in theory. As Perry states: "these policies imply that poor women were so commonly exploited economically and so easily duped into exploitative situations that the city government had to protect them from themselves and their men" (149).

Returning to the *Siete Partidas*, the only reference to women as panderer in the legal code is the brief reference "lo que dijimos en este título de los alcahuetes, aplíquese otrosí a las mujeres que trabajan en hecho de hacer alcahuetería" (129). Beginning in the fourteenth century, however, royal ordinances warn of false "monasteries" and "abbesses" who rent rooms to unlicensed prostitutes (Perry 142) and in seventeenth-century Sevilla, Padre Pedro de León wrote of "infernal stepmothers" who volunteered in orphanages feigning Christian virtue, but with the intent of teaching and recruiting the young orphans into prostitution. The crimes committed by these madams were seen

---

[1] As Perry indicates, noblewomen were prohibited from entering the sex trade, and when applying for the legal right to prostitute themselves, women had to affirm that they were not members of the upper classes. Prostitution was viewed as a desperate solution to the extreme poverty that many women in the lower income brackets suffered (145). Charitable organizations, in fact, were established for the purpose of collecting funds to provide dowries to poor women as well as to repentant former prostitutes to allow these women to marry (154).

somewhat differently than those committed by male pimps; crimes committed by women were frequently attributed to their poverty, and these women were viewed, paternalistically, as vulnerable victims of their circumstances, rather than corrupting influences, per se (Perry 152). In a similar fashion, perhaps, when Leonora threatens to disregard Sirena's honor if she does not help the Duchess with her plan to seduce Carlos, the older woman does so only because of the untenable situation forced upon her by her husband. Leonora would not have engaged in this type of behavior if it were not for her circumstances.

This notion of women being in need of protection or guidance to keep them on the straight and narrow is reflected not only in the legal treatises of the day, but also in Pinheiro's *Fastiginia o fastos geniales* written between April and July of 1605 as he reflects on his time in the Spanish Court at Valladolid.

> De suerte que imagino que de esta gente, los más no hacen caso de los cuernos y á lo que la honra alcanza es á no querer averiguarlos, y hay algunos que dan la ocasión con la mucha libertad y disolución con que dejan proceder á las mujeres (112).

Under consideration, here, is not a comment relating to *alcahuetería* per se, but rather to adultery. The sentiment is similar however, for without male vigilance and protection, and with too much freedom, women will fall into debauched living, and dissolution. The responsibility to keep women from evil falls to their male relations—in this case their husbands in particular— but the concept of honor, appears to be, in actuality, not a great concern to men in the Spanish court at Valladolid in the early 1600's.

Pinheiro's text mentions furthermore, several cases of actual *alcahuetería*, in which noble husbands acted as ruffians and did, in fact, pawn their wives for financial gain.

> Contóme además que no queriendo ella mandar pedir á un hidalgo que la enamoraba 500 reales prestados, él [marido] mandó á rogarle, en nombre de la mujer, que se los prestase sobre una prenda, diciendo: «y no es posible que, yendo el recado en tu nombre, pida él prenda, siendo tan honrado caballero.» Y me juró que le había dicho: «[. . .] y si él viniera acá, á cuenta de su dinero, y quisiere acostarse conmigo, ¿qué mandas tú que le responda, pues eres tal que esto haces?» Y que él contestó amenazándola. [. . .] y así le llamó ella Don Fernando Cornelio de Quirós (113).

When the wife in this instant does not want to request money from her suitor, her husband then demands it himself, while using her name and trusting in her lover's generosity. Rather than expressing jealousy or concern for his honor that another man is courting his wife, he seeks to capitalize on her extramarital relationship and appears to view his wife as a commodity from which to profit. That his wife's suitor might feel entitled to consummate their relationship as a result of this financial transaction does not concern him, and leads to his wife looking upon him with disdain and referring to him in ridicule as "Cornelio," an obvious play on words with *cornudo* or cuckold.

Another of Pinheiro's examples of a husband pandering his wife is rather reminiscent of Lazarillo de Tormes and his famous *"caso"* in which the rogue is married to the concubine of the Archpriest of San Salvador and happily profits from his spouse's infidelity.

> Aquí me mostraron á un infame del hábito de Montesa, que con ser muy noble consentía que la mujer viviese amancebada con un canónigo de Toledo, y porque ella se incline á otro, que tenía menos años y menos dinero, el canónigo le pidió que la atemorizase, por los celos que tenía, y convenido el precio, le acometió hallándole en casa y le mató (113).

In Pinheiro's example, however, the pandering husband is a knight of the Order of Montesa—rather than a lowly town crier like Lázaro—who, for financial gain, has pawned his wife to the Canon of Toledo. The inconvenience to this arrangement is not spousal jealousy, but rather the fact that the wife is attracted to a younger, less wealthy man. She favors him over the older Canon, and would prefer to take him as a lover. The husband objects to this younger man, not because he is in any way concerned with his wife's infidelity, but rather because of the money he would lose if she left the wealthy cleric. The husband feels he has the right to choose his wife's lover for her, based on the financial gain the lover can provide him. In addition, the Canon is jealous of the younger man, and asks the husband to intervene on his behalf. In collusion with the cleric, and for a price, the husband then kills the younger suitor that the wife prefers, in favor of the older, richer man from whom he can better profit.

Both of these examples from Pinheiro's *Fastiginia* would fall into the fourth category of *alcahuetes* from the *Siete Partidas*; these men are examples of what was legally regarded as the vilest type of panderer: he who sells his wife to another man for financial gain. In addition, under the sumptuary laws of 1570 Sevilla, these are both examples of men pawning their women, and were an explicitly prohibited form of prostitution. A woman could choose to sell herself, but a man was forbidden from selling her, particularly if she were a member of the nobility, as is the case in these examples. Interestingly, the *Siete Partidas*, from thirteenth century Spain, while providing the basis for the development of legalized prostitution in Spain, also recognized the reality of extramarital sexual activity, and thus created a legal distinction between concubines—women who engaged in extramarital sexual activity for financial gain with only one man—and prostitutes—women who had sex with many. By the fourteenth century, however, and in an effort to distinguish and protect chaste women from those who were not, royal ordinances eliminated this legal distinction between concubines and prostitutes. In the eyes of the new sumptuary laws, all women, no matter the number of their partners, who engaged in sexual activity in exchange for money, were one in the same (Perry 140-41). In all of the three cases cited above, both from Pinheiro and from *Lazarillo*, in legal terms, the wife is acting not as a concubine with her lover, but as a prostitute, with her husband as pimp.

Turning now to *El pretendiente al revés*, the Duque de Bretaña's situation is somewhat different from these cases, as his initial intention is not to pander his wife, but rather to have his wife procure Sirena for him. In his case, therefore, we have an example not of wife pandering—as was the case with Pinheiro's knight who pawned his wife to the canon—but of a pandering wife, whose role it would be to convince Sirena to accept her husband as her lover. His intention at the beginning of the play is the seduction of Sirena in order to cure himself of his love sickness, thus making room in his heart for his wife.

> Tú has de ser mi Galeno y mi bien todo.
> Haz, Leonora, de modo, aunque provoque
> tus celos, que yo toque esta pintura.
> Desengañar procura mi deseo.
> Sepa yo si es angeo comparado
> contigo, este adorado desatino.
> Sepa yo si es divino o es humano
> este ángel, porque, sano, como es justo
> te estime más mi gusto y la experiencia
> me enseñe la excelencia, mi Leonora,
> con que eres vencedora. (1739-49)

In the Duque's analogy, Sirena is the painting that he has only been able to admire from afar. Leonora is to be his Galeno—a reference to the Greek philosopher and physician—who can cure him of his obsession. His stated intention is to compare the two women to prove to himself Leonora's superiority and to change or "mudar" his feelings for Sirena, and replace her in his heart with Leonora.

As I have already stated, Leonora pretends to accept the Duque's plan, however, she determines to pay him back in his own coin, and trick him into procuring Carlos for her, as she states in the following aside:

> ¡Pon los ojos en Sirena,
> necio, que yo los pondré
> en quien venganza me dé
> de tu desprecio y mi pena!
> ¡Tu tercera hacerme ordena,
> que yo te haré mi tercero
> porque por tus filos quiero
> vengarme desta manera,
> para que tu honra muera
> con las armas que yo muero! (1792-1801)

Her stated goal is not simply to take revenge on her husband for his intended infidelity; rather her plan is to "kill" his honor metaphorically with the same weapons (armas) that are killing her: his disregard and her suffering.

By the end of the second *Jornada* the Duque's obsession for Sirena is now overwhelming him, and rather than leaving it up to Leonora, Filipo himself begins to pressure Carlos to procure his wife/cousin for him. The Duque's obsession now consumes him to the point he first offers to make Carlos his *cazador mayor*, and throughout the play, as the Duque's obsession continues to grow, so to do his bribes. After *cazador mayor*, he then names Carlos the Baron of Flor with a rent of 6,000 ducados—a rent that he will supplement in exchange for certain favors—, then the Marquis of Anguiana, until finally the Duque states that he will declare Carlos his heir if only the younger man will act as his procurer and assist him in satisfying his sexual desire for Sirena. He dismisses any objections that Carlos sets forth as immaterial, as his intentions, he claims, are honorable—at least in regard to Sirena—much less so for his poor wife. When Carlos protests that to act as *tercero* to the Duque is to dishonor his cousin, the Duque responds that if Carlos can convince Sirena to satisfy him he will kill Leonora and marry the younger woman instead.

> ¿Pues qué afrenta se te sigue
> de que cumpla mi esperanza
> tu prima y la goce yo,
> si cuando me satisfaga,
> dando a Leonora la muerte,

> la has de ver entronizada
> sobre mi silla ducal? (2507-13)

As the Duque sees it, rather than dishonoring Sirena, through this seduction he will actually honor her by helping her ascend the social ladder. Marriage to him would make her his Duchess, rather than a socially inferior Marchioness. This now becomes a case of *estupro bajo palabra de matrimonio*, or seduction by promise of marriage, although the promise the Duque makes is to her cousin rather, as is more common, than to Sirena herself.[2] Interestingly, in this case, the Duque will only kill his wife after consummating his relationship with Sirena. It is never made clear if the reason for this is because he does not want to commit uxoricide in case things do not work out, or because he will simply renege on his promise of marriage to Sirena afterwards.

Interestingly, these attempts to bribe Carlos are not the first time that the potential relationship between the Duque and Sirena has been described in monetary terms. In the *Primera Jornada*—whilst still in Belvalle, and well before the Duque had devised this plan to bribe Carlos into pawning his cousin/wife—the younger man had expressed to Sirena his concern about moving to the Court. Attempting to calm Carlos's fears that she will be swayed by the Duque's advances, Sirena replies with a metaphor based in the concept of supply and demand, claiming that her steadfastness will be worth more after they move to the palace; all goods—here referring to the Duque's sexual obsession—decline in value when they produce no profit (897-900). Her intention here is to imply that the Duque will eventually desist in his attempts to conquer her as he comes to realize that his efforts have not produced the desired effect. Rather than calming Carlos, and foreshadowing the theme of pandering that develops later in the play's action, her words provoke him to exclaim:

> ¿Ya habláis del valor? Temer
> puedo que saldréis ingrata,
> porque quien del precio trata
> no está lejos de vender. (905-08)

---

2 Abigail Dyer indicates, in seventeenth-century Spain the term *estupro bajo palabra de matrimonio* was somewhat unstable and depended in great part on the jurist's personal interpretation of the concept. It could mean either rape, or refer exclusively to seduction based upon a marriage promise. For women to prove a case of *estupro* in either an ecclesiastical or a secular court, she had to demonstrate that she was of good character or reputation—*estupro* could only be committed against respectable people—and that she had been a virgin prior to her seduction.

By the play's third act Sirena is, of course, fearful for her virtue, jealous of Leonora's flirting with Carlos, annoyed by her husband's distrust of her, and thoroughly fed up with the entire situation. When the villagers of Belvalle visit her at the palace she takes matters into her own hands, and uses this opportunity to flee from this "confuso infierno / donde son los pecados cortesanos" (3287-88) and to return to her simple life in the country, seeking refuge at Corbato's farm in the hopes that the Duque will not find her there. When Carlos discovers that she has escaped from the palace, he determines to follow her, and after a series of complications, Filipo, Leonora, and finally Leonora's father, the Duque de Borgoña¾who has arrived unexpectedly to intervene on behalf of his daughter¾also take shelter at the farm. They have all been caught in a tremendous cleansing downpour, which Galoppe interprets as a manifestation of divine ire at the goings-on at court (7), and now must exchange their silk for rustic clothing, further emphasizing the two underlying themes of *menosprecio de corte, alabanza de aldea*, and a world turned upside down that are present throughout the play.

In the countryside, away from the corrupting influence of the court, and safe in the presence of the Duque de Borgoño, Carlos can finally confess that he and Sirena are secretly married, and plead with Duque Filipo to forgive their daring. Before Filipo can respond, the Duque Enrico intervenes in his role as mediating father-figure to reestablish order at the play's end. As the two couples in this instance are already married, the Duque's role in this play is to reaffirm the validity of both unions, particularly Sirena and Carlos's clandestine marriage. More importantly, however, he reminds everyone involved, and Filipo in particular, of the sanctity of their marriage vows and the duties that these entail. As his peer and father-in-law, he reminds Duque Filipo that Sirena is his deudo, but that she is not a "deudo que se cobra / en ofensa de su fama / y agravio de vuestra esposa" (3807-09). He offers Carlos and Sirena safety in Borgoña away from Filipo's sphere of influence, and furthers grants Sirena the county of Aspurg as her dowry. Duque Filipo can finally recognize that he has been an "amante al revés" and wisely chooses not to protest. The play concludes with Cardenio, one of the shepherds, summarizing the moral of the story in *sayagués*: "Aprienda a hacer desde agora / el amante pretendiente / las diligencias que importan" (3847-49).

As this paper lays out, the theme of *alcahuetería* is a common one in Spanish literature, and was a topic of concern and debate to both ecclesiastic and secular authorities. Furthermore, it was a practice that was not uncommon in Spanish society, even at the highest levels of the social hierarchy, if Pinheiro is to be believed. Less frequent, of course, in both society and literature, is the case of the wife acting as the actual procurer for her husband. In *El pretendiente al revés*, Tirso takes the character of the *alcahueta* to an absurd extreme, and creates a play in which wives act as procurers for their husbands, and vice versa. This situation is further complicated, of coure, by Sirena's and Carlos's secret union. After the Council of Trent, although clandestine marriages such as Sirena's and Carlos's were no longer considered legally valid, they continued to be common. In her study of the issue of clandestine marriages in Tirso's plays, María Berta Pallares de Rodríguez Arias concludes that Tirso privileges individual freedom over the strict norms imposed by the Council. *El pretendiente al revés* supports this interpretation, as the young couple's union is recognized and supported in the end by the Duque Enrico as evidenced by his generous dowry for Sirena. Although their marriage might not be legally recognized, it is a union entered into by mutual consent and with honest intention on the part of both husband and wife. Unlike Filipo and Leonora, Sirena and Carlos love each other and fight to honor their marriage vows in spite of the other couple's increasingly desperate attempts to seduce them into infidelity. Their love, honor and constancy are recognized and rewarded in the end, while the other couple, particularly the Duque Filipo, is reprimanded for their lack of the same. The younger couple's union, while clandestine, is presented as more legitimate than Leonora and Filipo's, for theirs is a union based on love. In *El pretendiente al revés* Tirso calls to account unfaithful partners and husbands, such as Filipo, who would manipulate their wives, and abuse of their wedding vows, but he does so in a highly original and entertaining "carnaval de deseos." This play is an interesting addition to the corpus of *alcahuetas* and *alcahuetes*, and the Duchess Leonora can take her place alongside the Celestinas of the Spanish literary tradition.

Works Cited

Alfonso X el Sabio. "Partida Séptima, Título 22: De los alcahuetes." *Las Siete Partidas*, pp. 110-11, Biblioteca Universal Virtual, 2006, www.biblioteca.org.ar/libros/130949.pdf. Accessed 13 Apr. 2019.

Cervantes, Miguel de. *El ingenioso hidalgo Don Quijote de la Mancha*. Edited by Luis Andrés Murillo, Castalia, 1978.

———. "El rufián viudo llamado Trampagos." *Entremeses*, edited by Florencio Sevilla Arroyo and Antonio Rey Hazas, Alianza Editorial, 1998.

———. *Los baños de Argel y El rufián dichoso*. Edited by Florencio Sevilla Arroyo and Antonio Rey Hazas, Alianza Editorial, 1998.

Dyer, Abigail. "Seduction by Promise of Marriage: Law, Sex, and Culture in Seventeenth-Century Spain." *Sixteenth Century Journal*, vol. XXXIV, no. 2, 2003, pp. 439-55.

"*El pretendiente al revés*, el 'carnaval de deseos' de Tirso de Molina." *Eldiario.es*, 7 Feb. 2014, www.eldiario.es/politica/pretendiente-carnaval-deseos-Tirso-Molina_0_226427868.html. Accessed 13 Apr. 2019.

Evans, Peter W. "Sexo y cultura en *El pretendiente al revés* de Tirso de Molina." *El mundo del teatro español en su siglo de oro: ensayos dedicados a John E. Varey*, edited by José María Ruano de la Haza, Dovehouse Editions, 1989, pp. 267-74.

Fiadino, Elsa Graciela. "De amores y risas en los palacios de Tirso." *Hispanismos del mundo: diálogos y debates en (y desde) el sur*, edited by Leonardo Funes, Miño y Dávila Editores, 2016, pp. 95-104.

Galoppe, Raúl A. "El revés del pretendiente: Hacia una configuración del deseo en una comedia tirsiana de difícil clasificación." *L'Érudite Franco-Espagnol*, vol. 2, Fall, 2012, pp. 2-12.

Pallares de Rodríguez Arias, María Berta. "El matrimonio clandestino en la obra de Tirso de Molina." *Homenaje a Tirso de Molina*, special edition of *Revista Canadiense de Estudios Hispánicos*, vol. 10, no. 2, Invierno, 1986, pp. 221-34.

Palomo Vázquez, María del Pilar. Introducción. *Obras completas de Tirso de Molina*, edited by María del Pilar Palomo Vázquez and Isabel Prieto, vol III, Turner, 1997, pp. ix-xxiii.

Perry, Mary Elizabeth. "Deviant Insiders: Legalized Prostitution and a Consciousness of Women in Early Modern Seville." *Comparative Studies in Society and History*, vol. 27, no.1, January, 1985, pp. 138-58.

Redondo, Agustín. "De las *terceras* al alcahuete del episodio de los galeotes en el *Quijote* (I, 22). Algunos rasgos de la parodia cervantina." *Actas del X Congreso de la Asociación Internacional de Hispanista*, 21-26 August, 1989, Barcelona, edited by Antonio Vilanova, PPU, 1992, pp. 679-690.

Tirso de Molina. *El burlador de Sevilla*. Edited by Ignacio Arellano, Espasa-Calpe (Colección Austral 86), 1989.

———. *El pretendiente al revés y Del enemigo, el primer consejo (dos comedias palatinas)*. Edited by Eva Galar Irurre, Instituto de Estudios Tirsianos, 2005.

———. *El vergonzoso en palacio y El condenado por desconfiado*. Edited by Antonio Prieto, Editorial Plantea, 1982.

Well-Behaved Panzas Rarely Make History: Teresa Panza and the Metafiction of *Don Quijote*

G. CORY DUCLOS
Colgate University

> THE PROFESSOR. ... [M]y field includes Renaissance and baroque texts, theory, and culture, about which, as behooves me, I often argue for *constructedness* and equally often for *post-poststructuralist denconstruction*.
>
> DON QUIXOTE. This is incomprehensible to me, sir.
>
> SANCHO PANZA. And, as you can imagine, to me.
>
> THE STUDENT. Let's just say he is a man who reads, studies, teaches, and writes about books.
>
> DON QUIXOTE. *That* I can comprehend.
>
> – EDWARD FRIEDMAN, *Crossing the Line*

THROUGHOUT HIS LITERARY OEUVRE, Cervantes develops interesting female characters and comments on the gender dynamics of his time, often using fiction to give women a voice that society denied them. The various feminine figures within *Don Quijote* alone have provided fertile ground for scholarship and exploration from a feminist standpoint. As one exception to these women, Teresa Panza (the wife of Sancho who is given a few different names) has received relatively little scholarly attention. She does not, like other women in the novel, profess a proto-feminist outlook. Instead, her most notable appearance is a seemingly conservative argument that echoes a misogynistic line of thought, which may explain why the character does not always resonate with contemporary readers. Reducing Teresa's contribution to the face-value nature of one discourse elides her larger role within the work's narrative realism. Teresa Panza adds to Cervantes's metafictional enterprise in Part 2 by serving as the realist counterpart to Sancho's more active participation in Don Quijote's idealistic fantasy. Furthermore, an analysis of Teresa's arguments in Part 2, chapter 5, reveals her deep connection to a local, popular culture that resists the growing dominance of the early modern nation-state. Studying Teresa and her connections to the popular culture of a rural Spanish village provides insight into understanding Cervantes's mixing of literary fantasy and cultural realism that comes to define the modern novel.

In the realm of Cervantes scholarship, apart from some intrigue regarding her name,[1] Teresa Panza seems less compelling as an object of study than other female characters who more overtly challenge early modern social norms. Her minor role provides insights into early modern Spanish culture and helps explain Cervantes's use of metafiction, yet she has not been the subject of much critical inquiry (see Fanny Rubio's edited volume *El Quijote en clave de mujere/es*). In the larger studies of the women in *Don Quijote* where Teresa is mentioned, she understandably often takes a back seat to other important feminine figures in the work (see Martha García's *La función de los personajes femeninos en* Don Quijote de la Mancha *y su relevancia en la narativa* as well as Teresa Marín Eced's edited volume *Figuras femeninas en el Quijote*). Those who have looked at Teresa specifically have focused on her as a symbolic representation of early modern culture, including the realm of domesticity, traditional folkloric characterizations, and proverbial wisdom.[2] But she is most often analyzed purely in terms of her relationship with her husband or within the Dulcinea/Aldonza paradigm set by *Don Quijote* (Cialella 275-76).

Of the studies that focus primarily on Teresa Panza, few have discussed what exactly she adds to the novelty of *Don Quijote*, in part, perhaps, because she is often considered a fundamentally conservative figure. Louise Ciallella notes that, "In the rare cases of critical study of Teresa's presence, she has been described as showing a conservative and/or passive state of silent longing and prosaic resignation, as aggressively berating her husband, or as one

---

1   See, for example, Guillermo Serés, "El entremés de los Panza y el 'tío abad' de Sanchico (*Quijote*, II, 5-72)" and Juan Diego Vila, "Sombras para Sanchico: herencia, malestar familiar y olvido."

2   See Mauricio Molho's *Cervantes: Raíces Folklóricas*, which analyzes Sancho Panza's folkloric origins, including a discussion of Teresa Panza and an analysis of the other names gives to her and their relation to the bobo/sabio duality that Sancho represents (300-36).

part of a realistic 'common life' and/or 'the natural world'" (275).³ Building on the work of Patricia Heid, Ciallella goes on to analyze Teresa's discourse, specifically her use of proverbs and how they keep Sancho connected to his home. As I will explore in this article, this link between Sancho and Teresa is emblematic of larger socio-cultural issues at play. Beyond reminding Sancho of his Manchegan roots, Teresa's discourse pushes back against the culturally colonizing enterprise of Spanish imperialism and the rise of the modern nation-state. Teresa's presence underscores the nuance of Sancho's characterization and the economic realities of the lower class he represents.

Don Quijote captivates readers and draws them in by creating dynamic characters whose personal development is as important, if not more important, than the story itself. Unlike the characters of idealist fiction that preceded them, Don Quijote and Sancho have a complex and evolving relationship that provides insight into the dynamics of class and power of early modern Spanish society. Additionally, the interplay between knight and squire is a key factor that contributes to the development of a sophisticated metafictional text. The main characters' differing views about the ultimate goals of their chivalric mission come into conflict around the figure of Dulcinea. Don Quijote's devotion to the imagined lady seems to dissuade him from engaging in what Sancho believes will be monetarily profitable endeavors, such as saving and marrying the Princess Micomicona. Sancho's attempts to dissuade his master of his love for Dulcinea draw the squire into the world of idealism, making him a more active participant in the metadrama that comes to define the second part of the novel.⁴

---

3   Ciallella gives examples of such works from Ruth El Saffar (*Beyond Fiction: The Recovery of the Feminine in the Novels of Cervantes*), Ann E. Wiltrout ("Las mujeres del *Quijote*"), Sadie Edith Trachman (*Cervantes' Women of Literary Tradition*), Concha Espina (*Mujeres del* Quijote), Lidia Falcón (*Amor, sexo y aventura en las mujeres del* Quijote), and Washington Lloréns (*Dos mujeres del* Quijote: *la mujer de Sancho, Maritornes*).

4   When thinking of Sancho's role in the second part, the influence of Avellaneda's false sequel looms large. Carlos Romero Muñoz has studied how the apocryphal *Don Quijote* plays into the development of Sancho and his wife in "Genio y figura de Teresa Panza." For more on the importance that the Avellaneda version plays in the development of Part 2, see Friedman's "Insincere Flattery," which sheds light on Cervantes's approach to literary intrusion through comparison with Mateo Alemán's similar dilemma regarding *Guzmán de Alfarache*. See also Erich Auerbach's, "The Enchanted Dulcinea" in *Mimesis: The Representation of Reality in Western Literature*.

As Sancho Panza develops as a character, his importance within the formal aspect of the novel changes. In Part 1, Sancho appears as part of the mimetic representation of early modern Spanish society. Similar to his counterparts in the picaresque novel or the *comedia*'s *gracioso* character type, Sancho is a realistic representation of the Spanish lower class. Juxtaposing this base, simple figure with the idealism of Don Quijote is part of what makes the work funny, but also what makes it formally innovative. Edward Friedman describes this literary style as "periphrastic realism": "The early modern displays of realism could be said to delay—or in the parlance of post-structuralism, to defer—mimesis. That is, as mediated by metafiction, the imitation of reality is, on an initial plane, indirect—and inwardly directed—but never oblivious to the real world or to the society with which the characters interact" (*Cervantes* 16). Initially, the interplay between realism and metafiction is achieved principally through the interactions between the two main characters. The discovery that Part 1 has been published and widely read creates a whole new set of participants in this fantastical world, drawing Sancho deeper into his master's imaginary realm.

The role Sancho plays in the novel extends well beyond that of a typical squire. As Don Quijote sets off on his second sally, the addition of a partner allows for more dialogue. The narrator is able to provide more than the inner thoughts or lonely soliloquies of a madman, and can instead detail the back and forth between two companions. Unlike the typical squires of chivalric romances, however, Sancho is prone to speak his mind, often challenging Don Quijote, prompting the knight to comment that such a talkative squire is unprecedented in the tales of knighthood.[5] Sancho is not simply a passive sounding board through which Don Quijote can speak to the reader, but an active participant whose realistic worldview pushes back against Don Quijote's idealism.

The tension between idealism and realism serves to produce both the humor and metafiction of *Don Quijote*. Sancho's social class, physical embodiment, and worldview all consistently root the reader in the economic, social, and physical realities of early modern Spain. Sancho's changing role at the end of Part 1 and throughout Part 2 threatens to remove him from the realistic representation in which he was established. As the squire more fully embraces his role within Don Quijote's world and even goes on to fulfill his dream of obtaining a governorship, the participation of Teresa Panza in the

---

5 See Eduardo Ubrina's *El sin par Sancho Panza* for discussion about the literary precedents in the tales of knighthood that inspired Cervantes's own parodic version of a squire.

narrative action helps keep Sancho, and the reader, planted on the ground, so to speak. Teresa's role in Part 2 is essential for the metafictional nature of the novel, underscored by Sancho and Quijote themselves when they note Avellaneda's error in assigning to her a different name.

In *Cervantes and the Material World*, Carroll Johnson explains how Sancho represents a particular economic reality of early modern Spain. A close reading of Sancho's living and working conditions match up with historical records about the daily lives of working-class peasants of the time (Johnson 12-14). Cervantes provides an even more complex vision of Sancho's economic reality by pairing him with a master with an economically feudal mindset. As a squire, Sancho believes his labor should be rewarded with a pre-established payout, either in the form of a governorship or with a set salary. Don Quijote, on the other hand, sees the possibility of a regally bestowed reward as an afterthought that may or may not correlate to the amount of service he provides. This conflict, as Johnson notes, represents the greater social struggle taking place in Europe as mercantile capitalism began to challenge the economic supremacy of feudalism (25-26).

In this regard, the characterization of Sancho Panza gains importance beyond a simple representation of a Spanish laborer and indicates larger global changes taking place. One critical aspect of the rise of early modern capitalism was the expansion of European empires into the new world. John Tutino's *Making a New World: Founding Capitalism in the Bajío and Spanish North America* is emblematic of sociological studies that explain how the rise of global capitalism depended upon the wealth generated from new world expansion.[6] Todd Ahlman and Gerald Schroedle note that archaeologists generally concur that, concerning the Caribbean, "the colonization and exploitation by European powers from the sixteenth through the nineteen century created one of the epicenters for historical globalization and the expansion of capitalism throughout the world" (1). This global phenomenon has been studied within literary scholarship, but primarily with respect to its effect on the Americas. The rise of capitalism in the new world and its influence in Spain has had been much less studied. Diana de Armas Wilson, however, has shown that Cervantes's works reflect the reality that Spain's expansion of its borders into the Americas was redefining the social, cultural, and political realities of the Iberian Peninsula.

---

6   See Jefferson Dillman's *Colonizing Paradise* and Marco Meniketti's *Sugar Cane Capitalism and Environmental Transformation* for similar discussions about Spanish colonialism in the Carribean.

The development of the Sancho/Quijote relationship develops along the lines of a burgeoning class struggle that pitted old and new economic structures against each other. Although Sancho comes to embrace the fantastic world of the chivalric romance, he tries to wrest control from Don Quijote to infuse his own proto-capitalist mentality into this literary landscape. In simple terms, one might see Don Quijote as a conservative defender of feudalism and Sancho as an economic progressive seeking to establish a new market. Yet such an interpretation would suggest that Sancho is (at least tacitly) an advocate for the principles of colonial imperialism around which early capitalist enterprises were coalescing. Nevertheless, as is often the case, Cervantes's story is far more nuanced. As I have explained elsewhere, Sancho is a much more subversive figure. What can be added to this discussion is the way in which Sancho is tied to the popular cultural traditions of Spain that resist some of the negative aspects of the advent of imperialist capitalism. The inclusion of Teresa Panza as an active agent in the second part of *Don Quijote* helps to underscore this point by more explicitly tying Sancho to the realities of rural village life in Spain and by showing a different form of resistance to cultural changes. Her words and actions add depth to Cervantes's literary realism, complicating the interplay between imagined and embodied worlds.

The field of cultural studies provides a useful frame here. This interdisciplinary field focuses on culture in terms of studying how new and competing ideologies are formed and disseminated in a way that relates to creating, sustaining, or challenging social power structures. The early modern period is a particularly important moment, because it represents a major cultural shift away from the strictures of medieval philosophy and the economics of feudalism toward the beginning of the enlightenment and the birth of modern capitalism. Using the work of these cultural theorists can give us insight into how Teresa Panza's concerns for her family's welfare represent issues of historical social change affecting her.

The emergence of the modern nation-state required a change in how people viewed themselves in relationship to others. Local, popular cultural identities were replaced with a sense of national, mass culture. Whereas in the past, communities were defined by tangible interactions among individuals, a national identity depends on what Benedict Anderson calls an "imagined community." That is to say, people can identify as belonging to the same group, in this case, a country, without directly interacting with each other. This process includes a reshaping of social norms. Such a cultural transformation necessitates the rejection of prior epistemologies and creates new institutions to solidify a new way of thinking to coincide with the values of a developing mass culture.

In studying this cultural shift, Jesús Martín Barbero has focused on the most hotly contested sites of conflict. He studies the early modern period to understand how the emerging ideologies of the modern nation-state replaced prior modes of knowledge (89-91). Certain ways of thinking, and people who adhered to them, were stigmatized, marginalized, and ultimately rejected. Especially symbolic of this shift was the role that women played in the cultural context of the medieval and early modern periods. Women, and especially mothers, were seen as repositories of popular cultural knowledge. As opposed to what would become a nationalized (and ultimately globalized) mass culture, local cultures contained their own idiosyncrasies that kept smaller groups of people ideologically and economically separated from a larger population. If maintained, this detached existence would frustrate the expansion of a modern state that depends upon the tacit acceptance of a unified, although imagined, communal identity.

This pushback against women as propagators of popular traditions is evident in the growing fight against witches and witchcraft. Relabeling traditional practices as heretical witchcraft justified a rejection of their epistemological value. Trials and burnings of witches served as a physical and public representation of the destruction of past ideologies in favor of the new. Denouncing female knowledge as heretical and violently attacking those who possessed it was only one manifestation of this social shift. As Louis Althusser points out, there are two main forms of ideological suppression, each with its own particular repressive method: The repressive state apparatus, which uses force and violence, and the ideological state apparatus, which foments particular ideologies through instilling new knowledge (although, it should be noted, each state apparatus is prone to using the method of the other in particular contexts).

At the same time that women were marked as witches and vilified for possessing a feminine knowledge that resisted new ideologies, schools, and especially schools for the middle classes, became more prevalent across Europe. In prior centuries, formal education was reserved for the wealthy who could employ private tutors in the home. During the early modern period, as humanist and scholastic thought spread, schools appeared that gathered in a larger group of young boys to learn outside of the family structure. Taking these boys away from the home was economically more practical, which opened up educational opportunities for the upper-middle class. Richard Kagan has noted that the languages and subjects studied in these classrooms reflects the needs of the growing merchant class, with greater emphasis being placed on the learning of Latin, Greek, and Arabic, subjects that were useful for commerce but, for that reason, shunned by the aristocratic classes (33).

The ideological aims of these schools coincided with the spread of the modern capitalist state and a rising merchant class. In this sense, removing boys from the home environment also served another important practice: taking them away from their mothers. Outside of the matriarchal influence, boys were given a new set of ideological principles to follow: "The school followed two principles: teaching as a form of filling empty vessels and instilling morality as a means of rooting out vices. In the new society, learning began by removing the harmful influences of the parents, especially the mother who was seen as the one who conserved and transmitted superstitions" (Martín Barbero 91). Inherent within this new educational institution was a form of misogyny aimed at attacking the cultural values contained within a particularly feminine epistemology.

The female figure as a site of cultural conflict appears throughout early modern and medieval Iberian works. Many of the texts that continue to resonate with modern readers and scholars contain female characters with a subversive bent. Perhaps *La Celestina* stands as the best example of a literary figure that symbolizes a clash between two cultural ideologies, and I would argue that we are drawn to such characters because they represent the deep-seated tensions at the root of the ideological and economic models that have come to dominate today. The reappearance of Celestina-esque characters is common throughout early modern *comedia* and the picaresque, which, of course, has its own feminine tradition.[7] The feminine characters in *Don Quijote* who receive most of the critical attention do not pertain to that same lineage. Modern readers are justifiably more drawn to those women who espouse a proto-feminist outlook. Teresa Panza, on the other hand, exists within this realm and brings into the novel elements of the contentious nature of larger social changes taking place across the globe.

In Part 2, chapter 5, Teresa gives a nuanced and astute argument against Sancho's desire to once again venture out with Don Quijote. Many critics have seen in this argument a profoundly conservative woman, willing to repeat the overtly misogynistic refrain of "la mujer honrada, la pierna quebrada, y en casa." Nevertheless, an analysis of her discourse shows that Teresa's character is drawn from a subversive tradition and that she argues in favor of maintaining a popular cultural tradition increasingly considered anathema.

---

7 I also believe that picaresque works with male protagonists have an important connection to the feminine that has not yet been adequately studied.

Her part of the dialogue represents an attempt to keep her husband at home by tying him to a local tradition that his proto-capitalist vision threatens. In this sense, Pilar Monedero is correct in defending what might appear to be a conservative posture taken by Teresa as well as by Don Quijote's niece and housekeeper. Their desire to prevent Don Quijote and Sancho from leaving their homes does not come from an impulse to uphold the norms of a patriarchal society, it is the manifestation a desperate struggle for survival when they knew very well what it would mean to lose the male head of household: "Nuestras heroínas, más que conservadoras, son unas supervivientes, abandonadas a su suerte por los 'hombres de la casa' en una época y lugar (el Siglo de Oro español), en que ser fémina sin amparo de varón era bastante mala cosa... Y no digamos en qué situación queda Teresa Panza, sin un patrimonio ni unas rentas..." (64). Teresa's arguments in favor of Sancho remaining at home are, in this context, representative of a type of resistance to a new social order that devalues the power of the rural matriarch of a poor family.

In particular, Teresa's arguments for what she wants for her children, as opposed to Sancho's fantasy of a governorship, reveal her desire to maintain popular cultural traditions. Sanchico is the direct relation of the Panzas who receives the least mention throughout *Don Quijote*. Of her son, Teresa says, "Advertid que Sanchico tiene ya quince años cabales, y es razón que vaya a la escuela, si es que su tío el abad le ha de dejar hecho de la Iglesia." At first glance, Teresa seems to want to send Sanchico to school, sending him away from the home to be subject to new ideological forms, but there is more at play here. There is quite a bit of critical discrepancy about the exact meaning of Teresa's description of Sanchico's future. This uncle could be either a literal or figurative uncle, who may or may not have a wholesome relationship with Teresa (Vila, 312-17; Serés, 30-33). Likewise, "dejar hecho de la Iglesia," may refer to employment by the church rather than becoming a member of the clergy (Serés 29). Furthermore, sending Sanchico to study at fifteen years old is fairly late for starting school and not typical of early modern education, which generally began at six years old and ended at fourteen. One can conclude from this that Teresa is not speaking of the same education as the early modern humanists, and may not even be suggesting that her son learn even so much as to read, but rather that they trade on some family relations so that he might learn the basic functions necessary to earn a living as a type of church functionary.

This episode also calls to mind a debate in Spain about the literacy of the clergy. The debate goes back to the thirteenth century, when the papal envoy Jean D'Abbeville, a cardinal and scholastic philosopher, sought to impose more learning on what he believed was an overly ignorant clergy in Spain. Many resisted this new requirement that priests be educated according to the scholastic standards as part of larger reform efforts within the priesthood. Daniel Salas Díaz explains that Spaniards saw D'Abbeville's presence as foreign interference that did not coincide with their own set of local values: "los clérigos españoles deben de haberlo visto como un enviado entrometido e incapaz de enteder el contexto de la clerecía rural" (54). Evidence of the debate about the clergy's education is seen in Gonzalo de Berceo's *Milagros de Nuestra Señora* and the tale of "El clérigo simple" (109-12). The dimwitted priest is only capable of reciting a single mass: "non sabié decir otra, diciéla cada día, / más la sabié por uso que por sabiduría" (110). Due to his inability to read and general ignorance, he is banned by a Bishop from saying mass. Ultimately, the Holy Mother intervenes, chiding the Bishop and demanding that he reinstate the cleric. The maternal imposition opposing an outside, progressive voice for education correlates with the larger understanding that retaining feminine knowledge resisted new ideological structures. Although one might argue that the Catholic church as a whole adapted to new ideologies and, in many ways, help to spread them, the poem illustrates the way in which popular interpretations of church doctrine varied and provided space for local resistance.

It is within this context that Teresa's desire for Sanchico can be understood. She is not calling for his education in a humanistic sense. Instead, she is asking that he be more firmly rooted within the popular culture of his particular Catholic upbringing. She wants a son who, like the simple cleric, is free from the confines of "book learning" and devoted to the maternal values embodied by his earthly and spiritual mothers. She resists Sancho's belief that her son should go to court or that perhaps he might adhere more to Don Quijote's philosophy which places such great importance on literacy.

Teresa's desires for her daughter run along similar lines as she rejects the notion that life outside of her village holds greater benefit for their family. Teresa affirms that Sancho is wrong to want to take Sanchica away from her home and peers and into the larger world of the royal courts. Among a string of refrains typical of her and her husband's speech, she says, "Al hijo de tu vecino, límpiale las narices y métele en tu casa" (466; part 2, ch. 5). And she means this literally, having already picked out Lope Tocho as Sanchica's future husband. The name Tocho, meaning dumb, suggests that Lope is far from perfect, but perhaps a better match than the courtly suitors Sancho imagines. Teresa rejects Sancho's desire to move the family away from their home and marry off their daughter to some high lord. She sees much greater value in staying where they are, arguing that they are all better suited to the culture of their rural village.

Throughout, her argument is couched within the realm of clothing, drawing us into the world of female domesticity.[8] Teresa compares the rustic attire of which Sanchica is accustomed to the fine clothes which surely will fit her poorly or at least uncomfortably as a metaphor for the situation in which they would put their daughter by an unequal marriage. As a wife and mother, Teresa is aware of the realities awaiting a woman whose husband comes from more noble blood and would always have the ability to criticize and condemn his upstart wife. Thus she argues against taking on titles that do not belong to oneself, landing a damming blow against Sancho's employer: "Idos con vuestro don Quijote a vuestras aventuras y dejadnos a nosotras con nuestras malas venturas, que Dios nos las mejorará como seamos buenos. Y yo no sé por cierto quién le puso a él DON que no tuvieron sus padres ni sus agüelos" (466; part 2, ch. 5). In the face of global changes, Teresa sees Sancho and his master's retreat to the world of knight errantry as an act of cowardice. The dependence on an imagined ideal social order does not provide her any help in protecting the local traditions she holds dear.

In sum, Teresa's discourse in Chapter 5 adds to the realism of the novel by giving us a glimpse into the struggle to affirm the value of her popular culture. Set against Sancho's idealism, Teresa's outlook brings to the forefront the burdens of the real world and the harsh truths about the difficulties she and her children will face in his absence. But Teresa's function in part 2 goes beyond serving as a foil to Sancho's newfound belief in the merits of knight errantry. Her role highlights the importance of metafiction that Cervantes appears to have underlined in his first part, especially as a way of countering the perceived deficiencies of the false sequel of Avellaneda (Romer Muñoz 107-10).

In Part 1, Cervantes gives us very little information about Sancho's wife. As is the case with other characters, including Don Quijote himself, we are never given the actual name of this woman. In Part 1, almost in the same breath, Sancho refers to her as both Juana Gutiérrez and Mari Gutiérrez. Some attribute the name change to a Cervantes's carelessness, others to a subtle mockery of common mistakes in the tales of chivalry, while others still have found the folkloric roots of the names Juana and Mari to show that, like Sancho, his wife encapsulates both wisdom and folly (Molho 300-28). In any

---

[8] See Carlos Romero Muñoz's more lengthy explanation of the particular items of clothing Teresa mentions as well as their cultural significance in early modern Spain (125-29).

case, this ambiguity caused a small issue for Avellaneda, who felt the need to standardize the name of Sancho Panza's wife and does so by referring to her as Mari Gutiérrez. The specificity allows Cervantes to call Avellaneda out as a fake by moving the goalposts and choosing an entirely different name. In Part 2, chapter 59, Don Quijote and Sancho learn of the second book but dismiss it out of hand because it speaks of Mari Gutiérrez rather than Teresa Panza. Don Quijote mocks the false sequel: "yerra y se desvía de la verdad en lo más principal de la historia, porque aquí dice que la mujer de Sancho Panza mi escudero se llama Mari Gutiérrez, y no llama tal sino Teresa Panza. Y quien en esta parte tan principal yerra, bien se podrá temer que yerra en todas las demás de la historia" (790). The joke here is that Cervantes himself once made that same "mistake." But if Cervantes simply wanted to call out errors in Avellaneda's work by giving his unnamed characters different names, he could have chosen others, including Don Quijote's niece who Avellaneda refers to as Magdalena. But in his part 2, Cervantes leaves the niece out of his argument with Avellaneda, choosing instead to pick a fight over the true name of Sancho's wife.

The special attention Cervantes pays to Teresa, rather than other characters, highlights the importance of Sancho Panza's character development in Part 2 as he begins to take on a more active role in directing the action of the metadrama of Don Quijote's chivalric fantasies. Cervantes, from the prologue to part 1, makes it clear that Sancho is key to the work: "Yo no quiero encarecerte el servicio que te hago en darte a conocer tan noble y tan honrado caballero; pero quiero que me agradezcas el conocimiento que tendrás del famoso Sancho Panza, su escudero, en quien, a mi parecer, te doy cifradas todas las gracias escuderiles que en la caterva de los libros vanos de caballerías están esparcidas" (12; Part I, Prologue). And at the end of Part 2, when the duo meets Álvaro Tarfe, it is Sancho's behavior that convinces the character from the false sequel that he should sign an affidavit declaring these are the true protagonists.

Cervantes's choice to give Teresa more of a role in Part 2 and to include her within the metafictional response to Avellaneda's work falls in line with the character development of Sancho. Just as Don Quijote needed a realist squire, the more idealistic Sancho needs a realist companion off which to play. Teresa is Sancho's link back to the realities of home, but when she receives the letter and gifts from the Duchess announcing Sancho's governorship, she is drawn into the metatheater created by the scheming Duke and Duchess. It is here that her reaction differs from that of her husband. She responds to the Duchess by sending back two letters, one addressed to her newfound noble friend and the other to her husband (750-53; part 2, ch. 52). In these letters, we see how Teresa's character continues to function within the realm of cultural realism even when engaging with the idealism of the chivalric fantasy world of Don Quijote. It is important to remember the context in which we as readers see the content of Teresa's letters. Although she addresses the letters to two specific individuals, they are read to the larger audience of the Duke and Duchess's court by Don Quijote while Sancho is still away as governor. Although this was not the express intended audience of Teresa when writing the letters, it is the audience Cervantes chooses to receive and read the letters. They are also read side by side, urging the reader to compare their content.

Stylistically, we might assume that Teresa would use more formal language with the Duchess, but she cannot avoid the rustic speech that is her nature. She says that everyone in the village was shocked to learn that Sancho was a governor since they all consider him to be an unlearned "porro" (750; part 2, ch. 52). She tells the Duchess that "me están buellendo los pies por ponerme en camino" (750; part 2, ch. 52). Teresa responds to the Duchess's gift of a coral necklace by offering her some acorns. The juxtaposition is both humorous and symbolic. The coral, which must have been imported from the sea (likely near the Canary Islands), is both more valuable and timeless. The acorns are locally grown, of relatively little value, and seasonal, as Teresa notes. Each gift represents the aspects of early modern femininity that the women respectively represent. The discrepancy in value between the two gifts serves as a metaphor for how incongruent the Panza's arrival in the Duke and Duchess's court would be.

In contrast to the strong opposition to the idea of social mobility that she takes in chapter 5, Teresa is drawn, like her husband, into the world of possibilities that a governorship brings. She's eager to silence all the haters in the village who refuse to believe her good fortune. But unlike Sancho, Teresa does not jump wholeheartedly into the world of fantasy Don Quijote has created. Just as her arguments to keep Sancho home were rooted in her family's immediate necessities, so too is she focused in her letter to the Duchess on easing her material burden: "Y así suplico a vuestra excelencia mande a mi marido me envíe algún dinerillo, y que sea algo qué, porque en la corte son los gastos grandes: que el pan vale a real y la carne, la libra, a treinta maravedís" (751; part 2, ch. 52). What seems like a change in Teresa's convictions about social class when presented with the possibility of material wealth mirrors other moments of humor in the form of pot-shots at the lower classes. While the knight lies on his deathbed, for example, Sancho and the housekeeper are described as feeling somewhat happy, since to these simple folk, "esto del heredar algo borra o temple en el heredero la memoria de la pena que es razón que deje el muerto" (864; part 2, ch. 74).

Behind such laughter over Teresa's quick turn of character, readers might fail to recognize the sincerity with which she writes and the important way in which she reaffirms her commitments to her village and how she, as a woman, holds certain powers. In her letter to Sancho, she shows what is really important to her. After having gushed about the unforeseen good fortune of Sancho having achieved a governorship, she returns to thinking about her village and informs Sancho of what has been happening at home. Once again, Teresa replants the readers on the firm ground of realism. She resists the urge to get completely swept up by the metatheater of the Duke and Duchess through the care she shows for her village, including one of the final details she mentions: "Por aquí pasó una compañía de soldados; lleváronse de camino tres mozas deste pueblo; no te quiero decir quién son: quizá volverán, y no faltará quien las tome por mujeres, con sus tachas buenas o malas" (752; part 2, ch. 52). The sobering nature of this event seems to be lost on the fictional readers, who simply laugh about Teresa, but it would be hard to see how it could be passed over without care by early modern readers. Contemporary readers certainly see here signs of Cervantes's compassion for the plight of these women. Furthermore, Teresa's refusal to tell her husband the names shows her recognition of the importance of female solidarity and exemplifies the power women held within the rural popular cultures of early modern Spain.

The presence of Teresa Panza in Part 2 gives insight into the larger global changes taking place in early modern Spanish society. As part of the literary tradition of women who subversively assert a feminine mode of knowledge, Teresa reaffirms the value of her local culture in opposition to her husband's desire to engage in the broader imagined community outside their village. This dynamic illustrates the way in which individuals negotiated their place during an early modern form of globalization and the advent of a nascent capitalism. As Cervantes inscribes this conflict within *Don Quijote*, he further complicates the relationship between narrative realism and idealism. Teresa represents more than a folksy character who adds a few more humorous aphorisms to the novel. Cervantes inscribes within Teresa the underpinnings of a larger cultural debate set off against the newfound idealism of Sancho in Part 2. Studying Teresa Panza provides a glimpse into the social realities of early modern Spain and the ingenuity of Cervantes's work that pairs mimetic representation of his contemporary surroundings with the metafictional nature of his literary project.

Works Cited

Anderson, Benedict. *Imagined Communities*. Revised ed., Verso, 1991.

Ahlman, Todd M, and Gerald F. Schroedl. "Introduction: Contextualizing Caribbean Historical Sites through Colonialism, Capitalism, and Globalization." *Historical Archaeologies of the Caribbean: Contextualizing Sites through Colonialism, Capitalism, and Globalism*, edited by Todd M. Ahlman and Gerald F. Schroedl, U of Alabama P, 2019, pp. 1-9.

Althusser, Louis. *Lenin and Philosophy and other Essays*. Translated by Ben Brewster, Monthly Review, 2001.

Auerbach, Erich. "The Enchanted Dulcinea." *Mimesis: The Representation of Reality in Western Literature*, 1953, Princeton UP, 2003, pp. 334-58.

Berceo, Gonzalo de. *Milagros de nuestra señora*. Edited by Michael Gerli, Cátedra, 2003.

Cervantes, Miguel de. *El ingenioso hidalgo don Quijote de la Mancha*. Edited by Tom Lathrop, revised ed., Juan de la Cuesta, 2005.

Ciallella, Louise. "Teresa Panza's Character Zone and Discourse of Domesticity in *Don Quijote*." *Cervantes*, vol. 23, no. 2, 2003, pp. 275-96.

Dillman, Jefferson. *Colonizing Paradise: Landscape and Empires in the British West Indies*. U of Alabama P, 2015.

Duclos, G. Cory. "A Squire's Schooling: The Education of Sancho Panza." *Confluencia* vol. 30, no. 3, 2015, pp. 69-85.

El Saffar, Ruth S. *Beyond Fiction: The Recovery of the Feminine in the Novels of Cervantes*. U of California P, 1984.

Espina, Concha. *Mujeres del* Quijote. Renacimiento, 1930.

Falcón, Lidia. *Amor, sexo y aventura en las muejeres del* Quijote. Vindicación Feminista, 1997.

Friedman, Edward H. *Cervantes in the Middle: Realism and Reality in the Spanish Novel from* Lazarillo de Tormes *to* Niebla. Juan de la Cuesta, 2006. Print.

———. *Crossing the Line: A Quixotic Adventure in Two Acts*. Juan de la Cuesta, 2012.

———. "Insincere Flattery: Imitation and the Growth of the Novel." *Cervantes* vol. 20, no. 1, 2000, pp. 99-114.

García, Martha. *La función de los personajes femeninos en* Don Quijote de la Mancha *y su relevancia en la narativa*. Academia del Hispanismo, 2008.

Heid, Patricia. "Language and Gender in *Don Quixote*: Teresa Panza as Subject." *Lucero*, 1991-92, pp. 122-31.

Johnson, Carroll B. *Cervantes and the Material World*. U of Illinois P, 2000.

Kagan, Richard L. *Students and Society in Early Modern Spain*. Johns Hopkins UP, 1974.

Marín Eced, Teresa, coordinator. *Figuras femeninas en* El Quijote. U de Castilla-La Mancha, 2007.

Martín Barbero, Jesús. *Communication, Culture, and Hegemony: From the Media to the Mediations.* Translated by Elizabeth Fox and Robert A. White, Sage, 1993.

Meniketti, Marco G. *Sugar Cane Capitalism and Environmental Transformation: An Archaeology of Colonial Nevis, West Indies.* U of Alabama P, 2015.

Lloréns, Washington. *Dos mujeres del* Quijote: *La mujer de Sancho, Maritornes.* La Milagrosa, 1964.

Rojas, Fernando de. *La Celestina.* Edited by Dorothy S. Severin, Cátedra, 2005.

Romero Muñoz, Carlos. "Genio y figura de Teresa Panza." *Peregrinamente Peregrinos: Actas del V Congreso Internacional de La Asociación de Cervantistas*, edited by Alicia Villar Lecumberri, Associación de Cervantistas, 2004, pp. 103-149.

Rubio, Fanny, editor. *El* Quijote *en clave de mujer/es.* Complutense, 2005.

Salas Díaz, Daniel. "Mas la sabia por uso que por sabiduria: lenguaje, conocimiento y poder en el milagro del 'simple clérigo.'" *Divergencias*, vol. 5, no.1, 2007, pp. 49-58.

Serés, Guillermo. "El entremés de los Panza y el 'tío abad' de Sanchico (*Quijote*, II, 5-72)." *Anales Cervantinos*, vol. 33, 1995-97, pp. 27-38.

Trachman, Sadie Edith. *Cervantes' Women of Literary Tradition.* Instituto de las Españas en los Estados Unidos, 1932.

Tutino, John. *Making a New World: Founding Capitalism in the Bajío and Spanish North America.* Duke UP, 2011.

Urbina, Eduardo. *El sin par Sancho Panza: Parodia y creación.* Anthropos, 1991. Print.

Vila, Juan Diego. "Sombras para Sanchico: herencia, malestar familiar y olvido." *El* Quijote *desde su context cultural.* Coordinator, Juan Diego Vila, Eudeba, 2013, pp. 311-24.

Wiltrout, Ann E. "Las mujeres del *Quijote*." *Anales Cervantinos* vol. 12, 1973, pp. 1-6.

Wilson, Diana de Armas. *Cervantes, the Novel, and the New World.* Oxford UP, 2001.

Miguel Manipulated: Metatheater and Social Critique in Two Quixotic Puppet Operas

Timothy M. Foster

West Texas A&M University

Aʟʟ ɪᴄᴏɴɪᴄ ᴛᴇxᴛs, sᴜᴄʜ as Miguel de Cervantes's *Don Quijote*, suffer the fate (or fortune) of endless manipulation by other artists who seek to take advantage of the original's success, build off its cultural legacy, or put a new spin on its interpretation. Most cultural production inspired by *Don Quijote*—from classical music to graphic novels—concerns the memorable characters and humorous episodes of the novel. Yet as Edward H. Friedman is quick to point out, the tale of the knight errant tilting at windmills is only half the story. The parallel narrative of *Don Quijote* is the story of the writing of the novel itself (*Cervantes* 14), starring Cide Hamete Benengeli, readers of Part 1, and even characters from the false sequel. In this study, I discuss two adaptations of Cervantes's masterwork that rely on both narratives from the novel—the wanderings of Don Quijote and the composition of *Don Quijote*. Incredibly, both are puppet operas: *Vida do grande d. Quixote de la Mancha e do gordo Sancho Pança* (1733) by Lusophone playwright António José da Silva and *El retablo de Maese Pedro* (1923) by Spanish composer and librettist Manuel del Falla. Both works adapt elements of Cervantes's metafictional narrative, employing metatheatrical techniques such as self-reference and play within a play. As the puppet characters vocalize the struggle to assert their autonomy, lashing out against injustice and artifice, the spectator is prompted to reflect on the institutions and social conventions that trap human "characters" in the real world. Thus, both operas offer comparable "readings" of *Don Quijote*, using the novel's famed self-referentiality to offer poignant societal commentaries on their own times and places as well as broader philosophical reflections about the nature of reality and fiction.

The narrative complexity of *Don Quijote* has been one of the most prominent issues in twentieth-century criticism, often discussed in relation to the emerging genre of metafiction. Patricia Waugh defines metafiction as "a term given to fictional writing which self-consciously and systematically draws attention to its status as an artifact" (2). One central aspect of metafictional narrative is the "frame" or structure within which a story is contained and that can be broken to lay bare the conventions of fiction (30-31). In *Don Quijote*, the frame is constantly broken by stories within stories (such as the intercalated tales), contradictory situations (such as the hanging narrative broken off in Part 1, ch. 8, carried on in the "translation" of Cide Hamete Benengeli), and characters' self-awareness of their literariness (exemplified by Don Quijote's knowledge of the publication of Part 1 and of the spurious sequel, as well as his subsequent paranoia at the intervention of his "enchanters"). According to Friedman, metafiction formed an integral part of Cervantes's approach in breaking away from idealism: at the same time as Cervantes helped to define realism, he called attention to the very mechanisms of narrative fiction itself (Friedman, *Cervantes* 15). He locates Cervantes's work at the emergence of what he calls "*periphrastic realism*" (16), in which "the imitation of reality is, on an initial plane, indirect." Accordingly, he posits that at its core, "*Don Quijote* is about *the perception of reality*." While metafiction can be conceptual and heady, most critics agree that the blending of reality and fiction in *Don Quijote* is playful and compassionate (a Cervantine trademark). For Ruth El Saffar, Don Quijote's struggles come from his surprise that the world he has created has come to fruition in strange and unwelcome ways: "Don Quixote's world is ridden with enchanters and illusion because he insists on taking as real an image of himself that is of his own creation" (151). Other characters, on the other hand, are able to "turn illusion to their own purposes" (144) and thus experience the "immense freedom" that comes from understanding the true nature of reality and fiction.

Though different in scope, many metafictional techniques and concepts can operate on stage in drama. Richard Hornby defines metadrama as: "drama about drama; it occurs whenever the subject of a play turns out to be, in some sense, drama itself" (31). Lionel Abel similarly defines metatheater as: "theatre pieces about life seen as already theatricalized" (60), and focuses on characters who drive metatheater as "metadramatists." Hornby elucidates six types of metatheater: 1) "The play within the play" (analogous to the story within a story in narrative); 2) "The ceremony within the play" (such as a funeral, tournament, trial, or coronation); 3) "Role playing within the role" (similar to Abel's conception of a metadramatist); 4) "Literary and real-life reference;" 5) "Self reference" (or reference to the work of theater itself); and 6) "drama and perception," or those plays whose metatheatricality focuses overtly on human perception as a major theme of the work (32).

Attempting to adapt even a fraction of the narrative complexity of *Don Quijote* to the stage represents a formidable challenge. In addition, as Jesús G. Maestro notes, the novel already contains a great deal of metatheatricality. Of the six metatheatrical episodes Maestro cites from Part 2 of *Don Quijote* (42), Silva and Falla adapt four: from Silva, 1) the traveling theater troupe of angels and demons (ch. 11), 2) episodes with the Duke and Duchess (chs. 34-35), and 3) Sancho as "governor" (chs. 49, 51, 53); and from Falla 4) Master Peter's puppet show (chs. 25-26). That so many of these already metatheatrical episodes should be found in stage adaptations of the novel should not surprise the not-so-idle reader. In the novel, these scenes stand out both for how they add to the narrative complexity and for how they contribute a sense of surreal reality, of "distanciamiento [...] enajenación o suspensión" (Maestro 43). The reader can see in her mind's eye the cart full of actors and can picture the wax figurines on strings being manipulated by tavern firelight. Even so, these are among the most unbelievable scenes in the entire novel where the reader as "audience" becomes fully aware of the fictionality of the episodes. Carrying those same episodes onto a physical stage, then, allows for even more opportunity to engage with self-awareness.

The more surprising point of connection between Silva and Falla's adaptations is that both employed not human characters but puppets. As puppet theater was a popular and itinerant spectacle in Europe, for both Silva and Falla, the decision to bring puppet theater into the realm of high art was an intentional choice with interpretative consequences. The material reality of puppet theater is almost inherently metatheatrical, presenting enticing possibilities for adapting an already metatheatrical story. On one hand, puppets make the suspension of disbelief difficult, creating a certain distancing from the audience because the "communication of actions and emotions must proceed through the exaggerated gestures that the mechanical limitations of puppets impose" (Allen 331). On the other hand, puppets, unlike actors, are physically under the control of their operators (Haley 156), making their connection closer to the author or director and inviting speculation on the nature between literary creators and their creations.

This metatheatrical push and pull of puppets can be seen in *Don Quijote*—and subsequently in Falla and Silva's adaptations—reinforcing the metafiction. Helena Percas de Ponseti has pointed out the recurring presence of puppets and strings in the novel, such as Don Quijote's hanging from

Maritornes's window (Part 1, ch. 43), Sancho's dangling from the tree during the hunt (Part 2, ch. 34), or Don Quijote's capture in the net of the false Arcadia (Part 2, ch. 52). Of course, puppet theater was already present in the novel itself in the significant—and significantly metatheatrical—episode of Maese Pedro's puppet show, one that demonstrates all six types of metadrama categorized by Hornby (Olid Guerrero 71-72). George Haley, in a classic study, saw the Maese Pedro episode as a microcosm of the novel's "relationships among storyteller, story and audience" (163). In Haley's approach, the reader of *Don Quijote* is implicitly included in the listening public of the *retablo* (150). Hence, after seeing Don Quijote get drawn into the puppet show only to destroy it—literally "laying bare" the mechanisms of storytelling—readers take a closer look at their own grasp of fiction and reality (164-65), starting with the very book they are reading.

Percas de Ponseti argues that the prominence of puppets in the *Quijote* places special emphasis on the manipulations of Cide Hamete Benengeli or the "enchanters" of Don Quijote's imagination. This situation then creates a leitmotif of "the role of an author as architect of his characters' destinies" (51). After his niece's suggestion that an enchanter has made off with his study and his later self-awareness of an Arab chronicler erroneously narrating his adventures, Don Quijote conflates the two with an ever-increasing fatality. As Friedman states, "In Part 2, Don Quijote has difficulty freeing himself [. . .] from 'the book' that has brought him into the world beyond fiction but that now has situated itself into the continuation" ("Character-Building" 12). In this reading, Maese Pedro acts as a stand-in for Cide Hamete or the enchanters and Don Quijote's destruction of the stage becomes a symbolic lashing out against his own lack of freedom. Mary Malcolm Gaylord takes the project of Maese Pedro's puppet show further, demonstrating how Don Quijote's outburst is a reaction not only against the trap of his own narrative but also against the imposed societal master narratives in early modern Spain: "The *Retablo de Maese Pedro* reminds us that art is never 'only art', that our favorite *fictions,* even our myths, are always rooted in historical time" (143).

While Cervantes may approach the matter playfully, for many readers of *Don Quijote* and other self-referential texts, the repercussions of the questioning of reality and fiction can be destabilizing. Hornby notes, "self-reference has the effect of challenging, in a sudden and drastic manner, the complacencies of the audience's world view" (117). Likewise, Abel contends that the metatheater of Shakespeare and Calderón demonstrated the "essential illusoriness in reality [. . .] in the metaplay life *must* be a dream and the *world* must be a stage" (78-79). For Waugh, the questioning of reality and perception has led many to wrestle with the "problem of human freedom" that emerges from characters' realizations that they are "trapped within the novelist's script" (119). Hornby further observes that metatheater tends to be more prevalent in times of societal pessimism, such as the early modern period or the late twentieth century (46), corresponding with the "widespread feeling that life is false" (47). As will be shown, both Silva and Falla wrestled with social concerns of their age, and their metatheater can be read as a response to their environments. By adapting the Cervantine metafiction into marionette metatheater, Silva and Falla capture the narrative and ideological possibilities behind *Don Quijote*, highlighting—in both story and staging—the themes of authorial manipulation, human freedom, the division between fiction and reality, and the narratives of social artifice in everyday life.

I will first consider António José da Silva's *Vida do grande d. Quixote de la Mancha e do gordo Sancho Pança*. Born in 1705 in Rio de Janeiro to New Christian parents, Silva, known by antonomasia as "O Judeu," was forced to uproot to Portugal with his parents at age seven and suffered persecution by the Inquisition for "Judaizing." He went on trial in two separate autos-da-fé: the first resulted in imprisonment and renunciation of his beliefs and the second ended in his being burned at the stake in 1739, just six years after the premiere of his first opera. A lawyer by training, Silva is credited with reviving Portuguese drama which had been burdened by heavy influence from Spanish Golden Age *comedias* and Italian opera (Oliveira 11, 45). Silva's body of work consists entirely of eight puppet operas, innovative on two fronts: composition in prose instead of verse, and the use of puppets on permanent stages (78). He encountered so much success bringing his puppet theater to the diverse audience of Lisbon's Teatro do Bairro Alto that the theater was nicknamed "*Casa dos Bonecos*" (45).

Although Silva's other operas involve Greek mythology, the strong Spanish influence in Portugal makes Cervantes a logical choice for adaptation. In fact, *Don Quijote*'s emphasis on the questioning of reality and fiction found poignant political resonance in the intellectual currents of the day. According to Anthony Close, eighteenth-century interpretations of Cervantes broadened the scope of the satire to include social criticism, approaching the novel as a model for "how reprehensible *mores* and institutions should be entertainingly yet edifyingly castigated" (12). Scholarly analysis of Silva's operas has focused on his involvement with Enlightenment circles in Lisbon (Costigan 92; Pereira 16) and on his plays' critique of the Portuguese nobility and of institutions such as the Inquisition (Chartier 170). Roger Chartier notes bluntly about the playwright that, "No mundo do *Dom Quixote* de Antônio José da Silva, a justiça não existe" (171). Lúcia Helena Costigan also spots this "emphasis on the theme of justice" (96), and Friedman observes that the humor of the piece belies its seriousness: "Silva invents scenes that will encourage laughter but that cannot detach justice from its broader, and more personal, frame" ("The Fortunes..." 89), further noting that justice in Silva's opera replaces chivalry in Cervantes's novel as the main satirical target. Taking this criticism as a point of departure, I show that Silva uses Cervantes's story—and structure—to springboard social critique, placing "justice" on stage in a metatheatrical satire.

Silva's puppet opera, a broad retelling of episodes from *Don Quijote*, Part 2, incorporates a variety of metatheatrical devices: 1) references to the literary tradition of *Don Quijote*; 2) real-life references to puppets and self-referential fourth wall breaks; and 3) the use of the play within a play, the ceremony within a play, and role playing within the role to break the dramatic frame. From the very beginning, Silva plays the same game as Cervantes by interacting with literary history. The protagonists of *Vida*, D. Quixote and Sancho Pança, are very aware that they are characters in a stage adaptation of the novel (just as the characters of *Don Quijote*, Part 2, are aware of the presence of a narrative detailing their prior exploits). In the opening scene, D. Quixote and his barber friend are engaged in a lively debate about whether the knights of chivalry actually exist or not. D. Quixote fancies himself part of the literary tradition alongside Roland and Amadis of Gaul, invoking his epithet, "Cavaleiro da Triste Figura" (85), in a bit of self-referential self-fashioning. With the desire to prove that tales of chivalry are real, D. Quixote declares: "Não tem remédio: hei de ir, que não é justo que fique sem fim minha memorável história" (88). D. Quixote's self-awareness does not stop other characters from trying to question literary tradition and his very existence. The sly Sansão Carrasco uses knowledge of the first part of the story to fuel a baffling conversation with the knight, claiming that he already defeated a knight known as D. Quixote:

> Carrasco: Tão verdadeiro e tão o mesmo, que mais não podia ser.
> D. Quixote: Digo que tal não há; pois d. Quixote é este que vedes presente [...]
> Carrasco: Pois verdadeiro ou fingido, sempre o venci; tenho dito (100)

This self-contradictory statement demonstrates the perils as well as the humorous opportunities that come with self-referentiality, offering a very Cervantine comment on the representation of reality in fiction.

The Don Quijote of the novel and the D. Quixote of the play are concerned not only with continuing literary tradition but also with commenting upon it. Silva's equivalent of the scrutiny of the library comes in the fantastic journey to "monte Parnaso," echoing Cervantes's own *Viaje del Parnaso* (1614). Silva's version is somewhat more vituperative, as Apolo, guiding D. Quixote and Sancho, is seeking vengeance against certain "poetazinhos" (113). D. Quixote obliges, criticizing the poets as if they were his enchanters: "Diga-me, senhor Apolo; e como se chamam os poetas, que tanto o perseguem?" (114). When D. Quixote valiantly threatens Apolo's poetic foes, Sancho warns: "Senhor, não se meta a brigar com os poetas, que são piores que gigantes" (114), recalling D. Quixote's past failures with giants that has, of course, entered into literary consciousness.

The characters in Silva's opera are also aware of their presence in the theater itself. Repeated use of humorous self-reference and references to real life are made, almost exclusively by Sancho. For example, frightened by a lion that D. Quixote will soon defeat, Sancho reasons: "talvez que este leão seja amigo de árias" (103), flaunting the fact that he knows he is part of an opera whose convention is to sing musical numbers. Similarly, when D. Quixote makes a particularly poetic statement, the illiterate Sancho replies: "Boa metáfora" (98), undermining his rusticity and breaking the theatrical frame by calling attention to the literary qualities of the text. On several occasions, Sancho comments on the material presence of the set. For instance, when D. Quixote admires the sumptuous decor of Montesinos's palace, Sancho responds "Parece-me que tudo isto é pintado em tábuas de pinho" (105). Additionally, on the ascent to Mount Parnassus, D. Quixote remarks on the "diáfanos vapores" through which they are passing, while Sancho sees only "nuvens de papelão" (112).

Sancho's most metatheatrical fourth-wall breaks go so far as to recognize the specific work in which they are participating. Commenting on the supposed similarity between Sancho and Dulcinéia, Sancho remarks, "Cuido que nem na *Vida* de vossa mercê se conta semelhante desaventura" (111, emphasis in original). Invoking the first word in the play's title, Sancho's awareness of the play and its divergence from the novel defies logic. Similarly, a few scenes later D. Quixote asks an innocent question "Sabes aonde estamos?" to which Sancho replies "Sei muito bem [. . .] Estamos no Teatro do Bairro Alto" (118), further underscoring his satirical self-consciousness. Taken together, these seemingly innocuous breaks of the fourth wall, incorporating real life and self-reference, serve to establish Sancho's strong metadramatic presence, increasing the humor and intensifying the satire.

The final and most prevalent example of metatheater in Silva's opera is the frequent use of the play within a play, ceremony within a play, and role playing within a role, drawing heavily from similar situations in the novel.

The audience is primed to look for such metaplays after D. Quixote and Sancho's encounter with a theater troupe similar to the one from Part 2, ch. 11. D. Quixote comments on the recent appearance of the troupe: "Olha, não vês estes gigantes vivos? Pois logo os verás mortos" (97), possibly alluding to the comedy troupe played by human actors outside the stage ("gigantes vivos"), and not puppets. The actor dressed as the "Diabo" responds to D. Quixote: "Senhor, nós somos uns pobres representantes de comédia, que imos já vestidos para fazer um auto sacramental aqui a uma quinta." This wondrous appearance of one acting group on the stage of another live puppet performance comically forces the spectator to question the entire theatrical setup, preparing the public for the metatheatrical plays within plays that will follow.

Just as in the novel, the primary metadramatists of the second part of Silva's opera are the Duke and Duchess (Fidalgo and Fidalga). These idle nobles are faithful readers of the knight's escapades and are looking to have a laugh at the expense of D. Quixote and, especially, Sancho. Much of the knight and his squire's time with the Fidalgos is concerned with the feigned "desencantos" of Dulcinéia—who actually appears on stage held captive by Merlim—and that of the Condessa Trifalde who has been cursed to grow a beard (146). The "disenchantments" of these characters by D. Quixote creates a situation of metatheatrical irony: though D. Quixote and Sancho are aware of their own status as dramatic characters on stage, they fail to see that the actresses are taking on additional "roles within the role" through a double metatheater. The two women in the entourage of the Fidalgos are not only playing as Dulcinéia and Trifalde, but are also acting within those roles as "enchanted" versions of themselves. Thus, their "disenchantments" fail to actually reveal their true identities, adding yet another layer to the metadrama, as the now disenchanted Dulcinéia and Trifaldi are still part of the enchantment.

After several humiliating episodes with the Fidalgos, Sancho finally achieves his own metadramatic goal: the governorship of the *ilha dos Lagartos*, site of the opera's most important play within a play. The jocosity of Sancho's botched Latin and over-the-top arias belies the sharp criticism of this climactic scene. Far from showing prudence and good governance, Silva's Sancho Pança is vain and gluttonous. As "judge" in the ceremonial "court," the metadramatic Fidalgos bewilder Sancho with complex and impossible cases that show his base and simple-minded nature. He begins by explaining why Justice is allegorically depicted as a blindfolded woman holding a sword and scales, demonstrating a metatheatrical understanding of justice: "isto de Justiça é coisa pintada e que tal mulher não há no mundo, nem tem carne, nem sangue, como *v. g.* a senhora Dulcinéia del Toboso" (130). Sancho continues: "pintaram uma mulher vestida à trágica, porque toda a justiça acaba em tragédia; taparam-lhe os olhos, porque dizem que era vesga" (130). By comparing the immaterial Justice to Dulcinéia—who in fact has shown up in the play (as noted by Friedman, "The Fortunes . . . " 85)—Sancho admits the theatricality, the inherent fiction in the process of meting out justice. Additionally, by describing Lady Justice as cross-eyed and justice itself as ending in tragedy, Sancho prefigures his own tragic miscarriage of justice.

In the very first case Sancho adjudicates, an actor sent by the Fidalgos comes to air his grievances: "Peço justiça contra a mesma Justiça [. . .] Não me fez justiça [. . .] Peço recebimento e cumprimento de justiça" (131). Sancho responds, "E de que comprimento quereis a Justiça?" mistaking "cumprimento" [*enforcement*] for "comprimento" [*length*]. Instead of meting out a just decision, Sancho offers the man a figurine of Lady Justice, asking him which size he would like. The plaintiff responds "Senhor, eu não quero justiça pintada" (131). This description of "painted" justice recalls Sancho's earlier metatheatrical remark on the set design, "pintado em tábuas de pinho" (105), only further underscoring the theatrical components of the very idea of justice. No criticism in the opera is more biting than this first instance of (one might say) meta-criticism, in which a man seeks justice from Justice itself, only to discover that justice is just a cheap theatrical illusion. Though masked by humorous word play, the criticism during Sancho's extensive governorship keeps coming against the nobility, the justice system, the medical establishment, the royal court, and other institutions. After his experience governing the island Sancho is never again able to regain his previously cheeky and playful breaking of the fourth wall. Sancho is run out of the *ilha* by a staged coup and flees back to D. Quixote, who is soon defeated by Sansão Carrasco, thereby ending their own chivalric metatheater.

Hornby suggests that the use of the ceremony within the play (for example, a trial) can signal tragedy if it is not completed due to "ineptitude, interruption, or corruption" (55). Correspondingly, the ill-fated nature of Sancho's governorship speaks volumes about Silva's understanding of the tragedy of justice, suggesting the impossibility of justice in a world of false appearances. This strong presence of metatheater, and especially Sancho's role as the primary metadramatist, heightens the criticism of a playwright who tragically struggled against unjust tribunals his whole life. Framed this way, the highly theatrical court of Sancho could be seen itself as a "metatheater," transparently farcical, and reflecting Silva's own experience with the theatrical modes of (in)justice—such as forced recantation—used by the Inquisition.

Furthermore, the fact that Silva's operas were performed by puppets only serves to reinforce the metatheatrical stage of justice. While on the one hand, the use of puppets creates distance between the audience and the acting "figures," on the other hand, it emphasizes the degree to which all humans are manipulated by forces outside of their control. For Silva's characters, the world is quite literally a stage, the world in miniature. If Silva suggests, as does Abel, that "all the world's a stage," then his puppet court of justice suggests to the audience that someone else is pulling the strings. Silva criticizes the forces of power in a hierarchical society, seeing justice as a theater manipulated by powerful religious and social forces. Yet beyond staging open social criticism—which would have been imprudent for the persecuted playwright—the staging of veiled criticism in a highly self-conscious theater allows the audience to subtly make the association between stage and life, puppet and persona, word and world, in their own mind. More than a criticism about one institution, the metacriticism of Silva in this opera becomes much larger, involving philosophical concepts of the highest order ("all the world's a stage") applied to lived tragedy.

Two centuries later, Manuel de Falla wrestled with similar themes in *El retablo de Maese Pedro*, a work that used the specific dynamic of puppet theater to even more clearly break down the barrier between audience and actors. Falla's short operatic piece is a more direct adaptation of Maese Pedro's puppet show from *Don Quijote*, Part 2, ch. 26. It was commissioned by the American-born Winaretta Singer, later known as the Princess of Polignac, and was first staged with an all-puppet cast in 1923. For Falla (1876-1946), already a mature artist when he composed the piece, *El retablo* represented an experimental departure from earlier works as well as a homecoming, having recently moved to Granada from Paris.

Writing in the early twentieth century, Falla's opera is imbued with the philosophical spirit of Miguel de Unamuno and José Ortega y Gasset that was questioning Spain's backwardness in the modern political order. Many thinkers and artists of the early twentieth century looked to Spain's literary past for solutions to the "problem of Spain" (Close 135), as demonstrated in two iconic interpretations of the *Quijote*. Unamuno's *Vida de don Quijote y Sancho* (1905) treated the knight errant as a real person who embodied the idealism and spiritual values of Spain in the face of a materialistic Europe (Vandebosch 21). Responding to the crisis of 1898, Unamuno "seeks the ultimate solution for Spain's 'problem' in the deliberate defense of fiction, illusion and dreams" (24). However, not all fictions are created equal: Unamuno views Maese Pedro's puppet show as a "farándula" (298) or farce, a pernicious type of fiction that is not believable and has no instructive value (Vandebosch 29). Therefore, Unamuno lauds Don Quijote's smashing of the puppet show, saying, "¡Brava y ejemplarísima pelea! ¡Provechosa lección!" (298). The *retablo* serves as a model, offering a critique of societal pretense: "Hay que acabar con los retablos todos, con todas las ficciones sancionadas" (299). Unamuno even goes so far as to call for the need to cut the strings and break up the figurines of parliament (303), implying that the political body has become a farce akin to the puppet show. In tracing the impact of Unamuno on Falla, it must be mentioned that Unamuno's most impassioned plea on behalf of the knight errant is precisely the quotation from chapter 26 that Falla chose to bring his opera to a climax: "¡viva la andante caballería sobre cuantas cosas hoy viven en la tierra!" (299).

On the other hand, Ortega y Gasset, in *Meditaciones del Quijote* (1914), offers a different view, emphasizing the interplay between fiction and reality, two "continentes espirituales" (169) embodied by the *retablo* and the inn. Concretely envisioning the space, Ortega describes, "Nada nos impide entrar en este aposento: podríamos respirar en su atmósfera y tocar a los presentes en el hombro, pues son de nuestro mismo tejido y condición" (169). Ortega reads Don Quijote's destruction of the *retablo* as a cautionary tale of the "naïve" reader unable to distinguish fiction from reality, or the ideal from the real (Vandebosch 28). The way to move between reality and fiction, between what *is* and what *might be*, is through creative self-reflection, exemplified by metafiction. Ortega proposes the artistic self-consciousness inherent in Cervantes's novel as a "remedy for the problem of the nation" (Vandebosch 15). Close boils down Ortega's prescriptions for Spain to the following: "think more; dare to challenge tradition; take ideas from Europe; offer in exchange a certain quality of life" (177). If Don Quijote errs in taking fiction too seriously, for Ortega, his attempt at least showed an inkling of the possibilities of moving between the two "continentes" of the real and the possible, leaving the reader with a more optimistic and creative view of Spain's future.

The influence of Unamuno and Ortega y Gasset—both of whom dedicated extensive chapters to the Maese Pedro episode—can be felt in Falla's *El retablo*, starting with the complex staging. The use of puppets continues Falla's longstanding interest with the genre, having staged puppet versions of *autos sacramentales* with Federico García Lorca in 1923. Falla's libretto includes three singing characters: Don Quijote, Maese Pedro, and the Trujamán; as well as silent spectators such as Sancho, the Ventero, and the Estudiante. In a stroke of genius only Cervantes could have inspired, these "real" characters are also played by puppets. The operatic stage is to be divided into two clearly defined spaces, separating the "real puppets" in the upstage *retablo* from the larger "spectator puppets" in the downstage inn. As Michael Christoforidis has noted, Ortega's description of the *retablo* and the two "continentes" may have served as inspiration for Falla's staging (139-43). As the show begins, Maese Pedro takes up the *retablo*'s controls, the spectator puppets take their seats, and all that remains visible to the opera's audience are the *retablo*, the Trujamán, and the unnaturally large legs of Don Quijote, which are to stay in the periphery and show agitation at the appropriate points of the text (4n). As in the novel, Don Quijote stands up several times to dispute details of the narration, emerging onstage along with Maese Pedro for their operatic sparring. As the action of the *retablo* intensifies, Don Quijote cannot bear the tension, and, mistaking fiction for reality, he destroys the puppet theater and the audience becomes visible again to display their reactions.

The most obvious metatheatrical technique is the use of the play within a play, but with a twist due to Falla's staging. Both the disappearance of the audience and the fact that the spectators are also played by puppets helps to create uncertainty about which is the "true" play. At the outset, Maese Pedro proclaims "Siéntense todos. Atención, señores, que comienzo" (8), a text purely of Falla's creation (Torres Clemente 300). The opera's audience cannot be sure precisely to whom Maese Pedro is speaking: to the puppet spectators, the opera audience, or, perhaps, both. Falla's spectator accepts Ortega y Gasset's invitation that "[n]ada nos impide entrar en este aposento" (169). However, in Falla's rendition the spectators are not made of the "mismo tejido y condición" as the puppet Quijote. Falla's audience identifies with Don Quijote as fellow spectators of Maese Pedro's *retablo* but at the same time is consciously aware of the dehumanized difference created by their puppet nature (San José Lera 228; Hess 203-04). In this sense, it is unsurprising that Don Quijote is unable to tell reality from fiction and ends up destroying the *retablo*. The "mechanical limitations" (Allen 331) that affect Don Quijote as a puppet also symbolically affect his ability to recognize the theater as theater, blinding him to Ortega's remedy for an artistically self-conscious Spain. Thus, the play within the play that constitutes the very fabric of Falla's *El retablo* immediately engages with metatheater not only on a practical level but also a conceptual level.

In fact, the very puppet show itself demonstrates metatheatrical elements. As the *retablo* opens, Charlemagne is goading Gayferos into rescuing Melisendra, who has been trapped in the palace of Zaragoza and is brashly kissed by an enamored Moor. As the Moorish king punishes the scoundrel in a public flogging (a ceremony within a play), Gayferos arrives at the palace to steal away with his lost bride. Cervantes's (and later Falla's) decision to adapt a tale of Charlemagne, "sacada de las Crónicas francesas y de los Romances españoles" (Falla 9) demonstrates a literary awareness that plays a prominent role in *Don Quijote*'s metacommentary on books and narrative. Falla had become very interested in Spanish literary history, and did extensive field research on *romances* with Lorca in preparation for the musical composition of the work (Torres Clemente 357-60). In addition to literary references, Falla also incorporates references to Spanish guitar and vihuela tunes, liturgical music, and popular songs, paralleling Cervantes's own use of a variety of intertexts in the *Quijote* (San José Lera 234; Hess 207). Falla, echoing Cervantes, offers a few quotes from the *Romance de don Gayferos*, including one that achieves a level of metatheatricality. Don Gayferos, disguised on his rescue mission, approaches Melisendra's balcony where she thinks he is just "algún pasajero" (36) and sings him a song: "Caballero, si a Francia ides, por Gayferos preguntade" (37). Subsequently, Gayferos reveals his true identity, making clear that a literary allusion to the *romance* has just been made. This type of obvious reference, common in Cervantes's *Don Quijote*, has the effect of bringing the audience back to reality: "the imaginary world of the main play is disrupted by a reminder of its relation, as a literary construct, to another literary work" (Hornby 88). In Falla's rendering, this literary reference made by puppets inside a play within a play only adds to the metatheatrical connections to *Don Quijote*.

If metatheatrical techniques are baked into the staging of *El retablo* and into the story of the puppet show, a careful analysis of Falla's text selection from Cervantes's original also demonstrates a "reading" of *Don Quijote* that emphasizes themes of authorial manipulation, social artifice, and the blurring of reality and fiction. As reconstructed by Torres Clemente (300-01), the libretto follows Part 2, ch. 26 closely, with the bulk of the discrepancies centered on the finale. As Falla's Don Quijote slashes at statues and strings, he utters: "¡Non fuyades, cobardes, malandrines y viles criaturas [...]!" (53). This exhortation uses text taken from the novel's iconic windmill scene (Part 1, ch. 8), in which Don Quijote threatens the "giants," using characteristic archaic language. The inclusion of this scene in Falla's context serves to emphasize the extent of the hero's delusion (or metatheatrical idealism) that underlies his destruction of the *retablo*.

Another textual deviation stems from Maese Pedro's retort to Don Quijote: "Deténgase vuesa merced, señor don Quijote, y *advierta que estos que derriba, destroza y mata no son verdaderos moros, sino unas figurillas de pasta.* ¡Mire, *pecador de mí,* que me destruye *y echa a perder* toda mi hacienda!" (Cervantes 601). Though this text comes from Part 2, ch. 26, Falla's omission of the italicized portions in the libretto (54-55) is significant because without it, Don Quijote is never disabused of his fantasy that he was rescuing a real damsel. Unamuno explicitly references this passage in his chapter about Maese Pedro: "Y no servía que Maese Pedro advirtiese a Don Quijote que aquellos que derribaba, destrozaba y mataba no eran verdaderos moros sino unas figurillas de pasta, pues no por eso dejaba de menudear aquél cuchilladas" (298). The omission of Don Quijote's acknowledgment of his own error emphasizes Unamuno's interpretation of Don Quijote's noble purpose in breaking down the *retablo*, a symbol of artifice.

Finally, Quijote's closing line synthesizes the evolution of the contextual significance throughout Falla's meticulous system of textual clues:

> Dichosa edad y siglos dichosos aquellos que vieron las fazañas del valiente Amadis, del esforzado Felixmarte de Hircania, del atrevido Tirante el Blanco; del invencible don Belanis de Grecia, con toda la caterva de innumerables caballeros, que con sus desafíos, amores y batallas, llenaron el libro de la Fama! (Falla 64-67)

His speech is an amalgam of four distinct parts of the novel. The first part makes reference to the famous Golden Age speech from Part 1, ch. 11, while the middle section honors the heroes who became source material for the *Quijote* (Part 1, chs. 12, 20). In the final section, Quijote acknowledges his participation in the narrative tradition of knight errantry, mentioning the "book of fame" as in Part 1, ch. 18: "Éste es el día, digo, [...] en el que tengo de hacer obras que queden escritas en el libro de la fama por todos los venideros siglos" (Cervantes 125).

Such confident language emphasizes Falla's association of the *retablo* scene with Don Quijote's conscious awareness that his own deeds are to be written down. In doing so, Falla reinforces that in this moment Don Quijote finally realizes that his connection with the enchanters will never allow him to be totally free. Pushed to do deeds worthy of inscription yet constantly frustrated by the very same enchanters who are writing his stories down, Quijote's increasingly bombastic language seems ever more ironic as the context and sentiment behind them becomes more defeatist. After all, just after this "book of fame" speech, Quijote famously mistakes a flock of sheep for an enemy army. In this sense, it is fitting that Don Quijote's final triumphant "¡Viva, viva la andante caballería sobre todas las cosas que hoy viven en la tierra!" (Falla 67-68) ends in musical discord, in a different key than the preceding measures had anticipated. As Hess notes, "The dispassionate logic of Don Quijote's prior utterances is instantly undermined in this parting scene of havoc [...] all encapsulated in the miscarried final cadence" (217). Taken together then, the context of the quotes manipulated by Falla from throughout Cervantes's text show a growing sense of frustration by Don Quijote at his lack of autonomy.

Consequently, in Falla's reading, the episode of Maese Pedro forms the lynchpin of Don Quijote's progression toward self-awareness. In the novel, the episode of Maese Pedro ends anti-climatically with Don Quijote's repentance and the revelation of Maese Pedro's true identity as Ginés de Pasamonte (a metatheatrical character in his own right). At its conclusion, Don Quijote issues his most important observation about the nature of his enchanters: "Ahora acabo de creer [. . .] lo que otras muchas veces he creído—que estos encantadores que me persiguen no hacen sino ponerme las figuras como ellas son delante de los ojos, y luego me las mudan y truecan en las que ellos quieren" (603). Read in the context of Falla's opera, this statement contains a striking realization by Don Quijote that he is in fact a puppet at the mercy of his enchanter, just like the "figuras" controlled by Maese Pedro. In Falla's opera, this admission is not necessary, for Don Quijote is already a literal puppet on stage for all to see. Then, as Unamuno suggested, Quijote's lashing out against the *retablo* may represent the frustration of an imprisoned fictional character. This scene can be seen as a turning point in Quijote's attitude in Part 2, for just after he leaves the inn, he becomes involved with the Duke and Duchess who make him into a puppet in their own show.

In sum, Falla's careful textual selections emphasize Don Quijote's own self-referential frustration in the novel. Falla's opera naturally lends itself towards Hornby's sixth and most profound type of metatheater, those works that turn from being a *"means* of perception" into being *"about* perception" itself (121). *El retablo* is imbued with a psychological complexity due to its staging and text that provoke reflection on the nature of existence and fictional representation—Ortega's two "continentes espirituales" (169). Only in Falla's opera, there appear to be three continents: puppets "acting" on stage, puppets watching the puppet play, and humans watching them both, unsure of which is the primary drama and which is the secondary. As the spectators of the novel's *retablo* are portrayed as puppets in the opera, Falla's spectators—in early performances Spaniards facing the same questions Unamuno and Ortega addressed—must assume the possibility that they too can be transformed, dehumanized, and trapped in a world of their own creation, just like the spectator puppets. Falla's puppet theater warns of a degree of social artifice and control that the actor, reader, and audience alike are quick to reject—in this way Falla's Don Quijote exhibits the heroism in breaking up the *retablo* with which Unamuno imbued him. Nevertheless, Falla's setup is playful, and, just like the ending of Cervantes's novel, not pessimistic or defeatist. Read in a certain way, Alonso Quijano, the Good, has the last laugh as he renounces his alter ego and watches as the world he has created unfolds around him. The spectator is quixotically invited to take part in the puppet play, leaving the world of the real and entering into the ideal as Ortega had prescribed. In this way, Falla's opera blends Unamunian heroism and Ortegian fantastical discernment, suggesting a path forward for Spain and demonstrating the benefits of self-reflection and metatheatrical thinking.

In this article, I have shown that António José da Silva and Manuel de Falla both incorporate metafictional techniques and themes from Cervantes's *Don Quijote* into their operatic adaptations of the novel. For both composers, the use of puppets creates a distancing effect, allowing uncomfortable fictions to be placed on stage while at the same time establishing an indissoluble bond between puppets and spectators as they watch society reflected back at them in a strange puppetesque *mise en abyme*. The spectators of these puppet operas are encouraged to reflect on the confines of societal fictions that may or may not be mutable. If, for Silva, humans are puppets trapped in a world of theatrical injustice, for Falla, roles—and destinies—can change by seeing through fictions and engaging with the world of the ideal.

While in the novel, Don Quijote's antics are only available to the reader in her mind's eye, on stage, Silva and Falla play with complex ideas of agency, manipulation, and control through the very staging of their works as puppet operas. This staging is uniquely suited to the spirit of Cervantes's text, for, as Friedman has noted:

> The very idea of metafiction can be compared to a marionette performance in which the strings are clearly and intentionally visible. In analogical terms, the "strings" are there in realism, but the objective is to conceal or disregard them. From several angles, Don Quijote is a *construct*, a counterpoint to real human beings. As he moves through the narrative—and as the narrative progresses—he becomes more and more a fictional entity, a literary, rhetorical, and cultural sign, a facet of Cervantes's textual and conceptual design. (Friedman, "Character-Building" 10)

It is in precisely this Friedmanian sense that both Silva and Falla tap into the theatrical potential of staging their respective adaptations of *Don Quijote* as puppet operas. The spectators, entering the theater expecting to suspend their disbelief, instead see fictional characters suspended on strings for all the world to see their fabricated nature. The transparency of the spectacle, made obvious to the audience by both visual and textual cues, serves to provoke questions—both immediate and transcendent, local and global—about social conventions, freedom, justice, and the construction of reality and fiction.

Works Cited

Abel, Lionel. *Metatheatre: A New View of Dramatic Form*. Hill and Wang, 1963.
Allen, John Jay. "Melisendra's Mishap in Maese Pedro's Puppet Show." *MLN*, vol. 88, no. 2, 1973, pp. 330-35.
Cervantes Saavedra, Miguel de. *El ingenioso hidalgo don Quijote de la Mancha*. Edited by Tom Lathrop, Revised ed., European Masterpieces, 2005.
Chartier, Roger. "O *Dom Quixote* de Antônio José da Silva, as marionetes do Bairro Alto e as prisões da inquisição." Translated by Estela Abreu, *Sociologia & Antropologia*, vol. 2, no. 3, 2012, pp. 161-81.
Christoforidis, Michael. *Manuel de Falla and Visions of Spanish Music*. Routledge, 2018.
Close, Anthony. *The Romantic Approach to* Don Quixote: *A Critical History of the Romantic Tradition in* Quixote *Criticism*. Cambridge UP, 1978.
Costigan, Lúcia Helena. "*Vida do grande Dom Quixote e do gordo Sancho Pança* by Antonio José da Silva and Miguel de Cervantes's *Don Quixote de la Mancha*: Comparative Aspects." *Signótica*, vol. 21, no. 1, 2009, pp. 89-102.
El Saffar, Ruth. "Cervantes and the Games of Illusion." *Cervantes and the Renaissance: Papers of the Pomona College Cervantes Symposium, November 16-18, 1978*, edited by Michael D. McGaha, Juan de la Cuesta, 1980, pp. 141-56.
Falla, Manuel de. *El retablo de Maese Pedro/ Les Treteaux de Maître Pierre/ Master Peter's Puppet Show: Adaptación musical y escénica du* [sic] *un episodio de "El Ingenioso Cavallero Don Quixote de la Mancha" de Miguel de Cervantes*. Chester, 1924.
Friedman, Edward H. *Cervantes in the Middle: Realism and Reality in the Spanish Novel from* Lazarillo de Tormes *to* Niebla. Juan de la Cuesta, 2006.
———. "Character-Building in *Don Quijote*." *Cervantes: Bulletin of the Cervantes Society of America*, vol. 27, no. 2, 2007, pp. 7-21.
———. "The Fortunes of Chivalry: António José da Silva's *Vida do Grande D. Quixote de La Mancha e do Gordo Sancho Pança*." *Cervantes: Bulletin of the Cervantes Society of America*, vol. 17, no. 2, 1997, pp. 80-93.
Gaylord, Mary Malcolm. "Pulling Strings with Master Peter's Puppets: Fiction and History in *Don Quixote*." *Cervantes: Bulletin of the Cervantes Society of America*, vol. 18, no. 2, 1998, pp. 117-47.
Haley, George. "The Narrator in *Don Quijote*: Maese Pedro's Puppet Show." *MLN*, vol. 80, no. 2, 1965, pp. 145-65.

Hess, Carol A. *Manuel de Falla and Modernism in Spain, 1898-1936.* U of Chicago P, 2001.
Hornby, Richard. *Drama, Metadrama, and Perception.* Bucknell UP, 1986.
Maestro, Jesús G. "Cervantes y el teatro del *Quijote.*" *Hispania,* vol. 88, no. 1, 2005, pp. 41-52.
Olid Guerrero, Eduardo. "Donde lo verá el que lo leyere y lo oirá el que lo ecuchara leer: sobre el lenguaje metadramático de los títeres de maese Pedro." *Anales Cervantinos,* vol. 41, 2009, pp. 63-81.
Oliveira, José Luís de. *O teatro de bonifrates em António José da Silva, o* Judeu. 2010. Universidade de Trás-os-Montes e Alto Douro, Master's thesis.
Ortega y Gasset, José. *Meditaciones del Quijote.* Residencia de Estudiantes, 1914.
Percas de Ponseti, Helena. "Authorial Strings: A Recurrent Metaphor in *Don Quijote.*" *Cervantes: Bulletin of the Cervantes Society of America,* vol. 1, no. 1-2, 1981, pp. 51-62.
Pereira, Paulo Roberto. Introdução. *As comédias de António José, o Judeu,* edited by Paulo Roberto Pereira, Martins, 2007, pp. 13-68.
San José Lera, Javier. "Literatura y música: *El retablo de maese Pedro* de Cervantes a Falla. Los valores estéticos." *Visiones del* Quijote *en la música del siglo XX,* edited by Begoña Lolo, Centro de Estudios Cervantinos, 2010, pp. 221-36.
Silva, Antônio José da. *Vida do grande d. Quixote de la Mancha e do gordo Sancho Pança. As comédias de António José, o Judeu,* edited by Paulo Roberto Pereira, Martins, 2007, pp. 81-148.
Torres Clemente, Elena. *Las óperas de Manuel de Falla: de* La vida breve *a* El retablo de maese Pedro. Sociedad Española de Musicología, 2007.
Unamuno, Miguel de. *Vida de don Quijote y Sancho según Miguel de Cervantes Saavedra.* 2nd ed., Renacimiento, 1914.
Vandebosch, Dagmar. "Quixotism as a Poetic and National Project in the Early Twentieth-Century Spanish Essay." *International Don Quixote,* edited by Theo D'haen and Reindert Dhondt, Rodopi, 2009, pp. 15-31.
Waugh, Patricia. *Metafiction: The Theory and Practice of Self-Conscious Fiction.* Methuen, 1984.

La desordenada codicia de los bienes agenos: El doctor Carlos García ante la tradición picaresca aurisecular

Antón García-Fernández
The University of Tennessee at Martin

La del doctor Carlos García es, sin duda, una de las figuras más oscuras y desconocidas de las letras españolas de los Siglos de Oro. Oscura porque prácticamente nada sabemos de sus circunstancias vitales, que se hallan todavía envueltas en un aura de misterio que sólo se ha disipado parcialmente durante el siglo XX. Desconocida porque las dos obras que publicó a comienzos del siglo XVII en París—La *Oposición y conjunción de los dos grandes luminares de la Tierra* (1617) y *La desordenada codicia de los bienes agenos* (1619)—pronto cayeron en un olvido crítico que terminaría únicamente en el siglo XIX con su reedición y en el XX con las primeras ediciones críticas[1]. Y, sin embargo, pese a la aparente falta de interés de gran parte de los estudiosos por ellas, ambas obras nos revelan a un escritor que, desde la periferia de su exilio parisino, parece plenamente familiarizado con las corrientes literarias en boga en la Europa de su tiempo. En particular en la *Desordenada codicia*, García se decide a entrar en un diálogo lúdico con la tradición de la novela picaresca, de una manera no muy diferente a la que encontramos en el *Rinconete y Cortadillo* (1613) de Miguel de Cervantes. En el presente trabajo me acercaré a la figura del doctor García con objeto de presentarlo como un escritor innovador, preocupado por ampliar los horizontes genéricos de la

---

[1] La mejor de las escasas ediciones críticas que de la *Desordenada codicia* es la que corrió a cargo de Giulio Massano y que se detalla en la bibliografía del presente trabajo. Además de un interesante estudio introductorio, esta edición mantiene la grafía original de la *princeps* y todas las citas de la obra que se incluyen en mi estudio proceden de ella.

picaresca mediante la introducción de elementos extraídos de la tradición de los *rogue pamphlets* británicos, con los que García probablemente entró en contacto. Si bien quizá no en sus versiones originales inglesas, sí a buen seguro el autor las conocería a través de sus populares imitaciones francesas.

Durante siglos, la vida de Carlos García se asemejó un agujero negro que algunos críticos trataron de llenar mediante lecturas en clave autobiográfica de las dos obras suyas que se conservan[2], así como de meras suposiciones que, como las de Jose María Sbarbi y Osuna, se hallan completamente exentas de rigor crítico alguno. Ciertos estudiosos, ante la escasez de datos fidedignos sobre el autor, le negaron el título de doctor (Gutiérrez 9). Incluso llegaron a dudar de su propia existencia, arguyendo que su nombre no era más que un seudónimo utilizado por algún escritor de mayor renombre (Eguren v), tal vez incluso por Cervantes (Sbarbi y Osuna 17). Hoy sabemos que estos críticos erraban en sus hipótesis, particularmente gracias a las investigaciones llevadas a cabo por hispanistas canadienses y franceses como Jean-Marc Pelorson, y españoles como Joaquín López Barrera. Así, este último sacó a la luz un texto de un escritor contemporáneo a García, la *Olla podrida a la española* (1655), de Marcos Fernández, quien se refiere a nuestro autor, criticándolo por su vida disoluta con una gran dosis de sátira. Fernández menciona que el "Dotor Garcias" es responsable de la *Oposición y conjunción*. Asegura también que lo conoció en París y lo describe con verdadera inquina como "Medico sin grado, filosofo entre seglares, predicador de lo que el quiso, i boton con cola en oxal proivido, abotonador general, i Albeitar de agraçones, bodegonero de asaduras porque el relleno de la bolsa no admitia mas, i vecino de la bastilla" (cit. en Pelorson 543).

Por su parte, Pelorson descubrió un documento legal en francés relativo a un proceso llevado a cabo en París contra una tal Léonora Galigaï por unas supuestas prácticas de magia negra, en el cual Carlos García aparece como uno de los testigos que prestan declaración. Dicho documento, que se refiere al escritor como "Charles Garcia natif de Caesar Augusta" (Pelorson 575) resulta enormemente importante por cuanto parece probar la existencia de Carlos García, lo presenta como natural de Zaragoza, y menciona su condición de doctor en medicina y filosofía, como asimismo el hecho de que pasó ocho meses en prisión al ser víctima de una falsa acusación. Así pues, García probablemente conocía de primera mano el ámbito carcelario

---

2 Escasos son los críticos que han dedicado estudios e incluso comentarios breves a la obra del doctor Carlos García, pero los más relevantes, entre los que se han publicado hasta el momento, están detallados en la bibliografía del presente trabajo.

en el que se presenta la *Desordenada codicia*, pero no por ello debemos identificar al autor con el narrador ni con el protagonista de dicha obra.

Esto es lo que, precisamente, han hecho varios de los pocos críticos que se han interesado por la producción literaria del doctor García, especialmente en sus lecturas de la primera obra del autor. La *Oposición y conjunción* es una suerte de ensayo en el que García indaga en la ancestral antipatía que, en su opinión, se profesaban españoles y franceses. Si bien la mayor parte de este tratado está dedicada a una exploración de dicha rivalidad entre "los dos grandes luminares de la Tierra", aduciendo para ello pasajes bíblicos y trazando una comparación exhaustiva entre diversos aspectos de ambas naciones, el capítulo diez trata "[d]e algunas cosas que sucedieron al autor, tocantes la enemistad y ódio de entrambas naciones" (244). Colocada exactamente en pleno centro de un libro que contiene veinte capítulos, esta sección actúa como una especie de respiro frente a la aridez de las disquisiciones teóricas que preceden y que continuarán posteriormente. Varios críticos han querido ver en este capítulo un discurso autobiográfico, pues García así lo presenta. Pero si lo leemos con cuidado, podemos apreciar con facilidad los rasgos novelescos y picarescos de los sucesos relatados por el autor, que se presenta como víctima de burlas y engaños muy similares a los que encontramos en los *rogue pamphlets* de Gilbert Walker, Thomas Harman o Robert Greene, o en textos similares franceses como la anónima *Vie généreuse des mercelots*.

Este diálogo intertextual establecido entre el doctor García y la tradición de los *rogue pamphlets* británicos a través de sus homólogos franceses es infinitamente más evidente en la *Desordenada codicia*, publicada también en París dos años después[3]. Es ésta la obra en la que García experimenta con mayor profundidad con los parámetros genéricos establecidos por la tradición picaresca española, con ayuda de elementos extraídos de los textos criminales ingleses. Esta forma de literatura popular, salvo en este libro de García y, de manera tangencial, en alguna que otra obra cervantina, nunca llegaría a florecer en España. Desde el *Lazarillo de Tormes* (1554), y pasando por el *Guzmán de Alfarache* de Mateo Alemán (1599), las novelas picarescas españolas se distinguen por presentar una visión crítica de la sociedad española contemporánea a través de los ojos del pícaro protagonista, personaje de baja condición social que, a lo largo de un relato ficticio y normalmente

---

3   La *Desordenada codicia*, por lo que parece, quizá por haber sido publicada en Francia y no en España, conoció mayor popularidad y difusión en su momento gracias a sus traducciones al francés, al inglés y al holandés que en su versión original en español. Para más información sobre ediciones y traducciones, vid. Massano 59-76.

autobiográfico en primera persona, aparece utilizado como vehículo para la crítica social. Por contra, los panfletistas ingleses conciben sus obras como una especie de tratado sociológico que sirve para dos propósitos diferentes: por un lado, advertir al lector de los peligros que encierra el submundo criminal urbano que describen con todo detalle; por otro, entretener al lector mediante la exposición de los diversos trucos y prácticas de los criminales, descripciones a menudo exageradas y de todo punto inverosímiles. Descritos por Frank Wadleigh Chandler en su ya clásico estudio con el término de *anatomies of roguery*, la mayoría de estos *rogue pamphlets* revelan la tendencia de sus autores a vilipendiar y criticar al criminal, a quien culpabilizan de todo problema de índole social o económica de que adolece la Inglaterra isabelina. Si en las novelas picarescas españolas el pícaro es sujeto a través del cual se canalizan la sátira y la crítica social, en los panfletos británicos el *rogue* es objeto de las invectivas de los autores, que ofrecen una verdadera taxonomía de los diferentes tipos de criminales que pululan por los bajos fondos londinenses y de otras ciudades. Estos se presentan como una enfermedad social que debilita el sistema y que, por tanto, conviene extirpar. No es infrecuente encontrar, en estos poco estudiados opúsculos, alusiones a los criminales que los describen, como lo hace Harman en su *Caveat*, como "these ranging rabblement of rascals" (69), "most wicked knaves" (73) o "beastly people" (92).

En su *Desordenada codicia*, García se apropia de algunos de estos elementos, también presentes en obras galas como la *Vie généreuse*, pero los modifica y los invierte de manera que desempeñan en su novela un papel opuesto al que poseen en los panfletos. Así, la principal innovación de García en un texto picaresco *sui generis* como es la *Desordenada codicia*, consiste en la incorporación de elementos propios de los textos ingleses—taxonomías, jergas criminales, descripción de una criminalidad rígidamente organizada y regimentada. Pero al mismo tiempo, la significación de dichos elementos sufre una completa transformación. Al igual que los autores británicos, García introduce clasificaciones de criminales en distintos gremios, da cuenta de sus jergas particulares y desliza historias que ejemplifican las actividades de cada clase de malhechos. Pero al contrario que sus modelos ingleses, mantiene el relato autobiográfico en primera persona, dando voz al pícaro para que articule la crítica social sin juzgarlo personalmente en ningún momento.

Quizá por ello, la estructura de la *Desordenada codicia* es un tanto más compleja que la de los textos de Awdeley, Harman, Greene y compañía. La novela se inicia con la voz de un narrador cuyo nombre desconocemos que, por razones también oscuras, se encuentra entre las cuatro paredes de una prisión, donde entra en contacto con Andrés, uno de los criminales allí recluidos. El narrador pronto pasará a convertirse en narratario, pues en cuanto entabla conversación con Andrés, será ya el ladrón quien tome la palabra durante el resto de la novela. Así, detalla de manera plenamente autobiográfica aquellos sucesos que considera de mayor relevancia en su trayectoria vital. Hasta aquí, la *Desordenada codicia* no difiere de otras obras picarescas, que suelen incluir la figura del narratario, pero al estructurar su novela como un diálogo entre Andrés y el narratario, García busca dramatizar la oposición entre dos voces diametralmente contrarias: mientras Andrés representa a los criminales que viven al margen de la sociedad y que se ven rechazados por el orden social imperante, el narratario, que en más de un momento demuestra sentirse fuera de lugar en este contexto carcelario, adquiere el papel y el punto de vista de la sociedad respetable que ve una amenaza constante en el mundo criminal. Pero a medida que la novela avanza, resulta evidente que es la voz del rechazado, del fuera de la ley, la que realmente prevalece, hasta tal punto que el texto deviene un monólogo del ladrón que el narratario escucha en silencio. Como acertadamente sugiere Roncero López, el narratario actúa como "intermediario entre el lector y Andrés", pero es la voz de Andrés la que escuchamos, y desde el principio, el ladrón se nos aparece como víctima de un sistema social que lo rechaza y lo empuja a una posición marginal.

Como suele ser práctica habitual en el género picaresco, Andrés menciona su nacimiento al comenzar su historia, pero evita revelar los apellidos de sus padres y su lugar natal, prefiriendo concentrarse en un episodio de su infancia que determinará su vida: tras haber sido acusados falsamente de "aver sacrilegado una iglesia, saqueado la sacristía con los cálizes y ornamentos della, y [...] de aver cortado la mano de un S. Bartolomé [...] el qual decían ser de plata", sus padres son condenados a muerte. Haciendo gala de un sentido macabro de la justicia, el magistrado decide dar la oportunidad al pequeño Andrés de salvar su vida si accede a ser él quien ejecute a sus progenitores. Viéndose obligado a aceptar tal proposición, la ejecución de sus padres será un sambenito que Andrés llevará colgado el resto de su existencia, un estigma social que determinará inevitablemente su entrada en el mundo criminal.

Parece preciso subrayar aquí, pues, que es la propia disfunción del orden social prevalente la que obliga a Andrés a vivir de espaldas a la ley, algo que ha observado convenientemente Roncero López: "Andrés [...] no se halla preparado para afrontar [...] la vida en una sociedad en la cual todos deben estar alerta para luchar contra todos. [...] Andrés, contrariamente a lo que sucede con Pablos o con Lázaro, ni se separa voluntariamente de sus padres ni es abandonado por ellos, sino que se ve obligado a salir al mundo, consciente de su ociosidad y holgazanería" (23). Por ello, no resulta extraño que Andrés dedique parte de su discurso a probar, como el subtítulo de la obra ya indica, "la antigüedad y nobleza de los ladrones", y lo hace de una manera irónica y agriamente burlesca, arguyendo que el robo es nada menos que un arte, acaso "la más noble, más absoluta y privilegiada de quantas hoy ay en el mundo, tanto que no conoze ni respeta rey ni roque, ni se le da un maravedí de quantos monarcas ay sobre la tierra, ni del braço eclesiástico ni seglar" (118).

Andrés rompe, así, la linealidad de su relato autobiográfico para tratar de probar, apelando al principio de autoridad, con ejemplos extraídos de la Biblia y de la Antigüedad clásica —el Demonio, Adán, Caín y Abel, Paris y Elena, Teseo y Ariadna, Jasón y Medea— que el latrocinio es un arte noble practicado desde tiempos inmemoriales. Como Harman en el *Caveat* o Cervantes en el *Rinconete*, Andrés presenta el mundo como un espacio en el que la corrupción galopante no tiene que ver con la idea de pobreza, sino más bien con la de ambición: "De aquí infiero el engaño notable en que vive hoy el mundo, creyendo que la povreza fue inventora del hurto, no siendo otro que la riqueza y prosperidad... Y assí en estos ladrones la grande prosperidad y riqueza que tenían fue causa de su desordenado apetito e insaciable ambición" (136).

Además, de manera semejante a lo que encontramos en la novela ejemplar cervantina, Andrés argumenta también que las prácticas criminales no se reducen a los bajos fondos, sino que pueden observarse en distintas profesiones que la sociedad considera respetables (médicos, cirujanos, sastres, zapateros, etc.), en las que la respetabilidad no es más que una ilusión, una máscara que encubre los múltiples engaños que tienen lugar bajo la superficie. Andrés afirma, incluso, que esta corrupción forma parte ineludible de instituciones de gran tradición y prestigio como la monarquía o la Iglesia. En cuanto a esta última, el pícaro llega a distinguir entre tres personajes-tipo claramente diferenciados: el clérigo, el religioso y el predicador, todos ellos ampliamente versados en artimañas diseñadas para engañar a quienes les encomiendan labores espirituales como oficiar misas o predicar la palabra de los padres de la Iglesia (147).

Lejos de representar dos espacios mutuamente excluyentes, el submundo criminal y la sociedad supuestamente respetable conforman dos caras de la misma moneda y poseen fuertes lazos que permiten subsistir a ambas. Como Cervantes en el *Rinconete*, el *Coloquio de los perros* y varios pasajes del *Quijote*, y al igual que la mayoría de los novelistas de la picaresca española, García denuncia a través de Andrés la corrupción social e institucional que se nos presenta como uno de los principales escollos que aquejan a la España de su tiempo. García inserta en su *Desordenada codicia* taxonomías criminales y Andrés describe las prácticas de los diferentes gremios de malhechores, ilustrándolas a menudo con historias a modo de ejemplo que a veces presenta como autobiográficas. Son todos estos elementos procedentes de la tradición de literatura criminal inglesa de los siglos XVI y XVII, pero en la obra de García aparecen invertidos, al servicio de la crítica social que la picaresca española encierra. La *Desordenada codicia* no constituye una crítica abierta al criminal; más bien, Andrés no se arrepiente en ningún momento de su conducta criminal, tejiendo constantemente un discurso crítico frente a una sociedad en la que no siente que tenga reservado un lugar propio.

Finalmente, y tras todas estas disquisiciones que ocupan una buena parte de la novela, Andrés continúa su relato autobiográfico, narrando las funestas peripecias que lo han conducido a la prisión en la que se halla recluido en el momento actual. La obra, no obstante, no termina ahí, sino que incluye un último capítulo titulado "De los statutos y leyes de los ladrones" (201). Dicha sección es una suerte de apéndice que demuestra a las claras que García debía de conocer y manejar el *Rinconete* cervantino, ya que los ecos intertextuales con la novela ejemplar resultan aquí más que evidentes. Andrés presenta el submundo criminal como una sociedad perfectamente estructurada, caracterizada por una estricta jerarquía y regulada por "razón, estatutos, leyes y premática" (201). Al frente de la misma se encuentra el capitán, un hombre invariablemente mayor y bien experimentado en distintas artes criminales, cuya descripción, aunque mucho menos grotesca, recuerda vivamente al Monipodio de Cervantes: "Es este nuestro caudillo hombre viejo, prudente, experimentado, sagaz y, finalmente, jubilado en el arte, al qual, aviéndole ya faltado las fuerças y ligereza para hurtar, exercita la teórica con nosotros, enseñándonos el método y preceptos de hazello" (203).

Como en la Sevilla imaginada por Cervantes, en este submundo criminal al que Andrés se refiere como "nuestra república" (202), existe un noviciado para los recién llegados, se divide a los pícaros según sus habilidades, se celebran reuniones semanales y existen castigos severos para quienes se desvíen del camino marcado por el líder. A la manera cervantina, pues, García crea aquí una sociedad criminal de enorme eficiencia y regimentada organización, que existe bajo la superficie de la sociedad respetable y que la subvierte a la vez que interactúa con ella de un modo patentemente simbiótico. Como señala Andrés, "[d]e todos los hurtos se saca primeramente el quinto para satisfacer con él al que nos perdona los açotes, destierro, galera y horca" (203), lo cual equivale a una abierta crítica a las instituciones de la sociedad supuestamente respetable de su tiempo, cuyos oficiales y funcionarios hacen a un lado sus obligaciones a cambio de una cierta ganancia económica. En este contexto, para Andrés, los bajos fondos picarescos son una consecuencia directa de la corrupción, de la bajeza moral y del irracionalismo que aquejan a la sociedad de su época, elementos de los que su propia vida es una prueba fehaciente.

Como hemos podido observar a lo largo del presente trabajo, pues, la reducida y notablemente desconocida obra literaria del doctor Carlos García merece una mayor atención crítica de la que hasta ahora ha recibido. En su afán por experimentar con los parámetros genéricos establecidos de la novela picaresca, el autor aragonés crea, especialmente en su *Desordenada codicia*, un texto que en absoluto debe ser considerado menor dentro del canon de la literatura picaresca, por cuanto establece un fructífero diálogo con otras corrientes de literatura criminal populares en la Europa de principios del XVII. Particularmente con los *rogue pamphlets* británicos, por entonces virtualmente desconocidos en la Península Ibérica. García se apropia de ciertos elementos constitutivos de dichas obras, adaptándolos a las idiosincrasias de su texto y creando así una novela picaresca atípica y heterogénea que infunde nueva vida y descubre nuevas posibilidades dentro del género multiforme que se ha dado en llamar novela picaresca.

Bibliografía

Alemán, Mateo. *Guzmán de Alfarache*. 2 vols. Ed. José María Micó. Cátedra, 2006.

Awdeley, John. *The Fraternity of Vagabonds*. *The Elizabethan Underworld*. Ed. A. V. Judges. Octagon Books, 1965. pp. 51-60.

Bareau, Michel. "Pour une biographie de Carlos García." *La antipatía de franceses y españoles*. Carlos García. Alta P, 1979. pp. 61-80.

Carballo Picazo, Alfredo. "El doctor Carlos García, novelista español del siglo XVII." *Revista Bibliográfica y Documental* 5 (1951): pp. 426-66.

Cervantes Saavedra, Miguel de. *Novela de Rinconete y Cortadillo*. *Novelas ejemplares, I*. Ed. Harry Sieber. Cátedra, 2009. pp. 191-240.

Chandler, Frank Wadleigh. *The Literature of Roguery*. 2 vols. Houghton Mifflin, 1907.

Eguren, José María. "Advertencia." *La desordenada codicia de los bienes ajenos y La oposición y coniunción de los dos grandes luminares de la tierra*. Librería de los Bibliófilos, 1877. pp. v-xii.

García, Carlos. *La desordenada codicia de los bienes agenos*. Ed. Giulio Massano. José Porrúa Turanzas, 1977.

———. *La oposición y conjunción de los dos grandes luminares de la Tierra*. Imprimerie de François Huby, 1617.

Greene, Robert. *A Notable Discovery of Cozenage / The Second Part of Cony-Catching / The Third Part of Cony-Catching / A Disputation between a He Cony-Catcher and a She Cony-Catcher*. *The Elizabethan Underworld*. Ed. A. V. Judges. Octagon Books, 1965. pp. 119-247.

Gutiérrez, Fernando. "Prólogo." *La desordenada codicia de los bienes ajenos*. Carlos García. Ed. F. Gutiérrez. Selecciones Bibliófilas, 1959. pp. 9-20.

Harman, Thomas. *A Caveat or Warning for Common Cursitors, Vulgarly Called Vagabonds*. Ed. A. V. Judges. *The Elizabethan Underworld*. Octagon Books, 1965. pp. 61-118.

Lazarillo de Tormes. Ed. Francisco Rico. Cátedra, 2006.

Massano, Giulio. "Introducción a *La desordenada codicia de los bienes agenos*." *La desordenada codicia de los bienes agenos*. Carlos García. Ed. G. Massano. José Porrúa Turanzas, 1977. pp. 5-76.

Pelorson, Jean-Marc. "Le docteur Carlos García et la colonie hispano-portugaise de Paris, 1613-1619." *Bulletin Hispanique* 71: 3-4 (1969): pp. 518-76.

Roncero López, Victoriano. "Introducción." *La desordenada codicia de los bienes ajenos*. Carlos García. Ed. V. Roncero López. Ediciones de la Universidad de Navarra, 1998.

Ruby, Pechon de. *La vie genereuse des Mercelots, Gueuz et Boesmiens, contenant leur façon de vivre, subtilitez et gergon*. Variétés Historiques et Littéraires, Tome VIII. Ed. Édouard Fournier. P. Jannet, 1857. pp. 147-91.

Sbarbi y Osuna, José María. *In illo témpore y otras frioleras. Bosquejo cervántico o pasatiempo quijotesco por todos cuatro costados*. Imprenta de la Viuda e Hija de Gómez Fuentenebro, 1903.

Valbuena Prat, Ángel. "El doctor Carlos García y *La desordenada codicia*: Prólogo explicativo." *La novela picaresca española*. Ed. A. Valbuena Prat. Aguilar, 1956. pp. 1155-56.

Walker, Gilbert. *A Manifest Detection of the Most Vile and Detestable Use of Dice-Play, and Other Practices Like the Same*. *The Elizabethan Underworld*. Ed. A. V. Judges. Octagon Books. pp. 26-50.

Ynduráin, Domingo. "La desordenada codicia de los bienes agenos." *Boletín de la Biblioteca Menéndez y Pelayo* 55 (1979): pp. 343-54.

Atenea y Minerva en la temprana edad moderna: Teresa Sánchez de Cepeda & María Isidra de Guzmán[1]

MARTHA GARCÍA
University of Central Florida

> Intelligence is defined in terms
> of the ability to achieve success in life
> in terms of one's personal standards,
> within one's sociocultural context.
> – ROBERT J. STERNBERG

En honor al Profesor EDWARD H. FRIEDMAN.
Defensor del derecho a la educación
que posee tanto el hombre como la mujer en todo siglo.

I. INTRODUCCIÓN

SE HA OTORGADO ESPECIAL atención en años recientes al uso de las destrezas analíticas, creativas y aplicadas en el logro de objetivos individuales y colectivos. Se enfatiza el hecho de que no solamente el coeficiente intelectual determina el éxito personal, sino que también se requiere el ejercicio de prácticas asociadas a la adquisición de conocimiento y la capacidad creativa de materializar ideas (Sternberg 2003).

Al tomar en consideración la mitología clásica comprendida desde el siglo I a. de C. hasta el siglo VI d. de C., notamos que Minerva evoca la representación mítica romana del saber, de las artes y de la protección de lo que se estimaba de valor capital. Atenea, su equivalente en la mitología griega, se asociaba con la sabiduría, civilización y conocimiento científico. Aunque am-

---

[1] Este trabajo ha sido presentado en forma de comunicación en *The GEMELA Biennial Conference "Transatlantic Perspectives"*, Grupo de Estudios sobre la Mujer en España y las Américas (pre-1800), el 26 de octubre de 2018.

bas deidades poseen nombres femeninos, sus respectivas alegorías se afiliaban marcadamente al gremio masculino, el cual ejercía funciones más acorde al reconocido desempeño de estos atributos. Es necesario recordar que la mitología revela realidades anexas y, en los valores adyacentes de la cultura en la cual surge, se sustenta y se transmite el *mito*. Se debe reconocer entonces que ese mismo patrimonio cultural podría ser equivalente o servir de marco de referencia para entender otros contextos culturales, aunque estos se susciten en un espacio distinto al que nace y se asienta una determinada historia mitológica.

Teresa Sánchez de Cepeda y Ahumada (1515-1582) y María Isidra Quintina de Guzmán y de la Cerda (1767-1803), por lo tanto, materializan este simbolismo mítico al haber sido ambas elevadas a la categoría académica de erudición, la cual constituía un privilegio reservado hasta entonces exclusivamente para el profesorado masculino del mundo universitario. Teresa contribuye a la construcción de una teología femenina mediante su producción creativa dentro del contexto religioso del siglo XVI. María Isidra transforma el mundo académico a través de la obtención del título universitario de mayor distinción, durante el proyecto de Ilustración española, que le acreditó la Universidad de Alcalá de Henares en 1785.[2]

En este contexto, las siguientes interrogantes merecen escrutinio: ¿cómo se materializa con éxito la personificación mítica de Atenea dentro del mundo monacal del siglo XVI? ¿De qué forma María Isidra se convierte exitosamente en la Minerva humana en el contexto universitario de la Ilustración española?[3] La metodología a seguir consistirá en tres aspectos precisos que se yuxtaponen y complementan uno al otro: el primero se concentrará en

---

2   Robert J. Sternberg, por ejemplo, define el éxito de la inteligencia en la facultad del individuo de alcanzar metas personales significativas dentro de un contexto cultural dado o pre-establecido (*Successful Intelligence* 2003).

3   José Miguel de Toro Vial enfatiza que "[l]os intelectuales cristianos comenzaron a confeccionar epítomes de obras históricas clásicas y redactaron las primeras crónicas universales. En este empeño se enfrentaron a una historia llena de elementos provenientes de la mitología grecorromana. Los relatos se nutrían de las luchas entre los titanes, las hazañas de los semidioses, los logros artísticos de las musas y las construcciones maravillosas de artesanos dotados de una sabiduría propia de los númenes. Para lidiar con posibles problemas teológicos, los apologistas acometieron un largo proceso de depuración que ya habían iniciado los griegos de época helenística y que habían continuado los romanos, conocido como "evemerismo" por Evémero de Mesenia († c. 250 a.C.), quien postulaba que los antiguos dioses no eran más que personajes muy antiguos, divinizados en reconocimiento a su contribución a los pueblos (Bonnefoy, 482-484)" (78).

el análisis de la figura mítica de Atenea en correlación a la obra creativa de Teresa de Ávila; el segundo se dedicará al simbolismo de Minerva en concordancia con el trayecto académico de María Isidra de Guzmán; y el tercero considerará el entorno socio-cultural emergente como resultado tácito de la vida y obras de ambas precursoras en dos espacios determinados: el religioso y el académico. Es decir, dos espacios socioculturales en los cuales se observaba reiteradamente que la presencia femenina carecía del justo equilibrio simétrico.[4]

II. ATENEA: TERESA SÁNCHEZ CEPEDA DÁVILA Y AHUMADA

Teresa Sánchez Cepeda Dávila y Ahumada (1515-1582) se dedicó desde temprana edad, no necesariamente a las actividades propias de una niña típica del siglo XVI que crece en la ciudad avilesa de marcada tradición medieval, sino que, por el contrario, se consagraba junto con su hermano Rodrigo, a la ávida lectura de aventuras novelescas y caballerescas. Estos libros se alternaban con libros históricos y neo-testamentarios que la madre de Teresa, Beatriz de Ahumada, leía en la casa Cepeda (Crisógono 23-24). Tras la muerte de la madre, el padre de Teresa, Alonso de Cepeda, decide enviar a su hija al convento de religiosas agustinas de Gracia para evitar que las compañías no gratas de miembros de la familia desvíen el camino de su hija. El 13 de julio de 1531 padre e hija salen rumbo al convento donde Teresa realizará su internado, el cual sería procedido por su ingreso al convento de la Encarnación, donde se desarrollaría, de ese momento en adelante, su vida monjil.

El 2 de noviembre de 1536, Teresa, novicia vestida de blanco y en presencia de los miembros de su familia, monjas y beatos, que observaban con atención el ritual de iniciación, toma el hábito carmelita, el cual conformará su refugio interior por el resto de su vida.[5] En el caso de Teresa, su batalla se centra en erradicar la ignorancia y se ancla en la lucha incansable en contra de la exigüidad del saber y la carestía de conocimiento. Esta primera fase en la vida teresiana sentará las bases de lo que constituiría años después su vocación a la lectura y escritura femenina dentro del contexto abacial del siglo XVI.

---

4   Las teorías sobre el uso de la inteligencia de Robert Sternberg con particular atención en *Wisdom, Intelligence, and Creativity Synthesized* (2003) formarán parte esencial del proceso de análisis que se propone en este trabajo.

5   Se podría entonces crear un paralelo representativo con Atenea quien se entrega a la vida casta y se dedica a la misión patente de combatir la carencia de justicia. Refiero aquí al estudio "Mythology and the Images of Justice" de Jacques de Ville y a los trabajos contenidos en *Allusions and Reflections. Greek and Roman Mythology in Renaissance Europe*.

En medio de un ambiente de tensión reformista y contrarreformista, Teresa reconoce la importancia de su función en un medio histórico y cultural que transformaría el curso de la iglesia católica. Teresa, con un espíritu también reparador, comenzó su movimiento activista, *no* desde el mundo ajeno al convento, sino que, por el contrario, el tan necesario cambio se realiza desde el interior de su castillo monjil fundando la orden de las carmelitas descalzas a pesar de la oposición hermética de sus superiores. Es importante destacar que Teresa logra este cometido sin sublevar la orden a la cual ella misma pertenece y en la que funciona con denuedo, perspicacia e inteligencia.

De acuerdo a la definición de Robert Sternberg, en primer lugar, se percibe que Teresa demuestra poseer y hacer buen uso del talento que se requiere en su habilidad de individuo, y mujer, para alcanzar con éxito sus metas espirituales de acuerdo al estándar personal que ella misma ha fijado dentro del severo entorno del convento, el cual, asimismo, se encontraba sometido a la estructura eclesiástica imperante (42). El 24 de agosto de 1562, se inaugura el convento de San José de la Madre Teresa en un espacio pequeño y con una ceremonia modesta que incluye la misa del clérigo letrado Daza. Julián de Ávila se convierte en el primer capellán del humilde convento y asiste al evento un grupo reducido de conocidos y amigos de Teresa (Crisógono 63-64).

La reacción ante este logro no sorprende, teniendo en cuenta el contexto monacal del siglo XVI. Teresa es obligada a regresar al convento de la Encarnación y dirigir desde esa sede a las denominadas carmelitas descalzas e hijas de San José. No lo visitaría hasta un año después en el que se le concede entrar de nuevo al pequeño claustro que ella había fundado. Desde entonces, su labor de *Madre Reformadora* se centraría en brindar educación a sus profesas, la caridad dirigida hacia quienes la necesitan, y el aprender empíricamente a escribir como un proceso creativo de vida. Se requiere notar que, tal como lo indica la misma Teresa en *Libro de la vida*, la caridad incluía la enseñanza y la educación que se les había negado a sus propias monjas. Teresa reconoce que no se les debía de privar de este derecho, ni dentro ni fuera del mundo clerical y monástico del siglo XVI. Sin embargo este obstáculo social o la imperfección con la cual se perfilaba al género *débil* en la temprana edad moderna no constituyeron nunca un impedimento insuperable en el logro de las metas teresianas que se fructificarían con las *fundaciones* de conventos a lo largo del territorio de la España aurisecular.

Sternberg, en segundo lugar, advierte que la capacidad de obtener el éxito en una empresa dada depende en cierta medida de la fortaleza capital con que cuente el individuo (43). En el caso de Teresa, se trata de la monja carmelita en medio de las reformas religiosas que consigue transformar esas limitaciones en caminos viables que compensen las flaquezas con que la mujer era tradicionalmente esbozada en la temprana modernidad. Para Teresa, el proveer saber y conocimiento formaba parte de la caridad necesaria y que, señal de desnudez ante Dios, comenzaba por sus monjas descalzas, quienes necesitaban y eran aptas, al igual que monjes, clérigos letrados, y altos eclesiásticos, de aprender y propagar esa caridad a otros. Esta virtud se convierte en la simbólica rama de olivo que Atenea entrega a Cécrope, y que se consolida en las subsiguientes fundaciones de las carmelitas descalzas que extenderían, a su vez, esa misión de caridad teresiana: "[d]ejemos si hubiesen de predicar o enseñar, que entonces bien es ayudarse de aquel bien para ayudar a los pobres de poco saber, como yo, que es gran cosa la caridad y este aprovechar almas siempre, yendo desnudamente por Dios" (*Libro de la vida* 228).[6]

Se registran un total de 17 casas del saber denominadas fundaciones y distribuidas de norte a sur en la región geográfica central del territorio español del siglo XVI en el siguiente orden cronológico: Ávila (1562); Medina del Campo (1567); Valladolid; Malagón (Ciudad Real) (1568); Toledo (1568); Valladolid (1568); Pastrana (Guadalajara) (1569); Salamanca (1570); Alba de Tormes (Salamanca) (1571); Segovia (1574); Beas de Segura (Jaén) (1575); Sevilla (1575); Caravaca de la Cruz (Murcia) (1576); Villanueva de la Jara (Cuenca) (1580); Palencia (1580); Soria (1581); Granada (1582), y Burgos (1582).

Sternberg explica que el tercer atributo reside en el equilibrio de habilidades y destrezas que se ejercita con el propósito de adaptar, edificar y seleccionar ambientes que contribuyan a transformar la realidad inminente en una realidad exitosa (43). A pesar de la oposición, antagonismo, y ante la resistencia de fuerzas de mayor calibre a su posición y condición de mujer, Teresa, lectora y escritora, profesa su misión con perseverancia, y al igual que Atenea, ni siquiera Ares logra derrotar su tesón. La vida y erudición de Teresa culminan con el reconocimiento de este legado el día 27 de septiembre de 1970 en la capital pontificia de Roma otorgando a la fundadora de las carmelitas descalzas el título honorífico de Doctora de la Iglesia.

Quizás la obra teresiana que mejor ilustra el cuarto aspecto que enfatiza Sternberg en la obtención de logros perdurables lo constituye *Camino de perfección*, la cual ilustra la meta de la obtención del saber, de la sabiduría, y de la justicia social que anida en la simetría de géneros.[7] Escrito entre 1566 y

---

    6   Escrito en 1562 y re-escrito en 1565 en base a la primera versión perdida de 1562.

    7   Se recomienda aquí la lectura de "Santa Teresa y Ana Ozores: dos caminos de perfección" de Blanca Estirado García.

1567 con la finalidad de suplir la necesidad imperante de un grupo pequeño de monjas en el sencillo convento de San José, esta obra contiene en sus páginas la instrucción de Teresa[8] digerida de tal manera que pudiese llegar a su audiencia, las novicias de la orden.[9] En el primer capítulo de *Camino*, Teresa asocia la caridad con el derecho a la educación y al saber e incluso crea la metáfora de la necesidad de entendimiento vinculada a la alegoría del hambre de justicia y conocimiento:

> Al principio que se comenzó este monasterio a fundar—por las causas que en el libro tengo escrito están dichas con algunas grandezas del Señor, en que dio a entender se había mucho de servir en esta casa—, no era mi intención hubiese tanta aspereza en lo exterior ni que fuese sin renta, antes quisiera hubiera posibilidad para que no faltara nada; en fin, como flaca y ruin; aunque algunos buenos intentos llevaba más que mi regalo.
> (*Camino de perfección* 68)

Elena Carrera explica que, desde el principio de esta obra, la preocupación de Teresa no solamente radica en la necesidad de que las mujeres tomen parte en la lucha contra la Reforma Protestante[10] que se imponía en el norte de Europa, sino que su inquietud abarcaba un número de factores mayor relacionado con el funcionamiento de la Iglesia Católica (290-300). Teresa menciona también la situación que está teniendo lugar en Francia y las consecuencias de estos movimientos en el estado actual de la Iglesia en Europa.[11] *Camino de perfección* se convierte, por lo tanto, en la contraparte requerida para combatir las prácticas predominantes que no se encontraban acorde con las necesidades de las profesas bajo su tutela y cuidado.[12] Tanto Teresa como

---

8 La labor pedagógica de Teresa se ha estudiado con detenimiento en varias ocasiones siendo uno de los primeros trabajos al respecto "El retrato de Teresa de Ávila como maestra, visto por unas metáforas en *Camino de perfección*" de Sister Cleopha Cipar.

9 Al igual que *Libro de la vida,* Teresa lo escribe dos veces y se conservan ambas obras, la primera de 1566 y la segunda de 1567 respectivamente.

10 Se recomienda, en este contexto específico, la lectura de "Reconfigurations of Mythology in Sixteenth-Century Lutheran Collections of Aesopic Fables" de Erik Zillén.

11 Carrera indica que aunque no se mencionan los Países Bajos, sí se registra la situación de violencia contra las iglesias católicas en Francia (301-02).

12 El lenguaje afectivo en *Camino de perfección* se registra en el uso frecuente de diminutivos, tal como ya lo ha explicado Alison Weber en "Teresa's 'Delicious' Diminutives: Pragmatics and Style in *Camino de perfección*".

Atenea se enfrentan con denuedo ante el adversario, pero desde el interior del campo de batalla al que cada una de ellas pertenece: Atenea compite con Poseidón; Teresa entra en contienda contra las autoridades obispales regidoras de la Iglesia Católica.

Teresa rechaza el pre-determinismo social y de género a través de la sabiduría e inteligencia puesta en servicio a la caridad que exige la erradicación de la ignorancia. Esa virtud teologal, de acuerdo a las premisas teresianas, no se limita a aprender y olvidar lo aprendido o a no usar el conocimiento para una causa mayor. En el capítulo 13, la fundadora de las carmelitas descalzas ofrece el siguiente consejo a sus monjas: "¡Oh, qué grandísima caridad haría y qué gran servicio a Dios la monja que en sí viese que no puede llevar las costumbres que hay en esta casa, conocerlo e irse!" (*Camino de perfección* 127).

Tal como lo expone Carrera, el texto teresiano desafía las corrientes ideológicas de subyugación y brinda una avenida donde el libre albedrío y el sentido de agencia prevalecen en contraposición al sistema codificado de la vida monástica (300). Teresa se convierte en la asesora que muestra a las hijas de la orden cómo transitar el sistema impenetrable del mundo eclesiástico del siglo XVI, donde tanto el hombre como la mujer se encontraban sujetos a los rígidos estatutos de una Iglesia en estado de discordia y desunión, en plena discrepancia interna y en medio de conflictos externos. Evoca la habilidad de Atenea de aconsejar y adiestrar a Heracles quien vence la impermeabilidad del león de Nemea.

En el capítulo 42, el último de *Camino de perfección*, se manifiesta la prudencia de Teresa en medio de la batalla entre el bien y el mal en función al amor y a la caridad que otorga el camino de la sabiduría. Al referirse al Padre Nuestro, la monja lectora y escritora instruye a sus hermanas en la fe que "[p]ues si acá una que tenga caridad le es esto gran tormento, ¿qué sería en la caridad sin tasa ni medida de este Señor?" (268). En casi todos los ejemplos en los cuales se hace referencia a la caridad, esta virtud se asocia al amor de mujer, no desde una visión erótica o nociva, sino que, por el contrario, se enaltece la capacidad innata de amar del ser humano que Teresa canaliza a través de la fuerza de la fe y la vida de caridad.[13]

Esta disposición caritativa del género femenino la dota para distinguir no solamente la necesidad del *otro*, y de la *otra*, a un nivel material o concreto, sino que también a un nivel espiritual e intelectual que conlleva las ansias de conocimiento. De acuerdo a este ejemplo, el problema del mal *no* lo constitu-

---

13   Al respecto de la fe y el amor dentro de la perspectiva teresiana se recomienda la lectura de "Writing in Saint Teresa as a Dialogue of Faith and Love: 'Mental Prayer' in *Camino de perfección* (chapter 24)" de Roberto J. González-Casanovas.

ye Dios, el Señor, sino que la tradición en la que la Iglesia se encontraba sumida demarcando diferencias inexistentes de género, de capacidades, y hasta de funciones administrativas en las que la autoridad se reservaba exclusivamente al gremio masculino. La capacidad de amar al prójimo, tal como lo ha expuesto Carrera, viene de Jesucristo y por lo tanto el texto teresiano demuestra que esa misma capacidad no debería ser censurada en la mujer o redirigida a un plano netamente carnal (305).

Se convalidaría entonces la figura mítica de Atenea que trasciende la implacable fuerza de Poseidón. Teresa permanece fiel a sí misma y a su misión dentro de un sistema circunspecto en la batalla incesante entre luchas religiosas y de género. Ha triunfado, tal como lo propone Sternberg, en el cuarto apartado de la teoría de inteligencia exitosa dentro de un equilibrio simétrico de capacidad analítica, innovación creativa y práctica de las destrezas aprendidas y acertadamente desarrolladas (43).

III. Minerva: María Isidra Quintina de Guzmán y de la Cerda

María Isidra Quintina de Guzmán y de la Cerda (1767-1803), al igual que Teresa, se conoce como una niña y adolescente atípica. Fue estudiosa de filosofía, teología, griego, italiano, letras, artes y lectora asidua desde una edad temprana. Al igual que Teresa, constituyó una excepción de la norma, incluso durante las reformas carlistas, las cuales representaban un desafío para la superación de la mujer que deseaba formar parte del verdadero proyecto de Ilustración. Se sabe que el padre de María Isidra, el marqués Montealegre—al igual que el de Teresa—configuró un pilar importante en la educación de su hija. En la biblioteca del hogar de María Isidra, por ejemplo, se encontraban manuscritos del siglo XV de Rodrigo Ponce de León, marqués de Cádiz, obras clásicas en griego y latín, y hasta obras de Miguel de Cervantes y Saavedra (Vázquez Madruga 29).

María Isidra ha constituido un caso ejemplar en el sistema universitario de finales de la temprana edad moderna. La doctora de Alcalá representaría la validez de la Ilustración española dentro del espacio cronológico que le corresponde; sin embargo, su historia vitalicia y en los medios académicos, la ubicarían dentro del funcionamiento ambivalente y asimétrico de la temprana edad moderna. María Jesús Vázquez Madruga nos advierte que: "[l]a incorporación de las mujeres como sujeto y objeto de la Historia supone no sólo la formulación de nuevos modelos teóricos y cómo no metodológicos sino una gran contribución a lo que podemos llamar Historia total" (19).

María Isidra vive y se desarrolla como mujer e intelectual durante otro período reformista, el llamado "despotismo ilustrado" bajo el reinado de Carlos III. La Revolución Francesa estallaría en 1789 junto con la monarquía de Carlos IV después de la muerte de Carlos III. A pesar de este ambiente de violencia y discordia, también llega a España la revolución industrial y científica con representantes tales como Benito Jerónimo Feijoo y Jovellanos.[14] Paul Ilie observa que Minerva posee un lugar primordial en la cultura de Carlos III. Por ejemplo, en referencia al *Elogio de Carlos III*, Ilie destaca que Jovellanos[15] acredita los logros nacionales a la Ilustración y lo hace a través de metáforas en las que sobresalen la imagen mítica de Minerva (1).[16] Al igual que Teresa, María Isidra se vio obligada a luchar contra la oposición directa y, en su caso específico, a enfrentarse ante las autoridades que regían el mundo universitario de finales de la edad moderna.

El desenvolvimiento en la arena pública con su ingreso a la Real Academia de la Lengua Española en 1784 y a la Sociedad Económica Matritense en 1786, por ejemplo, le ocasionó serios percances con Francisco Cabarrús, quien opinaba lo siguiente sobre la participación femenina en sociedades administradas explícitamente por el gremio masculino: "califica a las mujeres de charlatanas e incompetentes y si jóvenes, coquetas, si casadas, con obligaciones sagradas, si mayores, amargadas" (Vázquez Madruga 24). Al igual que Minerva, la tenacidad y sapiencia de María Isidra logra superar estos obstáculos de naturaleza externa, mientras su erudición se acrecienta contribuyendo de manera interna a la emancipación que se forjaría dentro del ámbito universitario. De acuerdo a las premisas de Sternberg, en primer lugar, María Isidra, al igual que Teresa, demuestra la inteligencia que se requiere a nivel individual para alcanzar sus fines académicos conexos a su propia iniciativa personal, la cual ella misma ha determinado dentro del inestable ambiente universitario del siglo XVIII.

---

14   Vázquez Madruga menciona también las aportaciones reformistas de Jovellanos (23).

15   La preparación universitaria de Jovellanos se llevó a cabo en la Universidad Complutense de Alcalá.

16   En referencia a la competencia entre Marte y Minerva, Antonio y Adelaida Cortijo Ocaña notan que

"[l]os límites entre espacio real y espacio de representación han de imaginarse también lo suficientemente amplios como para entender la participación de estos personajes-personas reales que no dejan de tener sus nombres y apellidos en todo momento, además de para entender el hecho de que la repartición de los premios de los combates de la Aventura tenga lugar en el "sarao de Palacio" que se celebra con posterioridad a la representación, por la noche" (81-82).

Las metas personales de María Isidra se materializan a pesar de las tensiones internas por las cuales atravesaba la Universidad Complutense durante las monarquías borbónicas (42). María Isidra Guzmán se dedica a defender el derecho de la mujer de ingresar en el mundo universitario de la prestigiosa Universidad de Alcalá, una de las primeras universidades fundadas en Europa. En este ambiente de reformas progresistas, María Isidra infiere que las oportunidades que los hombres recibían, más allá de su función de esposo y padre, eran mucho más visibles en el espacio social, público y abierto, mientras que para la mujer se reservaba únicamente el espacio doméstico, privado y cerrado del hogar. Aquí habría que aclarar que el templo de Minerva no solamente se establece en lugares destinados al medio privado y hermético, sino que su alegoría de *monumento* sólido que Carlos III erige durante la monarquía de los ilustrados procura evocar la fortaleza romana de capitolio y palacio etéreo. Para Ilie, por ejemplo, en España "[e]l espíritu de Minerva impregna estos lugares tanto en las artes visuales como en la literatura del XVIII" (16).

En segundo lugar, Sternberg propone que la posibilidad de obtener el éxito se encuentra íntimamente ligada a la fortaleza interna con que cuente el individuo. Nos remitimos entonces aquí al ejemplo que María Isidra personifica quien, en medio de la reformas carlistas, logra superar los límites impuestos por el sistema vigente a través del permiso que le concede el mismo rey para ser examinada y doctorándose así en una de las universidades más prestigiosas de Europa. Este triunfo académico contrarresta las limitaciones con las cuales la mujer era tradicionalmente percibida, incluso en plena Ilustración española (43).

Se supera este desafío no necesariamente a través de la competencia discusiva, sino que, al igual que Minerva, el reto se supera con el talento que se requería y con la habilidad intuitiva necesaria que legitimara la presencia femenina en el entorno académico, con lo cual su mensaje revelaba que estas mismas oportunidades deberían ser ofrecidas sin distinción de género o condición social. Es decir, una visión evidentemente avanzada para la sociedad carlista. Se invita, de esta manera, a reflexionar sobre el verdadero teorema de la simetría, una función netamente aritmética y arquitectónica que procuraba crear de una manera pacífica, pero firme, un espacio *no* alterno, sino equitativo para la mujer ilustrada del Siglo de las Luces. Vázquez Madruga explica que es precisamente en el terreno de la razón donde se lleva a cabo la igualdad de género, puesto que de lo contrario la mujer se subordina a una posición de criatura irracional que hay que dominar (25).

Por fortuna, María Isidra *no* se dejó confundir por la única retórica admisible de su tiempo, sino que, por el contrario, concentró su energía, talento y erudición en demostrar lo ilógico de estos enunciados invalidando estos preceptos pre-deterministas con el estudio, examen, y defensa de tesis doctoral. Se hace acreedora del título en Filosofía y Letras el 6 de junio de 1785 pasando a la historia con su merecido grado de Doctora de Alcalá realizado en el acto vigente de ceremonia universitaria: la primera mujer en obtener tan alto mérito en la España del siglo XVIII durante la Europa de la Ilustración. Aquí se aplicaría el tercer atributo que Sternberg considera necesario en el logro del éxito, el cual reside en el equilibrio entre habilidades y destrezas que el individuo manifiesta con el objetivo de adaptar, edificar y seleccionar biósferas que contribuyan a transformar la realidad inmediata en una realidad exitosa (43).

María Isidra no solamente tuvo que superar obstáculos externos debido al ambiente de reformas carlistas, sino que también se vio obligada a vivir en medio de reformas universitarias internas en la Universidad Complutense bajo la rectoría de Pedro Díaz de Rojas, Abad de la Magistral. El ambiente de constante restructuración en el que tuvo que funcionar, además de su condición de mujer—a pesar de las buenas intenciones del rectorado en dirigir un plan de reforma más acorde con su momento actual—demuestran su entereza y aplomo en lograr sus metas académicas. Se ha sugerido incluso, explica Vázquez Madruga, que el doctorado comprobablemente acreditado y resultado tácito de su capacidad, entrega al estudio y firme perseverancia, había sido un regalo del rey o una evidencia de la decadencia por la que atravesaba el sistema universitario (154). Estos comentarios divergentes revelan, a su vez, el ambiente asimétrico y de tensión en el cual María Isidra triunfó, a pesar de los obstáculos afrontados, y que reflejan entonces un mérito más hacia su persona y capacidad intelectual: "[a]lcanzó un sueño que es seguro, no fue únicamente suyo sino también de otras muchas sabias mujeres. Es incuestionable que consiguió romper una barrera que durante siglos fue infranqueable: doctorarse en una Universidad" (Vázquez Madruga 157).

María Isidra, al igual que Teresa, defiende su fe mediante un cristianismo ilustrado. Vázquez Madruga nota en el capítulo IX de *Vid*, obra impresa de María Isidra, que "[ella] daba la bienvenida a los adelantos procedentes del extranjero que no supusieran peligro alguno para las tradiciones españolas, esto es, Monarquía, Iglesia y en definitiva el sistema estamental" (27). La vida eclesiástica, tal como se infiere en el contexto histórico, había comenzado a descuidar el aspecto de orden cultural o educativo. Tanto las misiones en ultramar como la Iglesia en España desatendían en muchos casos las necesidades inmediatas de los feligreses. Esta carencia de educación la suplían las órdenes religiosas masculinas: "disponían de colegios en las universidades más importantes del reino y en el caso de la Compañía de Jesús, ésta se convierte en la educadora de la élite de la sociedad española" (Vázquez Madruga 28).

La figura mítica de Minerva, de igual forma, conformaba parte importante de la literatura doctrinal y de la vida piadosa de la cultura del siglo XVIII en España. En algunos ejemplos, inclusive, se percibe que el mismo autor de las obras dogmáticas podía acudir a la diosa romana invocando su sabiduría y piedad o se podía utilizar su nombre para reprender o contrarrestar la ignorancia o dejadez en los asuntos relacionados con las obras cívicas de beneficencia pública (Ilie 5). María Isidra, por lo tanto, al igual que Teresa, reconocía la importancia de la caridad, la cual, como ya he manifestado, incluye la caridad educativa. La participación de María Isidra en obras benéficas y su generosidad se registran durante toda su vida en documentos oficiales e inclusive en su testamento donde se destina una cantidad considerable de su herencia a la propagación de la educación.

A diferencia de Ovidio quien perfila a Minerva como la diosa cruel en la fábula de Aracne de *Las metamorfosis*, observamos en María Isidra un paralelo un poco más cercano a la realidad del Siglo de las Luces que nos remite al signo artístico que Minerva emite dentro del proyecto de Ilustración del siglo XVIII en España. Ilie ha notado que "[a] lo largo del siglo borbónico, Minerva es la diosa rectora de la creatividad española" (3). María Isidra ha triunfado, de acuerdo a las premisas de Sternberg, en el cuarto apartado de la teoría de inteligencia exitosa dentro de un equilibrio simétrico de capacidad analítica, innovación trasformadora y habilidades prácticas en el rígido territorio masculino del recinto universitario (43).

IV. Conclusiones

Se responden entonces aquí las preguntas que han originado este estudio. Teresa de Ávila materializa con éxito la personificación mítica de Atenea en el mundo monacal del siglo XVI. La batalla metafórica que se lleva a cabo a un nivel intelectual no se reserva únicamente al hombre, sino que, por el contrario, la mujer participa de forma patente en su función de protectora, consejera, y pedagoga. Al igual que se asocia Atenea con la enseñanza de las artes y oficios dedicados a las mujeres, también la figura de esta diosa griega muestra su predisposición al mundo culto e intelectual representando la ciudad que escogió ser bautizada con su nombre.

Teresa recorre un camino a través de su escritura que la conduce a la perfección en un territorio mixto e híbrido en su funcionamiento monjil cotidiano del siglo XVI.[17] Desde esta perspectiva, nos encontraríamos observando a Atenea Partenos en un ámbito intermedio entre lo que se consideraba propio del gremio femenino, la caridad y la enseñanza, y lo que se destinaba para el papel masculino, el campo de batalla y la escritura. Teresa, Atenea virgen, nunca sucumbe ante el amor carnal de la adolescencia y consagra su pureza en sacrificio vivo hacia Jesucristo, su fuente de inspiración creativa y literaria. Teresa transforma las imperfecciones con que se asociaba al *género débil* en esa perfección que ofrece un sendero de éxitos y logros a pesar del sistema hierático en el cual ejercía sus funciones de mujer devota dentro del ambiente reformista de la temprana modernidad. *Camino de perfección* se convierte en el Partenón de la Acrópolis ateniense, es decir, su templo sagrado desde el cual imparte con inteligencia y creatividad la caridad que rescata a sus monjas de las terribles garras del león de la ignorancia.

María Isidra personifica a la Minerva humana que entra al templo de la sabiduría, supera su contorno inmediato y logra que el proyecto de Ilustración se materialice con éxito superando las divisiones de género a finales de la temprana edad moderna. Evoca el grabado alegórico de 1781: "España conducida por Himeneo al Templo de Minerva" (Ilie 1). Es verdad que María Isidra nunca pudo acudir a la aulas universitarias ni enseñar en salones de clases debido a su condición de mujer, lo cual revela el fracaso de la Ilustración en este sentido, pero con la obtención de su doctorado inició el camino en una vereda imperfecta, tal como lo hizo Teresa, hacia la comprobación de la igualdad intelectual de género. Vázquez Madruga lo expresa con exactitud: "[María Isidra] rompió barreras y abrió caminos para las mujeres de su época y para las del futuro" (158).[18] Simboliza, por lo tanto, la alegoría de Minerva en su facultad de "reflexionar sobre la historia y el destino colectivo" (Ilie 2). Al igual que Teresa, María Isidra representa un ser humano híbrido que funciona en un ambiente masculino, pero sin dejar de ser mujer.[19]

---

17   Carrera concluye que Teresa encuentra un sentido de identidad individual y colectivo que la diferencia y la posiciona, tanto a ella como a sus monjas, en un lugar que no permite la intrusión de estereotipos asociados con las limitaciones de género, pero lo hace sin obviar la diferencia que existe entre ambos y la realidad de la condición humana tanto del hombre como de la mujer (307).

18   "Mythology, Empire, and Narrative" de Jarad Zimbler ofrece una evaluación contemporánea de la significancia de la mitología y su intersección con la narrativa y los mecanismos de poder moderno.

19   Maja Ćuk en "Runaway: Munro's Rewriting of Greek Mythology from a Feminist Perspective" ha examinado la mitología desde una reinterpretación que enfatiza la óptica de la mujer en la producción creativa.

De acuerdo a las premisas de Sternberg, Teresa y María Isidra transformaron las *imperfecciones* en el *signo* de la *perfección* que reside en la fortaleza mediante el éxito individual y colectivo obtenido, a pesar de la rigidez del sistema sociocultural en el cual se desempeñaban—el monacal y el universitario—dos esferas sociales en las cuales se observaba marcadamente—dentro de este contexto histórico—que la presencia de la mujer carecía de la merecida simetría social.[20] En ambos ejemplos, tanto el de Teresa, Atenea y Doctora de la Iglesia, como el de María Isidra, Minerva y Doctora de Alcalá, nos encontramos, *no* ante entes llanos producto de una fábula prosista o figuras mitológicas reservadas exclusivamente al capricho de los dioses, sino que ante la presencia de mujeres de carne y hueso que demuestran—cada una en su respectivo ámbito histórico de acción y senda de vida escogida—que el triunfo también puede perfectamente existir en la creatividad e inteligencia femenina.

Obras citadas

Ávila, Teresa de. *Libro de la vida*. Editado por Dámaso Chicharro, Cátedra, 1997.
Ávila, Teresa de. *Camino de perfección*. Editado por María Jesús Mancho Duque, Espasa-Calpe, 1996.
Carrera, Elena. "Writing Rearguard Action, Fighting Ideological Selves: Teresa of Avila's Reinterpretation of Gender Stereotypes in *Camino de perfección*." *Bulletin of Hispanic Studies*, vol. 79, no. 3, 2002, pp. 299–308.
Cipar, Cleopha (Sister). "El retrato de Teresa de Ávila como maestra, visto por unas metáforas en *Camino de perfección*." *Santa Teresa y la literatura mística hispánica. Actas del I Congreso Internacional sobre Santa Teresa y la Mística Hispánica*, editado por Manuel Criado de Val, EDI-6, 1984, pp. 303–07.

---

20 "Creemos que la desmitificación o 'historización' de las fábulas entre los cronistas cristianos no responde únicamente al rechazo de lo mitológico en cuanto pagano y, por tanto, contrario a la religión revelada. Esta actitud, que se enraíza en un proceso de evemerismo consciente y de larga data, fue sobrepasada por la puesta en práctica de lo que podríamos llamar una incipiente metodología de la historia. Esta podría caracterizarse preliminarmente por los siguientes elementos: la búsqueda de una verdad histórica (que arrancaba para los cronistas de la verdad teológica sobre el mundo y el ser humano), la elaboración de una estructura narrativa en torno a la verosimilitud, y la aparición de una crítica historiográfica moderada pero real. Con esta metodología, muchas generaciones de cronistas procuraron sacar los relatos antiguos de la dimensión del mito y traerlos al espacio de la historia" (de Toro Vial 86).

Cortijo Ocaña, Antonio, y Adelaida Cortijo Ocaña. "La *Aventura de la roca de la competencia de Marte y Minerva*. Una folla cortesana desconocida del siglo XVII." *Bulletin of the Comediantes*, vol. 50, no. 1, 1998, pp. 79–92.

Crisógono, P. *Vida de Santa Teresa*. Editorial de Espiritualidad, 2010.

Ćuk, Maja. "Runaway: Munro's Rewriting of Greek Mythology from a Feminist Perspective." *Alice Munro and the Anatomy of the Short Story*, editado por Oriana Palusci, Cambridge Scholars, 2017, pp. 83–94.

Estirado García, Blanca. "Santa Teresa y Ana Ozores: dos caminos de perfección." *Cinco siglos de Teresa: la proyección de la vida y los escritos de Santa Teresa de Jesús. Actas selectas del Congreso Internacional «Y tan alta vida espero. Santa Teresa o la llama permanente. De 1515 a 2015»*, editado por Esther Borrego y José Manuel Losada, Fundación María Cristina Masaveu Peterson, 2016.

González-Casanovas, Roberto J. "Writing in Saint Teresa as a Dialogue of Faith and Love: 'Mental Prayer' in *Camino de perfección* (chapter 24)." *Studia Mystica*, vol. 13, no. 4, 1990, pp. 60–76.

Ilie, Paul. "El templo de Minerva en la España del XVIII." Trad. Andrés Zamora. *Hispanic Review*, vol. 59, no. 1, 1991, pp. 1–23.

Nivre, Elisabeth Wåghäll, editora. *Allusions and Reflection. Greek and Roman Mythology in Renaissance Europe*. Cambridge Scholars, 2015.

Sternberg, Robert J. *Wisdom, Intelligence, and Creativity Synthesized*. Cambridge UP, 2003.

Toro Vial, José Miguel de. "La mitología grecorromana en el discurso narrativo de las crónicas universales medievales." *ALPHA*, vol. 45, 2017, pp. 77–89.

Vázquez Madruga, María Jesús. *Doña María Isidra Quintina de Guzmán y de la Cerda, 'Doctora de Alcalá'. Biografía*. Río Henares Producciones Gráficas, 1999.

Ville, Jacques de. "Mythology and the Images of Justice." *Law and Literature*, vol. 23, no. 3, 2011, pp. 324–64.

Weber, Alison. "Teresa's 'Delicious' Diminutives: Pragmatics and Style in *Camino de perfección*." *Journal of Hispanic Philology*, vol. 10, no. 3, 1986, pp. 211–27.

Zillén, Erik. "Reconfigurations of Mythology in Sixteenth-Century Lutheran Collections of Aesopic Fables." *Allusions and Reflections. Greek and Roman Mythology in Renaissance Europe*, editado por Elisabeth Wåghäll Nivre, Cambridge Scholars, 2015, pp. 465–79.

Zimbler, Jarad. "Mythology, Empire, and Narrative." *Late Victorian into Modern*, editado por Laura Marcus, Michèle Mendelssohn, y Kirsten E., Shepherd-Barr Oxford UP, 2016, pp. 38–54.

Anacaona and the *areito*: A Generative Model for Pro-indigenous Discourse in Lope de Vega's *El Nuevo Mundo descubierto por Cristobal Colón*?

JEANNE GILLESPIE
The University of Southern Mississippi

WOMEN'S VOICES AND THE ENCOUNTER IN LOPE'S *NUEVO MUNDO*

Spanish playwright Felix Alvaro Lope de Vega y Carpio used the theatre as a platform to examine economic, moral, spiritual, and interpersonal interactions, commenting on historical and fictional events as well as contemporary sociopolitical currents. In the three acts of the comedia *El Nuevo Mundo Descubierto por Cristobal Colón* [*Nuevo Mundo*], Lope stages the mounting of Columbus's expedition, the first documented encounter between Amerindians and Europeans, and the tragic results of Spain's first colonial settlement in what would eventually be known as America.

Lope's dramatization of competing interests in Europe and Guanahaní—the Taino name for the island somewhere in the Bahamas on which the expedition first landed—skillfully blends the discourses related to the voyages of Christopher Columbus and the reception of the Europeans by the Amerindians. *Nuevo Mundo* interweaves the multiple and often contradictory motivations on the part of European powers to participate in the expedition with an allegorical trip into Columbus's imagination, internal conflicts within Columbus's crew and the Amerindian community, misperceptions and misinterpretations between the Amerindians and Europeans, and an ambivalent and violent finale. These elements are so complex that the critical reception of the play has vacillated from celebrating the glories of the Admiral and the Reyes Católicos in the Americas to fiercely condemning the work for anti-Spanish sentiments.

Lope's *Nuevo Mundo* has been an enigma over the centuries with scholars and playwrights offering quite divergent interpretations and perspectives on the quality and significance of the work, ranging from admiration to disdain. Neoclassical playwright Leandro Fernández de Moratín described *Nuevo Mundo* as:

> [la c]omedia de las más disparatadas de Lope. La scena [sic] es en Lisboa, en Santa Fe, en Granada, en Barcelona, en Guanahaní, y en medio del mar y en el aire. Entre los personajes de ella hablan el Demonio, la Providencia, la Religión Cristiana, la Idolatría y la imaginación de Cristóbal Colón. En la tercera jornada hay una confusa mezcla de fornicación y doctrina cristiana, teología y lujuria, que no hay más que pedir (133-34).

Over 100 years later, Marcelino Menéndez y Pelayo countered Moratín's commentary arguing that any drama about Columbus would have to take place in the lands he visited and that no play would encompass the time elapsed for those events (1949: 307).

Menéndez y Pelayo also commented that other critics, such as French translator and editor Jean Joseph Stanislas Albert Damas-Hinard, found the comedia at the other end of the critical spectrum (237):

> According to Damas-Hinard:
> [*Nuevo Mundo*] seems to me superiorly conceived from the Catholic and Spanish perspective. ... Whenever Columbus appears and speaks, we recognize in him the superior man; the man destined for great things. (308-09)

While Damas-Hinard celebrated the pro-Spanish and Catholic underpinnings he found in the text, Spanish novelist and literary critic Azorín (José Martínez Ruíz) actually placed Lope on the "malos españoles" list because of the "antiespañolista" nature he perceived in this work. The list included Fray Luís de León, Lope, Cervantes, Gracián, Moratín, Larra, and one honorary bad Spaniard, Teófilo Gautier.

> ¿Por qué es un mal español Lope? ¿Porque tiene, principalmente, un puesto en esta galería? Por su comedia *El Nuevo Mundo descubierto por Colón* ... Un consenso universal ha condenado nuestra conquista americana. Lope marcha en compañía, entre otros, de Voltaire, Montaigne, Herder, Andrés Chenier... (247)

Does Lope belong on the list of "Bad Spaniards"? Perhaps. An examination of Lope's use of the sources of the first encounter, with a special focus on the *areito* performed by the Amerindians and through the representation of the female characters, especially the *amerinda*, Tacuana, in the comedia may shed some light upon this conversation.

In *Making Subjects: Literature and the Emergence of National Identity* (1998), Allen Carey-Webb compares the three female Amerindian characters Tecue, Palca, and Tacuana to the multilingual negotiator and interpreter who accompanied Cortés and his forces, Malintzin (49). Carey-Webb maintains that "demythologizing Malinche has been an important undertaking in the critique of colonial discourse." In addition, Carey-Webb points out that

> Lope's sensitivity to the currents of the time is evident in his use of the Malinche story ... Although strictly anachronistic to a play about Columbus, Malinche is, nevertheless, the generative model for the development of the three *india* characters ... projecting it backwards in time to the very earliest encounter of Spaniards and Native Americans and reproducing it as testimony from the mouth of the depicted indigenous female subject (49-51).

In the case of *Nuevo Mundo*, I suggest that Malintzin, while a keen example of the participation of elite indigenous females, *amerindias*, in the discourses of the colonization of the Americas, is not the "generative model for the development of the three *india* characters" in *Nuevo Mundo* as Carey-Webb asserts, rather the generative aspect would be better assigned to the Taino *cacica* Anacaona, since she was one of the first *amerindias* cited in the accounts of the Americas and shares many similar characteristics with Tacuana. I also suggest that the reason that Lope is on the "Bad Spaniards" list is directly related to the representation of Tacuana as modeled on Anacaona.

Since Carey-Webb's publication, a significant amount of research signals that Malintzin was trained to serve in the capacity for which she was offered to Cortés and, at best, the expectations for the life of elite Amerindian women, like those of many aristocratic European women, were in service to the goals and projects of the ruling powers.[1] According to Carey-Webb,

---

[1] For more on these themes, see Frances Kartunnen's "Rethinking Malinche," Susan Kellogg's "From Parallel and Equivalent to Separate but Unequal: Tenochca Mexica Women, 1500-1700," Geoffrey and Sharisse McCafferty's "The Malinche Code: the Symbology of Female Discourse in Postclassic Mexico," and my works on Malintzin and Anacaona, "Malinche: Fleshing out the Foundational Fictions of

"[t]he Malinche model depends on the notion of *intelligent* submission, knowing full well who the Spanish are and what they desire, the *india* allies herself with the conquerors, opening soul, heart, and body to their designs" (52). Anacaona and Malintzin, like thousands of other Amerindian women over the centuries of conquest and colonization, were involved in similar negotiations, sometimes with and sometimes without their consent. Lope's construction of the composite character "Tacuana" captures many of the nuances of *amerindias*' participation in the Encounter. She also embodies and gives voice to the mutually-beneficial potential of the conquest (at least from a European gaze). Three specific moments in the comedia mark Lope's awareness of Anacaona in the chronicles of the first encounters: 1) the introductory *areito* as the Amerindians take the stage for the first time at the beginning of the second act; 2) the kinship relations and elite status of Tacuana as the daughter of a powerful *cacique*, wife of another *cacique* stolen by a third powerful ruler; and 3) the person who offers the possibility of *amerindias* as partners that carry the potential for Spanish success in the encounter and colonial endeavors.

This final moment which we will analyze in greater detail below is Tacuana's soliloquy in the third act narrating how the *amerindias* could be of benefit and facilitate success for the Spaniards. In terms of the potential for success of the Spanish colonial endeavor, it offers a stark contrast to an allegorical commentary of a scene in the first act that Sofie Kluge calls the "Tribunal Scene." The scene, analyzed in detail in "*Dios los juzga de la intención*: Questioning Conquest in Lope de Vega's '*El nuevo mundo descubierto por Cristóbal Colón*,'" offers Columbus a successful pitch with which to engage the *Reyes Católicos* after their victory against the Muslim forces of Granada.

Near the end of the first act, after Columbus and his brother have been turned down by the Portuguese and British Crowns and several important Spanish aristocratic houses, they arrive in Granada in time to witness the warrior "El Gran Capitán" Gonzalo Fernández de Cordoba take the city from its Moorish ruler, Mohammed XII, el "Rey Chico" and deliver it to the "Reyes Católicos." In the middle of this final event of the Reconquest, Columbus experiences an out-of-body experience in which he literally witnesses a trial between Idolatry (the religion of the Americas) and Religion (the Cristian religion) over whether the conquest of the Americas is just. Columbus witnesses the squabble over which Providence presides. These three

---

the Conquest of Mexico," and "In the shadow of Coatilcue's smile or reconstructing female indigenous subjectivity in the Spanish colonial record."

are represented as female characters, so, in fact, the juridical discourse takes place entirely in women's words.

In the end, Idolatry asserts that if she loses the Indies to Religion, covetousness disguised as Christianity will guide the Conquest:

> No permitas, Providencia,
> hacerme esta sinjusticia,
> pues los lleva la codicia
> a hacer esta diligencia.
> So color de religion
> van a buscar plata y oro
> del encubierto Tesoro. (770-76)

Despite Idolatry's protests, Providence rules that God will be the judge of whether the Conquest is just, and since the Christian King Ferdinand is the sponsor of the enterprise, there should be no doubts:

> Dios juzga de la intención.
> Si él, por el oro que encierra,
> gana las almas que ves,
> en el cielo hay interés,
> no es mucho le haya en la tierra.
> Y del cristiano Fernando,
> que da principio a esta empresa,
> toda la sospecha cesa. (777-84)

At this moment, when all appears settled, the Demon arrives at the door to offer his perspective on the potential for the success of Christian Conquest. First, he wonders where the tribunal plans to send Columbus:

> Oh! tribunal bendito,
> Providencia eternamente,
> ¿dónde envías a Colón
> para renovar mis daños?
> ¿No sabes que ha muchos años
> que tengo allí posesión? (788-93)

Then he makes fun of Ferdinand's penchant for war and conquest.

> No despiertes a Fernando,
> déjale andar en sus guerras,
> ¿las no conocidas tierras
> andas ahora enseñando?
> ¿En ti cabe sinjusticia? (794-98)

In a detailed and fascinating study of this allegory, Sofie Kluge argues that:

> [the Tribunal Scene] reveals that, beneath its homage to Columbus, *El nuevo mundo descubierto por Cristóbal Colón* entails a tentative revision of the politico-religious conquistador mentality in its capacity as unreflective and militant Christian Eurocentrism. Indeed, Lope's comedia can, I argue, be seen as a very subtle piece of cultural critique, spurred on by the fervent debate on Spanish conduct overseas and dominated by thoughtful meditation (108).

An examination of the Tribunal scene using Kluge's perspective is enlightening. In the tribunal, Columbus realizes that, like the Reconquest that led El Gran Capitán to glory in Granada, if Columbus can convert the people of "undiscovered lands"—ironic, since the allegorical characters and the audience already know they exist—to Catholicism, he can bring greatness to his patrons, Ferdinand and Isabella, and to Spain. Ambiguous as the discourse may be, the allegorical characters help him find the "hook" he needs to persuade the Reyes Católicos to support him. Columbus's desire for greatness is palpable, so the need for him to engage allies that will support his work is heightened. He is able to secure the backing of the Reyes Católicos and sets sail for America.

The subtlety of this message is especially marked because the pro-American discourse occurs in women's voices. Kluge and Carey-Webb are honing in to a pro-American discourse that remains subtle because it takes place in allegorical references and later in the discourse of an *amerindia*. I maintain that this is partially why some critics, and especially Moratín, found the comedia "*disparatada*" and why the Neoclassical playwright complained about the confusing mixture of fornication, religious doctrine, theology and lustfulness in the third act.

Lope's use of the *Areito* in *Nuevo Mundo*

The second act opens with Columbus's crew in full mutiny. As the mutiny scene is resolved, the action shifts to an Amerindian community's celebration on the beach of Guanahaní. A female Amerindian leads a song to the Sun God announcing the wedding of Dulcanquellín, a Taino cacique, and Tacuana, the wife of a neighboring cacique. The other Amerindians reply to each line the *india* sings with "*Hoy que sale el sol*:"

> Cante así una india y respondan otros:
> [INDIOS]
> Hoy que sale el sol divino,
> hoy que sale el sol,
> hoy que sale de mañana,
> hoy que sale el sol,
> se junta de buena gana,
> hoy que sale el sol. (1134-39)

The *india* expounds on the nature of the celebration while the chorus of Native Americans continue to repeat their refrain:

> Dulcanquellín con Tacuana...
> Él Febo y ella Dïana...
> A cacique tan hermoso...
> y a esposa de tal esposo,...
> nuestro *areito* glorioso,...
> consagre el canto Famoso... (1140-50)

The song identifies itself as the indigenous genre "*areito*" in line 1148. Lope's nod to Amerindian epic tradition suggests a familiarity with the fact that Taino females did compose and stage these compositions. As Mártir de Anglería explains, *areitos* were used for ceremonial celebrations as well as for historical commemoration, and in *Nuevo Mundo*, the composition is used for calling forth the celebrants to announce the wedding between the local *cacique*, Dulcanquellín and Tacuana. Nevertheless, Menéndez y Pelayo is correct that Lope's *areito* lyrics have a decidedly European feel. While Menéndez y Pelayo defends Lope's disregard for the unities in *Nuevo Mundo*, he critiques the comedia for its "inauthentic" representation of America, especially in Lope's use of the *areito*.

Menéndez y Pelayo asserts that Lope's use of the *areito*: "[t]ampoco parece muy americano aquel *areito* que Lope hace cantar a sus indios en los desposorios de Tacuana, ni mucho menos la idea de hacerle acompañar con panderos" (320). His observations are correct regarding the Classical references in the *areito* from *Nuevo Mundo*. Lacking an indigenous model, Lope draws on the Roman sources with an allusion to the Roman gods Phaeton and Diana in the *areito*'s text. Melissa Figueroa offers interesting insight into this allusion in "Courting the Female Body: Towards a Poetics of the Conquest." For Figueroa, these two gods represent an immoral liaison between brother and sister (12-13.) Nevertheless, we will find out later that Tacuana was married off by her father to Tapirazú (*Nuevo Mundo* 2141-48), and that, although Dulcanquellín has kidnapped her from her unconsummated marriage bed, he professes not to touch her until he has won her heart (1317-20).

Figueroa does explore the connections between Diana, the hunter, and a woman who vows not to take a husband. In indigenous societies, as in European royal families, couples with close kinship ties were not uncommon. I suggest however, that, again, Anacaona may be a model for this as she served with her brother, Behechio, as ruler of Jaragua until his death and became the *cacique* at that time. While this will be explored in more detail later, Figueroa observes that Tacuana's "final decision—to not marry and to convert to Christianity—makes her one of the most radical characters of the play and at the same time sheds new light on one of the passages that most puzzles critics: her concealed sexual interest for Terrazas" (13).

Additionally, Menéndez y Pelayo criticizes Lope further for not following the historical sources more accurately. The critic, who has studied the account of Columbus's voyage in great detail complains that:

> No parece haber conocido ni las Décadas de Pedro Mártir, ni la biografía del Almirante, que Alfonso de Ulloa imprimió en 1571 a nombre de su hijo D. Fernando Colón ... [n]i mucho menos tuvo acceso a los textos ... de Fr. Bartolomé de las Casas. (313)

I disagree with Menéndez y Pelayo on this account. By employing the *areito* as an element of indigenous performative discourse, I argue that Lope may indeed have consulted the *Decades*. It is Pedro Mártir de Anglería who makes one of the first mentions of the *areito* in the Spanish archive in 1516, and he indicates that he is quite impressed with the fact that "uncivilized men" would have a mechanism for history:

> Your Beatitude will no doubt ask with astonishment how it comes that such uncivilized men, destitute of any knowledge of letters, have preserved for such a long time the tradition of their origin. This has been possible because from the earliest times ... wise men have trained the

sons of the *caciques*, teaching them their past history by heart ... they carefully distinguish two classes of studies; the first is of a general interest, having to do with the succession of events; the second is of a particular interest, treating of the notable deeds accomplished in time of peace or time of war by their fathers, grandfathers, great-grandfathers, and all their ancestors. ... These poems are called *arreytos* (*De Orbe Novo* Decada III Book VII p.16).

As Mártir de Anglería explains, the *areito* itself is a discourse of power, prepared for a special occasion to commemorate significant events. It was also used as an offering of alliance or allegiance (16). Mártir de Anglería also explains, contrary to Menéndez y Pelayo's assertion, that drums were used in the *areito*, if not tambourines:

As with us the guitar player, so with them the drummers accompany these *arreytos* and lead singing choirs. Their drums are called *maguay*. Some of the *arreytos* are love songs, others are elegies, and others are war songs; and each is sung to an appropriate air. They also love to dance, but they are more agile than we are; first, because nothing pleases them better than dancing and, secondly, because they are naked, and untrammeled by clothing (Decade III, Book VII).

Fernández de Oviedo, who relied heavily on Mártir de Anglería's writings, describes the Anacaona's act of composition in greater detail:

En el tiempo que el comendador mayor don frey Nicolás de Ovando gobernó esta isla, hizo un *areito* antél Anacaona, mujer que fue del cacique o rey Caonabó (la cual era gran señora), e andaban en la danza más de trescientas doncellas, todas criadas suyas, mujeres por casar; porque no quiso que hombre ni mujer casada (o que hubiese conocido varón) entrasen en la danza o *areito*. (125).

From this analysis, it becomes clear that Anacaona's *areito* is an attempt to offer Taino wives to the Spaniards to bring them into the community and to cement an alliance.

We certainly see that Mártir de Anglería's treatment of the Amerindians casts them as "uncivilized," "naked, "and "without history." These are common tropes in the European gaze with regard to non-European, and especially Amerindian, subjects, but we do not see this aspect in Lope's treatment of the Amerindians. His narrative communicates the opposite of an uncivilized indigenous population. In fact, we will see that in several instances, the Tainos are represented as more "civilized" than the Europeans. This aspect reflects part of the subtle revisioning Kluge has highlighted in *Nuevo Mundo* concerning Spanish conduct overseas. While Anacaona's negotiations were perceived by many European chroniclers as immoral and uncivilized, this is precisely the action that happened in many indigenous communities as the Europeans marched through their lands and settled near their cities and towns. It was also how these communities established relationships with other Native settlements in their area and in their trade zones.

Alessandro Martinengo offers a detailed and convincing study showing that Lope did indeed incorporate aspects of Mártir de Anglería and Fernando Columbus; although the playwright did mold and model these details to his poetic and dramatic purposes. Martinengo cites critics including Raquel Minian de Alfie who recognized that Lope incorporated many colonial sources, but would often "contaminate" them with details of other sources (6-7) and the French editors and translators Jacques Lemartinel and Charles Minguet who approached their edition of *Nuevo Mundo* from the perspective that the poetic license Lope takes with the historic sources are justified since he was attempting to create a comedia that would engage audiences in 1600 and that was *"plus légendaire qu'historique"* (p. v) (See Martinengo 7).

Martinengo identifies several other elements in the comedia that further prove Lope's use of a wide variety of sources woven into a complex and entertaining narrative. These include a general derision of the Genovese found in Cervantes, Góngora, Quevedo, and others (8); the mutiny on the ship, which is treated in Mártir de Anglería and Fernández de Oviedo in detail; and the eroticism between the *amerindias* and the Spanish crew, which both Mártir de Anglería and Fernández de Oviedo also explore in detail (7-19).

Although Lope's encounter is definitely meant to represent the initial contact between Europeans and Amerindians in Guanahaní—an island in the Bahamas in 1492—it is clear, as Martinengo and others have signaled, that Lope is not aiming for historical accuracy. Several elements of Lope's indigenous story arc such as the inclusion of the *areito*, and the presence of the cacique Dulcanquellín, and his aide Auté support Menéndez y Pelayo's assertion that another one of Lope's main sources was Francisco López de Gómara's *Historia general de las Indias* (1554). Lopez de Gómara identifies "Dulchanchellín" as the *cacique* of the Timucua people of Florida who was met by Pánfilo de Narváez in 1527 near Tampa Bay. In López de Gómara's chapter on the Narváez expedition, the chronicler also mentions the region of Aute in Florida, although in

Nuevo Mundo Lope has adapted the place name Auté as the name of an *amerindia*. These elements further confirm Minian de Afie's discussion of how the sources for inspiration become woven into the literary and poetic construction of the comedia for more performative effect that any attempt at realism.

AMERINDIAS AND CROSS-CULTURAL DISCOURSE: PALCA AND TACUANA

Nuevo Mundo represents one of the first stagings of Amerindians and it is quite possible that the roles were played by actual Amerindians. The situation in which they are engaged is a familiar plot for Lope. Dulcanquellín, like many of Lope's powerful male characters, has fallen for another man's spouse. The celebration of the betrothal sets up a conflict between two Amerindian communities since Dulcanquellín has kidnapped Tacuana to wed. The bride, who is the daughter of a neighboring cacique is also already married, and she vehemently protests becoming Dulcanquellín's wife:

> Esta noche había de ser su esposa, ...
> Es tu enemigo mi esposo,
> supiste aquí nuestro trato,
> dístenos arma y rebato,
> y robásteme furioso. (1261-68)

Tacuana makes her request to her potential husband:

> Sirve, amigo galán,
> conquístame, gana el pecho ...
> Enamórame, no quieras,
> por dar rienda al apetito,
> perder el bien infinito,
> que de amar, amando esperas. (1289-96)

Tacuana, like many of Lope's female characters, is well-spoken and not afraid to exercise her agency. At the same time, Tacuana's word choice "conquístame" hints of hegemonic discourse that will return in the third act. Nevertheless, the *cacique* is swayed by Tacuana's argument and grants her the time it takes for their love to blossom:

> Esperaré un mes, un año,
> un siglo en esta conquista,
> que basta el bien de tu vista,
> para no sentir mi daño. (1317-20)

As Tacuana pledges to stay with Dulcanquellín on her honor to the Amerindian divinity, "Ongol," Dulcanquellín's advisor, Auté, calls for the cacique's attention. At this moment, Tacuana's husband, Tapirazú, breaks up the festivities and attempts to dispatch Dulcanquellín. For a moment, the audience sees two Amerindian communities in conflict, but this is punctuated by the sound of Columbus's crew exclaiming "¡[t]ierra, tierra, tierra, tierra!" (1449). Tacuana is able to call an end to the conflict:

> Cese ahora el desafío
> pues tendréis tiempo y lugar.
> En que le podéis hacer:
> prevenid este alboroto,
> que el cielo en sus ejes roto
> hoy se debe de caer, (1463-68)

which is punctuated by another round of: "¡Tierra, tierra, tierra, tierra!" (1468) and canon fire.

The Amerindians scatter as the Europeans disembark and, with another sardonic twist, begin to name all the things they see in Spanish. As the Spaniards make their way along the beach, an *amerindia* named Palca literally runs into them. She is frightened but engages with them and they begin to offer her gifts and trinkets. One of them offers her a mirror, and she shrinks back, at her reflection leaving Fray Buyl to comment: "Poco solimán vendieran, / si así del espejo huyeran / las mujeres de Castilla" (1705-07). Soliman was a toxic, mercury-based compound used in Early Modern Spain to whiten skin. Buyl's reference to soliman suggests economic interests, as well since Spain was exploiting the profitable use of mercury as a cosmetic in the XVI and XVII centuries. Celestina even carried it with her among here wares:

> Aquí llevo un poco de hilado en esta mi faltriquera, con otros aparejos que conmigo siempre traigo, para tener causa de entrar, donde mucho no soy conocida, la primera vez: así como gorgueras, garvines, franjas, rodeos, tenazuelas, alcohol, albayalde y solimán, hasta agujas y alfileres. (79-80)

After the interaction, the Europeans send Palca off to entice others with trinkets, and Columbus begins to plan how he should be remembered like a new Alexander. The inclusion of Buyl in the first encounter is another indication Lope was working from López de Gómara's narrative, which includes Columbus's first and second voyages. It also supports that Lope was extrapolating from the histories since Friar Buyl accompanied Columbus only on the second expedition. Buyl's perspective on Amerindian women also reflects an appreciation of what he imagines as a potential for restraint and decorum, which he contrasts with his own disdain for European women.

In the first act of *Nuevo Mundo*, the tribunal brings us juridical discourse in the voices of female allegorical characters. In Act Two, the first two scenes set in the Indies stage a celebratory indigenous song led by a female performer and another *amerindia* demands that her captor treat her with respect and earn her love. A third Native woman acts as negotiator in the first contact. It is interesting that a significant portion of the transformational action in the comedia is driven by the female characters, a very common occurrence in Lope's compositions. It is also significant that they are the intermediaries for the indigenous communities in the cross-cultural communication, and that, in Lope's version, even the priest sees potential in their conversion to Christianity.

TACUANA'S NEGOTIATIONS AND EUROPEAN GAZE.
In the third act, we arrive at the "confusing mix of fornication and Christian doctrine, theology and lustfulness" of which Moratín so forcefully complains. The audience finds out that the bride-to-be, like Anacaona, comes from Haiti as she negotiates with the Europeans for protection and she sets up a proposal that the Americas could be a place where the two cultures come together. Tacuana makes her argument that the Amerindians can be good Christians as Fray Buyl had suspected:

> así veáis esta tierra
> sujeta a vuestros pendones,
> y ese vuestro Dios y Cristo
> triunfador de nuestros dioses.

She continues:

> y la cruz que nos predica
> aquese bendito monje,
> que la trajo en sus espaldas
> por la redención del orbe,
> desde Haití a la hermosa Chile
> generalmente se adore,
> y la misa que esperamos
> mueva nuestros corazones. (2109-20)

Tacuana also imagines the Americas as a place where the sons of the Spaniards could wed the Amerindian daughters to forge alliances:

> y volváis a vuestras patrias,
> y que vuestros hijos pobres
> jueguen ricos al tejuelo
> con el oro de estos montes
> o los traigáis a casar
> con nuestras hijas, a donde,
> mezclándose nuestra sangre,
> seamos todos españoles. (2125-32)

This passage offers more evidence that Lope is familiar with Anacaona's plight and that his *cacica* is also searching for a way to protect herself and to establish an alliance with the Europeans.

As the third act unfolds, it appears that Lope cites more from Anacaona's interaction with Bartolomé de las Casas in which the priest uses the case of Anacaona, chief in her own right and composer of *areitos*, as one of the examples of the extreme violence that impelled him to write in protest of the Spanish colonization processes. Lope's treatment of Tacuana here incorporates some aspects of the sexual freedom outlined in Fernández de Oviedo's description of Anacaona, but Lope's *cacica* also reflects a preoccupation of her role in the colonial structure and certainly as a representative of her people as characterized by Las Casas. According to Las Casas we know that in 1498 Anacaona entertained the Spanish administration with her *areito*, buying her people four years of life in the Spanish colony, but in 1503, she was captured and executed at the hands of the Spanish governor Nicholas de Ovando. In *Las obras del obispo* Las Casas summarizes the event:

> Aquí llegó una vez el gobernador que gobernaba esta isla con sesenta de caballo y más trecientos peones, ... llegáronse más de trescientos señores a su llamado ... de los cuales hizo meter dentro de una casa de paja muy grande los más señores por engaño, e metidos les mandó poner fuego y los quemaron vivos. A todos los otros alancearon e metieron a espada ... e a la señora Anacaona, por hacerle honra, ahorcaron. (f. 9r.)

Fernández de Oviedo used the comportment of Anacaona and the Taino women as the justification for Ovando's violent massacre of the Taino leaders. Due to the nature of Anacaona's *areito* he perceived her as "una mujer que tuvo algunos actos semejantes a los de aquella Semíramis, reina de los asirios." (132). He clarifies the statement by explaining that the comparison was not because of "los grandes fechos que cuenta Justino, ni tampoco en hacer matarlos muchos con quien se ayuntaba, ni en haçer traer á sus doncellas paños menores en sus vergonzozas partes, como de aquella reyna escribe Johan Bocaçio." But because "fué, como tengo dicho, absoluta señora e muy acatada de los indios; pero muy deshonesta en el acto venéreo con los cristianos, e por esto e otras cosas semejantes, quedó reputada y tenida por la más disoluta mujer que de su manera ni otra hobo en esta isla" (132-33).

This treatment is also, I believe, related to the accounts of Anacaona since both Fernández de Oviedo and López de Gómara suggest that she is licentious and untrustworthy and liken her to the Assyrian warrior queen, Semiramis. Shades of Semiramis's history are also reflected in Lope's treatment of Tacuana. Like Tacuana, Semiramis was pursued by a powerful man who was not her husband, the Assyrian king Ninus. In the legend of the warrior queen, Ninus demanded that Semiramis's husband, the Assyrian general Onnes, trade his wife for one of the king's daughters. Ninus threatened to blind Onnes if he refused, so in despair, Onnes hanged himself, and Semiramis married Ninus. Upon Ninus's death, as regent for their son, Ninyus, she ruled a powerful empire. In some narratives, Semiramis is criticized for being licentious and loose, in others she is praised as a wise and valiant queen.

Lope's treatment is significantly different. The revelation that Tacuana has not been with either her husband or Ducanquellín reflects the offerings of "*doncellas*" for the purpose of marriage to Spanish soldiers as described by Fernández de Oviedo. Different from Anacaona, who offered 300 women for the delight of her Spanish guests, Tacuana offers only herself, but her considerations are of a much larger scale. She proposes a comprehensive unification of their forces throughout the Americas:

> Yo soy Tacuana, de Haití,
> que he vivido desde entonces
> sin mi esposo, a quien Dulcán
> me robó la misma noche
> que Clapillán, padre mío,
> me le dio para que goce
> del indio más generoso
> que hay desde el Sur a los Triones.[2] (2141-48)

---

2   The final line refers to the Northern Hemisphere that extends from the South to the Triones—the seven stars that form the constellation Ursa Major.

Tacuana chooses Columbus's crewmember, Terrazas, the one who led the mutiny and who has already declared he is there for the gold and the women, to protect her from her "kidnapper," whom she describes as a barbarian. The agency with which Tacuana expresses her desire later for a Spanish male companion and rejects both of her Amerindian suitors contributes to Kluge's hypothesis that Lope is offering a significant shift in the construction of and the politico-religious conquistador mentality:

> Que me libréis del tirano
> cacique, bárbaro, y torpe,
> que aquí me tiene cautiva
> entre sus brazos disformes. (2133-36)

Terrazas understands very well this offer:

> Lo más entendido tengo,
> Tacuana, de tus voces.
> Sígueme, y no tengas pena
> que tu pretensión estorbe,
> que por ser mujer es justo
> darte ayuda, y baste, y sobre,
> para que nadie te ofenda,
> que nuestra defensa escoges. (2169-76)

In the hopes of a mutually beneficial alliance, the Amerindians and Columbus's crew exist in peace for a brief moment, while Fray Buyl shows some success in converting the Amerindians with the assistance of Tapirazú. Although Dulcanquellín is harder to convince, all seems well until Dulcanquellín finds out through the Demon from the Tribunal Scene—who is also the Amerindian deity Ongol—that Terrazas, whom he has entreated to help him reconnect with Tacuana, has actually been hiding her.

> Éstos, codiciando el oro de los indios,
> se hacen santos, fingen cristiano
> decoro, mientras vienen otros tantos
> que llevan todo el Tesoro. (2678-81)

Dulcanquellín responds in fury:

> ¡Oh, gente vil inhumana,
> fuera de piedad desnudas,

> con pieles de ley cristiana!
> *¡Oh, españoles, o traidores!*
> *¡Armas, gentes! ¡*Indios, alarma! (2700-04)

A melee ensues as Dulcanquellín exclaims: "Con falsa relación y falsos dioses, / nos venís a robar oro y mujeres" (2730-31). To which Auté responds: "Muertos son los más de ellos" (2732). Dulcanquellín, who throughout the comedia has shown the most moral approach to his situation, appears lost. It is he who, with the goading of the demon, sees through the abuse of Christian rhetoric and the tricks of Terrazas and the other Spaniards that were predicted in the Tribunal by both Idolatry and the Demon himself. The Spaniards, exemplified by Terrazas, are not worthy of the Amerindian alliance. In protest, the Amerindians remove the cross planted by Buyl but miraculously, another grows in its place, causing them to become true believers. Tapirazú exclaims: "Hoy, palo, el cetro has de ser / del rey de aquestos vasallos. / Danos otra vez perdón" (2742-44). Dulcanquellín responds: "Sin duda, que es verdadera / la cristiana religión; / quien dijere que no, muera" (2745-47)

At the same moment that the Amerindians destroy the colony, Columbus is meeting with the Catholic Monarchs in Spain, showing them the bounty of the Indies and parading the Taino people he captured (like Anacaona's husband, Canoabó) in triumphant glory. The Accountant makes notation of all the riches Columbus has brought at the same time that the Monarchs have the Amerindians baptized:

> Vamos a dar el bautismo
> a estos primitivos dones,
> sacrificios y oraciones
> a Dios, y el corazón mismo.
> Hoy queda gloriosa España
> de aquesta heroica victoria,
> siendo de Cristo la gloria,
> y de un genovés la hazaña.
> Y de otro mundo segundo
> Castilla y León se alaba. (2901-09)

While the final stanzas indicate the "second world" is praising Castile and Aragón, as the audience witnesses the simultaneous massacre of Columbus's crew on stage, the critique of Spanish behavior abroad and the ambiguity of the praise would not be lost. Kluge indicated in "Dios lo juzgará," the success of the Spanish colonial enterprise as determined by the catechism of Amerindian communities remains, at the very least, questionable. Lope belongs on Moratín's *malos españoles* list because he fails to communicate the glory of the highly masculinized Spanish conquistadors and he communicates the most important socio-political commentary on colonial Spain in the words of women. Lope's dramatic intent, subtle as it may be, questions the Christian intent and potential for success of the conquest. Ironically, this commentary occurs more than 100 years after the actual events, so the results of Columbus's voyages, including his trial and imprisonment, would have been known to the audience.

The treatment of Tacuana and the other *amerindias* in *Nuevo Mundo* is not a backwards projection of Malintzin as Carey-Webb suggests, but a reflection of Lope's reading, and poetic interpretation of the narratives involving Anacaona, and other *amerindias*, from a variety of sources. While Carey-Webb was spot on that Lope used actual *amerindias* as models, very little scholarship had been done on Native women's interactions with Europeans. This is not the case now, however. Despite the perception that Malintzin was unique, her compatriots were performing similar efforts throughout the colonies. Some of their voices are accessible in the archives and it is important to seek them out and to study them as we have studied the voices of the conquistadors in order to develop a more complete perspective of the complexities and subtleties of life in the Americas.

I agree with Kluge that Tacuana is the character most transformed in the comedia. In Tacuana, Lope develops a character who offers herself to the Spanish invaders with the intent and potential to become one of the first American Christians, but because of the actions of the Spanish crew, this experiment fails. Tacuana, like Anacaona—and in contrast to Malintzin—is from Haiti. She is the daughter, wife, and sister of *caciques* from the island as well as a *cacica* in her own right. Like Anacaona, Tacuana offers an alliance based upon interconnected kinship in which the Europeans and the Amerindians could become a unified people. She articulates and performs what was expected of Amerindian women whenever new power structures emerged, even before the arrival of the Europeans. The goal for this type of interaction is to find a way in which the settled community and the new arrivals can live and work together. While Tacuana represents some agency in her endeavors with not only the Spanish crew, but also her indigenous community, most *amerindias* involved in encounters with Europeans are not that far removed from European elite women like Isabella of Portugal or Catherine of Aragón who were married off by their families, often to close relatives, to assure good political and economic relationships between regions or countries. In the case of *Nuevo Mundo*, however, Tacuana's offer of herself and her conversion to Christianity is betrayed by the lack of Christian actions on the part of Columbus's crew, despite the celebration of the Amerindian baptism at the feet of Ferdinand and Isabella. Meanwhile, also ironically, the Accountant makes a record of the gifts, including Native bodies, that Columbus bestows them. In the final count, Tacuana and Dulcanquellín are the most amenable to Christianity, casting them also as most open to Spain's colonial efforts while the members of Columbus's crew reflect the most damaging since their lack of moral comportment is the catalyst for the Amerindian uprising. It is no surprise that the critical reception of this piece has been so polemic.

Works Cited

Azorín (See Martínez Ruíz, Fernando)

Carey-Webb, Allen. *Making Subject(s): Literature and the Emergence of National Identity*. Garland, 1998.

Casas, Bartolomé de Las, *Las Obras del obispo D. Fray Bartolome de las Casas, o Casaus, obispo que fue de la ciudad Real de Chiapa en las Indias*.... Antonio Lacaualleria, *Biblioteca Virtual Andalucía* 1551, f. 9r, www.bibliotecavirtualdeandalucia.es/catalogo/es/consulta/registro. cmd?id=1002307.

Damas-Hinard, Jean Joseph. *Théâtre de Lope de Vega*. Charpentier, 1892, vol. 1, pp. 217-282.

Fernández de Oviedo, Gonzalo. *Historia general y natural de las Indias*. Toledo, 1526, www.biblioteca-antologica.org/es/wp-content/uploads/2018/03/FERN%C3%81NDEZ-DE-OVIEDO-Historia-general-y-natural-I.pdf.

Figueroa, Melissa. "Courting the Female Body: Towards a Poetics of the Conquest in Lope de Vega's *El Nuevo Mundo descubierto por Cristóbal Colón*." *The Other America: Female Amerindians in Early Modern Spanish Theater*, editor Gladys Robalino, Bucknell, 2014, pp. 9-28.

Gillespie, Jeanne, "In the shadow of Coatilcue's smile or reconstructing female indigenous subjectivity in the Spanish colonial record." *Women's Negotiations and Textual Agency in Latin America, 1500-1799*, editors Monica Diaz and Rocio Quispe-Agnioli, Routledge. 2016, pp. 85-105.

———. "Malinche: Fleshing out the Foundational Fictions of the Conquest of Mexico." *Laura Esquivel's Fiction: Re-imagining Identity, Gender, and Genre in Mexico*, editor Elizabeth Willingham, Sussex, 2010, pp. 173-196.

Kluge, Sofie. "*Dios los juzga de la intención*. Questioning Conquest in Lope de Vega's *El nuevo mundo descubierto por Cristóbal Colón*." *Journal of Re-

naissance Studies, Staging History: Renaissance Dramatic Historiography Questioning Conquest in Lope de Vega's El nuevo mundo descubierto por Cristóbal Colón, editors Sofie Kluge, Ulla Kallenbach & David Hasberg Zirak-Schmidt, vol. 13, 2018, offprint, pp. 93-117, Academia.edu, www.academia.edu/37506631/_Dios_juzga_de_la_intenci%C3%B3n_Questioning_Conquest_in_Lope_de_Vega_s_El_nuevo_mundo_descubierto_por_Crist%C3%B3bal_Col%C3%B3n_.

Kartunnen, Frances. "Rethinking Malinche." *Indian Women of Early Mexico*, editors Susan Schroeder, Stephanie Wood, and Robert Haskett, Oklahoma, 1997, pp. 291–312.

López de Gómara, Francisco. *La historia general de las Indias. Biblioteca Saavedra Fajardo del pensamiento público hispano*, translated by Miguel Andúgar Miñarro. Amberes: Casa de Juan Steelsio, 1554, www.saavedrafajardo.org/Archivos/gomarahis1.pdf.

Martínez Ruíz, Fernando. "Lope de Vega." *Azorín: Obras Completas*, Madrid, 1920, p. 243-248.

Mártir de Anglería, Pedro. *The Project Gutenberg EBook of De Orbe Novo*. vol. 1, translated by Francis Augustus MacNutt, Decade *3*, Book *7*, archive.org/stream/deorbenovovolume12425gut/12425-8.txt.

McCafferty and McCafferty "De-Colonizing Malintzin." *Postcolonial perspectives in archaeology: proceedings of the 39th Annual Chacmool Archaeological Conference*, edited by Peter Bikoulis, Dominic Lacroix and Meaghan Peuramaki-Brown, Chaacmool Archaeological Association, 2009, pp. 183-192.

Menéndez y Pelayo, Marcelino. *Estudios sobre el teatro de Lope de Vega. Crónicas y leyendas dramáticas de* España. *Biblioteca Virtual Miguel de* Cervantes, edited by Enrique Sánchez Reyes, 2008, www.cervantesvirtual.com/nd/ark:/59851/bmc4q8b2

Lemartinel, Jean, and Charles Minguet, editors. "Introduction." *El nuevo mundo descubierto por Cristóbal Colón: comedia de Lope de Vega Carpio: édition critique*. Lille, 1980, pp. i-xv.

Minian de Alfie, Raquel. "Lope, lector de cronistas de Indias." *Filología*, no. 11, 1965, pp. 1-21.

Moratín, Leandro Ferández de. *Obras póstumas de D. Leandro Fernández de Moratín*. Madrid, 1867, vol. 3, pp. 133-134.

Vega y Carpio, Félix Lope. *"El nuevo mundo descubierto por Cristóbal Colón." Obras completas de Lope de Vega*, vol. 8, Turner, 1994, pp. 921-1012. artelope.uv.es/biblioteca/textosAL/AL0779_ElNuevoMundoDescubiertoPorCristobalColon.

El gran prodigio de España: Joanna Theodora de Souza's Performative Convent *Comedia*

ANNA-LISA HALLING

Brigham Young University

ALTHOUGH VERY FEW NUNS occupy a place in the Portuguese literary canon, Soror Violante do Céu, who wrote and published poetry and plays, is arguably the most well-known Portuguese convent author. Celebrated by her contemporaries, students and scholars alike study her *Rimas Várias* today. In many early modern convents throughout the Iberian Peninsula, like the Convento de San Ildefonso in Madrid and the Convento de la Concepción del Carmen in Valladolid, the practice of literary production passed from sister to sister, such as the collaboration between Sor Cecilia del Nacimiento and Sor María de San Alberto. Similar traditions passed from Sor Marcela de San Félix to Sor Francisca de Santa Teresa and from Soror Maria do Céu to Soror Magdalena da Glória. In the case of the Mosteiro[1] de Nossa Senhora da Rosa da Ordem do Grande Patriarca Santo Domingos in Lisbon, Portugal, a lay nun[2] named Dona Joanna Theodora de Souza (b. late 1600s) inherited Soror Violante's important literary heritage.

Soror Violante's *villancicos*, as well as her lost *comedia de santo*, reflect a strong performance tradition present in the Mosteiro da Rosa.[3] Following

---

1 Although the terms "convent" and "monastery" are gendered in English (representing spaces exclusively for women and men, respectively), Spanish and Portuguese differentiates between the two based on size. In other words, in Portuguese a *convento* is smaller than a *mosteiro*.

2 Souza's text contains a postscript explaining that the author was "recolhida no mosteiro da Roza de Lisboa" (39).

3 Theatrical production in the convent was a widespread practice among early modern nuns as a way of educating the women religious while entertaining them during their designated hours of recreation within the convent. The *Ceremonial del*

Soror Violante's example, Dona Joanna wrote her own performative *comedia de santo*—*El gran prodigio de España, y lealtad de un amigo*—perhaps at the end of the seventeenth century or the beginning of the eighteenth century.[4] Fortunately, since Madre Ángela de la Luz, who lived in the same convent as the author, published this work,[5] it survived the catastrophic fires following the Great Lisbon Earthquake of 1755, even though the convent itself did not. Scholars can access *El gran prodigio* in Madrid's Biblioteca Nacional, yet no modern editions of this work exist and very few critics have read or studied this little-known play. Although neglect has relegated this work to the margins of history, it clearly reveals the author's understanding and mastery of *comedia* tropes and dramatic conventions. In spite of common assumptions that convent plays such as this one fall in the category of closet dramas, Dona Joanna penned her play for performance. While we have no evidence of its staging,[6] either in the convent or in a secular setting, the performativity of the play and the performance tradition in convents such as the Mosteiro da Rosa make it clear that the author intended *El gran prodigio* for the stage.

Dona Joanna's *comedia* contains many performative aspects, allowing for an analysis of her work in relation to contemporaneous stagings of plays in *corral* and *coliseo* theaters, and according to the tenets of performance criticism. This critical lens rightly treats theatrical texts as scripts for production, rather than literary texts meant for individual consumption, and takes into consideration the theatrical milieu in which they were written as well as the possibilities for their staging. The term "theatricality" refers to "performativeness in communication, skills of representation, invention of forms of presentation, [and] actual performances" (Fabian 212) as well as "a specific type of performance style or inclusively as all the semiotic codes of theatrical representation" (Postlewait 1). Kier Elam distinguishes between a "dramatic

---

Convento, a conduct manual for the Convento de San Ildefonso in Madrid, indicates that certain hours were set aside, with some exceptions, both daily and yearly for recreational activities.

4   The text itself contains no publication information; the Bieses database suggests an eighteenth-century publication date while Teresa Soufas's *Dramas of Distinction* suggest that the Dona Joanna wrote it during the seventeenth century.

5   The postscript to Souza's work also indicates that her work was "dada à imprenta pela Madre Angela da Luz Religioza no mesmo mosteiro" (39).

6   Since Genevieve Love insists that literary critics "attend to the possibilities of performance criticism that locates settings of theatrical desire independent of future or past productions" (133), a lack of evidence of staging should not keep us from exploring the possibility that a work was indeed performed.

text" (the written work) and a "performance text," or a staged dramatic text (3). Dona Joanna's dramatic text reveals certain "performance signs" (Stroud 27), or rather "the micro-signs or network of signifying systems that comprise the performance text" (Friedman 57). This signifying network clearly reveals the theatricality of the *El gran prodigio*, including evidence of staging, such as costuming and movement. These indications of performativity and theatricality demonstrate that *El gran prodigio* fits within the framework of the theatrical production and performance that was wildly popular throughout Iberia beyond the convent.

El gran prodigio is a three-act play that features a young San Pedro Gonçales (1190-1246)—also known as San Telmo—a medieval priest from Palencia destined for beatification[7] after an exemplary life in service of his king, the church, and all Iberian sailors. While those around him succumb to the temptations of earthly love, Pedro speaks against the emotion, comparing it to "prizion" and "esclavitud" (2). In fact, he defies his friends (the *galanes* Lidoro, Thimoteo, and Felicio) and a devil by leaving his life as a student behind and taking religious vows. He even repeatedly resists the amorous attentions of one of the *damas*, Belisa, who rejects Lidoro and declares her love to Pedro both before and after he becomes a priest. Early in the play, as Pedro travels to accept a canonry granted to him by the Pope (as a result of the petitions of Pedro's influential uncle), his horse trips and subsequently, and quite unceremoniously, deposits the young canon in the mud. This humbling experience forces Pedro to confront and give up his pride. Pardoned by an angel, the protagonist relinquishes his new position and becomes a humble Dominican friar. All the while, Lidoro, Felicio, Belisa, Leonor, and Laurino (a character who appears towards the end of the first act) struggle with the twists and turns of trials of their own making, the result of their devotion to worldly love. As Juana Ecabias Toro succinctly states, "[c]ada uno de estos cinco personajes desea a la persona que no le corresponde sentimentalmente, y es amado por alguien a quien no desea" (128). Their (mis)adventures mirror the love triangles, revenge, and lost honor of secular plays.[8] As the play's sequencing continues, Pedro, the "gran prodigio de España," also performs several miracles, includ-

---

7   A campaign to canonize San Pedro (San Telmo) began in 2016, supported by the Parish of San Telmo de Palencia, the bishops of Oporto, Tui-Vigo and the Dominican Order in Portugal as well as the Argentine Brotherhood of San Telmo. They made this appeal to Pope Francis, who was bishop in the San Telmo neighborhood in Buenos Aires.

8   The religiously-themed *comedia de santo* genre often caused polemics because of its overlap with the more secular *comedias de capa y espada*. For example, in

ing throwing himself into a fire but not burning up and saving a group of sailors by calming the seas.[9] Eventually, two angels and the Virgin Mary herself appear and carry the protagonist away to Heaven. Although they take place in a *comedia de santo*, Pedro's actions are interwoven with tropes most often found in the popular *comedias de capa y espada*, including confusing love triangles, exciting duels, and humorous *graciosos*.

In terms of staging, *El gran prodigio* utilizes the same conventions found in *comedias* performed in the secular sphere. These include props, acting, stage directions, music, sound, special effects, and costuming. In fact, the very first stage direction dictates what the protagonist should wear, stating, "[s]ale Pedro de Estudiante" (1). Pedro does not mention his occupation during his subsequent conversation with Felicio and Lidoro (the first and second *galanes*, respectively) until line 87. Therefore, this information must first be conveyed to the audience through wardrobe since costumes are a "visual presentation of character or idea through clothed physical appearance" ("Costume" 318). Edwin Wilson and Alvin Goldfarb note that costumes, like the clothes we wear, convey "messages and impressions" that allow the viewer to "form judgments" (86). As Robert Lublin explains, "[o]ne's sex, social station, occupation, nationality, religion, and more could be established by the clothes one wore, which produced an individual as a member and constituent of the body politic" (10). This element of performance helps set the tone of the play, locates it in a historical setting, reveals information about the characters, and even intimates the relationships between them.

Other instances of costuming include a huntress outfit worn by Beliza, the first *dama*, as she comes onstage and relates her tale of woe to her servant, Lizarda. Beliza reveals that although she made Lidoro her "dueño" (5), she has now fallen in love with the unsuspecting Pedro, whom she encounters while hunting. The stage directions indicate that she appears "de Caçadora" (5). Her dress as a huntress, a type of *mujer varonil*, reflects Beliza's intent to hunt love as one who pursues unwilling prey and foreshadows her violent interactions with other characters, particularly her original suitor, Lidoro. Beliza also wears a cape, a hat, and mask during a swordfight[10] against Lidoro,

---

El gran prodigio, the amorous exploits of the three *galanes* lead to the use of weapons to avenge wrongs and offenses. Lidoro suffers grave injuries as a result.

9   San Pedro Gonçales, or St. Peter Gonzalez, is considered the patron of Spanish and Portuguese sailors.

10   This duel occurs as a result of lost honor and a complex love triangle. It is further complicated by a case of mistaken identity, all common tropes in staged Golden Age plays.

all of which serve to hide her identity from her foe but not the audience. This costuming allows Beliza a dramatic reveal when she stabs her former lover, declares "és Beliza quien te afrenta" (24), removes her mask, and flees offstage. In addition to underscoring characterization and marking important moments in the play, the use of costumes can also provide a disguise not only for actors, but for characters, as well, since "[a]n individual [becomes] extraordinary, or [is] subsumed into an undifferentiated group, by using costumes" ("Costume" 318). For instance, in *El gran prodigio*, a devil takes advantage of this performative element by appearing "al paño en traje de camino," since "este disfrás" (that of a "pobre forastero") allows him to conceal both his physical form and his true nature as a way of gaining access to the other characters (31). Other stage directions mention shoes, a jacket, and a hat. All of these costuming elements not only impact the audience visually, they also communicate meaning, including social class, gender, education, and relationships between the characters while furthering the plot.

While costumes play an essential role in the staging of this play, the stage directions reveal the importance of props, as well, particularly the shotgun, which appears several times during the course of the play. Each of these items occupies an integral role in the staging of the play and the onstage actions of the actors. Sophie Duncan asserts that "[p]rops' stage lives and their consequences for characters depend, catalytically and excitingly, on the possibility of multiple agents (i.e. characters) interpreting and disturbing the cognitive loads they bear" (7). In other words, props, like costumes, function as necessary supplements for onstage action and convey meaning in and of themselves. This is exemplified towards the end of the play when Beliza appears onstage "de penitente con una calavera en la mano," which she then deposits "al pie de la Cruz" (33), alluding to her repentance and subsequent forgiveness. The skull that Beliza brings onstage creates a *memento mori* for the other characters as well as for the audience members. This placement of the two props juxtaposes a symbol of earthly death with the cross, a symbol of everlasting life.[11] Additionally, Beliza's weapons (a knife and the shotgun she appropriates after Lidoro attempts to use it against her) translate her intense emotions into physical actions as she swears to employ them in her quest to kill Lidoro in revenge ("oy su muerte sin defensa, y para mayor offensa con sus mismas armas sea" [23]).

The implementation of these weapons aligns with Duncan's argument that props "[give] characters' minds external, material form" (230). The stage directions mention other necessary props as well, including saddlebags, a wine-

---

11   When she places the skull at the foot of the cross, Beliza declares, "aqui la pongo que es bien esté unida la imagen de la muerte al de la vida" (33).

skin, and a chain. The chain creates a sense of comicity when the devil uses it in the second act to bind the two *graciosos* to each other while they drunkenly sleep. When they arise and try to go their separate ways, the chain prevents them from doing so and precipitates an entertaining argument between them, as each thinks the other holds him hostage. The deeper meaning of the chain is soon revealed as the devil, who uses it to restrict their movements and cause strife between them, attempts to bind their souls as well, stating that the prop will serve as "[l]aços para arrastrar al infierno aquestes hombres menguados" (22). The devil then expands the metaphor introduced by the chain as he explains that the "duras cadenas" serve to "arrastrar, y prender a los hombres [para que] quando se jusgan dichozos, ven a hallarse desdichados" (22). Fortunately for both servants, the angel appears and the stage direction states, "[d]ale com el alfange en la cadena, y le rompe" (22), thus representing the triumph of good over evil. The prop serves not only to further the plot, but also to underscore the central moral message of the text—that of freedom from sin. Both costumes and props form and inform the performative nature of this play.

In addition to these theatrical elements, evidence of movement and blocking (as indicated both by the explicit stage directions and stage directions implicit in the dialogue) enhances *El gran prodigio*'s stageability. Kinesics, the study of how the human body communicates meaning, help lay bare the meaning of onstage movement. Elaine Aston and George Savona insist that theater semioticians must read the human body because of "its centrality to the theatrical sign-system and the production of meaning" (116). As with other early modern *comedias*, the stage directions in *El gran prodigio* are rife with terms such as "entra" and "sale," thus indicating a constant flow on and off the stage as actors enter and leave at crucial moments in the performance. To illustrate, the third act includes a door that demarcates the stage as an indoor space occupied by Thimoteo and Lidoro. Stage directions indicate that these characters knock on the door, open it, and pass through it. We also see moments of even more detailed instruction related to physicality, including, "sale Leonor sin verse uno a otro" (29) at a moment when the second *dama* enters a stage already occupied by Lidoro and neither one sees the other as they declare their mutual love and lament the *galán* Lidoro's lack of fidelity, only aware that they share the stage when they simultaneously declare "[c]onstante te adoraré" (30). This complex and constantly shifting blocking is representative of the many misunderstandings and mishaps that plague the romantic relationships in this play.

In another instance of onstage movement, the author reveals, "[s]ale Fray Pedro atravesando el tablado" with Marino and Thimoteo dragging behind him at some distance, after which the stage directions read "[e]ntrase por una parte, y buelve a salir por otra, y los dos tras el" (34). This parading across the stage, exiting, and reentering not only gives Lizarda the opportunity to speak with Pedro out of earshot of the other characters, but also affords her a chance to avoid Thimoteo, since she fears he may lure her into bad behavior and get her into trouble with her *ama*. The physical distance between them parallels her desire to avoid temptation by also staying emotionally far from her counterpart. Later, as Beliza confesses her sin and her unrequited love to Pedro (she calls him "dueño mio," much to his dismay [25]), the stage directions indicate that he sits while she kneels. By imitating the positioning common in confessionals, this movement not only reinforces the physical distance between the two characters, it also places Pedro in a position of spiritual authority and superiority over Beliza and underscores her need to humble herself and repent of past wrongs.

Another important moment that demonstrates the importance of movement occurs in the third act. After the devil enters Lidoro's house in disguise, he declares his intention to sow so much discord between Lidoro and Felício that he fears one of the *galanes* may throw him from his chair. The stage directions here read, "[s]ientase en medio de los dos" (31), thus reinforcing through physicality both the characterization of the devil and his plan to create a wedge between the two friends in spite of their sworn friendship and allegiance. In these instances, onstage movement and blocking convey essential information about the characters and their motivations. Lidoro and Felício's actions reveal the complications and consequences of carnal love while the devil's undue attention to Pedro manifests the protagonist's holiness and foreshadows his eventual triumph over evil through sainthood.

The actors' onstage movements also help create a sense of comicity at important moments, as when the *gracioso* Thimoteo wanders onstage half-dressed while carrying clothing and shoes in his hands. As he complains about his master, who woke him for an as yet unknown reason, the stage directions indicate that he puts on his shoes while drowsily and distractedly narrating "[o]ra vamonos calzando" and then wondering aloud, "aora siguese ... que, que se sigue a los sapatos? Ah si, será la cazaca? Si será, mas como, quando, yo nó sé lo que és aquesto. Donde se viste este trasto?" (21). The *didascalia* that immediately follows notes, "[q]ueda con sapatos, y sin cazaca, y repara en Mar[ino]" (21). Thimoteo's comic onstage bumbling complements that of Marino, who, just moments before, took several swigs from a wineskin and drunkenly passed out onstage, thereby allowing Thimoteo to find the wineskin, polish off the rest of the alcohol, and fall asleep next to his counterpart. Later, after both *graciosos* suffer a shocking encounter with the supernatural,

Thimoteo insists, "amigo vamos de aqui" (23). When Marino asks, "[c]omo nos vamos?" Thimoteo responds with "[a]si" and the stage directions indicate "haze que se vá" (23), thereby creating a moment of comic relief for the audience. These carefully crafted instructions directing the staged movements of the actors reveal Dona Joanna's intent as she penned a work in which physical movement was clearly necessary for dramatic and comic effect.

Beyond movement, moments that break the fourth wall also reveal the performative nature of *El gran prodigio*. For instance, through the use of the phrase "à parte," the stage directions indicate many moments when an actor speaks directly to the audience without being heard by those onstage. These asides clearly indicate that Dona Joanna imagined an audience that would interact with her text. This occurs when Beliza accuses Lidoro, her former lover, of "infamia" and "traicion" for stealing her honor and then accusing her of loving another. He responds with "Señora ... que ... yo ... no hallo," after which he directs his speech to the audience in a confessional aside by adding "ni desculpa, ni respuesta" (18-19), thereby admitting his wrongdoings and allowing the public to share in his shame. At a later point, Leonor, the second *dama*, listens in to the onstage dialogue "al paño" (28), playing with the notion that the public can see her eavesdropping while the onstage characters cannot. The playwright also includes soliloquies, such as Pedro's lengthy lamentation of his fallen state in the first act or Beliza's post-duel speech, spoken "como hablando adentro" (25), complete with an aside directed to the public. At other points in the play, the audience would have heard several voices engaging in dialogue offstage, as in the second act when lines spoken by Leonor, Felicio, and Lidoro are all identified as coming from "Dentro" (19). These offstage voices play a central role in adding to the onstage characters' confusion, thereby heightening the dramatic tension. Moments such as these in which characters directly convey thoughts, feelings, and information to audience members reveal the expectation that spectators would attend the staging and underscores the performativity of the play.

Yet another theatrical element present in Dona Joanna's *comedia* is the use of music and sound. In the context of the theater, sound can "give information which is needed but not given in the dialogue," "affect audience mood," "provide an emotional stimulus," and "reinforce an onstage action" ("Sound and Sound Effects" 1263). In *El gran prodigio*, a character named "Muzica" echoes several characters' lines and sings at different points throughout the play. In these moments, Muzica reinforces the moral message of the work through song and manipulates sounds introduced by others to add meaning to the dialogue. For example, in response to Leonor's question, "Será de mi amor desdoro?" Muzica responds with the echo "Oro" (13). When Beliza repents at the end of the second act, Muzica echoes the *dama*'s refusal to give in to sin ("No desmayo") with words of encouragement ("No desmayes") (26). The playwright also employs music to denote good and evil, as when the *graciosos* note the presence of the devil when they hear instruments playing (most likely in a minor key) and smell sulfur. These characters also acknowledge the protection of an angel, who sings to reassure them toward the end of the second act. This music conveys meaning to the servants who appreciate the "lindo modo de cantar" and delcare "és del Cielo" (23). Music even foreshadows Pedro's eventual sainthood, as in the last scene of the third act when the stage directions note, "[s]uenan instrumentos blandamente" (37) as a precursor to the protagonist's last speech and his subsequent ascension into Heaven.

Aside from music, audience members would also have heard sounds that added to the dramatic nature of the *comedia* and furthered the plot. For instance, after one of the many moments in which the angel thwarts his hellish nemesis, the devil descends beneath the stage—by way of a trapdoor—and the sounds of thunderclaps and instrumental music punctuate his downward movement ("suenan truenos, y al mismo tiempo instrumentos" [22]). In another instance, a particularly heated discussion between Lidoro and Beliza ends with Lidoro's angry declaration, "[m]e hire dexandote muerta" (19). This serious death threat undoubtedly requires a loud, angry, and threatening tone of voice. The stage directions indicate that at this point Lidoro "dispara una escopeta, que traerá" (19), which causes Beliza to faint. The sound of the weapon underscores Lidoro's murderous intentions and causes a physical reaction in Beliza as well as the audience. Later, the dramatic tension is heightened as the audience hears a "ruydo de tempestad" (27) immediately preceding Pedro's miracle of calming the seas. Music and sound play an indispensable role in this play, not just as backdrop but also as dramatic device, the use of which is performative in its very nature.

Beyond sound, special effects also hold a privileged place in this *comedia*. Wilson and Goldfarb note that these "seem miraculous or unusual" (109) while *The Oxford Encyclopedia of Theatre and Performance* indicates that such an effect "is an unusual or unique event" that "hopes to make a strong impression upon the audience" ("Special Effects" 1269). In *El gran prodigio*, the author uses special effects almost exclusively in scenes that deal with the supernatural, particularly those in which a devil and an angel appear as well as during the marvelous moments in the text that serve to reinforce Pedro's saintly nature. Many of these effects make use of a trapdoor or a discovery space in order to facilitate the sudden appearances and disappearances of both actors and items. These devices facilitate such moments as when the angel "aparece en lo alto" (32) on a balcony[12] and then disappears or when the devil descends into hell amidst flames ("Hundese el Demonio por un escutillon de fuego" [22]). They also allow for the creation of a stunning scene in which Beliza declares her amorous intentions to Pedro in the guise of religious confession. In this moment, the stage directions note, "descubrese una sala en que estará una hogera" (26). The play requires not only the sudden appearance of both a room not previously visible onstage, but also a fire into which the protagonist enters and does not burn: "Echase en la hogera, y queda sin quemarse" (26).[13] In order to make a "strong impression" on the spectators, this effect must be sufficiently realistic while not dangerous to the actor, thus revealing Dona Joanna's deep understanding of the technical aspects of dramatization.

An even higher level of stagecraft is required in the shipwreck scene. Not only does the audience hear the sounds of the shipwreck, they also must see it: "aparece naufragando una Nave" (37). The use of the gerund "naufragando" and the word "aparece" in these instructions indicate a mobile set piece (perhaps resembling a *carro triunfal* used for Corpus Christi celebrations) that actors and crew can move onto the stage and off, since shortly after its appearance, we read "[d]ezaparece la Nave" (37). Further onstage revelations include "un altar con un crucifixo" (33) that appears in the moment of Beliza's profound penitence. Yet another miraculous moment requires the unveiling of "una peña onde hallaran pan, y vino" (35) that materializes at the beckoning of Pedro and provides sustenance to his famished friends. This mysterious food-bearing rock suddenly disappears shortly after being found ("Van buscar el pan, y vino, y no le hallan"), allowing the protagonist to reprimand those same friends for "abuzar de la piedad de Dios" (36). In each of these scenes, special effects are used for dramatic effect and serve as a kind of foreshadowing that anticipates Pedro's destiny as a saint.

The climactic last scene, in which Fray Pedro leaves this world for the next, is by far the most theatrical and performative of *El gran prodígio*. The stage directions indicate the simultaneous use of music, costuming, props, and special effects: "Apareceran dos Angeles, y en medio nuestra Señora con una Corona en la mano, y mientras canta la música subirá el Santo hasta onde

---

12 Balconies were common elements of early modern *corral* stages.

13 Pedro declares that this previously unseen room contains "el lecho" where Beliza can try to seduce him, if she dares. He throws himself into the fire in order to prove to her that he would rather die than give in to her advances and to show her that "las eternas hogueras, que el Infierno te promete" (26) are what await sinners such as her. It is this miraculous display that brings about Beliza's sincere repentance.

está la Señora, de manera que ella le ponga la Corona en la cabeça, y acabando de cantar se encubre la aparencia" (38). These instructions indicate that the women portraying the Virgin and the two angels appeared on a balcony above the stage and that the actor playing Pedro was lifted up to her level through the use of stage machinery. A female actress would be clothed as the Virgin Mary, most likely in a white tunic and a blue robe as artists often portray her. The angels accompanying her would also be dressed in a way that allows the audience to immediately recognize their characters and characterization by reading the costumes as semiotic signs. The crown as a prop references the eternal fate of the protagonist, clearly signifying his celestial reward for a devoted life. The singing points to the otherworldly nature of these sudden visitors as well as the need to worship God through music as exemplified in many Bible passages.[14] This mystical moment reveals the ingenious use of stagecraft by the playwright as a way to inspire awe in the spectators and to portray Pedro not as a simple Dominican friar, but as a future saint.

The awareness and utilization of theatrical tropes and conventions common to the secular stage show that Dona Joanna's *comedia* was not written as a closet drama; rather, the playwright intended it for performance. Records of convents in Portugal, Spain, and Latin America show that nuns often staged plays *intramuros*, which strengthens the probability that Dona Joanna's play was indeed staged. What is more, because of the author's association with the Dominican Mosteiro da Rosa, where Soror Violante do Céu also lived and authored plays, and because Dona Joanna was a contemporary of Soror Maria do Céu, a well-known nun playwright living in a different convent in Lisbon, we might imagine that *El gran prodigio de España* was either staged in the convent by and for the nuns or perhaps meant for a *corral* or *coliseo* theater. Regardless of whether or not this *comedia* was staged during the author's lifetime, it deserves the attention of both academics and theater practitioners. The performativeness of this play enhances and underscores its meaning and message—the holiness and eventual sainthood of San Telmo—through a deep understanding of stagecraft, including costumes, props, movement, music, sound effects, and special effects. Dona Joanna's *El gran prodigio de España, y lealtad de un amigo*, like the plays of all of her nun counterparts, offers a unique perspective of an understudied and underappreciated feminine literary tradition and begs to tread the boards once more.

---

14 For example, verses three through five of Psalm 150 state, "[p]raise him with the sound of the trumpet: praise him with the psaltery and harp. Praise him with the timbrel and dance: praise him with stringed instruments and organs. Praise him upon the loud cymbals: praise him upon the high sounding cymbals."

Works Cited

The Bible. Authorized King James Version, Intellectual Reserve, Inc., 2013.
BIESES. Bibliografía de escritoras españolas.
"Costume." *The Oxford Encyclopedia of Theatre and Performance*, edited by Dennis Kennedy, vol. 1, Oxford UP, 2003, pp. 318-27.
Duncan, Sophie. *Shakespeare's Props:* Memory and Cognition, Routledge, 2019. ProQuest Ebook Central.
Elam, Keir. *The Semiotics of Theatre and Drama.* New York: Routledge, 2001.
Escabias Toro, Juana. *Ana Caro Mallén: Reconstrucción biográfica y análisis y edición escénica de sus comedias.* 2012. Universidad Nacional de Educación a Distancia, PhD Dissertation.
Fabian, Johannes. "Theater and Anthropology, Theatricality and Culture." *The Performance Studies Reader*, edited by Henry Bial, 2nd edition, Routledge, 2007, pp. 208-15.
Friedman, Edward H. "Poetic Discourse and Performance Text: Toward a Semiotics of the *Comedia.*" *Approaches to Teaching Spanish Golden Age Drama*, edited by Everett W. Hesse and Catherine Larson, Spanish Literature Publications Company, 1989, pp. 56-69.
Love, Genevieve. "Performance Criticism Without Performance: The Study of Non-Shakespearean Drama." *New Directions in Renaissance Drama and Performance Studies*, edited by Sarah Werner, Palgrave McMillan, 2010, pp. 131-46.
Lublin, Robert I. *Costuming the Shakespearean Stage: Visual Codes of Representation in Early Modern Theatre and Culture.* Routledge, 2011.
Postlewait, Thomas, and Tracy C. Davis. *Theatricality (Theatre and Performance Theory).* Cambridge UP, 2003.
Soufas, Teresa Scott. *Dramas of Distinction: Plays by Golden Age Women*, U of Kentucky P, 1997.
"Sound and Sound Effects." *The Oxford Encyclopedia of Theatre and Performance*, edited by Dennis Kennedy, vol. 2, Oxford UP, 2003, pp. 1262-66.
Souza, Joanna Theodora. *Comedia nueva. El gran prodigio de España, y lealtad de un amigo. BIESES.* Bibliografía de escritoras españolas.
"Special Effects." *The Oxford Encyclopedia of Theatre and Performance*, edited by Dennis Kennedy, vol. 2, Oxford UP, 2003, pp. 1269-71.
Stroud, Matthew D. "The *Comedia* as Playscript." *Approaches to Teaching Spanish Golden Age Drama*, edited by Everett W. Hesse and Catherine Larson, Spanish Literature Publications Company, 1989, pp. 27-42.
Wilson, Edwin and Alvin Goldfarb. *Theater: The Lively Art*, McGraw-Hill, 1993.

De Lisbeth Salander a la Ertzaintza: Fantasías neoliberales en la serie procedimental de Eva García Sáenz de Urturi

SALVADOR A. OROPESA
Clemson University

LA TRILOGÍA DE EVA García Sáenz de Urturi (Sáenz de ahora en adelante) se llama *La Ciudad Blanca*, epónimo de Vitoria-Gasteiz, la capital del País Vasco. La conforman *El silencio de la ciudad blanca* (2016), *Los ritos del agua* (2017) y *los señores del tiempo* (2018). El protagonista es el inspector Unai López de Ayala, alias Kraken, llamado así por el mítico pulpo escandinavo. Junto a él están su superior inmediata, la subcomisaria Alba Díaz de Salvatierra, y su compañera, la inspectora Estíbaliz Ruiz de Gauna. En la primera novela, juntos investigan una serie de asesinatos rituales de parejas con ascendencia vitoriana. Las muertes ocurren en diferentes monumentos de la ciudad, siguiendo un doble patrón cronológico basado en la edad de las víctimas y la antigüedad histórica de los edificios. En el segundo volumen, el caso trata sobre varios asesinatos relacionados con la mitología celta, en el que se utilizan rituales de la Edad del Bronce. En el tercer libro, los crímenes siguen el orden de una novela histórica sobre las disputas señoriales en la Vitoria del siglo XII. Ésta se estructura a partir del neomedievalismo y del peligro de hacer una lectura nacionalista de la Edad Media.

La trilogía de Steig Larsson, cuyos protagonistas son la *hacker* gótica Lisbeth Salander (Sampaio 76-79) y el periodista independiente Mikel Blomkvist (Terjesen and Terjesen), revolucionó el estilo *noir* gracias a cuatro cambios sustanciales en la concepción del género. En primer lugar, lo sacó del punto muerto de detectives privados y policías desencantados, misóginos y con problemas de alcohol. Mikel es un apasionado de su profesión: el periodismo de investigación contra los comportamientos deshonestos, tanto de las grandes corporaciones como del estado sueco (Vid. Terjesen and Terjesen) y en lo personal, sus compañeras son mujeres fuertes y con carreras exitosas, diversas e inteligentes. Su físico no es amenazador y su sexualidad trasciende etiquetas fáciles. La bebida que más consume es el café, para trabajar más. Lisbeth es un personaje completamente nuevo e inédito en la literatura, una mujer a la que se le ha privado de su ciudadanía, a la que se le ha vejado con ignominia, y que, aun así, ha encontrado una manera de luchar. Es uno de los primeros personajes complejos, cuya vida virtual es tan relevante como la análoga. Además aquella le ayuda a reinsertarse en el mundo civil. Lisbeth es bisexual y sexualmente compleja. En sus relaciones homosexuales prefiere el *bonding* y en las heterosexuales es más convencional. Su belleza es de naturaleza andrógina y la pequeñez de su cuerpo le da un aspecto aniñado. Ambos personajes son inteligentísimos y determinados.

En segundo lugar, la trilogía incorporó temas nuevos como los cambios que la existencia del internet (Kenley) ha producido en nuestras vidas. No es solo que los personajes lo utilicen, sino que éste ocupa, a partir de ahora, un lugar protagónico en el desarrollo de la trama. En tercer lugar, se aprecia un nuevo ímpetu al formato trilogía, que permite que el autor desarrolle sus ideas literarias en profundidad y que la editorial maximice su labor de mercadeo. Este es un formato de desigual desarrollo, pero que en el caso español y en el género negro, ha proporcionado dos trilogías de gran éxito comercial y de crítica, la del *Valle del Baztán* de Dolores Redondo (Oropesa), y la de *La Ciudad Blanca* de Sáenz, que es la que nos ocupa. El cuarto elemento es el constitucionalismo, aunque lo desarrollaremos con detenimiento en su momento, este es el aspecto más relevante de nuestra propuesta. Defendemos que la deconstrucción por parte del posestructuralismo de las narrativas maestras llevó en el ámbito occidental a una desestabilización, tanto epistemológica como social del estado de derecho. Si bien era necesario deconstruir una serie de modelos sociales dominantes y anacrónicos, como el machismo o el racismo institucional, ha habido consecuencias negativas, fruto de la aculturación, como es la aparición del populismo. Intuimos que hay un paralelismo entre el anti keynesianismo del neoconservadurismo, que ahondó la suspicacia y merma en la confianza en las instituciones públicas, la izquierda anticapitalista ,que confunde capitalismo y democracia, y el posestructuralismo, que es una desconfianza de la centralidad y del racionalismo, del concepto de autor o de las relaciones de poder que surgen de los poderes públicos. La burofobia que compartieron la academia y los políticos neoliberales nos ha conducido a un vacío en el campo de la cultura de la representación del estado de derecho.

El final de la serie de Salander supone una reivindicación del constitucionalismo, la novela denomina el problema "crisis constitucional" (*Reina* 111,

354 y 482). El tribunal constitucional declara que Lisbezh fue víctima de la "vulneración de sus derechos constitucionales" (738) y en la sentencia que le devuelve a la protagonista sus derechos constitucionales la jueza le recuerda también sus derechos y obligaciones como ciudadana (*Reina* 781). El orden jurídico es el que unifica al Estado sueco.

En España, la revolución económica más importante desde el fin de la autarquía y la entrada en la OCDE en 1959 la trajo la llegada del PSOE al poder en 1982 que revolucionó la distribución de la riqueza con la literal universalización del seguro de salud pública, aumentando la educación obligatoria y gratuita hasta los dieciséis años, y la universalización del sistema de pensiones al incorporar al sistema las no contributivas reposicionando el PIB español (35). Esto trajo cuatro consecuencias inmediatas, la desaparición de la izquierda radical a la francesa dentro del PSOE, la normalización del monetarismo, la autonomía del Banco Central y el rigor fiscal (143). La trilogía de Sáenz se encuentra inmersa en este contexto político y económico. Hay una segunda definición cultural de neoliberalismo[1], mejor dicho, de su representación en la cultura popular, que se manifiesta en la aparición de profesiones creativas, ocio exótico, establecimientos de lujo y tecnologías punta (Sánchez Prado 69-70). En este contexto los modernos policías que aparecen en la serie de Sáenz se ajustarían a esta visión. Las modernas comisarías de policía, la academia, y la eficiencia y medios de la policía científica, forense e informática completarían este dibujo de país económicamente avanzado.

Los ejemplos de este neoliberalismo abundan y sirven de redundancia necesaria para la representación de la policía constitucional. En *La ciudad blanca* encontramos el restaurante Zaldiaran con una estrella Michelín (74), la perfección burguesa de la confitería Goya en la calle Dato (86), el Asador Matxete (98), una ilustradora de cuentos infantiles como profesión creativa (387), y turismo de escalada de riesgo en Pakistán como actividad de ocio

---

[1] Cornel Ban define el neoliberalismo español como uno que los economistas denominan neoliberalismo integrado, *embedded neoliberalism* en inglés, un sistema híbrido que amalgama la ortodoxia macroeconómica, desregulación, un sistema impositivo progresivo, privatizaciones primando empresas emblemáticas internacionales, servicios públicos sólidos, y un programa amplio de inversiones públicas (5). Ban cree fundamental, a la hora de definir el neoliberalismo, la triada de Peter Hall de la apertura institucional de las operaciones financieras, las finanzas públicas unidas a la credibilidad de los mercados financieros del país dado, y estrategias de crecimiento unidas a la competitividad relativa de la economía nacional. Se mantienen los principios de la socialdemocracia en el sentido de que el estado es intervencionista. Esto se debe a la influencia del ordoliberalismo alemán que siempre desconfió de la libertad de los mercados.

(411). En *Los ritos del agua* aparece la presencia del guionista de una serie criminal en EEUU para una cadena parecida a HBO (67), moteros españoles que van a la Isla de Man a reuniones internacionales (92), la madre de Alba resulta ser una actriz de primer orden, Aurora Mistral, aparece una trabajadora en una empresa de innovación tecnológica pionera en el desarrollo del internet (258), y Alba hizo en el pasado el Camino de Santiago para perder peso (202). En *Los señores del tiempo* continúa la glocalización neoliberal de las anteriores. Alba le explica a Unai sus planes para con el hotel que ha heredado de su madre: "Quiero hacer rutas por las bodegas subterráneas de la villa que terminen con una cata de vino en el hotel. Y paseos en *segway* por los viñedos. Y quiero colaborar en el Certamen del Pintxo Medieval de este año (184). En otro contexto: "La vieja ferrería ahora es un agroturismo con un taller que hace piezas de vidrio" (192).

Las niñas asesinadas son el ejemplo máximo de las nuevas tendencias en la sociedad española:

> Estefanía estaba estudiando Música (sic), quería ser concertista de violoncello (sic), como su madre. Este verano se iba a ir con su cuadrilla a Escocia. A Oihana le gustaba programar aplicaciones. Era una niña muy precoz, destacaba en los cursos de Robótica y los profesores dicen que tenía un futuro brillante. (Sáenz, *Señores* 331).

Como en la novela realista decimonónica, la ansiedad no viene de un defecto de modernidad, sino en el exceso de ésta. ¿A qué colegio asistía Oihana para recibir clases de robótica con doce años? En este contexto la hipermodernidad de la Ertzaintza se mimetiza en este paisaje neoliberal.

En el pasado reciente del noir español, como las novelas de Pepe Carvalho de Manuel Vázquez Montalbán, los casos se resolvían al margen del Estado y siempre desde una fuerte desconfianza hacia las instituciones democráticas. Sánchez Zapatero y Martín Escribà incluyen en esta tendencia del desengaño no solo a Vázquez Montalbán sino a Juan Madrid y a Jorge Martínez Reverte (58). El neoconstitucionalismo apareció con series procedurales como las de Lorenzo Silva, Alicia Giménez Bartlett y Domingo Villar ya en el siglo XXI y en éstas se representa la confianza en las instituciones democráticas del estado de derecho. En estas ficciones no es la etnia, la religión, el idioma (Villar se autotraduce del gallego al castellano), ni la historia lo que unifica España, es el orden jurídico (Bárcena y Tajadura, 35)

Si trasladamos el triunfo del constitucionalismo en la trilogía sueca a las trilogías de Redondo y Sáenz, tras 2500 páginas nos encontramos con el desarrollo del artículo 14 de la Constitución Española, que permite la incorporación de la mujer a la policía, lo que se traduce que en las nuevas trilogías *noir* peninsulares en las que las autoras son mujeres y las mujeres son las protagonistas o coprotagonistas. La misma existencia de la Ertzaintza, la policía autónoma vasca, y de la Policía Foral, su equivalente navarro en la serie de Redondo, es fruto del desarrollo constitucional del artículo 149 29ª.

La Constitución de 1978 optó por la fórmula tradicional de la organización de la identidad española, es decir, por la presencia de unas nacionalidades históricas, en la que los vascos juegan un papel protagónico. Esta visión tradicional recoge no solo derechos forales (Navarra, País Vasco—Vizcaya y Álava—y Valencia), sino especiales (Cataluña, Islas Baleares y Galicia), consuetudinarios (Asturias, Murcia, Extremadura) y sin adjetivo (Aragón) (Cobacho Gómez).

En la Constitución de 1978 encontramos que la disposición adicional primera dice lo siguiente:

> Primera (derechos históricos de los territorios forales).
> La Constitución ampara y respeta los derechos históricos forales. La actuación general de dicho régimen foral se llevará a cabo, en su caso, en el marco de la Constitución y de los Estatutos de Autonomía.

La Constitución proclama por un lado la igualdad entre los españoles (Artículo 14 de la Constitución), y por otro legitima, entre otros, los privilegios forales vasco y navarro. En el terreno político esta peculiaridad se dirime en el campo de las competencias y en el desarrollo de leyes orgánicas. En el campo de la cultura, desde la alta a la popular, se solventa con mitos e historias sesgadas que justifican ideológicamente la desigualdad legal del privilegio. Nuestra hipótesis es que se tiene que crear una tautología constitucional-foral-literaria en la que la legalidad vigente, los mitos, y el imaginario colectivo se retroalimenten los unos a los otros, apuntando hacia una verdad lábil que contenga forzosamente una dosis necesaria de irracionalidad, que haga que la relación entre el mito y la historia nacionalista sea continua. La Constitución abre la puerta a una infinita reactualización de derechos históricos, cuya ansiedad plasma bien la literatura de Sáenz. Juaristi ha calificado esta relación de esquizofrénica ya que exige la pertenencia a la nación española y su simultánea separación (Palmero).

Las novelas de Larsson, Redondo y Sáenz se corresponderían en lo literario con lo que Bruce Ackerman llamó "momentos constitucionales" (Ovejero 100), que son periodos de aceleración constitucional, de desarrollo de libertades latentes que la sociedad entiende como necesarias en un momento dado.

Sáenz, como Larsson y Redondo antes que ella, representa una sociedad democrática compleja que intenta acomodar fuerzas dispares en conflicto y que se simplifica mediante el común denominador jurídico constitucional. La democracia parlamentaria se obvia para representar solamente las instituciones que salvaguarden la convivencia, y la Ertzaintza es una de ellas Si en la serie sueca eran los fantasmas del comunismo y el fascismo, los efectos del patriarcado, la erosión del estado de bienestar, el neoliberalismo que socava la sociedad del bienestar y la sexualidad fluida percibida como amenaza por amplios sectores de la sociedad (Thomas), en Sáenz es el riesgo de la construcción mítica de la historia, la endogamia y la excesiva modernidad. Al mismo tiempo se obvian otros temas como el clientelismo nacionalista o el terrorismo etarra. Todos estos factores se desarrollan dentro de los nuevos parámetros de la industria del libro y sus demandas de márquetin. Cada una de las tres trilogías son gigantescas empresas literarias, que van desde 1.800 hasta 2.500 páginas. Todas reciben un importante apoyo de la industria, incluidas las giras para promocionar los libros que se complementan en las redes sociales de las autoras y de la editorial. Sáenz especifica en su portal de internet que es una experta en mercadeo de libros ("Acerca de Mí"). En su cuenta de Instagram (evagarciasaenz) anunció las traducciones de su serie en alemán, búlgaro, italiano, polaco y portugués, y los lanzamientos de su trilogía en México, Colombia y Argentina, amén de numerosas firmas de libros por toda España.

En las series españolas, el mal viene de la práctica de ritos ancestrales precristianos. No olvidemos que la serie de Redondo ocurre en su mayoría en la Navarra euskaldún, y la de Sáinz en Vitoria y Cantabria. Partimos de la advertencia de José Álvarez Junco: "Debemos catalogar el caso vasco como el de un triunfo verdaderamente espectacular de una invención de la identidad y de la tradición hoy asumida no sólo por la comunidad nacionalista sino por la mayoría de la sociedad vasca" (251). Es precisamente contra este espejismo y ensimismamiento del que nos previenen Redondo y Sáenz, aunque ambas dejan entrever su personal atractivo por esta realidad. Un dato clave que tenemos que tener en cuenta y que explicaremos más adelante es la dualidad lógica catolicismo/paganismo. En esta, el catolicismo es la norma, está naturalizado y es invisible, mientras que el paganismo se condena. Esto es relevante para entender las dos trilogías españolas dadas las simpatías neopaganas de los protagonistas y antagonistas.

Otra peculiaridad es que en las tres series los personajes principales mantienen relaciones sexuales entre ellos. Estas se dirimen tanto en el ámbito personal como público según parámetros literarios ya establecidos en la novela romántica y en la novela realista. Las relaciones amorosas complican la trama y ponen a los protagonistas en peligro de muerte, pero al final los conflictos se resuelven en una combinación entre lo sentimental y lo policial. Estas series son extremas, ya que en la Redondo la protagonista mantiene relaciones sexuales con el asesino y en la de Sáenz, el asesino es el esposo de la subcomisaria Alba Díaz de Salvatierra. En la de Larsson, Lisbeth es violada por su guardián legal. En la serie alavesa en cada una de las novelas uno de los protagonistas casi muere tras ser gravemente herido, el orden es Unai, Alba y Estíbaliz.

El silencio de la ciudad blanca
La acción ocurre en Vitoria-Gasteiz en el verano de 2016 donde suceden unos crímenes que remedan otros acaecidos hace veinte años, solo que el asesino convicto, Tasio Ortiz de Zárate, aun se encuentra en la cárcel. La novela se centra en tradiciones vitorianas como el Día del Blusa, la bajada del Celedón y la Procesión de los Faroles. En una entrevista en *El aventurero de papel* la autora afirmó: "Tenía muy claro que quería escribir de mi tierra, de las costumbres y de sus ritos ancestrales" (Granger). La trama de la novela se construye con dos acciones paralelas, una en el presente, contada en primera persona por Unai, y la segunda en el pasado por un narrador omnisciente. Los crímenes acaecidos hace veinte años ocurrieron en: "El dolmen de la Chabola de la Hechicera, el yacimiento celta de La Hoya, las salinas romanas de Añana, la Muralla medieval" (17).

Tasio Ortiz de Zárate, cuya profesión antes de entrar en la cárcel era la de arqueólogo y divulgador científico en la televisión, otro profesional creativo, le explica a Kraken la lógica de los crímenes:

> Los primeros asesinatos eran una representación de la cronología de Álava. El dolmen de la Chabola de la Hechicera: Calcolítico, hace cinco mil años. Los bebés eran recién nacidos. Como si fueran las primeras edades del hombre, ¿captas el paralelismo... (poblado celtíbero de la Hoya, 1200 a.C. niños de cinco años. El Valle Salado, siglo I a.C. niños de diez años. La Muralla Medieval, siglo XI. Un niño de quince años y una joven de la misma edad (42-3).

La cronología es académica: Paleolítico, Neolítico, Roma y Edad Media y coincide con el contenido del Museo Arqueológico de Vitoria, un museo moderno, ortodoxo en su contenido, en el que domina la ciencia[2] sobre el nacionalismo regionalista.

---

2   En la bibliografía sobre neolítico vasco es fácil encontrar títulos como *La Edad de Hierro. Los vascones y sus vecinos. El último milenio anterior a nuestra era*

La nueva serie de crímenes recomienza en la Catedral Vieja y continúa el orden cronológico de los monumentos. La novela nos advierte de que una lectura errónea de la historia conlleva una tragedia social. El asesino, con su interpretación y su elaborado espectáculo macabro, convierte los monumentos en escenarios del mal. En realidad, estos monumentos vitorianos son modélicos en su estado de conservación y las restauraciones a los que han sido sometidos. El proceso de museización ha sido impecable. Por ejemplo, la restauración de la catedral de Santa María o catedral vieja es un referente mundial y recibió el premio Europa Nostra de 2002, el máximo galardón europeo a la restauración de un edificio individual. Es una de las visitas catedralicias más espectaculares del mundo ya que se puede visitar la cimentación del edificio. Las visitas se celebran bajo el atractivo cartel de "Abierto por obras".

El crimen en la catedral, el primero en la segunda serie, corresponde a una pareja de veinte años y con un apellido compuesto alavés. Los apellidos compuestos remiten a la hidalguía vasca y a los privilegios que conllevaron en el pasado, extensible a la ciudadanía vasca actual gracias al fuero. Los crímenes asocian historia y violencia y ponen en primer plano la endogamia de la ciudad, solo los alaveses "ancestrales" son víctimas. Una primera lectura de estos crímenes apunta al peligro del ensimismamiento[3] de una sociedad cerrada estructurada en cuadrillas que impiden la apertura hacia el otro. Así lo explica Unai: "Las cuadrillas se forman cuando estás en el instituto; es complicado entrar en una si vienes de fuera. Todo es muy endogámico" (119).

La orientación de los cadáveres es noroeste "como lo han hecho los paganos desde la Prehistoria" (83). Se nos dice que todo está envuelto en "paganismo, ocultismo, sincretismo" (84), de un personaje se nos cuenta que era "radical con los términos paganos" (84). Diego Muro (y es un ejemplo entre muchos) afirma que el nacionalismo radical vasco aboga por la independencia de Euskadi por medios violentos (660), en este contexto el adjetivo 'radical' es un eufemismo de violento. En una entrevista en *Qué leer* la autora explica cómo es el hermano de Estíbaliz:

(2008) de Xabier Peñalver, un estudio muy bien documentado, erudito, pero marrado por el absurdo de imponerle al neolítico un anacrónico substrato nacionalista.

   3   El tema central de la segunda novela, *Los ritos del agua*, es el incesto, entre hermanos primero y entre padre e hija después. El incesto se presenta como epítome de la endogamia. De hecho la asesina es Rebeca Tovar cuyo padre la abusaba y la dejó embarazada. En la tercera novela el incesto desencadena la participación en los crímenes de dos de los antagonistas.

El Hierbas es un camello con aficiones esotéricas, muy radical, una mala influencia que le llevó por caminos muy oscuros (Zurdo 62).

Jon Juaristi explica cómo tras el Concilio Vaticano II el nacionalismo entró en una fase neopagana, si no directamente atea (1999: 48). Hay un capítulo de *El bucle melancólico* que se titula "La guerrilla imaginaria" (269-344) en el que se explica con detalle la relación entre el neopaganismo de mediados del siglo XX y su conexión con el nacionalismo vasco. Según Juaristi a partir de 1952 se articuló la necesidad en los pequeños movimientos nacionalistas europeos de fomentar las religiones precristianas, especialmente neocélticas, desafortunadamente unidas a un fuerte componente antisemita (303).

Volviendo a la novela, en el transcurso de la investigación Unai tiene una conversación con Lutxo, "miembro destacado de mi cuadrilla, era el encargado de sucesos de *el Diario Alavés*" (63). Lutxo, sospecha que el asesino es el ya mencionado Eneko Ruiz de Gauna, alias el Eguzkilore y el Hierbas, radical neopagano y traficante de drogas.

Lutxo también explica el por qué del uso de la Catedral Vieja:
La Catedral Vieja, por todo el simbolismo que tiene esta ciudad, no solo religioso, sino porque contiene las ruinas del germen de Vitoria, la primigenia aldea de Gasteiz (105).

Esta contiene la semilla cristiana de la ciudad, y la lógica que se establece es que lo que no sea cristiano va contra la esencia del lugar. Esta obsesión con los monumentos históricos y prehistóricos contrasta con lo que Joseba Zulaika ha llamado las vacaciones vascas de la historia, "holiday from history" (139). En sus palabras:

> The issue is not excessive fiction regarding historical stereotypes but, rather, more fiction is needed as a tool to subvert the present, fiction being the primary expression of desire and a precondition for action. In the task of demythologizing culture, fiction becomes a key ally of the critical writer. What is myth today turns into fiction tomorrow, but when the fiction aims at becoming a crusade or a totalizing concept, we must suspect that the writer is engaged once again in remythifying the historical remains. When, instead of being a conceptual tool or a symbol, fiction becomes the indexical sign of the existence of entities that the imagination demands they exist, it turns again into myth (140).

¿En qué lugar de este bucle se encuentra la trilogía de la Ciudad Blanca? Sáenz quiere legítimamente preservar el status quo de la presente museización de Vitoria-Gasteiz y de toda la provincia alavesa, y en lo político la doble pertenencia. El quiasmo es el presente constitucional y foral de una Álava vasca y española, próspera, que acoge a turistas nacionales en sus impecables monumentos e infraestructura y con la presencia de vasquismos atractivos a la vascofilia española como la elección por Unai y Alba como su canción de amor de *Lau Teilatu*[4] de Itoiz.

El recuerdo del terrorismo etarra pasea como un fantasma sobre la trilogía, también el pasado franquista de Álava. El abuelo de Kraken fue alcalde durante la dictadura y luchó en el bando nacional[5] (95), lo cual fue lo normal en la provincia de Álava según nos cuentan Ugarte y Rivera. La pregunta es si como afirma Zulaika, simplemente nos encontramos en un bucle de desmitificaciones y remitificaciones del que no podemos escapar.

Los asesinatos rituales de las novelas, entretenidos e inverosímiles, conducen a los lectores no al horror, dada su inverisimilitud, sino al turismo. Queremos visitar estos lugares sin los cadáveres ficticios. Pero estos cadáveres no existen en el vacío, ya que, desafortunadamente, en un pasado cercano el terrorismo etarra sembró de muertos las calles de Vitoria-Gasteiz. Hay varios portales de internet dedicados a la memoria de las víctimas de ETA[6] y a través de ellos se pueden recorrer las calles de la ciudad: De los Herrán, Cuadrilla de Vitoria-Gasteiz, la puerta de los Marianistas junto a la Catedral Nueva, la calle Ramiro de Maeztu junto a la Diputación Foral de Álava también cerca de la Catedral Nueva, y así hasta veinte lugares que se corresponden a los asesinados en la capital a manos de ETA, entre ellos el vicelehendakari Fernando Buesa, y el ertzaintza que lo escoltaba, Jorge Díez Elorza. En otro contexto en *Los ritos del agua* Unai dice: "solía evitar, como muchos vitorianos, aquellos puntos negros de mi ciudad" (259). Se refiere a los asesinatos de la primera

---

4   *Lau Teilatu* es una canción feliz sobre jóvenes despreocupados en la fiesta de un pueblo, tal vez compartiendo un cigarrillo de marihuana. La canción es un amable rock sinfónico anterior a la llegada del bronco rock radical vasco inmerso en el punk y en el ska y en lo social en las epidemias de la heroína y la kale borroka. https://es.wikipedia.org/wiki/Lau_teilatu y https://es.wikipedia.org/wiki/Rock_radical_vasco. Sobre la vascofilia española vid. Juaristi 1997, 44-45.

5   El abuelo al final de la trilogía le regala a su nieta "una boinica roja" (430). El pasado carlista del abuelo es transparente.

6   https://es.wikipedia.org/wiki/Anexo:Asesinatos_cometidos_por_ETA_desde_la_muerte_de_Francisco_Franco. https://www.arovite.com/es/

novela, pero no es difícil unir el significado oculto de estas palabras a las ya mencionadas vacaciones de la historia.

Volviendo a la novela el siguiente escenario para los asesinatos es la Casa del Cordón, construida en tiempos de los Reyes Católicos por un judío converso, más tarde el tercer asesinato ocurre junto a la Hornacina de la Virgen Blanca en la balconada de la Iglesia de San Miguel Arcángel, zona monumental del siglo XVIII. El cuarto y último es en la zona del Ensanche, en la calle Dato, la principal de la ciudad que se corresponde al siglo XIX. Como ejemplo del ritual seguido citemos el tercero.

> La pareja yacía a los pies de la Virgen Blanca, ahora casi con seguridad de treinta años, desnudos, con las manos consolando el rastro del otro, el veneno de la pureza de la abeja en sus gargantas, castigándoles por el Pecado Original y un triángulo isósceles formado por tres *eguzkilores* indicando el Ojo de la Providencia (242).

El espacio público católico, el centro de las fiestas patronales vitorianas, es profanado por un ritual radical neopagano que rompe el equilibrio social de la ciudad. El mensaje no necesita ser sutil, la irrupción del pasado espurio amenaza la convivencia. Nótese el desprecio con el que la autora habla de El Hierbas en su entrevista con *Qué Leer*.

Este antipaganismo merece una explicación. Si nos apoyamos en el trabajo seminal de Michael Herren en su monográfico *Anatomy of Myth* en el que analiza las implicaciones epistemológicas del desarrollo de los mitos occidentales y su impacto en la teología cristiana, Herren comienza su estudio con una premisa diáfana, griegos (y romanos) nos dejaron mitos. Otras civilizaciones también lo hicieron, pero los mitos griegos aun dominan nuestra cultura mientras que los de culturas anteriores, tartesios, iberos, celtas y fenicios, sólo para nombrar a aquellos con presencia en la Península Ibérica, han quedado prácticamente olvidados a menos que fueran asimilados por los romanos, como las ninfas. Herren demuestra que la principal diferencia entre los mitos griegos y los de otras culturas es que "they not only gave us their wonderful narratives, but they also provided the elementary tools for interpreting them" (2).

En la serie de *La Ciudad Blanca* se sigue al pie de la letra la tradición mítica occidental. En ambas series la dicotomía paganismo/catolicismo en tanto que par lógico presenta dos miembros desiguales en el que el catolicismo es la norma y la cultura dominante y el paganismo es el elemento marcado. El catolicismo es parte del paisaje, el escenario donde los actores se sienten cómodos, su práctica pública está naturalizada y toda la ciudad, creyentes o no, asisten a las fiestas de la Virgen Blanca, patrona de la ciudad. En este ámbito el paganismo siempre se asocia al mal y la presencia de antiguos demonios en el mundo contemporáneo. La serie sigue el axioma cristiano de que "pagans had myths, but Christians had truths" (162).

Los ritos del agua

Como en la novela anterior la novela se divide en dos partes, una en el pasado que ocurre el verano de 1992 contada por un narrador omnisciente y la trama principal en el presente de 2016 contada en primera persona por Unai. En la del pasado Unai y tres miembros de su cuadrilla, Lutxo, Jota y Asier viajan a Cabezón de la Sal en Cantabria a construir bajo la dirección de un arqueólogo, Saúl Tovar, las cabañas de un castro celta usando adobe y brezo.

La construcción de la tradición en este caso es literal. Existe esta idea redundante de que el pasado siempre está en construcción y de que un error en este proceso puede tener consecuencias fatales en el presente. Ya en este, la primera asesinada es Ana Belén Liaño, una dibujante de cómic *underground*, alavesa y embarazada. Nótese el leitmotiv de las profesiones creativas tan caro a la cultura neoliberal.

La matan siguiendo un ritual celta, colgándola de un árbol y sumergiéndola en un caldero sagrado, en este caso: "El Caldero de Cabárceno, encontrado en una mina de Peña Cabarga, Cantabria, hace un siglo. Está fechado en torno al 900-650 a.C., Edad de Bronce... siempre se ha pensado que la pieza estaba destinada a ser utilizada en ceremonias religiosas o similares" (54).

El rito se corresponde con el de la Triple Muerte Celta en el que a la persona se la colgaba, ahogaba y quemaba. El ahogamiento se corresponde con los sacrificios a Teutates (Tutatis) al ahogarlo, a Esus (Eso) el colgarlo y a Taranis el quemarlo (113). Tal como la novela indica hay una breve referencia en *La Farsalia* de Lucano a estos dioses. No se olvide que el poeta romano nació en lo que hoy conocemos como Córdoba. El poeta cordobés, con su enigmática referencia, abrió la puerta a la imaginación de sus comentaristas posteriores. La ignorancia que tenemos sobre estos dioses hizo que se abrieran interpretaciones sobre sus poderes. En el monográfico de Freeman de 2017 para Oxford University Press sobre mitología celta que compendia nuestro conocimiento sobre el tema hasta el presente, todo lo que se comenta sobre estos dioses viene de Lucano (5-7). La edición y traducción al español de *La Farsalia* de Jesús Bartolomé Gómez para Cátedra solo hace una vaga referencia a César en la *Guerra de las Galias* (177). La *Encyclopedia Brittanica* se ciñe también a la información de Lucano. La ausencia de fuentes le permite a Sáenz ampliar la magnitud de los mitos.[7]

Siguiendo el proceso de ansiedad sobre la museización, el segundo asesinato ocurre, o mejor dicho, es puesto en escena, en el centro de interpretación del estanque celtibérico de la Barbacana (164). Este es un antiguo depósito de aguas celtibérico descubierto en 1998, construido hace 2.100 años en la villa de Laguardia (Álava) para embalsar agua de un manantial. Como bien se indica en la novela se descubrió en sus proximidades un ara romana dedicada a las Matres, prueba del sincretismo hispanorromano en su proceso de absorción de los celtíberos, como explica la progresiva desaparición de los oppida celtas en cuanto avanzó la romanización. Este Centro de Interpretación es una instalación museográfica audiovisual. http://www.alavaturismo.eus/estanque-celtiberico/.

Las novelas no se oponen a este proceso de museización del pasado, pero se unen a la ansiedad por lo ancestral y la manipulación de la historia que se manifiesta en teóricos de lo vasco como Juaristi o Zulaika o en estudiosos de los nacionalismos en España como Álvarez Junco. La necesidad esquizofrénica de interpretar el pasado en clave nacionalista, incluido el vasco (lo que no deja de ser un mandato constitucional) y mantener el rigor científico se traduce en lo que ya nos advirtió Zulaika de que la ficción se limita a cumplir el mandato mitificador que la clase política demanda, en vez de la función moderna y crítica de desmitificar. Sáenz se debate entre este Escila y Caribdis. Citemos a Unai explicándole a Alba lo que están observando. Si pensamos que ambos son alaveses no tiene mucho sentido que ella no sepa lo que le cuenta Unai:

> —Los nativos tenemos la costumbre de llamar sierra de Cantabria a estos montes, pero la denominación antigua era sierra de Toloño, derivada del dios várdulo Tullonius. Es el dios padre para los celtas, Teutates. Incluso quedan las ruinas de un monasterio medieval dedicado a Santa María de Toloño (169).

---

7   El monográfico de la revista *Desperta Ferro. Arqueología e Historia* de octubre-noviembre de 2017 dedicado a los Oppida, las ciudades de la Europa céltica, no tiene ni una sola mención a las deidades celtas, las que se proporcionan ya lo son romanizadas. El libro nacionalista *Divinidades y genios de la mitología de Vasconia* de 2017 tampoco los nombra. Aparecen los más asiduos: Mari, Jentil, Akerbeltz y el Basajaun entre otros, pero no hay ni un solo dios celta. Juaristi en *El bosque imaginario* dice de los celtas "apenas sabemos nada, a través de las fuentes clásicas, de sus divinidades, salvo de la adoración a un dios con astas de ciervo, Cerunnos" (222).

Los saltos etimológicos de estos teónimos son más que dudosos. En un informe oficial de la Euskaltzaindia/Real Academia de la Lengua Vasca, Roberto González de Viñaspre dictamina que la sierra de Cantabria debe de pasar a llamarse Sierra de Toloño, lo que ocurrió oficialmente en octubre de 2018. Pero lo que nos interesa de su exhaustivo informe es que solo señala que Toloño es un topónimo de origen celta y no aventura interpretación alguna sobre su significado.

Esta parte de la novela es confusa porque aunque Unai se ha declarado agnóstico en otras ocasiones ahora reza: "Gracias, Tulonio. Por cuidar de los míos" (170). Estos dioses no son muy efectivos ya que recibe un disparo en la cabeza, su cuñada es asesinada y su hermano y Alba casi perecen a manos del asesino. Esta escena climática ocurre en las ruinas del monasterio de Santa María de Toloño. Como reconoce Unai en el tercer volumen: "pero lo cierto era que ni el hilo rojo ni el *eguzkilore* habían protegido a los que más me importaban en el mundo" (369). Tanto en la serie de Sáenz como en la de Redondo, el culto a dioses ancestrales es improductivo.

Uno de los antagonistas en esta segunda novela es el antropólogo Saúl Tovar de la Universidad de Cantabria, que siempre se está refiriendo a mitos celtas y teónimos precristianos. Observemos que en ambas trilogías, la de Redondo y Sáenz, los antropólogos mueren. Una posible explicación es que se les castiga porque creían, o al menos respetaban en exceso, los mitos paganos. Hay una diferencia entre estudiarlos y tener fe en ellos. Otra posibilidad es que utilizan su ciencia para fines espurios. Saúl utiliza su posición para abusar sexualmente de su hija y estudiantes, llegando al asesinato.

Los señores del tiempo

En este caso los asesinatos se relacionan con una novela histórica contemporánea *Los señores del tiempo* que reescribe un cronicón medieval sobre las luchas entre señores alaveses y castellanos en la Nova Victoria y la Gasteiz del siglo XII. Ambas historias están contadas en primera persona, la contemporánea por Unai ocurre a finales de 2019, y la novela medieval por el conde don Diago Vela. En las anteriores novelas, las analepsis estaban en tercera persona, contadas por un narrador omnisciente. En este caso es diferente porque lo que estamos leyendo es un texto autónomo, una novela que se ha publicado anónimamente al mismo tiempo que los asesinatos. La diferencia está en que algunos de los personajes de la novela policiaca han leído o están leyendo la novela histórica. Los asesinatos en la Álava contemporánea remedan los de la novela histórica.

Las muertes violentas comienzan de nuevo en la almendra medieval, el primero, en el Palacio de Villa Suso en la Plaza del Matxete. La víctima es Antón Lasaga, un rico empresario de la industria textil quien es encontrado en los baños, muerto por una intoxicación de cantárida, un peligroso afrodisiaco medieval, altamente tóxico. Las siguientes son Estefanía Nájera de diecisiete años y su hermana Oiahana de doce, que fallecen por emparedamiento en una casa entre la calle Cuchillería y el Cantón de Santa María. Más tarde es el *hacker* gótico, Samuel Maturana, conocido en el internet profundo como MatuSalem. No es difícil hacer la conexión entre la hacker gótica Elizabeth Salander y MatuSalem; sus físicos son parecidos, aspecto aniñado, andrógino, con cuerpos no completamente desarrollados y pelos teñidos de colores no naturales. A Maturana se le mata siguiendo el ritual medieval de la incubación, en el que el reo era metido dentro de un barril junto a una serie de animales vivos, un perro, un gato, un gallo y una serpiente y eran arrojados a un río, donde morían ahogados mientras la persona sufría las agresiones de los animales enloquecidos.

Aun así, Unai continúa con su religión neolítica. Le explica a su hija Deva:

> ¿Ves el monte Toloño? Tú viniste de allí. Tu madre y tú pasasteis unos días con el dios Tulonio y la Madre Tierra os protegió. Ella es otra diosa. La más importante de hecho. Su nombre primigenio en estas tierras era Lur (184).

Mientras tanto en la acción de la novela histórica ha sido asesinado también con cantárida el conde de Maestu, y el protagonista, don Diego Vela, sufre un atentado con espada. Las hermanas de Onneca, la amante del conde, Bonna y Favila, mueren es su emparedamiento cuando el sacerdote encargado de pasarles alimentos deja de hacerlo. Unai analiza la novela:

> Está escrita en primera persona. Desde que se publicó se han perpetrado varios asesinatos en la ciudad, todos ellos con un *modus operandi* medieval, exactamente igual que algunas muertes de la novela: la mosca española, el voto de tinieblas y un encubamiento (188).

Para el policía Unai es importante la observación de que la novela dentro de la novela se escribiera en primera persona ya que en su condición de perfilador implica una inversión emocional importante por parte del autor, quien, de alguna manera aun no clara para él, está involucrado en los asesinatos.

Unai necesita ayuda para entender la novela y poner en comunicación las dos Álavas. Para ello acude a Iago del Castillo, director del Museo de Arqueología de Cantabria, quien le explica cómo funcionaba el concepto de identidad en la Edad Media:

Las fronteras entre el reino de Navarra y Castilla eran prácticamente líquidas, cambiaron cinco veces durante ese siglo. El pueblo llano no tenía un sentimiento de pertenencia tal y como lo entendemos ahora, luchaban por la supervivencia de su día a día según el estrato social en que hubiesen nacido, y se posicionaban a favor o en contra del rey de turno según los privilegios que otorgaban a una villa y de si los favorecía o no. No tenía que ver con un sentimiento patriótico. La lucha por el territorio era una lucha por la conservación de un estatus, incluso para los reyes, que tenían que demostrar constantemente su fortaleza porque no se les admitía la debilidad (354).

Si la Constitución de 1978 consagra el privilegio, la respuesta es obvia. La trilogía se posiciona en este privilegio. El Toloño de Unai no es más que el lugar común de amor a las montañas del nacionalismo vasco. Juaristi ha analizado este amor a las cumbres omnipresente en la retórica nacionalista vasca (*Sacra* 50-51). En la segunda década del siglo XXI en la España democrática neoliberal y glocal, el mal se personifica íntimamente unido a dioses paganos resucitados. Pero si en *Dracula* de Bram Stoker lo derrota la Sagrada Hostia, en la España contemporánea a los asesinos los derrota la Constitución. Unai resume bien la situación: "Siempre presenté al juez instructor de turno los atestados más completos" (414).

La lección de estas trilogías es que el mal, mítico o real, puede ser derrotado por las fuerzas constitucionales del estado bajo la supervisión directa del sistema judicial y que la pertenencia a una comunidad está unida al privilegio.

Obras citadas

alijostes Bordagarai, Koldo. *Divinidades y genios de la mitología de Vasconia.* Amaroa, 2017.
Álvarez Junco, José. *Dioses útiles. Naciones y nacionalismos.* Galaxia Gutenberg, 2016.
Ban, Cornel. *Ruling Ideas. How Global Neoliberalism Goes Local.* Oxford UP, 2016.
Bronson, Eric. "Why Journalists and Geniuses Love Coffee and Hate Themselves." Larsson's Philosophy of Female Attraction." Editor Eric Bronson. *The Girl with the Dragon Tattoo and Philosophy*. John Wiley, 2011, pp. 65-74.
Cobacho Gómez, José Antonio. "Los derechos civiles forales o especiales tras la *Constitución de 1978*". Anales de Derecho, vol. 7, 1985, pp. 7-34.
Evagarciasaenz, cuenta de Instagram.

Freeman, Philip. *Celtic Mythology. Tales of Gods, Goddesses and Heroes*. Oxford UP, 2017.

García Sáenz de Urturi, Eva. "Acerca de Mí," www.evagarciasaenz.com/autora.

———. *Los ritos del agua*. Planeta, 2017.

———. *El silencio de la ciudad blanca*. Planeta, 2016.

———. *Los señores del tiempo*. Planeta, 2018.

González de Viñaspre, Roberto. "Informe sobre las denominaciones Sierra de Toloño y Sierra de Cantabria". *Euskera*, vol. 55, n° 1, 2010, pp. 447-486.

Granger, Ana. "Entrevista a Eva García Sáenz de Urturi". *El aventurero de papel*, 9 de julio de 2016. https://elaventurerodepapel.blogspot.com/2016/07/entrevista-eva-garcia-saenz-de-urturi.html

Juaristi, Jon. *El bosque imaginario*. Penguin Random House, 2014. Ebook.

———. *El bucle melancólico. Historias de nacionalistas vascos*. Espasa Calpe, 1997.

———. *Sacra Némesis. Nuevas historias de nacionalistas vascos*. Espasa Calpe, 1999.

Kenley, Nicole. "Hackers without Borders: Global Detectives in Stieg Larsson's Millennium Trilogy". *Clues. A Journal of Detection*, vol. 32, no. 2, 2014, pp. 30-40.

Larsson, Stieg. *La chica que soñaba con un cerillo y un galón de gasolina*. Translated by Martin Lexell and Juan José Ortega, Destino, 2010.

———. *The Girl Who Kicked the Hornets's Nest*. Translated by Reg Keeland. Vintage, 2012.

———. *The Girl who Played with Fire*. Translated by Reg Keeland, Vintage, 2011a.

———. *The Girl with the Dragon Tattoo*. Translated by Reg Keeland, Alfred A. Knopf, 2008.

———. *Los hombres que no amaban a las mujeres*. Traducido por Martin Lexell and Juan José Ortega. Destino, 2009.

———. *La reina en el palacio de las corrientes de aire*. Traducido por Martin Lexell and Juan José Ortega. Planeta Mexicana, 2011b.

Lucano. *Farsalia o Guerra Civil*. Editor y Traductor Jesús Bartolomé Gómez. Cátedra, 2003.

Martín Matos, José Antonio. "Glocalización en la *Trilogía del Baztán*: Elementos locales y globales en el universo de Dolores Redondo". Editores. Á. Martín Escribà y Javier Sánchez Zapatero. *El género negro de la marginalidad a la normalización*, Andavira. 2015, pp. 87-95.

Miguel Bárcena, Josu de y Javier Tajadura Tejada. *Kelsen versus Schmidtt. Política y derecho en la crisis del constitucionalismo*. Guillermo Escolar, 2018.

Muro, Diego. "The Politics of War Memory in Radical Basque Nationalism". *Ethnic and Racial Studies*, vol. 32, no. 4, 2009, pp. 659-678.

Oropesa, Salvador. "Mitología y terrorismo en la *Trilogía del Baztán* de Dolores Redondo." *Clásicos y Contemporáneos en el Género Negro*. Eds. Álex Martín Escribà y Javier Sánchez Zapatero. Andavira, 2018, pp. 121-27.

Ovejero, Félix. *La deriva reaccionaria de la izquierda*. Página indómita, 2018.

Palmero, Fernando. "Entrevista a Jon Juaristi". *El Mundo* 29 diciembre 2018.

Peñalver, Xabier. *La Edad de Hierro. Los vascones y sus vecinos. El último milenio anterior a nuestra era*. Txertoa, 2008.

Sampaio, Maria De Lurdes. "*Millennium Trilogy*: Eye for Eye and the Utopia of Order in Modern Waste Lands". *Cross-Cultural Communication,* vol. 7, no. 2, 2011, pp. 73-81.

Sánchez Prado, Ignacio. *Screening Neoliberalism. Transforming Mexican Cinema 1988-2012*. Vanderbilt UP, 2014.

Sánchez Zapatero, Javier y Álex Martín Escribà. *Continuará . . . Sagas literarias en el género negro y policiaco español*. Alrevés, 2017.

Terjesen, Andrew and Fenny Terjesen. "Why Are so Many Women F***ing Kalle Blomkvist?: Larsson's Philosophy of Female Attraction." Editor Eric Bronson. *The Girl with the Dragon Tattoo and Philosophy*. John Wiley, 2011, pp. 49-64.

Thomas, Bronwen. "Kicking the Hornet's Nest: The Rhetoric of Social Campaigning in Stieg Larsson's *Millennium Trilogy*'. *Language and Literature* vol. 21, no. 3, 2012. 299-310.

Ugarte, Javier y Antonio Rivera. "La Guerra Civil en El País Vasco: La sublevación en Álava". Universidad del País Vasco. http://www.ehu.eus/ojs/index.php/HC/article/viewFile/18731/16685

Zulaika, Joseba. "Anthropologists, Artists, Terrorists: the Basque Holiday from History". *Journal of Spanish Cultural Studies*, vol. 4, no. 2, 2003, pp. 139-150

Zurdo, David. "Entrevista con Eva García Sáenz de Urturi". *Qué leer,* n° 219, 2016, pp. 60-63.

Juanita Versus Cecilia: Competing Allegories of Cuba by Mary Peabody Mann and Cirilo Villaverde

JULIA C. PAULK
Marquette University

FAMOUSLY SEPARATED BY ONLY ninety miles, the United States and Cuba have a long history of political, economic, and cultural exchange. In the nineteenth-century, a considerable number of Cuban exiles lived in U.S. and wrote about their homeland. At the same time, scores of U.S. travelers to Cuba also wrote about the island. These works provide important glimpses into how each country viewed itself and also perceived the other. Two works that form part of this dynamic through telling images of slaveholding Cuba are Mary Peabody Mann's *Juanita: A Romance of Real Life in Cuba Fifty Years Ago* (1887) and Cirilo Villaverde's *Cecilia Valdés, o la Loma del Ángel* (1882). While both authors published their works in the U.S. at a temporal and physical distance from their subject, they offer in their novels competing visions as they allegorize nationhood through the negative example provided by colonial Cuba. While Villaverde's text is an exploration of the problems of colonialism, Mann's novel proposes abandoning Cuba in order to safeguard an idealized U.S.. The few existing comparisons of these two novels by scholars of Transnational American Studies suggest a pathway towards greater understanding of hemispheric literatures. However, a more thorough contextualization of Villaverde's novel and of the archetype of the *mulata trágica* within Cuban national literature is needed to in order to more fully understand the ways in which these two novels illuminate one another.

The Peabody sisters, Elizabeth, Mary, and Sophia, are figures of growing interest for literary scholars. However, little research has been published to date on the three sisters in their own right rather than as female relations (Elbert, Hall, and Rodier ix).[1] Mary Peabody Mann and Sophia Peabody Hawthorne have been traditionally known as the wives of famous men, Horace Mann and Nathanial Hawthorne, respectively. Nonetheless, the works and intellectual contributions of each of the three sisters have slowly begun to be studied in earnest.[2] Mary Peabody Mann's *Juanita* merits much further investigation not only as an antislavery allegory but also because of its illustration of the author's perception of the U.S.'s position in relation to the rest of the American hemisphere. In her novel, Mann projects an idealized version of a harmonious, female-centric, and Protestant New England that is further defined by its contrast to the corrupt, colonial slave society represented by Cuba.

Mary Mann's interest in Cuba dates from a stay on the island undertaken with Sophia, from 1833 to 1835, and paid for by Mary's labor as a governess.[3] The two sisters recorded their experiences in literary form. Sophia wrote fifty-six letters home later collected into what is now called "The Cuba Journal."[4] Like Sophia Hawthorne, Mann also wrote letters from Cuba and relied on them when composing her novel, *Juanita*, years later (Ard xi). Further, Mann also took notes while still in residence at "La Recompensa" coffee plantation (Marshall 277). Although it is not known exactly when *Juanita* was written, Ard asserts that most of it was completed by 1858 and finalized shortly before her death in 1887 (Ard xvi).[5] Elizabeth Peabody's "Explanatory Note" clarifies that Mann did not wish to publish her novel while any members of the Morrell family still lived in order to protect them from embarrassment, and the novel was not published until after the deaths of the Morrells, Mary Mann, and slavery in both the U.S. and Cuba (Peabody 223). While a late publication date means that Mann's novel did not participate in the public

---

1   Mary Peabody Mann also wrote a number of educational works, edited Sarah Winnemucca Hopkins' *Life Among the Piutes* (1883) and translated Domingo Faustino Sarmiento's *Life in the Argentine Republic in the Days of the Tyrants; or Civilization and Barbarism* (1868). Mann's long collaboration with Sarmiento is a greatly underexplored area. Barry L. Velleman's *"My Dear Sir": Mary Mann's Letters to Sarmiento (1865-1881)* is one of the few sources for more information.

2   Of the three sisters, Mary Mann is the least studied (Elbert et al xii). *Juanita* has very recently begun to attract some critical attention.

3   Marshall's biography of the Peabody sisters describes the Cuba sojourn in detail (268-303).

4   At least two of Nathanial Hawthorne's short stories were influenced by Sophia's accounts of her travel to Cuba (Hall cited in Elbert et al xiii; Marshall 362).

5   Ard bases this statement on the fact that passages of the novel were published by Mary's son George in 1858 (xvi).

debate over slavery, the text nonetheless offers insight into how the author, part of an influential group of intellectuals, perceived Cuba, slavery, and her own country. For Ard and other scholars of Mann's novel, the primary merits of the work are the insights it provides into "race sensibilities of Mann's New England intellectual circle" (Ard xii), the author's feminism, the development of Transcendentalism, and the theory of romance as a literary form. However, an important aspect of Mann's novel that has received much less attention until quite recently is the way in which it presents a fictionalized colonial Cuba as a foil to a Protestant New England figured as the idealization of democratic principles at work in the U.S..

For the subtitle of her novel, Mann chose *A Romance of Real Life in Cuba Fifty Years Ago*. Earlier commentary on the novel has demonstrated a general tendency to take this claim to represent reality at face value. The text's first commentator, Elizabeth Peabody, characterizes the novel as an accurate presentation of life in colonial Cuba (223). In a more recent example, Michaela B. Cooper characterizes Mann's novel in the following way: "Her novel, *Juanita* [. . .] is a vivid testimony – part fiction, part reality-of its author's experience" (146). Although she discusses the fictions at work in realism, Ard also suggests that there is much of "real life" in *Juanita* when stating, "Mann wrote not merely a romance but a romance of 'real life.' Her details of slavery's daily horrors distinguish her romance from those of Hawthorne, who sought 'license with regard to every-day' reality" (xx). Perhaps it is because Mann's topic is Cuban rather than U.S. slavery that her antislavery novel has been largely overlooked compared to other North American abolitionist narratives.

Like many other nineteenth-century antislavery novels, *Juanita* is a tragic love story, bringing to mind the Latin American novels that Doris Sommer analyzes as nation-building allegories in *Foundational Fictions*. Told from the perspective of Helen Wentworth, a Unitarian from New England who visits her old school friend in Cuba, Mann's novel not only describes life on Cuba's sugar and coffee plantations but also follows the curtailed romance between the Moorish slave, Juanita, and the eldest son of the slave-owning Rodriguez family, Ludovico. Like other thwarted young lovers of nineteenth-century foundational literature, Juanita and Ludovico are initially separated by race, religion, and class. Their differences suggest those dividing much of the Cuban population during centuries of slavery and colonial rule. Near the conclusion of the novel, Ludovico at last understands that he really loves Juanita, and, to quote Helen Wentworth, finally "conquer[s] the prejudice of caste" (213) by asking Juanita to marry him. Conforming somewhat to the model of the "tragic mulatta", Juanita refuses to "ruin" Ludovico's life by marrying him (Ard xxv-xxvii). Rather, she agrees to take care of his motherless child and return with him as a servant to Cuba, where he feels a duty to try to make improvements. Ludovico attempts the bold move of freeing his slaves; however, like the slaves on the Shelby plantation in Harriet Beecher Stowe's *Uncle Tom's Cabin* (1852), they choose to stay with him (221). Juanita is killed prematurely in a fire, but the union suggested by the love she shared with Ludovico projects a possible future for Cuba. In a conclusion that again echoes that of Stowe's novel, in which the main characters of color relocate to Liberia, Ludovico abandons Cuba at the end of the novel (Windell 306).

An important difference between Mann's novel and the Latin American foundational fictions that Sommer studies is that the author sets her work in a foreign colony and not in her own country. *Juanita* is narrated from the perspective of a Protestant woman from nineteenth-century Massachusetts. Both Helen and the novel's narrator are utterly convinced of the moral and political superiority of the free states of the northern U.S. over Cuba. Mann's narrator almost always uses the term "Spanish" rather than "Cuban" to refer to Cuban society, thereby subsuming Cuban identity into a Spanish one. This is in notable contrast to the Cuban writers, particularly those of Domingo Del Monte's *tertulia*, like Cirilo Villaverde, Anselmo Suárez y Romero, and Félix Tanco Besmeniel, who were beginning to explore a specifically Cuban, *criollo* identity in the 1830s. The novel repeatedly characterizes the island colony as corrupt and inferior to the U.S.. Speaking of General Miguel Tacón's governorship, the narrator remarks that Tacón "exercised his despotic power without regard even to the remonstrances of his nobility, which had hitherto been lawless" (Mann *Juanita* 16). To the Protestant narrator, Catholic Cuba appears to be a place without religion: "[L]ike all other religious observances, the vesper prayer ceased at the time when the revolutions in Spain produced anarchy [. . .] in the colonies. The Sunday morning mass would probably have followed, but the custom of going from that to the cock-fight kept up the observance. [. . .] [N]ational religion was at an end" (17). Of particular concern to Helen and the narrator are children's wellfare and attitudes towards marriage. The novel strongly criticizes the "corrupting" custom of assigning slaves and "negro nurses" to care for children and notes appreciatively that Helen's hostess does not follow that tradition (51). Further, the narrator believes that matrimony is treated as "a nominal thing" among Cuba's elite and that slavery worsens the problem: "[W]here married women are obliged to reconcile themselves to the facts of concubinage, prevalent in all slave communities, and this, of course, even without the excuse or sanction of affection, perverted though it may be, the fountains of all virtue are poisoned" (55). For Helen Wentworth, "all distinction between good and evil seemed to be obliterated" (14) in slaveholding Cuba.

When comparing the Spanish colony to the northern parts of the U.S. in the novel, the latter is without fail found to be loftier than the former. Helen Wentworth considers her Massachusetts home to be "in the freest nation of the earth, and in the most advanced portion of that nation" (14). The narrator characterizes Spaniards as lacking in innovation and inner resources, and as being indolent and uninterested in education (72, 57, 178). As DeGuzmán argues, the Spaniard of the Black Legend becomes racialized in U.S. discourse of identity in the late eighteenth and early nineteenth century, producing a third figure in the ordinarily binary, black versus white conception of racial identity. The "Spaniard" becomes the "not-right-white", "the *off-white*", and the "the blackened figure of alien whiteness" in this conception (DeGuzmán 1, 4). The comparison with the colony makes the higher character of the U.S. all the more clear: "The general elevation of society in the northern and middle states of America [. . .] can only be rightly estimated when compared with an opposite state of things, where public morals are so corrupt that no one can be trusted" (127).[6]

The narrator does not forget that slavery was also practiced in the southern states of the U.S., and that the debate over slavery in the northern country was gaining strength. Helen feels a duty to stay in Cuba despite her horror of slavery because her own country is infected by the same "plague-spot" (14). In this way, Cuba is established as a substitute for the southern states of the U.S., allowing for a more allegorical reading of the novel. At the same time, however, Helen also claims that slavery in Cuba is harsher than that practiced in the Southern U.S. When Fanchon, a free African-American woman from the U.S., is brought to visit, she is horrified that Cuban slaves have to sleep on a board on the ground: "[M]y own mother was a slave, but she had a bed to sleep on, and here these poor souls have not even that comfort" (100). Near the conclusion, Mann's narrator blames the colonial administration for the terrible nature of Cuban slavery: "The confusion created by a succession of rulers each following the policy his own self-interest suggests, gives rise to many evils that are not found in United States slavery" (209). John C. Harvard also points out that Mann's representation of the cruelty of Cuban

---

6   A contemporary of Del Monte, María de las Mercedes Montalvo y Santa Cruz, the Condesa de Merlin, reverses the *leyenda negra* by arguing that slavery in Spanish colonies is gentler than that found in other places: "España con su gobierno absoluto es la única nación que se ha ocupado en suavizar la suerte del negro" (57).

slavery echoes the *leyenda negra* (Harvard 510).[7] The narrator appears unable to fully equate Cuban with U.S. slavery, thereby weakening the novel's stated goal of opposing chattel slavery in the northern country. Furthermore, Cuba becomes a sliding signifier in the novel, at times standing in for the problematic U.S. South but in other instances representing the morally and politically inferior Latin American other.

Although she is in a few instances able to admit to the problem of the "plague spot" infesting her own country, including northern investment in slavery, Mann's narrator consistently idealizes institutions in the United States by way of contrast between New England and the purportedly decadent island colony. The fact that the U.S. Constitution permitted slavery and that the national economy was intertwined with both Southern and Cuban slavery do not appear to figure into Mann's sectarian vision. In a national allegory projecting an idealized Protestant and democratic way of life in the northern U.S., Cuba not only becomes a substitute for the southern slaveholding states but also helps to define the U.S. by way of its undesirable racial otherness. In the context of U.S. relations with Cuba in the nineteenth century, *Juanita* reflects beliefs about the northern country's moral and political superiority that have repeatedly been used to justify military and economic intervention into Latin American countries. More "romance" than "real life", Mann's antislavery novel imagines the United States for its reader just as it does Cuba.

Harvard and Windell's studies of *Juanita* reflect the movement in U.S. American Studies to transnationalize that field by engaging more profoundly with literature of the Americas, but a more thorough grounding in Cuban literary studies would benefit their analyses. As a Latin Americanist and comparatist, I support more comparative study of the interplay between literatures and cultures of our hemisphere. At the same time, I share the same concern with scholars from disciplines outside U.S. American Studies that this continuing trend does not do enough to engage with previously existing scholarship and that this gives the impression of a continued privileging of intellectual production focused on and in the U.S. while claiming to

---

[7] The propagation of the "leyenda negra" by other colonial powers served as a justification for invasion of Spanish colonies and prefigures the "Good Neighbor" approach to U.S. foreign policy in Latin America in the twentieth and twenty-first centuries. Harvard refers to the prejudice against Latin American people as "Hispanicism", modeled after Edward Said's Orientalism (513). I am not sure that academic Hispanists would support that usage although I agree with Harvard's efforts to expose the racialized bias against nations of Latin America.

do otherwise.[8] My initial motivation in comparing *Juanita* to *Cecilia Valdés* was spurred by a poorly conceived comparison between the avaricious Carolina, a white slaveowner, and Cecilia, the woman of mixed racial heritage at the center of Cuba's national novel, in Ard's introduction to Mann's novel (xxvii).[9] Windell's article represents a more concerted effort to engage with Villaverde's novel, yet her analysis does not recognize the essential role of slavery in the development of Cuban culture or fully contextualize *Cecilia Valdés* within the context of nineteenth-century Cuban literature. A more thorough look at Villaverde's canonical novel and the development of Cuban literature in the first half of the nineteenth century helps make clearer the ways in which Mann's vision of Cuba is reflective of prevailing U.S. attitudes at that time.

Critics may not agree as to which is the first Cuban novel, but all seem to concur that the earliest examples of Cuban national literature are the antislavery works that came into being in the 1830s and 1840s, particularly those authored by the writers in the Del Monte circle, which includes Cirilo Villaverde.[10] These are the first works to demonstrate an awareness of a Cuban identity that is distinct from a strictly Spanish one and also to critique colonial institutions such as slavery (Schulman "Reflections" 59).[11] The majority

---

8   While supporting the idea of greater recognition of that which has previously been marginalized in American Studies, scholars in other fields express serious concerns about apparent lack of awareness of work already done in comparative literary studies and in Latin American Studies and also insufficient preparation to engage with literary and cultural traditions from outside the U.S. (refer to González Echevarría, "Latin American and Comparative Literature", and Sommer, *Proceed with Caution*, for further reading). Finally, scholars of literature from nations that do not have the political or cultural power that the U.S. wields are not necessarily interested in abandoning the construct of a national literature (see, for example, Herb Wyile's "Hemispheric Studies of Scholarly NAFTA? The Case for Canadian Literary Studies"). As long as the field is called Hemispheric or Transnational *American* Studies, the U.S. cannot be decentered as the subject of study.

9   Cecilia's name is misspelled as "Cecelia" several times in Ard's introduction as well. This may seem to be a small point to make but it is indicative of the larger problem in Transnational American Studies.

10   Villaverde was born in Pinar del Río, Cuba, in 1812, on a sugar plantation where his father was the plantation doctor. He was educated to be a lawyer but was primarily a journalist, writer, and educator in Cuba.

11   Cuban criollos such as Del Monte, Suárez y Romero, and Villaverde considered themselves ethnically and culturally white and Hispanic. Typical U.S. observers at the time would consider them "Spanish" or "Hispanic", different in terms of

of Cuban antislavery texts, including the earliest version of *Cecilia Valdés*, were written by the participants of the Del Monte tertulia during this period, which also saw a boom in the Cuban sugar market and tremendous increases in the importation of slaves that put whites in the minority. The intellectual class belonged to the planter society, called the *sacarocracia* ("sugar aristocracy"). Thinkers like Del Monte feared the non-white majority in a literal sense and viewed both slavery and slaves as uncivilized and foreign impediments to the modernization of Cuba.[12] The financial dependence of these upper-class writers on sugar production made them unwilling to imagine an immediate end to slavery, although they did promote reforms considered threatening enough by colonial Spain that many were exiled from the island. It is in this context that the *blanqueamiento* promoted by Francisco de Arango, Antonio Saco, and Del Monte must be understood as a racist program intended to erase blackness and not as a sign of racial tolerance or reconciliation.

As the century progressed, Cuban writers, primarily working in exile, became bolder in their literary approach to abolition and connected it with the end of all colonial institutions. Following the developments in its author's approach to slavery and colonialism, *Cecilia Valdés* evolved over the decades, being published in three differing iterations, from 1839 to 1882. Critical commentary on *Cecilia Valdés* within Cuban literary studies addresses the effects of Villaverde's long exile from his homeland on the final publication of his novel as well as the national allegory the text suggests.[13] Villaverde himself explains that he left behind his literary life when he fled Cuba in 1849: "abandoné, en fin, las frívolas ocupaciones del esclavo en tierra esclava, para tomar parte en las empresas del hombre libre en tierra libre" (4). As an exile, Villaverde was very active in the movement to liberate Cuba from Spain. His political and journalistic activities took precedence over his work as an author of fiction, and the revision of *Cecilia Valdés* was neglected for decades. Upon his arrival in the U.S., the writer supported the move to annex Cuba to the U.S. as a slave state and served as secretary for the filibustering General

---

ethnicity and religious beliefs, and not place them in a category of whiteness occupied by themselves.

12 See *Escritos de Domingo del Monte* for examples of the writer's attitude towards slavery and slaves.

13 Lazo's article, "Filibustering Cuba: *Cecilia Valdés* and a Memory of Nation in the Americas" and book, *Writing to Cuba: Filibustering and Cuban Exiles in the United States* study, among other issues, the influence of Villaverde's political activities on his novel and the creation of Cuban literature within the national boundaries of the United States.

Narciso López. In the 1860s, however, Villaverde became disillusioned with the role of the U.S. in liberating Cuba after repeated attempts to free the island had failed. As Rodrigo Lazo puts it, "By the late 1860s, a sector of the Cuban exile community (and Villaverde in particular) viewed the United States as a power more interested in its own hemispheric ambitions than in Cuban independence" ("Filibustering" 12-13). By the time *Cecilia Valdés* was revised and published, Villaverde had allied himself with fellow Cubans who opposed slavery and annexation and agitated for a free Cuba. As Lazo proposes, "Villaverde's novel accomplishes what the filibusters of López's era could not: to successfully stake a claim on Cuban ground" ("Filibustering" 18).

Ivan Schulman also argues that Villaverde's presentation of Cuba is colored by his long residence in the U.S.: the author was surely impacted by "los conflictos raciales, la Guerra de Secesión, la libertad de prensa, la lectura libre y abundante de obras nacionales y foráneas, y la publicación de la novela *La Cabaña del tío Tom* por Harriet Beecher Stowe" in his adopted country ("Prólogo" xxi). Not an explicit part of the text, the culture of the United States is nonetheless a subtext and point of comparison (xxvi). Like that of other exiled authors, Villaverde's presentation of Cuba is also imbued with nostalgia for the land he left many years earlier (Schulman xxi).[14] Similar to *Juanita*, Villaverde's novel is a look back at a time long past. In contrast, however, the author of *Cecilia Valdés* wrote with a deep concern for the future of the plighted island and a history of promoting its liberation.

Cecilia Valdés is a tragic romance, although the love story here plays out somewhat differently from the other national novels outlined by Sommer. Cecilia Valdés is a free woman of mixed racial heritage who does not know the identity of her father and who is trapped in a vicious cycle of exploitation by colonial ideologies of race, gender, and class. She is passionately in love with the wealthy white *criollo*, Leonardo Gamboa, without knowing that he is her half-brother.[15] Unlike other novels in which incest threatens but is not carried out, Cecilia and Leonardo eventually establish a household and

---

14 Schulman explains that Cuban narratives of "lejanía" ("distance", or exile) share a constellation of values, "'nostalgia desde fuera (emigración)', 'anhelos reminiscentes' e 'intuición de lo otro'" (Schulman "Prólogo" xxi).

15 The families of each of these two main characters add to the development of Villaverde's national allegory. Leonardo and Cecilia's father is Don Cándido, a Spanish-born slave trader. His wealthy wife, Doña Rosa, inherited her father's sugar plantation. Cecilia's mother and grandmother were both also seduced by wealthy white men; each generation of the women in the family is lighter-skinned in appearance.

produce a daughter. Leonardo soon wearies of Cecilia and marries a socially more appropriate match, Isabel Ilincheta, who is the daughter of a coffee plantation owner. Upon leaving the church, however, Leonardo is killed by Cecilia's would-be lover, José Dolores Pimienta, a free man of mixed racial heritage, who Cecilia had sent to kill Isabel.[16] Like her mother before her, Cecilia is imprisoned and goes mad, leaving her daughter an unprotected orphan.

Villaverde's novel has achieved canonical status as Cuba's nineteenth-century national novel and has been widely read as an allegory of nationhood. Schulman proposes that in "la versión definitiva de *Cecilia Valdés* el novelista tiende a expresar en forma alegórica los atributos socio-étnicos y económicos de la colectividad en los personajes individuales, y a utilizar, como en los relatos antiesclavistas primitivos, el núcleo familiar y sus miembros individuales para representar los valores colectivos" ("Prólogo" xxv). Schulman focuses particularly upon the Gamboa family in his discussion of the allegory. Don Cándido represents the avaricious and stubborn colonial administration, Doña Rosa the affectionate but somewhat misguided older generation of *criollos*, and Leonardo the new generation of *criollos*, who are apathetic participants in an immoral society. The Gamboas exemplify the ways in which Cuba's ruling classes, supported by slavery, have fallen into moral decline and the younger generations are repeating the sins of their fathers. For Schulman, the novel is a moral diagnosis of the social and political ills facing Cuba under colonial rule. Villaverde's analysis of the moral state of colonial Cuba is shared by a number of his fellow Cuban authors who promoted colonial reforms.

In Sommer's discussion of the allegory of *Cecilia Valdés*, she states that the problem facing the young lovers is slavery: "This is a novel about impossible love, not because blacks and whites should not love each other [...] but because slavery makes it impossible" (*Foundational* 128). The exploitations made possible by the colonial institution of slavery conflict with modern morality and the bourgeois marriage contract. Cecilia's parentage must be kept a secret, yet it is an "explosive secret, a debilitating blindspot where the rule of masters' privilege (double-)crosses modern family ties" (129). If Leonardo were to have known the truth, he would not have pursued Cecilia and would not have been killed. However, secrets are kept, and Leonardo is cut out of the "pattern traced here for fashioning a nation from competing colors and

---

16   Sommer describes the mixed-race musician and tailor, José Dolores, as a "doubly promising [...] purveyor of an autonomous Cuban style" (*Foundational* 128).

tastes" after his betrayal of the prototypical Cuban beauty (128). Moreover, both Leonardo and Cecilia, who has interiorized the island's racial hierarchy, fail to listen to those who know and can tell the truth about who she is (129). The slave characters, María de Regla, and her husband, Dionisio, try to tell the truth to just about anyone who will listen, but they are ignored until it is too late to avert tragedy.

Both Schulman and Sommer characterize this national allegory as pessimistic and deterministic. Each generation of women in Cecilia's family has been subject to the same form of exploitation, and her unprotected daughter appears doomed to repeat it. Worse yet, unlike other ill-fated pairs such as Gertrudis Gómez de Avellaneda's Sab and Carlota and Mann's Juanita and Ludovico, Cecilia and Leonardo could never parent a new nation together because they are sister and brother. The suggestion is, then, that everything in Cuba must change. Colonial ideologies and institutions must be abolished. Radical action, suggested by José Dolores's murder of the dissolute Leonardo, must be taken. Until Cuba is liberated, it will continue to be subject to exploitation and abuse, just like the imperfect Cecilia.

While Mann's Juanita is little-known, Cecilia Valdés is an iconic figure in Cuban culture and occupies a complex but important role in the discourse of *cubanidad* ("Cubanness" or "Cuban identity"). In the words of Roberto González-Echevarría, Cecilia as a Cuban mulata represents "una especie de mito nacional al estilo del de la Malinche en México" ("Cervantes" 268). Although the terms *cubanidad* and *cubanía* were not in circulation until the twentieth century, the origins of these constructs are to be found in the nationalist discourse of the nineteenth century (Kutzinski 7). The literary figure of the *mulata*, a woman of mixed racial heritage, plays a central but complex role in this discourse.[17] Appearing frequently as a symbol of Cuban culture, the figure of the *mulata* is privileged and highly visible in cultural production and the national imaginary yet, in life, belongs to a socially underprivileged group (Kutzinski 7). As Vera M. Kutzinski phrases it, the "iconic *mulata*, then, is a symbolic container for all the tricky questions about how race, gender, and sexuality inflect the power relations that obtain in colonial and postcolonial Cuba" (7). Like the dualistic archetype of the Cuban literary *mulata*, Cecilia is irresistibly and uncontrollably seductive and beautiful but, at the same time, is also associated with the copper-hued

---

17 Kutzinski considers Rosario Alarcón, Cecilia's tormented mother, to be the first version of this literary type in Cuban literature (7). Rosario appeared in the original version of *Cecilia Valdés* from 1839. Cecilia takes on the role of the prototypical *mulata* in the 1882 version.

patron saint of Cuba, the Virgen de la Caridad del Cobre.[18] Cecilia represents the burgeoning Cuban identity but is a victim of the injustices of that society. Regardless of the paradoxes of the use of the *mulata* figure as a symbol in Cuban cultural production, Kutzinski argues that "*mestizaje* has been perhaps the principal signifier of Cuba's national cultural identity" (5).[19] As a reminder of nineteenth-century programs of *blanqueamiento*, Cecilia is both a sign of Cuba's "race problem" and a solution to it. She embodies both pride and shame in her heritage.

Mulatez occupies a principal space in Villaverde's novel through a range of characters, making it both central to and representative of nineteenth and twentieth-century discussions of Cuban identity. In contrast, black/white racial mixing plays only a minor role in Mann's novel. The narrator describes Juanita as having "singular, Moorish beauty, which bore no trace of the negro" (Mann 62). She is the child of an Arabic/white woman and a white man. For those familiar with Cuban antislavery literature, "Moorish" is a notably odd choice of racial identifier.[20] Like Cecilia, Juanita is the product of several generations of exploitation of women of color by white slave owners. However, not being "negro" places her in a category apart from other women of color in the novel, as the fictional Isabella Rodriguez explains, "Her grandmother was [...] a] Moor. They are not often enslaved. They have little resemblance to other negroes; indeed they are not negroes" (Mann 76). Windell argues that Mann initially categorizes Juanita as a "Moor" but characterizes her as a tragic mulatta, creating slippage in the novel between Moor, *mulata*, and mulatta and thereby eliminating the "racial unknowability" of the Moor figure (313; 316). Mann's labelling of Juanita, a Hispanic woman of mixed race, as a Moor also participates in the Orientalist tradition in the nineteenth-century U.S. of identifying Spanish-speaking mulattas

---

18   The Virgen de la Caridad del Cobre is a complex figure in Cuban culture. Not only is she the patron saint of Cuba, but she is also associated with the Yoruba *orisha* Ochún. For more information about Ochún's role in Cuban culture, see for example, Madeline Cámara's "Ochún: una metáfora incompleta en la cultura cubana".

19   I prefer "mulatez" to "mestizaje" in this context because "mestizaje" ofter refers to racial mixing between Spaniards and indigenous populations.

20   Characters in Cuban antislavery literature are rarely described as being Arabic, especially given that the vast majority of Cuba's slave population originated in West Africa. David T. Haberly asserts that Mary Mann had forgotten most of the Spanish that she learned in Cuba by the time she translated Sarmiento's *Facundo* to English (1868) and relied heavily on a French translation for her own work (Haberly "Reopening *Facundo*" 59).

with tales of captive "moras" from Spain of the Reconquista (312). Francine Masiello explains that Mann read *Don Quijote* before sailing for Cuba and thus would have been familiar with the extensive representations of Muslims in Cervantes' novel. Masiello further points out that Mann had trouble with Cuban Spanish (31-34). Mann's use of "Moor" reflects the English language meaning rather than the Cuban one, which is used to indicate a person of darker skin tone, and serves as an example of how Mann's limitations in communicating in Spanish could lead her to impose external cultural norms on what she observed on the island. Likewise, Helen Wentworth's confusion over Cuban racial categories indicates a struggle to understand and to name racial identities that she did not encounter socially in the northern U.S. In one of her rare encounters with mulattas, Helen categorizes them as Jewish until learning that they are a former slaves of mixed racial heritage. [21] However, the novel maintains throughout that is Juanita is a "Moor." Aside from being characterized as Arabic, Juanita's treatment is also distinct from the tragic mulatta trope in that she is not sexualized in the way that the tragic mulatta typically is.[22] She and Ludovico never consummate their relationship. Rather, the rejection of blackness for Juanita endows her to an extent with a privileged status within the novel as a woman of high moral character. Nonetheless, the author's choice of Islam as a religion further highlights Juanita's otherness; as with the "Jewess", Juanita's otherness may not be visible but it can still be perceived. The novel's categorizations establish a hierarchy of morality and religion in the novel, with Catholicism, Islam, and Judaism all serving as markers of undesirable difference.

Both Ard and Windell refer to *Cecilia Valdés* in their discussions of Juanita, and in doing so highlight a shortcoming of Transnational American Studies that has been critiqued by scholars operating in other literary disciplines. In this case, to discuss *Cecilia Valdés* and analyze it in conjunction with an antislavery novel from the U.S., one must also know how Villaverde's novel is perceived within Cuban literary studies. Windell's study makes a much more considerable effort to engage with scholarship about Cuba, yet *Cecilia Valdés*

---

21   Helen is intrigued by this mother-daughter pair but is not able to identify their difference. Helen Wentworth first observes "a splendid-looking woman, who looked like a Jewess, with a young lady by her side" with "deep interest" at the village ball (110-111), and notes that no one will have asked either of ladies to dance despite their finery. She can only understand their exclusion as meaning that they are Jewish. She later learns that they are "the freed slaves of a wealthy man" and unlikely to be able to marry white men because of the "suspicion of negro blood" (178).

22   Ard also makes this point (xxv-xxvii).

is not situated in the context of nineteenth-century Cuban literature as a whole in her analysis. Referring to Cecilia as "the Cuban mulatta", Windell appears to seek to dislocate Cecilia from the Cuban and Hispanic Caribbean tradition of the *mulata trágica* and from the context of antislavery literature when she states, "unlike the antislavery U.S. tragic mulatta, the Cuban *mulata* figure moved beyond the context of slavery to embody Cuba's culture and racial difference from Spain" (315). To separate Cecilia Valdés from the literary tradition in Cuban literature which she helps to define runs counter to much of the extensive scholarship on *Cecilia Valdés*. As Zaira Rivera Casellas reminds us, "El tropo de la mulata trágica suele coincidir en la literatura del Caribe por los rasgos recurrentes de ser hija bastarda del amo, amenazada por el incesto, desvalorizada moral y sexualmente, sobre todo agobiada por inseguridades psicológicas y desgracias que le impiden incorporarse a la sociedad civil de forma productiva. Este perfil de la mulata se presenta en el Caribe hispano, por ejemplo, en la novela *Cecilia Valdés*" (100).

Cecilia is the best-known nineteenth-century Cuban *mulata trágica*, but there are others from Cuban antislavery novels of the nineteenth-century which more closely resemble the U.S. stereotype and perhaps offer better points of comparison with Mann's self-sacrificing Juanita. A few key examples are Dorotea of Suárez y Romero's *Francisco*, Rosalía of Tanco's *Petrona y Rosalía*, and Camila of Antonio Zambrana's *El negro Francisco*.[23] In Cuban literary studies, Cecilia Valdés is typically understood to participate in this tradition, particularly since the earliest version of her story originates from the context of the Del Monte *tertulia* of the late 1830s, which connected the criticism of slavery and blackness with colonial reform. In the case of the final version of *Cecilia Valdés*, condemnation of slavery becomes connected with independence for Cuba rather than with reform or annexation. Cecilia's tragedy, which as Sommer argues is the product of slavery, is Cuba's tragedy as a "slave" to Spain. To propose that the Cuban *mulata* moves *beyond* slavery is to fail to take in to account the centrality of slavery to Cuban cultural production from the nineteenth-century to today. Rather, slavery and race are the defining issues of early Cuban nationality because of the centrality of slavery to every aspect of life in Cuba until abolition was finalized in 1886; contemporary Cuban cultural production continues to explore this history. The overt recognition of the role of slavery and its effects on Cuban demographics and culture is a key difference between the development of Cuban

---

23 Lorna Williams' *The Representation of Slavery in Cuban Fiction* and William Luis' *Literary Bondage: Slavery in Cuban Narrative* are landmark studies of Cuban antislavery literature.

and U.S. rhetorics of identity in the nineteenth century. Whereas a writer in the northern U.S. could imagine that slavery and race had nothing to do with his or her vision of the nation, Cuban writers, surrounded by slavery, could not pretend to do so.[24] Antislavery literature is not a subset of Cuban national literature but is rather the foundation of Cuban national literature, and it continues to be revisited and rewritten by a range of Cuban writers and film-makers.

The treatment of racial mixing is one of the primary differences between Mann's and Villaverde's portrayals of Cuba, yet the two novels coincide in several interesting ways that have not yet been explored. For example, both works highlight the problems resulting from the corrupting influence of Spanish colonial rule in Cuba. Slavery is the most obvious evil resulting from colonialism but it is not the only one mentioned in either novel. As we have seen, however, Mann's text does not distinguish between Spanish and Cuban, and the island's problems appear to result almost as much from essentialized, "Spanish" character flaws in line with the *leyenda negra* as from colonialism. In contrast, Villaverde's novel, even in its earliest form as a short story, demonstrates an awareness of Cuban *criolla* identity distinct from Spanish identity. Corruption on the island is the result of colonialism and exploitation rather than from perceived inferiority of Hispanics. The characters of Villaverde's novel who see themselves as white would in Mann's novel occupy a lower wrung on the ethnic ladder because of their Spanish heritage and Catholic religion. Finally, the characters in Mann's novel with the potential to redeem the colony morally, Ludovico's family, choose to relocate to Switzerland. Helen Wentworth, the true moral center of the novel, returns to New England. Villaverde's characters remain firmly rooted in Cuba, and the exposure of Cuba's problems is understood to be a protest intended to promote a better future for the island.

Analyzed in conjunction, *Juanita* and *Cecilia Valdés* present us with important questions regarding the nature of allegory, the role of slavery in the formation of national literature, concepts of race and identity, and the literary and cultural relationship between the U.S. and Cuba. Their vantage points within the U.S. made it possible for each of these authors to write about Cuban slavery. For Mann, a position akin to that of the *exploratrice sociale* whose extended stay in Cuba and position as a white writer from the U.S. authorizes her to comment on Cuban slavery even while she limits commentary on slav-

---

24 Cuban writers of color, who were limited in number, had to be much more careful than their white counterparts when addressing race and slavery in their works.

ery in her own country. As an allegory of nationhood, Mann's novel establishes a moral hierarchy from North to South, with Protestant New England representing the ideal "state of things" and in opposition to corrupt, Catholic Cuba, which weighs in even behind the slave-holding South. Villaverde, having been exiled from Cuba, found the freedom and inspiration to extensively re-imagine his early short story as a vast panorama of nineteenth-century Cuban society and as a condemnation of colonialism. The author exposes extensive corruption in his pessimistic national allegory but nonetheless suggests the possibility of a different way of life in Cuba. Analyzed within a more fully hemispheric framework than that which is currently in use in Transnational American Studies, *Juanita* and *Cecilia Valdés* together bring to the fore the complex relationship between the U.S. and Cuba with bearing on contemporary issues. Current U.S. domestic and foreign policy continue to be based on a hierarchical, racialized view of the Americas with the North being the apex. Strict censorship under the Cuban Revolution has made inquiries into contemporary racism taboo. The comparative study of novels that engage with articulations of national identity during the slavery era can help us better understand the origins of our current situation and perhaps improve the troubled relationship between two geographically close nations.

Works Cited

Ard, Patricia. Introduction. *Juanita: A Romance of Real Life in Cuba Fifty Years Ago*. By Mann, UP of Virginia, 2000, pp. xi-xxxviii.

Cámara, Madeline. "Ochún: una metáfora incompleta en la cultura cubana." *South Eastern Latin Americanist*, vol. 42, no. 2-3, 1998, pp. 21-28.

Cervantes Saavedra, Miguel de. *El ingenioso hidalgo Don Quijote de la Mancha*. Madrid, Espasa-Calpe, 1969.

Cooper, Michaela B. "Should Not These Things Be Known? Mary Mann's *Juanita* and the Limits of Domesticity." *Reinventing the Peabody Sisters*. Edited by Monika M. Elbert, Julie E. Hall, and Katharine Rodier, U of Iowa P, 2006, pp. 146-62.

DeGuzmán, María. *Spain's Long Shadow: The Black Legend, Off-Whiteness, and Anglo-American Empire*. U of Minnesota P, 2005.

Del Monte, Domingo. *Escritos de Domingo del Monte*. Vol. 1, introduction and notes by José A. Fernández de Castro, Havana, Cultural, S.A., 1929.

Elbert, Monika M., Julie E. Hall, and Katharine Rodier. "Introduction: Reinventing the Peabody Sisters". *Reinventing the Peabody Sisters*. U of Iowa P, 2006, pp. vii-xxi.

―――, editors. *Reinventing the Peabody Sisters*. U of Iowa P, 2006.
Gómez de Avellaneda, Gertrudis. *Sab*. Edited by Mary Cruz, Havana, Instituto Cubano del Libro, 1973.
González Echevarría, Roberto. "Cervantes en *Cecilia Valdés*: Realismo y ciencias sociales." *Revista Canadiense de Estudios Hispánicos*, vol. 31, no. 2, 2007, pp. 267-283.
―――. "Latin American and Comparative Literature." *Comparative Cultural Studies and Latin America*. Edited and introduction by Sophia A. McClennen and Earl E. Fitz, Purdue UP, 2004, pp. 89-104.
Haberly, David T. "Reopening *Facundo*." *Bulletin of Hispanic Studies*, vol. 85, no. 1, 2008, pp. 47-61.
Harvard, John C. "Mary Peabody Mann's *Juanita* and Martin R. Delany's *Blake*: Cuba, Urban Slavery, and the Construction of Nation." *College Literature*, vol. 43, no. 3, Summer 2016, pp. 509-540.
Kutzinski, Vera M. *Sugar's Secrets: Race and the Erotics of Cuban Nationalism*. UP of Virginia, 1993.
Lazo, Rodrigo. "Filibustering Cuba: *Cecilia Valdés* and a Memory of Nation in the Americas." *American Literature*, vol. 74, no. 1, 2002, pp. 1-30.
―――. *Writing to Cuba: Filibustering and Cuban Exiles in the United States*. U of North Carolina P, 2005.
Luis, William. *Literary Bondage: Slavery in Cuban Narrative*. U of Texas P, 1990.
Mann, Mary Peabody. *Juanita: A Romance of Real Life in Cuba Fifty Years Ago*. 1887. Edited and introduction by Patricia M. Ard, UP of Virginia, 2000.
―――, editor. *Life Among the Piutes*. 1884. By Sarah Winnemucca Hopkins. Introduction by Russ and Anne Johnson, Bishop, Chalfant P, 1969.
―――, translator. *Life in the Argentine Republic in the Days of the Tyrants; or Civilization and Barbarism*. 1845. By Domingo Faustino Sarmiento. New York, Collier, 1961.
Marshall, Megan. *The Peabody Sisters: Three Women Who Ignited American Romanticism*. Boston, Houghton Mifflin, 2005.
Masiello, Francine. "Diálogo sobre la lengua: colonia, nación y género sexual en el siglo XIX." *Casa de las Américas*, vol. 34, no. 193, 1993, pp. 26-36.
Montalvo y Santa Cruz, María de las Mercedes, Countess of Merlin. *Los esclavos en las colonias españolas*. 1841. Linkgua, 2014.
Peabody, Elizabeth. Explanatory Note. *Juanita: A Romance of Real Life in Cuba Fifty Years Ago*. By Mann, UP of Virginia, 2000, p. 223.
Pratt, Mary Louise. *Imperial Eyes: Travel Writing and Transculturation*. New York, Routledge, 1992.
Rivera Casellas, Zaira. "La poética de la esclavitud (silenciada) en la literatura puertorriqueña: Carmen Colón Pellot, Beatriz Berrocal, Yolanda Arroyo

Pizarro y Mayra Santos Febres." *Cincinnati Romance Review*, vol. 30, 2011, pp. 99-116.

Sommer, Doris. *Foundational Fictions: The National Romances of Latin America*. Berkeley, U of California P, 1991.

———. *Proceed with Caution, When Engaged by Minority Writing in the Americas*. Harvard UP, 1999.

Schulman, Ivan A. Prológo. *Cecilia Valdés, o La loma del Ángel*. 1882. Caracas, Biblioteca Ayacucho, 1981, pp. xix-xvii.

———. "Reflections on Cuba and Its Antislavery Literature." *Annals of the Southeastern Conference on Latin American Studies*, vol. 7, 1976, pp. 59-67.

Suárez y Romero, Anselmo. *Francisco, El ingenio o las delicias del campo. Novela cubana*. 1839. Miami, Mnemosyne Publishing, 1969.

Tanco Besmeniel, Félix M. *Petrona y Rosalía*. 1838. Havana, Editorial Letras Cubanas, 1980.

Stowe, Harriet Beecher. *Uncle Tom's Cabin*. 1852. Edited by Jean Fagan Yellin, New York, Oxford UP, 1998.

Williams, Lorna Valerie. *The Representation of Slavery in Cuban Fiction*. U of Missouri P, 1994.

Windell, Maria A. "Moor, *Mulata*, Mulatta: Sentimentalism, *Racialization*, and Benevolent Imperialism in Mary Peabody Mann's *Juanita*." *J19: The Journal of Nineteenth-Century Americanists*, vol. 2, no. 2, Fall 2014, pp. 301-329.

Velleman, Barry L. *"My Dear Sir": Mary Mann's Letters to Sarmiento (1865-1881)*. Buenos Aires, Instituto Cultural Argentino Norteamericano, 2001.

Villaverde, Cirilo. *Cecilia Valdés, o La loma del Ángel*. 1882. Caracas, Biblioteca Ayacucho, 1981.

Zambrana, Antonio. *El negro Francisco, novela de costumbres cubanas*. Edited by Salvador Bueno, Havana, Editorial Letras Cubanas, 1979.

La superficie cóncava del primer cielo. Sobre la liminalidad de los *periplos angulares* al Lago Español de Álvaro Mendaña, Isabel de Barreto y el don Quijote portugués, Pedro Fernández de Quirós[1]

Vicente Pérez de León
University of Glasgow

I. Introducción

A LA PREGUNTA AL descubridor Pedro Fernández de Quirós por parte de un indígena del sur del Pacífico sobre quién eran, de donde venían y qué querían, la respuesta fue que procedían del este, que eran cristianos y que pretendían que ellos también lo fueran (Kelly 21).

Gustavo Bueno, en su prólogo a la obra de Pedro Pisa, *Caminos Reales de Asturias,* titulado "Homo viator. El viaje y el camino," distingue que "La idea del espacio antropológico que utilizamos es, desde luego, la idea de un espacio o symploké tridimensional, organizada en torno a tres ejes (C circular, R radial y A angular)."[2] Bueno, uno de los filósofos más originales del siglo veinte español, describe así el primero de ellos:

---

1 Este ensayo ha sido posible gracias a una "Dyason Fellowship" de la Universidad de Melbourne, la cual me permitió investigar en la biblioteca de la universidad de Carolina del Norte, la Nacional de Madrid y la Estatal de Victoria. En forma de comunicación, este trabajo fue presentado en el XXX congreso de la AISO, en julio de 2017 en Madrid.

2 Bueno continúa:

Cuando se cree haber descubierto la esfericidad de la Tierra, el viaje máximo, o pleno, será el viaje de circunvalación, el periplo o revolución máxima. Parece ser que el primero que pudo intentar un viaje máximo fue Alejandro (según nos cuenta su biógrafo Arriano). De hecho, ni siquiera lo realizó; y por eso hay que dejar pasar casi diez y nueve siglos, los que van del siglo III antes de Cristo al

Es evidente que el viaje «revolucionario», el *periplo,* como figura del eje circular del espacio antropológico, se configura, en principio, en este eje circular, [...]. El viajero, al volver, ha de *contar* su viaje; y el *contar* o el *relatar* es tan importante o más como el retorno físico. [...] El viaje canónico consistirá por tanto en el alejamiento de un grupo respecto de su pueblo, del pueblo que permanece en la patria; el viaje es público: no es una huida, implica una despedida.

Bueno incluye los viajes de Mendaña y de Quirós dentro de los periplos:

Por supuesto, los viajes de circunvalación de la Tierra no son los únicos que se ajustan al canon; ellos son los que se ajustan en su sentido más pleno. Pero también son viajes canónicos los viajes de Colón, o los viajes de Alvaro de Mendaña por las islas del Pacífico (1567, 1595) o el viaje de Pedro Fernández de Quirós, desde El Callao (21 de diciembre de 1605) a Méjico y luego a Madrid (9 de octubre de 1607), al que vuelve para contar, en más de cincuenta memoriales, que ha descubierto *Austrialia.*

Las travesías angulares estarían conformadas por aquellas con un sentido espiritual transcendental:

En cuanto al momento angular cabría decir que, a través de él, los viajes pueden alcanzar una dimensión directamente religiosa [...]. Una perspectiva que no estaría presente en los otros casos, y ello sin perjuicio de que, oblicuamente, los viajes pudieran tomar connotaciones religiosas, por ejemplo, por las oraciones o ceremonias que los acompañan. Pero ahora los viajes no sólo alejan al viajero de su posada: le acercan al mundo en el que habita algún numen divino. [...] Por supuesto, los viajes poéticos que Dante nos describe en *La divina comedia,* el viaje a los infiernos o el viaje a los cielos, son viajes imaginarios pero intencionalmente religiosos.

Sobre los viajes españoles al sur del Pacífico que nos ocupan se acumuló tempranamente evidencia acerca de la ausencia de la abundancia material es-

---

siglo XVI, para que pudiera tener lugar el primer viaje real de circunvalación a la Tierra, el viaje de Magallanes y Elcano: viaje también de grupos, que tomaron contacto con otros grupos, que fueron prolijamente relatados por sus cronistas. El viaje de Elcano se ajusta plenamente al canon del viaje máximo, dentro del eje radial: *Primum circumdedisti me.*

perada, en unas legendarias islas que se suponían habían sido descritas en la Biblia. Estas travesías fueron originalmente concebidas como viajes transcendentales, con la intención de regresar para contarlo. La tendencia del primer al hipotético cuarto viaje variará desde un sentido inicial como periplo hacia los confines de los territorios correspondientes al imperio español, hasta un viaje angular, de misión espiritual, a medida que se iba conociendo mejor la zona explorada y la naturaleza de sus habitantes. Es decir, que un periplo en busca de lo idílico material se convirtió en un viaje en el que el destino era, eminentemente, una misión espiritual. Esta transición coincide con el encargo de la responsabilidad de la empresa de Álvaro de Mendaña a Isabel de Barreto, entre el primer y segundo viaje, tras lo que Fernández de Quirós organizará el tercero. De hecho, de entre la evidencia del cambio en el sentido de la motivación del tercer periplo destaca el deseo de Fernández de Quirós de crear una nueva orden de caballería, la cual se adaptaría al residuo del paraíso espiritual que creía haber encontrado. La causa del fracaso final de su periplo angular tiene que ver con el hecho de que, aunque para Fernández de Quirós la motivación de la aventura espiritual era suficiente, éste no era el caso para la mayoría de su tripulación.

En este ensayo se ofrecen interpretaciones de varios de los testimonios del conjunto de los tres viajes al Pacífico por parte de Álvaro de Mendaña, Isabel de Barreto y Fernández de Quirós de finales del siglo dieciséis y principios del diecisiete, a partir de su sentido como, lo que denominaremos, uniendo ambos conceptos propuestos por Bueno, *periplos angulares*.

En aras de ilustrar el estudio de la liminalidad de estos viajes al lago español, consistente en la dificultad de situarse entre el original periplo planeado, basada en la vana esperanza de encontrar legendarias tierras bíblicas y el realista viaje angular materializado en las tres empresas españolas durante los reinados de Felipe II y III, se aportarán detalles sobre la naturaleza de la cosmovisión neoplatónica cristiana que guiaba a los descubridores. La presencia subyacente de la asunción de los límites del universo tolomeico con los del cielo católico serán complementarios en los textos de las crónicas de estos primeros exploradores españoles al Pacífico desde el Perú. Ahondándose en el sentido transcendental de esta serie de viajes transcontinentales al sur de las Filipinas, se estudiarán también detalles que delatan cómo se entendía la estructura del universo conocido en el contexto ideológico de la colonización de la *Terra Australis Incognita*, algo concebido por un tipo de descubridores-misioneros creacionistas del perfil de Álvaro de Mendaña y Pedro Fernández de Quirós. Esto servirá para entender mejor la complejidad y diversidad de propósitos del sistema colonial español en este período histórico. Éste incluye condicionantes ideológicos como es una concepción del mundo asociada a una estructura clásica, tolomeica y pitagórica leída a lo sagrado, con la cual se aportaba un orden inapelable, a partir del cual se interpretaba, tanto la realidad conocida, como aquella que no lo era todavía.

Con la aquiescencia de la Corte y de Roma, tanto Mendaña como el propio Fernández de Quirós pudieron consumar un total de tres viajes, desde Perú a Oceanía, en busca de establecer contacto con la *Terra Australis Incógnita*. En el primer periplo, los españoles encuentran tierras que se identifican con el territorio legendario y paradisiaco lleno de aquellas riquezas que le llegaban al rey Salomón cada tres años. Este detalle se describía en el *Libro de los Reyes* y las *Crónicas* bíblicas, lo que llevará a darle el nombre del legendario monarca a esta serie de islas vírgenes del sur del Pacífico. El hecho de que la mítica fuente de la abundancia salomónica nunca se hará presente en el primer viaje no fue óbice para que no se financiarán dos más todavía, además de buscarse medios para realizar una cuarta expedición, la cual finalmente nunca se llevará a cabo. Y es que, tras regresar de su tercer periplo, Fernández de Quirós dedicará el resto de su existencia a convencer infructuosamente a Felipe III de la necesidad de financiar la colonización espiritual de lo que él pensaba que era la mítica *Terra Australis Incognita*. Atendiendo a su propio testimonio, su ferviente creencia religiosa y pasión por regresar al Pacífico le llevarán a escribir hasta cincuenta memoriales a su rey. Su intención era convencerle de lo necesario de su proyecto, convirtiéndose en un personaje más de la corte madrileña y coincidiendo en esos mismos años con otros escritores del período como el propio Cervantes. De hecho, su firme convencimiento y actitud infatigable recuerda, siquiera vagamente, a la del protagonista cervantino más popular, como han apuntado algunos estudiosos como Pinochet de la Barra. La relación entre la exploración de Quirós y Don Quijote tiene, por cierto, mucho sentido. De la misma manera que Don Quijote encuentra en La Mancha el no-espacio o utopía necesaria para la acción caballeresca que reside en su mente, Quirós creyó ver realizada su propia y paradisiaca utopía. Su acción fue dirigida por el deber de ordenar espiritualmente a los habitantes de estas tierras, situándolos bajo el orden católico, tras recordarles la palabra de Dios que habían olvidado. Desde 1606, hasta poco antes de su muerte en 1614 en Panamá, Fernández de Quirós, muy presente en la corte madrileña, hizo valer, a quien le quisiere escuchar, su relato sobre la existencia de habitantes sin cristianizar, en tierras que se prolongaban al sur de lo conocido, en lo que podía ser la mítica Java la Grande de Marco Polo.

En los memoriales de Fernández de Quirós se aprecia que el descubridor de origen portugués era muy consciente de la importancia espiritual de su periplo a una *Terra Australis Incognita* poblada por descendientes del paraíso terrenal. Por ello, decidió poner todo su empeño en volver y concretar así su misión espiritual. El desmedido afán de Fernández de Quirós en regresar a la *Terra Australis Incognita* encenderá acusaciones contra él por parte de otros expedicionarios que fueron testigos de sus acciones. El caso más llamativo fue el de Diego de Prado, el cual llegará a advertir a Felipe III en contra de financiar un nuevo viaje de Fernández de Quirós, recomendándole atarle por loco y mentiroso. Sobra decir que su naturaleza indiscreta no era del gusto de la Corte, por el peligro de que su plan pudiera llegar a oídos de potencias extranjeras.

De entre las fuentes sobre los tres viajes españoles al Pacífico sur desde Perú destacan las aportadas en las crónicas y memoriales de testigos como Torquemada, Luis Arias, Diego de Prado, Váez de Torres, Diego de Córdoba y Juan de Merlo, que han sido estudiados por historiadores como Justo Zaragoza, P. Celsus Kelly, Francisco Morales Padrón y más recientemente por Mercedes Maroto Camino, entre otros. Es de destacar el trabajo comparado de los principales documentos de los hechos acontecidos en los tres viajes por parte de Kelly. De entre los detalles más literarios de las aventuras españolas en el Pacífico sur llaman la atención dos en concreto, con reminiscencias cervantinas. Por un lado, el que varias relaciones del viaje de Fernández de Quirós fueran elaboradas por Luis Belmonte, autor de una perdida segunda parte del *Coloquio de los perros*, entre otros textos literarios que incluyen varias comedias. Por otro, la citada, recurrente y posterior a su muerte comparación de Fernández de Quirós con una especie de Quijote del Pacífico.

En el planteamiento de la colonización espiritual de la *Terra Australis Incognita*, España se adelantará a las potencias rivales del momento, principalmente a Inglaterra, Francia y Holanda. El deseo de viajar a este océano fue un hecho histórico lógico debido, tanto al progreso científico en el arte de marear, como al deseo de completar la misión de cristianizar a los pobladores de los rincones más recónditos del planeta, iluminando con la palabra de Dios a todo aquél que no la conociere. El que la mítica *Terra Australis Incognita* se asociara con tierras del Pacífico a partir del encuentro con culturas isleñas del norte convirtió esta parte del mundo en un objetivo atractivo para las potencias europeas más técnicamente preparadas en este tipo de viajes. Sin embargo, desde el viejo continente, la cantidad de medios necesarios para el empeño era muy superior al caso de que el periplo partiera desde el Perú. No sólo se hacía el viaje mucho más breve, acortado por la disminución de la distancia entre meridianos cuanto más al sur se dirigiera el barco. El descubrimiento del navegante Andrés de Urdaneta en 1564 de una corriente marina circular en el Pacífico posibilitaba el regreso favorable desde las Filipinas hasta las costas pacíficas españolas, en lo que se denominó el tornaviaje, otorgando una ventaja más a España. El dominar la mayoría de los territorios que costeaban el lado americano del Pacífico no sólo facilitaba la propia partida en busca de la *Terra Australis Incognita*, sino también el apoyo que necesitaba el barco después de su largo viaje de regreso a la América española, tras su llegada en una situación muy precaria.

A pesar de la reciente "pacificación" de gran parte de las zonas americanas en conflicto, posterior a la conquista de las Filipinas y con un sólido vínculo comercial gracias el Galeón de Manila, la expansión comercial de la parte del imperio español del Pacífico no fue tomada en mucha consideración. En parte se debió a la propia evidencia de los descubrimientos de las gentes y territorios del sur del Pacífico en islas que se llamaban Salomón, pero que se supo muy pronto que no gozaban de la riqueza mítica asociada a ellas. A pesar de todo, en ciertos españoles permanecía existiendo una especie de "obligación histórica" hacia esa parte del mundo. De hecho, los territorios explorados correspondían a los asignados en el tratado de Tordesillas, cuyo meridiano dejaba la, por entonces desconocida de Occidente, costa oriental de las tierras por entonces denominadas por los españoles, en honor a los Austrias, Australia. Ésta incluía entre sus meridianos lo que es hoy es Melbourne y Tasmania, como parte de las tierras que España había asumido la obligación de cristianizar.

En definitiva, el devenir natural de las primeras exploraciones al sur del Pacífico se produjo en un momento histórico favorable a que se pretendiera consumar el encuentro con la única parte de la tierra no explorada, la *Terra Australis Incognita*. Ante la imposibilidad de establecer lazos comerciales, por no existir una cultura comercial similar a la potencia colonizadora, como sí ocurría en Filipinas y China, junto a la obligación de otorgar derechos similares a los de los indios americanos, a los que no se les podía esclavizar, la principal motivación para continuar siendo parte de esta empresa para hombres como Fernández de Quirós será la de iluminar las almas de sus habitantes con la palabra de Dios. Existe evidencia de que éste fue el caso, no sólo en el trato otorgado a los nativos en su encuentro con los españoles, sino también por la inclusión en el tercer viaje de familias y animales para fundar asentamientos en los que se conviviera en armonía e igualdad con los aborígenes de esta zona del mundo.

En este sentido, el proyecto colonial español del sur del Pacífico no sólo fue muy distinto al original colombino, sino también a la posterior colonización del resto de potencias europeas en esta zona del planeta. En el momento en que Mendaña y Fernández de Quirós realizan sus viajes se respeta firmemente el libre albedrío en el consentimiento para ser convertido, al igual que ocurría con el matrimonio, como no se cansaba de repetir en algunos de sus famosos entremeses y novelas Cervantes, asunto respetado en las misiones para la conversión de los nativos del Pacífico en fieles a la religión católica. El trato de respeto obligado, consecuencia jurídica que tiene su origen en la controversia entre Bartolomé de las Casas y Sepúlveda, que fue implementado a partir de Carlos V, será respetado rigurosamente por los jefes de las expediciones transpacíficas, como se aprecia en los testimonios de los encuentros con los nativos durante los tres primeros viajes al lago español entre Perú y el Pacífico Sur. A pesar de que se dieron inevitables escaramuzas con heridos y muertos por ambos bandos, tanto Mendaña como Fernández de Quirós mantendrán unos códigos de respeto en sus encuentros con los nativos que incluían costumbres como el que sólo se permitiera emplear la fuerza cuando peligrara la propia vida de los exploradores, o que se prohibiera terminantemente subir mujeres al barco.[3] Esto marcará la diferencia entre esta exploración y las agresiones masivas llevadas a cabo por los marineros de las potencias europeas en viajes posteriores, en injusto pago a la, en la mayoría de los casos, amabilidad e inocencia indígena.[4] De hecho, las diversas

---

3   Concretamente, el trato otorgado a las mujeres indígenas del Pacífico Sur por parte de las expediciones peruanas fue humano y respetuoso, especialmente en relación al que se les dará más de un siglo después por parte de los marineros de otras potencias europeas: "Cook seemed to think that the economies established by his voyages drastically affected women's decisions to become what he perceived as sexual commodities, either of their own volition or from coercion within their own societies" (O'Brien 77), algo que confirma el propio capitán Cook:

> The gallantry of our people in general made them very anxious to pay some compliment to the young lady, as "twas the first female we had seen for many months, but the young gypsy did not seem at all inclined to repay them in the kind Indian women in general trade in and indeed the kind that's most welcomed I believe by all men after so long an absence from the sex." [...] The seamen were as eager as ever in purchasing curiosities, and as pieces of cloth were usually given in exchange, most of them, as the Captain remarks, were "stripped of the few clothes the ladies of Otaheite had left them." (Young 199)

4   Existen numerosas fuentes de los abusos llevados a cabo en el Pacífico: "The historian Greg Dening estimates that by the time the Bounty sailed for Pitcarin, more than 130 islanders had been killed at Tubuai and Tahiti" (Sturma 41). Igler resume su devastador efecto antropológico:

narraciones de estos tres viajes al Pacífico Sur que se conservan denotan una actitud altruista, que tiene muy en cuenta el lado espiritual y civilizador por parte de sus primeros navegantes. Estos testimonios evidencian la ausencia de cualquier referencia al objetivo de despojar y someter a los nativos de las islas del Pacífico por un interés puramente material. Tras estudiar el diario de Fray Martín de Munilla, junto a otros documentos relevantes sobre el viaje de Fernández de Quirós a los Mares del Sur, Kelly confirma que la prioridad de la misión española será siempre el bienestar espiritual de los nativos, por encima de cualquier afán de medro.[5]

> What conclusions can be drawn from these sexual encounters in the Pacific? First, sexual relations permeated contact situations throughout the region: sex was part and parcel of the unequal material, cultural, and epidemiological exchanges that transformed the region in the late 1700's and early 1800's. Second, while these intimate relations ranged in nature from consensual affairs to mass rape, some level of coercion led young women to employ their bodies for the satisfaction of foreign men. The promise of material gain—for themselves, their elders, or in the case of enslaved women, their masters—increasingly structured sexual dealings with outsiders. Finally and most important, these sexual relations held consequences for women's reproductive functions in society and catastrophic costs for indigenous health. Venereal diseases introduced to native women and men rapidly spread through families and communities. Fertility and birthrates plummeted, while disfigurement and chronic ill health became common. Infant mortality rates rose, as did adult mortality through combinations of other introduced diseases. (52)

5   Como defiende Kelly:

> [. . .] Mendaña and Quirós, who were at once misioneros and descubridores, the motives were in the best traditions of Spanish exploration. [. . .] How was the Spaniards' right to preach the gospel to be exercised in the Indies? The theologians approached this question again with the utmost deliberation. Force might justly be used against the Indians only if absolutely necessary to exact respect for the Spaniards' right to preach. The rejection of the gospel by those preached to confer no right to punish them or to occupy their lands. Those preached to were no subjects of the king of Spain so could not be forced even to listen to the preachers [. . .] Force would be licit only as a last resort. [. . .] The emphasis was always on the conversion of the natives of the Austral Lands to Christianity (which included their humane treatment) and their submission to the obedience of the royal crown of their own free will. [. . .] The pages of Quiros' narrative which record his dealing with the natives are imbued with a

La suma de la falta de motivación, tanto por parte de los regidores de las Indias como de la propia Corte, de seguir sufragando misiones como las propuestas por Fernández de Quirós, unida a la fama de fantasioso que se granjearía este navegante en la Corte española, se añadirá a la necesidad constante de mano de obra para trabajar en las Indias. Por estas razones, se impidió que el sueño utópico de la colonización española de la *Terra Australis Incognita* favoreciera la ansiada conversión de las almas de los indígenas de estos lares del Pacífico. La posibilidad de la existencia de Java la Grande o *Terra Australis Incognita* era antigua, legendaria, mítica, tal y como había quedado reflejada en las obras geográficas clásicas y mapas desde tiempos de los autores pitagóricos, principalmente tras Tolomeo. Después del descubrimiento de América, los avances en la técnica de la navegación conducirán inevitablemente a un renovado interés en tener noticia de la *Terra Australis Incognita* por parte de los europeos.[6] A pesar de las exploraciones llevadas a cabo entre el siglo dieciséis y diecisiete, continuará la confusión del descubrimiento de la Antártida con el de la actual Australia. Se llegará a considerar ambas como parte de un mismo territorio, cuyas costas quedarán mucho tiempo sin navegar y cartografiar, presunción que todavía se mantendrá al menos durante más de un siglo.

II. Periplos angulares al Pacífico

El estudio de textos de autores místicos como San Juan de la Cruz y Fray Luis de León, en el contexto de las crónicas de los dos viajes al Pacífico de Álvaro de Mendaña, Isabel de Barreto y el tercero protagonizado por Pedro Fernández de Quirós, confirma una serie de coincidencias en el modo en

---

warm humanity, springing from his religious convictions. The natives, whatever their colour, were God's creatures; [...] (19, 16, 18, 85)

6   Se han mencionado otras fuentes como las de Bartolomé Ruiz, Pedro Simón, Pedro de Aedo, Sarmiento de Gamboa y La Gasca (Morales Padrón 987). De hecho, este último creía que al bajar en el Pacífico al paralelo de Guinea se podrían encontrar riquezas similares a las de esas tierras africanas. El primer explorador español en aventurarse a intentar encontrar la *Terra Australis Incógnita* fue Alvaro de Mendaña, del cual se cree que tenía conocimiento de un relato que recoge Morales Padrón sobre "un indio llamado Chepo de unos 120 años (que) había contado al capitán Francisco de Cáceres que los indios de Arica e Ylo navegaban en dos meses alcanzando una isla despoblada llamada Coatu [...]." se aportarán numerosos detalles sobre el nombre de sus señores, sus animales, etc., que parecen ser confirmados por el explorador Juan Montañés que avistó tierra al Sur de América cuando viajaba de Chile a Perú (Morales Padrón 986).

que se aborda el conocimiento del Empíreo durante este período. Tanto la fantasía de los místicos, condicionada por su fe, como la imaginación de los exploradores, se eleva ante la ausencia de instrumentos necesarios para medir la distancia con las estrellas y por tanto los límites de la bóveda celeste. La creencia en un espacio indefinido entre el primer cielo y el ámbito divino no sólo despertó la fantasía de la fenomenología mística, sino también alimentó la imaginación narrativa en la descripción de inusuales fenómenos naturales en las relaciones de viajes. En la tradición bíblica se alude tan solo al primer y tercer cielo respectivamente; los que ocupan los planetas y galaxias por un lado y por otro aquél en el que se encuentra el paraíso. Cuando se menciona el lugar en el que habita Dios se alude tan solo al "cielo." En la tradición posterior se describe una clasificación de los niveles celestiales mucho más elaborada, con un primer cielo que incluye la luna, el sol y las galaxias, llegando hasta un tercer cielo que sería el paraíso, tras el que se encontraría Dios. Este tipo de descripciones culminará con la más somera, llevada a cabo por Dante.

En su proyecto de exploración de la tercera tierra, tanto Álvaro de Mendaña y en mayor medida Pedro Fernández de Quirós, navegante portugués siempre al servicio de la corona española, al estar unificados ambos reinos en el tiempo que le tocó vivir, se encontrarán con extremas dificultades. Éstas no les impedirán entregar su vida, como fue el caso del primero, o dedicar prácticamente toda su existencia, como le ocurrirá al segundo, a poder llevar a cabo su misión de salvar las almas de los habitantes de la *Terra Australis Incognita*.[7]

---

7   En una reciente entrevista a Enrique Vidal, investigador del programa *Carabela*, buscador de palabras en manuscritos marítimos en su contexto, relata el descubrimiento de un texto del padre Andrés Serrano donde, cien años después del viaje de Quirós, continuaba con su misión original de exigir a la Corona la organización de viajes al Pacífico Sur, tanto para salvar las almas de sus habitantes, como para repoblar esas tierras:

> Vidal relata que un día preparaba una presentación de «Carabela» para un congreso de informática en Australia y le dio por buscar «Austral». Y ahí apareció un documento relevante para rescatar la historia española del continente austral: la carta al rey escrita el 10 de junio de 1710 por el procurador jesuita de las misiones de Manila, padre Andrés Serrano. Está a punto de partir hacia las «otras islas australes» y le relata: «La tierra que azia esta parte Austral del mundo está debajo de la demarcación de vuestra Real Corona y Patronazgo es en su longitud tanta como Europa, Asia menor y hasta el Caspio y la Persia, con todas sus islas». Cita el jesuita a Luis Vaez de Torres y Fernando de Quirós como navegantes que avistaron estas tierras un siglo antes, y lamenta que no se hayan enviado armadas a explorarlas, «una materia de tan importantes consecuencias

Fernández de Quirós no sólo morirá con dudas sobre si los habitantes de las islas recién descubiertas estaban solos o eran parte de tierra firme, sino también con su creencia de haber encontrado evidencia de los descendientes del paraíso terrenal (Kelly 13-14).

Las acciones que Fernández de Quirós llevó a cabo cuando llegó a la Austrialia del Espíritu Santo se han de entender en el contexto de un "descubrimiento ritualizado" con el que se pretendía establecer unos nuevos fundamentos para la convivencia entre los seres humanos. Existen referencias similares más recientes, las cuales responden a las descritas por Gustavo Bueno como angulares, también llenas de un profundo sentido religioso. En cierto modo, se pueden identificar, al seguir pautas similares, casos como el de Joseph Smith, fundador de la iglesia de los mormones. Antes de juzgar si Fernández de Quirós tenía un exceso de imaginación o ingenuidad a principios del siglo diecisiete para llevar a cabo sus planes de colonización espiritual, hay que recordar que el profeta americano decía haber accedido a través de un ángel a un documento en el que se aseguraba que Jesús había visitado a los indígenas norteamericanos. Por esta razón se sintió con la responsabilidad de viajar por el oeste americano para fundar una Iglesia al respecto en el siglo diecinueve, la cual ha sido hegemónica en el estado de Utah en los EEUU hasta en nuestros días.

La ausencia de referencias a aspectos económicos y materiales—oro, plata y especias—, unida a la imposibilidad de hacer esclavos, confirma la misión de Fernández de Quirós y sus colonizadores del Pacífico como un periplo angular. Bien se quiera pensar que fue a fuerza de que no se encontró la riqueza material que se esperaba, bien porque se considere que este principio espiritual estaba latente desde el inicio. En este sentido, la contradicción del viaje de Quirós es que sus escritos son evidencia de que él mismo estuvo inspirado por un afán puramente espiritual, en contra de la mayoría de los participantes de su expedición, aunque la generación de exploradores a la que perteneció

---

espirituales y temporales» porque ha llevado a «la perdición eterna de innumerables adultos» que han muerto sin ser evangelizados.

El padre jesuita, que moriría un año después, en octubre de 1711 en un naufragio en las islas Palaos por las que viajaba, añade que esas "otras islas son una pequeña parte de la otra tierra Austral; y conquistadas estas no es difícil el hacer pie e ir penetrando poco a poco por la inmensa tierra firme, que corre hasta 34 grados de la banda del sur y aun se cree que pasa más adelante azia el polo Antártico." La descripción es bastante exacta. Lo que hace después es tratar de convencer al rey de la facilidad para construir armadas pequeñas para ir poblando la tierra Austral. (García Calero)

Fernández de Quirós estuvo imbuida de un respeto elevado hacia los habitantes del Pacífico (Kelly 82). Los descubrimientos de Mendaña y Fernández de Quirós no solo tienen importancia por el progreso que supone en la historia de los viajes al Pacífico, sino también por el hecho de que sus memoriales se tradujeran a varios idiomas. De hecho, su elocuente y elogiosa descripción del Pacífico Sur será la que prevalezca en la mentalidad europea, al menos hasta el siglo diecinueve. En su propio tiempo, sus hazañas alimentarán un interés creciente por parte de otros navegantes y misioneros a viajar al sur del Pacífico en busca del paraíso terrenal de la *Terra Australis Incognita* descrito en sus viajes.[8]

Se da la paradoja de que la mayoría de los estudios postcoloniales que tratan de los viajes de Mendaña y Fernández de Quirós apuntan a que su propuesta de colonización fue un "fracaso," (Maroto 36)[9] al no tenerse en cuenta que el interés principal de la misión no era tanto la colonización material, el abuso, el saqueo y el despojo, como podría haber sido la práctica de la colonización anterior al debate de la Escuela de Salamanca o la posterior de otras colonias europeas. Muy al contrario, como se ha apuntado, le guiaba el hecho transcendental de creer haber descubierto el último reducto en el que se encontraban descendientes de los habitantes originales del paraíso bíblico, unido al deseo veraz de querer hacerles formar parte de una comunidad espiritual, en igualdad con los católicos españoles.

---

8   De hecho, la vida y obras de Quirós tuvo enorme difusión, sirviendo para inspiración futura:

> Quiros' name became a legend after his death, and his spirit lived on to inspire Fray Juan de Silva in his plan to make the whole South Pacific one vast Franciscan mission [. . .]. For the next century and a half, through his *Memorial* or derived accounts, he inspired Dutch, English and French navigators in their search for his Austral Lands. (Kelly 5)

9   La percepción peyorativa de Quirós y de Mendaña continua hasta hoy en día, al interpretarse como fallida la aproximación espiritual de su misión:

> The presentation of Quirós in his own writings and memorials is mostly aimed at self-promotion and is also highly baroque and rhetorical. Quirós is often seen as more humane than some of his contemporaries, but his humanitarian bent is often qualified by references to his uselessness as a leader, his bizarre mysticism and his erratic behaviour, especially in the second journey to the Pacific in 1605-6. [. . .]. Mendaña is often portrayed as a weak, incapable although humane, leader. (Maroto 44, 50)

A pesar de varias opiniones vertidas en los ataques contra Fernández de Quirós por parte de los marineros de su expedición, el sentido humanista de la misión de los líderes de los periplos angulares al Pacífico está fuera de toda duda. Esto, a pesar de que el episodio de los rituales ordenados por Fernández de Quirós para investir de un tono espiritual el acto del encuentro con lo que suponía los habitantes de la mítica *Terra Australis Incognita* tuviera el rechazo mayoritario de los franciscanos, que junto a su tripulación se burlarán de detalles tales como el de ofrecer la libertad a los esclavos. Fernández de Quirós decidió que fueran libres, como los propios habitantes de la recientemente descubierta isla, para pasar así todos a formar parte del igualitario paraíso terrenal. Éste no deja de ser un detalle más que confirma la naturaleza altruista y el deseo de que esta expedición sirviera para experimentar con la convivencia real de diferentes culturas, bajo un régimen basado en principios del Humanismo católico, siempre inspirado en la descripción bíblica del paraíso terrenal.

En resumen, el sentido del viaje de Fernández de Quirós como empresa colonialista entró en conflicto con el de su idea del periplo angular, lo que se acentuó cuando el líder del tercer viaje español al sur del Pacífico desde Perú se opuso a imponer los criterios explotadores de saqueo y apropiación aplicados a los indígenas americanos de las primeras expediciones transatlánticas. Aunque la fama de Fernández de Quirós prevalecerá, inspirando a los colonizadores posteriores, que serán influidos por los originales o las traducciones de sus crónicas y memoriales, no será así la propia presencia de España en el Pacífico. Existe numerosa evidencia de la tradición de una negación cartográfica que evita reconocer el proyecto civilizador español en aquella parte del mundo,[10] el cual, de hecho, se interrumpirá prácticamente hasta la expedición científica de Malaespina a finales del dieciocho. Esto se deberá a varios

---

10   Como afirma Padrón:

> Spain's presence in the Philippines was problematic. Looking back on the colonial Philippines from a twentieth-century perspective, Katharine Bjork argues that they are better understood as a periphery of the Chinese world system rather than of an emerging European world system, one which remained "Spanish" only because of the commercial opportunities it presented for Mexican (not Peninsular Spanish) elites [. . .] any, Ortelius's Maris Pacifici may have had to López de Velasco's cartography, or some similar Spanish map, we must remember that the *Maris Pacifici* works to de-Castilianize the Pacific Ocean. Although it figures the Pacific with borders that are intriguingly close to those established by the line of demarcation and the antimeridian, it remains silent about both lines, and about Castilian claims. (50, 22)

motivos, de entre los cuales destacan tanto el alto coste de la empresa, como el tono altruista de los memoriales conservados y traducidos, todo lo cual no seducía a la monarquía para afrontar un proyecto que parecía carecer de una razón práctica para justificar el viaje. De hecho, mientras la inversión en estos periplos provenía de Perú y de España, el mayor beneficiario terminaría siendo el Virreinato de Nueva España y más concretamente Acapulco, que era donde recalaban las riquezas del comercio del Galeón de Manila.

III. Mística celestial y viajes al Pacífico

El primer viaje español al Pacífico Sur de finales del dieciséis por parte de Álvaro de Mendaña contará con el piloto mayor Hernán Gallego, veterano navegante, considerado uno de los mejores de su tiempo. Éste escribirá una relación en la que expone claves del laberinto que suponía la cosmovisión renacentista, ofreciendo detalles para comprender las diferentes posibilidades de imaginar la arquitectura de la realidad en este período. En el capítulo once de su crónica, titulado "De cómo se descubrió una isla y se reconoció la del volcán y la pérdida de la nao almiranta" (Mayor Zaragoza 58), se describe así el descubrimiento de un volcán.

> [...]; es todo pelado por no tener árbol ni cosa verde, sino una color de tierra y piedras de extraña sequedad; tiene algunas hendidas, en especial dos a la parte del Oeste, y por ellas y lo más alto del cerro sale con estruendo mucha cantidad de centellas y tanto fuego, que puedo decir con verdad que diez volcanes que he visto, todos juntos no echan tanto fuego cuanto solo este echaba. Cuando se descubrió no se vió echar fuego; tenía una punta muy bien hecha, que a pocos días que se tomó puerto en la isla, descoronó, reventando con muy gran temblor, que con ser diez leguas distante de él donde surgió, se oyó y sintió moverse el navío; y de allí adelante, de cuando en cuando, había muy grandes truenos dentro de él, **y esto al salir de él fuego, y en acabando salía tanto y tan espeso humo que parecía tocaba la superficie cóncava del primer cielo, y después quedaba ordinariamente pruñendo.** (Mayor Zaragoza 61, negritas mías).

Al igual que en otras narraciones de viajes similares, la especulación de Hernán Gallego, sobre el itinerario del fuego y humo de un resonante volcán delata su concepción del cosmos. Particularmente, cuando describe los cielos que se alzaban por encima de la tierra, a los que alcanzaba un humo que "tocaba la superficie cóncava del primer cielo, y después quedaba ordinariamente pruñendo." De hecho, la concepción Ptolomeica del cosmos en tiempos de los viajes españoles al Pacífico no variaba mucho de la descrita por Manzolli en su *Zodiacus vitae*.[11] Domínguez complementa esta descripción, asociándola a los diferentes elementos:

> Los principales representantes de la cosmografía renacentista coincidían en la centralidad de dichos elementos, pero diferían en la manera en la que ellos estaban dispuestos. Existían tres maneras de representar la disposición de los cuatro elementos: 1) por sus cualidades (caliente, seco, húmedo, frío), 2) por sus propiedades (pesado, ligero) o 3) por cómo eran percibidos (Heninger 32). La más común de las representaciones era la que disponía en capas los elementos según fueran percibidos. La visión geocéntrica del universo procedente de la tradición ptolemaica proponía la esfericidad de la tierra articulada en cuatro esferas concéntricas (una para cada elemento) y rodeando é as se encontraban las siete esferas planetarias (una para cada planeta). La esfera más remota era la que contenía las estrellas del firmamento y se dividía a su vez en doce segmentos que representaban el zodiaco. (147)

De entre aquellos asociados a la mística destacará el fuego:

> Una estimación de las frecuencias absolutas, sin embargo, conduce a la conclusión de que el elemento rey es el fuego, seguido, a cierta distancia ya, del aire. Ambos etéreos, inasibles, carentes de sustancia propia—a diferencia de la materialidad de agua y tierra—y prefiguradores del dinamismo sublimador del espíritu. Ambos, también, encarnan valoraciones de virilidad, en oposición a la femineidad asumida por la tierra y el agua, principios pasivos frente a la actividad creadora de los primeros. (Mancho Duque 8)

---

11   The universe described in *Zodiacus Vitae* is based upon the traditional astronomy, which combined the physical theories of Aristotle with the mathematical calculations of Ptolemy. The earth is definitively placed immovable in the center of the universe, surrounded by the nine spheres which are conceived as material bodies. Every part of the universe is inhabited; as one ascends through the successive spheres, one passes through regions where ever more and more perfect beings have their dwelling places. [...] the sphere of the primum mobile surrounded by infinite space, occupied by no material body but filled only with purest light, and inhabited only by God and the highest order of spirits. (Johnston 103)

De hecho, para Telesio, el calor es el elemento fundamental asociado al movimiento:

> Telesio aspires, in effect, to erect the philosophy or science of nature upon the bases of:
> 1) Natural principles themselves, independent of theology.
> 2) Sensory experience, which produces the said natural principles and, in general, all of the information pertaining to natural philosophy. Heat is the principle of movement, making the corporeal matter into which it penetrates tenuous, rarefield, and light; cold is the principle of immobility, and it renders the matter it influences dense and heavy. [...] the universe is finite and that the two principles are located in its two opposing regions: cold in the central, immobile Earth and heat in the peripheral, moving heavens which encircle it (De rerum natura, 1586, I.1-4)

> Telesio retains the celestial spheres, which he considered to be solid bodies composed of the same igneous matter as the stars (though less substantial and dense, and therefore not heat-emitting). He also believed them to be the true source of celestial motion, responsible for propelling the stars. This theory of comets (without the miraculous intervention of God) is only compatible with the existence of celestial spheres if these spheres are penetrable, a conception which Telesio necessarily had to accept. (Granada 271-72).

El volcán descrito por Hernán Gallego combinará, de hecho, la presencia del fuego con su alcance a la superficie cóncava del cielo, en un mágico momento en el que también se desvela su cosmovisión humanista.

Un recorrido sobre el concepto de la superficie cóncava de los cielos nos retrae tanto a una obra clave sobre la escatología de la *Divina Comedia* de Asín Palacios, como al místico sufí andalucí Abenarabi, el cual sitúa el final de la superficie cóncava como el techo del paraíso, sin olvidar a autores como San Juan de la Cruz, el cual emplaza por encima de ese entorno la esfera donde se encuentra el Espíritu Santo. En el mismo campo de la mística cristiana, en la Oda XIII de Fray Luis sobre la vida del cielo, se aprecia otra aproximación a la concepción mística de la superficie cóncava del Empíreo. Allí se lee que, tras la esfera alrededor de la cual circula el sol en su recorrido, alcanzando uno a llegar a oídos del creador, que está vestido de pastor.[12] De este

---

12 Alma región luciente,
 prado de bienandanza, que ni al hielo

ni con el rayo ardiente
fallece; fértil suelo,
producidor eterno de consuelo:

de púrpura y de nieve
florida, la cabeza coronado,
y dulces pastos mueve,
sin honda ni cayado,
el Buen Pastor en ti su hato amado.

Él va, y en pos dichosas
le siguen sus ovejas, do las pace
con inmortales rosas,
con flor que siempre nace
y cuanto más se goza más renace.

Y dentro a la montaña
del alto bien las guía; ya en la vena
del gozo fiel las baña,
y les da mesa llena,
pastor y pasto él solo, y suerte buena.

**Y de su esfera, cuando
la cumbre toca, altísimo subido,
el sol, él sesteando,
de su hato ceñido,
con dulce son deleita el santo oído.**

Toca el rabel sonoro,
y el inmortal dulzor al alma pasa,
con que envilece el oro,
y ardiendo se traspasa
y lanza en aquel bien libre de tasa.

¡Oh, son! ¡Oh, voz! Siquiera
pequeña parte alguna decendiese
en mi sentido, y fuera
de sí la alma pusiese
y toda en ti, ¡oh, Amor!, la convirtiese,

conocería dónde
sesteas, dulce Esposo, y, desatada

mismo autor es la Oda III sobre "La música de Francisco Salinas llega a oídos de Dios a través de las esferas."[13] También se ofrece una referencia a las esferas celestiales cuando Amadís de Gaula elogia a Don Quijote de la Mancha en un soneto preliminar de su primera parte.[14] De hecho, en la segunda mitad

> de esta prisión adonde
> padece, a tu manada
> viviera junta, sin vagar errada. [...] (40-42 negritas mías)

13 El aire se serena
    y viste de hermosura y luz no usada,
    Salinas, cuando suena
    la música estremada,
    por vuestra sabia mano gobernada.

    A cuyo son divino
    el alma, que en olvido está sumida,
    torna a cobrar el tino
    y memoria perdida
    de su origen primera esclarecida.

    Y como se conoce,
    en suerte y pensamientos se mejora;
    el oro desconoce,
    que el vulgo vil adora,
    la belleza caduca, engañadora.

    Traspasa el aire todo
    hasta llegar a la más alta esfera,
    y oye allí otro modo
    de no perecedera
    música, que es la fuente y la primera.

    Ve cómo el gran maestro,
    aquesta inmensa cítara aplicado,
    con movimiento diestro
    produce el son sagrado,
    con que este eterno templo es sustentado. [...] (15-16 negritas mías)

14 Tú, que imitaste la llorosa vida
    que tuve, ausente y desdeñado sobre
    el gran ribazo de la Peña Pobre,
    de alegre a penitencia reducida;

del *Quijote*, Sancho también habla de las esferas terrestres y celestes desde el punto de vista de la Astrología.[15]

IV. Conclusión

La concepción tolomeica a lo sagrado del cielo, en el caso de las exploraciones al Lago Español, servirá como escenario místico en el intento de fundar una nueva sociedad cristiana igualitaria, reflejando un espíritu similar, por ejemplo, al que originará las colonias guaraníes Jesuitas. El deseo de encontrar aquellas tierras, de las que se beneficiaba el rey Salomón y procedían las riquezas que portaron los tres reyes Magos, que además se consideraban bíblicamente paradisiacas, había sido originalmente una motivación para los periplos angulares al Pacífico español que se producen a fines de siglo dieciséis. El ejemplo de la descripción del volcán pruñendo confirma que la descripción celestial tolomeica había adquirido un tono místico, particularmente en la interpretación del comportamiento del fuego ante el hombre cristiano consciente de la existencia de los diferentes niveles de la superficie cóncava del cielo. Esta descripción, combinada con la intención de Fernández de Quirós

---

tú, a quien los ojos dieron la bebida
de abundante licor, aunque salobre,
y alzándote la plata, estaño y cobre,
te dio la tierra en tierra la comida,

**vive seguro de que eternamente,
en tanto, al menos, que en la cuarta esfera,
sus caballos aguije el rubio Apolo,**

tendrás claro renombre de valiente;
tu patria será en todas la primera;
tu sabio autor, al mundo único y solo. [...]
(versos preliminares, I, negritas mías)

15   Y volviéndose al ama, le dijo: —Bien puede la señora ama no rezar más la oración de Santa Apolonia, **que yo sé que es determinación precisa de las esferas que el señor don Quijote vuelva a ejecutar sus altos y nuevos pensamientos**, y yo encargaría mucho mi conciencia si no intimase y persuadiese a este caballero que no tenga más tiempo encogida y detenida la fuerza de su valeroso brazo y la bondad de su ánimo valentísimo. [...] planetas, signos, puntos, medidas, de que se compone la esfera celeste y terrestre; que si todas estas cosas supieras, o parte d'ellas, vieras claramente qué de paralelos hemos cortado, qué de signos visto y qué de imágines hemos dejado atrás [...] (II, 7, negritas mías)

de fundar una orden religiosa adaptada a la inocencia de los seres con los que se encuentra, confirma que la falta de evidencia de riquezas no fue óbice para que se emplearán energías y recursos en la colonización espiritual de las tierras del Pacífico sur, al menos en estas tres ocasiones.

Los viajes desde Perú al Pacífico Sur en forma de colonización espiritual suponen una novedad que no se suele tener muy en cuenta en el contexto de los estudios postcoloniales. Aún menos, la original propuesta de crear una colonia basada en un espíritu igualitario y puramente religioso mediante una orden religiosa creada ad hoc. Del contraste con otras misiones colonizadoras espirituales, en las que se reproducen y proyectan ideas o mundos descritos en la Biblia, destacan las posibilidades reales de la existencia de la alternativa humanista católica de Fernández de Quirós a la hora de aminorar el impacto natural de un encuentro entre dos culturas distanciadas, tanto en su progreso tecnológico, como en sus concepciones del mundo. Al ser considerados seres inocentes descendientes de los primeros habitantes del paraíso terrenal, Fernández de Quirós contribuyó a propagar la idea, que perdura hasta nuestros días, de la bondad primitiva del ser humano en el Pacífico Sur, que tenía como precedente obras como *El Reloj de Príncipes* de Guevara, en la que se describe al villano del Danubio dentro del contexto de lo que se denomina un humanismo renacentista cristiano que rescataba la voz de los oprimidos (ver Bartra).

El viaje original de Fernández de Quirós, cargado del significado transcendental de poder ofrecer una oportunidad única a la nación española de encontrar míticas tierras bíblicas como la de Ofin, fue un *periplo angular*. Como afirma Bueno, el periplo no acaba nunca con la llegada al destino, sino que se prolonga con el proceso de relatar lo ocurrido. De esto es un buen ejemplo la propia existencia de Fernández de Quirós, la cual dedicará a la difusión oral y escrita la noticia del descubrimiento de lo que consideraba la *Terra Australis Incognita* o Austrialia del Espíritu Santo. Juzgándole por sus acciones, Fernández de Quirós merece ser honrado y recordado como uno de los humanistas católicos más íntegros que han existido, aún tan siquiera por su veraz intención de aceptar pretender integrar honestamente como iguales a los descendientes de Dios, indígenas del Pacífico Sur. Su contribución al origen y perpetuación del mito de su bondad ha contribuido en parte a su supervivencia hasta nuestros días. Esto no se da en el caso de otras muchas aventuras coloniales anteriores y posteriores, las cuales se guiaron por el interés de un despojo sostenido que provocaría la práctica extinción de los aborígenes en los territorios sometidos.

Obras citadas

Asín Palacios, Miguel. *La escatología musulmana en* La divina comedia, Imprenta de Estanislao Maestre, 1919.

———. *El místico murciano Abenarabi*, Revista de archivos, 1928.

Bartra, Roger. *El salvaje artificial*, Destino, 1997.

Bueno, Gustavo. "Homo viator. El viaje y el camino." Prólogo a *Caminos reales de Asturias* de Pedro Pisa, Pentalfa, 2000, http://www.filosofia.org/aut/gbm/2000pisa.htm.

Cervantes, Miguel de. *Don Quijote de la Mancha*, dirigido por Francisco Rico https://cvc.cervantes.es/literatura/clasicos/quijote/edicion/parte1/versos_preliminares/ amadis_de_gaula/default.htm y https://cvc.cervantes.es/literatura/clasicos/ quijote/edicion/ parte2/cap07/cap07_02.htm.

De la Cruz, San Juan. *Poesía*, edición de Domingo Ynduráin, Cátedra, 1983.

De León, Fray Luis. *Obras del P. Fr. Luis De León: reconocidas y cotejadas con varios manuscritos auténticos*, edición de Antolín Merino y Conrado Muiños Sáenz, Compañía de impresores y libreros del reino, 1885.

Domínguez, Julia. "Coluros, líneas, paralelos y zodíacos": Cervantes y el viaje por la cosmografía en el *Quijote*," *Cervantes*, vol. 29, no. 2, 2009, pp. 139-57.

García Calero, Jesús. "La inteligencia artificial halla rastros del descubrimiento español de Australia." *Diario ABC*. Cultura. 15-10-2019. https://www.abc.es/cultura/abci-inteligencia-artificial-halla-rastros-descubrimiento-espanol-australia-201910130104_noticia.html.

Granada, Miguel Ángel. "New Visions of the Cosmos." Editado por Arthur S. McGrade. *Cambridge Companion to Medieval Philosophy*. Cambridge UP, 2007, pp. 270-86.

Igler, David. *The Great Ocean: Pacific Worlds from Captain Cook to the Gold Rush*, Oxford UP, 2017.

Johnston, Francis R. "Thomas Digges, the Copernican System, and the Idea of the Infinity of the Universe in 1576." *The Huntington Library Bulletin*, vol. 5, 1934, pp. 69-117.

Kelly, Celsus. *La Austrialia del Espíritu Santo: The Journal of Fray Martín de Munilla and Other Documents Relating to the Voyage of Pedro Fernández de Quirós to the South Sea (1605-1606) and the Franciscan Missionary Plan (1617-1627)*. Hakluyt Society, Cambridge UP, 1966.

Mancho Duque, María Jesús. "El elemento aéreo en la obra de san Juan de la Cruz: léxico e imágenes." *Criticón*, vol. 52, 1991, pp. 7-24.

Maroto Camino, Mercedes. *Producing the Pacific: Maps and Narratives of Spanish Exploration (1567-1606)*, Rodopi, 2005.

Morales Padrón, Francisco. "Los descubrimientos de Mendaña, Fernández de Quirós y Váez de Torres y sus relaciones de viajes." *Anuario de Estudios Americanos,* vol. 24, 1967, pp. 985-1044.

O'Brien, Patty. *The Pacific Muse: Exotic Femininity and the Colonial Pacific,* University of Washington Press, 2006.

Padrón, Ricardo. "A Sea of Denial: The Early Modern Spanish Invention of the Pacific Rim." *Hispanic Review,* vol. 77, no. 1, 2009, pp. 1-27.

Pinochet de Barra, Oscar. *Quirós y su utopía de las Indias Australes,* Cultura Hispánica, 1989.

Sturma, Michael. *South Sea Maidens: Western Fantasy and Sexual Politics in the South Pacific,* Greenwood Press, 2002.

Young, George. *The Life and Voyages of Captain James Cook,* Whittaker, Treacher, 1836.

Zaragoza, Justo. *Historia del descubrimiento de las regiones australes hecho por el general Pedro Fernández de Quirós,* Imprenta de Manuel G. Hernández, 1876.

"Melancólico espejo": From Garcilaso's "Églogas" to Luis Cernuda's *Égloga, elegía, oda*

DAVID F. RICHTER
Utah State University

I. INTRODUCTION

THE INFLUENCE THAT RENAISSANCE and Baroque Spanish poets had on later Iberian poetic movements is undeniable. Writers including Garcilaso de la Vega, Fray Luis de León, Fernando de Herrera, Luis de Góngora, and others provided the lyrical foundations for writers of the Romantic period, like José de Espronceda and Gustavo Adolfo Bécquer; for Avant-garde poets such as Pedro Salinas, Luis Cernuda, Federico García Lorca, and others; and also for writers of some of the most recent poetic promotions in Spain, including the "poets of experience" and contemporary poets like Juan Antonio González Iglesias and Aurora Luque, who also espouse core tenets of classical poetic traditions.

The poetic production of Spain's Golden Age is comparable in richness only with what critic José-Carlos Mainer and others have called Spain's *Edad de Plata*, that period of modernist and avant-garde expression of the first four decades of the 20th century. Notwithstanding the originality of those writers of the modern age, their innovations and experimentations with pure poetry, ultraísmo, and surrealism were firmly rooted in Spain's own lyrical traditions. This impact was so important for the Generation of '27 writers, for example, that many of them congregated at the Ateneo of Seville in 1927 in homage to and celebration of Góngora and his poetry. While for many of these poets, such as for Lorca, Góngora served as a literary father due to his ability to "*cazar* las metáforas" (García Lorca 60), for others, like Cernuda, it was Garcilaso's work that proved most inspiring and led him to declare that Garcilaso was the "maestro del lenguaje más sutil y penetrante que haya en nuestra lírica" (*Estudios* 17). Indeed, as a young writer Cernuda was seduced by what Edward Friedman calls Garcilaso's principal achievement: the combination of "radical stylization with emotional depth" ("Realities" 57).

Luis Cernuda (Seville, 1902–Mexico City, 1963) was first introduced to poetry in 1911 while just eight or nine years old through his readings of Bécquer, during the same period that the Romantic poet's remains were transferred from Madrid to the chapel at the University of Seville (Cernuda, *Prosa* 625–26). Cernuda later enrolled as a student at the University of Seville during the 1919–1920 academic year and continued his study of literature in courses taught by Pedro Salinas. The next five years were formative for the young poet as he participated in literary gatherings at Salinas's home and tried his hand at the writing and publication of some of his own poems. The role of Salinas during this time cannot be overstated. It is during this period that Cernuda "hace la lectura y relectura de Garcilaso" (Zuleta 403) and that Salinas "le guió en sus lecturas de la poesía clásica española: Garcilaso, Fray Luis de León, Góngora, Lope de Vega, Quevedo, Calderón" (Harris, "Introducción," *Perfil* 23). Cernuda would reflect on the impact of Salinas many years later in his 1958 autobiographical essay, "Historial de un libro," where he writes, "No sabría decir cuánto debo a Salinas, a sus indicaciones, a su estímulo primero; apenas hubiera podido yo, en cuanto poeta, sin su ayuda, haber encontrado mi camino" (*Prosa* 627). Still under the tutelage of Salinas, and following the appearance of a few of his own poems in *Revista de Occidente* in 1925, Cernuda published his first volume of poetry, *Perfil del aire*, in April of 1927.

Written between 1927 and 1928, Cernuda's second collection of poems, *Égloga, elegía, oda*, constitutes "ejercicios sobre formas clásicas" (Zuleta 419) that echo Golden Age lyrical motivations and owe a clear debt to both Fray Luis and Garcilaso.[1] Rather than an adherence to the exuberant *gongorismo* that so enchanted his colleagues, Cernuda's collection is more aligned with the somber lament and melancholy emblematic of the suffering shepherds of Garcilaso's "Églogas," all the while demonstrating a "milagroso dominio del lenguaje lírico" (Mainer 227). The engagement with these literary precursors was certainly influential for Cernuda and highlights his deep understanding of the literary tradition while at the same time recognizing his own re-vision of it. As poet and critic Luis Antonio de Villena suggests:

> Cernuda va *avanzando* a través de encuentros, relecturas, aquiescencias o remodelaciones de otros poetas (Mallarmé, Garcilaso, Bécquer, Hölder-

---

[1] In addition to the powerful influence that Garcilaso exercised on Cernuda, the poet from Seville was also affected by the works of poets from classical Greek and Latin traditions. The interested reader could refer to Jesús Bermúdez Ramiro's study "El mundo clásico en la poesía de Luis Cernuda."

lin...), lo que en ningún caso supone imitación—tal vez sí, *imitatio*—ni plagio, ni epigonismo... [...] La poesía—todo arte—no es cabriola en el vacío, sino la afirmación querida y singularizada de una tradición de palabra y cultura. (22)

Even though Cernuda's *Égloga, elegía, oda* does not tell the traditional eclogue story of tormented pastoral lovers, it employs other natural Renaissance motifs borrowed from Garcilaso such as the rose, the water, the wind, and the rain, which all tend toward darkness and silence—that Cernuda calls the "melancólico espejo" (106)[2] in his 130-line "Égloga" and what critic Gustavo Correa refers to as the "vacío cósmico en Cernuda" (75). The present study examines Cernuda's "Égloga" from *Égloga, elegía, oda* in the context of Garcilaso's second "Égloga," underscoring not only the young Cernuda's reliance on Garcilaso's classical forms, themes, and tones emblematic of Golden Age lyrical tendencies, but also Cernuda's modern innovation of poetic forms and expression in his earliest poetic endeavors. In fact, as I will demonstrate here, Cernuda's early poems serve as a type of melancholy mirror-image of Garcilaso's work, only to be followed by more rebellious and violent incarnations characterized by the surrealist image, uprooted exile, and socio-political protest in later texts such as *Un río, un amor, Los placeres prohibidos, Las nubes,* and *Desolación de la Quimera*.[3]

II. Garcilaso and the Poetics of Suffering

Like most poems written in the pastoral tradition, which "sought to imitate and celebrate the virtues of rural life" (Strand and Boland 207), Garcilaso's three Églogas tell the stories of love, desire, deception, loss, suffering, and death. In the first part of the 421-line first eclogue, we read of the lamentations of two pastoral lovers, first Salicio, then Nemeroso. Salicio sings a "dulce lamentar" (1),[4] a pain harder to bear than the strength of marble, due to Galatea, who has deceived him and fled with another man. Salicio's "quejas"

---

2   All references to Cernuda's poetry come from *Obra completa. Vol. 1. Poesía completa*, edited by Derek Harris and Luis Maristany. In-text parenthetical documentation of poetry throughout this essay refers to poetic line numbers.

3   James Verlander traces the beginnings of Cernuda's surrealist inclinations to his readings of André Breton and Paul Éluard, which occurred in 1927 while he was writing *Égloga, elegía, oda* (31–32). The melancholy and anguish noted in Cernuda's earliest poems is greatly amplified in his more aggressive and somber works often qualified as surrealist.

4   All references to Garcilaso's poetry come from *Obra poética*, edited by Bienvenido Morros.

(57) direct the reader to the surrounding environment that witnesses to his suffering: the sunshine, the trees, the birds, the mountains, the valleys, the green grass, and the white lilies—all aspects of the *locus amoenus* that has been lost. Salicio speaks in hyperbole to emphasize the gravity of his suffering ("estoy muriendo" (60)), and 11 consecutive stanzas all repeat the same *estribillo*, "Salid sin duelo, lágrimas, corriendo." This apostrophe suggests at once the "exteriorización irreprimible del dolor íntimo, del corazón o del alma," as Adrien Roig notes (166), as well as the lengthy temporal duration of the suffering, which appears to last nearly an entire day. In the second part of the first eclogue, we read of Nemeroso, whose lover Elisa has died. Nemeroso sings of the "corrientes aguas, puras, cristalinas" (239), the birds, and the green fields that attest to the "grave mal que siento" (246). Nemeroso's concern is rooted in the Renaissance theme of *ubi sunt*, the pondering of where the dead reside once they pass away. Like Nemeroso, the pain seems unbearable and the poetic narrator of the stories states that "Nunca pusieran fin al triste lloro / los pastores, ni fueron acabadas / las canciones que solo el monte oía" (408–10).

In the first eclogue, like in the two that follow, anguish is given intensity through the "balance of discourse and emotion," thus confirming Edward Friedman's assertion that, in Garcilaso's poetry, "the human side cannot separate itself from the poetic side, and suffering is made poetic" ("Afterword" 291). Dedicated to the "hermosísima María" (2) the poetic voice of Garcilaso's third and final eclogue recounts stories told by four nymphs that emerge from the Tajo river. The 376 lines tell stories of love, dedication, death, and sorrow, first from Filódoce, who tells of Orfeo and Erídice; then from Dinámene, who sings of Dafne and Apolo; then Clímene, who speaks of Venus and Adonis; and finally from Nice, who re-tells of Nemeroso's heartbreak due to the death of Elisa. In his lectures on the varied representations of material reality in Spanish poetry, Pedro Salinas suggests that Garcilaso's poems highlight "a society in which sensitive souls lament over the ruin of a twilight" (73). While Garcilaso's poems depict a persistent idealization of reality, in each case that yearning for beauty, harmony, and perfection is counterbalanced by themes of loss and suffering.

In the second eclogue, the longest and most ambitious of all of Garcilaso's compositions at 1,885 lines, we read initially of the tormented lover Albanio whose love goes unreciprocated by the beautiful Camila, and then the lengthy story and the "tan estraño cuento" (1830) of the supernatural powers of Severo and the exploits of the Alba family, as told by Nemeroso. Scholars have criticized this eclogue, written around 1533, for its apparent lack of unity and internal coherence, with its first half focusing on the anguish of Albanio, and the second half jumping to the story of the Duque del Alba. However, the two stories are intertwined in the final moments as Salicio suggests that they take Albanio from the initial narration to Severo from the other story to be healed of his discontent.[5]

From the initial lines of the second eclogue, Garcilaso presents a text based in continual longing and pain, all the while connected to the natural elements of his surroundings. When looking at the "agua dulce desta clara fuente" (2), Albanio recalls memories of past and present desire: "¡Oh claras ondas, cómo veo presente, / en viéndoos, la memoria d'aquel día / de que el alma temblar y arder se siente!" (4–6). The mirror image from the pond serves as the starting point for introspection and the memory of "aquel día," which induces bodily quivering and heat. The exclamation points emphasize the intensity of the memories as well as the seriousness of Albanio's paradoxical "dulce murmurar" (13) that is mimicked by the sounds of the "mover de los árboles al viento" (14) and the "suave olor del prado florecido" (15). The constant references to the natural environment are central to Renaissance lyrical motivations. In fact, for Salinas, "[b]ucolic poetry is supposedly nature poetry: its scene is the country; [. . .] Nature is a sort of agent of God" (78). Speaking on Garcilaso's *carpe diem* sonnet, "En tanto que de rosa y azucena," Edward Friedman reminds us of a core tenet in the Golden Age writer's oeuvre: "Garcilaso's sonnet contains a commentary on the paradoxical nature of change; nothing is constant but mutability, the poet informs us" ("Golden" 47). Oftentimes this representation of temporal change is portrayed metaphorically through the annual seasons and the recurrent cycles of nature, and Garcilaso's work is no exception. While Albanio's description of Camila is initially portrayed in naturalistic terms, this serves not only to suggest that her beauty is akin to the most idealized elements of the natural world, but also to intimate that, like nature, temporal processes will lead to decadence and loss; that is, the invocation "[¡]oh claros ojos, oh cabellos d'oro, / oh cuello de marfil, oh blanca mano!" (20–21) will later lead to "daño / que tiene mi alma casi consumida" (26–27).

Albanio's love for Camila is projected onto all the beauty that he sees in nature, the natural elements such as the "alto pino" (52), "alguna robusta y verde encina" (53), "el ganado contando" (54), and "la verde selva" (56), all of which witness of his immense heartbreak. Spent of his will to lament any more, Albanio, "cansado y afligido" (100), succumbs to sleep. After a brief moment when Albanio recounts his projected desires of reclining in the

---

5   For a brief history of the formal difficulties of this text, see Audrey Lumsden's assessment in "Problems Connected with the Second Eclogue of Garcilaso de la Vega," pp. 251–57.

green grass with Camila, she appears only to disappear once again, leaving Albanio tormented beyond repair, and as "los despojos / de un cuerpo miserable y afligido" (567–68). He enters into a state of terminal madness and the other shepherds, Salicio and Nemeroso, provide a sounding board for his cries. Throughout the Albanio and Camila story, Garcilaso uses a tone of loss and despair, which is emphasized repeatedly by use of hyperbole. For example, we could consider the gravity of agonic exaggerations from Albanio over the course of the second eclogue: Albanio's despair is such that the pain penetrates him "hasta el hueso" (145); Camila is "aquélla por quien muero" (163); he exclaims that, "solté la rienda al triste llanto" (562) and "¡Oh modo de matar nojoso y triste! / ¡Oh muerte llena de mortal tardanza[!]" (870–71); Albanio later cries that "el cuerpo se m'ha ido" (890) and "hice de mis lágrimas un río" (490); the suffering shepherd "en cadenas" (934) declares that, "[n]o hay bien ni alegre cosa ya que dure" (981), and Albanio finally asks desperately, "¿No me ves como un muerto? Pues ¿qué hago?" (1029). These hyperboles throughout the eclogue serve as a constant reminder of the desperation felt by Albanio in his memory of Camila and the lamentations caused by her rejection. Indeed, the lyrical subjects throughout Garcilaso's eclogues, and his other poems for that matter, give voice to the idealization, beauty, yearning, vigor, loss, and sorrow inherent to Spanish Renaissance poetry.

III. Cernuda between Longing and Loss

The poetic tradition of longing and suffering left by Garcilaso was integral in the poetic formation of the young Luis Cernuda. His mentor Pedro Salinas declared that "to no poet does Spanish poetry owe more than to Garcilaso. [...] Garcilaso is a poet of love. The same sentiment of melancholy and hopeless love pervades his whole work, a love that is ever aspiration and reminiscence, delicate and quivering, as though it were floating in the air and had no earthly domain on which to rest" (76, 77). Nearly 400 years later, and focusing on the bleak tone and hopeless state of Albanio, Cernuda praised Garcilaso as a starting point for his own youthful despair. According to one critic, "Cernuda había encontrado en el estilo poético de Garcilaso un símbolo para su concepción personal de lo clásico en la literatura española. [...] Lo que es innegable es que Cernuda nunca hablaría con tanto entusiasmo de la obra de otro poeta del orbe hispánico. Esto es inobjetable para quien lea la totalidad de sus ensayos críticos" (Muñoz Covarrubias 193, 196). Garcilaso's *églogas* afforded Cernuda a language of intense desire and longing, in conjunction with torment and anguish—persistent feelings that would permeate the Sevillian's work from its inception.

The four poems from Cernuda's *Égloga, elegía, oda* were written between July of 1927 and July of 1928, and they exemplify a clear homage to classical

Renaissance styles and authors such as Fray Luis and Garcilaso. Speaking of this collection of poems, and noting the stark contrast between Cernuda's work and that of the rest of the Generation of '27 writers, renowned Cernuda critic Derek Harris concludes that,

> [e]stos poemas largos añaden al estilo simbolista un tono clásico que viene directamente de Garcilaso, cuya fluidez y elegancia melódicas se oyen, sobre todo, en las estancias de la "Égloga" y la "Oda". La presencia de Garcilaso se destaca contrastada con el entusiasmo por Góngora que florecía en aquel momento. Cernuda tomó su pequeña parte en el homenaje a Góngora, pero aceptó como modelo a Garcilaso, como para señalar su individualidad y la independencia de la moda. La exuberancia metafórica de Góngora no iba bien con la melancolía adolescente de sus primeros poemas, mientras que la elegancia contenida de Garcilaso concordaba perfectamente. ("Introducción," *Poesía* 51)

Cernuda appreciated the emotion and sensitivity in Garcilaso's laments (in addition to the anguish and melancholy evident in his lines), and this appears most pronounced in Cernuda's "Égloga." In his 1958 essay, Cernuda stated that "[m]i amor y mi admiración hacia Garcilaso (el poeta español que más querido me es), me llevaron, con alguna adición a Mallarmé, a escribir la 'Égloga'" (*Prosa* 631). In his study of Garcilaso and Cernuda, Miguel García-Posada writes that Cernuda's homage to Garcilaso "[e]s una deuda profunda, de espíritu, de visión [...], que a veces emerge en forma de préstamos muy asimilados" (1).

Structurally, the eclogue by Cernuda is much more in line with Garcilaso's *second* eclogue than with his first or third. Cernuda follows the versification and rhyme scheme of Garcilaso's second eclogue, with the same consonant rhyme pattern, heptasyllabic and hendecasyllabic lines, and 13-line stanzas. However, Garcilaso's poem is much longer, with nearly 2,000 lines in comparison to Cernuda's 130 line poem (10 stanzas of 13 lines each), and Garcilaso's poem also contains numerous tercets and quartets, which Cernuda omits. Cernuda's poem also connects with the Renaissance themes of Garcilaso's second eclogue. In the 130 lines of the 1927 "Égloga," "no falta ninguno de los elementos que caracterizan el *locus amoenus*: sombra, agua, hierba, brisa, flores; incluso incorpora otros de los tópicos de la bucólica: por ejemplo, terminar el poema con la llegada del atardecer" (Márquez 290). But Cernuda's poem portrays a pastoral scene gone awry. Rather than telling of lovers' feuds, projected desires, and the fall to existential madness, Cernuda focuses on the melancholy tone of nature in decline, with virtually no connection to any metaphorical human relationship. As Miguel Márquez suggests, "en ese paisaje no aparecen los actores del drama bucólico; el paisaje está solitario" (290). Instead, this poem ignores self and other and, perhaps as a defense mechanism, it creates a distance between nature and the lyrical "I."

In Garcilaso, Cernuda finds a pastoral language and series of natural motifs that fit his youthful experimentation with poetic forms and his budding somber vision of reality. From the beginning of the "Égloga," one senses a cyclical pattern of rising to the Platonic heights in desire and aspiration, and then falling to the depths of silence and darkness, confirming Derek Harris's contention that the dominant emotion of Cernuda's early poems, "es la melancolía, que transforma el simbólico paisaje risueño y primaveral en una escena otoñal de tristeza y frío" ("Introducción," *Poesía* 59). Cernuda accomplishes this by portraying the natural consequences of plant growth, wind and rain, personified frustration of desire embodied by the plant life, and the subsequent silence, fall, and darkness. In the initial lines of the text, Cernuda discusses the architecture of a tree branch "tan alta, sí, tan alta" (1) that reaches for the sky. The upward reach of the "rama el cielo prometido anhela" (3) directs the attention toward upward yearning and desire for the heavens. On the upper branch of the tree, the rose flower "asume / una presencia pura / irguiéndose en la rama tan altiva" (14–16). But by the third stanza we notice the beginning of a downward fall that will end in complete darkness:

> Si la brisa estremece
> en una misma onda
> el abandono de los tallos finos,
> ágil tropel parece
> tanta rosa en la fronda
> de cuerpos fabulosos y divinos.
> ¡Rosados torbellinos
> de ninfas verdaderas
> en fuga hacia el boscaje!
> Aún trémulo el ramaje
> entre sus vueltas luce prisioneras
> de resistente trama
> las que impidió volar con tanta rama. (27–39)

After drawing our attention to the sky, this section and the rest of the poem focus on the forest floor as the wind catches the tree limbs and the rose petals scatter and fall downward. The image of the rose, so important in literary expression for centuries, appears here only to wither. For Emilia de Zuleta,

Cernuda's usage of the rose motif contains within it inherent contradictions of both perfection and destruction:

> A partir de la imagen de la rosa con su presencia pura, y del agua gozándose a sí misma, se va perfilando un ambiente natural animado y poblado de presencias fabulosas. El poeta enumera los signos que componen su cuadro de perfección, pero en ese gozo sin afanes parece que la vida se sofocara y que la gracia de las formas ocultara el germen mismo de la tristeza. (420)

The wind here denotes change and abandonment. Cernuda's "language of flowers" speaks of the imminent fall to oblivion.

Through a movement of descending climax, and with the gaze directed downward, Cernuda's poem now focuses on the pond below, an image similar to that of Garcilaso's second eclogue. Cernuda's poem reads:

> Entre las rosas yace
> el agua tan serena
> gozándose a sí misma su hermosura.
> Ningún reflejo nace
> tras de la onda plena
> fría, cruel, inmóvil de tersura.
> ....
> Plenitud sin porfía.
> Nula felicidad; monotonía. (40–45, 51–52)

Contrary to Garcilaso's ponds, here there is no reflection, suggesting at once the absence of human interaction and a lack of connection to another. Even after the falling rain, the only presence is "algún eco" (66), "ese vapor sonoro; fría vena" (68), and the "confuso hueco" (69)—each image invoking the empty spaces and vacated sounds of loneliness and the abyss.

The images here borrow the melancholy and suffering of Albanio in Garcilaso's text, but they amplify the darkness and emptiness that anticipate the surrealistic "hombre gris" (1) or "cuerpo vacío" (2) from Cernuda's "Remordimiento en traje de noche," which would appear just two years later in *Un río, un amor*. In this sense, and in line with the budding avant-garde tendencies in Cernuda's work, Gustavo Correa suggests that, "[l]a mirada contemplativa de Cernuda se separa, así, de la de Garcilaso, al introducir un proceso de abstracción que se halla de acuerdo con el arte contemporáneo de intención cubista" (83). After "la dicha se esconde" (92) in Cernuda's "Égloga," the reader is confronted with additional images of melancholy and loss. Rather than a reflection of memories of a heartbroken past, Cernuda outlines the pond like this in the penultimate stanza of the poem:

> Sobre el agua benigna,
> melancólico espejo
> de congeladas, pálidas espumas,
> el crepúsculo asigna
> un sombrío reflejo
>
> ....
>
> Tanta dulce presencia
> aun próxima, es ausencia
> en este instante plácido y vacío,
> cuando, altísimo monte,
> la sombra va negando el horizonte. (105–09, 113–17)

Through constant recourse to antithesis, Cernuda frames this scene in terms of the negation of pure forms: warmth turns to cold, light turns to shadow, presence turns to absence, and we witness the "afirmación absoluta de la soledad" (Márquez 290). The forest pond, seen here as a "melancholy mirror," only reflects the growing darkness that overtakes the natural space.

The downward movement of decay and shadow culminates in complete silence and darkness in the tenth and final stanza. Here the remaining light is consumed and the last bit of movement from the breeze ceases. For Correa, "[e]l paisaje desaparece, quedando la naturaleza sumida en el abismo nocturno" (85). All that is left is the melancholy void:

> Silencio. Ya decrecen
> las luces que lucían.
> Ni la brisa ni el viento al aire oscuro
> vanamente estremecen
> con sus ondas, que abrían
> surcos tan indolentes de azul puro.
> ¿Y qué invisible muro
> su frontera más triste
> gravemente levanta?
> El cielo ya no canta
> ni su celeste eternidad asiste
> a la luz y a las rosas,
> sino al horror nocturno de las cosas. (118–30)

In the final lines, we read that the heavens cease to communicate, and the light and flowers are separated from the eternities. The lack of human context in this poem, along with the distancing from reality, gives this text a more weighty despair than Garcilaso's second *égloga*, to which Cernuda pays direct homage. But what, in fact, is the poetic voice in Cernuda's eclogue lamenting? Could it be a lost love, a crisis of identity, the heavens withdrawn, the vague horror of the "cosas" from the final line?

Cernuda not only projects that relationships are failed, but the entire natural ambience is fallen; indeed, as Miguel Márquez writes, "llega la noche y el *locus amoenus* se transforma en *locus horridus*" (291). In his essay, "Historial de un libro," and with clear reference to his own homosexuality (according to James Verlander (32)), Cernuda himself states that he wrote these poems during a period when he felt "hostilidad hacia esa sociedad en medio de la cual vivía como extraño. Otro motivo de desacuerdo, aún más hondo, existía en mí; pero ahí prefiero no entrar ahora" (*Prosa* 632). Interestingly, the final images employed in this poem connect with motifs that appear in subsequent years in Cernuda's more aggressive surrealist poems as well as in texts written from exile, works where Cernuda is much more open about his sexuality and the persistent tension between reality and desire. In *Un río, un amor*, for example, the negation of the wind and the silent heavens seen in the "Égloga" appear as the empty wind (3) and "cielo implacable" (4) in "Remordimiento en traje de noche"; the "silencio" from the "Égloga" is shown "bajo la noche el mundo silencioso naufraga (9) in "Sombras blancas"; the darkness of this poem transforms into "la noche sin luz, en el cielo sin nadie" (40) in the final line in "Decidme anoche"; and the "invisible muro" that implies separation in the 1927 text appears in "Mares escarlata" as "Olvidado de todos, / su dolor contra un muro" (10–11). Similar motivations and images permeate *Los placeres prohibidos*, *Las nubes*, and *Desolación de la Quimera*, volumes that focus increasingly on the body, one's own truth, and the critique of modern society.

IV. Conclusion

A final intertext that seems relevant to the present conversation regarding Cernuda's dialogue with Garcilaso and the Renaissance themes that Cernuda incorporates into *Égloga, elegía, oda* is that of *Ocnos*, the Sevillian poet's collection of prose poems written primarily in 1940 and 1941 during his time in Scotland.[6] The texts of that collection "versan sobre la infancia y adolescencia del poeta," engage the memories and landscapes that influenced his youth, and

---

6   *Ocnos* was first published in 1942, later in an extended version in 1949, and finally in a definitive version in 1963, shortly after the poet's death.

concentrate "en la figura del Albanio, proyección del poeta con clara fuente en la 'Égloga Segunda' de Garcilaso" (Harris, "Introducción," *Poesía* 77–78). In prose poems including "Belleza oculta," "La catedral y el río," "Jardín antiguo," "El poeta," "La naturaleza," "El huerto," and others, the lyrical narrator recounts the experiences and concerns of Albanio, a suffering and anguished lover and alter ego of Cernuda himself. For Pablo Muñoz Covarrubias,

> [n]o debe resultar extraño que el personaje principal de *Ocnos* se llame Albanio, como uno de los pastores de la Égloga segunda de Garcilaso. La preferencia por aquel nombre seguramente se debe a su interpretación de lo bucólico: el mundo de las églogas del toledano lo remitía a un ámbito ideal, de perfección y de armonía incomparable, lo que fue un anhelo vital para Cernuda. (206)

Already in exile by the 1940s, Cernuda sought to recapture in *Ocnos* the remembrance of his youth in Seville, in conjunction with the nostalgia and melancholy that the recollection of his earliest years evoked. In these texts, we notice Albanio's first readings of Bécquer and Byron, his afternoons by the river, and the time he spent in his own *locus amoenus*, the lush gardens of the Alcázar of Seville.

The moments of satisfaction in *Ocnos* are tempered by loneliness and loss. In "Belleza oculta," for example, we read of Albanio's entrance into adolescence and the ensuing "aire de aquel campo entonces casi solitario," with the "habitación aún vacía," and "un sentimiento de soledad hasta entonces para él desconocido" (*Poesía* 565–66). Later, in "La catedral y el río," we learn of Albanio's afternoon next to the stream, where "en soledad de nuevo, el río era tan verde y misterioso como un espejo" (*Poesía* 567). In each of the poetic landscapes in the prose poems of *Ocnos*, Cernuda details the "destinos humanos ligados con un lugar o con un paisaje" (*Poesía* 568) and the natural environments that are evoked with nostalgia for the past idealization of nature. That beauty, however, is linked with the present sense of "melancolía y aislamiento que lo acompañaba" (*Poesía* 566).[7] By the end of Cernuda's "Égloga

---

7   Those interested in more information regarding the connection between Garcilaso's and Cernuda's usage of the Albanio figure can refer to the following resources: Mario Martín Gijón's article, "El poema en prosa como divinación autobiográfica en Luis Cernuda. De *Ocnos* a *Variaciones sobre tema mexicano*," especially pp. 556, 562, and 568; Aileen Anne Logan's recent dissertation, titled "Memory and Exile in the Poetry of Luis Cernuda," which focuses on Cernuda's poetry written in exile (see, in particular, pp. 103–28); and Julio M. de la Rosa's 2002 article in *El País*, titled "Albanio en el Edén."

from *Égloga, elegía, oda*, and throughout much of his poetic oeuvre, what remains as a result of longing and desire is a poetic environment centered on bleak absence, darkness, cold, and silence. The heavens are withdrawn and the subject remains in a barren wasteland. The melancholy mirror image of the pond in Cernuda's "Égloga" doubles all of this, as if the lyrical "I" were caught in the middle of the abyss that both rises above and descends below. If for Garcilaso the madness of Albanio is caused by the lover's lament of loss, for Cernuda, it seems that the anguish is brought on by more encompassing realities of one's identity and environmental surroundings, even the void created by existential melancholy, ever the impasse between reality and desire.

Works Cited

Bermúdez Ramiro, Jesús. "El mundo clásico en la poesía de Luis Cernuda." *Cultura, Lenguaje y Representación: Revista de Estudios Culturales de la Universitat Jaume I*, vol. 7, 2009, pp. 25–37.

Cernuda, Luis. *Estudios sobre poesía española contemporánea*. Ediciones Guadarrama, 1957.

———. *Obra completa. Vol. 1. Poesía completa*. Edited by Derek Harris and Luis Maristany, Ediciones Siruela, 2002.

———. *Obra completa. Vol. 2. Prosa 1*. Edited by Derek Harris and Luis Maristany, Ediciones Siruela, 2002.

Correa, Gustavo. "Mallarmé y Garcilaso en Cernuda: De *Primeras poesías* a la *Égloga* y la *Oda*." *Revista de Occidente*, vol. 145, 1975, pp. 72–89.

Friedman, Edward H. "Afterword: Redressing the Baroque." *Hispanic Baroques: Reading Cultures in Context*. Edited by Nicholas Spadaccini and Luis Martín-Estudillo, Vanderbilt UP, 2005, pp. 283–305.

———. "The Golden Age Sonnet: Metaphor and Metonymy, with a Difference." *Calíope: Journal of the Society for Renaissance and Baroque Hispanic Poetry*, vol. 5, no. 1, 1999, pp. 47–58.

———. "Realities and Poets: Góngora, Cervantes, and the Nature of Art." *Calíope: Journal of the Society for Renaissance and Baroque Hispanic Poetry*, vol. 8, no. 1, 2002, pp. 55–68.

García Lorca, Federico. *Obras completas. Vol. 3. Prosa*. Edited by Miguel García-Posada. Galaxia Gutenberg–Círculo de Lectores, 1997.

García-Posada, Miguel. "Cernuda y Garcilaso: Ecos garcilasianos en la elegía 'A un poeta muerto (F.G.L.)'." *Ínsula: Revista de Letras y Ciencia Humanas*, vol. 39, no. 455, 1984, pp. 1, 3.

Garcilaso de la Vega. *Obra poética*. Edited by Bienvenido Morros. Introduction by Rafael Lapesa, Editorial Crítica, 1995.
Gijón, Mario Martín. "El poema en prosa como divinación autobiográfica en Luis Cernuda. De *Ocnos* a *Variaciones sobre tema mexicano*." *Bulletin of Spanish Studies*, vol. 92, no. 4, 2015, pp. 549–69.
Harris, Derek. Introducción y estudio. *Perfil del aire. Con otras obras olvidadas e inéditas, documentos y epistolario*. By Luis Cernuda, Tamesis Books, 1971, pp. 11–101.
———. Introducción. *Poesía completa. Vol 1*. By Luis Cernuda, Ediciones Siruela, 2002, pp. 43–96.
Logan, Aileen Anne. "Memory and Exile in the Poetry of Luis Cernuda." Diss. University of St. Andrews, 2007.
Lumsden, Audrey. "Problems Connected with the Second Eclogue of Garcilaso de la Vega." *Hispanic Review*, vol. 15, no. 2, 1947, pp. 251–71.
Mainer, José-Carlos. *La Edad de Plata (1902–1939): Ensayo de interpretación de un proceso cultural*. Ediciones Cátedra, 1999.
Márquez, Miguel Á. "El *locus amoenus*: Ergon o Parergon en soledad." *Tropelías: Revista de teoría de la literatura y literatura comparada*, vols. 12–14, 2001–2003, pp. 285–92.
Muñoz Covarrubias, Pablo. "Garcilaso de la Vega y la crítica literaria de Luis Cernuda." *Anuario de Letras*, vol. 44, 2006, pp. 187–210.
Roig, Adrien. "Las lágrimas de Salicio en la 'Égloga primera' de Garcilaso de la Vega." *Actas de la Asociación Internacional de Hispanistas, 21–26 de agosto de 1995, Birmingham, Estudios Aureos II. Vol. 3*. Edited by Jules Whicker, U of Birmingham P, 1998, pp. 163–73.
Rosa, Julio M. de la, "Albanio en el Edén." *El País*, 20 March 2002, www.elpais.com/diario/2002/03/20/andalucia/1016580160_850215.html.
Salinas, Pedro. *Reality and the Poet in Spanish Poetry*. Translated by Edith Fishtine Helman, The Johns Hopkins UP, 1966.
Strand, Mark, and Eavan Boland, editors. *The Making of a Poem: A Norton Anthology of Poetic Forms*. W. W. Norton, 2000.
Verlander, James. "Luis Cernuda y el surrealismo: Primeras lecturas (1925–1928)." *I mondi di Luis Cernuda: Atti del Congresso Internazionale nel I centenario della nascita*. Edited by Renata Londero, Forum Editrice, 2002, pp. 31–41.
Villena, Luis Antonio de. Introducción. *Las nubes / Desolación de la Quimera*. By Luis Cernuda, Ediciones Cátedra, 1999, pp. 9–60.
Zuleta, Emilia de. *Cinco poetas españoles (Salinas, Guillén, Lorca, Alberti, Cernuda)*. Editorial Gredos, 1971.

Returning Home in Juan Ruiz de Alarcón's Plays
Gladys Robalino
Messiah College

THIS ESSAY IS ABOUT the representation of "retuning home" in the plays of Juan Ruiz de Alarcón. Though narratives about returning home are so old that they appear in both classical literature and the Bible, they have not been classified and studied as a literary genre until recently. In fact, serious studies of the phenomenon of human migration and counter-migration only began in the late twentieth and early twenty-first centuries. This is especially true when we observe the narratives of the diaspora of Spaniards to the New World and other places in the growing empire during the sixteenth and seventeenth centuries. The corpus of these narratives has been classified and studied as Colonial Literature with a focus on the encounter of Europeans and Natives as well as the hermeneutical process to make sense of that experience. Yet there are hardly any studies on the narratives about the reverse experience of returning to the homeland, Spain. The closest we get to seeing the experience of the returnees is in the caricatured representation of those returning from Indias (the "indianos") especially in minor literary genres like the *entremeses* and the picaresque. This stereotyped image of returnees shows how the locals perceived them and the kind of social issues they faced, but it does not provide the response and reaction of those returning home nor their own attempts to make sense of their experience. Maybe the destabilizing effect of the experience and the possibility of ending up even more alienated from the community restrained the returnees from speaking about it.

A peculiar case is that of Juan Ruiz de Alarcón. This playwright was born in New Spain in 1581. He experienced returning to his parents' homeland. He traveled to Spain in 1600 to continue his education in the Universidad de

Salamanca, returned to New Spain in 1608 and moved back to Spain permanently in 1613. He was able to experience what is called "roots migration"—a term accredited to Susanne Wessendorf to refer to the return settlement of second generation Italians in Switzerland, but later used by migration theorists to refer generally to second-generation return migration to the homeland. Ruiz de Alarcón's desire to continue his higher education in Spain reflected his career ambitions but also a desire to return to his cultural roots and recover his family ties with Spain. But, as explained by Helen Lee, while root migration can be for some a positive experience that "can reaffirm their sense of cultural identity," for others "[it] can have a negative impact, if they feel like 'outsiders' and perhaps even have their sense of identity challenged" (*Ties to the Homeland*, 20). As Lee points out, return migration can be more challenging for the second generation than for the first generation migrants "partly because they are inevitably perceived as 'different' from those remaining in the home country" (Conway and Potter 2007, cited in Lee, 21). While we can only speculate about how Ruiz de Alarcón felt upon going to Spain, the recurrent images of returning to the homeland and of the returnee as dramatic character in his plays offer a possible insight of the experience. Its reconstruction in the fictional space of the dramas can provide some patterns and consistencies around its emotional weight, its complexities, or the mechanisms to make sense of it. I propose this focus can reveal some of the issues, possibilities, and complexities of this experience of returning home. As Fatemeh Pourjafari and Abdolali Vahidpour have stated, literature is the best way to reflect on the "complex and ambiguous realities" around human experiences and particularly in migration where "the levels of ambivalence, of hybridization and plurality, of shifting identities and transnationalism are perhaps greater than in many other aspects of life." (679). The return to the homeland is an element of Ruiz de Alarcón's work that has not previously been explored, yet it is a theme that I believe deserves special attention in order to better understand how return migration destabilizes notions of home, belonging and cultural identity in his plays. To that aim, this essay centers on five characters from Ruiz de Alarcón's plays that return to Spain—the homeland—after a long sojourn abroad. It explores their particular characteristics and the circumstances that define their return, and it focuses on the emotional components that surround their experience and how these challenge each character's sense of cultural identity.

In Ruiz de Alarcón's plays, the emotional expectation for returning home is surrounded with an aura of joy. This is evident in *La culpa busca la pena y el agravio la venganza*[1] and *El semejante a sí mismo*.[2] In *La culpa*, the image of Spain that the returnee sees from the boat as he approaches is described in a happy, longing tone:

> Y un día, al correr su pabellón la aurora,
> que alegra a luces cuando a perlas llora,
> desde el tope, que sube
> a barrenar la más distante nube,
> un marinero experto,
> "¡Tierra, tierra!" en alegres voces dice;
> y a poco espacio el lusitano puerto
> felice vio quien le buscó felice; (431-38)[3]

In the background, we see the sunrise "que alegra a luces" and we can hear the sailor's voice setting the tone of the verses when he announces with "alegres voces" the sighting of the land. The words of the poetic voice end with the emotional effect this image causes in the viewer evidenced by the repetition of the word "felice" twice in the last verse. The sighting of the port produces an effect of excitement, joy, illusion, and hope that explodes in the shout "¡Tierra, tierra!" It is possible to note the intense happiness that the return home causes in the speaker. A similar tone appears in Sebastián's narration in *El semejante* when he recounts his return to Spain after being rescued from the ocean. The long and disconsolate account of the shipwreck contrasts with the anxious desire to return home that the narrator expresses in one verse, "vuelvo a España, y vengo a veros" (2730).

In contrast to the excitement associated with the expectation of returning home, a commonplace that we find in these plays is that the return itself results in disillusion, fear, threats, and danger. The homeland is not a place of safety for the returnees but rather a place that threatens them with loss of material possessions, social isolation, betrayal, and death. Nuño Aluaga, in *La crueldad por el honor*, for example, finds himself at the center of a major political crisis when he returns to Aragón, a crisis, which will ultimately result in his death. He had joined King Alfonso I of Aragón in the battle of Fraga. After the King's death and their defeat in battle, Nuño takes a pilgrimage to the Holy Land and returns to Aragón after 28 years. He finds out upon his re-

---

[1] I will refer to it as *La culpa* from here on.
[2] I will refer to it as *El semejante* from here on.
[3] It is necessary to clarify here that Portugal was part of the Spanish territories from 1580 to 1640 while these plays were written.

turn that "[t]odo en discordias se abrasa … " (93) in the city due to the long absence of the king. Several nobles were fighting over the throne of Aragón and Queen Petronila's hand in marriage. She had refused to marry again trying to save the throne for her own son, but ultimately causing more political unrest. Nuño gets at the center of the political upheaval when he decides to take advantage of the crisis and assume the identity of the King. He aims to both avenge his honor and place his own son in the throne of Aragón:

> NUÑO. Aparte (Vuestro valor
> anima, Sancho, mi intento.
> Nuño Aulaga, vuestro padre,
> hijo, os viene a levantar
> hoy al cielo, y a vengar
> la afrenta de vuestra madre.) (115-20)

This act of betrayal to his king and country will actually place Nuño in the opposite political faction of his son—who will stay loyal to the Queen and the heir prince—turning father and son into enemies. He not only fails to achieve his goal of gaining the throne for his son, but he is also unable to establish a relationship with him. Ultimately, Nuño dies at his son's hands, the son murders his father to avoid the dishonor that Nuño's treason would bring to the family.

Like Nuño, Garci-Ruiz from *Los favores del mundo* puts himself in a dangerous situation when he returns to Spain. Garci-Ruiz is a soldier who had been away fighting in Africa and other " … tan diversas partes" (65). He returns to Spain in secrecy to find Don Juan de Luna and avenge his honor after Don Juan slapped him with a glove believing the rumors that Garci-Ruiz had called him a coward. Their sea mates had prevented a fight between the two allowing Don Juan to escape. Garci-Ruiz had spent the next six years looking for him until he finally finds his enemy in Madrid. In the very first scene, he engages in a duel with Don Juan and wins, but ends up sparing his life when he hears Don Juan praying to the Virgin Mary. Because of this action, he receives the praise of the Prince and a habit (or knighthood status) from one of the military-religious orders of his choosing. The beautiful Anarda falls in love with Garci-Ruiz when she witnesses the fight. Anarda's affection however turns Garci-Ruiz into the rival of two powerful men in the court, the Prince and Count Mauricio. In the second act, Garci-Ruiz injures Mauricio in a fight, upsets the Prince and is a victim of Julia's lies about

Anarda. At multiple times, Garci-Ruiz expresses his confusion to the rapid changes of fortune in this world and the emotional effect this has on him:

> Hoy me vio el Príncipe, y hoy
> Me vi al más sublime estado
> De su favor levantado,
> Y ya derribado estoy
> En un infierno profundo
> De temor y de ansia fiera
> Paciencia: desta manera
> Son *Los favores del mundo*. (1625-32)

Garci-Ruiz articulates the feelings of fear and anxiety that he experiences as he tries to navigate the social conventions of this space and "el engaño y desengaño / de *Los favores del mundo*" (2410-11).

Also, Diego of *Los empeños de un engaño* finds himself in danger when he returns to Spain after being in the wars in Flanders. When he arrives in Seville, he meets Teodora. He follows her to Madrid where her suitor Don Sancho and Don Sancho's cousins gravely injure him during a fight when they find him in her home. Diego almost meets his demise in this adventure. Yet returnees are not always intentionally getting involved in dangerous situations. In some cases, danger finds them when they return to their homeland. Sebastián, in *La culpa*, had spent fifteen years in Indias when he received a letter from his father demanding his return. He interprets this demand as a bad omen: "cuando una carta de mi padre, ¡ay cielos! / cubrió tan clara luz de obscuros velos" (409-10). Indeed, he meets danger as soon as he sets foot on Spanish soil. In fact, his life is in danger twice while in the port of Seville. The first time, recounted by Sebastián's servant Motín, occurred when both went to swim in the Guadalquivir where Sebastián, "sin prevenir los azares / de su hondura, se arrojó" (661-62) and almost drowned. Don Fernando saves him by chance and they become good friends. The second time, while getting back to the inn, robbers attack Sebastián "... para quitalle / un diamante que traía / en el dedo..." (749-51). Again, Don Fernando saves him. Although these events help complicate the plot because, unbeknownst to Sebastian, he now owes his life to the one who insulted his father and injured his family's honor, both scenes emphasize the vulnerability of the returnee who comes into a world he does not know well. Sebastián is in danger as he tries to navigate a space that now seems new and alien to him.

Sebastián's risks do not end with these incidents. The threat to his life increases when Sebastián arrives in Madrid and falls in love with Ana, Fernando's sister. This immediately earns him Don Juan's animosity since he also loves Ana, though he is not reciprocated. Don Juan challenges Sebastián to a duel in Act II, scene III:

> en resolución sabed
> que si vos, como Faetón,
> el pensamiento atrevéis
> al sol que adoro, esta espada
> un rayo ardiente ha de ser,
> que en vuestras cenizas llueva
> escarmientos otra vez. (1084-90)

Fernando arrives in time to stop the fight forcing both of them to put their swords away. Nonetheless, this incident makes Fernando wrongly suppose that they were fighting over Lucrecia whom he loves. Fernando then starts to distrust Sebastián's friendship:

> Qué sospechas, qué recelos
> son estos, suerte crüel,
> con que a mi pecho abrasado
> tan dura guerra movéis?
> Con tantos y tan urgentes
> indicios di que es infiel
> a mi amistad [Sebastián],
> y que de Lucrecia es
> amante; ... (1153-61)

His suspicions increase because neither Sebastián nor Juan reveal that the cause of their fight is not Lucrecia but Fernando's sister, Ana. This leads to Fernando also threatening his life:

> ¡Vive Dios! Si lo averiguo,
> ....
> que he de quitarle la vida
> que le di, pues a perder
> el beneficio condena
> a los ingratos la ley. (1205-16)

The situation worsens with Lucrecia's lies. Thinking that Juan is now courting Ana, Lucrecia confirms Fernando and Ana's suspicions that her father is planning to marry her to Sebastián. Fernando then calls Sebastián to a duel, which tragically ends with Sebastián killing him. Not only Sebastián's life is continuously endangered as he returns to Spain but his later marriage to Ana, meant to be a joyous occasion, turns into a moment of mourning and sadness after the tragic murder of her brother.

Likewise, in *El semejante*, when Leonardo returns from surviving a shipwreck, he is overwhelmed with feelings of doubt, suspicion, and fear thinking his beloved Julia and his dear friend Juan have betrayed him: "Recelo alguna traición" (2740). These fears increase when Celio, Julia's brother, appears at Juan's house enraged and thinking that his sister is hiding there. Leonardo starts suspecting that Juan—who is under the guise of his cousin Diego—and Julia are having an affair. "¿Don Juan a Julia ha querido? / vive el cielo, que es traidor" (2809-10). Don Juan, trying to protect his honor and his false identity, tells Celio that Julia is there to see Leonardo. This only increases Leonardo's doubts and suspicions since he knows this is not true: "Mi sospecha es verdadera" (2825). Leonardo's confusion and anxiety increases when Julia goes along with Juan's lie, which makes him confront her: "Pues dime, Julia traidora, / ¿cómo tal engaño intentas?" (2841-42). Finally, Juan's cousin Diego intervenes to uncover the deceit and prevent Julia from marrying Leonardo. He breaks his silence and discloses the secret he had promised to keep for his cousin Juan, revealing that Juan has been posing as Diego all this time. When Juan's lie and Juan's and Diego's true identities are revealed, we also find out that Diego was the fiancé Julia thought she had lost ten years before. Because Julia had promised her hand in marriage to Diego first, she decides to marry him. Leonardo's absence from Spain determines his loss of Julia and, consequently, his loss of the social place he aspired to obtain by marrying her. In fact, Leonardo is the only *galán* excluded from the marital matches at the end of the play and he resigns to keep his promise to God to enter a monastery if he survived the shipwreck:

> Yo no lo puedo impedir,
> Puesto que en la mar soberbia
> De religión hice voto.
> Si Dios me librase de ella (2941-44)

Leonardo's exclusion from matrimonial bliss is symbolic of his final social isolation, which is marked by his seclusion in a monastery. Even his voice is reduced to short expressions of confusion, rage, disillusion, and resignation until its total obliteration when he takes the vows of silence in the monastery. The experience of returning to Spain is filled with feelings of doubt, fear, and anxiety caused by his friend and his lover's lies and betrayal.

In *Todo es ventura*, the risk of the returnees from Indias is built around economic loss, possible social isolation, and threats to their lives. The characters in this play are Don Enrique and his servant Tello—two retired soldiers. Both return to Madrid hoping to find economic security in the court. Since Don Enrique returns from Indias with some wealth, he settles comfortably in Madrid and even starts courting the noble and rich Belisa. On the other hand, Tello returns from Indias completely poor and tells Duke Albert that he arrived "a Madrid... buscando / la fortuna;..." (299-300). He complains that, after traveling to Nueva España three times as a soldier in the fleet, "... de sus tesoros" he has not seen any part (321-22). All Tello can hope for is a job with a good master so he is happy to be hired by Don Enrique and live in his house. Unfortunately, six months after their arrival to Madrid, Don Enrique runs out of money without having secured his marriage to Belisa. Finding himself broke, he is forced to fire Tello:

> ENRIQUE. Ya ha logrado
> la Fortuna su intención,
> pues mi larga pretensión
> me ha traído a tal estado,
> que no puedo sustentar
> los criados que solía (1-6)

This unfortunate financial twist leads to other possible loses for Don Enrique. Without money, Don Enrique has no possibilities to secure a convenient marriage in Madrid's court. Additionally, Don Enrique's financial problems also have an impact on Tello's security since his loss of the job leaves him homeless and penniless:

> ¡Bueno habéis quedado, Tello,
> Sin amo y sin un real,
> Sumado todo el caudal
> En un vestido y un cuello! (57-60)

This financial and material loss is not the only problem they face when they return to Madrid. In the first act, Don Enrique inadvertently becomes involved in a fight defending a woman. The scene takes place in El Prado where Don Enrique sees a man trying to force a woman to uncover her face. Don Enrique takes out his sword to rescue her thinking it could be Belisa. Tello also takes his sword out when he sees his old master in danger, but arrives too late because Don Enrique has killed the man. We hear the "muerto soy" (133) behind the curtain. Don Enrique and Tello come from behind the curtain holding their swords and Leonor—the woman hiding her identity under a veil—tells one of them (it is not clear who she is addressing) to escape: "Mirad por vos, caballero" (138). Both escape in the darkness of the night, the guards chase them and, in scene VII, we discover that the sheriff has captured Tello and put him in jail, while Don Enrique has managed to hide in the cloister of La Victoria's convent. Tello's imprisonment and Don Enrique's forced clandestine situation add to the image of danger and vulnerability that surrounds the returnee in this play. We can see again how Spain is represented as a place of danger, economic loss, and social isolation for the returnees as they are at risk of losing the possibility of economic stability and are instead confined in the convent and in jail.

Another common factor among the characters returning to Spain in Ruiz de Alarcón's plays is the sense of estrangement. Locals see and treat returnees as foreigners, which is stressed by their being insistently called "forasteros" [outsiders] or "indianos" if they had been to Indias. Ana and her maid Inés call Sebastián "forastero" and "indiano" in the first *jornada* of the play *La culpa*. Leonor calls Diego "forastero" in the very first verse of *Los empeños de un engaño* and the servants repeat this epithet multiple times to refer to him throughout the play. Tello and Don Enrique in *Todo es ventura* are referred to as "indianos." Anarda and Julia persistently call García "forastero" as they both contend for his love. These names emerge in the court women's gossiping, and the servants' exchange of information about them. The women show curiosity and attraction for the newcomers. The returnees cause what Julia Kristeva calls a sort of "fascination" (96) amongst the women, who immediately start calculating their potential as husbands. The term "forastero," according to the *Tesoro de la lengua castellana* is: "el que no es del mismo lugar, ni de la misma tierra, de *foras extra*, de donde se dijo extranjero, extraneus" (15). In fact, like actual foreigners, these characters rarely have any social ties in Spain and, even when they do, those relationships are broken or compromised. This collective perception of them as outsiders— they are not known or recognized—initially helps with the *enredos* in the *comedia*. Certainly this is the case with Don Enrique and Tello in *Todo es ventura* whom the police, Leonor, and even the Duke's servants get mixed up. Not being known in the court can offer an advantage from which some of the characters try to benefit. Diego in *Los empeños de un engaño* wants to make sure nobody knows his real condition of "pobre y forastero" (355) so he can court the noble and rich Teodora. In Garci-Ruiz's case, this allows him to move around secretly while he is looking for his enemy to avenge his honor. In some cases, a false identity or a disguise further impedes their recognition. Nuño Aluaga arrives in Aragón disguised as a beggar and, after he finds out about the details of the political unrest going on in the kingdom, he assumes the identity of King Alfonso I—who was believed to have died in the battle of Fraga—taking advantage of the many years that have passed and their relative likeness. His disguises make his recognition impossible, even at the time when he needs his son to recognize him and help him. Sebastián's father, in *La culpa*, asks his son to arrive in Spain under the false name of Rodrigo de Rivera, having to hide his true identity until—unbeknownst to him—the family honor is cleansed. It is under this false name that Sebastián and Don Fernando de Vasconcelos become friends, unaware their families are mortal enemies. Sebastián can only reveal his true identity to Don Diego de Mendoza, a very close friend of his father. This moment when he can claim his name and lineage is emotional for him. Don Diego not only recognizes Sebastián's rightful belonging to the Sosa lineage, but gives him an embrace which Sebastián calls " . . . el primer alivio que he tenido / en cuanto mar y tierra he discurrido." (387-88). Being recognized and accepted produces an emotional cathartic moment of "alivio."

It is notable that these characters are not only seen as outsiders, but some of their behaviors are also perceived by the locals as "strange" and at odds with those traditional of locals, most notably, those of the male courtiers in Madrid. In the eyes of the locals, they behave differently, strangely, oddly, which makes them stand out and threatens to alienate them. In *Todo es ventura*, Duke Alberto praises Tello for not having learned the "costumbres de la corte" [court manners]:

> En vos, Tello, no han entrado
> las costumbres de la corte;
> que en ella los lisonjeros
> que cercan a los señores,
> diciendo lo que no hacen,
> en obligación los ponen;
> y vos negáis lo que hacéis
> —prueba de valiente y noble (371-78)

Likewise, Garci-Ruiz in *Los favores del mundo* surprises everyone in the court, and steals Anarda's heart by bravely fighting Don Juan and, then, benevolently forgiving him when he hears him praying to the Virgin Mary for his life. In fact, the Prince is so impressed by Garcí-Ruiz' action that, though he calls it "strange," he praises it and says he would rather have done this action himself than be the Prince of Spain:

> Las más ilustres historias
> en vuestras altas victorias
> el *non plus ultra* han tenido;
> mas la que hoy ganáis, ha sido
> *plus ultra* de humanas glorias.
> Vuestra dicha es tan extraña,
> que quisiera, vive Dios,
> más haber hecho la hazaña
> que hoy, García, hicistes vos,
> que ser príncipe de España. (606-15)

Sebastián in *La culpa* also stands out for his physical and ethical superiority over his male rival, Don Juan de Lara. At the end of the first act, Ana Vasconcelos finds herself alone with Don Juan in her house, which is quite a compromising situation for her so she asks him to leave. Don Juan takes this rejection badly and not only refuses to leave but physically restrains Ana to force her to explain it. Sebastián, who has been on the street outside Ana's garden all this time, hears this scuffle and decides to stop Don Juan without creating a scandal by casually entering the house asking for Don Fernando. This scene shows the contrasting characters of these two rivals. While Don Juan de Lara is portrayed as violent, jealous and insecure, Sebastián—though jealous too—shows respect for Ana, restraint over his emotions, and sensibility to causing any harm to her honor if a fight between the two rivals were to occur in her house. Later in the play, the differences between these two characters is expanded favoring Sebastián. Don Juan confronts Sebastián for "interfering" [estorbarle] in Ana's house to which Sebastián responds with corrective admonitions:

> que decir que os estorbé
> cuando en casa de doña Ana
> los dos nos hablamos, es
> un lenguaje muy ajeno,

> don Juan, del que usar debéis
> por vos, por ella y por mí;
> porque ni a doña Ana, a quien
> mira con respeto el sol,
> os pudistes atrever,
> ni ella permitir que a solas
> con más licencia la habléis
> que en presencia de testigos,
> ni vos, conforme a la ley
> de noble, cuando eso fuera,
> lo debéis dar a entender,
> Ni a mí, que soy de su hermano
> tan estrecho amigo, es bien,
> cuando olvidéis lo demás,
> que de ese modo me habléis. (1031-52)

Sebastián lays out here how he understands a *caballero* must behave, particularly towards women. He tells Don Juan how he should not have dared to act in such a way towards Ana, "a quien con respeto mira el sol" nor should he have mentioned his intentions if she had in fact allowed him to be alone with her. Don Juan's response to these admonitions is only a sarcastic remark "Esas son caballerías / de Amadís y Florisel" (1053-54). Alluding that the code of behavior that Sebastián speaks about is only part of the fictional romances of chivalry but does not represent the actual code of conduct in Madrid's court. Don Juan uses this to mock Sebastián for showing how little he knows about the "costumbres de la Corte" and how this proves his foreignness:

> ... se os luce, don Rodrigo,
> lo recién llegado bien,
> pues ignoráis que en la corte
> la competencia es cortés,
> permitido el galanteo
> y usado el darlo a entender. (1055-60)

In these scenes, the newcomer's behavior is contrasted with that of the local males and explains why the locals place them in the cultural space of outsider. Even if what makes these characters different is a positive attribute, it still points to their alterity, their status of not belonging, and their disconnection from the group. By defining returnees through the negation (not knowing the community values, not following their customs, etc.),[4] the returnee is relegated to the place of outsider, denied a space within the community, and, possibly, even threatened with social and political exclusions. These threats cause in the returnee anxiety, tension, and resistance. We can see that when Don Juan mocks Sebastián for not understanding the ways of the court, he reacts angrily: "mal os ha informado quien / os dijo que los precetos / de noble y galán no sé" (1070-72). Sebastián not only refutes the accusation of not knowing the courtly ways, but is also ready to fight against being accused of it:

> Al fin me tratáis
> Como a forastero, pues
> Desconocéis este acero;
> *(empuñan)*
> Mas presto veréis en él
> Vuestro engaño y mi valor (1091-95)

Characters struggle with this sense of disconnection and the continued remarks about their foreignness.

While these characters might be considered outsiders to the social group of the court, they occupy the center in the structure of the drama. In fact, they have the male lead role. Furthermore, in their attempt to join the upper class through a marriage to a court lady, they become rivals to noblemen, who are presented as lower in moral conduct and character. By virtue of moral superiority, the returnees, in most cases, end up winning the ladies' hearts (Garci-Ruiz, Sebastián, don Enrique and Tello) and even the admiration of some. Tello, in *Todo es ventura*, aspires only to a post as servant due to his poverty yet he will too end up marrying a noble lady. Only old Nuño, in *La crueldad por el honor*, who decides to impersonate the king, ends up killed for his transgression. This positive representation of the returnees is quite different, in the absence of other examples, to the popular representation of the returnees from Indias. These plays not only place returnees at the center of the plots but also morally above other characters.

In conclusion, Juan Ruiz de Alarcón's dramas present an image of returning home as a threatening experience. These stories disrupt the idea of home as

---

4 Julia Kristeva in her book *Strangers to Ourselves*, proposes that the foreigner is "[t]he one who does not belong to the group, who is not "one of them," the other. The foreigner, as it has often been noted, can only be defined in negative fashion." (95).

a place of safety. Returnees are represented as vulnerable subjects who are continually at risk of possible material losses, threats of social isolation, and even death. While the dramas tend to idealize the returnees both in their virility and moral values, they also reveal a sense of disconnection, estrangement, and dislocation of the returnees, which destabilizes their identification with the group and its cultural values and creates feelings of fear and anxiety. The response is an intense desire of the returnees to belong and be accepted, a desire that usually takes shape in a "pretensión" to marry into the upper class, which, even when it happens, is accompanied by possible danger (Garci-Ruiz's marriage to Anarda leads to exile) or a dark tragic aura (Sebastian's marriage to Ana happens at the same time as her brother's funeral). Assimilation is either impossible or complex and problematic for the returnees.

Works Cited

Covarrubias Orozco, Sebastián. "Forastero." *Tesoro de la lengua castellana o española*. Melchor Sánchez, 1673, p. 15. https://archive.org/details/tesorodelalenguaoocovauoft/page/1. Accessed 29 April 2019.

Kristeva, Julia. *Strangers to Ourselves*. Columbia UP, 1991.

Lee, Helen M. *Ties to the Homeland: Second Generation Transnationalism*. Cambridge Scholars, 2008.

Pourjafari, Fatemeh, and Vahidpour, Abdolali. "Migration Literature: A Theoretical Perspective." *The Dawn Journal*, vol. 3, no. 1, January-June 2014, pp. 679-692. https://thedawnjournal.in/wp-content/uploads/2013/12/2-Fatemeh-Pourjafari.pdf. Accessed 5 November 2014.

Ruiz de Alarcón, Juan. *La culpa busca la pena y el agravio la venganza. Obras completas de Juan Ruiz de Alarcón*. Ed. Agustín Millares Carlo, vol. 3, Fondo de Cultura Económica, 1957, pp. 1-80.

———. *El semejante a sí mismo. Obras completas de Juan Ruiz de Alarcón*. Ed. Agustín Millares Carlo, vol. 1, Fondo de Cultura Económica, 1957, pp. 295-382.

———. *Todo es ventura. Obras completas de Juan Ruiz de Alarcón*. Ed. Agustín Millares Carlo, vol. 1, Fondo de Cultura Económica, 1957, pp. 613-99.

———. *La crueldad por el honor. Obras completas de Juan Ruiz de Alarcón*. Ed. Agustín Millares Carlo, vol. 2, Fondo de Cultura Económica, 1957, pp. 359-464.

———. *Los favores del mundo. Obras completas de Juan Ruiz de Alarcón*. Ed. Agustín Millares Carlo, vol. 2, Fondo de Cultura Económica, 1957, pp. 359-464.

El poder de las palabras: la percepción de los conversos en la literatura del Siglo de Oro
Tugba Sevin
Southwestern Oklahoma State University

El año 1492 no fue la fecha en la que resolvió el problema judío que existía en la realidad histórica y cultural de España desde la antigüedad.[1] Aunque con la conquista musulmana en 711 los judíos empezaron a vivir un período considerado como la "Edad de Oro" de la convivencia, esta atmósfera pacífica fue siempre interrumpida por la hostilidad que se sentía hacia la población judía. Los hebreos españoles, aunque vivían en la Península desde el siglo I de la era común[2], fueron considerados siempre el "otro" en la conciencia española. El judío fue diferenciado del resto de la población española por algunas imágenes estereotipadas, como sus rasgos físicos y sus profesiones.

En este ensayo propongo revelar la imagen del judío converso en la literatura del Siglo de Oro, a partir de una exploración del antisemitismo de *Las paces de los Reyes y judía de Toledo*, comedia escrita por Lope de Vega en 1610-1612 y señalando la perspectiva conversa en *El diablo cojuelo* de Luis Vélez de Guevara. Opino que con el análisis de una perspectiva de un escritor católico y otra de un autor converso, será posible ver una imagen representativa del "problema" converso de la época. Los dos autores usaron el poder de las palabras para describir la imagen del converso que querían reflejar dentro de la sociedad española del siglo XVII. Por ejemplo, si analizamos la comedia de Lope de Vega, *Las paces*, considerando la rea-

---

[1] "El problema judío se planteó cuando aún no está definitivamente conformada la sociedad hispano-visigoda; la legislación antijudía de Sisebuto (612-21) constituye el primer paso en un proceso que condujo, en fases sucesivas, a la discriminación ... y al destierro ... de los judíos. See Montenegro 14.

[2] See Beinart 6.

lidad histórica y socio-cultural española en que los judíos y los conversos eran considerados el mal absoluto que afectaba la unidad del reino español, notamos un sentimiento antisemita en esta obra. En este ensayo sugiero también que el contexto anti-judío de *Las paces* depende de su escritor, Lope de Vega, que como afirma en su "Arte nuevo de hacer comedias en este tiempo", al escribir sus comedias buscaba el aplauso del vulgo. Por esta razón, yo sostengo que Lope, especialmente en esta obra, empleó, de una manera implícita, imágenes antijudías, porque era consciente de la mentalidad española que había alimentado la expulsión a la mayoría de los judíos de su país y todavía tenía problemas con los conversos. Por otra parte, Luis Vélez de Guevara utilizó su única obra en prosa, *El Diablo Cojuelo*, para mostrar simbólicamente la realidad y los problemas que lo rodearon como converso en España del Siglo de Oro.

Los judíos existieron en la Península Ibérica desde la antigüedad; desde los primeros tiempos vivían juntos en juderías, casi siempre bajo la protección directa de los emperadores. Empezando de los siglos bajomedievales, los judíos en la Península Ibérica fueron el blanco de muchas presiones externas y persecuciones. Cuando los musulmanes gobernaron la Península Ibérica por 800 años empezando en el 711, los judíos y cristianos tuvieron una vida tolerante porque ellos, según las leyes musulmanas, eran "la gente del libro". Pero a mediados del siglo XII, a consecuencia de las presiones de los Almohades, muchos judíos tuvieron que emigrar a las zonas gobernadas por los cristianos. Se establecieron en muchas ciudades, pero la más famosa era Toledo, por ser conocida como "el Jerusalén de los hispano-judíos" (Fromm 146) donde se ocupaban de labores mercantiles, fiscales y usurarias[3]. También trabajaban en la corte cristiana sirviendo de médicos. Durante la Edad Media, las tres culturas y religiones que vivían en Toledo coexistían en armonía y por eso este período fue considerado el "Siglo de Oro" de la convivencia. La situación pacífica empezó a cambiarse en el siglo XIV, ya que el sentimiento hostil latente en la realidad histórica española resucitó y los judíos fueron considerados otra vez los protagonistas de todas las maldades y se convirtieron en chivos expiatorios. Se les culpaba por ser responsables de la muerte de Jesucristo y de aumentar sus riquezas con facilidad (Hinojosa 27). Los rumores se convirtieron en ataques crueles a las juderías y en destrucción de los edificios civiles y religiosos.

---

3 Bobes, Jesús Maire, *Judíos, moros y cristianos,* Akal, 2008, pp. 16.

El clima de hostilidad se resolvió con la expulsión de los judíos de Sepharad[4] donde se había formado la mayor comunidad judía del mundo.[5] En la decisión de desterrar a miles de hijos e hijas nativas del país no hubo excepción para nadie; las órdenes se aplicaban a todos los judíos que no se convertían al cristianismo. Los que no convirtieron empezaron un viaje trágico hacia países que no conocían.

En la Península, los judíos que no querían, o no podían, abandonar sus casas y sus pasados se convirtieron al cristianismo, pero aún así, sufrieron las consecuencias de trato hostil. A estos judíos les llamaron 'marranos', 'conversos', 'cristianos nuevos', 'criptojudíos' y '*anussim*' (en hebreo 'forzados', 'violados'[6]). Muchos de los conversos empezaron a vivir dobles vidas; al parecer eran católicos, pero en sus casas practicaban su religión judía, aunque había entre ellos los que habían abrazado la religión cristiana en libre albedrío. La Inquisición empezó a perseguirlos. Algunos, para protegerse de las consecuencias de la Inquisición, entraron en los monasterios para estar en un lugar seguro[7]. La hostilidad hacia los conversos continuó en la sociedad y por la Inquisición. Como afirma Jesús Maire Bobes, los falsos testimonios adquirieron gran peligro por los conversos, porque se les culpaba por todos los asesinos y ataques sucedidos en la sociedad (24). Muchos conversos que no pudieron soportar este tipo de opresión social encontraron la solución en esconderse detrás de nuevos nombres, casamientos o títulos que compraron (57) y empezaron a vivir una vida ficticia en la cual tenían que actuar siempre, porque la vida era un teatro para ellos.

En esta situación de confusión social, Lope de Vega reescribió una leyenda de amores del siglo XII entre el rey Alfonso VIII y una judía llamada Raquel. La obra dramática parece ser una reelaboración inocente de una leyenda nacional, pero al analizar los detalles de los diálogos y el final de la obra, es posible llegar a la conclusión de que la obra refleja la perspectiva antisemita del período. Además de *Las paces de los Reyes y judía de Toledo*, Lope escribió otras piezas como *El Brasil restituido* y *El niño inocente de la Guardia* que reforzaron el antisemitismo de la época. (Faverón Patriau 361). Por eso, aunque el contenido histórico de *Las paces* se basa en el siglo XII, según Jesús Cañas Murillo, la reescritura de esta leyenda en el siglo XVII por Lope "demuestra el sentimiento de aversión hacia los judíos que existía después de la expulsión,

---

4 Sepharad es una palabra derivada del hebreo y significa España.
5 Kamen, Henry. *The Disinherited: Exile and the Making of Spanish Culture 1492-1975,* Harper Collins, 2007, pp 15.
6 *Ibid.*, pp 23.
7 *Ibid.*, pp 22.

esta vez a los conversos o sea a los cristianos nuevos, aunque el tema principal de la obra no sea el problema antijudaísmo." (77)

Las paces de los Reyes y judía de Toledo refleja la percepción de los conversos en la mentalidad de la sociedad española. La obra se basa en una leyenda en la cual el rey Alfonso VIII se enamora a primera vista de una bella judía Raquel que se bañaba en el río Tajo. Con ella vive siete años, rechazando a su familia y su reino, causando la derrota de Castilla por los moros en Alarcos en 1195. Por el orden de la reina Leonor, los nobles de Castilla asesinaron a la judía. Alfonso prometió vengarse, pero apareció un ángel ante él que le hizo convertirse otra vez en buen marido, padre y rey, recibiendo el galardón de Dios con la victoria hacia los moros en la guerra de las Navas de Tolosa en 1212.

La protagonista de la obra es Raquel y el marco escénico de la trama es Toledo, ciudad conocida en el siglo XII por su vasta comunidad judía. Todos los símbolos antisemitas que se atribuyen a la protagonista Raquel pueden asociar con toda la comunidad judía de Toledo y de toda España porque "Raquel es . . . un nombre genérico de las mujeres judías en el ámbito vulgarizado y también en el figural . . . actúa como madre de judíos" (Concepción Argente Del Castillo Ocaña 37). En esta obra, la protagonista Raquel es identificada con imágenes negativas como "hechicera", "Circe", "Medea", "Elena". La sangre impura de Raquel y sus vestidos diferentes son signos que la diferencian del resto de la población. Por ejemplo, cuando el rey Alfonso ve por la primera vez a Raquel, se entristece y dice, "¡Oh nuevo mal, ¡Oh extraña desventura" (1260), porque Garcerán, amigo y consejero del rey, señala que Raquel es una hebrea por su manera de vestir (1268-69). Según Gustavo Faverón Patriau, "las ropas de Raquel le dicen al rey una verdad simbólica que es una mentira en lo real: ésta es una judía, no una mujer" (362). A Alfonso no le importa la ascendencia de Raquel, y decide buscar su casa. Pregunta por su domicilio a dos hortelanos quienes otra vez le recuerdan al rey (o al público espectador/lector) la falla de esta comunidad que es ser judía (1390). El hortelano Belardo, que es la personificación del escritor, advierte al rey que hay que huir "treinta leguas" (1429) de ella, porque la judía es "una mujer mal nacida" (1432) y sería gran error estar junto a una judía porque es "una mujer sin fe" (1454) y "en su ley, es bajeza" (1447). Raquel también reconoce el conflicto entre los cristianos y los judíos señalando "vemos los cristianos / huir de la sangre nuestra" (1147).

En la obra, el amor de Raquel no se considera sincero, como se sospechaba de la sinceridad religiosa de los conversos en el Siglo de Oro. Todas las imágenes negativas atribuidas a Raquel son en realidad, las imágenes estereotipadas asignadas a todos los judíos (en este caso, a los conversos). Pero, en esta comedia, Raquel se convierte en chivo expiatorio y se representa como la causa de todas las maldades, porque Raquel se retrata como una mujer provocadora que desvía al rey de sus responsabilidades causando daño a toda la comunidad.

Raquel es un miembro del mosaico cultural español, y ella se identifica como "no... cristiana" pero enfatiza que es "española" (1141). Con esta afirmación, Lope demuestra al lector que tampoco él no puede negar la realidad española formada de la variedad de culturas y creencias. Pero, a continuación, como para contradecir esta opinión, termina la obra a manera muy española y cristiana, porque cuando Raquel y Alfonso están pescando en el Tajo, Alfonso saca del agua una calavera que él identifica inmediatamente con la muerte (2243) y Raquel pesca un ramo de oliva (2259). Belardo explica el significado de estos símbolos:

> La muerte que el rey sacó
> Para Raquel, claro está
> Que muestra su muerte ya;
> La oliva que ella pescó
> Para el rey, muestra que, muerta
> Esta afición pertinaz,
> Quedará este reino en paz. (2301-07).

Como se notan en estos versos, Belardo, el álter ego de Lope de Vega, afirma que con la muerte de Raquel se establece la paz en la nación y también en el matrimonio de los Reyes, porque la Circe, la Medea, la Cava Raquel no va a existir en sus vidas. La afirmación de Belardo también se puede interpretar de manera antisemita, porque si Raquel simboliza toda la comunidad judía, ¿es posible pensar que Lope de Vega, personificado en Belardo que es un personaje "antisemita irreductible"[8], haya querido sugerir que con la "muerte" de la comunidad judía, España tendría la paz eterna? La respuesta depende de la interpretación de cada lector, pero hay que recordar que Lope mata a su protagonista judía, convirtiéndola en cristiana. Creo que la conversión de la judía es un mensaje muy importante para los espectadores o lectores españoles de esa época, porque sugiere que España tiene que ser un país cristiano y el "otro" va a ser siempre definido por su

---

8   Menéndez Pelayo, Marcelino. "Las Paces de los Reyes y judía de Toledo", 63.

diferencia de creencia y conducta. A pesar de las informaciones acerca la posición cercana de Lope a los conversos, propongo que, en mi lectura de *Las paces de los Reyes y judía de Toledo* de Lope, es posible notar que el dramaturgo siempre afirma los valores fundamentales de la sociedad, además los menciona en *El arte nuevo de hacer comedias*, donde defiende un teatro dirigido al placer del vulgo. Pienso que esta obra y algunas otras obras de Lope son testimonios de su capacidad de satisfacer las demandas antijudías de su audiencia.

En contraste, Luis Vélez de Guevara, en *El diablo cojuelo (1641)*, con el poder de su pluma, demuestra la perspectiva y las preocupaciones de los conversos como él. La obra empieza en Madrid. El protagonista, un estudiante joven, llamado don Cleofás Leandro Pérez Zambullo, huye de la justicia por unos problemas por su relación con una doncella. Se esconde por casualidad en el desván de un astrólogo que tiene encerrado a un diablo en una botella. El diablo le pide que le dé la libertad y Cleofás lo acepta. Una vez liberado, el Diablo Cojuelo lleva al hidalgo a un viaje mágico por Madrid, Toledo y Sevilla. En este viaje los dos (y también los lectores) tienen la posibilidad de observar las vidas reales de la sociedad española, porque pueden ver desde las alturas el interior de las casas. Al final, los dos son capturados. Cleofás continúa sus estudios en Alcalá y el diablo cojuelo, aunque entra en la boca de un escribano que bostezaba, no puede escapar del diablo que le perseguía y es llevado al infierno con el escribano.

Esta obra en prosa, aunque parece ser una narración de un viaje fantástico de un estudiante y del diablo Asmodeo (cojuelo), es en realidad una obra que contiene muchos mensajes dirigidos al lector. *El diablo cojuelo* ofrece el panorama de la sociedad española del siglo XVII, enfocándose en los valores, la hipocresía de la sociedad, especialmente de la nobleza (de la Villa y Corte de Madrid y de Andalucía). Vélez de Guevara en esta obra demuestra también la sensibilidad de la sociedad española hacia los conversos. Él siendo un judeoconverso, sufría las consecuencias de su ascendencia judía en una sociedad que categorizaba a toda la gente según su limpieza de sangre. Aunque de Guevara se consideraba uno de los escritores importantes de la "escuela de Lope de Vega" y se conocía por su posición cercana de la corte, nunca pudo obtener el elogio merecido por parte del pueblo y de la corte. Nacido en 1579 en Écija de padres conversos, Vélez de Guevara se alistó en el ejército y sirvió en Italia y en Levante. En 1596 entró en el servicio del Cardenal Don Rodrigo de Castro, que era el Arzobispo de Sevilla. Estuvo en su servicio por cuatro años durante los cuales asistió a muchas actividades en la Corte; una de estas fueron las bodas de Felipe III en Valencia. A mediados de 1602 regresó a Sevilla donde vivió un tiempo y luego se mudó a Valladolid y a Madrid. Su propósito era estar cerca de la Corte y de la nobleza, por eso se quedó allá hasta su muerte en 1644. Como señala George Peale, en la Corte, Vélez de Guevara fue siempre un observador que nunca pudo recibir elogios como Calderón y Lope de Vega (*Spanish Dramatists* 244). Él escribió muchas comedias sobre diferentes temas. Sus comedias religiosas eran las más conocidas. Fue un gran comediante que tenía talento en todas las formas literarias, escribió poesía, comedia y prosa, y se consideraba uno de los escritores más importantes de la comedia española. Tuvo una popularidad enorme durante el siglo XVII en los diversos niveles sociales, como el ambiente comercial y el cortesano. Por eso, existían muchas ediciones sueltas de sus obras. A pesar de esta fama, sus obras nunca fueron recopiladas como las de Lope, Tirso y Calderón (Manson y Peale 17-18). Sus obras eran tan originales que incluso Quevedo, que se conocía por su actitud intolerante hacia los judíos conversos, lo citó entre los más famosos escritores junto a Calderón y Lope de Vega (Peale, *Spanish Dramatists* 249). Por ejemplo, una comedia suya, *Las virtudes vencen señales*, se parece a *La vida es sueño* de Calderón en su contenido y caracterización de los personajes. Sus contemporáneos alabaron el éxito de Luis Vélez de Guevara en muchas ocasiones; por ejemplo, Cervantes escribió los versos siguientes:

> Topé a Luis Vélez, lustre y alegría
> y discreción del trato cortesano
> y abracéle en la calle, a medio día. (Profeti 1)

Lope de Vega mencionó la originalidad de Vélez así:

> El florido Luis Vélez de Guevara
> … nuevo Apolo,
> … pudo darle sólo,
> y sólo en sus escritos,
> … flores de concetos inauditos …,
> así sus versos de oro
> con blando estilo la materia esmaltan. (Profeti 2)

Aunque Luis Vélez de Guevara escribió sobre temas religiosos católicos y demostró a la sociedad su devoción a la religión católica, como todos los conversos, tuvo que cambiar su apellido paterno a de Guevara para alejarse de los efectos de su ascendencia judía. Según señala Mary G. Hauer, "At that period in Spain, the last thing anyone wanted to admit was that a member of his family had been punished by the Inquisition and least of all Vélez" (15). En la sociedad española de aquel periodo, aunque un converso se comportaba según las reglas de la sociedad dominante, siempre estaba relacionado con su genealogía judía por una razón u otra. Luis Vélez de Guevara a lo largo de su vida quiso ser parte de la nobleza y servir en una de las "Órdenes caballerescas" (Hauer 16), pero, aunque había cambiado su apellido para ocultar su origen, no pudo ser miembro de esta orden porque el primer requisito era tener sangre limpia.

En el prólogo de la obra, Vélez de Guevara prefiere escribir una carta corta al lector llamándolo "lector amigo" y menciona que lo que ha escrito se ha atrevido "llamarle libro, pasándo[se] de la jineta de los consonantes a la brinda de la prosa." En esta frase Vélez de Guevara demuestra su modestia y al mismo tiempo, señala que ha empezado a escribir en prosa, que es un estilo más libre en comparación con la poesía, porque en la poesía hay que seguir las reglas y contar sílabas. Escribiendo en prosa, él define también a su designado lector. Con el lenguaje peculiar que él usa a lo largo de la obra, Vélez de Guevara señala que su lector es educado, alguien que conoce la Corte y su forma de vida. La obra está formada de vocabulario relacionado con el vestimento y las profesiones relacionados con la Corte. Por eso, solo el lector que conoce estos ambientes puede entender mejor esta obra; en efecto, éste era el propósito de Vélez de Guevara: criticar la sociedad culta usando el poder de sus palabras. En el prólogo, él informa al lector también sobre la división de los capítulos, a los que llama trancos como innovación suya. El prólogo termina con el agradecimiento del escritor al lector por su lectura de la obra. Lo que es interesante, es que Vélez de Guevara firma este capítulo de otra forma innovadora, "El autor y el texto," y al hacer esto, difiere de muchos escritores anteriores que pensaban que la única autoridad era el escritor. Pero Vélez de Guevara considera al escritor y el texto como dos personajes distintos, dando alma y vida al texto mismo.

El tranco primero empieza en Madrid "por los fines de julio, las once de la noche en punto, hora menguada para las calles" (11). El escritor ofrece una visión pesimista de Madrid por la noche mencionando sus lugares famosos como el Prado y los Manzanares "por faltar la luna, jurisdicción y término redondo de todo requiebro lechuzo y patarata de la muerte. El Prado boqueaba coches en la última jornada de su paseo, y en los baños de Manzanares los Adanes y las Evas de la Corte" (11). Para él, la falta de la luna se asocia con la muerte, y parece que todo en esta grande ciudad tiende a morir volviendo a su origen. En este ambiente, el estudiante Cleofás Leonardo Pérez Zambullo huye de la justicia por estar con una "doncella" llamada Tomasa de Bitigudiño y llega al ático de un astrólogo, y Vélez de Guevara asocia la astrología con "embustera ciencia" (14). El estudiante oye un suspiro que "pareciéndole imaginación o ilusión de la noche" (14), pero lo oye por la segunda vez y dice un refrán "¿Quién diablos suspira?" haciendo alusión al carácter principal de la obra. Recibe una respuesta de "una voz entre humana y estranjera" de una botella de vidrio. El estudiante empieza a hablar con esta voz extraña que le pide que lo libere de esta botella porque el que habla dice que había pasado mucho tiempo "sin emplear[se] de nada, siendo [él] el espíritu más travieso del infierno" (15) y esta manera, el escritor empieza a informar al lector quién es este segundo personaje de la obra. Esta voz afirma que se llama Diablo Cojuelo porque "le pusieron este nombre, a diferencia de los demás, habiendo todos caído desde tan alto" (17) y todos se cayeron sobre él y no pudo resistir el peso y por eso se le quebraron las piernas. El diablo pide a Cleofás que le saque "deste Argel de vidrio" (18) haciendo referencia a Argel donde muchos españoles fueron presos como cautivos. Entonces, Cleofás rompe la botella con un "instrumento astronómico gigote" (19) y rescata al diablo. Pero lo que ve lo sorprende mucho porque el aspecto físico del Diablo Cojuelo no era lo que esperaba:

> vio en él un hombrecillo de pequeña estatura, afirmado en dos muletas, sembrado de chichones mayores de arca, calabacino de testa y badea de cogote, chato narices, la boca formidable y apuntalada en dos colmillos solos, que no tenían más muela ni diente los desiertos de las encías, erizados los bigotes como si hubiera barbado en Hircania; los pelos de su nacimiento, ralos, uno aquí y otro allí, a fuer de los espárragos, legumbre tan enemiga de la compañía, que si no es para venderlos en manojos no se juntan. ... (19)

Esta descripción monstruosa del diablo recuerda la descripción de los conversos dada en el *Tratado de Alborayque*, obra anónima impresa en 1545. En esa obra, el converso se pinta como un ser medio humano y medio animal para señalar las cualidades malas que supuestamente tuvieron los conversos en la época. El talento de Vélez de Guevara yace en el uso de un lenguaje peculiar que se nota en los detalles que nos proporciona; por ejemplo, en lugar de escribir directamente las partes del cuerpo del Diablo, nuestro escritor usa imágenes para suavizar y para satirizar el aspecto de esta criatura extraña. Por ejemplo, en vez de decir "cabeza," el escritor emplea "calabacino de testa" y el "pelo" está relacionado con "espárragos". Esta técnica sirve animar la lectura, y los lectores pueden también visualizar el Cojuelo.

Luis Vélez de Guevara, en su única obra en prosa, critica la sociedad española usando un lenguaje decorativo y conceptista. Como otros escritores conversos que temían del control constante de la Inquisición, Guevara también usó palabras con doble significados o imágenes para criticar los valores obsesionados de la sociedad. Por ejemplo, la fuga constante del protagonista y del diablo cojuelo es un símbolo importante, porque demuestra la psicología de los conversos que tenían que escapar de la realidad y actuar constantemente para alejarse de los prejuicios de la sociedad y de los castigos de la Inquisición. La huida de nuestro escritor empezó con el cambio de su apellido. Sabemos que la compra de títulos y casamientos falsos también eran otras formas de huida entre los conversos. El tópico literario barroco *theatrum mundi*, en la vida de los conversos se convirtió en una forma de vida. Los conversos tenían dos opciones: o vivir en la sombra o actuar constantemente. En esta obra, de Guevara se enfoca mucho en la teatralidad y critica la sociedad por condenar los conversos a actuar en la vida diaria y por dar importancia en la apariencia. Por ejemplo, en el tranco (capítulo) segundo el diablo cojuelo promete enseñar al estudiante "el teatro donde tantas figuras representan" (22). En el tranco tercero el escritor sugiere que en la sociedad (especialmente en Madrid) "hombres y mujeres . . . pretenden engañar los unos a los otros, levantándose una polvareda de embustes y mentira, que no se descubría una brizna de verdad por un ojo de la cara" (35).

Luis Vélez de Guevara escribió *El diablo cojuelo* desde su perspectiva. Observó y criticó la sociedad que ha dejado fuera de la esfera social a los conversos como él. Quiso reflejar una realidad social en la cual el converso vive en un mundo encerrado como el diablo Asmodeo (cojuelo) y aunque escape o actué mucho, al final va a ser siempre escogido por la sociedad o capturado por la Inquisición. Lope de Vega por otro lado, usó la fuerza de su pluma para describir una realidad deseada por sus espectadores. *Las paces de los Reyes y judía de Toledo* de Lope de Vega y *El diablo cojuelo* de Luis Vélez de Guevara son obras ficticias y en este ensayo están interpretadas desde mi lectura. Pero no hay que olvidar que como señala Edna Eizenberg "even if the tales are not real, they are true in the sense that they mirror and heighten situations, perceptions, and tensions inherent in a society" (Nirenberg 18).

Obras citadas

Beinart, Haim. "¿Cuándo llegaron los judíos a España?." *Estudios* 3, 1962, pp. 1-32.

Bobes, Jesús Maire, *Judíos, moros y cristianos*. Akal, 2008.

Del Castillo Ocaña, Concepción Argente "La hermosa Raquel: del imaginario barroco al imaginario neoclásico." *Homenaje a la Profesora Ma. Dolores Tortosa Linde,* edited by Remedios Morales Raya, Granada UP, 2003, pp. 35-46.

Faverón Patriau, Gustavo. "Siete años en el purgatorio: judíos y cristianos en *Las paces de los Reyes y judía de Toledo* de Lope de Vega." *Bulletin of the Comediantes*, vol. 58, no. 2, 2006, pp. 359- 83.

Fromm, Annette B. "Hispanic Culture in Exile." *Sephardic and Mizrahi Jewry: From the Golden Age of Spain to Modern Times*, edited by Zion Zohar, New York UP, 2005, pp. 145- 67.

Hauer, Mary G. *An Addendum to Luis Vélez de Guevara: A Critical Bibliography*. Biblioteca Virtual Miguel de Cervantes, 2013.

Hinojosa Montalvo, José. "Los Judíos en la España medieval: de la tolerancia a la expulsión." *Los marginados en el mundo medieval y moderno*. Universidad de Alicante, 1998.

Kamen, Henry. *The Disinherited: Exile and the Making of Spanish Culture 1492-1975*. Harper Collins, 2007.

Menéndez Pelayo. "Las Paces de los Reyes y judía de Toledo." *Estudios sobre el teatro de Lope,* edited by Enrique Sánchez Reyes, Madrid, 1949, pp. 57-75.

Montenegro, Enrique Cantera. "La imagen del judío en la España medieval." *Espacio, tiempo y forma, Serie III, Ha. Medieval*, vol. 11, 1998, pp. 11-38.

Murillo, Jesús Cañas. "Las paces de los Reyes y judía de Toledo, de Lope de Vega, un primer preludio de Raquel." *Anuario de Estudios Filológicos*, vol. 11, 1988, pp. 59-81.

Nirenberg, David. "Deviant Politics and Jewish Love: Alfonso VIII and the Jewess of Toledo." *Jewish History*, vol. 21, 2007, pp. 15-41.

Peale, C. George. *Antigüedad y actualidad de Luis Vélez de Guevara: estudios críticos*. Benjamins, 1983.

Peale, C. George, y William R. Manson. *El espejo del mundo*. Juan de la Cuesta, 2002.

Family Functions and Dysfunctions: Secrecy in *La vida es sueño*

GWEN H. STICKNEY
North Dakota State University

PEDRO CALDERÓN DE LA BARCA'S *La vida es sueño* has been read as a play about such themes as kingdoms and kingships, philosophy and knowledge, and reality and dreams, but it is also a timeless exploration of family interaction. As Edward H. Friedman reminds us, "The theater transforms human events and discourse into plays, analogues, imitations" (41). Challenging family relationships were not unfamiliar to early modern audiences, or even Calderón himself.[1] In *La vida es sueño*, Calderón portrays the functions and dysfunctions of several family units, with the fate of an entire kingdom depending on their successful functioning. In this essay, I draw from Family Systems theories, approaches used in contemporary counseling, to analyze this play as the intertwined story of young adults seeking to establish their identities and assume adult roles, with the actions of each family member affecting those of others. Along the way, the families in this *comedia* attend to tasks faced by families today, such as entry into the family unit; integration and self-differentiation of members; maintenance of family agendas; handling secrets; and coping with death. Although seemingly quite

---

[1] Don W. Cruickshank discusses some possible connections between Calderón's life and art, including family challenges: "Perhaps the safest explanation is that years later, as he constructed plots from problematic family relationships, the poet became aware of the potential for disaster which had existed in his own family, and developed in his imagination a situation which had not come about in reality" (53). Alexander A. Parker analyzes the actions of Calderón's strict father (102-05). Darci L. Strother discusses circumstances in Calderón's biological family, including the deaths of both parents when he was a teenager, that may have shaped the author's perspective on families ("Loving Parents" 82).

different at first glance, the two main nuclear families in this *comedia* are similar in many of their functions, but the nature of their dysfunctions poses special challenges for Segismundo. The characters' conduct and the keeping of family secrets function as part of family systems that offer insights into family interactions that cut across centuries while suggesting worrisome repercussions for their country's leadership.

In his study of the family in Spain since the seventeenth century, David S. Reher finds it "difficult to overestimate the importance of the family for Spanish society" (2). Although seventeenth-century families were somewhat different from contemporary ones, many of their purposes are similar, such as providing practical, economic and emotional support; facilitating procreation and childrearing; and maintaining family name and property through inheritance and family alliances. Due to high infant mortality rates and the frequency of the premature death of a spouse, nuclear families could be small then, as now, and economic or political considerations, such as inheritance and family alliances, often motivated marriages. Although divorce, annulment, and separation were rare, remarriage was permitted after a spouse's death (Anderson 163). Steven Ozment specifies between 1100 and 1500, before Calderón wrote, as when parent-child relations became more affectionate, citing parents' responses to a child's death from period images and archives and letters to children staying with relatives to avoid the plague (58-61,78-79). In *Family Matters: A Study of On- and Off-Stage Marriage and Family Relations in Seventeenth-Century Spain*, Darci L. Strother opines that parent/child relationships were changing: "Despite the diversity of possible forms of family structure, whether nuclear or extended, with or without domestic help, with or without a *paterfamilias*, historians have indicated a move toward the strengthening of the bond between parents and children, and toward according childhood the distinction of being a special and separate life-stage from adulthood" (137). In *Family and Community in Early Modern Spain*, James Casey points to the belief of early modern Spanish thinkers about the connection between family man and citizen: One comes to govern a community successfully, which is a source of honor, by learning within and leading a family, an idea rooted in Roman thought (1, 5, 7, 145). Calderon's play was created within this historical context.

Previous research about *La vida es sueño* mentions the family relationship between Basilio and Segismundo. In "The Father-Son Conflict in the Drama of Calderón," Alexander A. Parker explores the author's "psychological obsession" with rebellious sons and tyrannical fathers in Calderón's early plays. In "El 'mito de Uranos' en *La vida es sueño*," Francisco Ruiz Ramón compares Basilio to some of Calderón's parental figures and determines that he is the only parent who leaves his child completely unaware of his identity and distances himself, emphasizing Basilio's fear and violence in the father/son conflict (549, 53). Frederick A. de Armas has utilized mythological symbolism to analyze the relationship between Basilio and Segismundo in a variety of ways. For example, de Armas reads the father and son within the tradition of the pagan god Saturn, who devoured his children, and son Jupiter in "El planeta más impío," suggesting certain human tendencies in family relationships in very early narratives. De Armas also observes a parallel between the father/son rivalry and the anxiety of influence Calderón felt towards Lope de Vega ("Critical Tower" 5-6). C. A. Merrick points to Basilio's and Clotaldo's similar roles that form part of Calderón's consideration of the moral responsibilities of parents (257).

Critics have utilized and rejected psychoanalytical approaches to illuminate the father/son relationship in this play. Parker considers and then dismisses the Oedipus complex as not taking into consideration Calderón's other plays and life experiences. Ruiz Ramón favors the Uranus over the Oedipus Complex because Segismundo does not marry his mother (561). Willian Egginton highlights problems inherent in using psychoanalysis to read literature before analyzing how Segismundo achieves a sense of skepticism from his father. Ruth Anthony parallels Basilio's concealment of his son with the king's repression of his own passion and sexuality. Henry W. Sullivan uses Greek myth, Freud, and Lacan's account of the Oedipal structure to explore knowledge in dreams and their misinterpretation, such as those of both Clorilene and Segismundo. Matthew D. Stroud moves beyond the Oedipus myth, using Lacanian psychoanalysis to examine Segismundo's and Rosaura's searches for identity and the Name-of-the-Father, considering many kinds of lack and Basilio's pursuit of truth and knowledge in light of competition with his son and ultimately death.

Since classic works speak to readers across time and circumstances, it stands to reason that *La vida es sueño* offers insight to a modern public about family functions through portraying the interactions of early families. In *Ancestors: The Loving Family in Old Europe*, Ozment reminds readers of our intimate bond with past and future: "The centuries that lie behind us are a deep, clinical record of human behavior, while the lessons still to be learned about ourselves from centuries to come exist only in our imaginations. From this perspective, the greater temptation for every generation is not slippage back into the past, but belief that past, present, and future constitute absolutely distinct types of humanity" (2). When one reads *La vida es sueño* as a play about single parents raising children on their own, a situation common in the twenty-first century, it invites the application of modern theoretical knowledge to this classic, making use of counseling's more advanced and varied tools. Having come into existence from seeds planted in the 1930s and 40s that blossomed in the 1970s, Family Systems approaches are more recent than this *comedia* (Becvar and Becvar 14), yet they serve to analyze the familial tensions present throughout the play.

While considering Freud's work valuable, psychiatrist Murray Bowen objected to the shortcomings of Freudian analysis, which he saw as lacking basis in science (Papero vii). Bowen and others have since offered new Family Systems approaches that provide alternative explanations for some of the same issues considered in previous literary criticism by examining family relationships holistically instead of psychoanalyzing the mental workings of fictional characters. These theories consider a family as an interrelated system in which each member's actions affect those of the others, according to Stephen A. Anderson and Ronald M. Sabatelli in *Family Interaction: A Multigenerational Developmental Perspective* (6). Although Family Systems theory originated in the United States in the twentieth century, it is used by counselors in other countries, including Spanish-speaking ones. In "Viability of Family Systems Theory for Latin America," Sara E. Cooper surveys the Spanish-language studies of family psychology and therapy from before 1988 and indicates that more than 150 of the bibliographical entries either include Family Systems in the title, have been published in a Family Systems journal, or have been authored by proponents of the approach (189). Cooper adds that more work is being done in the field and that Family Systems perspectives have proven adaptable to Hispanic culture (194). Despite clear differences between modern and early modern families, Family Systems theory is flexible enough to offer insight into human tendencies in social interaction that perhaps have not changed so much throughout the centuries. For example, in "Dysfunction, Discord, and Wedded Bliss," Donald D. Miller utilizes Family Systems research to analyze the families in *Don Quijote* that contrast sharply with early writings about model families, such as *La perfecta casada* (1583).

La vida es sueño vividly portrays family interaction from the start of the play. Among the listed speaking roles, two nuclear families, adoptive relationships, and an extended family are represented. Only the unnamed soldiers, guards, and musicians are not part of the families in the play. In the ninth line of the *comedia*, there is a reference to Phaethon, who tragically insists on driving his elder's chariot through the sky to prove his lineage, foreshadowing the parent/child interaction in the work. *La vida es sueño* portrays the dysfunctions of multiple family units, both nuclear and extended: a deceased mother and a royal father who has secretly imprisoned his son Segismundo, leaving his subjects uninformed about the heir to the throne; a father who is unaware of the existence of his daughter Rosaura, and thus has not participated in her upbringing, until she arrives on the scene to restore her honor; and ambitious cousins who desire to ascend the throne.

On the surface, there are obvious differences between Segismundo's and Rosaura's situations. One is a motherless son and the other a fatherless daughter, with their different gender expectations. Segismundo is the heir to the throne born in wedlock, while Rosaura is the illegitimate daughter of an unmarried mother. Segismundo has been raised almost in isolation with little family interaction, except that provided by a faithful servant. Rosaura has been nurtured by her mother, who gave her the sword for her protection and sent her off to discover the secret of her birth. E. M. Wilson opines that although Segismundo is humbled by disillusion, Rosaura, whose actions are driven by honor, provides a contrast (78, 85). Yet a closer look at the two characters points to striking similarities, even in their familial situations. As children, both are associated with secrets related to their birth, but now Segismundo and Rosaura are young adults of marriageable age trying to make sense of their lives. Additionally, both are separated from their real parents, accompanied by employed substitute parental figures, and are unhappy (1.2.250-75). *La vida es sueño* establishes a parallel between the two characters, presenting them in transitional states: Rosaura as man/woman, and Segismundo as man/beast caught between real life and a dream (3.10.2716-27, 3.10.2902-20, 1.2.211-12). In this play, both children are hidden to protect a family agenda and seek to kill their fathers metaphorically. However, their fathers eventually serve as part of their rite of passage into adult identities.[2] Many, including de Armas ("Planeta" 907, 910), Rafael Lapesa (99), Ellen C. Lavroff (486, 489, 494), Barbara Mujica (190, 231-36), Thomas Austin O'Connor (20, 23), José María Ruano de la Haza (29, 34), and Stroud (39), have noted that Segismundo and Rosaura's similar plots are intertwined among various parallel structures in the play, but we might also ask how the similar youths' development differs. To expand upon the comparison of these two characters, Segismundo's cousins are also young adults who are undertaking a journey to individuate, or form a distinct identity, and to assume their adult roles, although fewer details are given about Astolfo's and Estrella's upbringing. In fact, all these youths have unusual relationships with their fathers. Neither Segismundo nor Rosaura have much knowledge of their fathers early in the play, and readers are

---

[2] José María Ruano de la Haza observes that the actions of both fathers deny the children their rightful social identity and that Rosaura's honor and identity depend upon Segismundo's actions and vice versa (34).

more aware of Astolfo's and Estrella's lineage through their mothers than their fathers. Family Systems perspectives offer a way to compare the interactions in these coming-of-age story lines.

According to John V. Knapp's "Family Systems Therapy and Literary Study: An Introduction," one significant function of a family is "differentiation," or support for the process of family members' development into independent selves (16). Ozment indicates that "preparing a child to live and work independently was a parent's highest duty and chief obsession" for early families, too (73). E. T. Aylward considers *La vida es sueño* a *Bildungsroman* that traces the theological, political, and social development of Segismundo, but there are three other unmarried young adults in the play who also undergo the process of differentiation.

The first act provides insight into Segismundo's progress toward independence. When Rosaura, a *mujer vestida de hombre*, enters the scene complaining of her fate, she discovers Segismundo, a beastly man dressed in skins and bound by chains in a tower, lamenting his birth. Described as a "vivo cadáver" (1.2.94), "esquelto vivo" (1.2.201), and "un hombre de las fieras / y una fiera de los hombres" (1.2.211-12), Segismundo is trying to make sense of his life: "qué delito cometí / contra vosotros naciendo" (1.2.105-06). Due to his limited experience with the world, Segismundo is forced to use what he can observe—nature—to attempt to understand who he is (1.2.131-62). Like his father who keeps secrets, Segismundo attempts to hide his shortcomings, threatening to kill Rosaura who overheard his monologue, which provided her an insider's view like that often held by family members (1.2.180-82; Berg-Cross 119). Despite almost complete isolation and little worldly knowledge, Segismundo seeks to grasp his raison d'être.

Segismundo's natural attempt at self-differentiation is interrupted by his father when Segismundo is finally freed from the tower in a test of his competence to shoulder the responsibility of managing a kingdom. Following the king's order, the son is drugged and brought secretly to the palace so that he can be observed in a carefully controlled experiment without the young man knowing the truth. As if set up to fail by his father, the heir apparent overreacts during the test, treating his cousins with extreme discourtesy, killing a man who suggests a correction to his behavior, and threatening to kill others. However, Segismundo metaphorically becomes aware of who he is: "informado estoy / de quién soy" (2.6.1545-46). Segismundo's public attempt to take on adult commitment alarms those around him, and probably overwhelms him, fitting Linda Berg-Cross's description of some young peoples' first experience with autonomy in the book *Basic Concepts in Family Therapy*:

"[A]utonomy is often felt as a frightening experience of suspended animation instead of a secure push into an area of desired personal fulfillment" (47). Berg-Cross notes this reaction when youth mature in "disengaged families," where "family members move in isolated orbits for long periods" and lack shared experiences and meaningful connections (47).

Rosaura's first attempt to take on adult responsibilities, although less violent, likewise, breaks with accepted social norms. The audience or readers do not directly witness Rosaura's interaction with Astolfo, but they observe the consequences as Rosaura arrives in Poland to regain her lost honor. Although Rosaura did not show wise judgment with her earlier action, she has assumed responsibility for her reputation, is on a journey, and seems to handle the situation well. In fact, critics have viewed Rosaura as Segismundo's guide.[3] William M. Whitby argues that Rosaura's presence—not Basilio's plan—awakens Segismundo's consciousness (102), while Ruano de la Haza describes Rosaura as the key that allows Segismundo to create coherence from what he had believed to be a fragmented existence (34).

Less is known about Astolfo's and especially Estrella's differentiating from their families. Like Rosaura, these two young adults are on a journey with the hope of assuming the adult responsibility of governing a kingdom. Since Basilio seems willing to grant them leadership of his kingdom if Segismundo proves unfit, Estrella does not seem incompetent to carry out the demands of leadership. A little more is known about Astolfo's transition into maturity: Unlike Basilio, Rosaura and the audience are conscious of Astolfo's dalliance with and desertion of a young woman who had accepted his promise of fidelity. Despite this lack of judgment, Astolfo seems more prepared for adult challenges than Segismundo.

The contrast between Rosaura's, Estrella's, Astolfo's, and Segismundo's progress toward adulthood raises the question of what has led them to where they are. Although the two cousins and Rosaura seem to be advancing toward adulthood quite well in comparison, Segismundo's childhood experience conflicts with the kind needed for healthy transformation: "Psychologists universally acknowledge that the child's ability to bond successfully with the parent lays the foundation for successfully exploring and affecting their environment. Children with a secure attachment are able to separate from the parent and find ways of satisfying their own needs" (Berg-Cross

---

3   Lavroff reads Rosaura theologically as divine grace, redeeming Segismundo. In "Segismundo/Philip IV," de Armas states that Rosaura is a later version of Astraea, who "comes to guide the prince towards perfection" (83). Ven Serna states that Rosaura leads Segismundo to his self-discovery at various times (692).

43). The differences among Segismundo's, Rosaura's, Astolfo's, and Estrella's attempts at differentiation seemingly reflect their parental bonds.

According to Knapp, a significant task of a family system is providing support for a new member's "integration into a solid family unit" (Knapp 16), which would create a parent/child bond. Rosaura, who seems to be a more mature example for Segismundo, has been integrated quite differently by her mother Violante. An example of the mother/daughter bond is described in the play: Although Rosaura failed to live up to the social convention of maintaining purity before marriage, Violante lovingly comforts her, recognizing that the daughter erred in the same way that the mother had years earlier (3.10.2820). In fact, it is Rosaura's mother who initiates the young woman's journey into adulthood to discover her identity and restore her honor by giving her daughter the sword and telling her to go to Poland to be seen (3.10.2839-48), unlike Segismundo's father who drugs his son to control the youth's search for identity. Rosaura quite easily accepts Clotaldo as her substitute father figure when he tries to help her, and she quickly earns Estrella's trust as her attendant (2.12.1790). Rosaura's more loving integration and resulting warm bond with her mother enable her to separate from her parent, seek her own identity, and form relationships with others during her journey to Poland. Although less is known about Astolfo's and Estrella's childhoods, they, like Rosaura, travel independently to Poland, separating from their families to make adult lives.

From a Family Systems perspective, Segismundo's behavior can be traced to a lack of family connections.[4] Integration should begin at the time of a child's birth to initiate parent/child ties, but Segismundo's negative perception of birth parallels his lack of integration in his nuclear family. In the beginning of the play, Segismundo is unaware of his mother's death and his father's existence. In fact, between Basilio and Segismundo, there is no evidence of closeness shared in the categories of contact time, personal space, emotional space, informational space, conversation space, and decision space (Berg-Cross 55). Clotaldo, a sort of adopted substitute father, who does not raise even his own daughter, is responsible for Segismundo's limited integration. Segismundo himself seems instinctively aware of the problems that his upbringing has caused. In fact, he repudiates his father for educating him like a beast. Not hugging him doesn't matter since he hasn't been treated like a man (2.6.1478-86). Anderson and Sabatelli indicate that a poorly differentiated individual may attempt to compensate for the lack of a sense of self

---

4 Everett W. Hesse pinpoints the cause of Segismundo's violence in "the lack of parental affection, his unjust incarceration, his unknown identity and the cruelty of his tutor" (8).

by interacting only with people he or she can control (62).[5] Basilio has created this kind of situation with his son by imprisoning Segismundo and then drugging him to place him in the "dream." Likewise, Segismundo threatens violence in order to control others.

After a very limited integration of Segismundo by Clotaldo in the tower, the arrival of outsiders in Poland brings about Basilio's overdue attempt to integrate Segismundo into the palace, a father/son relationship, and social norms as the audience wonders whether nature or nurture will win. When Clotaldo tells him that he is the heir apparent, Segismundo threatens to kill his tutor for mistreating him for years, even though Clotaldo was following the king's orders. Astolfo corrects Segismundo when the heir to the throne does not recognize his cousin and treat him with the courtesy befitting his rank. Instead, Segismundo emphasizes his own superior social status (2.4.1353-72). Estrella rebukes her cousin for not treating a woman properly when seeking to kiss her hand (2.5.1404-07). Angry after these bewildering encounters, Segismundo eliminates the second servant, a voice that has tried to integrate Segismundo by suggesting correct behavior. After this incident, Segismundo's father arrives, but he gives his son a stern lesson: "[M]ira bien lo que te advierto: / que seas humilde y blando, / porque quizá estás soñando, / aunque ves que estás despierto" (2.6.1528-31). After his father leaves, Segismundo figuratively continues the natural process of differentiation into an independent adult that was occurring in the first act as he exclaims "informado estoy / de quién soy" (2.6.1545-46). In another interaction when Segismundo could learn how to interact respectfully with a woman, Segismundo threatens Rosaura's honor and disrespects the aged Clotaldo before his father has him taken back to his tower.

Although it appears that the prophecy about Segismundo has come true from these scenes, one might also read these episodes as Segismundo's long-postponed attempts at integration into his family and society. Because his social maturity does not match his adult stature and age, Segismundo's actions appear more improper to onlookers. Moreover, Segismundo suddenly finds himself in a position where a family secret is being revealed to him, and difficult secrets often lead members to act out. Furthermore, Segismundo has little time in the palace to adapt because he is quickly drugged and returned to the tower, where he resumes the maturational process of differentiation. Differences in how children are integrated in the play result in distinct levels of differentiation.

---

5   De Armas compares Basilio to Saturn who eats his children to "avoid being challenged" ("Planeta" 908).

Another essential family function is maintaining equilibrium in the system. At times, families find themselves having to cope with changes, which can cause profound upheaval and mean both short- and long-term lifestyle modifications. Unhealthy family systems find it difficult to adapt to change, while functional systems adapt, balancing continuity with the past with new circumstances to promote growth in family members (Walsh 29). Death is an example of a change that strongly affects families, and the death of Basilio's wife, Clorilene, in childbirth could be a particularly difficult kind of death because it was a traumatic loss of a young spouse in an "off-time" death that was not preceded by an illness that would give time to prepare and grieve (Anderson and Sabatelli 264, 265, 269, 273). In "Loving Parents or Cruel Jailers?" Strother discusses Basilio's strange imprisonment of his son as the action of a first-time parent and grieving widower (82, 86-90). Based on a reading of images from alchemy, de Armas suggests that Clorilene may have become pregnant with Segismundo during an extramarital relationship ("Planeta" 907, "King's Son" 4). Whether their marriage was happy or not, a wife's death is likely to dredge up some emotions for the husband, even if it is only an awareness of his own immortality, and cause change.[6] For children who lose a parent, besides causing anxiety, depression, and feelings of abandonment, unresolved grief can "affect the individual's capacity to form meaningful intimate relationships" in the future, according to Anderson and Sabatelli (277). Segismundo lost not only his mother, whom he does not know about, but also his father, who withdrew from him, and no one modeled for Segismundo how to cope with their absence.

Casey indicates that it was important for families to honor the dead: "Keeping alive the memory of the dead was the first and most serious obligation of the heir" (206). Anderson and Sabatelli list four essential tasks necessary for the healthy functioning of a family after a death: "Shared acknowledgement of the reality of the death," "Shared experience of the pain of the grief," "Reorganization of the family system," and "Reinvestment in other relationships and life pursuits" (267-68). The family consisting of Basilio and Segismundo, who experienced a loss, does not show evidence of having managed the first task successfully, about which Anderson and Sabatelli

---

[6] In *Family Matters*, Strother argues that marriages in the seventeenth century, although different from those in the twentieth, lasted long enough that they were not formed only for reproduction and childrearing (82). Bowen's theories were influenced by scientific studies of animal behaviors. Even male and female animal pairs develop attachment and divide tasks related to their maintenance and survival, becoming interdependent, so that one "pays a price of some sort" when the other has not completed a task (Papero 28-9, 31).

caution: "Efforts to protect children or other vulnerable family members by keeping secrets or withholding information are likely to inhibit resolution of the loss and may lead to the development of ineffective coping strategies such as denial, minimization, and avoidance" (267). Failure of family members to express and accept the emotions of relatives after a death also leads to behavioral, health, and psychological problems (Anderson and Sabatelli 267). Lorrain M. Wright and Jane Nagy add that a mother's death has different consequences than that of a father because of long-held beliefs about feminine nurturing (126). Although Basilio has invested significant effort in his studies, which is an example of the coping style of withdrawal into isolation or work, according to Anderson and Sabatelli (276), it seems as if family tasks carried out by Clorilene and Basilio have not been reorganized or assigned because Segismundo has been locked in the tower. Given that none of the tasks of mourning have been completed effectively by the entire remaining family unit, it is unlikely their energy is "available for new activities and experiences" (Anderson and Sabatelli 268) or that the family has been able to change its life strategies to meet changing circumstances.

Although he claims that locking Segismundo in the tower was to protect Poland, Basilio has chosen secrecy, a common strategy for lessening pain, which, if used long-term, prevents families from maintaining cohesiveness and managing conflict (Anderson and Sabatelli 281). To further analyze Basilio's choice, Sullivan offers that the horoscope followed by Basilio is really "subjective projections of the King's own unconscious fears and misgivings reflected back to him" since Basilio and his wife imagine their son's future before his birth from her dream and his reading of astrology (40, 42). Unconsciously, through his prolonged denial, Basilio may be protecting his kingdom from Segismundo, protecting Segismundo from his circumstances, or protecting Basilio himself from grief, change, or the inevitability of death. When Segismundo is in the tower, as Mujica states, it enables Basilio to "remove the constant reminder of his own failure as a father" (201). According to Jo-Ann Krestan and Claudia Bepko, denial, which is often unconscious, protects a person or family from pain and despair (143). In contrast to the father/son unit, Rosaura's family did not experience the death of a family member, although Clotaldo's unexplained long-term absence must have influenced the family. Less information is provided about how Violante and Rosaura were affected by the lack of a husband and father, but it appears that Rosaura and her mother adapted to the situation enough so that the two could develop a loving mother/daughter bond, reorganize their family system, and reinvest in other pursuits despite that fact that they may not have acknowledged the loss and shared their grief.

Both parent/child systems appear to be dyadic, or composed of only two members, but, in each case a third member is needed to create a triangular structure. Triangles often develop at times when a family system is under too much stress (Berg-Cross 120). Basilio employs his loyal servant Clotaldo to assume the function of the third person and raise his son, and Rosaura travels with her protector, the *gracioso* Clarín, until Clotaldo chooses to enter rightfully into her family system, first as a secretive paternal figure and finally as her real father. The absent third person and the adopted replacement play a significant role in the balance and behavior of the systems.

These families illustrate two more functions of family systems, which are interrelated, in this play. The functions are maintaining the family agenda and protecting secrets, but there are factors in the last function that appear to affect integration, and thus differentiation, as well as the equilibrium of the systems. The families of Segismundo and Rosaura both carry out their family agendas. The agenda established by Basilio, and supported by the extended family represented by cousins Estrella and Astolfo, is to govern the kingdom of Poland. The agenda set by Rosaura's mother was a different one: to protect the family's honor. The agendas of both of these families are intimately connected with the final family function of keeping secrets, where there is a noticeable difference between these two family units.

Throughout the ages, families have struggled with decisions about secrecy and openness that have significant long- and short-term effects on interactions among family members. Berg-Cross outlines the kinds of secrets that are kept by families, dividing them by events or personal facts (156). Rosaura's family secret is of the former kind because they hide her illegitimate birth and her mother's premarital sexual activity. On the other hand, Basilio keeps secret personal facts about his son's presumed behaviors and attitudes (Berg-Cross 156). Not much is known about the kinds of secrets most common in families, but more is known about their functions, which include supportive, protective, manipulative, and avoidant secrets (Berg-Cross 157-60). The secret of Rosaura's birth, as kept by her mother, who also does not tell her the origin of the sword, falls into the category of protective secrets, which aim for the family to present a positive image to the extended family and/or community, but protective secrets are not always healthy. In "Secrets in Families and Family Therapy," Evan Imber-Black analyzes a family, whose dysfunctions originate from the long-kept half-century-old secret that the first daughter was born before the parents' marriage (4, 8). Imber-Black points out that the same first daughter and her daughter both became pregnant before marriage, a three-generation repetition which "may be seen and framed as a misguided attempt to finally open the family secret" (10). Although Rosaura does not become pregnant in the play, she could have repeated the act.

The secret of Segismundo's birth does not appear to have the same function since the residents of Poland would likely be pleased to know of a legitimate male heir to rule. By not admitting this, Basilio promotes the idea that he has disappointed his subjects by not engendering and raising their future king. Basilio's secret is multifunctional, with a variety of meanings. Hiding his son's existence may be protective because Basilio judges it in the best interest of his subjects. Not telling Segismundo about his origin also makes this secret manipulative since it withholds knowledge from the son so that the father may maintain his advantage. Avoidant secrets, with which Basilio's secret also has points of contact, are of the kind that allows a family system to avoid dealing with problematic or annoying knowledge, such as the existence of a son, in this case, or possibly an extramarital affair, as de Armas suggested. Anthony argues that the secret is Basilio's (and Clotaldo's) sexuality and contact with the feminine (169). Because (1) Basilio's wife and sister share the same name, Clorilene, (2) Basilio's sister's husband is not named, (3) the play ends with the marriage of cousins, and (4) similar names, such as Segismundo's aunt and Basilio's sister Recisunda, repeat in the family, Roberto González Echevarría suggests a metaphorical hint of a family history of incest, which is a serious secret for families (62-63). This kind of secret often causes severe anguish to the victim (who may act out this hurt in variety of ways) and utter turmoil throughout the family as members consciously or unconsciously gain awareness of and then keep or reveal the secret of the sexual exploitation. Family systems often keep secrets, but some are more helpful to the members than others. Through the comparison of the secrets of these two families, Basilio's secret functions in more destructive ways than that of Violante, who initiates her daughter's journey to uncover her secret. In "Shame: Reservoir for Family Secrets," Marilyn Mason states that it is not always the content of the secret that is destructive, but the resistance of the family to discussing and passing on the secret among family members, which causes the family to become mired in shame (31). Because of how these secrets affect the equilibrium of the family systems and their ability to change, their integration of the child, and, thus, the child's successful differentiation, Rosaura and Segismundo find themselves more prepared and less prepared to transition into the adult world.

Despite the hardships Segismundo faces as he prepares to assume his adult identity and role, the end of the second act and the third act present Segismundo's process of differentiation. After being returned to the tower, Segismundo reflects on his experiences in the castle, where he observed through his missteps the differences between social classes, men and women, kings and subjects, and the authority of fathers and sons, and he seems to regret his inappropriate actions. Segismundo also philosophizes about the relationship between life and dreams: "que toda la vida es sueño, / y los sueños, sueños son" (2.19.2186-87). While dreaming after his return to the tower, Segismundo imagines that Clotaldo will die by his charge's hand, but Segismundo later chooses not to kill his tutor, instead recognizing him for raising him, which is a father's role, and then freeing him to fight on his father's side (3.4.2396-97).

The third act includes the doubling of Segismundo's and Rosaura's conflicts with their fathers, which are peacefully resolved in the end, showing the two young people taking on adult roles. Assuming responsibility for her betrayal, Rosaura decides that she must kill Astolfo to restore her own honor since Clotaldo will not do so, so she joins Segismundo's supporters. Segismundo articulates his new agenda of doing good deeds: "Mas, sea verdad o sueño, / obrar bien es lo que importa" (3.4.2423-24). In the end, a presumably wiser Segismundo forgives his father's error in his use of prophecy, and Clotaldo is forced to admit to his premarital sexual encounter with Violante so that Rosaura can be honorably married. The character of Segismundo has shown growth, but the success of his differentiation is owed to stressors from outside his family system that liberate him from the tower at two different times.

By the end of the play, the secrets are out, and the audience enjoys a seemingly happy ending since the youths are matched, supposedly prepared to begin their adult lives, have families of their own, and assume their responsibilities as king and nobility. The young peoples' attempts at differentiation appear to have proven successful. Fortunately, research indicates that some children can individuate more than their parents, depending upon if the child must focus on parental tensions or has more freedom to participate in "age-appropriate tasks" (Anderson and Sabatelli 65). Yet the matches at the end are unsatisfying. Despite obvious attraction, Segismundo gives up Rosaura for Estrella. This may be a noble gesture that reestablishes Rosaura's honor, but it may also be that Segismundo is marrying the less self-reliant of the women or, as González Echevarría suggests, that Segismundo solidifies his right to rule by marrying another heir, which weakens Astolfo's bid to the throne, pairing him with an a illegitimate bride who is no longer a virgin (70). Anthony views Segismundo's decision as a rejection of lust and disorder (170). Rosaura is left to marry Astolfo, who may have never planned to marry her because of her unknown lineage (May 124), even though he had recognized his love interest in Poland and had saved her portrait.

Family Systems theories make apparent another concern that dampens the young couples' futures in the unwritten fourth act. Family functions and dysfunctions are part of a legacy that is handed down from generation to generation, which Froma Walsh succinctly summarizes: "The capacity to function as a spouse and a parent is seen as largely determined by family-of-origin experiences" (36). For example, Rosaura's premarital relationship is reminiscent of her mother's, and, as May points out, Rosaura has chosen a husband more like her father than she knows because both men abandoned their supposed love interests (124). Critics have puzzled over Segismundo's decision to confine the rebellious soldier who had freed him to the tower, suggesting many motivations for Segismundo's pronouncement. From the perspective of Family Systems theories, the son's action seems similar to his father's tactic for controlling a problem, a behavior associated with people who have not successfully differentiated, which is a troubling quality in a ruler. Like father, like son, this parallel between Segismundo's and his father's actions[7] raises the question of Segismundo's ability to rule. When comparing Basilio's governance of his country to his leadership of his family[8] a concern emerges that may repeat with Segismundo because public leadership reflects family life, according to psychiatrist Bowen: "the same processes of dysfunction observed in the family can be seen in the larger society... Under conditions of chronic stress, both the family and society will lose contact with their intellectually determined principles and will resort to an emotional basis for decisions that offer short-term relief" (Becvar and Becvar 139). Likewise, Friedman sums up the interaction between life and stage: "The stage serves as a mirror to the world, while at the same time the world may be viewed as a stage that reflects performance conventions and motifs" (41). In art and life, if one does not learn leadership within a family or other system and cannot lead the system wisely in a sustained fashion, it does not seem auspicious for a country's gov-

---

7 A. Robert Lauer also notes the similarity between father's and son's actions (139-40). Mujica highlights father's and son's "arrogance, their insistence on intellectual certainty, their tendency to systematize, their unwillingness to see beyond appearances" as well as a "craving for self-assertion" (199).

8 In contrast to the view that kings in the *comedia* were honorable men representing the dramatist's moral outlook, Dian Fox writes of the ironic fallibility of monarchs in Calderón's plays (217), noting that Basilio keeps secrets from his subjects, rules absolutely, and pays more attention to his studies than his kingdom (220), in addition to his shortcomings as a father.

ernance. Segismundo's and Rosaura's life experiences may have given them the wisdom to avoid future dysfunctions and create new agendas for their futures, such as Segismundo's call to do good deeds. However, if not, reflecting family systems in life and literature, Segismundo and Rosaura might find themselves again repeating past patterns aggravated by their legacy of family secrets.

Works Cited

Anderson, Stephen A., and Ronald M. Sabatelli. *Family Interaction: A Multigenerational Developmental Perspective*, 4th ed., Pearson, 2007.
Anderson, James M. *Daily Life during the Spanish Inquisition*. Greenwood, 2002.
Anthony, Ruth. "Violante: The Place of Rejection." de Armas, pp. 165-82.
Aylward, E. T. "A Question of Values: The Spiritual Education of Segismundo in Calderón's *La vida es sueño*." *Bulletin of the Comediantes*, vol. 54, no. 2, 2002, pp. 339-72.
Becvar, Dorothy Stroh, and Raphael J. Becvar. *Family Therapy: A Systemic Integration*. Allyn and Bacon, 1988.
Berg-Cross, Linda. *Basic Concepts in Family Therapy: An Introductory Text*. Haworth, 2000.
Calderón de la Barca, Pedro. *La vida es sueño*, edited by José María García Martín, Castalia, 1984.
Casey, James. *Family and Community in Early Modern Spain: The Citizens of Granada, 1570-1739*. Cambridge UP, 2007.
Cooper, Sara E, editor. *The Ties That Bind: Questioning Family Dynamics and Family Discourse in Hispanic Literature*. UP of America, 2004.
———. "Viability of Family Systems Theory for Latin America." *The Ties That Bind: Questioning Family Dynamics and Family Discourse in Hispanic Literature*, edited by Cooper, UP of America, 2004, pp. 185-96.
Cruickshank, Don W. *Don Pedro Calderón*. Cambridge UP, 2009.
de Armas, Frederick A. "'El planeta más impío': Basilio's Role in *La vida es sueño*." *Modern Language Review*, vol. 81, 1986, pp. 900-11.
———. "Segismundo/Philip IV: The Politics of Astrology in *La vida es sueño*." *Bulletin of the Comediantes*, vol. 53, no. 1, 2001, pp. 83-101.
———. "The Critical Tower." *The Prince in the Tower: Perceptions of La vida es sueño*, edited by de Armas, Bucknell UP, 1993, pp. 3-14.
———. "The King's Son and the Golden Dew: Alchemy in Calderón's *La vida es sueño*." *Hispanic Review*, vol. 60, no. 3, 1992, pp. 301-19.
———, editor. *The Prince in the Tower: Perceptions of La vida es sueño*. Bucknell UP, 1993.

Egginton, William. "Psychoanalysis and the *Comedia*: Skepticism and the Paternal Function in *La vida es sueño*." *Bulletin of the Comediantes*, vol. 52, no. 1, 2000, pp. 97-121.

Fox, Dian. "Kingship and Community in *La vida es sueño*." *Bulletin of Hispanic Studies*, vol. 58, no. 3, 1981, pp. 217-28.

Friedman, Edward H. "Deference, *Différance*: The Rhetoric of Deferral." de Armas, pp. 41-53.

González Echevarría, Roberto. "Los dos finales de *La vida es sueño:* una lectura cervantina." *Literatura y pensamiento en España: Estudios en honor de Ciriaco Morón Arroyo*, edited by Francisco La Rubia-Prado, Juan de la Cuesta, 2003, pp. 55-75.

Hesse, Everett W. "*La vida es sueño* and the Paradox of Violence." *Revista de Estudios Hispánicos*, vol. 5, 1971, pp. 3-17.

Imber-Black, Evan, editor. *Secrets in Families and Family Therapy*. W. W. Norton, 1993.

Imber-Black, Evan. "Secrets in Families and Family Therapy: An Overview." Introduction. *Secrets in Families and Family Therapy*, edited by Imber-Black, W. W. Norton, 1993, pp. 3-28.

Knapp, John V. "Family Systems Therapy and Literary Study: An Introduction." Introduction. *Reading the Family Dance: Family Systems Therapy and Literary Study*, edited by Knapp and Kenneth Womack, U of Delaware P, 2003, pp. 13-36.

Knapp, John V., and Kenneth Womack, editors. *Reading the Family Dance: Family Systems Therapy and Literary Study*. U of Delaware P, 2003.

Krestan, Jo-Ann, and Claudia Bepko. "On Lies, Secrets, and Silence: The Multiple Levels of Denial in Addictive Families." Imber-Black, pp. 141-59.

Lapesa, Rafael. "Consideraciones sobre *La vida es sueño*." *Boletín de la Real Academia Española*, vol. 225, no. 62, 1982, pp. 87-102.

Lauer, A. Robert. "El leal traidor de *La vida es sueño* de Calderón." *Bulletin of Hispanic Studies*, vol. 77, 2000, pp. 133-44.

Lavroff, Ellen C. "Who Is Rosaura?: Another Look at *La vida es sueño*." *Tijdschrift voor Levende Talen*, vol. 42, no. 5, 1976, pp. 482-96.

Mason, Marilyn. "Shame: Reservoir for Family Secrets." Imber-Black, pp. 29-43.

May, T. E. "Rosaura." *Hispanic Studies in Honour of Frank Pierce*, edited by John England, Department of Hispanic Studies, University of Sheffield, 1980, pp. 123-26.

Merrick, C. A. "Clotaldo's Role in *La vida es sueño*." *Bulletin of Hispanic Studies*, vol. 50, no.1, 1973, pp. 256-69.

Miller, Donald D. "Dysfunction, Discord, and Wedded Bliss: Baroque Families in *Don Quijote*." Cooper, pp. 63-78.

Mujica, Barbara Louise. *Calderón's Characters: An Existential Point of View*. Puvill, 1980.
O'Connor, Thomas Austin. "*La vida es sueño:* A View from Metatheater." *Kentucky Romance Quarterly*, vol. 1, no. 25, 1978, pp. 13-26.
Ozment, Steven. *Ancestors: The Loving Family in Old Europe*. Harvard UP, 2001.
Papero, Daniel V. *Bowen Family Systems Theory*. Allyn and Bacon, 1990.
Parker, Alexander A. "The Father-Son Conflict in the Drama of Calderón." *Forum for Modern Language Studies*, vol. 2, no. 2, 1966, pp. 99-113.
Reher, David S. *Perspectives on the Family in Spain, Past and Present*. Clarendon, 1997.
Ruano de la Haza, José María. "Teoría y praxis del personaje teatral áureo: Pedro Crespo, Peribáñez y Rosaura." *El escritor y la escena V: Estudios sobre teatro español y novohispano de los Siglos de Oro. Homenaje a Marc Vitse*, edited by Ysla Campbell, Universidad Autónoma de Ciudad Juárez, 1997, pp. 19-35.
Ruiz Ramón, Francisco. "El 'mito de Uranos' en *La vida es sueño*." *Teatro del Siglo de Oro: Homenaje a Alberto Navarro González*, Edition Reichenberger, 1990, pp. 547-62.
Serna, Ven. "Rosaura: mujer, varón y monstruo." *Actas del Sexto Congreso Internacional de Hispanistas celebrado en Toronto del 22 al 26 de 1977*, edited by Alan M. Gordon, Evelyn Rugg, and Rafael Lapesa, Dept. of Spanish and Portuguese, U of Toronto, 1980, pp. 691-93.
Strother, Darci L. *Family Matters: A Study of On- and Off-Stage Marriage and Family Relations in Seventeenth-Century Spain*. Peter Lang, 1999.
———. "Loving Parents or Cruel Jailers? Towards an Understanding of Calderón's Basilio and Liríope." *Bulletin of the Comediantes*, vol. 45, no. 1, 1993, pp. 81-92.
Stroud, Matthew D. *The Play in the Mirror: Lacanian Perspectives on Spanish Baroque Theater*. Bucknell UP, 1996.
Sullivan, Henry W. "The Oedipus Myth: Lacan and Dream Interpretation in *La vida es sueño*." *New Hispanisms: Literature, Culture, Theory*, edited by Mark I. Millington and Paul Julian Smith, Dovehouse Editions Canada, 1994, pp. 37-52.
Walsh, Froma, editor. *Normal Family Processes: Growing Diversity and Complexity*, 3rd ed., Guilford, 2003.
Whitby, William M. "Rosaura's Role in the Structure of *La vida es sueño*." *Critical Essays on the Theatre of Calderón*, edited by Bruce W. Wardropper, New York UP, 1965, pp. 101-13.
Wilson, E. M. "On *La vida es sueño*." *Critical Essays on the Theatre of Calderón*, edited by Bruce W. Wardropper, New York UP, 1965, pp. 63-89.
Wright, Lorraine M., and Jane Nagy. "Death: The Most Troublesome Family Secret of All." Imber-Black, pp. 121-37.

Copying the Unreal: The Multiple Imitations in the Balcony Scene of *Don Gil de las calzas verdes*

ROBERT L. TURNER
University of South Dakota

"it is not what is behind the codpiece
but what is behind the forehead that counts"
– EDWARD FRIEDMAN[1]

THE *COMEDIA* IS A genre replete with misdirection, disguise, false identities, cross-dressing, and numerous elements that raise questions regarding identity and the self. The Mercedarian playright, Tirso de Molina, was a prodigious manipulator of these elements as seen in *El vergonzoso en palacio, La celosa de sí misma, El amor médico, Bellaco sois Gomez, Esto sí que es negociar,* and other works. Tirso typically employs these techniques in a straight forward manner: a covered face, a misgiven name, or the creation of an alter ego. In contrast, *Don Gil de la calzas verdes* is distinctive in the degree in which Tirso creates a proliferation of identities. Not only does he provide the audience with four different versions of the fictitious Don Gil, Ellen Frye's "greatest non-character of the Spanish baroque *comedia*" (136), but he also multiplies the names associated with the other leading characters within the play, creating a veritable cloud of possible identities tied to the various characters. This multiplication of names and identities is a form of mimetic act which in turn is based on the mimesis of the theatrical construct itself. The reader or viewer becomes a participant in a self-replicating baroque world which, as Jesse M. Syllepsis Molesworth

---

[1] From "Clothes Unmake the Woman: The Idiosyncrasies of Cross-Dressing in Ana Caro's Valor, agravio y mujer." *Confluencia*, vol. 24, no. 1, 2008 pg 170.

states, "mim[es] imitation rather than attempting to counterfeit verisimilitude" (417) anticipating the Derridean view of constant deferment.

The play opens with a situation common to the *comedia*. Our heroine, Doña Juana Solís, has arrived in Madrid chasing her wayward lover, a Don Martín de Guzman, who, in a similarly common manner, has promised marriage and then abandoned her. The first indication that this is not a standard by-the-numbers scorned bride plot comes as we learn that Don Martín's abandonment comes not from his own fickle nature, but at the command of his father. When Don Pedro, Doña Ines' wealthy father, offers to marry her to Don Martín with a dowry of 70,000 ducats, Martín's father jumps at the proposal. However, since his son is already committed to Doña Juana, he offers an invented Don Gil de Albornoz in his place. Doña Juana, commenting on this betrayal, tells her criado, and the audience:

> JUANA. No se atrevió a dar el sí
> claramente por saber
> que era forzoso salir
> a la causa mi deshonra...
> [H]izo a mi esposo partir
> a esta Corte, ...
> Díjole que se mudase
> el nombre de don Martín,
> atajando inconvenientes,
> en el nombre de don Gil, (164-67, 170-71, 173-76).

It is the Elder Guzman who is the source both of Doña Juana's dishonor and of the name Don Gil, and not his son Don Martín.

This is noteworthy for multiple reasons. First, I wish to emphasize that Tirso departs from the more typical narrative of a faithless lover and instead points his condemnation towards the greed of old men. There is something particularly chilling in the cold calculation by Don Martín's father that trades Doña Juana's honor for familial wealth. This change in the common spurned woman narrative makes Don Martín less of a villain and more into a pawn for his father's desires. This early impression is further reinforced by Don Martín's constant ineffectuality throughout the play and is indicative of his role as a secondary character, a puppet to be manipulated, not a person embodied with agency.

Likewise, the initial creation of the Don Gil persona differs from other invented or assumed names common in the *comedia* due to its origin. Don

Gil is invented for Don Martín, but it is not his own invention and therefore he fails to completely embody the name, contenting himself with a letter of introduction. In practical terms, this results in the identity of Don Gil being initially undefined, or at least under-defined. Isabelle Bouchiba-Fochesato puts it in these terms: "Simbólicamente, don Martín acepta vaciarse de lo que le define social y religiosamente: su estatuto de hijo y su estatuto de marido para entrar en una identidad vacía que, además, le van a denegar tanto doña Juana como casi todas las damas y galanes de la obra" (13).[2] This failure on Don Martín's part, and the fact that Doña Juana has learned of the plot, means that the name Don Gil becomes a reflection of "la inestabilidad *real*, la que existe fuera de la escena, en la realidad previa a ella" (Ramos, 60). This instability creates a contested space that Doña Juana usurps before the rising of the curtain and that provides her the opportunity to oppose Don Martín and his father's plans. While María Eugenia Ramos sees this instability as causing Juana's transformation, I understand it in terms of creating an opportunity for Doña Juana to exercise her agency. Unlike Doña Leonor in *Valor, agravio y mujer*, there is no "Mi agravio mudó mi ser" (510) moment. Instead, Doña Juana states: "Saqué fuerzas de flaqueza, dejé el temor femenil, dióme alientos el agravio" (209-11). Doña Juana's "determinación cuerda" (213) is a key element in her character and is reflected in her ability to assume the name of Don Gil and to manipulate events throughout the course of the play.

Tirso highlights the unfulfilled and incomplete nature of the Don Gil persona as Doña Juana hires a new criado, Caramanchel, as part of her efforts to complete her disguise. When he asks her name, the answer "Don Gil no más" (518), acts as a verbal castration, a removal of the Lacanian name of the father, that is reemphasized in the following line when Caramanchel dubs his new master "Capón" (519). The author further stresses the incomplete nature of this pseudonym in the two juxtaposing scenes that follow. The first brings Don Martín to the stage as he presents himself to Inés' father conveying his own father's recommendation and bearing the full name Don Gil de Albornoz. Here Tirso further concretizes this version of Don Gil by tying his name to his clothing. As L. Carl Johnson points out, the Albornoz was a "hooded, woolen cloak of Moorish origin" (135). This fictitious last name literalizes the role of Don Martín's new name in covering up his identity. The Albornoz conceals the Guzmán who cannot ethically marry Doña Inés.[3]

---

2   Numbers refer to paragraph.
3   In a different work, Tirso puts this ethical dilemma in these terms "yo no he de ser mujer / de quien ya para con Dios / está casado con vos" (*La Huerta de Juan Fernández*, 3182-84).

The second, complementary, scene presents Doña Juana in the moment in which she meets and begins to woo Doña Inés. In contrast to Don Martín's introduction, Doña Inés' naming of Doña Juana's iteration of Don Gil (996) serves to emphasize his "bare" nature. This Don Gil is bereft of name, beard, and, unbeknownst to Doña Inés, phallus. Thus, the addition of "de las calzas verdes" becomes an ironic echo of Don Martín's Albornoz. Since there is nothing else to grasp, Doña Inés chooses a descriptor. These paired scenes highlight the core distinction between our two primary Gils. The first comes with a letter of introduction, a last name, and the approval of both sets of fathers, the second appeals directly to the contested woman, lacks a name, and is clearly feminine in "his" bearing and figure.[4]

As can be expected in a play where inversion and misdirection reign, Doña Juana is considered the more attractive of the two, and her performance of Don Gil rapidly becomes the primary version of the identity "by manipulating the re-characterization of 'Don Gil' so that only she best embodies the reconstituted horizon of expectations associated with that identity" (Johnson, 137). From this point on, Doña Juana's avatar serves as the focus of desire for the various would-be lovers. With this dynamic now established, let us away to the balcony scene in the third act to consider how this contested name duplicates and reduplicates itself.

The final act of the play revolves around the extended balcony scene which will quickly devolve into a wild melee of competing Gils as the play tends towards its chaotic conclusion where "La apariencia de don Gil y su actuación como tal crean la realidad de varios 'don Giles'" (Ramos, 67). During the course of the play, Doña Juana has employed every strategy available to thwart Don Martín. This includes adding distractions such as introducing her true history under the name of Doña Elvira, including a version of Don Martín, who she names as Don Miguel (1293-1314). As the false Don Gil, promising to marry Doña Inés' cousin Doña Clara (2459-61), having Quintana tell Don Martín that she died in childbirth (2046-85), and sending a letter to her father telling him that Don Martín murdered her (2320-40). These various manipulations, what Everett W. Hesse called a "play within a drama" (391), serve to create a chaotic state in which objective reality becomes suspect with the proliferation of so many potential truths. Each of these tactics serves to complicate matters for Don Martín, but they also generate confusion for everyone else.

---

4   In just the first act, Doña Juana's version of Don Gil is described using such terms as "capón" (519) and "hermafrodita" (724), with Doña Inés making multiple comments on "his" face (793, 839).

This confusion comes to a crisis point as Doña Inés accuses Juana/Gil of betraying her and preferring her cousin Doña Clara. When Doña Inés confronts Don Gil with evidence linking him both to Doña Elvira as well as to Doña Clara and to herself, Doña Juana drops the Don Gil mask exclaiming:

> JUANA. ¡Que soy Elvira!
>   ¡Lleve el diablo a don Miguel!
> INÉS. ¿Quién?
> JUANA. Doña Elvira ¿En la voz
>   y cara no me conoces?
> INÉS. ¿No eres don Gil de Albornoz?
> JUANA. Ni soy don Gil....
> JUANA. Su vestido
>   y [semejanza] hizo el daño.
>   Si esto no te ha persuadido,
>   averigua el desengaño. (2554-59, 2562-65)

All of the elements which will shortly be evident in the balcony scene are present here. As the play builds towards the balcony scene, Tirso has created a multiplicity of identities that are all tied to Doña Juana. These embark both the multiple identities she creates for herself and others and the multiple versions of Don Gil that spring to life due to her actions. Because Doña Juana has created such a tangle of names and stories, she becomes simultaneously, Doña Juana (her actual, original identity), Don Gil de las Calzas Verdes (the charming stranger who presented himself in the garden), the "true" Don Gil de Albornoz (the legitimate choice of Inés' father as evidenced by her possession of Martín's letters [1792-1880]), and Doña Elvira (The wronged woman). This multiplying effect serves to split our perception of identity and to highlight the arbitrary nature of naming since as Johnson observes, there is "no absolutely fixed point of reference" (139) that connects name, identity (characteristics), and an individual.

Several critics have addressed this proliferation of selves. The aforementioned Johnson describes this multiplication as part of "an intricate web of overlapping contexts that resist easy analysis" (133), while Johnathan Thacker observes that "Tirso seems to challenge himself to produce a love intrigue of such complexity that it becomes almost impossible to follow except in performance" (64–65). Discussing this phenomenon, Nadine Ly argues that Tirso creates both multiple iterations of Don Gil (304) and also multiple levels of theatricality. In her schematic (314-16), the spectator is presented with the following levels: 1) Doña Juana (person), 2) Doña Juana as actor playing Don Gil, and 3) Don Gil as actor playing Doña Elvira (308). I must respectfully disagree. I see a level 0), the actor, and behind her, the text. Therefore, I argue we need to consider the following scheme: Level -1) the text, 0) the actor playing the role, 1) Doña Juana, 2) Don Gil, and then 2.5) Elvira. Elvira is not Doña Juana playing Don Gil playing Elvira. This element is covered, in part, in the charts in Ly's article, but not developed in the same way that I understand it. What we see is Doña Juana playing Elvira, who coincidentally happens to resemble Don Gil.[5] It is worth noting, as Ly does in the footnote on pp 310-11, that Doña Juana's "ghost" acts as a further level of creation and is the only "real" Doña Juana until the conclusion of the play. At the same time, Doña Juana's ghost is the creation of Don Martín's imagination and so should be considered a step-sibling to the proliferation of Gils. It is a fantastic representation of the original and not under the control of the creator or embodier of the role. These multiple roles and levels are highlighted in the run up to the balcony scene as a means of emphasizing the emerging chaos in the play, as well as the slippery nature of identity that so often is central to Tirso's work.

This scene underscores both the feminine and masculine aspects of Doña Juana's personas: elements that as Christopher Weimer observes (102), are present from the beginning of the work. Her masculine aspects are presented as objects of desire, both as a slightly forbidden love in the form of Calzas Verdes, and as a realistic choice, if she is indeed the "true" Albornoz. The feminine aspects represent, in the form of Doña Elvira, and underneath it all, Doña Juana, the hopeful lover and wronged woman, emblematic of female concerns in this theatrical world. As Doña Juana plays Don Gil, one of her important accomplishments is that she maneuvers Doña Inés into a position of empathy. Her description of how Don Miguel wronged Doña Elvira and then became Don Gil not only echoes her actual situation, but also provides Doña Inés with the opportunity to imagine herself as the victim of a false lover. This is a parallel of her treatment of Don Martín. As Everett Hesse observes, she provokes his empathy by "making him suffer that jealousy, fear and harassment that she endured when he abandoned her for another woman" (393). This pattern of repeated parallelism is a significant feature of the work. Doña Juana thus becomes the hermaphrodite that Caramanchel labeled her in the first act as she simultaneously plays the role of the scorned lover and the faithless suitor.

---

5   A closer approximation to Ly's vision is seen in *El Amor Médico* where Gerónima deliberately layers herself in multiple, nested, identities.

Doña Inés's reluctance to believe that the object of her affection is in fact a woman leads her to place Juana/Gil/Elvira in a dress (2604). After the change of wardrobe, she comments: imagina / mi amor en ése fingido / que eres hombre, y no vecina (2608-10), citing Doña Juana's "voz, presencia y cara" (2615). Even after she is persuaded that Doña Juana is female, her longing remains: "don Gil quisiera que fueras, / que yo adorara tu engaño" (2665-66). This is not the only time that the play flirts with homosexual desire, but this forced un-crossdressing of Doña Juana and Doña Inés' following commentary, starkly highlight the fluid nature of desire and act as part of Tirso's larger commentary on identity itself.[6] Doña Juana's portrayal of Don Gil is inscribed with feminine characteristics in addition to the lack of a history and name. It is these attributes that attract Doña Inés and Doña Clara and which the various sub-Gils will attempt to mimic. The same focus on clothing and voice that confounds Doña Inés will likewise dominate the following scene.

The balcony scene begins with the appearance of Don Juan, one of Doña Inés' suitors. By this point in the play, he is so frustrated with the two Don Gils that he swears: "¡Vive Dios, que aunque me cueste / vida y hacienda, tengo de quitarla / a todos cuantos Giles me persigan!" (2657-60). Arriving on his heels is the *gracioso* Caramanchel. His role in the balcony scene is to act as a surrogate audience member and provide a metatheatrical commentary, constantly reminding the audience of the artificiality of the Don Gil construct.

The action begins once Don Juan approaches the balcony and the various characters on stage set their expectations. Doña Inés speculates as to whether the person below is Don Gil de Albornoz while Caramanchel wonders aloud if his missing master has arrived. In both instances, the following line is the same: "habla," as a command (2767, 2770). With the dark evening hiding faces and bodies, the voice, including its timbre and tone, becomes the conveyer of meaning and the sign of the desired Don Gil, as we see immediately when Caramanchel rejects this first version of Don Gil because his master has a high-pitched voice (2780). Doña Juana, hearing Don Juan's masculine tenor, assumes him to be Don Martín (2786-87), while Doña Inés explicitly inquiries of Don Juan how her desired Don Gil suddenly has a lower pitched voice (2789-98). In each case, the characteristics of the voice signal as much or more than the actual content of speech.

---

6   Raúl Galoppe and David Dalton explore the gender and sexual aspects of the play in their translation and production *of Love's a Bitch* as discussed in their article "(Un)faithful Renditions: Gender Dynamics in an Adaptation of *Don Gil de las calzas verdes*".

The next entrant into this farcical landscape is Don Martín. Although Don Martín is already employing the name Don Gil, he arrives dressed in green in an attempt to emulate his rival, thus abandoning his previous iteration as Don Gil de Albornoz. Stating: "he de andar / como él y me han de llamar / don Gil de las Calzas verdes" (2824-27), he bemoans the usurpation of "his" name (2805), oblivious to the irony his own imitation creates. In doing so, Don Martín once again proves his buffoonish nature. He has belatedly understood the power of Doña Juana's Don Gil, but his imitation is futile since he duplicates her clothing while trying to court Doña Inés in the dark. This act is in fact a double imitation, where Don Martín copies the copy of his false identity. This pursuit of a receding "real" opens a labyrinthine hall of mirrors in which, "[w]e are faced then with mimicry imitating nothing; faced, so to speak, with a double that doubles no simple, a double that nothing anticipates, nothing at least that is not itself already double. There is no simple reference" (Molesworth, 417). This parallels Doña Juana playing Doña Elvira playing Don Gil and is another example of Tirso's tendency to create scenes where Don Martín's and Doña Juana's activities echo each other.

Upon his arrival, Don Martín immediately manages to both mistake Don Juan for Don Gil and to simultaneously imagine that this Don Gil is in fact the ghost of Doña Juana (2831-38). Martín's confusion is characteristic of the underlying structure of this scene and the play as a whole. His supposition is both correct and incorrect. Correct that his rival Don Gil is Doña Juana, incorrect that she is dead, and completely misplaced as he identifies Don Juan as the supernatural Gil. This constant displacement of identity is the key element of the third act, creating what Everett Hesse has termed a "pseudoreality" (392). In this we see an anticipation of postmodern mimesis in which the copies are copying copies of copies all the while blurring original identities creating an "endless hall of mirrors ... by explicitly drawing attention to its status as representation" (Nelson, 150). Yet this is not an endless deferment that leads to nowhere. Instead, Tirso points to the hidden truth buried underneath the multiple layers of representation. Metaphorically, Doña Juana is dead: "Quintana: Misas va a decir por ti / en fe que eres alma que anda / en pena. Doña Juana: ¿Pues no es así?" (2316-18). Don Martín's abandonment has left her stripped of her previous life and hopes. This is one of the reasons why Doña Juana-as-herself doesn't appear until the end of the play. This also explains why she sends her father a note saying Don Martín killed her (2320-40) and why Quintana tells Don Martín that she died bearing his child

(2046—85).⁷ In a very real way, Doña Juana's life in society has ended and her transformation into Don Gil de las calzas verdes becomes an ironic echo of the biblical command to become "one flesh" (Gen 2:24) as she shares her new name and identity with Don Martín. This metatheatrical moment in which Tirso explicitly evokes Doña Juana's presence and overlays it on Don Juan, while she is elsewhere onstage, is a reminder to the audience of the nestled layers of performance they are seeing all the while highlighting its artificiality.

When Don Martín approaches the balcony, Don Juan manages to make the only correct identification of the evening, immediately recognizing him as Don Gil de Albornoz (2847-49), which is the only name he knows for Don Martín. Assuming that no mortal creature could pierce his clever disguise, Don Martín becomes further convinced that he is speaking with Doña Juana's specter (2857-61). All the while, Caramanchel keeps the count for the audience.

> CARAMANCHEL. ¿Don Gil estotro se llama?
> A pares vienen los Giles.
> Pues no es mi don Gil tampoco,
> que hablara a lo caponil" (2865-68).

Hearing the two masculine voices, Doña Juana tells Inés that the second Gil must be Don Miguel. Thus, in a matter of minutes Don Juan has become Don Gil, Don Martín and Doña Juana's Ghost, while Don Martín is now Don Gil de Albornoz, Don Gil de las calzas verdes and Don Miguel. This multiplying of roles works in parallel with the proliferation of Gils. While there are only two self-proclaimed Gils on stage at this moment, they have already been marked with a total of six identifiers.

The attractive power of the idea of Don Gil is such that it captivates all the major players in the piece. Because Doña Juana's representation is an idealized one, and only superficially connected to the realities of courtship and marriage, she, or her avatar, can embody the desires of Doña Clara and Doña Inés without real commitment. In discussing this scene, Raúl A. Galoppe and David Dalton astutely note the tremendous value of the mask created by the *calzas* and the name Don Gil: "[It is] a mask that veils sexual differ-

---

7 I find it significant that the information about Doña Juana's supposed death opens the third act. The first act starts with her new life as Don Gil, the second with "his" absence and the fear that Don Juan has killed "him" (1085-86), now the final act includes the definitive death of Doña Juana just as Don Gil becomes ubiquitous. This reflects Tirso's leitmotiv of presence and absence in the work as well as the completed transition to imagination over concrete reality as a motivating principle.

ence and exposes desire beyond the social constraints attached to sex and its practices. By hiding identities in an explicit way, a mask adds confusion and generates desire by defying us to sort out the confusion it creates. Quintessentially Baroque and quintessentially queer, the green breeches as masks of desire serve as crucial elements in exploiting comedic situations" (144). Although speaking explicitly about their queered version, *Love's a Bitch*, this observation holds true for the original text as well. In this contested space, Don Martín and Don Juan each try to lay claim to the identity of the charming, attractive Don Gil since it is he who holds Doña Inés' favor. In contrast, the women listening to the tenor of their male voices label them as Albornoz or Miguel, associating them with the less attractive and deceptive versions of the role, while the men attempt and name each other in a struggle for control of the desired identity. In this struggle, it is the two men who come closest to the truth, hidden by the night and concealed in green tights. Don Juan correctly identifies Don Martín but still errs in naming him since he is unaware of the existence of Don Martín de Guzmán. Likewise, Don Martín's conviction that Don Gil de las calzas verdes is Doña Juana is accurate but misdirected onto Don Juan. This conviction is enough to frighten Don Martín and he abandons the stage unable to come to terms with Doña Juana's ghost and his own feelings of guilt. Doña Juana still dressed as Doña Elvira, chooses this moment to excuse herself and makes her way to the street.

If the first half of the scene highlighted the male pretenders to the Don Gil name, the second half is a chance to showcase the women. Our third Don Gil arrives when Doña Clara approaches the balcony with the desire to see if "her" Don Gil is courting Doña Inés. This prompts the overwhelmed Caramanchel to exclaim "Don Giles llueve Dios hoy" (2982). Once again, the voice acts as the sign of identity as Doña Inés tells us "Éste es mi Don Gil querido, / que en el habla delicada / reconozco" (2983-85), and once again the sign misleads. Doña Clara's arrival prompts a quick reordering of names as Doña Inés deduces that the other Don Gil must be Don Juan while Don Juan, addressing Doña Clara, repeats his claim to the name of Don Gil, denying that he is Don Miguel. Doña Juana, our primary Don Gil also joins the crowd, prompting the incredulous Caramanchel to exclaim "Ya son cuatro, y serán mil." (3021). Caramanchel's observation is more correct than he knows. If the creation of one Don Gil requires an elaborate ruse, helped along by a letter of introduction from Don Andrés de Guzmán and vouchsafed by witnesses (571-73), the second act of creation is much easier. Doña Juana's version is identified by clothing, lack of a beard, and her voice, not by name or family. The third and fourth Gils produced rely on little more than darkness and a willingness to claim the name. As each Don Gil tries to copy an imaginary creation, each copy is less and less "real" and more and more abstract, like a faded photocopy, or as Caramanchel puts it, a ghost.

What are we to make of such a strange scene? There are farcical moments to be sure, but the creation and proliferation of Gils is more than just a game. As Everett Hesse observes: "each masquerader wants to achieve a similar goal in deadly earnest" (391). The original iteration of Don Gil was part of a stratagem to gain Doña Inés and her money for Don Martín, at the expense of Doña Juana and her honor. Doña Juana's creation is also serious. As we see literally written out for us in her letters, Doña Juana's choices are the nunnery or death. The fact that she plays upon these fears to reach her goals doesn't remove their very real possibility if her plans fail. Don Juan and Doña Clara make use of the name because of the attractive power that it holds. For them, Don Gil may open otherwise closed doors. For Doña Clara, marriage to a charming youth, and for Don Juan a second chance to win Doña Inés's favor. Most of all, Don Gil represents freedom. For Don Martín, it is a freedom from his commitments; for Doña Juana, it means freedom from the cloister. Doña Inés sees the freedom to love an exotic and tantalizing stranger instead of one "tan lleno de barbas" (979) as well as an outlet for her potential homosexual desires. Don Juan sees the name as a way to freely express his feelings for Doña Inés, while for Doña Clara, the name holds the same attraction as it does for Doña Inés but additionally, it allows her the opportunity to walk the city alone at night (2959-62). As a result, all the major characters are willing to invest in the name since it provides each of them with something they desire.

The paired counterpoint to the multitude claiming the same name is how individuals attract multiple names within the scene. I have remarked on the fact that both Don Juan and Don Martín are burdened with multiple identities, just as is Doña Juana in the run up to the balcony scene. If picking the right name brings freedom, the multiplication of names acts, in this instance, as a limiting agent. Don Miguel is a faithless lover. Being tied to that name reduces one's attractiveness, as does being tied to the name of the boorish Don Gil de Albornoz.

The final moments of the balcony scene result in an irreducible conflict over the identity of Don Gil, as the three remaining pretenders to the name state their claims. "Juan: Don Gil el verde soy yo" (3027). "Clara: Don Gil de las Calzasverdes / soy yo sólo" (3032-33). "Juana: Yo soy / don Gil el verde o el pardo" (3035-36). This confrontation provokes an attack by Don Juan which Quintana defeats, wounding Don Juan in the process and providing us with a "fifth Gil" as Doña Juana takes credit for the wound and tells Don Juan "di que te hirió a doña Inés / don Gil de las Calzasverdes" (3045-46). The night ends inconclusively. Each imitation Don Gil has attempted to make their claim without success. As a result, Don Martín is now thoroughly convinced that he is being punished for his sins (2891-94) and Don Juan has lost a fight and been wounded in the act (after line 3042). Doña Clara's adventure ends with confirmation that she has been lied to by Don Gil and with a threat to her life (3003-04, 3047-49). Only Doña Juana finishes the night successfully. She has convinced Don Martín of his guilt and kept all other threats at bay.

The following morning Tirso wraps the strands together, first placing Don Martín in triple jeopardy for having supposedly killed Doña Juana (3122-26), wounded Don Juan (3181-86), and failed in his promise to marry Doña Clara (3153-57). Even his claim that it is Doña Juana's ghost that is at the root of all the confusion, is taken as an admission of guilt (3199). Only when Don Martín is hemmed in does Doña Juana appear to set things right. Her self-naming "doña Juana / hija tuya" (3206-07), is done in context of a reconnection to her family and place in society as well as confirming her claim upon Don Martín.

To conclude, I wish to discuss some of the questions that this text raises and to suggests some possibilities. First, there is the way in which Tirso presents power structures within the play itself. Similar comedias generally function within a power vacuum where the symbolic power of society, represented by the father, is absent or avoided. Furthermore, once the lovers have their way, they integrate back into the same society, returning to the dominant social order. Fathers in the *comedia* are usually a force of order and law. In this case, the entire plot is set into motion by Don Martín's father. Instead of modeling virtuous behavior he explicitly encourages and, in fact, orders his son to abandon Doña Juana for financial gain. I am unaware of another play in which a father countermands a consummated promise of marriage, without being clearly portrayed as a villain. In this case, it is a simple fact of life, condemned, perhaps in desperate resignation, by Doña Juana as "codicia" (155). The conclusion also echoes this disturbance of the normal pattern, since it is Doña Juana who deliberately brings her father to Madrid to enlist his aid, and it is Doña Juana, not her father, who emerges in the final scene to restore order. In the play, Tirso makes an effort to present the violation of social norms as more than the act of one, immature, young man. Instead, the entire violation of the social order comes from someone who typically represents it. This suggests that in the world of *Don Gil de las Calzas verdes*, the division is not generational, but rather factional, a division between love and greed.

The second element I wish to address is the way disguise and identity, particularly in the Balcony scene, are proliferated and weakened. Tirso's general tendency with disguise seems to be towards an identification with the mask, such as in *El vergonzoso en palacio*, *El amor médico*, or *La celosa de sí misma*. In this play, the disguise, perhaps a better term is alternate identity, becomes so copied that it loses coherence and becomes something that anyone can claim. While Doña Juana is easily able to manage her version of Don Gil, the other imitators struggle to either embody the Don Gil that Doña Juana creates or to self-define themselves. Don Martín is never comfortable as Don Gil de Albornoz and never controls his circumstances; Don Juan and Doña Clara try on the mask as well, but without effective results. Instead, the idea of Don Gil becomes paramount and the physical representation is of secondary importance. In a similar fashion, the overnaming of individuals is effective for Doña Juana, but not for anyone else. Her portrayal of Doña Elvira effectively furthers her goals. In contrast, by linking Don Martín-as-Gil to the fictitious Don Miguel, Don Martín becomes locked into the very situation that the name Don Gil de Albornoz was created to avoid.

Finally, what we see in the balcony scene of *Don Gil de las calzas verdes* is a questioning of the power of naming in and of itself. Tirso takes the stance that naming is both vital and simultaneously unreliable. When L. Carl Johnson comments: "The events dramatized illustrate the not so obvious fact that only a tenuous relationship links a given individual, the characteristics that define that individual, and the linguistic sign which indicates that person's identity" (138), he astutely describes the inherent slippage between the self, the name, and external perceptions of the two. Prior to the start of the play, the name Don Gil serves as a convenient way to hide the fact that Don Martín cannot legitimately marry Doña Inés. It is only when Doña Juana imbues the name with desirable characteristics that the name carries any importance. This gap between self and name affects the workings of desire as well. Doña Inés and Doña Clara express clear preference for an effeminate Don Gil. Neither the name, nor Juana herself, are as attractive as the combination of the two.[8] It is in the gap between the name and the performance that Doña Juana is able to thrive.

---

8 I have not dedicated much space to the homoerotic elements of the play, but it is certainly possible to read the work in that light.

Works Cited

Bouchiba-Fochesato, Isabelle. "Poética del deseo femenino en *Don Gil de las Calzas Verdes* de Tirso de Molina." *Criticón*, vol 128, 2016, pp 9-21. doi:10.4000/criticon.3142. Accessed 10 March 2019.

Caro, Ana. *Valor agravio y mujer* in *Women's Acts: Plays by Women Dramatists of Spain's Golden Age*. Edited by Teresa Soufas, UP of Kentucky, 1996, pp 163-194.

Frye, Ellen. "Meta-Imitation in the Comedia: Don Gil de las calzas verdes." *Comedia Performance*, vol. 1, no. 1, 2004, pp 126-42.

Galoppe, Raúl A and David Dalton. "(Un)faithful Renditions: Gender Dynamics in an Adaptation of *Don Gil de las calzas verdes*." *Bulletin of the Comediantes*, vol. 67, no. 1, 2015. Pp 131-48.

Hesse, Everett W. "The Nature of the Complexity in Tirso's 'Don Gil'", *Hispania*, vol. 45, no. 3, 1962, pp 389-94.

Johnson, L. Carl. "The (ab)Uses of Characterization in Don Gil de las calzas verdes." *Tirso de Molina: His Originality Then and Now*, Edited by Henry W. Sullivan and Raúl A. Galoppe, Dovehouse, 1996, pp 133-43.

Ly, Nadine. "Descripción del estatuto de los personajes en Don Gil de las calzas verdes, de Tirso de Molina." *Criticón*, vol. 24, 1983, pp. 69-103.

Molesworth, Jesse M Syllepsis. "Mimesis, Simulacrum: *The Monk* and the Grammar of Authenticity." *Criticism*, vol. 51, no. 3, 2009, pp 401-23.

Molina, Tirso de. *Don Gil de las calzas verdes*, edited by Esther Fernández Rodríquez, LinguaTetxt, 2013.

———. *El amor médico*, edited by Blanca Oteiza, Madrid-Pamplona, Instituto de Estudios Tirsianos, 1997.

———. *El vergonzoso en palacio*, edited by Everett Hesse, 7th edition, Cátedra, 1990.

———. *La celosa de sí misma*, edited by Gregorio Torres Nebrera, Cátedra, 2005.

———. *La Huerta de Juan Fernandez*, http://www.comedias.org/tirso/huerta.html. Accessed 4 April 2019.

Nelson, Brian. "Realism: Mirage or Model?" *Romance Studies*, vol. 30, no. 3-4, 2012, pp 149-52.

Ramos, María Eugenia. "Don Gil de las calzas verdes: Tirso y el prejuicio antiteatral en el siglo XVII." *Revista de Humanidades*, vol. 3, no. 1, 1997, pp 55-71.

Thacker, Johnathan. *A Companion to Golden Age Theatre*, Tamesis, 2007.

Weimer, Christopher. "Ovid, Gender, and the Potential for Tragedy in Don Gil de las alzas verdes." *Prismatic Reflections on Spanish Golden Age Theater: Essays in Honor of Matthew D. Stroud*, edited by Gwyn E. Campbell and Amy R. Williamsen, Peter Lang, 2016, pp 101-11.

La comunidad morisca del siglo dieciséis se enfrenta a los horrores de la tumba
Miguel Ángel Vázquez
Florida Atlantic University

LA LITERATURA ALJAMIADA, ESCRITA en romance hispano, pero transliterada en caracteres árabes, ofrece al investigador una fuente directa para examinar las creencias y actividades religiosas de los moriscos en la España de la época pre-moderna. A lo largo del siglo dieciséis, al mismo tiempo que Garcilaso se entronizaba como el gran poeta de la era, que *La vida de Lazarillo de Tormes* denostaba al clero y que San Juan de al Cruz cantaba al gozo de la unión mística, los moriscos, en silencio, desarrollaron un corpus literario que logró sobrevivir oculto varios siglos después de su expulsión en 1609. En 1884, a raíz del descubrimiento en Almonacid de la Sierra de un gran depósito de manuscritos, Serafín Estébanez Calderón afirmará esperanzado que la literatura aljamiada era "por decirlo así, las Indias de la literatura española, que están casi por descubrir, y que ofrecen grandes riquezas a los Colones primeros que las visiten" (López-Baralt 121). Si bien la literatura de los moriscos no ofreció a los investigadores las tan ansiadas joyas literarias[1], sí abrió a los investigadores una amplia ventana por la cual

---

1   La gran mayoría de los textos aljamiado-moriscos son, o bien traducciones de textos que son parte de la literatura popular árabe de la época medieval (relatos de las primeras batallas del islam, relatos que salen de las mil y una noches como el de Bulūqiya o Tamīm al-Dār, y otros relatos que salen de la tradición oral), o textos doctrinales destinados a enseñar a los moriscos todos los aspectos del islam (traducciones del Corán, colecciones de plegarias, tratados sobre ley musulmana). Eso dicho, hay que llamar la atención a importantes excepciones que son ejemplos de una literatura morisca original como la poesía de Mohamed Rabadán o Ybrahīm Taybilī (Vázquez, "Poesía morisca") o el importantísimo texto alegórico *Tratado de los dos caminos* (Galmés de Fuentes).

echar una mirada tanto al universo espiritual de los moriscos, como a sus avatares. ¿Cómo practicaban los moriscos el islam en un contexto socio-político que los obligaba a la clandestinidad más estricta? Aquellos ritos que otrora se llevaran a cabo en público, como el llamamiento a la oración, escuchar el sermón de los viernes, o la fiesta de la ruptura del ayuno al final del mes de Ramadán ya no podían celebrarse de la manera tradicional. Los edictos reales que se sucedieron a lo largo del siglo dieciséis prohibiendo un extenso catálogo de actividades que las autoridades religiosas consideraban musulmanas, no solo forzaron el ocultamiento de los textos aljamiados, sino también forzaron a la práctica de un islam clandestino. En este sentido es bien conocida la fetua que el muftí de Orán emitió con respecto a cómo los moriscos podían modificar sus practicas religiosas sin que éstas se invalidaran (García Arenal 43-45).

En este ensayo quiero examinar un aspecto de las prácticas religiosas moriscas según se desprende de varios manuscritos: las cartas moriscas para el muerto. Tal vez el primer investigador en describir estas cartas fuera Pedro Longás en su *Vida religiosa de los moriscos* de 1915, donde explica que:

> Escribíase esta carta en árabe, con azafrán, en pergamino o papel, y se colocaba a todo muerto, hombre o mujer, ya en su mortaja, ya fuera de esta, pero dentro de la misma fosa: en el primer caso, debajo de la cabeza o en el costado derecho, a veces entre el sudario y la mejilla derecha; en el segundo caso, a la cabecera de la fosa, bajo la tierra. Este segundo rito se permitía, como menos expuesto a denuncias. Se creía que era de gran mérito para el muerto, que le servía de descanso y aun de compañía en el sepulcro, y le prestaba fortaleza para responder a los ángeles Móncar y Naquir en el juicio a que el difunto había de ser sometido aquella misma noche; asimismo se pensaba que quien la leía en vida obtendría alta recompensa de parte de Dios en vida y en muerte, en el sepulcro y al tiempo de ser pesadas sus acciones en la balanza de la justicia divina. (295)

Antes de examinar el texto íntegro de una de estas cartas (de las que he estudiado unos catorce ejemplares) y para entender de dónde sale la necesidad de este rito mortuorio, convendrá pasar revista sobre la concepción de la muerte en el islam. El corpus escatológico morisco a nuestra disposición está compuesto de historias o anécdotas pías que describen al lector diferentes aspectos de la muerte y el proceso de morir. En términos generales, los textos escatológicos moriscos son herederos de una antiquísima tradición textual musulmana que tuvo sus orígenes en la tradición oral, pero que rápidamente se codificó en importantes disquisiciones teológicas y que cuenta con un enorme número de anécdotas y leyendas. Conviene, por lo tanto, pasar revista rápida de esa tradición para contextualizar mejor los textos aljamiados.[2] Tal vez sorprenda al lector saber que los árabes del siglo séptimo a los que Mahoma llevó el mensaje del islam no concebían la idea de otro mundo o vida espiritual más allá de la muerte. Para ellos, la muerte era el final de todo y no había más. Aunque la idea de la vida eterna no les era desconocida—eran conscientes de las creencias de los judíos y los cristianos—el propio Corán recogió para la posteridad las objeciones que le hicieron a Mahoma cuando éste les prometió no sólo otra vida después de morir, sino también una recompensa o castigo según su conducta en la tierra.[3] La relativa novedad de la idea de una vida eterna llenó de todo género de interrogantes a aquellos que finalmente acabaron por aceptar el mensaje coránico.[4] ¿En qué consistía el proceso de morir? Cuando el Corán[5] dice: "Él [. . .] envía sobre vosotros a custodios. Cuando, al fin, viene la muerte a uno de vosotros, Nuestros enviados le llaman, no se descuidan" (6:61), ¿quiere decir esto que hay ángeles que intervienen en el proceso de morir? ¿Cuántos y quiénes son? Cuando el Corán dice: "Los ángeles dirán a aquellos a quienes llamen '¿cuál era vuestra situación?'" (4:97), ¿quiere esto decir que los ángeles sostienen una conversación con el difunto y lo interrogan? ¿Es que acaso los muertos despiertan y conversan? Y cuando el Corán dice: "Si pudieras ver cuando estén los impíos en su agonía y los ángeles extiendan las manos: '¡Entregad vuestras almas! Hoy se os va a retribuir con un castigo degradante'[. . .]"(6:93), ¿quiere decir que la muerte es dolorosa? Éstas serían algunas de las tantas interrogantes que la falta de detalles del libro sagrado sobre la muerte inspiraría en aquellos

---

2   Me limitaré aquí, por consideraciones de espacio, a bosquejar en unos cuantos párrafos las razones que llevaron al desarrollo de toda una literatura islámica ultramundana, sus autores y textos más importantes. El lector curioso que quiera más detalles, puede consultar el primer capítulo de mi *Desde la penumbra de la fosa. La concepción de la muerte en la literatura aljamiado morisca.*

3   Véanse los siguientes pasajes coránicos que ilustran lo dicho: 17:49, 17:98, 22:5, 23:35, 23:82, 30:80, 32:10, 36:78, 37:16, 37:53, 44:35, 45:24, 56:47.

4   Para más información sobre la muerte según el islam, véase el clásico estudio de Eklund; y para un estudio más al día es indispensable consultar el libro de Jane Idleman Smith e Yvonne Yazbeck Haddad, en el que las autoras, en lugar de limitarse sólo al islam clásico, dedican toda la segunda parte de su estudio al mundo musulmán contemporáneo.

5   Cuando cito del Corán lo hago siempre a partir de la traducción de Julio Cortés., *El Corán*, Madrid: Planeta, 1986. El resto de las traducciones del árabe son mías a menos que se indique lo contrario.

primeros musulmanes. El Corán, sin embargo, nunca respondió de manera directa a esas preguntas y se limitó sólo a describir vagamente el proceso de morir.

Esto, sin embargo, no fue óbice para que surgiera un abundante acervo textual basado en los *aḥādiz* [= tradiciones del profeta Mahoma] que detallaba para los creyentes las minucias del proceso de morir. Al asomarnos a los textos que componen ese corpus, los lectores que venimos de un trasfondo religioso-cultural judeo-cristiano no podemos más que asombrarnos ante el despliegue de una imaginación que en muchos casos produjo episodios verdaderamente aterradores. Para un cristiano, los muertos descansan en la tumba hasta el día de la resurrección; para un musulmán, las primeras horas después de la muerte no constituían el final de una vida dedicada a la salvación del alma, sino que, todavía en la tumba, en la propia antesala al otro mundo, tendría que enfrentarse a otra dura prueba que bien podía poner en peligro de condena al creyente más pío. Tan temprano como el siglo IX de la era común (siglo II del calendario musulmán de la hégira) ya, contamos con varias colecciones que recogen un sinnúmero de anécdotas sobre el proceso de morir, en las que se nota que la mayoría de los temas, imágenes y tópicos más recurrentes asociados a la escatología musulmana ya estaban sólidamente codificados en la cultura popular. Dos colecciones pioneras son *Kitāb al-mawt* [Libro de la muerte] y *Kitāb al-qubūr* [Libro de las tumbas] de Ibn Abī al-Dunyā.[6] Éste último, proverbial por la vida ascética que cultivó, fue un prolífico escritor bagdadí (823-894 de la era común) y además fue maestro de varios príncipes abasíes e incluso de califas como al-Muʿtaḍid y al-Muqtafī. Ibn Abī al-Dunyā se interesó muchísimo por los temas del más allá, como bien lo demuestran no sólo los citados tratados, sino otros tantos con títulos como *Man ʿāsha baʿd al-mawt* [Quien vivió después de morir] o *Kitāb al-ayāt wa man takallama baʿ d al-mawt* [Libro de los milagros o de quien habló después de morir]. Ávido lector de los tratados de Ibn Abī al-Dunyā fue el famosísimo al-Ġazālī (1058-1111) quien en su más importante obra (*Iḥyāʾ ʿulūm al-dīn* [Revivificación de las ciencias de la religión]) dedica el libro número 40, titulado "*Kitāb dikr al-mawt wa mā baʿdahu*" [El recuerdo de la muerte

---

6   Estos tratados, aunque se han perdido para siempre, quedaron conservados en las citas que de ellos hicieron importantes escritores de la talla de al-Ġazālī y al-Suyūṭī. Leah Kinberg, quien editó ambos textos en árabe, se dio a la tarea, nada fácil, de recoger cuantas citas pudo de los tratadistas que citan de Ibn Abī al-Dunyā para tratar de reconstruir en la medida de lo posible el texto original del *Kitāb al-mawt* (143 citas) y del *Kitāb al-qubūr* (121 citas).

y el más allá] al tema de la muerte.[7] Otro famoso texto que se le atribuye a al-Ġazālī es *Al-durra al-faḫīra fī kashf ʿulūm al-āḫira* [La perla preciosa sobre la revelación del conocimiento del otro mundo],[8] aunque T. J. Winter advierte que la autoría de al-Ġazālī sobre este texto ha sido puesta en entredicho.[9] También importa destacar *Al-taḏkira fī aḥwāl al-mawtā wa umūr al-āḫira* [Recordatorio sobre el estado de los muertos y asuntos del otro mundo] del famoso comentarista coránico cordobés al-Qurṭubī (muerto en 1273); *Kitāb al-rūḥ* [Libro del espíritu] de Ibn al-Qayyim al-Ǧawziya (1292-1350); y el importante *Kitāb šarḥ al-ṣudūr* [La expansión de los corazones] de Ǧalāl al-Dīn ʿAbd al-Raḥmān al-Suyūṭī (1445-1505).

Por las páginas de todos estos clásicos de la escatología musulmana vemos desfilar imágenes francamente impresionantes. Uno de los temas más destacados que se nos ofrecen una y otra vez es la idea que el proceso de morir es profundamente doloroso y traumático: "Šaddād ibn Aws dijo: 'La muerte es para el creyente el más terrible horror en este y el otro mundo. Es peor que ser serruchado con sierras, o cortado con tijeras, o hervido en pucheros. Si el difunto saliera y le contara a la gente de este mundo sobre la muerte, no les aprovecharía la vida, ni encontrarían deleite en el sueño.'"[10] Otro elemento constante en estos textos es el Ángel de la Muerte que curiosamente sólo se menciona explícitamente de manera muy escueta y una sola vez en el Corán,[11] pero que pasa a ser uno de los personajes más importantes de todos estos tratados escatológicos. Junto al Ángel de la Muerte, e igualmente importantes, encontramos a los temibles Munkar y Nakīr,[12] ángeles, sobre los que volveré más adelante, descritos de manera hiperbólica y de apariencia horrorosa, cuya misión es interrogar al difunto en su tumba sobre su fe islámica. El resultado del interrogatorio deter-

---

7 T. J. Winter, en su introducción a su traducción del *Kitāb ḏikr al-mawt* (*The Remembrance of Death and the Afterlife*, indica que por lo menos el veinte por ciento de las citas o anécdotas que al-Ġazālī presenta en su *Kitāb ḏikr al-mawt* las tomó de Ibn Abī al-Dunyā (pág. xix).

8 Estudiado y traducido al francés por Lucien Gautier en 1878, y más recientemente por Jane Idleman Smith en 1979 como *The Precious Pearl*.

9 Winter, op. cit. pág. xxvi-xxvii, nota 40.

10 Al-Ġazālī, op. cit. pág. 1773.

11 Ver Corán 32:11: "Di: 'El Ángel de la Muerte, encargado de vosotros, os llamará y luego seréis devueltos a vuestro Señor".

12 A propósito de sus nombres (*munkar* quiere decir 'abominable' y *nakīr* 'detestable'), algunos de los miembros de la *muʿtazila* (escuela de pensamiento musulmán que utilizó la lógica y la filosofía para entender la religión), aunque aceptaban la idea del interrogatorio no concebían que Dios creara unos ángeles con nombres tan desagradables. (Eklund 5-6).

minará si el tiempo que pasará en la tumba será uno placentero o tortuoso. En ese sentido, la misma tumba, que le habla al difunto, también emerge como un personaje importante en estos textos. En primer lugar, llama la atención la llamada *ḍaġṭa* o doloroso estrechamiento de la fosa que, según muchas fuentes, sufrirán todos los difuntos, en mayor o menor medida, aunque según otras fuentes, sufrirán sólo los pecadores. Además, como un atisbo a la pena eterna, se habla sobre el ʿ*adāb al-qabr* [= castigo o tormento de la tumba] que sufrirá el pecador en la misma por tiempo indefinido hasta el día de la resurrección.[13] La tumba, en sí misma, también forma parte del eje discursivo de los autores clásicos que instan al creyente a recordar y pensar mucho en la muerte, para no olvidar que esta vida es pasajera y que es importantísimo obrar rectamente para ganarse el premio de una vida eterna en el Paraíso. En ese sentido, no hay más que recordar que Ibn Abī al-Dunyā tituló uno de sus tratados *El libro de las tumbas*. Las 121 citas, anécdotas o fragmentos poéticos recogidos en ese texto giran todos en torno al tema de la tumba, convirtiéndola en el *memento mori* ideal para el creyente, pues le recuerda siempre cuál será su morada final.

A partir de lo resumido arriba queda claro que los textos medievales musulmanes utilizados por los moriscos para dilucidar asuntos del más allá, concebían el proceso de morir como difícil y profundamente agónico. Pensemos, por un momento, en los moriscos españoles del siglo dieciséis. Ellos se encontraban aquejados por una consciencia culpable por el lamentable estado del islam en España. Ya se sabe que a lo largo del siglo dieciséis no pudieron adherirse estrictamente a los ritos que su religión les imponía. Las conversiones forzosas, las visitas de los cristianos para examinar a los neoconversos en materia de su nueva religión, la obligación de ir a misa, entre otras imposiciones, resultó en la erosión no sólo de la religiosidad musulmana de los moriscos, pero también de su identidad arabo-musulmana. El acogerse a

---

13 Importa añadir que los *muʿtazilíes*, no aceptaban la idea del castigo de la sepultura y ponían como prueba el que cuando se desenterraba a alguien, no se encontraban en la tumba ni serpientes, ni alacranes, ni fuego, ni el cuerpo parecía haber sido atacado por tales. A esto responde al-Ġazālī en su citado *Kitāb ḏikr al-mawt* que el castigo de la fosa ocurre al nivel de otro orden de las cosas que pueden percibir sólo unos pocos escogidos, como el profeta a quien le fue dado ver más allá del mundo visible. A ese nivel alterno de la realidad accedemos a través de estados alterados de consciencia, como el sueño. Se trata de uno de los planos de la existencia a caballo entre el mundo material que se percibe con los sentidos y el mundo inteligible que se percibe sólo con el intelecto. Al-Ġazālī arguye que el tormento de la tumba se experimenta del mismo modo que un hombre sueña que una serpiente lo muerde: éste siente el dolor de la mordedura, aunque en la realidad tangible no haya tal serpiente (1813).

la doctrina de la *taqiyya*, que les permitía profesar otra religión para proteger sus vidas, les facilitó aparentar ser cristianos en público, mientras seguían siendo musulmanes en secreto, pero esta estrategia les costó cara, pues con el tiempo, la minoría religiosa acabó por olvidar, no solo el árabe, sino la práctica apropiada del islam. Así un anónimo autor se queja acremente de que

> [...] ni uno solo de nuestros correligionarios sabe algarabía en que fue revelado nuestro santo alcorán, ni comprende las verdades del adin [= religión] ni alcanza su excelencia apurada, como no le sean convenientemente declaradas en una lengua extraña, cual es la de estos perros cristianos, nuestros tiranos y opresores[14].

Con igual frustración se expresará el poeta aragonés Mohamed Rabadán, al comentar el mal estado de la religiosidad morisca. Cito a partir de la edición de Lasarte López del poemario de Rabadán:

> la Inquisision [*sic*] desplegadas
> con grandes fuersas y apremios,
> hasiendo con gran rigor
> cruesas y desafueros,
> que casi por todas partes
> hacía temblar el suelo;
> aquí prenden, allá prenden
> a los batisados nueuos,
> cargandoles [*sic*] cada dia [*sic*]
> galeras, tormento y fuego,
> con otras adbersidades
> que a solo [*sic*] Allá es el secreto;
> pues entre tantos trabaxos
> e intolerables tormentos,
> ¿qué luz se puede tener
> del adin y su simiento?
> Si en el seruisio de Allá
> andan tibios y perplexos
> de cosas tan encumbradas,
> no es mucho que estén agenos
> tubiendo tantos contrarios (72)

---

14   Este pasaje apareció originalmente en las notas a la traducción al castellano que hizo Pascual de Gayangos de *History of Spanish Literature* de Ticknor, p. 420.

Por otro lado, el anónimo autor del *Tratado de los dos caminos*, irá todavía más lejos, al celebrar con un magnífico soneto, la expulsión de los moriscos decretada por Felipe III:

> Dios, que a los suyos padeciendo mira
> muerte en la bida y en el cuerpo ynfierno,
> por pecados de padres sin gobierno
> o por la causa que a su globo admira,
>
> alça la ardiente espada de su yra,
> y como criador y amante tierno
> no es, siendo eterno, en la bengaça eterno
> que al descanso, piadoso la retira.
>
> Del Faraón de Spaña ablanda el pecho,
> y a su pesar les da en el mar camino,
> que stá de berdes flores prado hecho;
>
> y en su buestro yngenio raro y peregrino,
> dándole luz de Dios tanto probecho,
> que ya no soys mortal sino dibino. (Galmés deFuentes 199)

Podría resultarle extraño al lector que este poema fuera escrito nada menos que para Felipe III (el "Faraón de Spaña" que menciona el poema). Pero para el autor, que ha venido a ser conocido como "exiliado de Túnez", aunque los moriscos fueron exiliados de su patria, el encontrarse en tierras del islam supone una bendición pues así podían practicarlo sin miedo a ser perseguidos.

A partir del estado de cosas, descrito anteriormente, con respecto al islam en la España del siglo dieciséis, cabe imaginarse la ansiedad que provocaría en los moriscos la idea de la muerte, según se desprendía de los manuscritos aljamiados, donde se aprecia, no importaba cuán pío fuera un creyente, acabaría experimentando el doloroso proceso de morir. De particular interés son los ángeles Munkar y Nakīr, mencionados anteriormente. Éstos tenían la tarea de acercarse al difunto durante su primera noche en la tumba para interrogarlo en cuanto a su espiritualidad. Si el finado podía contestar correctamente las preguntas de los dos ángeles, descansaría apaciblemente en la tumba hasta el día del juicio final, cuando Dios lo reviviera para juzgarlo. Según al-Tirmiḏī en su Ǧāmīʿ:

Nos lo refirió Abū Salama Yaḥyā ibn Ḥalaf al-Baṣrı: Nos dijo Bišr ibn al-Mufaḍḍal según ʿAbd al-Raḥmān ibn Isḥāq según Saʿīd ibn Abī Saʿīd al-Maqburī según Abū Hurayra que dijo: Dijo el profeta, bendígale Dios y lo salve: "Cuando el difunto es enterrado (o cuando uno de ustedes es enterrado) se le acercan dos ángeles negros y azules, al uno se le llama Munkar y al otro Nakīr, y le preguntan: '¿Qué solías decir acerca de este hombre?' Y el difunto dice lo que solía decir: 'Él es el siervo de Dios y su enviado. Doy fe que no hay más dios que Dios y que Mahoma es su siervo y su enviado'. Y dicen Munkar y Nakīr: 'Sabíamos que ibas a decir eso'. Entonces se le ensancha la fosa a un ancho de setenta por setenta codos y se le ilumina. Luego le dicen Munkar y Nakīr: 'Duerme'. Y dice el difunto: '¿Puedo volver a los míos para darles noticias?' Y le contestan los ángeles: 'Duerme como el novio al que nada lo despierta excepto el amor de su esposa por él'. Y así permanece hasta que lo revive Dios de este su lecho".

"Y si el difunto era hipócrita, contesta: 'Oía a la gente decir, y decía lo mismo. No sé'. Y dicen Munkar y Nakīr: 'Sabíamos que ibas a decir eso'. Y se le dice a la tierra: '¡Estréchate sobre él!' Y se estrecha la tierra sobre él hasta que sus costillas se confunden unas con otras y permanece atormentado así hasta que Dios lo revive de este su lecho" (*Ǧamīʿ al-Tirmiḏī* vol. 2, pág. 267).

Al-Tirmiḏī, como se ve, no se detiene tanto en la descripción física de los ángeles como lo harán varios manuscritos aljamiados, que cargan las tintas en el aspecto terrorífico de los enviados. Así, Çilmān al-Fāraçī, sale de su tumba para contarnos el momento en que vio a los dos ángeles:[15]

---

15 Sería prolijo describir aquí en detalle mi sistema de transcripción para los textos aljamiados. El lector interesado en esos detalles puede consultar las notas a mi edición de los textos aljamiados que presento en mi *Desde la penumbra de la fosa*. El sistema de transcripción que utilizo es básicamente el mismo que utiliza la escuela de aljamiadistas de Oviedo (expuesto en Galmés de Fuentes, *Dichos de los siete sabios de Grecia*, pp. 35-40) pero sigo las mismas modificaciones que introdujo Consuelo López-Morillas en su *Textos aljamiados sobre la vida de Mahoma*, pp. 35-38. Entre las modificaciones más importantes que propuso López-Morillas están 1) la supresión de "vocales y semiconsonantes epentéticas que no representan una pronunciación real, sino que obedecen a la estructura de la sílaba árabe" (p. 35); la eliminación de guiones "cuando dos palabras españolas se escriben juntas [. . .] y están presentes todas las letras, se separan con un espacio" (35); y 3) cuando la *yīm* "aparece sin *tašdīd*, pero correspondiendo al sonido *ch* se transcribe como J" (p. 37).

> i-abrí mis ojos i vid dos almalaques [=ángeles] negros, zarcos [= azules][16] sus ojos i-en [la] mano dell uno una maça de fierro que si feriesen con ella sobre el más grande monte del mundo, lo tornaría polvo menudo. I cridaron a mī cada uno dellos un crido de apagança [= alegría] que voló mi coraçón i se escureçió mi vista i se espartieron mis junturas i yo quedé estordido [= aturdido]. (Ms. BNE 5313, fols. 190r – 190v).

En otro manuscrito, un muerto revive para contarle a un querido amigo su experiencia con la muerte, y describe a Munkar y a Nakīr así:

> I estando así entraron sobre mí dos almalaques i no me demandéis por su ḥaleqamiento [= hechura], yā [= oh] mi ermano, i su fuerte vista. I traían en sus manos maças de fierro calientes que si fueran puestas sobre la tierra derrocaríanla; i si no [fuera] que la piadad de Al.lah baxó sobre mí, yo era de los perdidos. I solté mi lengua i respondíles a todo lo que me demandaron i después salieron de mí. (Ms. BNE 5301, fol. 8r)

Finalmente, una calavera que Jesucristo había revivido para interrogarla sobre la muerte, le cuenta al profeta que

> Yo estando ansí veos que vinieron sobre mí otros dos almalaques muy fieros que fazían tremolar la tierra debaǰo de los piedes y eran sus nonbres Munkar wa Nakir [sic] y en su mano del uno una maça de fierro que si por ventura se ajuntasen todos los de la tierra, personas y alǧinnes [= genios], para debantarla no abrían poder—i-era en su mano como un grano de mostaçia—i díšome a mí: —¿Quién es tu señor i quién es tu alquibla? (Manuscrito misceláneo de la Escuelas Pías de Zaragoza, fol. 84v.)[17]

---

16 Los ojos azules son considerados de mal agüero entre muchos árabes.

17 En la Biblioteca de las Escuelas Pías de Zaragoza hay dos voluminosos manuscritos aljamiados de materia misceláneo. A ninguno de los dos manuscritos se les ha asignado una catalogación oficial, aunque uno de ellos lleva en el primer folio la notación "Códice 26". Cuando Alberto Montaner preparaba su catálogo sobre los materiales aljamiados en esa biblioteca, a este manuscrito le había asignado el número 11. En cuanto al otro, no lleva ningún tipo de número o código, aunque los folios sí están numerados. Es en el primer manuscrito aquí mencionado que se encuentra la historia de Jesús con la calavera.

Nótese que, en los ejemplos anteriores, los ángeles son representados igualmente temibles tanto para el pío como para el pecador, mientras que Idleman Smith y Haddad notan que "some narratives omit these terrible details entirely, while others indicate that they appear un such frightful image only to those who are destined for the Fire" (42). Lo que importa subrayar aquí es que la literatura de los moriscos insiste más en los detalles mórbidos del proceso de morir.

¿Cómo podía, entonces, un morisco del siglo dieciséis, sobrecogido por la idea de una muerte tan difícil, conjurar la amargura de ese proceso? La respuesta la ofrece la carta de la muerte, con la que se enterraba al difunto para ayudarlo en su paso al otro mundo. En el Apéndice a este ensayo, el lector encontrará mi edición de una de estas cartas que aparece en el manuscrito RESC 8 de la Biblioteca Tomás Navarro Tomás del Consejo Superior de Investigaciones Científicas en Madrid. Se trata de uno de los ejemplares más completos porque viene precedido de una corta introducción seguida de la carta del muerto propiamente que está escrita en árabe. La introducción empieza con una explicación que no está del todo clara:

> Aquesta es una decla[ra]çión muy virtuosa de una virtuosa ale'a [= aleya del Corán] a petición que vino con ella Ǧibrīl [. . .] al annabī [= profeta] Muḥammad [. . .] departe de Al.lah para que fuese piadad sobre todo creyente o pecador con que fuese derremisión [= redimido] de sus pecados i alimpiamiento de su a'rruḥ [= espíritu]. I todo creyente de buena ventura que la querrá leir o tener consigo apiadará Al.lah sobr-él en este mundo i en el otro. (fol. 66r)

En el texto citado se indica que el texto que sigue es una explicación ("declaraçión") de una "ale'a" o aleya coránica que Dios envió a Mahoma a través de su mensajero, el ángel Gabriel. Se añade también que quien lea ese texto recibirá la misericordia de Dios en este mundo y el otro. A todas luces, el texto parece decir que la carta de la muerte es una aleya coránica, pero el problema es que el texto de la carta de la muerte que sigue no está en el Corán, así que no puede tratarse de una aleya enviada por Dios a Mahoma. Creo que el sentido queda más claro si se recurre a los otros significados de la palabra árabe "aya" que también quiere decir 'señal', 'presagio', 'milagro', o 'mensaje'. Si suponemos que aquí "ale'a" quiere decir 'mensaje', el texto parece afirmar que la carta del muerto es de origen divino—aunque no parte del Corán—, lo que explica las virtudes asociadas a su posesión y lectura. En ese sentido es de notar cómo la "carta del muerto" no solo es de utilidad para el difunto, sino que el vivo puede acceder a la protección divina al copiarla y leerla de modo que Munkar y Nakīr no atormentarán al difunto el día de su muerte. Se hermanan así la religiosidad (el texto como parte de los ritos funerarios) y la magia (el texto como amuleto protector). Esta combinación de magia y religiosidad no debe sorprender ya que, tanto en la tradición judeo-cristiana como en la musulmana, es común ver en la confección de amuletos protectores tanto de pasajes bíblicos como de pasajes coránicos (Labarta 164-65; Lara y Montaner).

Por último, la introducción incluye las instrucciones de dónde poner la carta del muerto al enterrarlo y lo que pasará con el difunto que ha sido enterrado con ella. En esta parte del texto se encarece de manera especial la protección que la carta dará a su poseedor: verá su última morada en el Paraíso, será visitado por ángeles, no sufrirá los espantos del Día del Juicio, y su rostro brillará como la luna llena[18], entre otros privilegios. Cabe notar que el texto indica que "salrrá con su carta a su (a su) man derecha" (fols. 66v – 67r) lo que parecería ser una referencia a la carta del muerto, pero no creo que este detalle se refiera a la carta del muerto que me ocupa aquí, sino de un listado o catálogo en el que se han consignado las buenas o malas acciones del difunto cuando estaba vivo. Esta otra "carta" o escrito parece tener su origen en el Corán 17:14: "¡Lee tu escritura! ¡Hoy bastas tú para ajustarte cuentas!". Según muchas tradiciones, este "escrito" es un catálogo de las obras buenas y malas que llevó a cabo el ser humano antes de morir. Estas obras eran cuidadosamente consignadas por dos ángeles que tenían la tarea de anotar, uno las buenas obras, las malas el otro. El que los textos aljamiados que describen el proceso de morir hablen de una "carta" y no de un "escrito" o "testimonio" escrito puede tratarse de un equívoco de traducción puesto que *kitāb* se puede traducir como 'escrito', 'libro' o 'carta'. El documento puede aparecer de varias maneras, pero siempre en el contexto de la tumba y de los sucesos que allí le ocurren al muerto. También el hecho de si la carta (o catálogo de obras) se sostiene en la mano derecha o izquierda es significativo. En el caso del interlocutor de Çilmān (citado anteriormente), las buenas obras le dicen que le darán su carta en su mano derecha. En el caso del diálogo de Jesucristo con la calavera (también citado anteriormente) ésta narra lo que le dijeron:

> Yā [= oh] enemigo de Al.lah y enemigo de tu persona, toma tu carta en tu mano la yzquierda por de çaga [= detrás] de tus espaldas.

---

18 Muchos textos aljamiados afirman que el Día del Juicio los rostros de los condenados se ennegrecerán, mientras que los rostros de los que han alcanzado la recompensa divina se blanquearán.

—I tomé mi carta por de çaga de mıs espaldas en mi mano la izquierda i leí mi carta i no fallé en ella solamente una alḥaçana [= buena obra]. (fols. 84r-84v)

El que la calavera hablara del no haber encontrado en su "carta" más que una sola buena obra deja claro que la "carta del muerto" morisca y la carta a la que hacen referencia los relatos aljamiados son dos cosas distintas. La carta de la muerte, como se verá, es una petición de piedad que identifica al difunto como buen musulmán, mientras que la "carta" de los relatos es un listado de las buenas y malas acciones que llevó a cabo el difunto en este mundo.

Tras la introducción, sigue el texto de la carta del muerto[19]. Lo primero que salta a la vista es que la lengua del texto pasa del romance hispánico del siglo dieciséis al árabe culto. El cambio de lengua probablemente responde a que el proceso de morir conllevaba el mencionado interrogatorio de los ángeles Munkar y Nakīr, que de seguro se llevaría a cabo en árabe. Solo tengo noticia de una carta del muerto escrita en romance hispánico (Ms. RESC 43 del CSIC[20]) y se trata, más bien de una traducción de otra carta en árabe. Del mismo modo que había en la literatura aljamiada traducciones del Corán y de otras plegarias para la conveniencia del musulmán que no dominaba el árabe, también debió haber traducciones de la carta del muerto. Pero hay que subrayar que el texto en romance no sustituye el texto en árabe, y de la misma manera que un musulmán tiene que orar y recitar el Corán en árabe aunque no lo entienda, también la carta del muerto, como rito, tenía que copiarse en árabe para que fuera válida como rito funerario. A los moriscos del siglo dieciséis que ya habían perdido el uso del árabe les preocuparía cómo contestar a los temibles ángeles una serie de preguntas que determinarían su destino en el más allá. Todas las cartas del muerto tienen casi el mismo texto, y aunque hay variantes, las cartas siempre empiezan por atestiguar la šahāda o profesión de fe musulmana ("No hay más dios que Allāh, y Mahoma es su enviado"), que de inmediato identificaba al portador del texto como musulmán. La šahāda habría sido suficiente para satisfacer las preguntas de Munkar y Nakīr, pero la carta del muerto va más allá incluyendo luego de la profesión de fe, una serie de jaculatorias en alabanza a Dios, un ruego a Dios en la que el difunto pide no ser abandonado en medio del tormento de la fosa, y que en el día del juicio se le conceda la recompensa del Paraíso.

---

19   En el apéndice he incluido el texto en árabe exactamente como aparece en el manuscrito y luego incluyo mi traducción al español.

20   Le agradezco al colega Pablo Roza Candás haberme llamado la atención a este documento.

Importa llamar la atención a un importante detalle que aparece en todas las cartas del muerto: todas están escritas en primera persona, como si fuera el propio difunto el que recita la *šahāda* y pide misericordia y protección. El detalle no es insignificante, porque una carta en tercera persona implica que otro puede conseguir la salvación por uno, pero esto no puede ser así. Un tema muy recurrente en la literatura escatológica musulmana, es que el día de su muerte, el difunto está solo ante Dios y únicamente sus obras lo acompañan. El propio Corán advierte una y otra vez contra la idea de interseción (*šafāʿa*): "Temed un día en que nadie pueda satisfacer nada por otro, ni se acepte la intercesión ajena, compensación ni auxilio" (2:48). Con todo, otros exegetas, basados en Corán 53:26 o 43:86, han sugerido que la intercesión es posible, siempre que el intercesor tenga permiso de Dios para ello. Esta "ventriloquia ritual" (la del texto que habla por el difunto) podría ser la respuesta al problema de la intercesión, pues el texto ayuda al difunto en su paso al trasmundo, sin correr el peligro de pedir la salvación a través de la intercesión.

La carta morisca del muerto es producto de una cultura religiosa que concebía el proceso de morir como uno difícil, físicamente doloroso y emocionalmente agónico. En este sentido está vinculada a otras tradiciones religiosas que también concebían la muerte como un proceso peligroso para el finado y que requería de mecanismos rituales que lo protegieran y lo ayudaran en su paso al otro mundo. Así, por ejemplo, los antiguos egipcios anticipaban una serie de pruebas, obstáculos, y enfrentamientos con seres peligrosos que el alma del muerto tenía que superar. Para su socorro, el difunto contaba con el *Libro de los muertos* o *Libro de la salida*, que contenía plegarías, sortilegios e instrucciones que guiaban al muerto a llegar a salvo al Aaru en la otra vida (Wasserman *et al*). Por su parte, los órficos de la antigua Grecia pensaban que, al morir, el alma del difunto estaba en peligro de olvidar quién era y lo que había aprendido en vida, para poder escapar el "ciclo de aflicción"—¿una referencia a la reencarnación? Como remedio, enterraron a sus muertos con unas laminillas de oro que funcionaban como instrucciones para que el espíritu pudiera moverse con seguridad en el inframundo (Bernabé y Jiménez San Cristobal; Graf y Johnston). Otro tanto tenemos entre los budistas del Tibet, según los cuales, la lectura del *Bardo thodol* o *Libro tibetano de los muertos* le provee al alma del difunto una serie de instrucciones para viajar por el trasmundo y tratar de evitar renacer y tener que volver al *samsara* (Coleman, *et al*). No quiero decir con esto que las cartas del muerto moriscas fueran influidas por estas tradiciones, sino apuntar a la actitud que han compartido varios grupos religiosos sobre la importancia de desarrollar una tradición textual que ayude a sus muertos a encarar las vicisitudes que suponía el paso a la otra vida. Es decir, estos textos iban más allá de las plegarias y servicios litúrgicos por el alma del difunto el día de su funeral. Tomando en cuenta que en la España del siglo dieciséis no les sería fácil a los moriscos llevar a cabo todo un funeral musulmán en público en medio del cementerio, la carta del muerto convenientemente les permitía identificar a sus difuntos como musulmanes ante los ángeles Munkar y Nakīr. De ese modo cumplían con su deber como comunidad religiosa de despedir ritualmente a sus seres queridos en la antesala a la vida eterna.

***

APÉNDICE
Edición de la carta del muerto del manuscrito RESC/8 del CSIC[21]

[65v] بسم الله الرحمان الرحيم

[En el nombre de Dios, el Clemente, el Misericordioso.]

Esta es la declaración de la carta de la muerte[22] i su muy gran[de][23] alfaẓīla [= mérito] para los muertos en sus mortasas o en sus fuesas. Conforme agora tenemos el tienpo i la libertad ponerle an[24] al muerto en la cabeçera de la fuesa debaso la tierra que Al.lah ya ve por qué se faze [66r] aquello.

Aquesta es una decla[ra]çión muy virtuosa de una virtuosa ale'a [= aleya del Corán] a petiçión que vino con ella Ǧibrīl, la salvaçión de Al.lah sea sobre él i sálvelo, al annabī [= profeta] Muḥammad ṣᶜm [= Dios lo bediga y salve] departe de Al.lah para que fuese piadad sobre todo creyente o pecador con que fuese derremisión [= redimido] de sus pecados i alimpiamiento de su a'rruḥ [= espíritu]. I todo creyente de buena[25] ventura que la querrá leir o tener consigo apiadará Al.lah sobr-él en este mundo i en el otro. Diso el annabī Muḥammad, ṣᶜm, esta es la promesa que mostró a mī Ǧibrīl i diso yā [= oh] Muḥammad

---

21 En este texto han intervenido por lo menos tres manos diferentes. La primera ha escrito el texto en aljamía, la segunda y tercera el texto árabe de la carta de la muerte como tal. La letra es clara en los tres casos pero se nota que las últimas dos estaban claramente habituadas a la escritura árabe pues se trata de una escritura elegante. La tercera mano es la que resulta más agradable a la vista pues incluso utilizó un cálamo con bisel bastante grueso que resultó en una escritura caligráfica.

22 "muerta" en el manuscrito.

23 Lectura conjetural. La tinta ha corroído el folio.

24 "ponnerlendan" en el manuscrito.

25 "puena" en el manuscrito.

quien leirá esta carta de tu alumma [= comunidad de creyentes] una vegada [= vez] adebedeçele [= le promete] Al.lah para él el alǧanna [= el Paraíso], i arredarlo a [= lo retirará/ salvará] del fuego i cuando entrará en la fuesa apercurarl-a [= le procuará] Al.lah setenta almalaques que le-scusarán [66v] a él su razón i no será guerreado de Munkar wa Nakīr en la fuesa ni será avergonçado dellos cuando le demandarán cuenta [= lo interroguen] en la fuesa. I es la promesa aquella que la nonbró Al.lah en su onrrado al-qurʾān que diso no enseñoreará la rogaría sino quien tomará en poder del piadoso promesa.

I sea escrito en papel o pergamino i séale puesto debaso de su cabeça en su fuesa i será dicho "duerme como duerme el novio cuando se casa que no ay sobre tī miedo ni tristeza". I no salrrá su aʰrrūḥ de su cuerpo hata [= hasta] que vea su lugar en l-al-ǧanna i vesitarlo an setenta almalaques apercurados con él i vernán con aʰtabaques [= bandejas] del al-ǧanna i presentes i albriçi[a]rlo an i cuando salrrá el día del ǧudiçio salrrá con su carta a su [67r] (a su) man derecha i su cara como la luna de catorçe noches su claredad andará entre sus manos i serle a dicho "no ayas miedo ni tristeza". No pasará con espanto de los espantos del día del ǧudiçio que no sea estorçiado [= que no los evada] dellos i serle a dado su carta a su man [= mano] derecha. I las ǧentes en la cuenta que los abrá enfrenado el sol i el sudor çerca de las cabeças de los ḥaleqados [= las criaturas / los creados] hata que hervirán los meollos de los ḥaleqados i el que terná aquesta carta será en sonbra [bajo] el alḥarš [= el trono] del señor del mundo con los aʰnnabíes i verdaderos pros i pasará el ṣirāṭ[26] qomo el relánpago pasante i entrará en el al-ǧanna sin cuento ninguno i con [67v] viene sobre todo muçlim que deprenda[27] esta rogaría y amostradla a vuesas muǧeres i hisos. I quien no alca[n]sará a saberla leʾir o a saberla de coraçón escríbala en un papel o pergamino[28] i póngasela debaso de su cabeça en su fuesa cuando murra que Al.lah no le menospreçiará su walardón i aproveǧarl[e] a con aquello por su poder i su onra i con Al.lah es la concordança. Y es esta la carta de la muerte:

بِسْمِ اللهِ الرَّحْمَانِ الرَّحِيمِ

اَللَّهُمَّ اِنِّي عَهَدتُّ اِلَيْكَ فِي دَارِ الدُّنْيَا بِأَنِّي اَشْهَدُ اَن لاَ [sic] اِلَهَ اِلاَّ اَللهُ وَحْدَهُ[68r] لَا شَرِيكَ لَهُ وَاَشْهَدُ اَنَّ مُحَمَّدًا عَبْدُهُ وَرَسُولُهُ صَلَى اَللهُ عَلَيْهِ وَسَلَّمْ وَاَنَّ الدِينَ عِنْدَ اَللهِ كَمَا وَصَفَ

---

26   Puente delgadísimo que pende entre el cielo y el infierno. Los salvados lo cruzarán rápidamente, mientras que los condenados se precipitarán al fuego del infierno.

27   "debrenda" en el manuscrito.

28   "pargamino" en el manuscrito.

وَاَنَّ اَلاِسْلَامَ كَمَا شَرَعَ وَاَنَّ اَلْقَوْلَ كَمَا قَالَ وَاَنَّ اَلْقُرْءَانَ كَمَا نَزَلَ وَاَنَّكَ اَنْتَ اَللهُ لَا اِلَهَ اِلاَّ اَنْتَ اَلْحَقُّ اَلْمُبِّيْنُ جَزَاءَ اَللهُ مُحَمَّدًا خَيْرَ اَلْجَزَا وَحَيَا مُحَمَّدٌ نَبِيَّنَا بِالسَّلَامِ. كهيعص.

اَللَّهُمَّ اِنِّي اَسْئَلُكَ يَا غِيَاثِي عِنْدَ كُلِّ كُرْبَتِي وَيَا صَاحِبِي عِنْدَ وَحْدَتِي وَيَا وَلِيٍّ فِي غُرْبَتِي وَيَا مُونِسِي[29] فِي اَلْقَبْرِ وَوَحْشَتِي وَيَا اِلَهَ اَلْآوَّلِيْنَ وَاَلْآخِرِيْنَ اِلَهَ اِبْرَاهِيْمَ وَاِسْمَاعِيْلَ وَاِسْحَقَ [sic] وَيَعْقُوبَ وَالْاَسْبَاطِ عَلَيْهِمُ اَلسَّلَامُ. كهيعص والْقُرْءَانِ الْحَكِيمِ[30] يَا شَاهِدَ [كل نجوى ويا منتهى][31] كُلِّ [68v] شَكْوَى وَيَا عَالِمَ كُلِّ خَفِيَةٍ وَيَا كَاشِفَ كُلِّ بَلِيَةٍ وَيَا مُجِيرَ اَلْمُسْتَجِرِينَ وَيَا صَرِيخَ[32] اَلْمُسْتَضْرِخِينَ وَيَا اَمَانَ اَلْخَائِفِينَ وَيَا غَنِيَّ كُلِّ فَقِيرٍ وَيَا قَوِيَّ كُلِّ ضَعِيفٍ وَيَا مُحْيِ الْعِظَامَ وَهِيَ رَمِيمٌ اَسْئَلُكَ يَا رَبِّ اَلَا تُكِلْنِي اِلَى نَفْسٍ وَاَصْرِفْ[33] عَنِّي الشَّرَ وَلَا تُبَعِّدْنِي مِنَ اَلْخَيْرِ.

اَللَّهُمَّ اَجْعَلْ لِي عِنْدَكَ يَوْمَ اَلْقِيَامَةِ عَهْدًا مَنْشُورًا تَفَنَى بِهِ [عند موتي وتونسني به][34] فِي الْقَبْرِ مِنْ وَحْشَتِي. فَاِنَّهُ يَا رَبِّ لَا يَضُرُّكَ مَعْصِيَتِي وَلَا يَنْفَعُكَ طَاعَتِي.

[69r] وَلَا حَوْلَ وَلَا قُوَّةَ اِلَا بِاللهِ الْعَلِيِّ الْعَظِيمِ.

[Traducción del texto en árabe]

En el nombre de Dios, el Clemente, el Misericordioso.

¡Dios mío! Me comprometí contigo en este mundo testificando que no hay más dios que Dios, único, sin asociado y testificando que Mahoma es su siervo y su enviado—Dios lo bendiga y salve—y que la religión está en Dios como prescribió y que el islam es así como instituyó y que la doctrina es así como dijo y que el Corán es así como lo reveló y que Tú eres Dios, no hay otro dios sino Tú, verdad manifiesta. Que Dios recompense generosamente a Mahoma y que preserve la vida de Mahoma con la paz. KHY‘Ṣ[35].

---

29 Dividió la palabra entre dos renglones: "muwa / nisī".

30 Esta palabra aparece tachada lo que resulta curioso, porque efectivamente "al-ḥakīm" es un adjetivo que comúnmente sigue a la palabra "Corán".

31 Añado estas palabras a partir de lo que dicen las otras cartas de la muerte. Se entiende mejor que Dios sea el "término de toda queja" a que sea el "testigo de toda queja".

32 Dividió la palabra entre dos renglones: "sari / yḫa".

33 "اَضْرِبْ" en el manuscrito. Corrijo según las otras cartas de la muerte.

34 Estas palabras también las añado a partir del texto de las otras cartas de la muerte, pues sin ellas no tiene sentido la oración.

35 Referencia a la sura 19, la de María, que comienza con estas letras. KHY‘Ṣ son parte de las llamadas *muqaṭṭa‘āt*, o letras aisladas, que en diferentes combina-

¡Dios mío! Te pido, oh socorro en mi aflicción, oh camarada en mi soledad, oh amigo en mi nostalgia, oh compañero en mi fosa y en mi desolación. Dios de los primeros y de los últimos, dios de Abraham, de Ismael, de Isaac, de Jacob, y de las tribus, sobre ellos sea la paz. KHY‘Ṣ, ṬH, YS y el sabio Corán. Oh testigo de todo secreto, oh término de toda queja, oh conocedor de todo misterio, oh descubridor de toda desgracia, oh protector de los indefensos, oh auxilio de los que gritan pidiendo socorro, oh sosiego de los temerosos, oh riqueza de los pobres, oh fuerza de los débiles, oh vivificador de los huesos aún cariados, te pido, oh Señor, que no me abandones a mí mismo, aparta de mí el mal y no me alejes del bien.

¡Dios mío! Concédeme el día de la resurrección un pacto público con el que me avales en mi muerte y con el que me consueles en la fosa de mi desolación pues, oh Señor, ni te perjudica mi desobediencia ni te beneficia mi obediencia.

Y no hay fuerza ni poder sino en Dios, el Alto, el Grandioso.

Obras citadas

Bernabé, Alberto y Ana Isabel Jiménez San Cristóbal. *Instrucciones para el más allá. Las laminillas órficas de oro*. Ediciones Clásicas, 2001.
Coleman, Graham y Thupten Jinpa (eds); Gyurme Dorje (trad.). *The Tibetan Book of the Dead*. Penguin, 2007.
Eklund, Ragnar. *Life Between Death and Resurrection according to Islam*. Almqvist & Wiksells Boktryckeri, 1941.
El Corán. Trad. Julio Cortés. Tahrike Tarsile Qur'an, 2009.
Galmés de Fuentes, ed. *Tratado de los dos caminos por un morisco refugiado en Túnez. (Ms. S2 de la Colección Gayangos, Biblioteca de la Real Academia de la Historia)*. Instituto Universitario Seminario Ramón Menéndez Pidal / Seminario de Estudios Árabo-Románicos, 2005.
———. *Dichos de los siete sabios de Grecia. Sentencias morales en verso*. Gredos, 1991.
García Arenal, Mercedes. *Los moriscos*. Editorial Nacional, 1975.
al-Ġazālī, Abū Ḥāmid Muḥammad bin Muḥammad. *Iḥyā' ʿulūm al-dīn*. Dār al-Maʿarifa, 2004.
———. *The Precious Pearl. A Translation with Notes of the Kitāb al-Durra al-Fakhira fī Kashf ʿUlūm al-Ākhira*. Trad. Jane. I. Smith. Scholars Press, 1979.

---

ciones, encabezan 29 suras del Corán. Se les ha llamado también "letras misteriosas" porque nadie sabe a ciencia cierta su significado. ṬH y YS que aparecen más adelante son referencias a la sura 20 y 36 respectivamente.

Graf, Fritz y Sarah Iles Johnston. *Ritual Texts for the Afterlife. Orpheus and the Bacchic Gold Tablets*. Routledge, 2007.

Ibn Abī al-Dunyā, Abū Bakr ʿAbd Allāh ibn Muḥammad ibn ʿAmr. *Kitāb al-mawt wa kitāb al-qubūr*. Ed. Leah Kinberg. U de Ḥayfa, 1983.

Ibn Qayyim al-Ǧawziyya. *The Soul's Journey after Death*. Trad. A. Bewley. Dār al-Taqwa, 1987.

Idleman Smith, Jane e Yvonne Yazbeck Haddad. *The Islamic Understanding of Death and Resurrection*. SUNY UP, 1981.

Labarta, Ana. "Supersticiones moriscas". *Awrāq*, vols. 5-6, 1982-83, pp. 161-90.

Lara, Eva y Alberto Montaner, eds. *Señales, portentos y demonios. La magia en la literatura y la cultura españolas del Renacimiento*. SEMYR, 2014.

Lasarte López, José Antonio. *Poemas de Mohamed Rabadán. Canto de las lunas. Día del juicio. Discurso de la luz. Los nombres de Dios*. Diputación General de Aragón, 1991.

Longás, Pedro. *Vida religiosa de los moriscos*. Imprenta Ibérica, 1915.

López-Baralt, Luce. *Huellas del Islam en la literatura española. De Juan Ruiz a Juan Goytisolo*. Hiperión, 1985.

López-Morillas, Consuelo. *Textos aljamiados sobre la vida del profeta Mahoma: El profeta de los moriscos*. CSIC, 1994.

al-Qurṭubī, Abū ʿAbd Allāh Muḥammad bin Aḥmad bin Abī Bakr ibn Farḥ. *Al-taḏkira fī aḥwāl al-mawtā wa umūr al-āḫira*. Dār al-kitāb al-ʿarabī, 2004.

al-Suyūṭī, Ǧalāl al-Dīn ʿAbd al-Raḥmān. *Kitāb šarḥ al-ṣudūr bi šarḥ ḥāl al-mawtā wa al-qubūr*. Dār al-Kitāb al-ʿArabī, 2001.

Ticknor, M. G., *Historia de la literatura española*, Pascual de Gayangos (trad.) y Enrique de Vedia (ed.), M. Rivadeneyra, 1856.

Vázquez, Miguel Ángel. "Poesía morisca (o de cómo el español se convirtió en lengua literaria del islam)". *Hispanic Review*, vol. 75, no. 3, Summer 2007, pp. 219-42.

———. *Desde la penumbra de la fosa. La concepción de la muerte en la literatura aljamiado morisca*. Trotta, 2007.

Wasserman, James, et al. *The Egyptian Book of the Dead. The Book fo Going Forth by Day*. Chronicle Books, 1998.

Winter, T. J. (Traductor). *The Remembrance of Death and the Afterlife: Book XL of the Revival of the Religious Sciences*. The Islamic Texts Society, 1989.

Poéticas profanas de lo sagrado. Intersecciones culturales en torno a la construcción del predicador barroco. Dos propuestas teóricas

JUAN VITULLI
University of Notre Dame

CUANDO LOS EDITORES DE este volumen amablemente me escribieron invitándome a participar en un homenaje a Edward Friedman, no lo dudé un instante y acepté de inmediato. La alegría fue inmensa, ya que iba formar parte de una celebración colectiva en torno a una persona que tanto hizo, intelectual y emocionalmente, por aquellas personas que tuvimos la suerte de compartir tiempo con él. Esta algarabía inicial, lo admito, dio paso a una preocupación mayor ya que la responsabilidad no era pequeña. Como casi todo lo que sucede en este mundo que aún debería seguir llamándose Barroco, esta alegría fue poco a poco extinguiéndose, dejando paso a una melancólica pregunta, difícil de responder: ¿qué tipo de ensayo podría yo escribir que representara todo lo que Edward Friedman significa para mí como investigador y como profesor de literatura española? ¿De qué manera podría el ensayo ser un verdadero homenaje a lo que Friedman hizo en el campo de estudios de la temprana modernidad española y no un mero artículo de ocasión que iba a engrosar mi no tan voluminoso CV? Es por eso que me pareció ideal encontrar una aproximación que lograra transmitir la profundidad de sus aportes como maestro y como investigador. Ese espacio creo haberlo encontrado en una de las intersecciones intelectuales que mejor representan a Friedman, esto es, su devoción repartida entre la investigación y la enseñanza. Como todos sabemos, Edward Friedman es el autor de varios libros decisivos para nuestro campo de estudio. También ha escrito un corpus importante de ensayos que conectan la literatura del Siglo de Oro con la teoría literaria. Simultáneamente, la labor de Friedman se ha extendido a las aulas, a los salones de clase, donde siempre realizó un ejercicio intelectual profundo, generoso e incansable. Es por eso que mi ensayo tendrá como eje dos propuestas teóricas recientes para introducir el estudio de la predicación del Barroco en el salón de clases. Mi aporte a este volumen tiene como objetivo pensar en la oratoria cristiana barroca desde dos enfoques teóricos innovadores: la cultura material y los estudios sónicos. Creo firmemente en la necesidad de introducir en los seminarios de nuestros departamentos el estudio de la predicación barroca ya que es un artefacto cultural de múltiples aristas que necesitan ser constantemente revisadas. Pero al mismo tiempo reconozco que surgen dificultades de todo tipo (textuales, culturales) para atraer doctorandos a este campo. Sostengo que, si pudiéramos estudiar este fenómeno histórico a la luz de nuevos aportes, se podría avanzar mucho en la divulgación y en el estudio de este importante aspecto de la cultura barroca, que aún hoy en día permanece a medio descubrir.

Mi ensayo está dividido en dos secciones. En la primera abordaré la predicación a la luz de la historia material. Específicamente, voy a estudiar el estatus del púlpito y su compleja inserción dentro de discusiones mayores en torno a la liturgia y la predicación efectiva. Mi interés se concentrará en testimonios que provienen de artes de predicar donde el púlpito se presenta como un objeto cultural dual. Por un lado cumple un rol específico en la esfera simbólica de la liturgia católica (buscando reafirmar lo que Brian Larkin llamó su "sacred immanence"). Simultáneamente se introducen numerosos elementos vinculados con lo estrictamente material que parecerían contraponerse, o al menos dificultar, la función esencialmente litúrgica antes mencionada. En la segunda parte de mi ensayo conecto lo que se ha dado en llamar el giro sónico en los estudios de la temprana modernidad y su presencia en los discursos sobre la predicación. Para ello, voy a analizar una serie de testimonios, donde el aspecto sonoro de la predicación es puesto en primer plano, a través de las reflexiones que los autores realizan sobre su incidencia. Al destacar estos momentos, me interesa demostrar que existe una clara conciencia de lo sonoro como parte fundante de la oratoria católica.

Una breve escena rescatada del olvido me ayudará a explicar con mayor claridad la plena correspondencia entre lo material y lo sonoro dentro de la práctica de la predicación. En una carta escrita por un anónimo jesuita el 15 de abril de 1643, se cuenta un asombroso caso ocurrido en la Iglesia Catedral de Córdoba. Se narra allí el "... singular conflicto que ocurrió entre el Tribunal de la Inquisición y el Cabildo catedralicio..." durante la predicación de un sermón el domingo cuarto de Cuaresma. El jesuita Juan de Armenta, encargado de predicar ese día, fue advertido por un canónigo que durante el sermón había de preferir en la venia "... al tribunal de la Inquisición respecto del Cabildo, aunque asistiese el prelado . . ." (*Cartas 346*). Esta instrucción sorprendió al predicador ya que era "cosa que se salía de la común práctica y ceremonial." (*Cartas 346*) Aún mayor fue su sorpresa cuando, la mañana del Domingo, escuchó, de boca del Deán, que sería excomulgado si al salir a predicar no cumplía el mandato de pedir la venia al tribunal. El predicador buscó amparo en el Rector de su orden, quien insinuó tratara de actuar con prudente cautela para no disgustar al Tribunal ni desairar al Cabildo. Cansado y confundido, el pobre Armenta no tuvo otra opción que subirse al púlpito y hacer lo que ya había hecho en otras oportunidades: predicar un sermón. Al momento de llevar a cabo la venia, y viendo que el predicador no cumplía con lo requerido, se cuenta que . . .

> yendo a tomar la bendición el predicador, entonó el preste el *Credo* y respondió al punto el coro, con que fue fuerza le llevasen los secretarios de la Inquisición sin bendición al púlpito, y al mismo tiempo fue otro a notificar al que presidía el coro alguna excomunión de parte del Tribunal; pero muy de acuerdo con los prebendados, fijos todos en sus sillas altas, sin hacerle mal de acción, todo prorrumpieron en gritos y demonstraciones ruidosas, con que no pudo notificar nada, como ni otros secretarios que subieron al púlpito a notificar al pueblo, porque los órganos, instrumentos y campanas se hundían, y las sillas del coro se deshacían a golpes, con que no pudieron notificar nada por ningún camino. (346-47)

La confusión y el caos se apoderaron del espacio litúrgico, suspendiendo la misa y generando consecuencias en el propio predicador. Los gritos, los ruidos, las personas y las cosas, se mezclan, se agitan, y vuelan por el aire objetos que modifican el espacio y la disposición de los cuerpos en la iglesia. Lo que antes era un espacio litúrgico ordenado y preparado para comenzar a emitir un mensaje sacro (el sermón) se transforma literalmente en un campo de batalla, donde nadie está a salvo de las fuerzas en pugna. Lo material y lo sonoro están en el centro de esta escena tragicómica y cobran singular importancia para poder entenderla: las personas en el coro se ponen de pie, los órganos, instrumentos y campanas (todos índices de lo acústico en el espacio eclesiástico) se mezclan con el ruido de las sillas y las maderas que parecen crujir debido a la pelea que está a punto de ocurrir. Los objetos materiales no dejan de producir sonidos y ganan protagonismo. Así mismo, el espacio material del púlpito ya no se presenta tampoco como un lugar de protección donde el predicador está a salvo y desde donde puede pronunciar su sermón, sino que es un espacio transgredido por la ira de la audiencia. En suma, esta escena singular, donde el espacio de la iglesia parece volverse una plaza pública en pugna, permite observar la plena participación de lo material y lo sonoro en el espectacular evento del sermón. Estos dos ámbitos se pueden observar cuando los elementos pertenecientes al sermón se salen de su lugar, de su rol y abandonan su función asignada debido al caos pero dejan rastros, índices precisos para que el investigador puede reconstruir sus funciones. El significado de la anécdota, claro está, excede su dimensión inmediata y puede también leerse como una imagen precisa sobre la actualidad de los estudios sobre la predicación en el Barroco. Como el confuso Juan de Armenta, los que estudiamos este fenómeno cultural, observamos que la predicación parece atrapada en una red de oposiciones binarias: lo textual /lo espectacular, lo teológico/lo teatral, lo ideológico/lo religioso, lo dogmático/lo desafiante, la imposición vertical/ la crítica al estatus quo.[1] Justamente, mi lectura hoy busca evitar esta trampa epistemológica y aprovechar dos intersecciones culturales. Me refiero a la cruce entre el espacio material de la prédica (el púlpito) y la dimensión sónica de este evento.

Púlpitos materiales e imaginados

La influencia del púlpito como objeto en la predicación no puede minimizarse, ya que en su dimensión material, el púlpito combina y sintetiza los grandes temas debatidos en torno al valor, la función y la efectividad del discurso homilético. En su valioso estudio sobre el origen, la evolución, los cambios y la significación del púlpito en el Renacimiento, Ben-Aryeh Debby señala la importancia de pensarlo inserto dentro del espacio litúrgico. Debido a su naturaleza como objeto tecnológico y simultáneamente artístico, el púlpito presenta numerosas aristas que conviene explorar para poder reconstruir su valor y funcionalidad. Debby nota que "both pulpit and sermon are rheto-

---

[1] La evolución del estudio del sermón dentro del contexto del Barroco fue analizada por Francis Cerdan, quien ha destacado los cambios de percepción frente a esta práctica cultural. Dentro de la revalorización de la cultura barroca, la oratoria sagrada ha sido una de las últimas manifestaciones discursivas que ha captado la atención de la crítica. Cerdan, en su "Introducción crítica" a los *Sermones cortesanos* de Fray Hortensio Paravicino, presenta un somero y agudo análisis de la evolución de esta forma literaria. Miguel Ángel Núñez Beltrán en su *La oratoria sagrada de la época del Barroco* ha explicado de manera convincente la función social y simbólica de la predicación en este período de la historia española. Ambos estudiosos utilizan como clave interpretativa los aportes historiográficos realizados por José Antonio Maravall. Por otra parte, los estudios de Fernando R. de la Flor intentan (como mi ensayo también pretende) revisar este marco teórico para brindar un panorama más completo y complejo de este crucial fenómeno del Barroco.

rical modes working together to convey certain religious and cultural messages" (11). Es necesario primero recordar que el espacio mismo de la iglesia constituyó un elemento de cierta estabilidad arquitectónica y simbólica, ya que en cada edificio sacro se repiten un conjunto limitado de objetos y muebles que cumplen con las actividades sacramentales y pastorales: altares, confesionarios, tumbas, pilas bautismales y púlpitos se encargan de regular las acciones de los cuerpos que habitan este espacio. Sin embargo, como Evonne Levy señala al hablar de los interiores eclesiásticos de la España barroca, esta estabilidad se veía afectada debido a que su efectividad estaba estrechamente vinculada a las técnicas sobre los sentidos. Se creaba así un espacio interior hecho de diferentes capas conceptuales que apelaban a captar la percepción del auditorio, a partir de constantes estímulos visuales, sonoros, olfativos y táctiles. Se intentaba entonces evitar la fragmentación del mensaje evangélico propuesto desde la arquitectura y la decoración interior de la iglesia, proyectando una serie de significados estables por medio de objetos reconocibles.[2]

Debby observa que, desde la Edad Media, la prédica se ejercía a partir de la introducción de dos ambones móviles, cuya su ubicación se fundamentaba en el tipo de mensaje que se predicaba desde ellos. Es por ello que sobre el costado sur de la nave principal se ubicaba el ambón desde donde se dictaba la lección, mientras que el evangelio se predicaba desde la parte norte (54). El primer cambio que se percibe se origina alrededor del siglo XIII, cuando se propone y codifica el uso de púlpitos fijos en el espacio eclesiástico localizado en la parte central de la nave, delante del coro y más cerca de la congregación: así se comienza a pensarlo como la plataforma desde la cual el predicador va a dar su mensaje y tiene que enfocarse en la comunidad sobre la cual quiere intervenir. (54) Otro cambio de considerable importancia fue la construcción de púlpitos fijos que se proyectaban desde los pilares o la pared de la nave como un balcón hacia el público que asistía a la iglesia. Este hecho respondía a la necesidad de diferenciar dos eventos verbales cruciales en la ceremonia religiosa: la lectura de los evangelios se hacía a la manera tradicional desde los ambones móviles; mientras que para la oración se usaba el púlpito. Así la prédica del sermón adquiría cierto grado de autonomía dentro del rito. La palabra del predicador estaba enmarcada dentro de un espacio obsesivamente reglamentado, ya que el acto oratorio debía formar parte de una unidad mayor, debía insertarse dentro de una economía simbólica del espacio que respondía a procedimientos estrictamente litúrgicos. Curiosamente, con la llegada del Renacimiento, se observa una variación de singular importancia: el

---

2   Una buena síntesis del tema puede encontrarse en el artículo "Church: Interior" en *Baroque Lexicon*.

púlpito se comienza a ubicar hacia los costados de la nave central para evitar el eco generado por el transepto, relegando el valor litúrgico y buscando un espacio adecuado dependiendo fundamentalmente de cuestiones materiales cuantificables, clasificables y controlables, me refiero, claro está, al sonido y sus efectos en el edificio.

Examinando el vínculo entre geometría y arquitectura en el Siglo XVII, se percibe un cambio en la manera de concebir la función del púlpito, ya que se lo vincula con estrategias para incrementar y aprovechar su capacidad tecnológica, en lugar de priorizar su función litúrgica. La ya estable posición en la nave central, en conjunción con la suma de elementos con finalidad tanto visual como sonora, hacen que se le dé mayor importancia a la dimensión material (lo que el auditorio ve, escucha y toca) en lugar de la simbólica—lo que el objeto representa dentro del evento litúrgico. A partir de los avances en torno al estudio de la acústica, se codificó el uso del tornavoz como pieza clave del púlpito, pues debido a su ubicación sobre el cuerpo del predicador, ayudaba a que la palabra del orador llegara de manera efectiva a su auditorio vía la refracción, la concentración y el aumento de la voz. Algo similar sucede en torno al diseño de la cátedra y el respaldo en función de los valores espaciales y visuales. La primera opera como un filtro que controla el cuerpo del predicador, mostrando y escondiendo al auditorio el *decente gobierno de la acción*. El segundo, es el eje rector desde donde proyectar la mirada, los movimientos y las palabras. Estas nuevas variables que combinan lo arquitectónico, lo acústico y lo visual, son ejemplos del grado de especialización que tanto los diseñadores como los mismos predicadores y tratadistas tuvieron de la materialidad de los púlpitos barrocos. El púlpito es una herramienta que promueve y hace más efectiva la palabra del predicador, pero, simultáneamente, el púlpito aparece mencionado como un obstáculo que el orador católico deberá superar cuando las condiciones materiales de este foco de enunciación no sean las ideales. Hay una tensión constante entre la idea del púlpito como el medio más adecuado para emitir el mensaje y su imagen como una materia resistente sobre la cual el orador deberá reflexionar si busca que su actuación sea efectiva.

En su *Avisos para los predicadores*, fray Agustín Salucio (1523-1601) reflexiona en torno a la materialidad haciendo distintas alusiones al espacio desde donde la predicación se lleva a cabo y cómo el agente de la misma deberá adaptarse a este medio. El tratadista asevera que "el púlpito conviene que sea un poco ancho; y cuando yo lo he hallado tal que dentro pueda retraerme o adelantarme en ocasión un paso, ha sido muy a propósito." (188) Esta conexión entre espacio y cuerpo, confiere a la condición material del púlpito (su tamaño y amplitud) un valor importante ya que puede interferir (positiva o negativamente) en la actuación del orador. Salucio incorpora esta temática a lo largo de todo su tratado haciendo referencias a condiciones generales/abstractas o singulares/particulares. El tratadista conecta su ideal sobre el púlpito y los límites que ha encontrado al ejercer su labor pastoral, cuando señala que, ante la falta de púlpitos construidos siguiendo las normas geométricas, es necesario "acomodarse a lo que se hallare, como suelen los que caminan en cabalgaduras alquiladas. En todo el arzobispado de Toledo son los púlpitos importunamente angostos y demasiadamente altos, no sé por qué descuido." (188) La falta de atención al diseño del espacio oratorio ("descuido") está íntimamente vinculada con una falla en la construcción del púlpito material, aludiendo a dos elementos geométricamente determinados (angostura, altura) que presentarían problemas de índole sonoro y óptico al momento de realizar el ejercicio del sermón.

Esta primera mención a dos elementos mensurables (sonido, óptica) vuelve a mostrar la interdependencia entre dos variables materiales ya mencionadas (cuerpo, púlpito) y su compleja relación al momento de la prédica cuando Salucio señala otra de las ventajas que se observan a partir de un púlpito racionalizado: "Conviene que sean tan anchos que, quien tuviere necesidad, pueda escupir dentro; porque fuera no es lícito, aunque yo lo vi hacer a un gran predicador cortesano. Los que no lo somos, no debemos atrevernos a tanta descortesía." (188) El púlpito será entonces una plataforma desde donde mejor predicar, pero también puede ser visto como un obstáculo que es necesario superar por el experimentado predicador, curiosamente funcionará también como un objeto capaz de disimular una práctica (escupir) a evitar. La relación entre la localización del púlpito y la audiencia será también importante para Salucio:

> Los púlpitos no han de ser tampoco tan terreros y bajos que con la mano se llegue a las cabezas de los oyentes; ni tan altos que se desvanezca quien en ellos sube y esté fuera de conversación. También cumple que sean proporcionados al cuerpo, de modo que lleguen al principio del pecho, porque es cansadísima cosa si se descubre mucho del cuerpo, y muy ahogada, si se está hundido. (188)

En la búsqueda de un justo medio efectivo, el tratadista proyecta una imagen del púlpito que debe ajustarse proporcionadamente al cuerpo del emisor del mensaje evangélico a partir de tres acciones: regular visualmente lo que el predicador debe mostrar su audiencia; medir la distancia con el público y conectar la acción suasoria con el campo de lo sonoro. Salucio finaliza esta sección mostrando otra intersección entre corporalidad, sonoridad y visualidad en torno al objeto púlpito:

> Después de puesto bien el cuerpo, levantadas algo ambas partes de la capa sobre el borde del púlpito, las manos plegadas — o como mejor a cada cual le estuviere —, se mira con modestia y gravedad al auditorio, sin notable detenimiento, pues esto no es para más de saber dónde se ha de enderezar el razonamiento, de modo que, sin volver demasiadamente a una parte ni a otra el cuerpo, pueda bien de todos ser oído. (189)

La imagen final presenta una composición completa, donde cada uno de sus elementos está totalmente integrado en función del objetivo central: el mensaje evangélico. Esta interdependencia de sujetos y objetos se aprecia a través del énfasis en el cuerpo (representado a partir de la disposición de las manos, el uso de la mirada y la postura erguida), lo sartorial (la capa) y el objeto material donde ambos descansan y significan (el púlpito). También es importante la conexión entre el cuerpo erguido que representa desde el púlpito y el deseo por "enderezar el razonamiento" para alcanzar mejor a su auditorio. La injerencia de la materialidad del púlpito en el discurso del tratadista manifiesta la interacción constante de los distintos elementos que operan en el acto oratorio dentro del espacio litúrgico. Por último, la forma en que el religioso piensa la materialidad del púlpito coincide, punto por punto, con las trasformaciones históricas del objeto y su función: me refiero a la tensión entre la función tecnológico/ pragmática del púlpito post Trento, versus la función litúrgica tradicional. Esta tensión es una de las claves para entender con mayor claridad que la construcción del predicador barroco debe entenderse como un proceso inacabado, en constante desarrollo y pleno de paradojas. Así mismo, es indispensable observar la predicación más allá de lo textual, buscando insertarla dentro de un contexto cultural mayor.

"CON CIERTA HAMBRE DE OÍR": LO SÓNICO EN LA CONSTRUCCIÓN DEL PREDICADOR BARROCO

En su obra *Pliego de cartas en que ay doze epístolas escritas a personas de diferentes estados y oficios* (1594), el doctor Gaspar Salcedo de Aguirre incluye un texto donde explica la labor del predicador. En esta extensa carta, Salcedo de Aguirre combina buena parte de la información contenida en las más populares artes de predicación a los que le suma un número de anécdotas basadas en experiencias personales que conectan la teoría con la práctica. Al momento de definir la labor del predicador Salcedo de Aguirre establece dos características fundamentales en su labor. La primera, es la que busca convencer y transmitir el mensaje evangélico a la audiencia y de allí buscar la conversión, el arrepentimiento, la corrección o directamente la reafirmación de un credo. (181) Inmediatamente, después de esta declaración de principios doctrinales y litúrgicos, el autor asevera que "el segundo oficio del predicador es deleitar los oyentes, diciendo tales cosas de tal manera, con tal estilo y lenguaje, que les tenga suspensos, y vayan oyendo con mucho gusto sin violencia, sin pesadumbre, antes con cierta hambre de oír." (181) Esta última frase pone de manifiesto un claro interés por la dimensión sonora del evento comunicativo del sermón: el tratadista utiliza una imagen compleja que se estructura a partir de la correlación entre una necesidad biológica/natural (el hambre) y un fenómeno plenamente acústico/sónico donde el sustantivo elegido (oír) pone en primer plano la dimensión material del lenguaje versus lo que podría definirse como la esfera semántica del discurso (escuchar). En otras palabras, ya desde la primera definición del trabajo del orador católico, Salcedo de Aguirre nos indica la necesidad de recuperar este aspecto crucial en la constitución de identidades culturales durante el Barroco y que no ha sido del todo estudiado en conexión con la predicación.

En la introducción a un esclarecedor volumen sobre la conexión entre sonido y cultura en la temprana modernidad europea, Daniele Fillippi y Michael Noone explican la importancia de adoptar una perspectiva de análisis amplia al momento de reflexionar sobre lo que se ha dado en llamar el giro sónico en los estudios de la cultura post-Trento. Específicamente, estos autores, siguiendo las propuestas de John O Malley, establecen la categoría de "Catholic sounscape" (paisaje sonoro católico) para poder integrar toda una serie de actividades y fenómenos sonoros propios de la cultura europea de este período. De esta forma, la predicación participa de este paisaje sonoro junto con otras prácticas culturales recurrentes en la época tales como la música, el canto, las celebraciones, las campanadas, etc. Todas estas manifestaciones de lo sonoro van formando diferentes capas de sentido que contribuyen visibilizar numerosos fenómenos vinculados a lo sónico que cumplieron una función importantísima en esta sociedad. El objetivo de los autores antes mencionados es tratar de explicar qué tipo de cultura sónica se desarrolló en este contexto y cómo esta cultura contribuyó a la formación de identidades individuales y comunitarias. (14) Fillippi y Noone afirman que ...

> Sound, to begin with, emerges as a decisive factor in the shaping of individual and collective identities, and in the building of Catholic com-

munities. It had the power of uniting as well as that of differentiating. It marked time and space, helping Catholics to construct and experience their *sacral geography*, and to navigate the daily, weekly, and annual cycles specified in the liturgical calendar. Sound, moreover, dramatically entered into play at many crucial moments in the faithful's life cycle. Sound and music were fundamental in almost every public aspect of Catholic life, well beyond the confines of the liturgy. Through sound and music, groups and communities represented themselves in the public arena; they articulated, organized, and disciplined their presence during events, gatherings, and festivals of religious, civic, or mixed character. (15)

Teniendo en cuenta justamente esta intersección productiva entre individuo, comunidad, imaginación y sonido, me interesa señalar aquellos elementos propios del paisaje sonoro que jugaron un rol preponderante en la construcción del perfecto predicador barroco. En los tratados de predicación abundan numerosas y recurrentes referencias directas e indirectas a aspectos pertenecientes a la esfera sónica. Estas reflexiones ayudan a entender que en el largo y heterogéneo proceso de constitución de este agente cultural (el predicador) existe un interés puntual por reglamentar lo sonoro. Para ello, resulta fundamental entender a este último concepto como una problemática que abarca diferentes niveles. Por un lado, lo sonoro se define a partir de la conexión entre el aspecto material del sonido y el espacio litúrgico donde se celebra el acto oratorio. En otras oportunidades, lo sonoro emerge a partir de ciertos comentarios, sugerencias y reglas que los tratadistas incluyen en sus artes de predicar mostrando la plena conciencia que de la esfera sónica tienen estos escritores cuando reflexionan sobre la forma más adecuada para la predicación.

En este extenso corpus (desde el fundamental *Modo de predicar* de Fray Luis de Granada publicado en 1576 hasta el *Operario instruido y oyente aprovechado* del jesuita Miguel Pascual de 1698) los preceptistas elaboran una serie de reglas que involucran tanto lo verbal como lo no verbal, lo espacial, lo corporal, lo visual y lo gestual. Al presentarse una serie de micro-disciplinas se genera un sujeto producto de saberes, normas y reglas que exceden el ámbito de la palabra (mores, según O'Malley). Esta constante intersección de los distintos aspectos que hacen al predicador, culmina en el deseo por construir un sujeto sólido, sin fisuras, homogéneo y partícipe de un discurso con el cual mantiene una relación de reciprocidad: si él es el producto de todos estos dispositivos culturales, simultáneamente asumirá el rol de intermediario ante el público que asiste al evento litúrgico para recibir el mensaje eclesiástico (ya que será el canal a través del cual se efectivice este último, siguiendo la fórmula maravalliana de interpretación de la cultura barroca). Pero es justamente en estas relaciones de mediación donde es posible hallar elementos que se resisten a ser regulados, y así observar que en torno a la construcción del predicador barroco persiste un estado de reforma permanente, un proceso incompleto y continuo que pone en juego mucho más que una batalla en torno a un llamado "estilo culto" versus un "estilo llano".

Tomemos por caso ejemplar la que quizás sea la retórica cristiana de mayor alcance que se haya publicado luego de Trento: *Los seis libros de la retórica eclesiástica o modo de predicar* de Fray Luis de Granada. En un fundamental ensayo para entender la relación entre musicología y predicación, Todd Borgerding señalaba cómo ya en este seminal tratado sobre oratoria podían notarse las constantes conexiones entre la retórica y lo audible. Para Borgerding no era casualidad que las reflexiones más explícitas sobre la implicación de lo sonoro en la predicación aparecieran en las secciones de los tratados dedicadas a la pronunciación o acción porque "the fact that all of these references to music appear in discussions of pronunciation and never in conjunction with tropes, figures, or disposition points out that, for these preachers, music was heard as variations in sound closely related to the affective style of oratory that they promoted." (588) La plena integración de lo sonoro en las reglas que pretendían delinear el modelo más adecuado para el predicador comprueban las hipótesis de Fillippi y Noone sobre la capacidad de crear identidades a través de la regulación de lo sónico en el mundo católico post Trento. Reflexionando sobre la necesidad establecer un conjunto sólido de técnicas específicas en torno al púlpito, Granada decide insertar una serie de recuerdos que funcionarán como ejemplos de su propia actividad:

> Hace pocos días que he topado con un libro en francés que disertaba sobre la técnica y método de la cinegética, y que baja tanto a cada uno de los preceptos de esta técnica y método que, con las mismas notas con las que los cantores apuntan en sus libros la melodía que entonan a coro, insinúa con qué sonido y con qué inflexión vocal deberían los perros ser llamados por los cazadores y azuzados a cazar. De cierto que me tiene maravillado la diligencia de las gentes que no sólo se han inventado preceptos para esta cuestión, sino que incluso intentaban transmitirnos una especie de tipo de canto y de tono con el que se tendría que llamar a los animales. Conque, si éstos han sido tan afanosos con una nadería, ¿a qué nos vamos a dejar superar por ellos al transmitir nosotros la parte más sobresaliente de todas y la que le es más necesaria a los predicadores?" (641)

Para Granada, su trabajo es presentar un estudio sistemático de los elementos básicos que componen la figura del predicador y para hacerlo decide investigar los aspectos materiales de la lengua (el sonido, los tonos) presentes en el evento comunicativo, ya que Granada observa que estos últimos pueden estudiarse en sus unidades mínimas de sentido y así desentrañar los misterios de este arte, de la misma forma que se puede hacer lo mismo con sus acciones y gestos. Al equiparar el entrenamiento del animal con el proceso de formación del perfecto predicador, Granada parece sugerir que la figura del predicador puede reducirse a una serie limitada de axiomas que interactúan como partes de una máquina mayor. Este carácter maquínico (como Fernando de la Flor lo llama) de la figura del orador se traduce en la idea de que puede estudiarse en su totalidad analizando los distintos mecanismos que constituyen a este sujeto. Casi como si estuviera calibrando los resortes más ínfimos de un autómata, en este discurso sobre la predicación, Granada presenta una serie de oposiciones en constante tensión y de difícil resolución. Si por un lado se plantea la posibilidad de estabilizar los elementos que intervienen en la construcción del predicador (al profundizar el conocimiento del sujeto, al clasificar las casi ilimitadas situaciones ante las que se va a enfrentar y al catalogar los múltiples modos del decir y del moverse de acuerdo al espacio que se ocupe en el acto suasorio) el tratadista introduce también en su reflexión una visión de lo sonoro donde habita lo inesperado, lo transitorio y lo que presenta resistencias frente a una meditada disciplina. Entonces, ¿cómo será posible controlar el aspecto lo sónico de la predicación? Para Granada, la respuesta está en la plena interacción entre diferentes esferas de la vida sónica, a saber, lo religioso y lo secular. El tratadista, nos recuerda Borgerding, va a incluir una anécdota que poco parce tener que ver con el ámbito litúrgico de la prédica pero que, curiosamente, posee un significado suplementario que será preciso visibilizar:

> Así, para tener más eficacia para dar a entender qué pienso yo en esta parte, señalaré qué nos ocurrió a mí y a un predicador novicio. Pidióme él que escuchara a uno para luego darle consejo si se me antojaba que había algo digno de advertir; él pronunció la prédica entera, la cual se había aprendido palabra por palabra, sin ninguna variación del tono de voz, tal y como si recitara de memoria algún salmo de David. Y acabada la prédica, al volver a casa, vi por el camino a dos mujerzuelas que discutían y se peleaban con acritud, y así como hablaban ellas aguijoneadas por auténticas emociones, también mudaban a renglón seguido, de acuerdo a la variedad de sus emociones, las diferentes formas e inflexiones de la voz,

y entonces yo al compañero que venía conmigo le dije: Si aquel predicador hubiera escuchado a estas mujerzuelas e imitara esta misma forma de pronunciar, en modo alguno le faltaría nada para la perfecta acción de la que totalmente andaba privado. (647)

La construcción del predicador debe abandonar el campo de lo estable/predecible y adentrarse en las complejidades de lo transitorio de la experiencia social que lo circunda—aun cuando esa misma circunstancia presente sujetos y acciones que a primera vista nada tendrían de modélico. El predicador que quiera suplir todo eso de lo que "andaba privado" deberá escuchar e imitar también a esas mujerzuelas que se pelean en un camino arrabal oscuro para poder corregir una carencia de la técnica. Esto demuestra cómo también la experiencia del sonido fuera de la liturgia y del espacio eclesiástico forma parte de una experiencia mayor, de una comunidad que los contiene y los define a partir de lo que Fillippi y Noone definieron como el paisaje católico de la temprana modernidad. Esta reversibilidad del hecho sónico marca una serie de conclusiones productivas: en primer lugar, se percibe a través de indagar el plano sónico el grado de cohesión y continuidad que existía en este aspecto; además, queda claro que para aprender a usar el sonido dentro del espacio litúrgico será necesario oír el espacio público en todas sus variedades; y también se deduce que es importante señalar la activa conexión entre la esfera secular y la religiosa al momento de fundar las bases del modelo perfecto de predicador. Granada saca su conclusión a partir de una experiencia urbana y es esa experiencia urbana la que va a cimentar su visión sobre cómo predicar. Hay en esta anécdota un ida y vuelta, un movimiento de vaivén entre lo litúrgico y lo social que parece hallar el punto de intersección máximo en la experiencia sónica compartida.

Este complejo vínculo entre lo interno y lo externo, entre lo sólido y lo que se disuelve, puede observarse también en otro tratado clave para entender la predicación del XVII, me refiero al *Arte de orar evangélicamente* de Agustín de Jesús María (1648). En su tratado, el erudito comienza declarando la importancia del decir elocuentemente en la predicación y su conexión con el resto de la sociedad. Si bien asevera que es importante "sanar" los vicios del auditorio con la potencia de la palabra divina, inmediatamente después sostiene que esto sólo puede hacerse si se conoce el arte de la elocuencia. Para el padre de Jesús,

Todas las mayores calamidades de la república se originan de mal disciplinados ingenios. Y siendo este dicho en todas las materias en que los buenos ingenios carecen de magisterio, en materia de hablar elocuentemente le hallo más cierto por ser más general el peligro y no menos dificultoso el remedio. (2)

Para el religioso, el proyecto de fundación del perfecto predicador no ha florecido como debía y esto se debe a la falta de disciplinamiento de los sujetos, fundamentalmente de aquellos que deben predicar. Su arte de sermones viene entonces a remediar este problema que establece las reglas del perfecto predicador, quien podrá dedicarse a ejercer su rol y sanar el cuerpo enfermo del reino. En el capítulo V, sección primera del *Arte*, el carmelita propone una clasificación de las cualidades sonoras/estilísticas de las vocales y las consonantes del castellano y sus correspondientes efectos en el auditorio. Esta reflexión me permite conectarla con las preocupaciones ya expuestas de Granada en torno a la conexión exterior/interior a través del lenguaje, las cosas y los cuerpos. Para el religioso, la clave de toda la predicación está en conocer el interior de las palabras precisas que podrán causar el efecto deseado. Para ello, Santa María ofrece una taxonomía de las palabras (sublimes, grandes, medianas e ínfimas) siguiendo un singular razonamiento:

> las palabras grandes y sublimes en la pronunciación son aquellas que contaren de sílabas más hinchadas, y estas son las que de las letras vocales tienen más aa y oo, y de las consonantes, más mm y tt teniendo más larga la pronunciación; las que tienen más breve con estas vocales ii y uu, constituyen palabras ínfimas. Las ee son medianas y juntas con la ii se hacen ínfimas. (folio 60)

La superficie del lenguaje será analizada con el mismo fervor y la misma curiosidad con que se estudia el "decente gobierno de la cara" o el "teatro de los gestos" (todas frases que aparecen recurrentemente en las retóricas cristianas): la palabra, unidad básica del discurso suasorio, proferida en el púlpito deberá seguir el mismo impulso y compartir el mismo orden que el movimiento de una mano, la inclinación del cuello, la dirección de una mirada o la inflexión de un tono—buscando el modelo perfecto que ser aproveche de este conocimiento en pos de la efectividad. Sin embargo, la materialidad de las palabras adquiere en éste (y en muchos otros tratados) un significado mayor si la conectamos con las disputas en torno al proyecto de construcción del perfecto predicador y a la dimensión sónica que, junto a otros significantes presentes que, a medida que se enuncian, parecen jugar en contra de este mismo proyecto. Santa María orienta su tratado a anticipar los efectos inesperados producidos por los sonidos de las palabras, y aflora en su propuesta una clara ansiedad por intentar controlar todos los aspectos del evento comunicativo que se lleva a cabo durante el sermón.

Algo similar puede también verse en lo escrito por Francisco de Ameyugo en su *Rethorica sagrada y evangélica* (1667) donde el interés por dominar el cuerpo se conecta con la ansiedad por clasificar los problemas de la esfera sónica. En el Capítulo III del Libro VI de la *Rethorica*, Ameyugo comienza estableciendo una clara continuidad entre el uso del cuerpo en el púlpito y la forma adecuada de administrar la voz como herramienta para una predicación efectiva. Este vínculo, claro está, se encuentra enmarcado dentro de una discusión de mayor alcance: Ameyugo dedica estas últimas páginas de su tratado a clasificar los distintos elementos que componen lo que tanto en la retórica clásica como en la cristiana se denominaba actio o pronunciación. Resulta importante señalar que el religioso propone la necesidad de inventar, a través de un discurso plagado de reglas y sugerencias, una natural artificialidad en la apariencia del predicador. Es así como los movimientos del cuerpo deberán responder a una serie de normas establecidas por el tratadista y que se deben aplicar al momento de predicar el sermón y así emitir un significado suplementario a lo expresado a través de lo verbal. El uso normativo de las manos, las pautas esenciales para mantener al cuerpo erguido y hasta las mejores estrategias para disimular una tos, un catarro o un estornudo serán partes fundamentales en la creación de un estilo al que podríamos llamar total de la predicación.

Dentro de este paradigma, la voz del predicador será también pensada de una forma similar, en tanto elemento material que puede y debe ser controlado con anticipación por la voluntad del orador. Todo el capítulo III estará dedicado a proponer las propiedades que todo predicador deberá seguir si pretende "gobernar graciosamente la voz" (73), poniendo singular atención en aquellos aspectos que hoy podríamos clasificar como pertenecientes al ámbito de lo sónico en la temprana modernidad europea. Una de las propiedades más importantes de la voz es su carácter "enmendada", esto es:

> que carezca de todo vicio: es vicio que sea o muy baja o muy alta y desentonada; que hay algunos Predicadores que como algunos llevan las cosas a palos, ellos las llevan a gritos, dando clamores desentonados; y dando a entender también que tienen mal pleito, pues que lo meten a voces. La voz pues se ha de acomodar a la capacidad del lugar y concurso del audi-

torio; de suerte que ni sea tan baja que no se perciba, ni suene más de lo que es necesario. (73)

El tratadista propone una plena conexión entre el espacio, la voz y los efectos sonoros que de esta intersección se deducen. Cuando Ameyugo afirma que la voz se debe acomodar al lugar y el concurso está señalando, de manera implícita, los efectos cambiantes de lo sonoro de acuerdo a la acústica del lugar donde se predique y la asistencia (o no) masiva de público al evento religioso. Esta simple indicación, que podría pasar desapercibida en una lectura rápida, confirma la plena conciencia de que, para poder establecer con mayor profundidad qué tipo modelo dominante de predicador se propuso en el Siglo XVII, es necesario rescatar aspectos y fenómenos culturales varios, heterogéneos y pertenecientes a diversos campos de la experiencia cultural. Algo que puede conectarse con la tensión antes descrita entre lo irrepetible y lo cotidiano, entre el misterio y el ministerio, y entre lo objetivo y lo subjetivo. Toda la serie de retóricas cristianas que evalúo en mi estudio, apuntan a un tipo de relación paradójica similar que oscila entre lo celestial y lo terreno, lo sacro y lo profano, lo político y lo poético y que no termina nunca de hacer resonar sus ecos en ese diálogo, aporético e inacabado, que es la producción del predicador barroco.

En resumen, en el ensayo he buscado incorporar un aspecto no del todo estudiado (lo sonoro) al debate en torno a la formación del predicador en el Barroco. A través de esta forma de aproximarme a un fenómeno cultural tan importante como la predicación, he destacado los vínculos existentes entre las diferentes esferas que constituyeron esta cultura. He analizado primero la dimensión material del púlpito porque permite observar continuidades y rupturas en el estado de reforma permanente que habitó la sociedad de la temprana modernidad española después de Trento. Me interesó mostrar cómo, tanto en arquitectura y en manuales de oratoria cristiana, se observa un interés similar por las variables litúrgicas y materiales que intervienen en el acto comunicativo del sermón. Así mismo, he incorporado testimonios de tratadistas que de forma explícita aportan ideas sobre la dimensión material del lenguaje empleado desde el púlpito. Esta serie de testimonios buscaron hacer que se perciba la predicación sagrada no como un hecho aislado que solo importa al investigador especializado, sino que prefiero entenderla como una práctica cultural que no puede disfrutarse en profundidad si no es examinada dentro del complejo marco epistemológico del que surgió.

Obras citadas

AAVV. *Cartas de algunos padres de la compañía de Jesús*. Madrid: Imprenta Real, 1861.
Agamben, Giorgio. *Opus Dei. An Archeology of Duty*. Stanford University Press, 2013.
Barnes, G. *Sermons and the Discourse of Power: The Rhetoric of Religious Oratory in Spain (1550-1900)*. UMI, 1988.
Ameyugo, Francisco de. *Rethorica sagrada y evangélica. Ilustrada con la práctica de diversos artificios rethoricos para proponer la palabra divina*. Juan de Ybar, 1667.
Borgerding, Todd. "Preachers, Pronunciation and Music: Hearing Rhetoric in Renaissance Sacred Polyphony." *The Musical Quarterly*, vol. 82, no. 3-4, 1998, pp. 586–598.
Cerdan, Francis. "Historia de la historia de la Oratoria Sagrada española en el Siglo de Oro, Introducción crítica y bibliografía." *Criticón* no. 32, 1985, pp. 55-107.
———. "La emergencia del estilo culto en la oratoria sagrada del siglo XVII." *Criticón* no. 58, 1993, pp. 61-72.
———. "Actualidad de los estudios sobre oratoria sagrada del Siglo de Oro (1985 - 2002)." *Criticón* No. 84, 2002, pp. 9-42.
Debby, Nirit Ben-Aryeh. *The Renaissance Pulpit. Art and Preaching in Tuscany 1400-1550*. Brepols Publishers, 2007.
De Jesús María, Agustín. *Arte de orar evangélicamente*. Imprenta de Salvador de Viader, 1648.
De la Flor, Fernando. "La oratoria sagrada del Siglo de Oro y el dominio corporal." *Culturas en la Edad de Oro*. Editorial Complutense, 1995, pp.123-47.
Fillippi, Daniele, and Michael F. Noone. *Listening to Early Modern Catholicism: Perspectives from Musicology*. BRILL, 2017.
Fumaroli, Marc. *L'Age du l'Eloquence: rethorique et res literaria de la Renaissance au seuil de l'epoque classique*. Droz, 1980.
Granada, Luis de. *Los seis libros de la retórica eclesiástica, o método de predicar*. Traducción e introducción de Manuel López-Múñoz, Instituto de Estudios Riojanos, 2010.
Herrero Salgado, Francisco. *La oratoria sagrada en los siglos XVI y XVII*. Fundación Universitaria Española, 1986.
Hersey, George L. *Architecture and Geometry in the Age of the Baroque*. The University of Chicago Press, 2001.
Howard, Peter Francis. *Beyond the Written Word. Preaching and Theology in the Florence of Archbishop Antoninus. 1427-1459*. Casa Editrice Leo S.Olschki, 1995.

Larking, Brian. *The Very Nature of God. Baroque Catholicism and Religious Reform in Bourbon Mexico City*. U of New Mexico P, 2010.
Ledda, Giussepina. *La parola e l'immagine. Strategie della persuasione religiosa nella Spagna Secentesca*. Biblioteca di Studi Spanici, 2003.
Levy, Evonne and Kenneth Mills, eds. *Lexicon of the Hispanic Baroque. Transatlantic Exchange and Transformation*. University of Texas Press, 2014.
Maravall, José Antonio. *La cultura del Barroco*. Ariel, 1975.
Núñez Beltrán, Miguel Ángel. *La oratoria sagrada en la época del Barroco. Doctrina, cultura y actitud ante la vida desde los sermones sevillanos del XVII*. Universidad de Sevilla, 2007.
O'Malley, John W. *Trent. What Happened at the Council*. Harvard UP, 2013.
Orozco Díaz, Emilio. *Introducción al Barroco I*. Universidad de Granada, 1988.
Salzedo de Aguirre, Gaspar. *Pliego de cartas en que ay doze epístolas escritas a personas de diferentes estados y oficios*. Juan Batista de Montoya, 1594.
Salucio, Agustín. *Avisos para los predicadores del santo evangelio*. Estudio preliminar, edición y apéndices de Álvaro Huerga, Juan Flors, 1959.
Smith, Hillary. *Preaching in the Spanish Golden Age. A Study of Some Preachers of the Reign of Philip III*. Oxford UP, 1978.

Tilting at Relevance: The Quixotic Enterprise of Portuguese Authors of the Iberian Union

JONATHAN WADE
Meredith College

> "Apropriar-se da figura de Dom Quixote,
> no sentido em que agora uso o termo,
> é interiorizá-lo, fazendo-o nosso
> ou com ele dialogando,
> em tudo ou em muito
> a nós semelhante.
> É, enfim, re-criá-lo,
> re-apresentá-lo,
> re-escrevê-lo"
> – MARIA FERNANDA DE ABREU
> (Introduction 16)

WHILE MANY PORTUGUESE AUTHORS writing in Spanish during the Iberian Union (1580-1640) enjoyed a certain degree of celebrity both during their lifetimes and in the decades that followed, by the late nineteenth century they had all but been erased from Iberian cultural history. The critical consensus was that these authors were not Spanish or Portuguese enough to be admitted into either canon; the idea being that there was no room for them in the case of the former, and no place for them in the case of the latter. As a result, literary critics and historians have, with few exceptions, marginalized Portuguese literature of the Dual Monarchy, casting it off for its perceived impurity and lack of artistic merit. The twentieth century offers some important exceptions to this trend: Hernani Cidade, Edward Glaser, Eugenio Asensio, and Pilar Vázquez Cuesta, for example, are among those who dedicated considerable effort to rethinking the place of Portuguese authors of the seventeenth century. Asensio is not wrong to point out the overzealous nature of Cidade's *A literatura autono-*

mista sob os Filipes and how it casts many Portuguese authors of this time in the same nationalist light.[1] What remains underappreciated is Cidade's effort to fashion a narrative that rescues seventeenth-century Portuguese letters from cultural oblivion. His framing is still important precisely because an over-arching narrative that adequately captures the richness and complexity of Portuguese literature of the Dual Monarchy remains elusive. Heightened interest in Iberian Studies since the turn of the century has resulted in many relevant publications, although most focus on individual authors/works and not the period as a whole. In this essay I would like to explore some of the ways that Alonso Quijana's transformation during the opening chapters of Miguel de Cervantes's *Don Quixote* can inform how we read, understand, and appreciate the texts produced by many seventeenth-century Portuguese authors and the unique context in which they lived.

You will not find authors suiting up in the aged armor of their ancestors among the Portuguese of this time, nor will you find such characters in the literature they produced. But what many early modern Portuguese authors do offer is a way of writing and being that is not unlike Don Quixote's approach to knight errantry. Just as Alonso Quijana refashions himself by assuming a new name, establishing a purpose for his life, electing a source of inspiration, and identifying a model to follow; a generation of Portuguese authors redefined themselves during the Dual Monarchy by spreading the glories of Portugal in a borrowed language, taking inspiration from their motherland just as their literary model, Luis de Camões (c.1524-80), had done the century previous. Through poetry, theater, literary criticism, and historiography, many writers fashioned an intelligible rhetoric of nationhood that sets them apart from many of their Iberian contemporaries. Similar to the fanciful world of Don Quixote, the Portugal these authors cast and celebrated in their writings was a construct made by and through texts. Within the familiar frame of *Don Quixote*, then, this essay reimagines the literary legacy of the Portuguese of early modern Iberia, highlighting the quixotic nature of their enterprise.

Extant criticism includes several sources on the subject of Cervantes and Portugal. In some instances these studies center on specific references to Portugal and the Portuguese within Cervantes's complete works,[2] however

---

1   See Asensio's "España en la época filipina" for more information.

2   In *Don Quixote*, for example, Portugal (by name) comes up seven times, including when the priest and barber decide to preserve *Palmerín de Inglaterra* from the fire (64; part 1, ch. 6) and when Sansón tells Don Quixote and Sancho where the first part of their adventures has been published (567; part 2, ch. 3). Additionally,

more often the focus is on reception, influence, and legacy. A number of articles, for example, look at Portuguese translations of *Don Quixote*, the first of which appeared almost two centuries after its publication.[3] In *Cervantes no romantismo português* (1994), Maria Fernanda de Abreu traces the presence of Cervantes within the writing of Almeida Garrett and Camilo Castelo Branco, among others. More specifically, her work establishes the "sebastianização de Dom Quixote e à quixotização de Dom Sebastião" in nineteenth-century Portuguese literature.[4] In the decades preceding Abreu's work, trailblazers of comparative Iberian Studies such as Fidelino de Figueiredo, José Ares Montes, Glaser, and Asensio, among many others, also took up the subject of Cervantes and Portugal.[5]

In two separate articles, Glaser examines Cervantes's fame within seventeenth-century Portugal and keys in on the ways Portuguese authors of that time, with their "too simplified a picture of *Don Quixote*" (156), appropriated the figure of Don Quixote for satirical ends; by parodying a parody they could have fun at the expense of their Iberian neighbors. Vanda Anastácio unpacks this particular strategy even further in her analysis of what she calls "*os papéis* da Restauração": a catch-all for the variety of texts in circulation following the Restoration. While she agrees with Glaser's assertion regarding the satirical use of *Don Quixote*, in her analysis of *Cartel de desafío y contesta-*

---

the narrator mentions "la famosa ciudad de Lisboa" in the prologue to part 1 (12) and the Canon makes reference to Lusitania (504; part 1, ch. 49). Two of the most celebrated Portuguese authors of the sixteenth century also enter the narrative: Jorge de Montemayor (originally Montemor), whose *Diana* is also spared a fiery finish by the priest and barber (66; part 1, ch. 6); and the "excelentísimo Camoes," whose work two costumed shepherdesses have learned as part of their performance of the pastoral (991; part 2, ch. 58). In "Portugal en la vida y obra de Cervantes," Miguel Ángel Teijeiro Fuentes reviews examples from *Novelas ejemplares, Persiles, Galatea*, and *Viaje del Parnaso*, connecting them to what we know of Cervantes's biography.

3   See Cobelo, Dotras Bravo, and Abreu (*Cervantes*) for more information.

4   In an article published almost two decades later, Abreu traces the same theme as it appears in a twentieth-century play by Carlos Selvagem ("1943").

5   Alexia Dotras Bravo describes Figueiredo as perhaps "el primer divulgador de Cervantes en Portugal en el siglo xx" (136). As Xosé Manuel Dasilva explains, Figueiredo's *Pyrene* (1935) puts forward a number of promising subject areas on the topic of Cervantes and Portugal, including "El tema del *Quijote* en la literatura portuguesa de los siglos XVII a XX" ("Abreu" 379). Until Abreu's work appeared in the 1990s, the most substantive contribution to the subject of Cervantes and Portugal came by way of a series of articles by Ares Montes in *Anales Cervantinos* that traces, among other things, Cervantes's influence in Portugal across several literary genres.

cion cavalleresca de Don Quixote de la Mancha Cavallero de la triste figura en defension de sus Castellanos (1642), Anastácio identifies something more subversive at play.[6] Rather than the comical casting of the Spanish in the likeness of Don Quixote that was common among Portuguese-authored works at the time, in *Cartel de desafio* the errant knight is "caracterizado como um partidário dos portugueses, que apresenta a Restauração como uma 'pena justa' enviada por Deus para punir a 'soberbia, embustes, y tyrannias' de Castela e chama aos castelhanos 'gallinas'" (Anastácio 132). What's more, Don Quixote relinquishes the Knight of the Lions title in favor of Knight of the Chickens, since, by his own admission, Castile has traded its castles for chicken coops. Rather than a trope of idiocy or the absurd, in *Cartel de desafio* Don Quixote personifies good judgment in aligning himself with the Portuguese and, as the story goes, seeing the Spanish for who they really are. This iteration of the famed knight fuels the propaganda war that characterized the relationship between Spain and Portugal for the better part of three decades following the Restoration. This and other examples reveal how a "funny book" (see Russell) could be re-purposed for socio-political gains.

Although much has been made of the relationship between Cervantes and Portugal over the last hundred years, what remains underappreciated is the way that *Don Quixote* helps to tell the story of many seventeenth-century Portuguese authors. While some have examined what Manuel de Faria e Sousa, Jacinto Cordeiro, António de Sousa de Macedo, Francisco Manuel de Melo, and others have said about Cervantes and his beloved character,[7] I am interested in the ways that the *Quixote* illuminates the lives of these Portuguese authors by providing a fictional frame within which to see their place within early modern Iberia. Eugenio Asensio, for instance, once referred to Faria e Sousa as the "Don Quixote del camonismo" (qtd. in Dasvila 10 and Méndez 645). Faria e Sousa's monumental commentary on *Os Lusíadas* is unparalleled, widely considered the greatest of its kind. The same, of course, is often said of Cervantes's novel. There is much more, however, to Asensio's description. In reference to a passage from volume 4 of his commentary in which Faria e Sousa describes the pathetic state he was in following a half-century of tireless reading and study of *Os Lusíadas*, Asensio makes an acute observation: "Faria y Sousa recuerda al Caballero de la Triste Figura, tanto por su traza física como por su espléndida obsesión" ("Fortuna" 319). The

---

6 As Dotras Bravo points out, *Cartel del desafío* has been the focus of a number of studies. Aside from Anastácio's, both María Cruz García de Enterría and José Montero Reguera have written on the subject.

7 This is well-chronicled by Nicolás Marín, Ares Montes, and Glaser.

interplay of the real and the fictional is what most interests me about these observations. Nobody familiar with Faria e Sousa's complete works would hesitate to describe him in terms of Quixotism, yet there is ultimately something more deeply quixotic about Faria e Sousa and many of his Portuguese contemporaries.

The opening chapter of *Don Quixote* introduces the reader to a middle-aged man who finds something unexpected in the books that he consumed, and consumed him, both day and night. What had been his leisurely escape gradually becomes his lived reality. As the line blurs between the real and the fictional, so does Alonso's need for the actual books, since he now embodies them. In creating himself anew, he undertakes a transformation patterned after his fictional predecessors, with Amadís de Gaula as his North Star. His makeover begins externally, with the donning of a new name and a refurbished look: "Y lo primero que hizo fue limpiar unas armas que habían sido de sus bisabuelos, que, tomadas de orín y llenas de moho, luengos siglos había que estaban puestas y olvidadas en un rincón. Limpiolas y aderezolas lo mejor que pudo" (31; part 1, ch. 1). After baptizing his old horse Rocinante, he settles on a title for himself after days of careful consideration. Now Don Quixote de la Mancha, the self-made knight moves inward with his interests, adding a lady of his fancy and a mission of his making to his persona. The outmoded knight errant's overall quest is straightforward: "irse por todo el mundo con sus armas y caballo a buscar las aventuras y a ejercitarse en todo aquello que él había leído que los caballeros andantes se ejercitaban, deshaciendo todo género de agravio y poniéndose en ocasiones y peligros donde, acabándolos, cobrase eterno nombre y fama" (31; part 1, ch. 1). Over the course of just a few pages, this very ordinary *hidalgo* becomes something altogether extraordinary. In what follows I will use the beginnings of this familiar story to tell another.

Many Portuguese authors of the Dual Monarchy constructed their identity much like Alonso Quijana constructs his. Part of the shared experience of these authors, for example, was their relationship to the Spanish language. While Portuguese was their mother tongue, for many of them Spanish was also part of their cultural inheritance.[8] This was especially true of literature, wherein Spanish maintained a position of prestige for the better part of two

---

8   In the case of Francisco Manuel de Melo (1608-66), Spanish was actually his mother's tongue, she being a native of Alcalá de Henares. Marriages between the Spanish and Portuguese were not uncommon at the time. The children of these marriages could lay claim to biculturalism without leaving the walls of their home. For many others, contact with Spanish would have come through the university.

centuries. The cultural practice of writing in Spanish that began to flourish in response to the inter-dynastic marriages of the early sixteenth century, became so ubiquitous by the seventeenth century that most Portuguese-authored texts of the Iberian Union are written in Spanish. It would be reductive to assign a single motive to this cultural practice. It would also be a mistake to ignore it altogether considering that the authors themselves often address the language of the text in the introductory sections, if not in the work itself.[9] As Pilar Vázquez Cuesta summarizes, Portuguese authors offered many different reasons for using Spanish: "Melhor adequação do castelhano para determinados géneros ou estilos, maior universalidade, que devia aproveitar-se para dar a conhecer no Exterior as glórias portuguesas, superiores qualidades de clareza e compreensibilidade, são alguns dos múltiplos argumentos utilizados pelos escritores desse tempo" ("Bilinguismo" 814). Language, in general, and Spanish, in particular, functioned for them as Don Quixote's armor did for him. It had its imperfections, but it did the job. What is more, just as Don Quixote could not conceive of himself as a knight without looking the part, there was no way for a Portuguese author of the Iberian Union to be successful without writing in Spanish.[10] In his study of medieval, renaissance, and baroque polyglot poetry, Leonard Forster explores, among other things, the connection between language and dress. After quoting a passage from the English writer Thomas Gawen (1612-84), he explains the relationship: "one clothes one's thoughts in different linguistic garments according to the requirements of 'decorum' on the one hand (that is, what the formal occasion demands) or of the audience on the other (that is, what language they understand) . . . . One can change one's language as one changes one's clothes, as circumstances may require" (28). By writing in Spanish, therefore, the Portuguese could stand with the lettered elite of

---

Numerous Spanish professors taught at Portuguese universities, not to mention the countless Portuguese who studied in Spain (Martínez-Almoyna 29-30).

9 It would not be wrong to categorize many of these explanations as a form of apologetics. Sousa de Macedo's prologue to the reader in *Flores de España* often gets cited for its particular defense of Spanish as the *lingua franca* of the text, as does Faria e Sousa's commentary on *Os Lusíadas*. Bernarda Ferreira de Lacerda's *Hespaña libertada* (1618) addresses the same issue in the opening stanzas of her epic poem. There is something both conventional and confessional about the way Portuguese authors talk about writing in Spanish. It is widespread enough to merit its own sustained treatment in a separate monograph.

10 António Ferreira may very well be the only Portuguese author of some prominence to never write in Spanish during the sixteenth and seventeenth centuries.

the Peninsula and reach a broader audience. On balance, the road to literary acclaim was paved in Spanish. Hence, just as Don Quixote's self-appointed office required the unexpected revival of his ancestor's armor, in order to perform the literary role they desired, Portuguese authors donned the dominant language of early modern Iberia.

Even though the language question is critical to understanding Portuguese literature of the Dual Monarchy and its reception then and since, there is something ultimately more profound guiding many of the texts produced during those decades. Armor, after all, represents only the first of many changes that would see an uncertain someone from an undetermined somewhere become "el famoso don Quijote de la Mancha" (171; part 1, ch. 19). Beneath the surface of Don Quixote's character appear the two dominant figures of his inner world: Dulcinea and Amadís de Gaula (the former motivating him to action and the latter modeling what action to take). Among Portuguese authors the particulars change, but the principle remains the same. Many Portuguese works of the Dual Monarchy are characterized by two constants: Portugal and Camões. Their patriotic writings are motivated by the *patria*, and the model that they frequently cite is none other than Portugal's most celebrated poet. Throughout *Don Quixote*, we find our favorite knight paying tribute to Dulcinea, invoking her name at every turn. Everything about her is superlative, which he wants everyone to know and in some cases openly acknowledge (e.g., the merchants from his first sally). Within many Portuguese-authored works written in Spanish during the Iberian Union something similar occurs, only the inspiration comes from an imagined community rather than an imagined lady.[11] In some instances the references to Portugal are obvious, while at other times more subtle; but Portugal is always there, described in virtually the same superlative way every time.

Perhaps the best illustration of the Dulcinea-Portugal analogy is António de Sousa de Macedo's *Flores de España, Excelencias de Portugal* (1631). Nowhere is early modern Lusophilia more prominently displayed than here. In the prefatory letter to Philip IV he describes the work as "lo mejor de Portugal en lengua castellana," words that we might use to describe the entire subset of Portuguese texts that motivate this essay. The point here is not to

---

11   I agree with Onésimo Almeida that "cognitive community" may be a more accurate way to describe the Portuguese since Portugal, in this case, extends beyond mere mental projection (13). The Dulcinea comparison, then, is analogous only so far as the comparison is understood in terms of motivation and absence. Benedict Anderson's *Imagined Communities* provides a complete picture of the concept I have employed.

hold up the individual over the collective (i.e., my writing is the best Portugal has to offer), but to use Spanish to celebrate the *patria* in all its glory (both real and imagined). The titles of the twenty-four chapters are enough to make this point. They include, "De la hermosura de los campos, rios [*sic*], y fuentes de Portugal" (ch. 2), "De la verdad de los Portugueses" (ch. 12), and "De lo mucho que Portugal ha sido siempre estimado de Dios, y de los hombres" (ch. 23), among others. Over the course of five hundred pages, Sousa de Macedo catalogues Portugal's supremacy with the detail and hyperbole of a Petrarchan sonnet. He eventually concludes the work not because he has run out of things to say, but because he trusts that the reader gets the point: "Estas son *parte* de las Excelencias de Portugal, porque muchas son tan claras, que por no gastar tiempo en lo que no es necessario [*sic*], no las escrivo [*sic*], algunas por muy superiores no he podido alcançar" (fol. 249, ch. 24; my emphasis). Like the omnipresent absence of Dulcinea in *Don Quixote*, Portugal is always there; not just in works with an unmistakable rhetoric of nationhood such as *Flores de España*, but also in more understated ways such as the three *comedias* penned by the Portuguese dramatist Ângela de Azevedo, each one situated in Portugal and with significant traces of her homeland.

As important as Dulcinea was to Don Quixote's emerging identity, the primary reason for his belief that a knight even needed a love interest was his general commitment to knight errantry and specific devotion to Amadís de Gaula, the pinnacle of knight errantry. As he explains to Sancho, "el famoso Amadís de Gaula fue uno de los más perfectos caballeros andantes. No he dicho bien, *fue uno*: fue el solo, el primero, el único, el señor de todos cuantos hubo en su tiempo en el mundo" (234; part 1, ch. 25). Don Quixote models all of his behavior on what he knows of Amadís de Gaula. It would not be too much to say, in fact, that his chivalric gospel could be summed up in the question, "what would Amadís do?" Portuguese authors of the Iberian Union were not without their own Amadís. Indeed, it is impossible to overestimate the importance of Luís de Camões to the Portuguese imaginary then and since (Mattoso 35). Less appreciated, however, is the role that Portuguese annexation authors played in elevating Camões to the status of national deity.

Camões punctuated the latter part of the sixteenth century with perhaps the single most important Portuguese work ever written: *Os Lusíadas* (1572). The fact that thirty-six editions of his epic were published over the course of the Dual Monarchy speaks volumes of its importance on the Iberian Peninsula as one of the foundational narratives of *Portugalidade*. As Portuguese authors paid tribute to their homeland in the decades of the Dual Monarchy, Camões's name inevitably turns up. He is scattered throughout Sousa de

Macedo's *Flores de España*, for example, as well as Francisco Manuel de Melo's *Hospital das letras*. Notwithstanding the many works that could be cited for the ways they invoke the name of Camões, no work exalted Camões and solidified his place in the Portuguese imaginary more than Faria e Sousa's critical commentary *Lusíadas de Luis de Camoens, principe de los poetas de España* (1639). Faria e Sousa completed his multi-volume edition over the course of twenty-five years of intense study, writing, and revision. In his "Elogio al comentador," Lope de Vega agrees with Faria e Sousa's assessment that Camões is unsurpassed in poetry, adding that Faria e Sousa is no less accomplished as a commentator (*Lusíadas*).[12] His edition not only includes a reproduction of the poem in Portuguese, but also a Spanish prose translation, thereby reaching a larger audience with both his annotations and Camões's original work.

From the outset of his masterwork, Faria e Sousa makes his allegiance to Portugal and Camões very clear. His patriotic agenda begins with the title: *Lusíadas de Luis de Camoens, principe de los poetas de España*. Whereas the first part of the title quietly passes, what follows thereafter calls for attention. There is an important precedent for using the designation "Prince" in reference to a poet. It appears on the Peninsula as early as 1555 in *Los doze libros de la Eneid de Vergilio, principe de los poetas latinos*. Thereafter, the Renaissance writer Garcilaso de la Vega received the same distinction among Castilian poets. In 1622, for example, Tomás Tamayo de Vargas titled his critical edition *Garcilasso de la Vega, natural de Toledo: Príncipe de los Poetas Castellanos*, only to be echoed four years later in Luis Brizeño's *Obras de Garcilasso de la Vega, Príncipe de los Poetas Castellanos*. While Virgil was given preeminence among authors who composed in Latin, Garcilaso assumed the same role in Spanish. Rather than name Camões heir to the same title among Portuguese poets, however, Faria e Sousa surpasses Tamayo de Vargas and Brizeño's scope, increasing Camões's poetic reign to the entire Iberian Peninsula in the title of his commentary. In "Vida del Poeta" (section 24), one of the introductory sections of the work, Faria e Sousa confidently affirms his position on the matter, extending the sphere of Camonian superiority even further: "A los que estuvieron congoxados con el titulo que en la fachada deste volumen dimos al Poeta, de Principe de los de España; no fuera mucho si dixeramos de todos los de Europa (que viene a ser de todo el mundo [. . .]) ya que el Poeta se aventajó a todos" (*Lusíadas* 49-50). Faria e Sousa treats Camões with the same esteem that we see throughout *Don Quixote* and the many passages in which the protagonist makes reference to his knight in shining

---

12 "Como Luis de Camoes es Principe de los Poetas que escrivieron en idioma vulgar, lo es Manuel de Faria de los Comentadores en todas lenguas."

armor, Amadís de Gaula. While Faria e Sousa's commentary is unsurpassed in the depth and breadth of its exaltation of Camões, references to the poet and his epic abound in Portuguese literature of the Iberian Union. Camões was, for them, a guiding light during a time of uncertainty, a reminder of the potential reach and influence of the written word.[13]

When it came time for the young Portuguese dramatist Jacinto Cordeiro (1606-46) to write the prologue to what would be the first of many *comedias*, he not only wrote it in Portuguese, but therein made a clear statement of intent: "tenho de eternizar grandezas de minha patria" (*La entrada*). In Glaser's estimation, this is "a literary program worthy of more attention" (Glaser, "More" 144). One of the stated purposes of many of the Portuguese-authored works written in Spanish during the Dual Monarchy was to celebrate Portugal by spreading her glories across the globe in a language that could effectively reach all four corners. During the course of the play, Cordeiro lays bare the virtues of his native soil, including Portugal's divine election, love, obedience, loyalty, grandeur, and general superiority. These same characteristics recur over and over again in Portuguese literature of the Iberian Union. Cordeiro's stated objective, therefore, is indicative of a wider trend within Spanish language writings by the Portuguese from 1580 to 1640. For many of them, this was their quest. With Portugal as their inspiration and Camões as their lead, they dressed in the language of the empire and set out to prove to the world that Lusitânia was not lost, even if its Golden Age was. As a familiar literary reference, Don Quixote can connect readers to the widely unfamiliar world of the Portuguese authors of the Dual Monarchy by highlighting the constructedness and textuality of their reality. Many of them adapted to the unique conditions of the early seventeenth century by clothing themselves in the language of the empire, finding purpose in the Portugal that was and the Portugal that could be, and looking to Camões as a model of how this could be done. Neither Don Quixote nor the Portuguese were entirely consistent in carrying out the identity they had fashioned for themselves, but that is part of what makes their (hi)stories so intriguing.

Although marginalized and maligned by many critics and historians over the centuries, this essay highlights a subgroup within early modern Portuguese literature that advances a rhetoric of nationhood with identifiable characteristics and that also aligns with Don Quixote's early development as a character. For Eduardo Lourenço, who sees both Don Quixote and San-

---

13   Parts of this paragraph also appear in chapter 3 of the author's forthcoming study, *Being Portuguese in Spanish: Re-imagining Early Modern Iberian Literature (1580-1640)* (Purdue UP, 2020).

cho as innate expressions of Portuguese identity, this alignment may be more than mere coincidence: "Poucos povos serão como o nosso tão intimamente quixotescos" (23). Within the conversation of Cervantes and Portugal, perhaps there is a place not only for what Faria e Sousa, Cordeiro, Sousa de Macedo, and their Portuguese contemporaries said about Cervantes and his works, but also for the ways that they tilt at the impossible together with the Man of La Mancha.

Works Cited

Abreu, Maria Fernanda de. "1943. Don Quijote sebastianizado. En un lugar de Europa, que el autor quiso poner Tristiânia." *Anales Cervantinos*, vol. 45, 2013, pp. 341-54.

———. *Cervantes no romantismo português*, Estampa, 1994.

———. Introduction. *Dom Quixote de la Mancha*, by Miguel de Cervantes, Dom Quixote, 2005, pp. 15-59.

Almeida, Onésimo Teotónio. *National Identity — A Revisitation of the Portuguese Debate*. NUI Maynooth Papers in Spanish, Portuguese, and Latin American Studies, no. 5, National University of Ireland, 2002.

Anastácio, Vanda. "'Heróicas virtudes e escritos que as publiquem'. D. Quixote nos papéis da Restauração." *Iberoamericana*, vol. 7, no. 28, 2007, pp. 117-36.

Anderson, Benedict. *Imagined Communities*, Verso, 1991.

Ares Montes, José. "Cervantes en la literatura portuguesa del siglo xvii." *Anales Cervantinos*, vol. 2, 1952, pp. 193-230.

———. "Don Quijote em um romance português." *Anales Cervantinos*, vol. 11, 1972, pp. 155-58.

———. "Don Quijote en el teatro portugués del siglo xviii." *Anales Cervantinos*, vol. 3, 1953, pp. 349-52.

———. "Don Quijote en tres poetas portugueses." *Anales Cervantinos*, vol. 25-26, 1987, pp. 67-73.

Asensio, Eugenio. "La autobiografía de Manuel de Faria y Sousa." *Arquivos do Centro Cultural Português*, vol. 13, 1978, pp. 629-37.

———. "España en la épica filipina." *Revista de Filología Española*, vol. 33, 1949, pp. 66-109.

———. "La fortuna de *Os Lusíadas* en España." *Estudios portugueses*, Fundação Calouste Gulbenkian, Centro Cultural Português, 1974, pp. 303-24.

Azevedo, Ângela de. *Dicha y desdicha del juego y devoción de la Virgen*. In *Women's Acts: Plays by Women Dramatists of Spain's Golden Age*, edited by Teresa Soufas, UP of Kentucky, 1997, pp. 4-44.

———. *La margarita del Tajo que dio nombre a Santarén*. In *Women's Acts: Plays by Women Dramatists of Spain's Golden Age*, edited by Teresa Soufas, UP of Kentucky, 1997, pp. 45-90.

———. *El muerto disimulado*. In *Women's Acts: Plays by Women Dramatists of Spain's Golden Age*, edited by Teresa Soufas, UP of Kentucky, 1997, pp. 91-132.

Cervantes, Miguel de. *Don Quijote de la Mancha*. Edited by Francisco Rico, Real Academia española, 2015.

Cidade, Hernani. *A literatura autonomista sob os Filipes*. Livraria Sá da Costa, 1950-1959.

Cobelo, Silvia. "A tradução tardia do *Quixote* em Portugal." *TradTerm*, vol. 16, 2010, pp. 193-216.

Cordeiro, Jacinto. *De la entrada del Rey en Portugal*. Lisboa, 1621.

Dasilva, Xosé Manuel. "Camões y la cultura española." *Límite: Revista de Estudios Portugueses e de la Lusofonía*, no. 9, 2015, pp. 9-14.

———. Review of *Cervantes no romantismo português*, by Maria Fernanda de Abreu. *Anales Cervantinos*, vol. 33, 1997, pp. 379-82.

Dotras Bravo, Alexia. "La recepción de Miguel de Cervantes en el Portugal contemporáneo." *Edad de Oro*, vol. 35, 2016, pp. 135-47.

Faria e Sousa, Manuel de, editor. *Lusiadas de Luis de Camões comentadas por Manuel de Faria e Sousa*. 1639. Imprensa Nacional-Casa da Moeda, 1972.

Ferreira de Lacerda, Bernarda. *Hespaña libertada*. Lisboa, 1618.

Forster, Leonard W. *The Poet's Tongues: Multilingualism in Literature*. Cambridge UP, 1970.

Glaser, Edward. "The Literary Fame of Cervantes in Seventeenth-century Portugal." *Hispanic Review*, vol. 23, no. 3, 1955, pp. 200-11.

———. "More about the Literary Fame of Cervantes in Seventeenth-century Portugal." *Anales Cervantinos*, vol. 5, 1955, pp. 143-57.

Lourenço, Eduardo. *Nós e a Europa ou as duas razões*. Imprensa Nacional-Casa da Moeda, 1994.

Marín, Nicolás. "Camoens, Faria y Cervantes." *Homenaje a Camoens: estudios y ensayos hispano-portugueses*, Universidad de Granada, 1980, pp. 239-46.

Martínez-Almoyna, Julio, and Antero Viera de Lemos. *La lengua española en la literatura portuguesa*, Imnasa, 1968.

Méndez, Sigmund. "La alegoría humanista y el reto hermenéutico del *Quixote*." *eHumanista*, vol. 23, 2013, pp. 622-86.

Montero Reguera, José. "*Don Quijote* en 1640: algo más que un libro de burlas (historia, política y algo de literatura)." *Cervantismos de ayer y de hoy. Capítulos de historia cultural hispánica*, by José Montero Reguera, Universidad de Alicante, 2011, pp. 17-24.

Russell, P. E. "'Don Quixote' as a Funny Book." *The Modern Language Review*, vol. 64, no. 2, 1969, pp. 312-26.

Sousa de Macedo, António de. *Flores de España, Excelencias de Portugal*. Lisboa, 1631.

Teijeiro Fuentes, Miguel Ángel. "Portugal en la vida y obra de Cervantes." *Revista de estudios extremeños*, vol. 62, no. 2, 2006, pp. 683-700.

Vázquez Cuesta, Pilar. "O bilinguismo castelhano-português na época de Camões." *Arquivos do Centro Cultural Português*, vol. 16, 1981, pp. 807-27.

———. "La lengua y la cultura portuguesas." *Historia de la cultura española: El siglo del* Quijote, vol. 2, Espasa, 1996, pp. 577-680.

The Importance of Humor in Recent Translations of *Don Quijote*

STEVEN B. WENZ
The University of Maine at Farmington

ONE COULD LIST MYRIAD reasons why *Don Quijote* holds a central place in the Western canon, yet perhaps the work's most noteworthy feature has been the breadth of critical interpretations that it has elicited over the centuries. As Carroll B. Johnson once observed, "[e]very generation of intellectuals has seen its own preoccupations and its own most cherished discoveries anticipated in Cervantes' text" (18). Enlightenment thinkers praised Cervantes for denouncing folly and providing a model of decorum, while the Romantics viewed the novel's protagonist as a misunderstood genius waging a tragic struggle against societal constraints. Realist authors of the nineteenth century admired Cervantes's depiction of the physical world, whereas twentieth-century critics would find in *Don Quijote* a celebration of relativism and of the linguistically contingent construction of "reality" (18). To these readings, of course, one must add the important recent studies on metafiction, gender and sexuality, and racial and ethnic identity that have enriched our understanding of the work; and the next generations of *Quijote* scholars will surely call our attention toward a new and unforeseen array of valuable critical approaches.

Even so, ever since the publication of Part I in 1605, humor has played an equally crucial role in *Don Quijote*'s identity among readers. We are all familiar with the anecdote according to which Philip III, upon seeing a boy laughing with a book in his hands, remarked that "Aquel estudiante o está fuera de sí o lee la historia de don Quijote." This mindset survives in today's universities, as professors of Spanish literature, when assigning the *Quijote* to undergraduate students, mention the work's humoristic moments in order to overcome resistance to tackling a four-hundred-year-old text. If one were to consult the general population, regardless of whether respondents had read Cervantes's work, a majority would likely associate *Don Quijote* with the windmill scene of part 1, chapter 8, interpreting that image in humorous fashion. From the perspective of literary scholarship, humor has served as an implicit focal point for many of the dominant interpretations over the centuries. Renaissance thinkers emphasized the therapeutic effects of laughter, Enlightenment critics stressed its power in correcting aberrant behavior, Realist authors understood humor as reflecting the historical context, and contemporary scholars have pointed out the carnivalesque subversion of hierarchies and the role of language-games in deconstructing philosophical and social preconceptions.

Yet *Don Quijote* has always been a global text, and humor is a culturally-specific phenomenon, whose efficacy depends on a set of shared experiences and presuppositions: when the differences between text and audience have stretched too far, humor will fail. Such potential barriers were less likely to arise in the years immediately following the work's publication, when copies of *Don Quijote* began to spread across the Spanish Empire and translations made their way into other European languages. As time passed, however, and the gap grew ever wider between the context of production and the manifold contexts of reception, humor posed an increasing challenge for translators. After all, if Spanish readers in the twenty-first century, for whom the *Quijote* remains the national text, notice that their opinion of what is humorous differs from that of Cervantes, what is one to say for modern-day readers of a *Quijote* in other languages? If humor has held and continues to hold a significant position in the critical and popular identities of *Don Quijote* throughout the Spanish-language tradition, we should seek to understand to what extent humor plays a similar role in other linguistic and cultural contexts.

This essay attempts to contribute to that project by studying the role of humor in recent translations of *Don Quijote*. I examine the frequency and the importance with which humor has appeared as a topic of interest for literary critics and popular reviewers when evaluating the success or failure of the new versions. In order to establish some of the possible points of interest, I begin by discussing the significance of humor within the critical tradition and by summarizing the various forms of humor that *Quijote* scholars have considered essential features of the work. Next, drawing upon Translation Studies, I consider the challenges that translators face when attempting to convey the humoristic aspects of literary texts in general and of *Don Quijote* in particular. In the final section of the essay, I offer a survey of scholarly and popular reviews of selected recent translations of *Don Quijote* into English, Portuguese, French, and Italian, with the goal of providing a glimpse into the current place of humor in the *Quijote*'s critical identity across diverse communities of readers.

Humor in *Don Quijote*

In Book XI of the *Confessions*, when exploring the nature of time, St. Augustine distinguishes between intuitive understanding and philosophical reasoning: "If no one asks me, I know; if I want to explain it to a questioner, I do not know" (242). Humor functions in much the same way. Individual and cultural sensitivities vary, but we all have an intuitive grasp of what is "funny" and believe to recognize "humorous" material as distinct from its "serious" counterparts. Upon closer inspection, however, humor proves more difficult to define. Psychologists and philosophers have approached the question from a variety of angles, but most perspectives fall into two broad categories. One group of explanations focuses on the stimulus of humor and seeks to identify the features in a given situation or text that provoke a certain mental state; another group of explanations focuses on the response and argues that, if this mental state arises, the stimulus should be considered "humorous," regardless of its particular features. Both of these approaches grapple with the question of what makes the cluster of perceptions, emotions, and physical reactions that we call "humor" different from other experiences (Vandaele, "Introduction" 153-54). Even if we manage to trace such a distinction, humor remains a problematic concept. As Jeroen Vandaele points out, there are many sub-categories of humor, each with its particular origins and effects: "[s]atire, for instance, can be defined as humour with a further critical effect and caused, for example, by an exaggerated imitation of social norms. Similarly, parody can be seen as humour with an equally sharp edge but is provoked, for instance, by an exaggerated imitation of *aesthetic* norms" (155, italics in original). From all of these considerations, we can conclude that it is necessary to make at least three clarifications when discussing humor: 1) whether we are considering the cause of humor, its response, or both; 2) what types of reactions in the listener or reader we identify as responses to humor; and 3) what sub-categories of humor we are including within this term.

Readers and scholars of *Don Quijote* have long understood humor as both stimulus and response. P. E. Russell's well-known description of the work as a "funny book" depends on each side of the equation, in that, for Russell, authorial intention successfully produced a humorous effect among contemporary readers. Russell argues that Cervantes wrote *Don Quijote* "with the object of occasioning that boisterous laughter from the spectators which Cervantes so frequently describes. ... [R]eading the tale, he tells us, the melancholic is to be made to laugh and he whose disposition is naturally merry is to be made to laugh louder" ("Funny" 312). According to this logic, *Don Quijote* is a humorous text because it induces laughter among its readers, and the reactions of characters to situations within the story provide a model for such behavior. Russell extends this description to more subtle responses, mentioning the author's "conspiratorial wink" toward readers whenever the knight and squire find themselves in ironic situations (*Cervantes* 84). A similar focus on stimulus and response appears in the work of Anthony Close, who, like Russell, has studied authorial intention and the reception of the text among its earliest readers. Close argues that seventeenth- and eighteenth-century audiences considered *Don Quijote* "hilarious" (*Romantic* 15) and that, as evinced by the Prologue to Part I, Cervantes's "primary aim is incitement to laughter" (*Comic* 8). Adrienne Martín has continued this interpretation, arguing that "[h]umor is so fundamental to Cervantes' conception of prose fiction that he opens his novel with a brief yet unmistakably explicit comic *ars poetica*" (160). Critics have observed that this humor manifests itself in various ways. Alan Trueblood, for whom laughter is a significant feature of the work, follows Russell in pointing out that "en la risa que Cervantes se proponía suscitar en el lector, apuntaba él a algo más que la bronquedad de la carcajada" (6). This type of reflexive or intellectual humor corresponds to what Michael Scham, in a sophisticated reading of "epistemological humor" in the *Quijote*, has called "the generous light of Cervantine laughter" (41), which invites readers to recognize their own errors in the folly of the protagonists.

If humor in *Don Quijote* provokes a variety of reactions, it is because "humor" characterizes an immense variety of situations throughout the work. P. E. Russell, when analyzing the first translations of the novel, centers on the role of *burlas* and slapstick. As his discussion of the epithet "El Caballero de la Triste Figura" makes clear, early readers and translators understood this description as inspiring not pathos and admiration but rather ridicule and schadenfreude: the protagonist's disfigured countenance is a subject worthy of mockery ("Funny" 316). Russell would go on to highlight the linguistic components of Cervantine humor, mentioning the author's use of unexpected words or phrases to achieve ironic or ridiculous effects (*Cervantes* 88), his exaggerated or absurd manipulation of clichés (90), and his penchant for "extremely forced metaphorical comparisons" (92). Anthony Close views *Don Quijote* as a burlesque novel in that it ridicules another literary style (chivalric romance) through a "ludicrous combination of baseness and nobility," employs "a grand style for an incongruous subject," attributes "base language or sentiments to supposedly noble characters," and adopts "an aggressively banal style for a grand subject" (*Romantic* 19). The critic has also called attention to Cervantes's playful treatment of the "verdad de la historia" and his ironic and mocking portrayal of Cide Hamete (*Comic* 151-52). Alan Trueblood's analysis of laughter follows that of Close in regard to the burlesque but also cites several examples of physical and situational humor, "la chanza grosera, burda y hasta—para el concepto moderno—cruel" (6).

More recent scholarship has provided an even more nuanced typology of humor in *Don Quijote*. According to Michael Scham, the novel's humor "ranges from farcical to linguistic" and depends on "epistemological games" (46). Laura Gorfkle offers a superb reading of that linguistic humor and argues that "the scope of word play is so extensive that it can easily be considered one of the primary features in the style of the work" (102). Her analysis includes such examples as alliteration, assonance, rhyme, litotes, pleonasm, repetition, plays on word roots, neologisms, corruption in pronunciation or syntax, and misuse of rhetoric. Gorfkle also represents an important recent tendency in *Quijote* scholarship to emphasize, drawing upon the work of Bakhtin, the carnivalesque inversion of roles within the text. Adrienne Martín adopts a similar perspective and underlines the characters' "ludic transvestism" (168) and subversion of social hierarchies. Martín's useful overview of the critical tradition underscores the breadth of humoristic elements that scholars have identified: irony, burlesque, parody, satire, "fool literature," jokes, wordplay, violence, slapstick, "Sancho's prolixity and prevarications," and the author's "subtle allusions and personal invective" (162). *Don Quijote*, then, encompasses nearly every type of humor imaginable, spanning from the physical to the intellectual and from the specific to the general.

While there is no guarantee that readers of *Don Quijote* in Spanish today will recognize and appreciate every instance of Cervantine humor, the potential for multiple interpretations grows exponentially through translation. Translators read the original work, form a certain idea of how the text functions, and attempt to convey that meaning to readers in another language. A translator's attitude toward humor, therefore, will determine whether readers identify the work as attempting to be humorous and, depending on the translator's skill, whether the author has succeeded. Translation is itself a critical intervention, as translators advocate for a particular reading of the novel through their transformation of the text. To cite the most well-known instance, the Romantic perspective has skewed modern translations of *Don Quijote* away from the comic tradition, in that word choice and the treatment of tone have encouraged sympathy toward the protagonist rather than an ironic detachment (Russell, *Cervantes* 100). Any recent translation that downplays the humorous components of the *Quijote*, whether by design or as a result of translator error, will continue that trend and will reinforce the Romantic approach among new communities of readers. Conversely, translations that emphasize humor will facilitate association with the comic, opening up an array of readings based on whichever humorous features receive the greatest attention and the most effective rendering in the new version.

Translation and Humor

A central idea in Translation Studies is that of translation as interpretation. Lawrence Venuti has argued that "[m]eaning is a plural and contingent relation, not an unchanging unified essence, and therefore a translation cannot be judged according to mathematics-based concepts of semantic equivalence or one-to-one correspondence" (13). Interpretation governs our connection with all discourse, including that within our "own" language and culture, and translation extends this process across semiotic systems. It is for this reason that, in Roman Jakobson's classic tripartite distinction among intralingual translation (rewording), interlingual translation (translation proper), and intersemiotic translation (transmutation), each category involves the interpretation of signs by means of other signs (233). In the case of "translation proper," translators interpret the verbal signs of one language through the verbal signs of another language. The same emphasis on interpretation underlies George Steiner's "hermeneutic motion," in which the translator "invades, extracts, and brings home" (298). For Steiner, translation "aims to import and to naturalize the content of the source-text and to simulate, so far as it is able, the original executive form of that content" (333). Implicit in this definition is the translator's particular understanding of the original text, awareness of the formal differences between languages and of the cultural differences between groups of readers, and expectations of which new responses will emerge as a result of certain linguistic constructions. It is not that translation seeks to "say the same thing in a different language." This, at any rate, would be impossible, given that linguistic form itself already provides a unique space for the creation of meaning. Rather, translation depends on the translator's personal and contingent interpretation of a source text and on the attempt to produce that interpretation in new readers through the forms of another language: translation is always a creative act.

Perhaps more than any other cultural phenomenon, humor reveals the interpretative nature of translation. Even within a single language, when the meanings of the words themselves are unlikely to pose a barrier to comprehension, successful humor depends on a variety of shared experiences and expectations that lead the audience toward a particular reaction: laughter. In Argentina, for example, where popular humor depicts Galician immigrants as foolish, speakers of Spanish from other regions might fail to see why the antics of a Galician should be a cause for mirth. A similar phenomenon occurs across generations, as undergraduate students often make humorous references to popular culture that mystify their professors. In this sense, Jakobson's concept of intralingual translation or rewording becomes necessary when humor fails: an effective joke should be immediately intelligible, because "if you have to explain it, it isn't funny." These potential obstacles to humor only multiply when crossing linguistic boundaries. In addition to the probable lack of a shared cultural context, one now faces the task of achieving a similar connection among ideas through a new system of signs. Content-based humor with a wide sphere of reference, such as jokes regarding well-known traits of famous politicians, athletes, or entertainers, may hold a greater likelihood of succeeding. In contrast, a particular challenge arises for wordplay and other types of self-reflexive humor, in which speakers achieve a humorous effect by manipulating the relations among sounds, forms, and meanings. As this correspondence rarely obtains across different languages, humor "is often seen as a paradigm case of 'untranslatability'" (Vandaele, "Humor" 149), in that readers and translators alike must resign themselves to either a weak approximation or a complete omission of this textual feature.

Yet ample evidence suggests that humor is indeed translatable, if one takes that adjective to mean that a work elicits laughter across linguistic boundaries. Whether we consider English renditions of *Astérix* and of Japanese *anime* or foreign-audience reactions to dubbed Hollywood comedies, it is clear that, general pessimism notwithstanding, it is possible to achieve a similar reaction in different languages and cultural contexts. At the heart of the matter lies the problematic definition of correspondence. A strict approach to the issue requires parallelism between the source language and the target language, in that only the existence of the appropriate forms in each language would guarantee the existence of humor. Salvatore Attardo's discussion of translating puns, for example, relies on the mapping of form and function: "[t]hose puns that exhibit in the SL [source language] a set of features which is consistent with a set of features in the TL [target language], such that the pragmatic goals of the translation are fulfilled, will be translatable. A pun that does not will be untranslatable" (190). From this perspective, if the "pragmatic goal" is to elicit laughter, each language must allow for a humorous play on words, presumably in the same way. English homophony, for example, between *see* and *sea* would prove impossible to replicate in Spanish, in which the words *ver* and *mar* bear no resemblance to one another. Any humor that depended on this relationship would, in fact, seem to be untranslatable.

Nonetheless, a broader approach to correspondence leads to a more optimistic conclusion. David Bellos, whose commentary focuses on the supposed impossibility of translating jokes, has questioned the criterion of "matching" in successful translation. He argues that "[h]umorous remarks, shaggy-dog tales, witty anecdotes, and silly jokes are untranslatable only if you insist on understanding 'translation' as a low-level matching of the signifiers themselves. Translation is obviously not that" (280). If one understands humor as a perlocutionary effect, as the production of laughter in response to linguistic form, it no longer becomes necessary to preserve every detail of the original text. When the end justifies the means, translators acquire greater freedom to modify the source in order to draw out the same reaction. Translators may decide to compensate a loss in one area through addition in another: as long as a character remains noteworthy for his or her verbal dexterity, for instance, it appears not to matter how readers of the translation arrive at this impression. Returning to the previous lack of correspondence between *see/sea* and *ver/mar*, one could easily imagine a context in which minor modifications would achieve a humorous effect. If humor in the original work depended on a character growing weary of sightseeing during a trip, the dialogue might include the utterance "I don't want to *see* anything else. I'm *seesick*." This turn of phrase could then appear in Spanish as "No quiero *ver* nada más. Tengo *vértigo*." To be sure, the lexical components of this relationship have changed, but the translation fulfills the "pragmatic goal" of conveying humor and of indicating that this humor is a result of a play on words.

The difficulty when translating literature, however, is that a translated text faces pressure on multiple fronts. On one hand, as Lawrence Venuti has explained at length, publishing houses often encourage translators to produce a "natural" or "transparent" text, as though the new version were the "original" (1). This approach to translation would seek to erase stylistic and linguistic peculiarities that would mark the text as "foreign," and translators would reshape the work in accordance with the linguistic and cultural codes of the target-language audience (1). Commercial considerations and the need for popular acclaim, therefore, would take precedence over the sensitive portrayal of difference. On the other hand, even when translators adopt what Venuti has called "foreignizing translation" and attempt to convey the myriad nuances of the source text, the interpretative nature of all translation will require countless personal interventions, each of which opens up its own space for further interpretation by readers. To use the present example, there are as many *Quijotes* as there are translations, and all of them allow for a particular set of responses. This consequence seems of little importance as long as we restrict critical judgment of a text to readings in the original. Yet contemporary society is ever-more global and interconnected, while the digital distribution of texts and the ubiquity of social media have democratized access to culture. Readings in translation contribute to the overall critical identity of a work, and it is essential that we understand the relationship between interpretations of the original and interpretations of its counterparts in other languages, particularly with texts such as *Don Quijote*, whose enduring popularity and historical significance have led to myriad translations across the world.

While some humorous aspects of *Don Quijote* would indeed seem to pose a challenge for translators, the previous theoretical considerations suggest a more nuanced conclusion. There appear to exist two broad categories of humor in the *Quijote*: 1) situational humor, which depends minimally on linguistic form; and 2) verbal humor, which depends significantly on linguistic form. If we leave behind problematic concepts such as "authorial intention" or "true meaning," the relationship between original text and its translations will depend on verbal signs and the spaces for interpretation that they open up for readers of each version of the novel. *Quijote* scholarship has established a more-or-less accepted array of plausible readings of the work, and critics, bringing their own opinions to bear, will denounce "translation failure" whenever the translated version either makes unaccepted readings possible or makes accepted readings impossible. Therefore, with the two categories of humor above, critical judgment of translations will rely on whether translators, as evidenced by the new text, have "noticed" the humor that critics detect in the original.

With this in mind, it would appear that situational humor would be easy to translate, particularly when translators are familiar with the scholarly tradition. A given scene or character trait may fail to provoke laughter today, but translators who understand its historical value will attempt to give readers the opportunity to attain a similar insight. Referring to the categories mentioned earlier, slapstick and *burlas* would require the least dexterity from translators, as they often need only to make clear to readers that certain actions have taken place. One could list countless examples from throughout the work, such as Don Quijote's lost teeth in part 1, chapter 18; Sancho's flatulence in part 1, chapter 20; or the episode of the cats in part 2, chapter 46. Humor based on Don Quijote's madness or Sancho's foolishness will be equally simple to translate, in that it results from an evident lack of correspondence between ideas and reality. Examples here would include the adventure of the windmills (part 1, ch. 8), the Cave of Montesinos (part 2, ch. 22), Maese Pedro's puppet show (part 2, ch. 26), and Sancho's dream of ruling an island. The humor in such episodes occasionally depends on linguistic features, as in the battle with the Biscayan (part 1, ch. 8), the encounter with the enchanted Dulcinea (part 2, ch. 10), or Sancho's misunderstanding of the archaic term "ínsula," but, even if translators fail to transmit the particular speech of these characters, readers will grasp the humorous tone of the overall event. A similar logic applies to Sancho's prolixity. Although, as will be seen, his specific word choices pose a challenge for translators, it is easy to convey the idea that Sancho speaks excessively or at inappropriate times, especially in those cases when the judicious side of Don Quijote serves as a foil.

Humor resulting from parody, satire, irony, metafiction, and the subversion of hierarchies should also transcend language barriers, as it depends more strongly on extratextual knowledge than on any particular linguistic form. In these cases, in which readers' familiarity with literary and cultural history will often prove decisive, translators may wish to provide a safety net through explanatory comments. For example, in order to notice Cervantes's humorous references to knights errant, giants, and enchanters, readers must understand the conventions of chivalric romance, the rudiments of which could be summarized in a translator introduction or with a footnote on their first appearance in the novel. The role of Cide Hamete, in similar fashion, would become clear through an explanation of the ironic term "Arab historian," while the epistemological humor, multiple authors, and missing manuscripts would likewise benefit from a brief scholarly clarification. After this point, readers will be aware that this humor arises from the features of the original text rather than from any errors or obscurities in the translation. To be sure, one could argue that readers of any literary work, whether in the original or in another language, will base their interpretation on knowledge of such conventions and should be responsible for reaching informed critical judgments. Yet in order to prevent critics from attributing "incomplete" readings to translator error, translators would do well to explain the nonlinguistic features that make *Don Quijote* a humorous text.

Whereas situational humor causes few problems for translators, verbal humor requires both a keen understanding of the source text and considerable creativity in the target language. Malapropisms, except when the specific error introduces a noteworthy connotation, present the least difficulty within this category. The protagonists' interactions with the peasant women in part 2, chapter 10, for instance, need only to convey the idea that these are not the fair ladies whom Don Quijote imagines. Translators' decisions will vary according to the audience, but, as long as the peasant women speak in what readers will interpret as a "lower-class" manner, the translation will have succeeded. A special case in this regard appears in the humorous neologism *baciyelmo* (part 1, ch. 44), with which Sancho reconciles conflicting viewpoints and reinforces the concept of multiperspectivism. Translators into English, for example, have opted for various renditions: "basin-helmet" (Raffel), "basinelmet" (Rutherford and Lathrop), and "basihelm" (Grossman). As before, however, the crucial task will be to express the confluence of opposing worldviews. If translators wish to provide additional clarity, a footnote will suffice; after all, this is the solution that Francisco Rico adopts in his Spanish-language edition of the *Quijote*. Other linguistic features that should prove easy to translate include litotes, repetition, pleonasm, and misuse of rhetoric. It is true that the target language, especially outside the Indo-European family, may lack the corresponding structures or cultural parameters. Even here, however, translators may draw upon other features of the language to create a similar effect: should the rules for negation make litotes impossible, translators can attempt to convey understatement or irony in culturally meaningful ways, perhaps through recognized syntactical or lexical features.

Verbal humor poses the greatest challenge for translators whenever it depends on a close connection between meaning and form. At times, the logic of the text calls attention to this type of humor and eliminates the problem of "noticing," leaving only the task of finding a suitable version in the target language. For example, during the episode of the enchanted ship (part 2, ch. 29), Don Quijote orders Sancho to inspect himself for lice as a way of confirming whether they have crossed the equator. When Don Quijote asks him "has topado algo?", Sancho responds with the celebrated phrase "Y aun algos." Situational humor is evident from the context, insofar as Sancho both calls attention to his master's madness and demonstrates his own lack of hygiene, and all that remains is to convey the verbal humor of Sancho's creative plural form. Regardless of whether translators stay within the conventions of the language ("lots of things") or decide to innovate ("somethings"), a certain degree of verbal humor will come across.

In contrast, there are myriad instances throughout the novel in which linguistic humor proves more nuanced and subject to interpretation, as a result of which it would be more appropriate to speak of a gradual cumulative effect than of a single brilliant moment. Laura Gorfkle's valuable analysis of word play in the *Quijote* contains many examples from this category (105–09). Some depend entirely on sound, such as the priest's use of *a caballo* and *acaba* (part 1, ch. 29), and would be impossible to reproduce in most languages if translators adhere to a strict definition of correspondence. Even were translators to find a functional equivalent, the humor is so subtle as to leave readers wondering whether the feature was present in the original. Alliteration and assonance follow a similar logic, as they are easy to notice in the original but difficult to express in translation without altering the lexical referents. Puns, as we have seen, will depend especially on the translator's attitude toward what Bellos has called "matching." Strict correspondence will require a considerable amount of luck. For every positive outcome, such as the possibility of translating "desvalijando a la valija" (part 1, ch. 23) as "ransacking the sack" or Sancho's *faux pas* "vuestra altivez" as "your haughtiness" (part 2, ch. 10), there are countless occasions on which no equivalent seems possible. The pun between "sin costas" and "sin costillas," for example (part 1, ch. 15), would force translators either to seek other types of connections between damages and body parts or to elide the problem altogether. If the translation privileges the lexical referent, the phrase "without costs" and "without ribs" will pass unnoticed in the best case and strike readers as unnatural in the worst. On the other hand, a significant lexical modification for the sake of humor will please readers but may frustrate scholars, particularly if the new version appears to go against established interpretations of the novel. As before, one must decide which features of the text merit emphasis and what consequences the translator's choices will have for the overall critical identity of the work.

Humor in Reviews of Recent Translations

In order to test out these theoretical reflections, I will end by surveying a number of scholarly and popular reviews of recent translations of *Don Quijote* into English, Portuguese, French, and Italian. My goal is to determine how much attention the problem of translating humor has received and whether the presence of humor was a significant criterion in the evaluation of each version. The translations used were those of Edith Grossman (2003) and Tom Lathrop (2007) into English; Carlos Nougué and José Luis Sánchez (2005) and Ernani Ssó (2012) into Portuguese; Claude Allaigre, Jean Canavaggio, and Michel Moner (2001) and Aline Schulman (1997) into French; and Angelo Canale (2012) and Botta et al. (2015) into Italian.

The first conclusion that emerges from this sample is that reviews in popular publications tend to focus on word choice and rhetoric. Michael Dirda's *Washington Post* review of the Grossman edition, for example, describes the translator as "terrific in emulating Don Quixote's high-flown diction when he's at full chivalric throttle." Carlos Fuentes's comments for the *New York Times* take a similar approach, mentioning Grossman's "plain but plentiful contemporary English" and remarking that she "can highlight Don Quixote's flight into heroic rhetoric with great comic effect and meaningful emphasis." Ilan Stavans, in his *LA Times* review, acknowledges criticism toward Grossman but concludes that her translation "has a je ne sais quoi that makes this reader confident," calling attention to the stylistic parallels between her English and the Spanish of Cervantes. This emphasis on diction is equally forceful in popular assessments of the Portuguese translation by Nougué and Sánchez. Reviewers seem to have followed the translators' concern with preserving the text's original flavor while making it accessible to a modern Brazilian audience: "como escreveria Cervantes o *Quixote* no português de sua época, mas de modo tal que não perdesse o sabor hispânico de então e fosse compreensível para o leitor de hoje?" (Bernardo). Reviewers of French translations, for their part, have associated diction with readability. Jean-Charles Gateau's review for *Le Temps* praises the Allaigre/Canavaggio/Moner edition for its "vocabulaire plus contemporain et plus précis," as a result of which "l'amélioration est indiscutable, la lecture plus aisée, le plaisir plus grand." An even more strident perspective characterizes Jean-Didier Wagneur's review of the Schulman translation for *Libération*, in which he attacks "cette myopie qui fait préférer l'érudition philologique à l'évidence" and affirms that "[l]e *Quichotte* d'Aline Schulman n'est ni une adaptation ni une restauration mais une traduction 'pour une oreille d'à present,' aussi précise que claire."

When popular reviews mention humor, they rarely connect it with the quality of the translation, presenting it instead as an intrinsic quality of the original that may or may not resonate with contemporary readers. Dirda states that "much of Cervantes's humor no longer seems funny: The jokes that once made people laugh now strike us as callous and cruel." James Wood's review in the *New Yorker* calls attention to many of the humorous aspects that *Quijote* scholars have studied, and he praises Grossman for capturing the humor across linguistic registers, but he makes little mention of specific translator choices that convey this feature of the original. An underlying assumption is that Cervantes's humor either succeeds or fails on its own, depending on whether it aligns with modern-day expectations. The same assumption emerges from Olivier Le Naire and Cécile Thibaud's comments on the Schulman translation. Citing the famous anecdote on contemporary reception, the reviewers observe that "Ah! qu'il est loin, hélas! le temps où Philippe III d'Espagne, voyant un courtisan s'esclaffer devant lui, aurait lancé: 'Soit il est fou, soit il lit Don Quichotte!'" According to this perspective, translators bear no responsibility for a lack of humor, as changing attitudes among readers necessarily produce a different experience.

Scholarly reviews, in contrast, tend to focus on specific areas of translation, among which humor only occasionally holds a privileged position. Michael J. McGrath's evaluation of the Grossman edition, for instance, praises the translator for capturing irony, but the scholar's primary interest involves accuracy in translating names, cultural references, or potentially unclear situations. Tom Lathrop, in the same vein, celebrates the popular success of Grossman's translation but provides an analysis based on academic criteria, which leads him to suggest that "serious students of literature in translation" use a different volume (240). Lathrop points out translation errors through a series of nuanced lexical references and criticizes some of the footnotes that Grossman has borrowed from the Riquer edition (243). Didier Souiller's survey of French translations likewise focuses on the consequences of specific translator choices. He discusses different translations of the problematic concepts *desengaño* and *discreto*, for example, showing their relationship with authorial intentions and scholarly interpretations of crucial scenes from the novel.

The problem of translating humor has received the closest attention from translation scholars and the translators themselves. In an interview with *Sul 21*, Ernani Ssó explains that dissatisfaction with the portrayal of humor in previous Portuguese versions led him to retranslate the *Quijote*: "sentia que o livro perdia muito de sua vida e humor. Daí minha vontade de tentar recuperá-lo até onde fosse possível." Ssó goes on to argue that humor is fundamental to Cervantes's work and that translator decisions play a crucial role in the success or failure of the new version. Tracing a connection among cultural references, wordplay, and jokes, he concludes that "no caso do Cervantes, há jogos de palavras, há piadas em cima de referências culturais. Se não se recriar tudo isso, a coisa fica insípida, achatada. Ou nem faz sentido nenhum." Mariarosa Vidoni, in her analysis of the Canale edition, praises the translator for "il mantenimento della polifonia del linguaggio cervantino che riprende e parodia la lingua alta della prosa cavalleresca, di quella pastorale e dell'arte oratoria, così come la lingua bassa del popolo, i proverbi e le sentenze colte" (226). These comments establish a clear link between translator intervention and the possibility of arriving at interpretations that *Quijote* scholars have considered fundamental. Vidoni likewise calls attention to the difficulty of translating proverbs, particularly when "non esiste una corrispondenza tra la lingua di partenza e quella di arrivo ed è impossibile restituire alla cultura ricevente i concetti di un'altra" (227). Although one might question, along with David Bellos, this narrow definition of translation matching, Vidoni's comments reveal a keen awareness of how translation opens up spaces for cross-cultural interpretation. This perspective also characterizes the work of Silvia Cobelo, who has studied

Brazilian editions of *Don Quijote*. Cobelo argues that the rendering of proverbs offers a glimpse into whether translators seek to preserve the strangeness of the original or attempt to produce a "national" version for contemporary readers.

The most noteworthy example of attention to humor appears in the essay "Escollos de traducción en el *Quijote* (I)," in which Patrizia Botta and Aviva Garribba discuss the challenges that Botta et al. faced when preparing their recent Italian edition. Within the authors' impressive list of potential difficulties, one finds many of the features that *Quijote* scholars have associated with the comic tradition, such as polysemy, rhetorical games, contrasting linguistic registers, playful neologisms, and Sancho's proverbs and malapropisms (172-73). The authors insist on the role of translators in interpreting the original, in understanding how this interpretation depends on linguistic form, and in attempting to allow for the same interpretation in the forms of the target language. Botta and Garribba emphasize "un constante humorismo confiado a la lengua que no hay que perder vertiendo al otro idioma" (173), as well as "juegos retóricos y sonantes simetrías de repeticiones que un traductor ha de reconocer y saber mantener" (173). This analysis refers back to the problem of "noticing" mentioned earlier, in that Botta and Garribba depict translators as sensitive readers and informed literary critics who also possess talent for eliciting humor.

Three broad conclusions emerge from this survey of popular and scholarly evaluations. First, popular reviews of translations tend to take humor in the *Quijote* for granted, as though it were an intrinsic feature of the text that readers may or may not appreciate in accordance with their cultural background. From this perspective, should *Don Quijote* no longer prove to be a "funny book," it is because attitudes toward humor have changed, not because translators have failed to recognize or convey Cervantes's wit. Second, when literary critics assess translations of the novel, humor occupies an ancillary role at best. Only in discussions of Cervantine irony does the topic receive particular attention. Perhaps this occurs because, as we have seen, many facets of humor in *Don Quijote* are gradual and cumulative, whereas scholarly commentary tends to focus on specific problems of interpretation, often in connection with polysemic concepts like *desengaño*. Along the same lines, scholarly evaluations frequently insist upon a correct understanding of the novel's historical background: hence McGrath's detailed remarks, for instance, on the translation of numismatic and culinary terms (24-26). Finally, as one might expect, it is translators themselves who offer the most nuanced reflections on translating Cervantine humor. In this sense, translators underscore the fundamental role of interpretation, as they must, above all, be attentive readers of the original work. Unlike popular reviewers, translators cannot take humor for granted, because at each point of the text they are keenly aware of the connection between linguistic form and the production of laughter. Implicit in the translator's mind is the question of how to achieve a similar effect in the target language. Even before the actual work of translation has begun, translators already perceive which structures will permit easy approximation and which will require significant dexterity or perhaps even omission. For scholars, "translation failure" almost always entails a lack of correspondence between interpretations considered valuable in the original and the interpretations made possible by the translation. As a result, the passages in each text where these interpretations emerge tend to receive the bulk of scholarly attention. Translators, in contrast, face a vast array of problems on every page, and this perpetual need for close-reading brings forth a sharper awareness of subtle cumulative effects, such as the verbal humor that poses so many challenges in the *Quijote*.

No translation will please everyone. Translators who adopt what Venuti has called the "domesticating" approach, producing a "fluent" text that is accessible to a diverse public, will earn the text broader recognition but may draw the ire of scholars. Within English-language versions of the *Quijote*, this appears to have been the fate of Raffel and, to a lesser extent, Grossman. On the other hand, "foreignizing" translations that emphasize cultural differences may fail to attract a wide readership. In the best case, such versions will receive praise from scholars, and in the worst case they will fall prey to the same type of criticism as the popular publications, albeit with a greater degree of erudition. Occasionally, these scholarly translations seem almost to denounce their own inadequacy and to point readers toward the original. This logic seems to govern, if only implicitly, bilingual editions such as Canale's in Italian and that of Nougué and Sánchez in Portuguese.

Although much work in Translation Studies, the present essay included, calls attention to challenges and problems, there is a persistent silver lining in this field: every rendition provides a fresh approach to the text, and by translating our most-cherished works, we invite new communities of readers to discuss their meaning and value. Translation, then, when understood as interpretation and creative re-imagining, keeps literature alive. This is particularly true of *Don Quijote*, as over four centuries later, new editions continue to appear across the globe. Not every version will be funny, and not every reader will laugh, but the enduring popularity of knight and squire, in all their varied manifestations, would surely have brought a smile to Cervantes's face.

Works Cited

Attardo, Salvatore. "Translation and Humour: An Approach Based on the General Theory of Verbal Humour (GTVH)." *The Translator*, vol. 8, no. 2, 2002, pp. 173-194.

Augustine, Saint, Bishop of Hippo. *Confessions*. Translated by F.J. Sheed. Hackett, 2006.

Bellos, David. *Is That a Fish in Your Ear? Translation and the Meaning of Everything*. Faber and Faber, 2011.

Botta, Patrizia, and Aviva Garribba. "Escollos de traducción en el *Quijote* (I)." *Tus obras los rincones de la tierra descubren: actas del VI congreso internacional de la Asociación de Cervantistas*. 2008, pp. 167-190.

Cervantes, Miguel de. *Don Quijote de la Mancha*. Edited by Francisco Rico. Alfaguara, 2015.

Close, Anthony. *Cervantes and the Comic Mind of His Age*. Oxford UP, 2000.

———. *The Romantic Approach to* Don Quixote. Cambridge UP, 1977.

Cobelo, Silvia. "Os tradutores do *Quixote* publicados no Brasil." *Tradução em Revista*, no.1, 2010, pp. 1-36.

Dirda, Michael. "The great knight's tale in a new translation." Review of *Don Quixote*, translated by Edith Grossman. *Washington Post*, 9 Nov. 2003.

Fuentes, Carlos. "Tilt." Review of *Don Quixote*, translated by Edith Grossman. *New York Times*, 2 Nov. 2003.

Gateau, Jean-Charles. "Don Quichotte régénéré." Review of *Don Quichotte précédé de La Galatée*, edited by Jean Canavaggio. *Le Temps*, 19 Jan. 2002.

Gorfkle, Laura J. *Discovering the Comic in "Don Quixote."* North Carolina Studies in the Romance Languages and Literatures, 1993.

Jakobson, Roman. "On Linguistic Aspects of Translation." *On Translation*. Edited by Reuben A. Brower. Harvard UP, 1959, pp. 232-239.

Johnson, Carroll B. "*Don Quijote* Turned 400. Did Anybody Notice?" *Cervantes: Bulletin of the Cervantes Society of America*, vol. 30, no. 2, 2010, pp. 15-32.

Lathrop, Tom. "Edith Grossman's Translation of *Don Quixote*." *Cervantes: Bulletin of the Cervantes Society of America*, vol. 26, no. 1, 2006[2008], pp. 237-255.

Le Naire, Olivier, and Cécile Thibaud. "Don Quichotte ou l'éternelle chevauchée." *L'Express* 28 Feb. 2005.

Martín, Adrienne L. "Humor and Violence in Cervantes." *The Cambridge Companion to Cervantes*. Edited by Anthony J. Cascardi. Cambridge UP, 2002, pp. 160-185.

McGrath, Michael J. "Tilting at Windmills: *Don Quijote* in English." *Cervantes: Bulletin of the Cervantes Society of America*, vol. 26, no. 1, 2006[2008], pp. 7-40.

Ribeiro, Milton. "O engenhoso tradutor e sua longa batalha com Cervantes e o Quixote." *Sul 21*, 21 Oct. 2012.

Russell, P.E. *Cervantes*. Oxford University Press, 1985.

———. "*Don Quixote* as a Funny Book." *Modern Language Review*, vol. 64, no. 2, 1969, pp. 312-326.

Scaramuzza Vidoni, Mariarosa. "Il primo *Don Chisciotte* bilingue in Italia." *Tintas. Quaderni di letterature iberiche e iberoamericane*, no. 3, 2013, pp. 221-227.

Scham, Michael. "*Don Quijote* and the Art of Laughing at Oneself." *Cervantes: Bulletin of the Cervantes Society of America*, vol. 29, no. 1, 2009, pp. 31-55.

Souiller, Didier. "Quelques remarques concernant les traductions françaises de Don Quichotte." Société française de littérature générale et comparée. http://sflgc.org/agregation/souillerdidier-quelques-remarques-concernant-les-traductions-francaises-de-don-quichotte/.

Stavans, Ilan. "A new Sancho Panza speaks for the knight-errant." Review of *Don Quixote*, translated by Edith Grossman. *Los Angeles Times*, 14 Dec. 2003.

Steiner, George. *After Babel. Aspects of Language and Translation*. Oxford UP, 1975.

"A tradução do *Quixote*." www.ugfpos.com/17301/18001.html. Accessed 31 Mar. 2019.

Trueblood, Alan. "La risa en el *Quijote* y la risa de don Quijote." *Cervantes: Bulletin of the Cervantes Society of America*, vol. 4, no. 1, 1984, pp. 3-23.

Vandaele, Jeroen. "Humor in Translation." *Handbook of Translation Studies, Vol. 1*. Edited by Yves Gambier and Luc van Doorslaer. John Benjamins, 2010, pp. 147-152.

———. "Introduction: (Re-) Constructing Humor: Meanings and Means." *The Translator*, vol. 8, no. 2, 2002, pp. 149-172.

Venuti, Lawrence. *The Translator's Invisibility. A History of Translation*. 2nd ed. Routledge, 2008.

Wagneur, Jean-Didier. "Quichotte Nouvelle Manche." Review of "*L'ingénieux hidalgo Don Quichotte de la Manche*," translated by Aline Schulman. 6 Nov. 1997.

Wood, James. "Knight's Gambit." Review of *Don Quixote*, translated by Edith Grossman. *New Yorker*, 22 Dec. 2003.

Don Quijote and the Construction of Dulcinea

HABIB ZANZANA
The University of Scranton

1.0 INTRODUCTION

THE LITERARY CONVENTIONS AND the aesthetic traditions of the Spanish Golden Age often stress beauty over a woman's participation in the public discourse and present texts in which female characters function as objects of men's desire. Dulcinea inspires love and heroism in *Don Quijote de La Mancha* as the knight often claims in the novel. The female icon is always present in Don Quijote's literary imagination and in his discourse on love and chivalry although she never appears physically in the novel. Her absence is widespread, enigmatic, and significant in the overall structure of the novel. Dulcinea is not a speaking subject in *Don Quijote* and does not intervene directly in the public discourse, while the passion she inspires follows literary conventions and the sublimation of sexual desire. It would be hasty, however, to state that Cervantes fabricated through *Don Quijote* a literary model that reflects the male psyche and masculine fantasies about women.

This essay demonstrates that the construction of Dulcinea is based upon a collection of idealized traits derived from the chivalric code, and that Don Quijote's quest represents a search for truth. Furthermore, Dulcinea serves as a central device binding the entire novel together through three means. Firstly, she embodies the chivalric ideal and the truth that justifies and motivates Don Quixote's quest. Secondly, the frequent challenges to her existence and beauty create momentum and continuity throughout the novel. And lastly, she mediates and links the unfinished story of Don Quijote and the found Arabic manuscript by making her mark on the page and in the history of Don Quijote de la Mancha.

Similar to the narrative structure, which calls attention to the importance of language and truth when chronicling the history of Don Quijote de la Mancha, the knight is often asked to prove Dulcinea's identity, origin, and manifestations. Put another way, Don Quijote must gather pieces of evidence throughout the narrative, considered elements of the truth, to bear witness that Dulcinea is his beloved princess and that no woman surpasses her in beauty and virtue because the concern for truth affects the discourse on *Don Quijote* and the construction of Dulcinea. Cervantes may be reflecting on the debates of the period that centered on the notions of truth, fiction, metafiction, story, and discourse. The construction of Dulcinea mimics the loosely woven structure of the novel in which embedded stories, characters and narrative elements occupy an important space within and outside the text.

2.0 A Gendered Construction

My analysis begins with Arthur Efron's definition of Dulcineism as "the belief that human life is satisfactorily conducted if it is lived out in close accord with the prescribed ideals of the received culture," and expands its scope to interrogate theories of representation, story, discourse, and the effects of Cervantes's narrative techniques on the gendered construction of Dulcinea. It situates the female character within the aesthetic conventions of the period and explores the innovative methods Cervantes develops to create, situate, and integrate the character into the narrative fabric.

Anne Cruz keenly observes that Cervantes is often sympathetic to his female characters and willing to carve a space for their personal growth and self-realization: "Cervantes often portrays women in a positive light... It is clear that his female characters are increasingly liberated from objectification of solely erotic conflicts" (200). Dulcinea, thus, represents a dynamic literary construct that invites the reader to reconsider traditional notions of gender and representation. Dulcinea embodies the fragmentation of the narrative structure and prompts the reader of *Don Quijote* to participate in the process of gathering and piecing together text and forms of representation while partaking in the humor, irony, and the play of absence and presence. In his study of the structure of the novel, Edward Friedman explains that:

> Adhering to a poststructuralist model centuries before its conception, Cervantes decenters Don Quijote from his own narrative, and the margins provide the ideal perspective from which to consider and to reconsider the stories behind the story joined at the hip to history. Don

Quijote becomes a metonym for the reader and Miguel de Cervantes a metonym for the writer. To some extent, the two are indivisible, but alternates between a comfortable synthesis and the setting up of barriers. (4)

Jane Flax argues that gender is an indispensable mode of inquiry and that the feminist critic must determine if there are essentially male or female categories of thought and social relations. Flax maintains that gender is "a central constituent in each person's sense of self and in a culture's idea of what it means to be a person" (26). Julia Kristeva moves away from Saussure's focus on "langue" to offer a model that recognizes the heterogeneity of language and the importance of the subject defined as "the place, not only of structure and its repeated transformation, but especially, of its loss, its outlay" (24). In *The Pleasure of the Text*, Roland Barthes observes that Kristeva changes the place of things. "[she] always destroys the latest preconception, the one we thought we could be comforted by, the one which we could be proud of. She observes authority, the authority of monological science" (29). Cervantes introduces a conception of gender that embodies the dynamic nature of the construction of identity and embraces the instability of the sign. The truth professed by Don Quijote on the existence and representation of Dulcinea calls upon the reader first to reconsider already established categories of gender, self, language and power and, second, to take into account the semantic and semiotic properties associated with the idealized construction of Dulcinea. *Différance* resides in the reversal of binary oppositions and particularly in the reversal of the correspondence between the writing, thought, logos, and the play of absence and presence of Dulcinea in the text.

3.0 The Chivalric Code and Dulcinea

The construction of Dulcinea by Don Quijote finds its inspiration in the chivalric code of conduct and the conventions of courtly love in the novel. María Jesús Fuente denotes that "Cervantes parece conocer bien las características del amor cortés, y así, lo dibuja en los sentimientos de don Quijote y el comportamiento hacia su dama y de la dama hacia él" (212). After reassembling rusty old parts of an armor and choosing his steed Rocinante, Don Quijote decides on a lady to love and honor as Cervantes writes "se dio a entender que no le faltaba otra cosa sino buscar una dama de quien enamorarse; porque el caballero andante sin amores era árbol sin hojas y sin fruto y cuerpo sin alma" (40). The quest for justice and truth is the knight's raison d'être; it serves to demonstrate his courage and noble heart and bring, in the end, greater renown to the woman he loves. In *The Chivalric World of Don Quijote*, Howard Mancing states that "in order to understand Don Quijote, it is necessary to appreciate the concept of himself as a knight-errant in imitation of the literary heroes of the sixteenth-century romances of chivalry. The reader of Cervantes should bear in mind that the world in which Don Quijote lives is a world of chivalry ... He was obviously attracted by these books' artificial chivalric world where a man of courage and ability could gain honor and fame by sustaining right in the face of injustice and evil and could thereby win the admiration of other men and the love of a beautiful woman" (11).

The creation of Dulcinea, beginning with the first chapter of the novel, operates through the prism of Aldonza Lorenzo, a young farm girl Don Quijote has quietly loved and admired for twelve long years. Don Quijote acknowledges the affective bond linking him to Aldonza Lorenzo. However, in an effort to comply with the strict rules of chivalry, he alters her name to Dulcinea del Toboso and rejoices in the fact that it is not only beautiful but also "músico y peregrino y significativo" (41; part 1, ch. 1). Don Quijote's decision to change the name of the peasant girl from Aldonza to Dulcinea may strike the reader, at first blush, as an innocent and inconsequential transposition. However, naming entails a deliberate act of will. Cheris Kramarae asserts that naming imparts authority and makes clear that "those who have the power to name the world are in a position to influence reality" (165). Toril Moi concurs with this view and claims that naming expresses a will to be and to regulate reality according to pre-established categories (158).

Some critics (Efron, Parker, and Roberts) have minimized the importance of Alonso Quijano's distant love for Aldonza Lorenzo. They argue that, in view of the fact that the aging hidalgo did not reveal his feelings to the peasant girl and that she never reciprocated his love, we should conclude that Dulcinea is a fictional creature borne out of Don Quijote's literary imagination. Emilio Goggio considers Don Quijote's love for Aldonza conventional and unconvincing. He observes that "Aldonza has no feminine charms. She holds no warm place in Don Quijote's heart" (286) and was chosen simply to comply with a chivalric purpose. In *Coming to Terms: The Rhetoric of Narrative and Film*, Seymour Chatman notes that naming contains an implicit description at the smallest level (210). For Don Quijote, the peasant girl ceases to function as such in his immediate reality, to be replaced by a new literary transfiguration called Dulcinea del Toboso.

Don Quijote adopts a distant, idealized construction of Dulcinea couched in fictional terms and that conforms to the fanciful female subject in his mind. The reader and critic, on the other hand, could determine that Dulcinea is an ornate reconstruction of Aldonza Lorenzo and interpret her idealization as evidence of Don Quijote's madness and his inability to allow a "real" woman to enter the written account of his life. The emphasis on the heroic and the idealized helps to explain, for example, what happens, in *Don Quijote* part 2, chapter 10, when the knight gazes at a peasant girl whom Sancho claims is the true Dulcinea. Don Quijote is quick to dismiss Sancho's assertion as false; he does not recognize in the rustic farm girl standing before him manifestations of the ideal and the sublime embedded in his psyche.

4.0 Don Quijote's Quest and the Search for Truth

The representation of Dulcinea must conform to the principle of the truth in the novel even when the literary and the imaginary coalesce to create a female icon contained solely in Don Quijote's mind. At the end of part 1, chapter 8, for instance, the text is marked by two dramatic events: firstly, an abrupt break in the narrative, and, secondly, the unexpected purchase of a manuscript in the market place. The newly found narrative document, miraculously, picks up right where the battle between Don Quijote and the Biscayan had left off at the end of the preceding chapter. However, readers discover the new authorial voice of Cide Hamete Benengeli, an Arab historian who is credited for this continuation of the story *Don Quijote de la Mancha*. They are also advised to read carefully and critically because the text is likely to contain numerous falsehoods, for it is well known that Arabs are liars: "si a esta se le puede poner alguna objeción cerca de su verdad, no podrá ser otra sino haber sido su autor arábigo, siendo muy propio de aquella nación ser mentirosos" (95; part 1, ch. 9). The Arab chronicler, we are led to assume, could have diminished or distorted some of the knight's heroic accomplishments and cast a doubt on Don Quijote's courage and, most troubling, he may have lied about his chivalric quest and his chaste love for Dulcinea del Toboso.

The commitment to the truth has not vanished entirely from the narrative. The young Morisco receives money to provide a faithful, word-for-word translation of the original text. However, now that the document claims a different authorship, doubt and ambiguity have infiltrated the text. Reading thus becomes a doubly self-conscious act that involves interpreting and evaluating events, characters and discourse, because truth operates in a constant state of deferral and displacement. The construction of the novel follows the dialectical scheme that results from placing an imaginary figure such as Dulcinea in a state of presence (as a female icon) while also emphasizing her condition of prolonged absence and indeterminacy. Friedman remarks that in *Don Quijote* Part I, the knight errant "invents or fabricates a chivalric frame for the characters, situations, and chance meetings on his path toward glory as a righter of wrongs, as a defender of the weak, and as a loyal subject of Dulcinea del Toboso." Moreover, the absence of a flesh and blood Dulcinea in *Don Quijote* strengthens her status as a female representation and literary construction and positions her character as a decentering presence in the novel. The construction of Dulcinea by Don Quijote mirrors the fragmented nature of the novel and emphasizes the elasticity of her textual representation. *Don Quijote* is a novel that displays the loosely woven narrative fragments that have come to epitomize the self-conscious text. In a similar fashion, the knight-errant bravely defends his elevated construction of Dulcinea and demands that others support the truth of the terms of her representation. His construction of Dulcinea is idealized, heroic and chivalric, and expands as the narrative unfolds and other forms of representation come into focus.

An important female character emerges in the world of *Don Quijote* at the end of part 1, chapter 1. Dulcinea enters the narrative propelled by the power of Don Quijote's imagination, his chaste love and chivalric purpose. However, the reader must wrestle with Dulcinea's evasive nature and the fact that the female character never appears in the text. Her absence has led many critics to dismiss the function of Dulcinea in Don Quijote's chivalric universe. Anthony Close claims that Dulcinea's contribution to Don Quijote's heroic pursuits is secondary. He argues that Dulcinea fulfills one of the requirements Don Quijote must meet in order to become a knight-errant, "love, for him, is a sort of professional obligation, like the need to carry a slide-rule if one is a draughtsman" (146). Close considers Dulcinea a literary convenience, a mere pretext for Don Quijote's obedience to the precepts of chivalry. Arthur Efron, on the other hand, points out that Don Quijote's approach is irreparably flawed. The critic argues that by centering first on his person, then on Rocinante and finally on Dulcinea, Don Quijote implicitly dictates the order and importance of the elements themselves and their sequence. That is to say, if Don Quijote had been truly concerned with Dulcinea and genuinely interested in making her a meaningful part of his chivalric ambitions, the knight would have first selected a beautiful maiden rather than spent time gathering bits and pieces of an old armor.

A complete dismissal of Don Quijote's love for and dedication to Dulcinea based solely on the fact that she does not come first in the process of selection may be unwarranted. We should reconsider, perhaps, Efron's contention that Dulcinea functions as an afterthought mainly because she appears last in the sequence of chivalric requirements. The order of selection followed by Don Quijote does not reflect an established hierarchy or his own set of priorities, in my opinion. It may signal, instead, that the narrative voice is being cautious and timely when disclosing Don Quijote's enduring passion for Aldonza Lorenzo. Timing is crucial as Don Quijote takes the first few steps toward realizing his ambition to become a knight and roam the world in search of adventures. The latter reference to Dulcinea reflects a concern with revealing too much and too soon to the reader. Viewed in this light, an untimely statement on Don Quijote's love for Aldonza would project the knight's most secret longing into the public sphere and carry the risk of eliciting the reader's scorn and ridicule. Thus, far from an insignificant afterthought, Dulcinea's final entry into the text is the result of long and careful deliberations. More important, Don Quijote's quiet love for Aldonza and his acknowledgment that Dulcinea now embodies all of his chivalric ideals suggest that Cervantes is willing to entrust the reader with intimate aspects of the knight's inner conflicts, aspirations, and desires.

5.0 The Construction of Dulcinea as a Universal Truth
Having just released Andrés from the grips of a cruel master in part 1, chapter 4, Don Quijote prepares for a second confrontation. This time, however, instead of intervening to restore moral order and justice, the knight defends his representation of Dulcinea. Don Quijote asks a group of Toledo traders on their way to Murcia to stop in the middle of the road and make a statement of truth, "todo el mundo se tenga, si todo el mundo no confiesa que no hay en el mundo todo doncella más hermosa que la emperatriz de la Mancha, la sin par Dulcinea del Toboso" (59). It is worth wondering about Don Quijote's request and questioning the meaning behind his insistence on a public consensus on Dulcinea's beauty. If Don Quijote had previously praised himself and Dulcinea by calling her the most fortunate of all maidens, he now seeks a shared acknowledgment of the superiority of her beauty. However, why such an assertion? What would the proclamation reveal about him and his relationship with Dulcinea?

We must keep in mind that the readers of the novel share a privileged status at this point in the narrative: they know that Don Quijote has just inscribed Dulcinea into his chivalric destiny, and they recognize the affective bond that connects Aldonza to Dulcinea in the trajectory of his life and adventures. A public statement of the maiden's beauty by the traders would sanction, on the one hand, Dulcinea's entry into the chivalric world of Don

Quijote and mark, on the other, her transition from an abstraction (contained solely in Don Quijote's mind) to that of a character and a participant in the overall discourse. A knight cannot pursue his heroic vocation if he is unable to make his passion and glory known to the woman he loves and to the world at large. For Don Quijote, great deeds (and delivering Andrés is one of them) are meant to honor Dulcinea, make her name resonate all over the world, and spread the news of her beauty.

The fact that the traders travel from town to town and interact with large crowds makes them the ideal transporters of a newly professed truth and female inscription. An isolated statement could not possibly convey the splendor of Dulcinea's beauty. Don Quijote demands a unanimous agreement: "todo el mundo" must accept that Dulcinea is the most beautiful of all maidens and the empress of La Mancha (and, of course, the most celebrated of all women). Rescuing the young Andrés from the hands of a brutal master has filled Don Quijote with pride and exhilaration just hours before. It has also embolden him and proven the righteousness of his new chivalric enterprise. Consequently, the unequivocal affirmation that Don Quijote solicits from the traders attests to the power and significance of Dulcinea in Don Quijote's sentimental imaginings that have been derived from his literary universe.

Don Quijote's response to the traders' refusal to reiterate and confirm his bold statement illustrates the clash between various forms of representation. The traders do not necessarily deny the existence of Dulcinea; they simply ask for a piece of evidence. Two separate signs precipitate the conflict: the verbal and the visual. For Don Quijote, the two signs are independent and unrelated, but for the traders the existence of one conditions the presence of the other. In other words, in the traders' opinion, Dulcinea cannot function as a signifier, with the corresponding properties assigned to her by Don Quijote, without a visual confirmation. Consequently, they insist on a portrait of Dulcinea to assess Don Quijote's pronouncement and the veracity of his claim. The knight replies that no portrait of Dulcinea could shine a greater light on the truth of his words that she is the most beautiful maiden in the world: "Si os la mostrara, replicó Don Quijote ¿qué hiciérades vosotros en confesar una verdad tan notoria? La importancia está en que sin verla lo habéis de creer, confesar, afirmar, jurar y defender; donde no, conmigo sois en batalla, gente descomunal y soberbia" (59; part 1, ch. 4).

The traders' judgment may follow the old adage that "seeing is believing," but for Don Quijote the confirmation of Dulcinea's beauty must be an act of faith and, like all firmly held beliefs, taken as truth regardless of proof.

Rosilie Hernández-Pecoraro recognizes that "[w]ithout question, Dulcinea-the perfect object of desire-is the impetus that drives Quijote's imagination. Her idealized absence is a constant presence for the knight. She anchors his chivalric imagination and provides a justification and motivation for his actions. In the critical corpus, the pair Dulcinea and Aldonza is typically interpreted as a set of radical opposites that showcases the comedic and parodic irony that nurtures the ethos of the Quijote . . . I propose we also think of the Dulcinea-Aldonza coupling precisely through the axis of fiction and economic landscape that is reproduced and reimagined in the *Quijote*" (170-74). Don Quijote projects his love for Dulcinea in a public and geographical space called La Mancha where his beloved empress reigns even if the traders have never heard her name. Don Quijote's request carries out an even more grandiose purpose; it constitutes an attempt to transform Dulcinea into a female character of heroic and universal dimension.

The discord between the knight and the traders arises from Don Quijote's refusal to attach a fixed signifier to Dulcinea. The conflict intensifies as Don Quijote insists that the traders fully agree with his representation of Dulcinea. The traders may deem Don Quijote's unexpected delay amusing at first; however, for Don Quijote, this marks a crucial moment because the confirmation of Dulcinea's existence and beauty is essential to his identity as a knight errant. In an analysis of realism in *Don Quijote*, Erich Auerbach uses the French expression *idée fixe* or obsessive fixation to characterize Don Quijote's chivalric ambition. Auerbach does not relate Don Quijote's quest for adventures to the woman who inspires and guides his heroic ambitions. I propose that the notion of *idée fixe* be expanded to include not only Don Quijote's chivalric mission but also his commitment to love and defend Dulcinea and her name. While all knights-errant embrace a common chivalric code, the expression of their love for a beautiful maiden can vary significantly. Therefore, Don Quijote is free to invent for himself an image of Dulcinea's unmatched beauty. He can also demand that others confirm his belief that Dulcinea and her unparalleled beauty strengthen his commitment to truth and his defense of chivalric ideals. Her beauty is an indisputable fact, he claims, that everyone in the world should know, express approval of, and give support to by public statement.

For Don Quijote, both the power of his declaration and the strength of his arm should compensate for the lack of a portrait of Dulcinea. Ironically, he fails to convince a crowd of men to agree with his representation of Dulcinea and to support his statement. Dulcinea's instability as a sign operates through the absence of a portrait and the traders' refusal to literally take his word for it. To make matters worse, the traders begin mocking Dulcinea's origin and phyical appareance. They enrage Don Quijote further by painting a hideous portrait of his beloved princess, "aunque su retrato nos muestre que es tuerta de un ojo y que el otro le mana bermellón y piedra azufre con todo complacer a vuestra merced, diremos a su favor todo lo que quisiere" (60; part 1, ch. 4). The distortion of Dulcinea's image produces a fury in Don Quijote, who charges against the men. The merchants ask Don Quijote for a small piece of evidence, the size of a grain of wheat. They introduce the grotesque with a reference to Dulcinea's eyes, one blind and the other oozing vermilion and sulfur. Don Quijote replies by contesting the image with a softer, more delicate representation of the female character drawn in ambergris and civet in cotton.

A battle of signifiers takes place and moves the men from a verbal confrontation to physical assault. The portrait of Dulcinea (even the size of a grain of wheat), the main piece of evidence missing to prove her existence and extraordinary beauty, leads to a dispute that leaves Don Quijote badly beaten: "a despecho y a pesar de sus armas, le molió como cibera. ¿cómo lo haría, molido y casi deshecho?" (61; part 1, ch. 4). There is a play on the words, eyes, wheat, and civet and milled, which is significant with respect to the way the representation of Dulcinea functions in the episode. The traders may be asking Don Quijote the following question: how could the dry plains of La Mancha produce a beautiful grain of wheat in the splendor of Dulcinea? These are men accustomed to trading and manipulating language to conclude a deal to their advantage. It is therefore not entirely surprising that they object to the absence of a visual representation of Dulcinea and taunt him with its opposite. The grotesque deformation of Dulcinea reflects the need to deconstruct Don Quijote's idealized image by the traders. It illustrates also an attempt to degrade and dehumanize Dulcinea and, consequently, provoke the knight's anger. Equally important, it may serve to underscore that Quijote and his amorous vision have been blinded to the reality around him. This idea is conveyed through the image of Dulcinea's eyes: one is "tuerto" or blind and bathed in darkness; and the other, obscured by a thick film composed of a greenish and whitish substance. The emphasis on darkness and decay suggests that no grain of wheat could possibly grow in the absence of light. Similarly, without a portrait, Don Quijote cannot make his idealized representation of Dulcinea reproduce and flourish in the world at large.

6.0 Dulcinea and the Sound of Silences Breaking

It is worth considering that in part 1, chapter 8, the continuation of the story of *Don Quijote de la Mancha* is mediated through a reference to Dulcinea in the margin of newly found manuscript authored by Cide Hamete Benengeli. The Morisco hired to translate the pages of the handwritten document reads an annotation and burts out laughing, "Está, como he dicho, aquí en el margen escrito esto: Esta Dulcinea del Toboso tantas veces en esta historia referida, dicen que tuvo la mejor mano para salar puercos que otra mujer de toda la Mancha" (6). The position of Dulcinea in the margin of a text cannot be considered purely incidental. It is a reflection of the play of absence and presence, writing and difference. The placement of her name outside the page of the found manuscript gestures toward her central function in *Don Quijote de la Mancha*. Put another way, the reference to Dulcinea signals that the female character plays a preponderant role in the development of the novel and in the discourse of love and chivalry. Her presence and place in the margin of the text make possible the recognition, retrieval, and continuation of the story. Without her meaningful intervention, the narrative account of Don Quijote de la Mancha would have remained shrouded in darkness and silence.

Myra Jehlen characterizes gender as "a quality of the literary voice hitherto masked by the static of common assumptions." She argues that "as a critical category, gender is an additional lens, or a way of lifting of the curtain to an unseen recess of the self and society" (265). Dulcinea becomes a catalyst and a recognizable center in the discourse despite her lack of a physical presence. She breaks the silence associated with her absence by serving as a link from the unfinished story to the found Arabic manuscript. Without the reference to Dulcinea, the written history of Don Quijote's life may never have been spotted, recovered, authenticated, and translated into Spanish. In addition, all of his heroic actions would have remained lost and unvoiced. Dulcinea helps break the silence inside the archives of la Mancha and prevents the story from lapsing into oblivion at the end of part 1, chapter 8. She functions as a sign placed purposefully in the margin of the text to facilitate its identification and to ensure the preservation of writing, history, and her story.

The reader may object to the amusing note about Dulcinea that appears in the margin and claim that the reference to salting pigs undermines the importance of the female character. In *Don Quijote as a Funny Book*, Peter Russell invites readers of Cervantes's novel to enjoy the text for the humor contained in the chivalric adventures of Don Quijote (180). Russell notes that the Romantic approach favored by writers such as Miguel de Unamuno can overshadow the text's comic elements and, more important, overlook Cervantes's generous blend of humor in *Don Quijote*. The annotation in the margin does not constitute a fragment of the text per se. The previous (original) text ceases to exist as such and becomes a joint production. It belongs to both the Spanish and Arabic literary traditions since Cide Hamete confirms his contribution to and authority over the text by attaching his name to the manuscript. It is the story of Don Quijote de la Mancha and of Dulcinea del Toboso; ultimately, it is an invitation to read.

At the end of part 1, chapter 9, the Biscayan declines to go to El Toboso to surrender to Dulcinea afer Don Quijote defeats him. In spite of his refusal, the narrative pays tribute to the female character by acknowledging her influence over Don Quijote's chivalric quest and the destiny of writing. Two large fragments of a manuscript are placed next to each other and subsequently reunited and, joined together, they form a complete life story. In the process, Dulcinea has acquired the authority of a literary mediator. Put another way, Dulcinea is a character marked by absence that peels away one layer of presence to show another. Dulcinea participates in the construction of the text while remaining an evasive and decentering representational figure.

7.0 The Intersection of Desire and the Construction of Dulcinea

The idealized portrait of Dulcinea diverges significantly from the description of other female characters in the novel such as Maritornes in part 1, chapter 16. Maritornes's physical description recalls the grotesque portrait of Dulcinea painted by the traders earlier in the novel, "ancha de cara, llana de cogote, de nariz roma, del un ojo tuerta y del otro no muy sana" (143). Once again, Don Quijote, inspired by his literary imagination, alters the reality of his surroundings. He takes the inn for a castle and conceives an improbable love intrigue between himself and the daughter of the lord of the castle. However, the terms of this fabricated love affair operate through a reversal of the traditional model of courtship. That is, instead of the knight errant falling in love with a young maiden, the girl is enamored of him right from the start. Unable to contain her love for Don Quijote, the daughter of the lord plans a nocturnal visit to the knight's chamber. Don Quijote feels anxious and vulnerable at first; still, he intends to remain strong and steadfast regardless of the circumstances: "y propuso en su corazón de no cometer alevosía a su señora Dulcinea del Toboso, aunque la misma reina Ginebra con su dama Quintañona se le pusiesen delante" (147). The tension grows when Maritornes, quietly searching for the mule driver in the dark, falls into Don Quijote's arms. This is, presumably, the moment that Don Quijote had been dreading all along, and yet his reaction is not of shock or horror. On the contrary, he welcomes the young woman into his arms and relies on his imagination to guide his senses.

An extraordinary transformation of the peasant girl accompanies the clumsy movement of Don Quijote's hands. At his touch, Maritornes's coarse gown feels like soft silk, the glass beads around her wrists, oriental pearls, and her hair, gold of Arabia that rivals the sun, and her breath, sweet fragrance. This portrayal reaches beyond the domain of literature to include manifestations of the erotic, Orientalism, and the luminous beauty of Renaissance paintings. The narrative deflates, however, Don Quijote's attempt to fabricate a fantastic tale out of this delightful encounter. It consistently accentuates the opposition between the peasant girl in Don Quijote's arms and the beautiful damsel he imagines himself holding. In *The Dialogic Imagination*, Mikhail Bakhtin argues that in *Don Quijote,* Cervantes has deliberately established stark contrasts between characters and their speech. The critic maintains that Cervantes "is dragging what is being compared down to the dregs of an everyday gross reality congealed in prose, thereby destroying the lofty literary plane that had been achieved by polemical abstraction" (386). Don Quijote confesses that he cannot accept the damsel's invitation to indulge in the pleasures of the flesh, first, because he is badly bruised, but more important, because he is entirely devoted to Dulcinea. Chaos and confusion soon follow the brief interlude between Don Quijote and Maritornes, and the charming secret rendezvous gradually transforms into a riotous carnivalesque tableau.

8.0 Don Quijote and the Affective Bond between Aldonza and Dulcinea

In part 1, chapter 25, the letter Don Quijote writes Dulcinea stirs up a conflict in terms of her representation. Don Quijote explains to Sancho that Aldonza Lorenzo is at the origin of his love for Dulcinea del Toboso. He adds that Dulcinea can neither read nor write. He has loved and admired her a long time and without her knowing, "osaré jurar con verdad que en doce años que ha que la quiero más a la lumbre destos ojos que han de comer la tierra, no la he visto cuatro veces" (239). The reader may question Don Quijote's decision to disclose the affective bond connecting Aldonza and Dulcinea. The truth is that Don Quijote had no choice in the matter: Sancho must know where and to whom he should deliver the letter. Don Quijote does not declare directly that he is in love with Aldonza Lorenzo; he supplies the name of her parents to clear up any doubt. Sancho cannot believe his ears, "¿Que la hija de Lorenzo Corchuelo es la señora Dulcinea del Toboso, llamada por otro nombre Aldonza Lorenzo?" (244). Don Quijote responds affirmatively. However, his answer makes clear that he has distanced himself from Aldonza Lorenzo, and that Dulcinea is the only woman occupying his heart and mind: "Ésa es y es la que merece ser señora de todo el Universo" (244). Carroll B. Johnson draws attention to the contrast between Don Quijote's idealized image of Dulcinea and Sancho's competing description of the plain farm girl he pretends to have visited in El Toboso, "Sancho makes up a story (generates a discourse) about Dulcinea based on his knowledge of Aldonza Lorenzo and what Aldonza would probably be doing when he arrived and how she would react to Don Quijote's message. Sancho's story is unacceptable to Don Quixote because Aldonza is not Dulcinea... Don Quixote needs a story about a princess, but Sancho is telling him one about a farm girl" (84).

Sancho's focus on Dulcinea's rustic appearance, after he presumably returned from his journey in part 1, chapter 31, may respond to the squire's need to adjust to the new reality that Aldonza Lorenzo is the inspiration for Dulcinea del Toboso. He describes her body and gestures as unattractive, manly, and rough, "Lo que sé decir... es que sentí un olorcillo hombruno; y debía ser que ella, con el mucho ejercicio, estaba sudada y algo correosa" (312). Sancho engages in a critique of the knight's idealized image of Dulcinea. He does so by substituting an equally overdetermined portrayal of Aldonza that accentuates the coarse nature of her traits, strong body odor, and her lack of grace. The zeal that accompanies Sancho's unflattering depiction of Dulcinea bears little with his concern for the truth. Instead, it sheds a light on Sancho's distinct inability to understand the play of absence and presence of Dulcinea in the narrative account of Don Quijote's life as he had demonstrated earlier in part 1, chapter 25 when he declared, "que hasta aquí he estado en una grande ignorancia; pensaba bien y fielmente que la señora Dulcinea debía de ser alguna princesa de quien vuestra merced estaba enamorado" (244). Don Quijote does not contest vehemently Sancho's attack on his idealized representation of Dulcinea because no ill words could ever change his construction of the female icon who animates his love and the purpose of his chivalric quest.

9.0 Dulcinea and the Parameters of Fiction and Metafiction

Michel Foucault argues that, in part 2, Don Quijote's meeting with the duke and duchess marks an extraordinary event. They enjoy an opportunity and a privilege rarely granted readers of fiction: they meet, in flesh and blood, the character whom they had read so much about, the famous Don Quijote de la Mancha (48). At this moment, the boundaries between fiction and reality subside as Don Quijote steps forward to greet the duchess and the duke. Roland Barthes's distinction between the "scriptible" and the "lisible" turns blurry as the knight symbolically exits the realm of fiction to enter a shared reality with his readers. E. C. Riley contends that "Cervantes's ironic vision enables him to put within the pages of *Don Quijote* things that are normally outside books automatically; but also to manipulate the story so that the principal characters are actually conscious of the world outside the covers of the book ... He brings his public into fiction ... Part II is full of characters who have read part I and know all about the adventures of Don Quijote and Sancho ... He makes Quixote and Sancho conscious of themselves as literary heroes of a published work and therefore conscious of the world outside their story" (129).

Don Quijote's entrance into the world of the real, a place and space he rarely inhabits, recalls the manifestations of the presence of Dulcinea in the text. Until their encounter with Don Quijote, the duke and duchess had always regarded the knight of la Mancha and his beloved Dulcinea as imaginary constructs, fictional entities contained and constrained by the limits of fiction. Don Quijote's intrusion into the world of the "real," or into their fictional world, could be a deception like the enchantment of Dulcinea, a mockery played on unsuspecting readers of fiction. At the level of narrative discourse, the noble couple welcomes Don Quijote into their literary domain: he has symbolically exited one level of fiction and entered another, undergone a mise en abyme, and they acknowledge his safe passage from one fictional terrain onto another, without a breakdown in the narrative. By the end of the process, he has become a visible character standing before the duke and duchess, who associate him with the story of a madman they had read about in a work of fiction. A. J. Greimas notes that "unlike Isolde for Tristan, Dulcinea does not prepare a soft bed of moss for [Don Quijote]: he does not care about happiness: what he seeks is the full realization of his life, justifying it and fulfilling it with meaning, thereby creating his personal honor for himself" (177).

This sudden shift in the knight's perception of himself and in how others view him underscores the absence of a fixed signifier and opens a space for elements of fiction and metafiction. Mercedes Alcalá Galán argues that the self-referential quality of *Don Quijote* and the emphasis on fiction and metafiction extend to the character of Dulcinea who:

aparecerá en digresiones de corte retórico sobre su perfección sin cifra, el noble amor que inspira Don Quijote, traducido en valentía, o los inefables dones que su persona atesora ... Al no ser un personaje "directo" o "indirecto," estará siempre mediado el discurso o la actuación metateatral de los otros. Es un personaje que se sitúa en un nivel más profundo de la ficción y que sale de la fantasía de don Quijote para convertirse en fantasía no solo colectiva sino colaborativa. En definitiva, podría decirse que Dulcinea es un metapersonaje. (24)

Don Quijote's exit from one level of fiction and his subsequent entry into the duke and duchess's shared reality (or other level of fiction) are a symbolic reenactment of his descent into the cave of Montesinos. When he enters the cave and meets literary figures such as Montesinos, Lady Belerma, the enchanted Dulcinea and a host of other enchanted creatures, Don Quijote stands halfway between dream and reality, the heroic and the material, beauty and distortion. Don Quijote follows the same itinerary when he meets the duke and duchess. This time, however, he is welcome as a literary character who steps out of a book about the history of a knight by the name of Don Quijote de la Mancha. Don Quijote, who had never doubted the legitimacy of his chivalric quest, becomes unsure of his place and space in the play of absence and presence. He seems to stand out as an anomaly, to have initiated estrangement, and to belong to a world in which fiction and reality fuse and confuse readers and characters. It is precisely this shared experience with Dulcinea, (and indirectly with Marcela), that forms the basis for his decision to defend his ideals of love and chivalry by means of language, thought, and arms. John J. Allen states that "Dulcinea es una creación consciente sin las restricciones de una presencia viva dentro de la acción, así como el sueño de la cueva de Montesinos es una creación inconsciente" (849).

10.0 Don Quijote and the Enchanted Dulcinea

Don Quijote uses absence to disengage from the grotesque representation of the enchanted Dulcinea. The knight refuses to provide the duke and duchess with a detailed description of Dulcinea, blaming his lack of rhetorical and stylistic refinement. Don Quijote shows restraint in speech to avoid another verbal assault on his female ideal. He knows that the duke and duchess have read the first part of the narrative account of his life and that they are familiar with his construction of Dulcinea. The knight hopes to keep his idealized Dulcinea (the one before enchantment), at a safe distance, secured in his heart and mind. Simply put, Don Quijote uses silence to shield and defend his paragon of beauty from misrepresentations and distortions. The construction of Dulcinea, like the construction of the text, appropriates a space in which signs, signifiers, forms of representation and discourses lay bare the textures and patterns of the narrative fabric. Don Quijote protects Dulcinea's image by rebelling against her grotesque tranformation and by highlighting a series of contrasts between his angelic princess and the ugly work of enchanters: "Halléla encantada y convertida de princesa en labradora, de hermosa en fea, de ángel en diablo, de olorosa en pestífera, de bien hablada en rústica, de reposada en brincadora, de luz en tinieblas, y finalmente, de Dulcinea del Toboso en una villana de Sayago" (776; part 2, ch. 32).

In *Don Quijote*, part 2, The duke and duchess attempt to destabilize the construction of Dulcinea by placing Don Quijote in events and situations in which the heroic, the symbolic, and the libidinal clash to test the limits of absence. The duchess begins the process of fragmenting and detailing Dulcinea as text. First, she examines Don Quijote's approach to and understanding of the female representation. She evaluates its significance, its patterns and designs. Second, the duchess points to the gaps and contradictions apparent in Don Quijote's evasive ideal and his construction of Dulcinea. Stacey Triplette contends that

> The Dulcinea question in the ducal household shows that inscribed readers all too easily become author figures, competing with the implied author and source text in the process of creating meaning. In conversations with Don Quijote and Sancho, the duchess returns to a particular detail, the image of Dulcinea winnowing grain... Evidently the duchess does not like this passage ... The duchess's vision of Dulcinea shows that what she values in the romance of chivalry is nobility and archetypal femininity. The memory of Aldonza does not fit the duchess's hierarchical notion of chivalry, and all trace of it must be expunged. (99)

In the end, the results of the duchess's probe suggest that Dulcinea exists beyond the strict parameters of the text. To understand Dulcinea's absence, the reader must accept a plurality of meanings and signifying practices that form the basis of her representation. Instead, the duke and duchess's form of inquiry, their method of decomposing the terms of Dulcinea's representation, and their partial grasp of Don Quijote's amorous discourse gesture toward absence and presence as narrative dimensions located strictly within the limits of fiction. In *Don Quijote*, Cervantes demonstrates that coherence, incongruity, voice, silence, and presence and absence should not be strictly defined and set off against one another in binary oppositions.

While it is true that Dulcinea does not appear in the text as a character who speaks for herself, her absence is not synonymous with lack but rather with the breaking of silences and with shifting origins. Ruth Anthony El Saffar has argued that:

> only through a parodic representation of the hero and the society whose conflicts the hero embodies can Cervantes declare his disengagement from its dynamics. Don Quijote is "about" neither rebellion nor social conformism. Rather, it is a work that speaks at every level of analysis, in the direction of silence, toward that which, despite the words, remains irrevocably unsaid. (221)

Unlike Dorotea, Dulcinea does not enjoy a detailed narrative account of her life and actions. There is no script available to articulate the manifestations of her presence in the literary universe Cervantes creates in *Don Quijote*. The construction of Dulcinea is an open text that grants a place and a space to literary inscriptions marked by absence and the shifting properties of her identity. Personhood, subjectivity, and agency may, however, enter into the construction of Dulcinea and bring to the fore Cora Kaplan's notion that "the fractured and fluctuant condition of all consciously held identity, the impossibility of a will-full, unified and cohered subject reader" (181). Dulcinea's position in the text resists closure, the stability of the sign and the imposition that logos can exert upon her representation and identity. Dulcinea upholds her literary and symbolic significance in Cervantes's *Don Quijote* by renouncing narrative authority, coherence, and organic unity.

11.0 CONCLUSION

Dulcinea embodies the Other and thus defeats the reader's (and the critic's) attempt to impose a unified approach to her representation in the novel. The play of absence and presence underscores the notion that knowledge and meaning are dynamic and shifting properties of the narrative structure. Her physical absence constitutes an integral part of Cervantes's narrative strategy and reminds us that, in the words of Geoffrey Hartman, "There is no absolute knowledge but rather textual infinites, an interminable web of texts or interpretations" (230). The dynamic construction of Dulcinea often compels many individuals to fill her absence with a complex canvas of textual representations such as Sancho's crude and offensive depiction of Dulcinea; and the duke and duchess's elaborate mise-en-scène of the enchanted Dulcinea. Prado de Arai claims that the absence of Dulcinea is an enigma that the reader can either ignore or take into consideration in the process of reading. Her character and absence articulate the contradictions inherent in language, meaning and interpretation. If the reader renounces a unified approach to narrative structure and to Dulcinea, her construction becomes synonymous with textuality, intertextuality and with the shifting properties of language and representation. In the end, the construction of Dulcinea resembles the construction of a text in the making. All the elements of language, story, discourse, subjectivity, and gender coalesce to position Dulcinea as a central character to our understanding of the structure and meaning of *Don Quijote de la Mancha*. The play of absence and presence of Dulcinea in the novel reflects the tension between truth, falsehood, and madness. Without Dulcinea, Don Quijote would lose his central purpose for the quest. Notwithstanding her absence, Dulcinea as an ideal; she symbolizes modernity, truth, and chivalric code and binds together the history of Don Quijote de la Mancha.

Works Cited

Alcalá-Galán, Mercedes. "El *Cancionero* de Dulcinea en el *Quijote* o la creación coral de un metapersonaje en evolución / Dulcinea's *Cancionero* in *Quijote* or the Choral Creation of an Evolving Metacharacter." *Calíope*, vol. 22, no. 2, 2017, p. 19.

Allen, John J. "El desarrollo de Dulcinea y la evolución de Don Quijote." *Nueva Revista De Filología Hispánica (NRFH)*, vol. 38, no. 2, 1990, p. 849.

Arai, Emma Prado de. *Dulcinea, protagonista invisible del Quijote*. Ediciones CLICH, 1947.

Auerbach, Erich. *Mimesis: The Representation of Reality in Western Literature*. Trans. William R. Trask. Princeton: Princeton UP, 1953

Bakhtin, M. M. *The Dialogic Imagination: Four Essays*. University of Texas Press, 1996.

Barthes, Roland. *Pleasure of the Text*. Notting Hill Editions, 2012.

Cervantes Saavedra, Miguel de. *Don Quijote de La Mancha*. Ed. Martín de Riquer. Barcelona: Editorial Juventud, 1985.

Chatman, Seymour. *Story and Discourse: Narrative Structure in Fiction and Film*. Ithaca: Cornell UP, 1978.

Close, Anthony. *The Romantic Approach to Don Quijote*. Cambridge: Cambridge UP, 1978.

Cruz, Anne. "Studying Gender in the Spanish Golden Age." *Cultural and Historical Grounding for Hispanic and Luso-Brazilian Feminist Literary Criticism.* Ed. Hernan Vidal. Minneapolis, MN: Institute for the Study of Ideologies and Literature, 1989, 195-222.

———. "Don Quijote, the Picaresque, and the 'Rise' of the Modern Novel" Gabriele, John P. 1605-2005: Don Quixote Across the Centuries: *Actas del Congreso celebrado en el College of Wooster* (Ohio, EE. UU.) Del 7 Al 9 de abril de 2005. Iberoamericana, 2005.

Efron, Arthur. *Don Quijote and the Dulcineated World.* Partners Press, 1985.

El Safar, Ruth Anthony. "In Praise of what is Left Unsaid: Thoughts on Women and Lack in Don Quijote." *MLN* 103 (1988): 205-22.

Flax, Jane. *Disputed Subjects: Essays on Psychoanalysis, Politics and Philosophy.* Routledge, 1993.

Foucault, Michel. *The Order of Things.* Routledge, 2002.

Friedman, Edward. "Reading Inscribed: Don Quijote and the Parameters of Fiction." *On Cervantes: Essays for L. A. Murillo.* Ed. James A. Parr. Newark, DE: Juan de la Cuesta, 1991. 63-84.

———. "Metafictional Crossings - Edward H. Friedman, Guest Editor." *Vol 2 (2005): Metafictional Crossings - Edward H. Friedman, Guest Editor | Vanderbilt e-Journal of Luso-Hispanic Studies,* ejournals.library.vanderbilt. edu/index.php/lusohispanic/issue/view/160.

Fuente, María Jesús. "La desconstrucción de Dulcinea. Bases medievales de los modelos femeninos en el Quijote." *Espacio, Tiempo y Forma,* 17, 2004, pp. 201-221.

Goggio, Emilio. "The Dual Role of Dulcinea." *Modern Language Quarterly* 13 (1952) 285-91.

Greimas, A. J. "Cervantes and His Don Quixote." *Cervantes: Bulletin of the Cervantes Society of America,* 36, 1, 2016, pp. 171-79.

Hartman, Geoffrey H. *Criticism in the Wilderness.* Baltimore: Johns Hopkins UP, 1980.

Hernández-Pecoraro, Rosilie. "Cervantes's Quixote and the Arbitrista Reform Project." *Romance Quarterly,* vol. 57, no. 3, 2010, pp. 169-182.

Jehlen, Myra. "Archimedes and the Paradox of Feminist Criticism." *Signs* 6, (1981): 592-95.

Johnson, Carroll B. *Don Quixote. The Quest for Modern Fiction.* Boston: Twayne Publishers, 1990.

Kristeva, Julia. *Desire in Language: A Semiotic Approach to Literature and Art.* Trans. Thomas Gora. New York: Columbia UP, 1980.

Kromarae, Cheris. *Women and Men Speaking. Framework for Analysis.* Newbury House, 1981.

Mancing, Howard. *The Chivalric World of Don Quijote. Style, Structure, and Narrative Technique.* Columbia, U of Missouri Press, 1982.
Moi, Toril. *Sexual, Textual Politics.* Routledge, 2008.
Newton, K. M. "Jacques Derrida: 'Structure, Sign, and Play in the Discourse of the Human Sciences.'" *Twentieth-Century Literary Theory*, 1997, pp. 115-120.
Parker, Alexander A. "El concepto de la verdad en el Quijote." *Nueva Revista de Filología Hispánica* 32 (1948): 287-305.
Riley, Edward C. *Don Quixote.* London: Allen and Unwin, 1986.
Roberts, Gemma. "Ausencia y presencia de Dulcinea en El Quijote." *Revista de Archivos, Bibliotecas y Museos* 4 (1979): 810-26.
Russell, Peter E. "Don Quijote as a Funny Book." *Modern Language Review* 64 (1969): 312-26.
Saussure, Ferdinand de, and Roy Harris. *Course in General Linguistics.* Bloomsbury Academic, an Imprint of Bloomsbury Publishing, 2013.
Triplette, Stacey. "Chivalry and the Female Reader in Part Two of Don Quijote." *Cervantes: Bulletin of the Cervantes Society of America*, vol. 38, no. 1, 2018, pp. 81-119.
Unamuno, Miguel de. *Vida de Don Quijote y Sancho.* Madrid: Austral, 1975.

Tuits/Tweets dedicados al Profesor Edward H. Friedman

Ed: Thank you for helping me shape a career that I love. I am fortunate to work in a profession that I find fulfilling. I have benefitted so much from your wisdom, your generosity, your kindness, and your support. I wish you all the best.
@Mindy Stivers Badía

Ed Friedman taught us (and continues to teach us) to be open-minded but committed, intellectually honest but persistent, rigorous but accommodating and inclusive.
@Robert Bayliss

Modern historians have chosen to record several early modern authors as having quoted one Cide Hamete whose words, roughly translated, read: "The *sin par* grace and wit of Ed Friedman have done more to revive the spirit of chivalry than any vain ambition of the famed Don Quijote."
@Cory Duclos

As I sat writing this note of thanks, worried about choosing just the right tone and sentiment, a friend came into my office and suggested that I simply make something up, borrowed from a foreign idiom or old master. So, here goes: *"Bien predica quien bien vive." Vale. Y gracias.*
@Timothy M. Foster

And again, one of the highlights of my years at VU was the chance to work with Ed, not just because of his help and guidance, but also because I found we had many things in common, particularly a love of

the Great American Songbook and Broadway musicals—not just Man of La Mancha!
@Antón García Fernández

Profesor Friedman: su erudición, generosidad, enseñanzas, humanidad y consejos inigualables nos han encaminado a alcanzar nuestras metas académicas y a sobrepasar la medida de nuestras propias y limitadas aspiraciones. ¡Muchas gracias por todo y enhorabuena!
@Martha García

I am deeply grateful for Ed Friedman's caring and wise guidance as well as his unwavering support as my mentor and my friend. Not only a highly respected academic, Ed is also the epitome of a gentleman scholar and one of the kindest human beings I have ever had the pleasure to know. I hope someday to emulate him in some small way.
@Anna-Lisa Halling

Noble, generous, kind; available and willing, exemplary yet unassuming; pleasant wit, accessible wisdom; a master teacher, who inspires the best in all. To think of him fills the heart with gratitude, and each of us are sure we are his favorite. Thank you, Ed!
@Eric Kartchner

El profesor Friedman trajo los estudios del Siglo de Oro de la estilística a la crítica literaria contemporánea sin caer en postmodernidades innecesarias o deconstrucciones anacrónicas. Esta base epistemológica ha sido vital en mi carrera.
@Salvador Oropesa

Unique as a Winter Solstice Full Moon Shadow on the Clyde. Eternal thanks for sharing your cosmic wit. A mi maestro y amigo Ed, siempre agradecido.
@Vicente Pérez de León

Dear Ed, I can't thank you enough for your mentoring and kindness throughout the years. I am grateful that our paths crossed at Vander-

bilt and I often reflect on my own growth as a scholar and instructor as a result of your influence. I am indebted to you for this and so much more. Un fuerte abrazo.
@David Richter

Prof. Friedman is the kindest, most generous, person I have met in my years in Academia. I had the fortune to have him as my advisor during graduate school in Vanderbilt University and I am grateful for all the ways he has supported me personally and many people I know.
@Gladys Robalino

Quiero dar las gracias a Dr. Friedman por apoyarme e inspirarme en mi disertación sobre la Diáspora sefardita y por estar siempre a mi lado en guiarme a la dirección correcta. Ha sido un honor colaborar con Dr. Friedman en mi proyecto de investigación. Sé que soy una persona privilegiada por ser la alumna de Dr. Friedman. Estoy orgullosa de tener a un mentor como él.
@Tugba Sevin

Para el profesor Friedman. Ejemplo de rectitud y responsabilidad académica. Por cuidarnos siendo sus estudiantes y por ayudarnos siempre quiero ofrecerle mi eterno agradecimiento a este invencible y solidario maestro de las letras.
@David M. Solodkow

With their labor, encouragement, and example, scholars and educators sow seeds for their students and colleagues to discover, nurture, prune, and reap. Thank you, Ed, for the groundwork you have laid for so many to harvest.
@Gwen H. Stickney

Estimado Ed, has sido un modelo de profesionalidad y de dedicación a tus estudiantes. Muchísimas gracias por tu apoyo durante mis años como estudiante graduada en IU y desde entonces durante mi carrera como profesora. Te deseo todo lo mejor. Un abrazo muy fuerte.
@Celia Tonkinson Dollmeyer

To a great man with the well-deserved reputation as the nicest person in Spanish literature. Thank you for all that you have done for me.
@Robert L. Turner

Una de tus citas favoritas de Gracián, y que incluías en tus prontuarios, era: "Lo bueno, si breve, dos veces bueno". Ahora yo también lo hago con mis estudiantes. Así se crean los legados basados en la generosidad intelectual. Gracias.
@Miguel Ángel Vázquez

Dear Ed, I send you my warmest thanks for your guidance and support over the past ten years. Your erudition, wit, sense of humor, and—most importantly—genuine kindness and concern for others are an inspiration and example to us all.
@Steven Wenz

It has been an honor and a privilege to be your student at Indiana University. I would like to thank you for your love of literature, your passion for teaching, and your commitment to research in all fields but especially in Spanish Golden Age literature. I am also grateful for your mentoring and generosity of heart and spirit.
@Habib Zanzana

Tabula gratulatoria

The editors of *Cosmic Wit* would like to express our gratitude to the University of Glasgow, to the Robert Penn Warren Center for the Humanities of Vanderbilt University, and to the Bulletin de Comediantes for their generous support to this volume in honor of Prof. Edward H. Friedman.

Mindy E. Badía
Robert Bayliss
Kathleen Costales
Timothy M. Foster
Anton Garcia-Fernandez
Jeanne L. Gillespie
Anna-Lisa Halling
Eric Kartchner
Connie Lathrop
Patricia W. Manning
Salvador Oropesa
Julia C. Paulk
David F. Richter
Gladys A. Robalino
Tugba Sevin
Gwen H. Stickney
Robert L. Turner III
Miguel Ángel Vázquez
Juan Vitulli
Jonathan Wade
Steven B. Wenz
Habib Zanzana

CPSIA information can be obtained
at www.ICGtesting.com
Printed in the USA
LVHW111107070223
738140LV00001B/2